ESSAYS ON FREGE

GOTTLOB FREGE, 1848-1925

Essays on Frege

EDITED BY E. D. KLEMKE

University of Illinois Press
Urbana, Chicago, and London
1968

To

GUSTAV BERGMANN

PREFACE

Gottlob Frege was born in November, 1848, at Wismar. He studied at Jena and at Göttingen and received the Doctorate of Philosophy at Göttingen in 1873. He then taught at Jena from 1874 to 1914. He died in July, 1925. "At the time of his death," writes William Kneale, "I was an undergraduate, already interested in logic, and I think that I should have taken notice if there had been any speeches made or articles published that year in his honor. But I can recollect nothing of the kind."[1] Frege's importance was acknowledged by Russell in *The Principles of Mathematics* and by Russell and Whitehead in *Principia Mathematica*. But Frege's own works were read by only a few philosophers and mathematicians, and hence he received little recognition in his own lifetime.

The situation has radically changed. During the past fifteen to twenty years, there has taken place a great revival of interest in the writings of Frege, especially with the publication of translations by Geach and Black.[2] Their volume was preceded by a translation of Frege's *Grundlagen* by J. L. Austin and followed by a partial translation by M. Furth of Frege's *Grundgesetze*. Some of the essays were also trans-

[1] William Kneale, "Gottlob Frege and Mathematical Logic," in A. J. Ayer, *et al.*, *The Revolution in Philosophy* (New York: St. Martin's Press, 1956), 26.

[2] For this and the other items mentioned in this preface, see the Selected Bibliography at the end of this volume.

lated and published individually in journals. As Frege's writings became more widely read, a number of articles were written about various aspects of Frege's work—his ontology, semantics, logic. Many of these papers are of great value for the study of Frege, and it was thought desirable to assemble some of them in a single volume. I have divided these essays into three main categories: (1) Frege's ontology, (2) his semantics, and (3) his logic and philosophy of mathematics. To some extent, these labels are not quite accurate. Thus a paper included in the section on semantics may have something to say regarding Frege's ontology as well. The categorization is a matter of emphasis; if a paper is chiefly about, say, Frege's ontology, then it appears in that section.

Two of the papers that are included in the volume have not been previously published. These are "Frege, Concepts, and Ontology," by Prof. Moltke S. Gram of Northwestern University (who so generously offered to write it for its appearance here), and my essay, "Frege's Ontology: Realism."

I have included as appendices three important essays by Frege, none of which were included in the excellent collection of translations by Geach and Black, but which are valuable for the study of Frege's thought. These are "The Thought: A Logical Inquiry" (translated by A. M. and M. Quinton), "Compound Thoughts" (translated by R. H. Stoothoff), and "On the Foundations of Geometry" (translated by M. E. Szabo).

I would like to express my gratitude to all of the writers, translators, editors, and publishers who so kindly granted their permission to allow these essays and chapters to be reprinted in this volume. I would also like to express my appreciation to all who gave encouragement and advice or who helped either with the selection of the items to be included or with the task of getting the manuscript prepared for publication. I am particularly indebted to Professors Gustav Bergmann, Charles E. Caton, H. L. Golding, and Moltke S. Gram; Mr. H. L. Schollick; Mr. G. Moor, for his assistance in preparing the bibliography and the index; and Professor Donald Jackson of the University of Illinois Press. But above all, warm thanks are especially due to Professor Herbert Hochberg, who first aroused my interest in Frege; Dean Otto Wirth, of Roosevelt University; and Professor Peter T. Geach, who helped in so many ways that I can hardly hope to acknowledge my gratitude adequately.

Finally, I wish to express my deep gratitude to the one to whom this volume is dedicated, one to whom I owe an enormous debt and one from whom I never cease to learn.

E. D. Klemke

Roosevelt University
Chicago, Illinois
October, 1967

CONTENTS

PART ONE

Frege's Ontology

1

Frege's Ontology

RULON S. WELLS

I. Frege's Significance for Ontology

§1. *Frege's primary contributions.* We remember Gottlob
Frege (1848-1925) for three primary contributions. He made
proof in mathematics and logic more precise and airtight, he
showed how the basic notions of logic and mathematics could
be assimilated to each other, and he produced a workable philosophy of mathematics. The ideals toward which he was
working were common in his day, particularly in Germany,
but he took them with supreme and unique seriousness.

It is Frege's third contribution that makes the point of departure for the present paper. Not merely did Frege show how
to manipulate symbols more exactly; he also gave a searching
account of what these symbols mean. Consider a philosophical
problem that arises out of the simplest arithmetic. When we
say that $5 = 2 + 3$, what do we mean? Do we mean that 5
is identical with $2 + 3$? But in some ways 5 and $2 + 3$ are
obviously different. Or do we mean that 5 and $2 + 3$ are equal
but not identical, equality being a relation that falls short
of complete identity? But in that case, some ordinary ways
of speaking in mathematics must be false. Suppose a pupil is

Reprinted with the kind permission of the author and the editor from
The Review of Metaphysics, IV (1951), 537-573.

asked for the positive square root of 25. The phrasing of the question implies that there is one and only one. No doubt he may answer, '5'. But then it follows that the answer '2 + 3' is not allowable, since ex hypothesi 5 and 2 + 3, though equal, are not identical. Yet ordinarily the answer '2 + 3' would be regarded as strange but not as wrong.

So it is not easy to say what we mean by '=' in arithmetic. Now consider the question, What do we mean when we say that $x^2 - 4x = x(x - 4)$? Here we have not only the problem about '=', but the further problem, What sort of things are $x^2 - 4x$ and $x(x - 4)$? Whether we are asserting identity or only equality, what are we asserting it between? Most mathematicians would say that these two things are functions, but what are functions? They are not simply numbers; what, then? And for that matter, what are numbers?

§2. *Implications for semantics.* By way of illustration, two questions about mathematical equations were raised in the previous section. The first of these Frege answers by saying that '=' denotes complete identity. Now this answer, and indeed any answer to the question, has implications for semantics, the science that describes meaning-relations. That is, there are certain semantical theories with which it would be incompatible; for instance, any theory which held that the sign '=' does not denote at all, but has meaning in some other way. Similarly, Frege's answer to the second question above has such implications. His answer (*Function* 9)[1] is that in

---

[1] The following system of reference is used. (a) Books and articles are cited by italicized title, usually abbreviated; the full title is given in the bibliography. (b) Many citations give not only the page but the paragraph and sometimes even the lines. E.g. 'Frege *Grundgesetze* 1.VIaI' identifies Frege's *Grundgesetze der Arithmetik,* volume 1, page VI, the first line of the first paragraph, i.e. the top line of the page. When it is convenient to count from the bottom rather than the top, the letter indicating the paragraph or the numerals indicating the lines will be italicized. E.g. 'Frege *Grundgesetze* 1.13a4' identifies the fourth line (counting from the top) of the first paragraph counting from the bottom. When a page is divided into columns, the left one is indicated by superscript 'a' and the right one by superscript 'b'. E.g. 'Frege

'$x^2 - 4x = x(x - 4)$', the left member and the right member denote ranges (*Wertverläufe*, see §11). This doctrine obviously entails that the two members denote *something*, i.e. enter into the denoting-relation; and this is an implication for semantics.

In like manner, any doctrine of what certain symbols mean, no matter what or how few these symbols are, has semantical implications. Even if a semantical theory be conceived as purely general, not concerned with details, still it must be *compatible* with all details. In this quite obvious way, Frege's and anybody's ascription of any kind of meaning to any symbol has semantical implications. In Frege's philosophy of mathematics there are many such.

There is a second way in which his philosophy of mathematics has semantical implications: He develops an explicit and general semantical theory. This theory is primarily designed to accommodate his philosophy of mathematics, but he gives it much more general application. In his essay *Ueber Sinn und Bedeutung* (1892)[2] he begins by posing the problem of identity, and works out the answer that, for instance, the expressions '5' and '2 + 3' denote the same number, but differ in 'sense'. (See §14 for a discussion of his notion of sense.) Then in the same essay he shows how his distinction between sense and denotation is workable and illuminating not only in mathematics but quite generally; and thus he arrives at a general semantical theory. According to it, there is no difficulty in saying that 5 and 2 + 3 are completely identical; the obvious differences between them mentioned in §1 turn

---

Grundgesetze 1.27^{b}a6' identifies the sixth line from the bottom of the page, in the right-hand column; this line reads 'Man darf ein Unterglied mit'. Because this entire column happens to contain only a single paragraph, with many symbols which would make line-counting difficult, it is easier to identify the line in question by counting from the bottom.

[2] For discussion of this famous essay, see Carnap *Meaning;* Church, all articles cited in bibliography; Jones *Objections;* Russell *Principles* Appendix A, *On denoting,* and *Knowledge* 225 et seq.; and Wienpahl *Sinn.* See also §§14-19 of the present essay.

out, on more careful scrutiny, not to be differences in the numbers themselves but merely in the expressions. Consequently, a meticulous and unwavering distinction between expressions and what they denote is enjoined (Cf. §26, (A)); and Frege proves (cf. fn. 28) that though this vital distinction is obvious when so stated, many abstruse reasonings obliterate it. His emphasis on the distinction is itself a semantical contribution.

§3. *Implications for ontology.* Frege's philosophy of mathematics has implications for ontology, as well as for semantics; and his semantical doctrines themselves have ontological implications in turn. However one may conceive ontology, it surely includes the task of describing the major kinds of being. That is, every ontological system will include a list of categories—or will be incomplete. And while an ontologist need not, in addition to listing his categories, list the things categorized, still all things to be categorized must admit of being relegated to one or another category in his list. If Frege says that the sense of the expression '2 + 3' is an entity, and a certain ontologist's list of categories makes no provision for such an entity, then either Frege or that ontologist is wrong. If the ontologist is wrong, he might be wrong either by expressly denying that the sense of '2 + 3' is an entity, or by being incomplete—by neglecting to pronounce on the matter one way or the other.

In the same way, Frege's entire semantics has ontological implications. To a limited extent, Frege himself develops these into an explicit contribution. For instance his essay *Ueber Begriff und Gegenstand* (1892) explains his two basic categories of being, function and object, and the grammatico-semantical basis on which they rest. (Cf. §12.) But there is room for a systematization of his ontology, based upon his own declarations and hints, yet going considerably beyond any exposition that he has left us. Such a systematization is the more in order, as Frege's ontology has been neglected in favor of his semantics. His contribution to semantics has attracted more attention not because it is more extensive — although it is — but because (a) our age is in general more interested in semantics than in ontology, and (b) the indispensable qualification for studying his contribution to either subject, viz. an interest in symbolic logic and a fair acquaintance with it, is considerably more common among semanticists than among ontologists.

In this paper I shall concentrate on Frege's ontology. The ontological implications of his mathematical philosophy and his semantics will be explicated; and the resulting statements, together with the ontological doctrines that he himself makes explicit, will be integrated into a system. This is the exegetical part of my task.

§4. *Further ontological relevance of Frege's system.* Frege's ideas have two further relevances for ontology, which will not be discussed in this paper but must be mentioned for the sake of clarity. (1) According to traditional Aristotelian doctrine, speculative philosophy is comprised of metaphysics (first philosophy), mathematical philosophy, and the philosophy of nature. Ontology in the Wolffian sense is general metaphysics. Now the second of Frege's three contributions mentioned in §1 breaks down the sharp distinction between mathematics and logic,[3] and this breakdown may well have repercussions in ontology. (2) Frege's ontological contribution is mainly concerned with abstract entities such as functions, senses, ranges, and so on. Many ontologists today, especially moderate realists in the Aristotelian tradition, would regard all these as beings of reason (*entia rationis*). Frege takes a more extreme-realistic view of them, but that is irrelevant to the point I wish to emphasize here. The whole subject of ab-

---

[3] Though it does so by introducing into logic the novel notion of range (cf. §11). Concerning this notion, Frege says (*Grundgesetze* 1.VIIb near end): "I regard it as purely logical." In any case it is surely far too general to be purely mathematical.

stract entities is suffering comparative neglect from most ontologists.[4] Frege's categories should command their attention.

§5. *Frege's ontological method*. Frege concludes that his system of semantics and ontology is not merely an adequate foundation for mathematics, but the best and only adequate foundation. Somewhat like Kant, he takes certain beliefs for granted and asks what they presuppose, i.e., under what conditions they could be true. In arriving at his conclusion, he makes a mistake that is extremely significant. He establishes the adequacy of his own system and the inadequacy of sundry others that have been previously propounded; and by an amazing leap in the argument he infers that his system is the only adequate one. Now in Part V, where this mistake of Frege's is analyzed in detail, it will be suggested that although the mistake seems egregious, it is committed to one extent or another by nearly all philosophers.

II. Exposition of the System

§6. *A table*. Frege's ontological system lends itself to schematic presentation. All entities may be classified as:

A. Objects
  1. Ordinary denotations
     a. Truth-values
     b. Ranges
     c. Function-correlates
     d. Places, moments, time-spans
     e. Ideas
     f. Other objects
  2. Ordinary senses

---

[4] Lack of preoccupation with the abstract entities of logic and mathematics seems to be correlated with Aristotelianism, as contrasted with Platonism over the issue of the status of 'ideas'. It appears that one can be an Aristotelian on this issue without being an unqualified Aristotelian. All that I ask readers of the present paper to grant is that the topic of logical and mathematical entities is, whether a central or a subordinate part of ontology, still genuinely a part of it.

B. Functions
  1. Functions all of whose values are truth-values
     a. With one argument (concepts)
     b. With two arguments (relations)
  2. Functions not all of whose values are truth-values
     a. With one argument
     b. With two arguments

§7. *Functions.* The notion with whose exposition it is best to begin is the notion of function. The notion itself is taken over from mathematics; but Frege rejects all previous accounts of it, for he holds that all of them involve confusion between expressions and their denotations. In particular, all of them give a hopelessly wrong account of variables. (Cf. §21.) To analyze what we mean by a function, it is best to study a concrete example (*Function* 6).[5]

The notion of function is inseparable from the notions of argument and of value. The following three expressions exhibit the same *function* but with different *arguments* (*Function* 6): (a) '$2.1^3 + 1$'; (b) '$2.4^3 + 4$'; (c) '$2.5^3 + 5$'. Furthermore, each of these three expressions has a *value*. Frege proposes to analyze 'has' here [6] as meaning 'denotes'. The argument of (a) is the number 1; of (b), 4; and of (c), 5. The value denoted by (a) is the number 3; by (b), 132; and by (c), 255. (Incidentally, Frege would say that both the compound numerical expression '$2.1^3 + 1$' and the simple numeral '3' have the same value, i.e. denote the same object: the number 3.) Moreover, Frege would say that the expression '$2.1^3 + 1$' does not literally contain an argument; it contains an expression '1', occurring twice, which denotes an argument. The argument is thus not a symbol but something symbolized. Now because of

---

[5] Cf. fn. 1.

[6] Not everywhere; for instance, when we say 'this expression has a sense', 'has' means in effect not 'denotes' but 'expresses'. Cf. §14. Frege's terminology is to say that an expression *denotes* its denotation but *expresses* its sense. Of course the sense in which *expressions* have values is different from the sense in which *functions* have them.

parallel considerations, and for further reasons to be stated in §26, he takes the same view of functions; they are not (in general) symbols but are what certain symbols symbolize.

If expression (a), (b) and (c) exhibit the same function, what does 'exhibit' mean here? Presumably, Frege reasons, that there is some component expression, present in all of them, that denotes the function. It should be whatever is left after we strike out the argument expressions, sc. '2. ^{3} + '; or as Frege would write it, '2.ξ^3 + ξ'.[7]

§8. *Analysis of values into functions and arguments.* Frege would say that the function denoted in isolation by '2.ξ^3 + ξ' and the argument denoted by '1' combine to produce the value denoted by '2.1^3 + 1', i.e. 3. But it is important to realize, and his exposition — especially in *Begriff* and *Verneinung* — makes the point sufficiently clear, that, given a complex expression such as '2.1^3 + 1', there is no unique answer to the question 'What function and what arguments are denoted in this expression?'. What one can say is that *if* 2.ξ^3 + ξ is the function, 1 is the argument; if 2.ξ^3 + ζ is the function, 1 and 1 are the respective arguments; if ξ.1^3 + ζ is the function, 2 and 1 are the respective arguments; if 2.1$^\xi$ + 1 is the function, 3 is the argument; if ξ is the function, 2.1^3 + 1 is the argument; etc. To put the matter in another way, '2.1^3 + 1' can be regarded as exhibiting the same function as '2.4^3 + 4', or as '2.4^3 + 7', or as '4.1^3 + 8', or as

---

[7] The introduction of a letter such as 'ξ' serves two purposes: (i) it is visually clearer than the use of blank spaces; (ii) it makes possible a differentiation between, for example, the two functions 2.ξ^3 + ξ and 2.ξ^3 + ζ. To show that these are different functions it is sufficient to note that the former is a function requiring one argument and the latter a function requiring two arguments. Again, $\xi = \xi$ is a different function from $\xi = \zeta$; for (i) the former is a function of one argument, the latter a function of two; (ii) the former has only one value — the True, no matter what the argument, whereas the latter has this value for some pairs of arguments but the False for others.

The function 2.ξ^3 + ξ like the function $\xi = \xi$, is a function of *one* argument although the same argument occurs twice. Cf. *Grundgesetze* 1.8 §4.

'$2.1^9 + 1$'; etc. Given an expression and the function that it denotes, one can ascertain the arguments; given the expression and the arguments, one can determine the function.

So far it seems as if a function, though not identical with an expression, is identified by it. In other words, it seems as if no two expressions identify the same function. It appears that Frege does not mean to admit this extreme consequence; on the other hand, he is prepared to admit that there can be functions that are different from each other even though they have precisely the same values for the same arguments. (*Function* 9a-b, to mention a single example, says that $\xi(\xi - 4)$ and $\xi^2 - 4\xi$ are different functions even though they have the same range, i.e. the same values for the same arguments.) This is tantamount to rejecting so-called extensionality of functions. We can only say that Frege has not laid down for us conditions under which different expressions identify the same function.[8]

§9. *Mathematical generalization.* So far, in our discussion of functions, we have only been describing how Frege clarifies the notion as it is used in mathematics, and not how he generalizes it. But a process which we shall call mathematical generalization (cf. §28) is one of Frege's major techniques. We so name it, not because mathematics has any prerogative over it, but because it is a recognized method in mathematics and because in applying it elsewhere Frege consciously takes

---

[8] Similarly, he does not lay down complete conditions under which different expressions with the same denotatum have the same sense; cf. §14 and fn. 14. It is not clear that Frege has any good reason for rejecting extensionality of functions. And in fact some of the functions he introduces *are* extensional; namely, all functions defined by specifying their range, i.e. by specifying their values for all possible arguments. Intensionality of functions appears all the more superfluous, since the sense-denotation distinction could be invoked as follows. Every function-name has a sense as well as a denotation; so the function-expressions '$\xi (\xi - 4)$' and '$\xi^2 - 4\xi$' could be held to denote the same function but to have different senses. It appears that Frege simply neglects to articulate his sense-denotation distinction with his concept of function; cf. *Sinn* 27b where he expressly refrains from integrating them. Cf. also Church *Introduction* 22b-3a §03.

mathematics as his model. And by applying this mathematically inspired method to some mathematical notions—function and correlative notions, Frege arrives at the keystone of his ontological system.

§*10. The notion of function generalized.* Frege proposes (*Function* 12b ff.) to generalize the notion of function beyond the sphere of mathematics. In mathematics or at least in arithmetic and algebra, the arguments and the values of functions are numbers. But according to Frege's generalized conception, any entity — whether object or function — is fit to be an argument of some function, and a value of some function. For example, Eve is the value of the function the mother of ξ, for the argument Cain.

In particular, truth-values (see §18) are fit to be values of functions; and the functions of which they are values are what are commonly called concepts and relations. So, by clarifying and mathematically generalizing the mathematical notion of function, in the light of the common-sense assumption that functions cannot be mere expressions, Frege is able to encompass the common-sense notions of concept and relation and give an account of them.

It is inherent in the nature of a function that a certain fixed number of arguments is required to satisfy it,[9] and that by or in itself it is unsatisfied (*ungesättigt, unerfüllt*).[10] The function ξ^3 requires one argument, the function $\xi > \zeta$ requires

---

[9] Frege does not quite fully state what he manifestly means. ξ^2 is a function of one argument; $\xi + \xi$ and $\xi = \xi$ are functions of one argument also; $\xi + \zeta$ and $\xi = \zeta$ are functions of two arguments. Now it is *not* required that ξ and ζ be distinct; $2 + 2$, for instance, is a value of $\xi = \zeta$ for the arguments 2 and 2 respectively. But to get from '$\xi + \zeta$' to '$2 + 2$' requires *two* substitutions: '2' for 'ξ' and '2' for 'ζ' (the order of substitution is here immaterial). Whereas, to get from '$\xi + \xi$' '$2 + 2$' requires only *one* step: substitution of (an occurrence of) '2' for (each occurrence of) 'ξ'. So it is misleading to speak of the number of arguments required to satisfy a function as fixed. It is more accurate to say that the maximum number is fixed.

[10] This does not mean (cf. Church *Anticipation* 151d) that functions are not full-fledged entities; it is more or less what Aristotle and the scholastics mean in speaking of accidents as 'existing in another'.

two; the function ξ is between ζ and η requires three. Functions all of whose values are truth-values Frege calls concepts (*Begriffe*) if one argument satisfies them, relations if two or more are required.[11] The function of one argument denoted by 'the mother of ξ' has the value Eve for the argument Cain, also for the argument Abel; since Eve is not a truth-value, this function is neither a concept nor a relation. The function denoted by 'Eve is the mother of ξ', which is a function of one argument and which has the value the True for the argument Cain, is a concept. The function denoted by 'ζ is the mother of ξ', a function of two arguments, has the value the True for the respective arguments Eve and Cain. Whatever arguments one chooses, its value is either the True or the False; so it is a relation.

§11. *Ranges of functions.* The table of §6 listed ranges among the kinds of objects. The notion of range (*Wertverlauf*) is perhaps the obscurest of all Frege's basic notions; and yet it is important because it is his nearest approach to the modern notion of class. Frege himself gives three different inklings of what he means by it. The cause of its obscurity is the fact which he points out in *Grundgesetze* 1.7, §3, that what he primarily defines is not range but identity of ranges. He stipulates certain circumstances (*Grundgesetze* 1.VIIIb; 14 §9; 36 §20 Grundgesetz V; cf. 2.253 et seq., 'Nachwort') under which two expressions will be said to denote the same range. Now in *Grundgesetze* 1.16-8 §10, Frege shows at length that such a stipulation does not suffice to determine what kind of a thing a range is. He there investigates the possibility of identifying certain ranges with truth-values, shows that with-

---

[11] There are also functions whose *arguments* are truth-values; expressions denoting these are his counterparts of the so-called operators of statement-composition, or truth-functional operators. In his formal system, material implication and negation are primitive (undefined) functions whose arguments and whose values are truth-values, and disjunction, conjunction, etc. can be defined in terms of these (*Grundgesetze* 1.20-5). Furthermore, the word 'the' denotes a function (*Grundgesetze* 1.18-20); and quantifiers too he treats (*Grundgesetze* 1.36-9, especially 38[b]e) as denoting functions—namely, second-level functions (cf. fn. 12).

out violating his fundamental stipulation "it is always possible to identify any range one pleases with the True, and
any range one pleases with the False" (17a8-5), and for reasons that are not clear immediately decides to do so. This is
one of his three determinations or narrowings of the notion
of range.

The second narrowing is that in some informal passages
he identifies certain ranges with classes. Namely, he defines
a concept as any function of one argument all of whose values
are truth-values; and he (*Grundgesetze* 1.8 §3; cf. Xa2-3)
calls the range of any concept a scope (*Begriffsumfang*). Then
in two later passages (*Grundgesetze* 2.159a, 253 et seq.; cf.
Peano 368b) he identifies scopes with what others have called
classes. Thus the elucidation (Carnap *Meaning* 126-7, etc.) of
scopes — and hence of all ranges — in terms of classes origi-
nates with Frege himself.

The third narrowing is given in a revealing passage in
Function (8d-9; cf. *Grundgesetze* 1.5a7-3), where he draws an
illustration from analytic geometry. Given a function of x,
say a parabolic function, the range is the resulting curve; in
this example, the parabola itself.

Now it is evident that in any case Frege's notion of range
is more comprehensive than the modern notion of class, since
not all ranges but only scopes are identified by Frege with
classes. But the third inkling shows us that even this identification is misleading. Frege may say (*Grundgesetze* 2.158-9)
"We will, for brevity's sake, say 'class' instead of 'scope of a
concept' "; and he may identify 'class' in this stipulated sense
with 'class' as understood by Russell and others; but it does
not follow that what Frege means by scope is virtually what
we today, following Russell, mean by 'class'. And what the
comparison with a geometric curve reveals is that Frege
means, rather, something more like what we today would
call a relation. The function x^2 determines a curve; now
analytic geometry teaches us to think of each point on the
curve as an ordered pair or couple of numbers. The curve

itself could be identified with the class of all and only these ordered pairs. And consequently the modern conception of a dyadic relation taken extensionally, as a class of ordered pairs, permits us to think of the curve defined by the function x^2 as a dyadic relation. The curve defined by x^3 is a different dyadic relation. A function of two variables such as $x^2 + xy + y^2$ has a range that is a triadic relation; and so on.

Now let us consider a function that is a concept. $x^2 = 4$ is such a function. Its range correlates the possible arguments of this function with the respective values. For the argument $- 2$, the value is the True; for the argument 0 it is the False (i.e. '$0^2 = 4$' denotes the False); for $+ 2$, the True; for $+ 3$, the False; and so on. The range of this function consists of an infinite number of ordered pairs, the first member of each pair being any entity (not necessarily a number; cf. §20) and the second member being either the True or the False. Moreover, there are precisely two ordered pairs whose second member is the True: (i) $[- 2$; the True] and (ii) $[+ 2$; the True].

Now contrast this with a class in the modern (Russellian) sense. The function $x^2 = 4$ determines the class $x(x^2 = 4)$; and this class contains not an infinite number of members but just two: $- 2$ and $+ 2$. Neither of these is an ordered pair. So the scope of the function $x^2 = 4$ is very different from the class determined by it.

Nevertheless, this class and the corresponding scope have certain properties in common; that is why Frege could interpret Russell's 'class' as his 'scope'. For instance, classes are identical if and only if the corresponding scopes are identical.

Accordingly, we may reduce Frege's three different determinations to two. His identification of scopes with classes need not be taken literally; it was merely feasible insofar as scopes and classes formally resemble each other. And even the remaining two determinations or narrowings may not be incompatible. Frege never *defines* 'the True' and 'the False' but once (*Sinn* 34a; cf. §18), and then ambiguously; so even though some ranges are truth-values, still all ranges may be classes of ordered pairs or trios or *n*-ads, i.e. relations taken in extension. The latter, then, is apparently Frege's fundamental conception of range.

§*12. Function and object.* We turn now to the contrast between functions and objects. In spite of the current interest in Frege, this his basic distinction has received scant attention, the reason being that it is not so directly relevant as the notions of sense, denotation, proposition, and truth-value to the semantic problems with which discussions of Frege have been most concerned. In expounding the distinction it seems advisable to follow Frege's own procedure in *Begriff*; viz. to begin by explaining the distinction between concept and object, and then show how what is true of concepts is true of all functions.

Roughly, in any true or false sentence (as opposed to a declarative sentence that is neither — cf. §18) that can be divided into a subject and a predicate, the subject denotes an object and the predicate denotes a concept. If a division is made in such a way as to yield two or more subjects, what remains denotes a relation. Frege neither affirms nor denies the existence of relations requiring three or more arguments, but the only relations he has occasion to discuss require two arguments only. Relations and concepts both differ from objects in being unsatisfied (cf. §10); but (*Grundgesetze* 1.37ᵃa4-ᵇa) relations are as fundamentally different from concepts as concepts from objects.

According to Frege's conception, it is in the very essence of concepts that they cannot be objects.[12] This is seen most

---

[12] There are, nevertheless, functions of functions (*Grundgesetze* 1.36-42 §§21-5); but (37ᵃa8-10) these second-level functions treat first-level functions as functions, not as objects. As Russell puts it (*PM* 1.xivf, xxixb, 659-66), first-level functions appear in second-level functions only through their values. *Grundgesetze* 1.41ᵃc, 41ᵇb admit third-level functions.

Geach *Subject* has recently revived and defended Frege's distinction between concept and object.

compellingly by trying to treat them as objects. What happens is that one gets an object, all right, but it is no longer the concept that one was originally trying to objectify. For instance, in 'Cæsar conquered Gaul', 'Cæsar' denotes an object and 'conquered Gaul' denotes a concept. Suppose we treat this concept as an object; grammatically, this involves treating its name as a grammatical subject. But to say, 'Conquered Gaul is a concept' is simply ungrammatical, while to say 'The concept of conquering Gaul is a concept' is grammatical but false. This is a surprising result, because at first sight one would think that 'The concept of conquering Gaul is a concept' is not merely true but truistic, even trivial. What Frege's doctrine amounts to is that 'conquered Gaul' and 'the concept of conquering Gaul' do not denote the same entity, and so are not mere grammatical variants of each other; and that furthermore it is the former expression and not the latter that denotes a concept. The radical difference in the grammar of the true expressions betokens an equally radical difference between the entities that they respectively denote. No sentence of the form 'x is a concept' is true; in Frege's terminology, the function, ξ is a concept, has the False as its sole value.

What then does 'the concept of conquering Gaul' denote? An object of a special kind; since Frege has no name for such objects, although he recognizes their existence (*Begriff* 201a), I shall call them concept-correlates. They are a species of what may be called *function-correlates*.

§13. *Kinds of objects.* No function is an object, then, and (*Function* 18b) an object may be defined as whatever is not a function. Since Frege uses no term to apply to whatever is either a function or an object, I shall introduce the term 'entity'. Frege nowhere gives a classification of objects;[13] in the table of §6 I have drawn up an inventory of the kinds of entities that he specifically calls objects. The first part of

---

[13] Except that *Gedanke* 69c-d posits, in addition to ideas and to things of the external world, a third realm, to which propositions belong.

this list comprehends truth-values (*Function* 18c); ranges (*Function* 19a); function-correlates (*Begriff* 201a); places, moments, and time-spans (*Sinn* 42b); ideas (no specific reference, but it is evident that this is where they belong); and of course in addition many other kinds that he has no occasion to discuss, or at least not to categorize.

§*14. Sense and denotation.* To explain the second part of the list it is necessary to turn to Frege's now famous distinction between sense and denotation. (*Sinn* gives the fullest exposition; cf. also *Peano* 368c-70a. See also §27 on the rationale of the distinction.) In the doctrine of sense and denotation, both ontology and semantics are involved.

Frege's distinction between the sense of an expression and its denotation is quite like the familiar distinction between connotation or intension and denotation or extension. Commonsense realism leads one to distinguish expressions from their meanings. But the meaning of an expression cannot be simply identified with its denotation, for we can find pairs of expressions that have the same denotation and yet somehow differ in meaning. There are at least two further factors to be considered. First, there are the private and variable meanings that an individual user of an expression attaches to it; Frege technically calls these ideas (*Vorstellungen*), and points out that by their very privacy they are irrelevant for logic and science. Second, there are standard, objective meanings: senses (*Sinne*), publicly knowable and such that two expressions may coincide in denotation and yet differ in sense. The expressions 'the morning star' and 'the evening star', though in point of fact they denote the same entity, obviously differ somehow in meaning; and since the meaning-difference is presumably objective, at least in part, it is to that extent a difference in sense and not merely in idea.

To say that an expression has a sense is only to say it has a meaning that is (a) objective, like the denotation, yet (b) distinct from the denotation. Frege imposes the following further conditions on sense: (i) he ascribes a sense to expressions which would not, according to Mill, have connotation; i.e. 'sense' is broader in extension than 'connotation'; (ii) he posits that every expression having a denotation has a sense (but not conversely); (iii) he posits that if two expressions have the same sense they have the same denotation, but that there are pairs of expressions identical in denotation but differing in sense; (iv) he apparently assumes that there are pairs of expressions, such as '5' and '2 + 3', differing in sense even though the identity-statement joining the two expressions (e.g. '5 = 2 + 3') is necessarily true. All of these conditions together may be thought of as an 'implicit definition', or 'definition by postulation', of the term 'sense'. But they do not suffice to justify one in speaking of *the* sense of an expression. Frege's conception of sense is a generic, determinable conception, and its power in dealing with present-day problems is largely due to the fact that, given the problem, one can add further assumptions — sometimes ad hoc — that determine a more specific conception.[14]

As for Frege's conception of denotation, its chief peculiarity is his assumption that no expression denotes more than

[14] Cf. fn. 8. Some people have proposed to recognize a kind of meaning such that no two expressions have the same meaning (e.g. Goodman *Likeness* 6d). Apparently Frege does not intend to impose so strict a requirement on his 'sense'. There are a number of passages in his writings where he expressly or implicitly ascribes the same sense to two different expressions, belonging to the same or different languages: *Function* 11a, *Sinn* 27d, 39f (cf. 42a3-1, 42b5-1). *Begriff* 196 fn. 1 points out that if no two expressions had the same sense, "every definition would have to be rejected as false"; and 199b states that "different sentences can express the same proposition" (and propositions are a species of senses). Similarly, Church *Formulation* permits different expressions to have the same sense, under certain circumstances. See also Church *Introduction* 19b.

On the other hand, there are pairs of expressions logically equivalent to each other, and yet to which Frege ascribes different senses; e.g. left and right members of true mathematical equations. And *Verneinung* 157 bottom seems to ascribe different senses to any sentence and the negation of its negation.

For Church's discussion of the sense-denotation distinction in general, see all of his items cited in the bibliography, and especially *Introduction* fn. 14.

one entity. (Cf. §16.) The denotation-relation that he is talking about is simply a different relation from the relation — commonly called 'denotation' — that obtains, for instance, between the word 'horse' and each horse that has existed or will exist.

§15. *Ordinary senses and ordinary denotations.* Entities are of two kinds, that are most directly distinguishable by their semantical properties. In Frege's semantical system, every expression that has a denotation has a sense; and some expressions that do not have a denotation have a sense. Moreover, every expression which when used ordinarily (*gewöhnlich*) in direct discourse has a sense (whether or not it also has a denotation), may be used in two other ways, in each of which it has both a sense and a denotation (*Sinn* 28b-c, 36b4-1): as a name of itself when used in the first way, and as a name of the sense it has when used in the first way. The second use we may call the autonymous use (cf. Carnap *Syntax* 17, 156), and the third use Frege calls indirect use — because, on his view, it is the way in which expressions are used in indirect discourse. To put the matter symbolically and more clearly: Let E be an expression which when used ordinarily has sense S and perhaps also denotation D. The denotation of E when used autonymously is E as used ordinarily, and the denotation of E when used indirectly is S. What the respective senses are, or how they may be identified (since in general specifying the denotation of an expression does not thereby specify its sense), Frege does not say.

Let us define an ordinary sense (relative to a given language) as any entity that is the sense of some expression (of that language) in its ordinary use; and an ordinary denotation as an entity that is the denotation of some expression in its ordinary use. Then it is a fact of Frege's ontology — never pointed out by himself — that the classes of ordinary senses and ordinary denotations are mutually exclusive; and furthermore, that all functions, if signified at all in a language, are ordinary denotations, not ordinary senses. For this reason it is needful to introduce the sense-denotation dichotomy only within the class of objects, not within the class of functions.

§16. *Is the sense-denotation distinction ontological?* This fact poses a speculative question. Could there be expressions, either incorporated in new languages or instituted in already existing natural or artificial languages, such that they would have ordinary denotations as their senses? For instance, could there be an expression whose sense would be a truth-value?

So far as I can see, there is no reason in Frege's system why there could not be such expressions, even if Frege himself never has occasion to take cognizance of them. But they would all have a certain property in common, which is the reason why they would never find a use in Frege's system; namely that they all necessarily lack a denotation.

To explain the point of the word 'necessarily' here, it is necessary to discuss a relation that is never mentioned by Frege and cannot properly be said to be part of his explicitly developed system. And yet its introduction seems to be an extrapolation that is entirely in harmony with his system. I will call it the *correspondence-relation*. Frege assumes the principle [15] that every expression with one sense has at most one denotation, and apparently regards this principle not as a convention but as a fact about the nature of senses. In consequence, it will be legitimate to speak in terms of a direct correspondence between a sense and its correspondent denotation, to which relation mediation via an expression that 'has' the sense and the denotation is inessential. To each sense, then, there corresponds at most one denotation; on the other hand, one denotation may correspond to more than one sense.

On the basis of the correspondence-relation senses may be classified into four kinds: (1) those that necessarily (essentially, inherently) lack a correspondent; (2) those that accidentally (i.e. as a sheer matter of fact) lack one; (3) those

---

[15] "The principle of univocality" (Carnap *Meaning* 98). Cf. Church *Introduction* fn. 6.

that accidentally have one; and (4) those that necessarily have one. Fictional names (e.g., 'Ulysses') are of kind (2); cf. also *Gedanke* 68b.

Although this fourfold classification is not Frege's, it seems to me to be virtually utilized by him. (And I further ascribe to him the epistemological view that we know immediately (intuitively, innately, a priori, by inspection of meanings) to which of the four kinds any particular sense belongs.) Let us call expressions whose senses are of kind (2), (3) or (4) *eligibles,* meaning that these expressions are eligible to have a denotation even if they do not have one; in parallel manner, expressions of kind (1) may be called *ineligibles.* Then one requirement that Frege imposes (e.g. *Grundgesetze* 1.45 §28) upon a properly constructed language is that all eligible expressions shall have ordinary senses of kind (4).

Now, to return to the speculative question with which this section began, we may say very compactly: there could be expressions whose senses are ordinary denotations, but they would all be ineligibles.[16]

Thus the sense-denotation distinction is not *merely* semantical; it is ontological as well. Whatever is a sense of some expressions, is also a denotation of some (possible) expression; but there are denotations which, if treated as senses, have no correspondent denotation.[17]

---

[16] Carnap *Meaning* 130 has pointed out — and Frege would accept the conclusion, I do not doubt — that from every ordinary sense there issues an infinite series of indirect senses. (Unlike Carnap, he would not regard this consequence as militating against his system.) The fact that ordinary senses have no correspondents means that these series of senses are not infinite in both directions; they have no end, but they have a beginning.

[17] Even so, one might think to banish the distinction *from semantics,* by showing it to be superfluous. The attempt might take these lines: whatever is a sense is also a denotation (of some expression or other); hence denoting can be taken as fundamental, and the relation of a term to its sense can be defined in terms of denoting. But the attempt would fail, for two reasons:

(1) Let S be the sense of expression E; then S is distinct from the denotation D of E if E has a denotation. And S will be the denotation

§17. *Senses and denotations of complex expressions.* Frege assumes four semantical principles about complex expressions:

(Ia and Ib) A grammatically permitted complex expression has a $\left\{\begin{matrix} \text{a. sense} \\ \text{b. denotation} \end{matrix}\right\}$ if and only if there is at least one way of dividing it into component expressions each of which has a $\left\{\begin{matrix} \text{a. sense} \\ \text{b. denotation} \end{matrix}\right\}$; [18] for example, into a function-expression and an appropriate number of argument-expressions (cf. *Sinn* 32b-3b).

(IIa and IIb) If two complex expressions A and B differ only in that in a place where A has component expression E, B has component expression F, and E and F have the same $\left\{\begin{matrix} \text{a. sense} \\ \text{b. denotation} \end{matrix}\right\}$, then A and B have the same $\left\{\begin{matrix} \text{a. sense} \\ \text{b. denotation} \end{matrix}\right\}$ or else both lack a $\left\{\begin{matrix} \text{a. sense} \\ \text{b. denotation} \end{matrix}\right\}$.

Principles (Ia) and (Ib) speak of there being 'at least one way' of dividing complex expressions. As noted in §8, there is in general more than one way.

---

of some term F — F being either E itself, used indirectly, or some other expression. But F will have *its* sense T; and T must be distinct from S, for if they were the same, their correspondent denotations S and D would be the same. Thus a vicious infinite regress begins; the sense of E has been defined, but not all senses. At every step in the recursive definition of 'sense', there will remain senses that have not been dealt with.

(2) How would we define the sense of E? By finding a term F whose denotation is the sense of E; but how could we find and specify such an F? The most obvious way would be by means of the correspondence-relation: the denotation of E is the correspondent of the denotation of F. But apart from difficulties when E has no denotation, admission of the correspondence-relation is tantamount to giving up denotation as the sole undefined semantical relation.

The above remarks do not show that semantics cannot get along with denotation as its sole undefined relation, but only that sense cannot be reduced to denotation in any way here envisioned.

[18] It is not clear whether Frege would assume that, if a complex expression has a sense, every possible way of dividing it yields components each of which has a sense.

Frege comes closest to a general and explicit statement of these principles in *Peano* 369-70.

§18. Senses and denotations of sentences. Frege treats sentences as complex expressions that conform to the above four principles. The sense of a sentence he calls its proposition (*Gedanke*); the denotation, if any, its truth-value. *Sinn* gives his fullest justification of this analysis. Frege treats sentences not only as expressions but as eligibles; accordingly, those of them that are analyzable into component eligibles all of which denote must themselves denote, by (Ib); and with the premiss available that a sentence denotes if and only if it is either true or false, the proof that all true sentences have the same denotation and all false sentences have the same denotation follows readily from (IIb). The object denoted by all true sentences Frege calls the True (*das Wahre*), and the one denoted by all false sentences he calls the False (*das Falsche*) (*Function* 13a, *Sinn* 34a, et alibi).

Not every indicative sentence denotes; for instance, the sentences of poetry and fiction do not. Such sentences are neither true nor false (*Sinn* 33; note how I. A. Richards's account of poetic statements is anticipated); they are, however, still eligibles. E.g. (*Sinn* 32b), 'Ulysses was set ashore at Ithaca while in deep sleep' is neither true nor false — lacks a denotation — if, as is probably the case, 'Ulysses' lacks a denotation. (It is assumed that there is no other way of dividing this sentence such that each component expression has a denotation.)

§19. A later modification. On one minor point *Gedanke* and *Verneinung* modify Frege's earlier ontology. In *Sinn* 39c he ascribes to imperative and interrogative sentences senses that are not propositions, i.e. that are not the senses of any indicative sentences, but are like them. Moreover he analyzes an indicative sentence, standing by itself and asserted to be true, as containing in effect two parts: an expression signifying a content (*Inhalt*), and an expression signifying [19] asser-

---

[19] I use 'signify' to be ambiguous as between 'express', 'denote', and some other kind of meaning that Frege does not analyze.

tion (*Behauptung*) of this content. Correspondingly, a judgment consists of an act of asserting a content. The content consists in turn of a proposition and a truth-value (*Grundgesetze* 1. X a). In his own symbolic language, he takes care (*Grundgesetze* 1.9) to make every asserted sentence consist of two parts: an assertion sign, and an expression expressing a proposition and denoting a truth-value. When Frege speaks of the sense of an indicative sentence, he must mean the sense of an unasserted sentence; otherwise the sense of an indicative sentence could not be simply a proposition, but would have to also involve the sense of the assertion sign (if it has a sense — see fn. 19). The innovation of *Gedanke* and *Verneinung* is (e.g. *Verneinung* 145a) to identify the sense of a question [20] with the sense of its indicative counterpart; e.g. of 'Is 2 the only even prime number?' with that of '2 is the only even prime number'. Presumably, then — Frege does not quite crystallize his doctrine — interrogative and imperative sentences differ from indicatives only in virtually containing an interrogation-sign or an imperation-sign in place of the assertion-sign.[21] If this is Frege's analysis, it is substantially similar to such present-day analyses of verbal moods as Beardsley's (*Imperative*), Lewis's (*Analysis*), etc.

§20. *Fundamental similarity of all objects.* To conclude this exposition, we return to our starting-point: the distinction between functions and objects. There is evidence that Frege regards all objects as being more like each other than like any function; namely, a requirement that he imposes on every properly constructed language. The requirement is (*Peano* 374a*16-5*a) that if a certain function admits some object as its argument, (i.e. has a value for that argument), then it must admit every object as an argument.[22] The requirement departs from mathematical practice, where it is quite usual to limit

---

[20] Frege only deals with questions that can be answered 'yes' or 'no', not with so-called complement-questions like 'What time is it?', that contain interrogative pronouns.

[21] It is this definitive, through very late doctrine, that is expounded in §18.

[22] And must not admit functions as arguments.

the arguments of such a function as ξ^2 to numbers. Frege requires that if ξ^2 takes some object, e.g. the number 3, as an argument — for which it has the value 9 — , then any object must be a fit argument for it. Frege's example is the sun; letting 'SUN' denote the sun, then 'SUN^2' must also denote, and hence, of course, have a sense. That is, ξ^2 must have a value for the argument SUN. What this value shall be, is unimportant; we can pick arbitrarily on any object and assign that as its value.

This requirement is a formation-rule of any properly constructed language, according to Frege.[23] And he is careful to make all the functions that he himself introduces conform to it. It may seem needlessly and complicatingly general when he (*Grundgesetze* 1.9 §5) introduces ————ξ, a function with one argument whose value is the True when the argument is the True, and the False when the argument is anything other

---

[23] There are two senses of 'meaningless' in which Frege would describe certain expressions as meaningless: (i) Any expression E is meaningless$_1$ if it violates the grammatical rules (formation-rules) of the language to which it belongs, otherwise meaningful$_1$; (2) A sentence S which is meaningful$_1$, and which has a sense, is meaningless$_2$ if it lacks a denotation, i.e. if it is neither true nor false; otherwise it is meaningful$_2$. Frege virtually assumes that any expression of any language that is meaningful$_1$ has a sense. And he requires of any properly constructed language (PCL) that every expression in it which has a sense have a denotation if its nature permits it to do so; in other words, that every eligible expression have a denotation. Furthermore, it is clear, though not pointed out by Frege, that every meaningful$_1$ sentence in any PCL is meaningful$_2$; this could be shown by canvassing the possible varieties of meaningful$_1$ sentences in any PCL, bearing in mind Assumption (Ib) and the requirement that every eligible expression have a denotation. And the converse, that every meaningless$_1$ sentence is meaningless$_2$, is obvious.

Consequently, Carnap's historical statement (*Syntax* 138b) that "It was Russell who first introduced the triple classification into true, false, and meaningful expressions" had better be amplified so as not to be misleading. Frege introduced the trichotomy both in precept (though not so forcefully as Russell) and in practice; only (i) he did not exploit its philosophical possibilities as Russell and his successors did, and (ii) he did not impose *sufficiently strict* formation-rules to render meaningless$_1$ the sentences that give rise to the logical antinomies.

than the True;[24] it seems odd to have a function such that
————2 = 4 is the False but also such that ————2 is the
False; but on Frege's view it is perfectly rational, because
both 2 = 4 and 2 are objects.

§21. *Variables.* A last remark about Frege's ontology. In
analyzing the notions of function, argument, range, and value,
one must naturally also analyze the notion of variable.
Frege's analysis disproves the charge (cf. Part III, §23) that
his abstract entities are inferred by mechanically projecting
the structure of language onto the world. Frege does indeed
hold that function-expressions denote functions, argument-
expressions denote objects, and value-expressions denote objects; but he draws the line at variables. Variables, he says,
must be construed as expressions, not as denotations. Vari-
able-expressions do not, contrary to the prevailing account
of them, denote variable entities. They do not denote anything at all.[25] And his reason for this view (*Was* 659b6) is an
ontological principle: every entity is determinate.

III. *Strangeness of Frege's Ontology*

§22. *Strangeness recognized by Frege.* Most people acquainted with Frege's ontology feel that it goes against the
grain. Frege is perfectly well acquainted with the feeling;
concerning his entire system he remarks (*Grundgesetze*
1.XIa), "I myself can in some measure estimate the resistance

---

[24] Had Frege introduced 'the True' (which let us abbreviate 'T') into
his formal system, he could have defined the function ————ξ as ξ = T.
The fact that the former function is taken as primitive shows that the
only context in which Frege would use 'T' in his formal system is in
identity-statements. And he has no use for 'the False' in his formal
system at all. The expression 'the False' could not be defined in Frege's
system either in terms of '————ξ' or in terms of 'T', because of peculiarities in his way of introducing negation. It is easy in his formal system
to build expressions denoting the False, either in terms of 'T' or of
'————ξ', but none of them would have the same *sense* as 'the False'.

[25] The details of Frege's account do not concern us here, but he
analyzes quantification in terms of second-level functions rather than
of objects. Cf. fn. 11.

that my innovations will encounter, because I too had to overcome similar resistance in me in order to make them. For it is not haphazardly and out of a quest for novelty, but under constraint from the very subject that I have arrived at them." He is particularly aware (*Sinn* 34ᵃ, *Grundgesetze* 1.Xa *9-8*, *Peano* 368c) that his assumption of truth-values, and his view that all true sentences denote the same entity, seems odd. And speaking of his definitions, he says (*Grundlagen* XIa), "I advise those who would regard my definitions, say, as unnatural, to reflect that the question here is not whether they are natural but whether they get at the heart of the matter and are logically unobjectionable."

So Frege claims that more compelling advantages of his system outweigh its strangeness. It will be clarifying if, before investigating this claim in Parts IV and V, we analyze as penetratingly as we can the features causing the appearance of strangeness.

§23. Parsimony. Many philosophers today would spontaneously object on the ground of parsimony. Frege sets up his ontology to make logic and mathematics intelligible; these philosophers would maintain that he has posited more entities than is necessary for that purpose. (Of course, Frege has the ready answer that he has been at pains *not* to infer any superfluous entities; but see §28.) A variant of this criticism is the objection that all Frege's beings are mere projections of language, "phantoms due to the refractive power of the linguistic medium" (Ogden and Richards, *Meaning* 96b).

But the maxim of parsimony is formal; it counsels elimination of superfluous entities, but indicates no way of determining which entities are superfluous. And on the other hand, Frege himself accepts a version of the maxim (see §28), as *Verneinung* 149-50 explicitly states. Consequently the issue between him and his objectors cannot be described as the issue of whether or not to conform to the maxim, but must rather be analyzed as the issue of whether or not certain particular assertions, asserting the existence of certain entities, *do* conform to the maxim.

Now it is generally agreed that no existence-statement based solely upon observation of the datum is to be ruled out by Ockham's Razor; so that conceivably one issue between Frege and opposing ontologists would be, whether the abstract entities whose existence he asserts are directly given or not. I suppose Frege would say that some of them, finite numbers for instance and at least some propositions, are directly given, but that the existence of others, e.g. truth-values, is inferred.

§24. *Some other objections.* I suspect that the basic commonsensical objection to Frege's ontological system, the inarticulate but firm objection that we feel whether or not we are in a position to defend it, is the conviction that there just *aren't* all these odd, queer, obscure entities that Frege invents. A similar objection might be urged by various realistic positions, that are willing to grant some abstract entities but would balk at truth-values, function-correlates, and so on.

Now all of the objections so far mentioned consist of denying some of Frege's existence-statements; e.g. they assert 'there are no abstract entities' or 'there are no truth-values' or 'there is no denotation of the negation-sign'. To that extent the strangeness of Frege's system consists in making such and such existence-assertions, and objections consist in denying these assertions.[26] But not all objections can be cast in this form; not the nominalistic objection, for example. Frege says that proper names, descriptive phrases, numerals and so on denote; and he also says that true and false sentences denote. Now one might in the first place deny that there is any such denotation-relation comprehending among its referents both numerals and sentences, and *this* denial would be the denial of an existence-statement. But a nominalist could not use this way of putting his objection, because it would not cut sufficiently deep. He would have sweepingly denied all relations anyway, even, for instance, a denotation-relation between numerals and numbers. To express in his own terms the objection I am imagining, the nominalist would have to say

---

[26] Dialectical difficulties about such denials have recently been discussed by Quine *On what.*

something like this: It is incorrect, or misleading, or not ultimately satisfactory, to build a language in which one and the same verb is used to fill the blank in (i) 'Sentences——truth-values' and (ii) 'Numerals——numbers', if both the resulting statements are to be asserted as true.

IV. Rationale of Frege's Ontology

§25. *Frege's method of argumentation.* Frege doesn't merely present his system; he argues it. In the following exposition it will be possible to go somewhat further than he does in formulating, assembling, and systematizing his basic arguments.

His basic method of argumentation is akin to the Kantian: taking certain beliefs for granted, he inquires into the conditions of their possibility, i.e. into their presuppositions. What he takes for granted is a commonsensical realism: a belief (a) that there is an objective reality which is independent of but accessible to human knowledge; (b) that though human error is abundant, we do in fact already possess much genuine knowledge of this reality, including the standard parts of mathematics; (c) that all knowledge is a cognition of timeless, objective truths; and (d) that not only the natural sciences but logic and mathematics have objective truths as their subject-matter.

Frege's method of inferring presuppositions, rather like the scientific method of verifying a hypothesis,[27] consists of two parts: (1) devising a view that accounts for the assumed beliefs; (2) showing that no other possible view accounts for them. In science it is never possible to do the second task conclusively, because there is no effective way of reviewing all possible theories. In Part V we shall see that Frege's execution of the second task must be similarly inconclusive, for similar reasons. Here in Part IV our concern is with the first task. I will first briefly state the rationale of Frege's

---

[27] In *Sinn*, the comparison is explicit; e.g. 35b end.

entire ontological system, and then discuss some of the details at greater length.

§26. *The overall picture.* In fixing the basic concepts of his system, Frege uses the method of mathematical generalization (cf. §9). Since he aims to deal with the notions of mathematics, he would in any case have to give an account of the notions of function, argument, and value. His thought runs along these lines:

(A) Frege's realism (which involves a rejection both of psychologistic and of formalistic theories of mathematics) leads him to make a sharp distinction between expressions and what they denote.[28] Applying this distinction to mathematical notions, he infers that function-expressions denote functions, just as argument-expressions denote arguments. Mathematically generalizing the notions of function (realistically interpreted), argument, value, and range — this latter notion itself generalized from the notion of a curve in analytic geometry — he finds that the notion of function can encompass the logical notions of concept and relation, *if* these be thought of as functions whose values are truth-values. The notion of function cannot, however, be generalized to include arguments,[29] values, and ranges, the very grammar of the expressions denoting these showing them to be radically different from functions.

(B) Frege arrives at the notion of truth-values from another direction also. Many mathematical statements are identities; if identity-statements assert identity of denotations, some other kind of meaning besides denotation must be reckoned with. In line with his realism, Frege distinguishes two kinds: a subjective kind (idea) and an objective kind

---

[28] E.g. *Function* 3; *Grundgesetze* 1.IXb, XIIIb, 4; *Was* 662-3. See further Carnap *Syntax* 156-60 and Quine *Mathematical Logic* 23-6. For a few examples of philosophical errors resulting from failure to draw the distinction clearly, see Quine *Whitehead* and Church *Review C* 302d.

[29] Except, of course, that functions of one level may be arguments of functions of a higher level.

(sense). Now sentences can be regarded as value-expressions, having both sense and denotation like other value-expressions; thus the notions of sense and denotation have been mathematically generalized, and have proved to solve other problems too, such as the analysis of indirect discourse.

(C) The doctrine that sentences have senses as well as denotations finds further corroboration from the realistic analysis of judgment (*Sinn* 34[a], *Grundgesetze* 1.Xa, *Gedanke*) into (a) a human, private, transitory act of judging or asserting and (b) an objective, eternal content judged, which is, or includes, the sense and the denotation of some sentence. This analysis is corroborated in turn by the observation that to assert a content is not the only thing we can do with it; a content may, instead or as well, be questioned, (in special cases) commanded, or (as in antecedent and consequent of a conditional sentence) merely contemplated.

Now a few comments on sundry points in the preceding sketch.

§27. *Psychologism and formalism.* Frege defended his realism by incessant and elaborate polemicizing against psychologism and formalism, which — in his day at least — were its chief rivals in the philosophy of logic and mathematics. Psychologism says that what we are studying in logic and mathematics is ideas in our minds; formalism says that what we really study is the expressions themselves that we employ in the study.

Anti-formalism is the reason for Frege's distinction between expressions and what they denote. Common sense contrasts symbols with what they are about or what they mean; Frege makes the contrast more exact by distinguishing three kinds of meaning — two of them objective, one subjective. The common-sense notion of what a symbol is about amounts, so far as it can be expressed in Frege's terms, to his notion of the denotation of an expression.

So far Frege's notion of sense follows pretty well along commonsensical paths. Now he mathematically generalizes the notions of sense and of denotation; in particular, he inquires whether they may not be applied to sentences as well as to other expressions. After an argument too complicated to expound here,[30] he concludes that all true sentences have the same denotation and all false sentences have the same denotation, which denotations he calls the True and the False, respectively. Sentences that are neither true nor false, such as those of fiction, have no denotation. Thus sentences resemble noun-expressions in that some have a denotation and some do not.

One of the strong recommendations of the sense-denotation distinction to Frege's mind is (*Grundgesetze* 1.Xa19-20) that it offers a ready explanation of indirect discourse. Since the phenomenon of indirect discourse falls under the purview of the semantics of natural languages, not of logic or mathematics, Frege's interest in it suggests that he intends to be outlining a semantical system that will be adequate to the former field as well as to the latter two. But I have no light to throw on either the reasons or the causes that directed Frege's concentrated attention to this particular phenomenon in the first place.

§*28. Parsimony again.* In Part III (§23) I mentioned objections to Frege's system on grounds of parsimony. The notion of parsimony or economy or simplicity is a complicated one, and to date nothing approaching a definitive analysis of it has been published. Nelson Goodman has made a notable contribution in three articles,[31] in which one of the important points is that a system-builder may have to choose between different kinds of simplicity or parsimony that are incompatible with each other. Frege too is confronted with choices of this kind, though without stating the fact and quite possibly without realizing it.

---

[30] Church *Review C* gives a "reproduction in more exact form" of the argument (*Review C* 301b). Cf. §18.

[31] *Simplicity, Logical Simplicity,* and *Improvement.* See Wells *Facts* for my viewpoint on the philosophical import of simplicity.

The kind of parsimony Frege strives for is not parsimony of entities, nor even of kinds of entities, but parsimony of a kind that can be effected by mathematical generalization. Thus, he has no hesitation about inferring an infinity of senses of expressions; [32] but, once having concluded the necessity of distinguishing sense from denotation, he tries to apply the distinction not only to 'terms' but also to sentences. Again, a certain economy [33] would be effected by treating functions extensionally; i.e. by assuming that if ϕ and ξ have the same range, $\phi = \xi$; but apparently he has no interest in such an economy. (That Frege is careless about laying down identity-conditions in general has been remarked in §8.) Is there not something in common between this indifference and his indifference to brevity or compactness of proofs (*Grundgesetze* 1.VIIa)? Similarly, although Frege thinks of definitions as abbreviations (*Grundgesetze* 1.VIb end), he does not seem especially eager to minimize the number of primitive signs in his system. (Cf. *Peano* 366a-7 on policies in definition.) On the other hand, one particular economy — reduction of numerical equality to identity — he treasures very highly (*Grundgesetze* 1.IXb). Yet another instance of Frege's parsimony is found in his discussion (*Verneinung*) of negation; he analyzes judging (*das Urteilen*) as the act of asserting a content (*Behauptung eines Inhalts*), and declines to posit a distinct, unanalyzable act of denying a content (*Verneinung eines Inhalts*) on the ground that in such a case we can equally well consider that the negation of the denied content is being asserted. This is an economy because negation of contents must be admitted even when there is no judging — for example, in the antecedent or consequent of a conditional sentence.

---

[32] Nor would he demur at the infinite series of senses mentioned in fn. 16.

[33] Which however cannot be described as a reduction in the number of entities of a certain kind, in case the number both before and after reduction is infinity, and infinity of the same order.

V. The Fallacy in Frege's Argument

§29. *Adequacy and exclusive adequacy.* In §5 I mentioned a certain important fallacy in Frege's defense of his system. It is one thing to show that a system is adequate, another to demonstrate that it is exclusively adequate. For the latter demonstration involves showing that no other possible system (dealing with the same subject-matter) is adequate. Yet in *Grundgesetze* Frege seems to think that he has accomplished both demonstrations.

Now we know today that not even adequacy can be claimed for the system; that is, for his formal and informal logical-semantical-ontological system taken as a whole. (1) Its most conspicuous inadequacy is the fact pointed out by Russell in 1901, in a letter to Frege, viz. that it leads to logical antinomies; an inadequacy which Frege unsuccessfully [34] tries to surmount in *Grundgesetze* 2.253-65. But this inadequacy does not vitiate such basic conceptions as function, sense, truth-value, etc.; and Church (*Formulation*) sketches a rehabilitated version of Frege's system upon which a 'simple theory of types' is imposed. There are two other sorts of inadequacy that might be pressed. (2) The system is certainly incomplete; for instance, as we have seen (fn. 8), Frege does not lay down exhaustive conditions under which two expressions have the same sense, nor exhaustive conditions under which two function-expressions denote the same function. Frege might fairly describe inadequacies of this sort as matters of detail. (3) Basic philosophical objections to it might be raised. Some of these were mentioned in Part III. One might argue against Frege's 'Platonism' or extreme realism, for example.

However, the topic of the present Part V is not the adequacy of Frege's system but its exclusive adequacy. Of the two demonstrations that Frege seems to think he has accomplished, it is the second that will here be our concern. That

---

[34] Sobocinski *Antinomie* discusses Frege's attempt and Lesniewski's proof that it is unsuccessful. See Frege *Notes* 251 for philosophical discussion.

Frege has not demonstrated the exclusive adequacy of his system can be shown in two ways, negatively and positively; negatively by showing that his arguments are inconclusive, and positively by producing an alternative but equally adequate system. The negative approach is used in §30; in §31 a very small and fragmentary contribution of the positive or constructive variety is presented.

§*30. Frege's arguments for exclusive adequacy.* It is worthy of note that Frege devotes far more space to establishing the adequacy of his system than to establishing its exclusive adequacy. In behalf of the latter he offers three kinds of arguments: he (1) makes bare assertions of his claims, (2) criticizes sundry previously proposed views, and (3) challenges others to produce a better system.

Of (1), one can only remark (a) that Frege indulges in it quite often, and (b) that it has very little weight. It would be a mistake to set it aside as having no weight at all; it may be thought of as informing us that Frege, a man to whose meticulousness and subtlety we can testify on other grounds, is unable to envisage any system superior to the one with which he presents us.

Number (2) is the technique that occupies the most space in Frege's writings. *Grundlagen* is largely given over to it, as also the Foreword to volume 1 and Part III.1 of volume 2 of *Grundgesetze*,[35] as well as most of his shorter writings. If thought of as an inductive method, it is excellent, and Frege handles it brilliantly; but if thought of as apodictic, it must fail unless it is somehow demonstrated that the theories refuted are all the possible alternatives to the theory being defended. Frege does not essay any such demonstration; he merely reviews the existing theories. And that is why he employs (3).

As for technique (3), he has shown his system to be the best of those in existence at the time of his writing, and the

---

[35] §§55-164. §§86-137 are translated by Black *Formalists.* Cf. Linke *Frege.*

burden of proof properly passes to anyone who would maintain that a still better one can be worked out. There is of course a certain presumption that it will not be easy to devise a better one. "It is radically improbable," he says (*Grundgesetze* 1.XXVI, speaking of Part II of that treatise), "that such a structure could be erected on an uncertain, defective basis. Indeed, whoever has different persuasions can try to erect a similar structure on them, and he will realize, I believe, that it cannot be done, or at least not so well. And I could acknowledge that I had been refuted only if someone showed concretely that a better, more tenable structure could be erected on different fundamental persuasions, or if some one showed me that my axioms led to obviously false theorems. But that no one will succeed in doing." (Russell disconfirmed this last prediction in 1901; cf. §29.)

Here Frege imposes unreasonably strong conditions on a refutation. Would it not be sufficient to produce an alternative system that is not 'better and more tenable' but merely *as* good and *as* tenable? And second, Frege apparently regards as insufficient any merely destructive criticism of his logical, semantical, and ontological foundations,[36] although as we have seen above in number (2), it is a kind of argument that he himself uses most liberally.

§*31. Sketch of a positive refutation.* To intimate that systems alternative to Frege's can be developed, I will very briefly sketch a tiny fragment of one such system. The fragment is obtained by elaborating on a passing remark of Quine's. In *Mathematical Logic* 32c Quine concludes that "it . . . seems well to adhere to the common-sense view that statements are not names at all," i.e. that sentences do not denote anything.

So Frege says that every sentence that is either true or false denotes a truth-value, whereas Quine favors the view

---

[36] Such as Russell's in *Principles* Appendix A, *On denoting,* and *Knowledge* 225 et seq. Frege is defended by Jones *Objections,* and by Church *Sense* and *Review C* 302d.

that no sentence denotes anything at all. This sounds like a flat disagreement, a mutual contradiction. Yet it need not be so. Let us see whether we can take the view that both Frege and Quine are right. This could be, if they are talking about different things. (I do not commit myself as to whether this is the *sole* condition under which both could be right.) Developing this supposition, let us call the denotation that Frege is talking about F-denotation, and the denotation that Quine is talking about Q-denotation. Then Frege says that every true or false sentence F-denotes a truth-value, and Quine says that no true or false sentence Q-denotes anything. So construed, the appearance of contradiction vanishes. Such a supposition does not definitively settle the question, for various objections might be raised against it. But at least one prima facie objection may be dismissed. Frege, it might be argued, would want to maintain not only that true sentences F-denote, but also that they Q-denote truth-values; while from the other side someone might contend that not only do sentences not Q-denote anything, they do not F-denote anything either. The reply to this argument is that since it is part of the very nature of Q-denotation that sentences do not belong to its domain of referents, it would be a self-contradiction to affirm that sentences Q-denote truth-values; and since it is included in the definition of F-denotation that, among the ordered couples that it relates there are couples $[x;y]$ such that x is a sentence and y is a truth-value, it would equally be a self-contradiction to say that no true or false sentence F-denotes anything. Thus, if those who speak in terms of F-denotation and those who talk of Q-denotation want to express their disagreement with each other, they must do so in some other way.

From this short illustration it may perhaps be discerned how a system very different from Frege's could be erected, namely the system of Quine's *Mathematical Logic*.[37] And with

---

[37] Logical antinomies have turned up in this system too, and have been corrected in subsequent reprintings; but they appear to have nothing to do with Frege's and Quine's diverse conceptions of denotation.

this insight the vista of an alluring line of inquiry opens up. Could it be that many of the apparent disagreements in philosophy and elsewhere are illusory, and can be dispelled, like the one between Frege and Quine, by proper analysis? Could they be transformed from disagreements into simple diversities? The thought is an ancient one, but it has certainly not yet been brought to its apotheosis. Could it be that Frege is right in what he affirms, wrong in what he denies; right in holding that we *may* regard sentences as denoting truth-values, wrong in holding that we *must* do so? If so, it may well turn out that his error, so far from being egregious (§5), will be one of the most common errors in philosophy.

BIBLIOGRAPHY

Beardsley, Elizabeth L. [*Imperative*] "Imperative sentences in relation to indicatives," *Philosophical Review* 53.175-85 (1944).

Black, Max [*Formalists*] "Frege against the formalists," *Philosophical Review* 59.77-93, 202-20, 332-45 (1950).

Carnap, Rudolf [*Syntax*] *The Logical Syntax of Language* (1937).

——— [*Meaning*] *Meaning and Necessity* (1947).

Church, Alonzo [*Anticipation*] "Schröder's anticipation of the simple theory of types," preprinted from *Journal of Unified Science* 9.149-52 (1939).

——— [*Sense*] "On sense and denotation," *Journal of Symbolic Logic* 7.47 (1942).

——— [*Review C*] Review of Carnap's *Introduction to Semantics*, *Philosophical Review* 52.298-304 (1943).

——— [*Review Q*] Review of Quine's "Notes on existence and necessity," *Journal of Symbolic Logic* 8.45-7 (1943).

——— [*Review S*] Review of Smart's "Frege's logic," *Journal of Symbolic Logic* 10.101-3 (1945).

——— [*Formulation*] "A formulation of the logic of sense and denotation," *Journal of Symbolic Logic* 11.31 (1946).

——— [Review WB] Review of papers by M. G. White and M. Black, *Journal of Symbolic Logic* 11.132-3 (1946).

——— [*Introduction*] *Introduction to Mathematical Logic*. Unpublished, dated October 1948 with corrections to November 1949; all references are to the first chapter of this treatise, entitled "Introduction." May be obtained from Fine Library, Princeton University, directly or by interlibrary loan.

——— [*Logic*] "A formulation of the logic of sense and denotation,"

Structure, Method and Meaning (edited by H. M. Kallen, P. Henle, S. K. Langer) (1951).

Frege, Gottlob [*Grundlagen*] *Die Grundlagen der Arithmetik* (1884).

—— [*Function*] *Function und Begriff* (1891).

—— [*Begriff*] "Begriff und Gegenstand," *Vierteljahrsschrift für wissenschaftliche Philosophie* 16.192-205 (1892).

—— [*Sinn*] "Ueber Sinn und Bedeutung," *Zeitschrift für Philosophie und philosophische Kritik* (N.F.) 100.25-50 (1892).

—— [*Grundgesetze*] *Grundgesetze der Arithmetik* 1 (1893), 2 (1903).

—— [*Peano*] "Ueber die Begrisschrift des Herrn Peano und meine eigene," *Berichte über die Verhandlungen der königlich sächsischen Gesellschaft der Wissenschaften zu Leipzig,* Mathematisch-physische Classe, 48.361-78 (1896).

—— [*Was*] "Was ist eine Funktion?," *Festschrift Ludwig Boltzmann gewidmet* 656-66 (1904).

—— [*Notes*] Notes written in 1910 to Philip E.B. Jourdain, "The development of the theories of mathematical logic and the principles of mathematics," *Quarterly Journal of Pure and Applied Mathematics* 43.219-314 (1912). The notes are printed as footnotes to the section on Frege, pp. 237-69.

—— [*Gedanke*] "Der Gedanke," *Beiträge zur Philosophie des deutschen Idealismus* 1.58-77 (1918).

—— [*Verneinung*] "Die Verneinung," *Beiträge zur Philosophie des deutschen Idealismus* 1.143-57 (1919).

Geach, P. T. [*Subject*] "Subject and predicate," *Mind* 59.461-82 (1950).

Goodman, Nelson [*Simplicity*] "On the simplicity of ideas," *Journal of Symbolic Logic* 8.107-21 (1943).

—— [*Logical simplicity*] "The logical simplicity of predicates," *Journal of Symbolic Logic* 14.32-41 (1949).

—— [*Likeness*] "On likeness of meaning," *Analysis* 10.1-7 (1949).

—— [*Improvement*] "An improvement in the theory of simplicity," *Journal of Symbolic Logic* 14.228-9 (1950).

Jones, E. E. Constance [*Objections*] "Mr. Russell's objections to Frege's analysis of propositions," *Mind* 19.379-86 (1910).

Lewis, C. I. [*Analysis*] *An Analysis of Knowledge and Valuation* (1947).

Linke, Paul F. [*Frege*] "Gottlob Frege als Philosoph," *Zeitschrift für philosophische Forschung* 1.75-99 (1946-7).

Ogden, C. K., and I. A. Richards [*Meaning*] *The Meaning of Meaning* (fifth edition, 1938).

Quine, Willard V. [*Mathematical Logic*] *Mathematical Logic* (1940).

—— [*Whitehead*] "Whitehead and the rise of modern logic," *The Philosophy of Alfred North Whitehead* (ed. P. A. Schilpp) 127-63 (1941).

—— [*On what*] "On what there is," *Review of Metaphysics* 2.21-38 (1948).

Russell, Bertrand [*Principles*] *Principles of Mathematics* (1903; second edition 1938).

—— [*On denoting*] "On denoting," *Mind* 14.479-93 (1905).

—— [*PM*] *Principia Mathematica*, by A. N. Whitehead and B. Russell. The reference is to the second edition (1925) of volume 1; the new matter in the second edition is by Russell.

—— [*Knowledge*] "Knowledge by acquaintance and knowledge by description," *Mysticism and Logic* 209-32 (1918).

Sobocinski, Boleslaw [*Antinomie*] "L'analyse de l'antinomie russellienne par Lesniewski," *Methodos* 1.94-107, 220-8, 308-16 (1949).

Wells, Rulon S. [*Facts*] "The existence of facts," *Review of Metaphysics* 3.1-20 (1949).

Wienpahl, Paul D. [*Sinn*] "Frege's *Sinn und Bedeutung*," *Mind* 59.483-94 (1950).

2

Frege's Hidden Nominalism[*]

GUSTAV BERGMANN

Some philosophical pieces are like symphonies, others like quartets. This one is merely an ontological theme with variations. After I have introduced the theme, it will be seen that *Exemplification versus Mapping* is a very good name for it. The phrase does not signify, though, except to one already familiar with the theme. That is why I did not choose it as a title. All but the last of the variations are comments on Frege's ontology, though as such they are highly selective.[1] This is one reason for the title I chose. The other is that I hope to draw expository advantage from its shock value.

I

In ontological discourse two clusters of very ordinary words are used philosophically. First of all, therefore, I shall state how I propose to handle these words. One cluster contains 'thing', 'object', 'entity', 'existent'. When I do not wish to

---

Reprinted with the kind permission of the author and the editor from *The Philosophical Review*, LXVII (1958), 437-459.

* I have profited from discussions with Mr. Reinhardt Grossmann, who will elaborate some of the points in this paper as well as some related ones in his doctoral dissertation.

[1] An excellent detailed exposition may be found in R. Wells, "Frege's Ontology," *Rev. Metaphys.*, IV (1957), 537-573. References to this study are by page number, preceded by the letter *W*.

indicate anybody's ontological commitment, I use *entity*. When I wish to speak of what philosophers, speaking philosophically, assert to "exist," I use *existent*. Frege uses both 'object' and 'function' philosophically; and he holds, either explicitly, or very nearly so, that every entity (not, existent!) is either an object or a function.[2] The other cluster contains 'naming', 'denoting', 'designating', 'referring'. Nor are the philosophical uses of the two clusters independent. Some philosophers, for instance, maintain that an existent is what is or could be named (denoted, designated) by a word or expression. When I wish to speak without indicating ontological commitment, I avoid all these verbs and borrow instead Frege's *standing for*. If they followed this use, the philosophers just mentioned could say that a name is a word or expression which stands for an existent.

Consider 'This is green'. On one occasion, 'this' may stand for an apple; 'green', for its color. Some hold that, on another occasion, the two words could stand for what they call a sensum and one of its qualities, respectively. Others disagree. The difference makes no difference for my purpose. So I shall entirely ignore it in calling the sort of thing 'this' and 'green' stand for, on all occasions, an *individual* and a *character*, respectively. Also, I shall in this essay use the two words without ontological commitment even though, in the case of 'individual', that is admittedly unusual. For Frege, individuals are one kind of object; characters, one kind of function. But there are in his world still other kinds of objects and of functions.

Some ontologists, including Russell (and myself) though not Frege, make much of a distinction between simple and complex characters. For what I am about it is irrelevant, so I shall disregard it. There is also the distinction between types

---

[2] In rendering Frege's terms I follow the well-known *Translations from the Philosophical Writings of Gottlob Frege* by M. Black and P. Geach (Oxford, 1952). References to this volume are by page number, preceded by the letter *F*.

of characters and functions. Both Frege and Russell pay attention to it. But again, with one glancing exception, it is irrelevant for what I am about, so I shall virtually ignore it. This shows how selective I shall be in my remarks about Frege.

Even in ontological discourse the terms *realism* and *nominalism* are used in two ways; once strictly, once broadly. The ontologist's first business is to list all kinds of existents (not, all existents). If he discerns many kinds, perhaps too many, one calls him a realist. If he lists but few, perhaps too few, one calls him a nominalist. This is the broad use. In the strict sense, an ontologist is a realist if he counts characters, or at least some characters (for example, simple ones), as a kind of existent. A nominalist in the strict sense holds, conversely, that no characters are existents. In this essay, unless there be a qualification to the contrary, both terms are always used strictly.

Two things about Frege are beyond reasonable doubt. Had he used 'existent' as I do (as far as I know he did not use it at all), he would have agreed that everything he calls an object is an existent. This is the first thing. Of objects there are in his world many kinds. Nor are the distinctions among them "ordinary," like that between cats and dogs. They are even more sweeping than that between physical and phenomenal objects, which surely is sweeping enough and, according to some, anything but ordinary. His distinctions are so sweeping indeed that, if the word is to have any meaning at all, one cannot but call them ontological. This is the second thing beyond reasonable doubt. Specifically, Frege distinguishes (at least) the following (ontological) kinds (of objects): individuals, numbers, truth values, value ranges (classes of objects), senses, propositions (thoughts), concept correlates.[3] Many philosophers think that with the sole exception of individuals all these kinds are odd. Or, to say the same thing

---

[3] As far as I know, the term is Wells's.

differently, they refuse to consider the odd kinds of entities as existents. Still differently, these philosophers (including myself) reject Frege's exaggerated realism (broad sense). It is not my purpose to rehearse their arguments, or to improve on them, or to invent new ones; even though I shall permit myself, *en passant*, to call attention to two oddities about truth values. As far as Frege is concerned, my purpose is rather to give some reasons for my belief that, for all his exuberant realism in the broad sense, he was in the strict sense at least implicitly a nominalist. My primary concern, though, is neither biographical nor textual. What I shall really argue, therefore, is that the structure of Frege's ontology though not, as will transpire, of Church's emendation of it,[4] is nominalistic.

Everything said so far is merely preliminary. I shall proceed as follows. In the next section the theme is introduced and used to exhibit what I take to be the root of Frege's nominalism. In the third section I shall show that in one case this very nominalism forces upon Frege that multiplication of entities (or rather of existents) which is so characteristic of his ontology. In the fourth section I shall show that what is, broadly speaking, the most serious as well as the most obvious intrinsic flaw of the system is but another consequence of its author's hidden nominalism. I say intrinsic because this flaw is of course not that exuberant realism (broad sense) which, as I said, I shall not question except once and incidentally. In the last section I shall vary my theme, very briefly and very sketchily, by sounding it as a background for the siren songs of a more recent nominalism.

II

Where one arrives depends in part on where he starts. A philosopher's starting point depends in part on his basic paradigm. Frege's is very different from the realist's. My theme builds on this difference or, rather, contrast. I present

---

[4] A. Church, *Introduction to Mathematical Logic* (Princeton, 1957).

first the realist, because it helps to bring out the contrast more forcefully. Some realists, including myself, propose an explication of the philosophical use of 'exist' upon which all individuals and (some of) their characters but no higher characters are existents.[5] The realist I present is of this sort. My case does not depend on the limitation. But again, it helps to bring out the theme more clearly by freeing it from some bywork that otherwise would have to be introduced.

The realist starts from individuals and their characters. That is, he starts from entities Frege calls objects (and from their characters), though not from those objects which with Frege's critics I called odd. 'Peter is blond' may thus serve as the realist's paradigm. What claims does it suggest to him? What do and what don't these claims imply? What reasons can he give for them? I shall take up the three questions in this order.

First. 'Peter' and 'blond' both stand for existents. Generally, both individuals and characters are existents. This is one major claim. Many realists, including myself, also hold that every existent is either an individual or a character; but for the purpose at hand that does not matter. What 'Peter is blond' stands for comes about if two existents, one of each kind, enter into a certain "relation," or, as I would rather say, nexus. This nexus the realist calls *exemplification.* Obviously it is a very fundamental feature of his world. This is another major claim. To see that it is not independent of the first, notice that to say of something that it does or may enter into a nexus is to presuppose that it exists. Notice also that when I spoke of a sentence "standing for" something, I quite deliberately paid with clumsiness for the agreed-upon neutrality of the phrase.

Second. (a) An individual may or may not exemplify a character. To say that a character exemplifies an individual is nonsense. The very nexus between the two kinds is thus

---

[5] See "Elementarism," *J. Phil. and Phen. Res.*, XVIII (1957), 107-114.

asymmetrical. This alone shows that individuals and characters are not alike *in all respects* which concern the ontologist. Nor do the realist's claims imply that they are. Obviously not, I should say. For, if they were, what point would there be in distinguishing between them? (b) In the paradigm, the copula or, as I prefer to say, the predicative 'is' stands for exemplification. In a much larger number of cases, to say the least, the verbal image of this nexus between things is predication, that is, the grammatical relation between subject and predicate. That follows from the realist's claims.

Third. An articulate realist has of course many reasons for the position he takes. Fortunately they do not all matter for my purpose. What matters is that every time he discovers *some respect* in which individuals and characters are alike, he has discovered *a* reason. I shall state two such reasons, the two which I think carry most weight. (a) Just as we are never presented with an individual that is not qualitied, that is, does not exemplify a character, so we are never presented with a character that is not exemplified by some individual with which we are also presented. Notice that I speak of entities being presented to us, that is, as one says, epistemologically. Had I not promised to keep out the distinction between simple and complex characters and had I limited myself to the former, I could have spoken ontologically: Just as there is no individual that is not qualitied, so there is no character that is not exemplified. This is one fundamental likeness. (b) Consider the three entities that 'Peter', 'blond', and 'Peter is blond' stand for. The differences among them are ontologically significant. With that Frege agrees. For, if he did not, he would not, as an ontologist, either distinguish concepts from objects or set aside truth values as a kind of object. The realist says the same thing differently. Neither an individual nor a character is the kind of entity (notice the noncommittal word!) a sentence stands for. This is a second likeness. (b') The reader is assumed to be familiar with Frege's distinction between saturated and unsaturated expressions. 'Blond' or, as he would really have to say, 'is blond', is unsaturated. 'Peter' is saturated. (So is, very importantly, 'Peter is blond'; but that does not yet enter into my argument.) Primarily at least, the dichotomy is between expressions, not between entities. If one wants to apply it to entities, one must specify what in this case the two terms are to mean. For instance, one may propose "Individuals and characters are equally unsaturated" as an alternative way of stating the second fundamental likeness. An unsophisticated realist may object to this on the ground that, since individuals and characters are both existents, they really are both equally saturated. We know that he merely proposes another meaning for one(!) of the two terms as applied to entities. But his proposal has the merit of showing not only that this application serves no purpose but also the dangers that beset it.[6]

The realist's gambit has a further consequence, which gives rise to an objection, which in turn leads to a clarification. It will pay later if in introducing this matter I change the paradigm to 'Peter is a boy'. The objector points out that one who takes the predicative 'is' to stand for exemplification ought to admit that the paradigm and the sentence 'Peter exemplifies *the* character of being a boy' stand for one and the same entity. After a fashion, the realist does admit that. He even admits it for the sentence 'The individual (object) Peter exemplifies the character (concept) of being a boy'; and, if he used the two words in parentheses, he would also admit it for the further variations they make possible. Now the objector taunts the realist with a Bradleyan regress. It seems, he says, that in order to grasp what exemplification is, he must first grasp what it means for the (relational) character of being exemplified to be exemplified. The realist answers as follows. Exemplification is a very peculiar character. (That is why I called it a nexus and only once, in quotation marks, a relation.) Its peculiarity is the same as that of such "charac-

---

[6] See "Propositional Functions," *Analysis*, XVII (1956), 43-48.

ters" as being an individual or a character. To be an individual, for instance, is not to be of an "ordinary" kind, as is being a cat or a dog, but to be the sort of entity expressions of a certain grammatical kind stand for. The expressions for these peculiar kinds are therefore all expendable and the several alternatives for the paradigm need not be considered unless one speaks in a language containing them about another language and what its expressions stand for. I need not on this occasion endorse this answer. Nor would I on any occasion endorse it in this crude form. (That is why I said the realist admits what I made him admit "after a fashion.") I merely mention this answer because, being familiar and thus permitting me to communicate quickly about what does not matter for what I am about, it helps me to prepare the ground for what does. So much for the realist.

Frege starts from numbers and their functions. 'x^2' may thus serve as his paradigm. That numbers are objects and therefore existents he takes for granted. Questionable as that is, I need not question it. My concern is with functions, mathematical and otherwise. The current mathematical name for the crucial idea is *mapping*. The square function, for instance, maps each number onto another, namely its square. Generally, given two classes of entities which may but need not coincide or overlap, a function is a mapping rule, mapping each member of one of the two classes upon one (and, in the paradigmatic case, only one) member of the other. Let me now for a moment speak as a poet might, using some very loaded words very freely. A rule is a thing totally different from the things to which it applies. A mapping rule, in particular, is a thing much more shadowy, much less real, less palpable, less substantial than the things mapped and mapped upon. This more and these less, rather than the questionable status of numbers, is the heart of the matter. So I shall try to state it, not as a poet but as a philosopher might.

Numbers and their functions differ from each other in the two fundamental respects in which, as we saw, individuals and characters are alike. (a) Just as there is no unexemplified character, so there is no unqualitied individual. But there are of course numbers whether or not they be either arguments or values of functions. (b) The two notions of an individual and of a character, containing or presupposing each other to exactly the same extent, are equally "saturated" or "unsaturated." The notion of a number neither contains nor presupposes that of a function. The latter, however, contains and presupposes that of the two ranges (of numbers). (c) The realist's basic paradigm involves two entities, an individual and a (nonrelational) character. So does a function of one variable, which is Frege's basic paradigm. Or, rather, this is so after an argument has been chosen and the corresponding value computed by means of the function. The need for this additional step, which Frege never tires of emphasizing, increases the "ontological distance" between objects and functions. In Frege's paradigm, moreover, though not in the realist's, the two existents involved, the argument and "its" value, are existents of the same kind. This further increases the impression of disparity between them and the entity which is the function.

Still another circumstance subtly undermines the ontological status of functions. What mathematicians say about the latter often has a *subjective* ring. As they speak, it is they who do the mapping or, as it is often put, establish the correlation. 'Rule' itself, in most of its uses, has the same ring or tinge. This is an occasion for comment. *First.* Dangerous as that subjective ring or tinge may be philosophically, it is of course quite harmless as long as the mathematicians attend to their own business. What makes it even more harmless is that in fact mathematicians are not at all busy establishing or making functions. The vast bulk of their work consists in demonstrating what further properties a function has, assuming that it has some others. *Second.* The realist pulls the fangs of this potentially dangerous talk by construing functional expressions as, in the *Principia* sense, indefinite descriptions,[7] either mathematical or otherwise (the square of x, the father of x.) Descriptions in turn contain expressions standing for characters. And there is nothing subjective about characters (including, of course, relations), least of all in the case of numbers. As Russell put it, in a justly celebrated passage about the order relation, "we can no more 'arrange' the natural numbers than we can the starry heavens."[8] Notice, though, that even if starting from numbers in one sense, one who accepts this clarification starts in another sense from the realist's paradigm. *Third.* I spoke quite deliberately of the subjective tinge or blur from which some of the mathematicians' phrases suffer. My purpose was to give an objector his opportunity. Frege, this objector reminds us, insists over and over again that not only his odd objects but also functions, though they are not objects, are yet *objective.* I know that this is one of his guiding ideas. And I admire the steadfastness with which he wielded it as a weapon against the psychologism rampant in the Germany of his day. One may appreciate all this, as of course I do, and yet consistently hold, as I also do, that while within his system at least Frege succeeded in securing full ontological status for his odd objects, he did not so succeed, even within the system, in the case of functions. That is what I mean by his hidden nominalism. Notice that I call it hidden or implicit. Remember, too, that in this section I merely undertook to state it and to trace it to what I take to be its root, namely, the contrast between exemplification and mapping. The evidence will be found in the next two sections. But I am not quite done with the business at hand.

---

[7] *'The* father of x' is in this sense an indefinite description; '*a* son of Peter' is not, irrespective of how many sons, if any, Peter has. A. J. Ayer's "Individuals," reprinted in his *Philosophical Essays* (New York, 1954), makes one wonder whether he appreciates the distinction. What he calls indefinite descriptions seem to be predicative expressions which *happen* to be true for several subjects.

[8] B. Russell, *Introduction to Mathematical Philosophy,* p. 30 of the 1919 edition. The whole page repays reading in this context.

Nominalism is a thesis about characters. Nothing will be lost if we limit ourselves to nonrelational ones. Frege calls them *concepts*. What, then, does he have to say about concepts? The realist, we just saw, construes functions in terms of characters (concepts). Frege, proceeding in the opposite direction, as it were, construes concepts as a kind of function. In this way, the nominalism I have shown to be implicit in any analysis that starts from mapping is spread to concepts (characters). This is the point. Or, if you please, this is the last bar of my theme.

Frege's execution of the idea is familiar. If 'Peter is blond' is to be construed in analogy to 'the square of 3', then we must look for an object that goes with Peter as the value 9 goes with the argument 3. This object is the truth value of the sentence. This is one motive for Frege's "creation" of the two odd objects T and F. It fits nicely with another. He wants every saturated expression to stand for an object; sentences are saturated expressions; so the truth value of a sentence can serve as the object it stands for. Though Frege had still other motives for the "reification" of T and F, structurally these two are undoubtedly the most important. I should like to suggest that the first, that is, the need to make good the precarious analogy between concepts and functions, goes even deeper than the second.

I turn from things to words. The alleged analogy between characters and functions is not reflected in our language. If it were, we would have to say 'blond *of* Peter', just as we say '*the* square *of* 3', and not, as we do, 'Peter *is* blond'. (The reader who can anticipate the sequel will be struck by the irony of our propensity, if we consider such verbal violence at all, to say '*the* blond(-ness) of Peter'.) The culprit in the case is the predicative 'is'. From where the realist stands, we remember, it reflects very nicely the nexus of exemplification and is *a*, if not perhaps *the*, fundamental use of 'is'.[9] For Frege

---

[9] It becomes *the* fundamental use if the Leibniz-Russell explication of identity is considered adequate.

it is but a clumsily disguised 'of'. In 'Peter *is* the father of John', on the other hand, as in '$3^2 = 9$' and, alas, in 'Peter is blond $=$ T', 'is' reflects very nicely, from where Frege stands, what it is used to speak about. To express identity thus becomes *the* or at least *a* fundamental use of 'is'. In the last section I shall give some reasons why I believe that all nominalists are forced to consider it, more or less covertly, *the* fundamental use of 'is'.

This is the place to call attention to two oddities about truth values. First, let '*P*' stand for a sentence and consider the series

$$P = T, \quad (P = T) = T, \quad [(P = T) = T] = T, \quad \ldots$$

If P is true, so are all members of the series. If the arithmetical analogue were to hold, the members of the series

$$3^2 = 9, \quad (3^2 = 9) = 9, \quad [(3^2 = 9) = 9] = 9, \quad \ldots$$

would also all be true. Yet they are not even well formed. This is odd. Second, senses and propositions (thoughts) are in the system two kinds of objects, kindred in that a proposition is, as it were, the sense of a sentence. This is familiar.[10] Now there is a passage (*F* 64) in which I take Frege to assert, as I believe consistently he must, that '*P*' and '*P* $=$ T' have (express) the same sense. If the arithmetical analogue held, so would therefore '3^2' and '$3^2 = 9$'. Yet the former denotes a number, the second, T. Thus they do not even denote the same kind of object. This, too, is odd. If one has already accepted the system, he will probably not boggle at such oddities. But if he hasn't, they may make him even more averse to the reification of T and F and to what, as we saw, is at the bottom of it all, Frege's analysis of exemplification in terms of mapping.

III

A nodding acquaintance with Frege's work, or even with what is currently being said about it, leaves two impressions.

---

[10] See Sections III and IV.

The first is of the multiplication of entities due to his distinction between *reference* and *sense*, that is, between the objects *denoted* and the objects *expressed* by such saturated expressions as, say, 'the Morning Star' and 'Peter is blond'. The second impression is that *the* main intellectual motive for the multiplication is the hope that, by means of it, it will be possible to conquer the difficulties that arise in intensional contexts, that is, in contexts mentioning either modalities or propositional attitudes, such as believing, knowing, and so on. Considering the system as a whole, that certainly is *a* motive. But if the two impressions are as widely spread as I believe them to be, then it is probably worth pointing out that Frege was first forced into that business of multiplying entities by the very logic of his nominalism in a case much simpler and more fundamental, which has nothing whatsoever to do with either modalities or propositional attitudes. This is the case of *classes* (extensions, value ranges). Corresponding to each concept, which according to him is not an object and (if I am right) at least implicitly not an existent, Frege "creates" another entity, which according to him is an object, namely, the class of all objects which, as he says, fall under the concept.[11] In this section I shall give two reasons why his nominalism, made explicit, forces him to do just that. Such reasons, if sound, are of course the kind of structural evidence one must accumulate in order to establish that the system is, at least implicitly, nominalistic.

Consider the two functional expressions 'x^2' and '$x^2 - x + x$' and the equation '$x^2 = x^2 - x + x$'. After a fashion, we all know what the equation stands for. Practicing mathematicians, without giving the matter much thought, say either that the two functions have the same extension, that is, the class of ordered pairs $[(1,1), (2,4),...]$, or, alternatively, that the two functions are equal (the same, identical). Strictly speaking, from where Frege stands, the second alternative

---

[11] The limitation to first-level concepts which this formulation entails does not affect my purpose.

makes no sense. A function is a mapping rule. Following one of the two rules mentioned, one obtains the value by squaring the argument. Following the other, one first squares the argument, then subtracts it from the square, then adds it to the intermediate result. Considered as rules, the two functions are thus not the same. Generally, two rules are never the same, in a sense both strict and intelligible, unless they are, as one says, two tokens of the same type. All one can mean by calling them so is, therefore, that they yield the same result (have the same extension). I conclude that, if he wants to be consistent, Frege cannot, as in fact he does not, specify conditions of identity for concepts and functions. Or, rather, he would have to hold that an assertion of identity between two (concepts or) functions is true if and only if the two expressions mentioned are different tokens of the same type. Of this more later. For the moment we notice that had he stopped at this point, Frege could not have preserved what as a mathematician he surely wanted to preserve, namely, the equation '$x^2 = x^2 - x + x$' and the truism for which it stands. His way out is to interpret it as an identity not between the two functions but, rather, between their extensions. (Technically, he introduces a special notation for the latter and rewrites the equation as a statement of identity between them.) The *possibility* of this interpretation he thinks is *indemonstrable*. So he appeals to a *fundamental law of logic*. The words and the phrase italicized are his (*F* 26). This is the first reason I undertook to adduce. It shows how the nominalism implicit in any analysis that starts from mapping creates the need for the new entities. The second reason will show that they must be objects.

Frege does not specify the fundamental law of logic to which he appeals. What then is it? Does he use the phrase merely to dignify what is done in this case? Or is there a general principle involved? Even though his words at this place seem to suggest the first alternative, the second is I believe the right one. Consider the following three propositions. 1. To be a name and to be an expression standing for an existent is one and the same thing. 2. For a statement of identity, '$\alpha = \beta$', to be true, 'α' and 'β' must denote existents. 3. For '$\alpha = \beta$' to be a statement (to be well-formed, or to be meaningful), 'α' and 'β' must denote (or purport to denote) existents. Obviously, 3 is stronger than 2. Many ontologists endorse either 2 or 3, depending on the stand they take on issues which do not concern us. I would not even endorse 2.[12] That, however, is beside the point. The point is that either 1 and 3 or, perhaps, 1 and 2 follow deductively from the way many ontologists tended and still tend to use 'existent', 'name', and 'identity'. Add now, as a fourth proposition, that every saturated expression is a name; in the first three propositions replace 'existent' by 'object', and you obtain four principles, or four aspects of one principle, which underlie, either explicitly or very nearly so, all of Frege's analysis. This, I believe, is quite uncontroversial. Assume now that this principle is the fundamental law of logic to which Frege appealed. It follows that extensions (value ranges, classes) must be objects. This is the second reason I promised to adduce. Moreover, I have made it plausible, to say the least, that Frege uses 'object' as many ontologists use 'existent'. Concepts and functions in general, we remember, though objective, are not objects. It follows that, at least implicitly, the system is nominalistic. This concludes the main argument of the section. I proceed to four comments.

First. Let a_1, a_2, ... be all the objects that are blond; b_1, b_2, ... all those that are not. The class one ordinarily associates with the character blond is that of the a,[a_1, a_2, ...]. It can be argued that the class Frege associates with the concept blond is that of all ordered pairs (a, T) *and* (b, F). If so, in his world what sort of object is an ordered pair

---

[12] To this point I hope to return on another occasion. See "Sameness, Meaning, and Identity," in the *Proceedings of the Twelfth International Congress of Philosophy* (Venice, 1958). Reprinted in *Meaning and Existence*.

of objects? Probing deeply in some such directions, one is eventually led to the Russell paradox and the question as to what, if anything, Frege can do about it. I realize all that. Clearly, these subtleties do not matter for what I am about. That is why I proceeded as I did. But it may hurt my thesis if I appear ignorant where I am merely selective. That is why I mention the matter.

Second. Frege (*F* 50) feels the need to distinguish "the relation of an object to a first-level concept that it falls under . . . from the (admittedly similar) relation of a first-level concept to a second-level concept." So he proposes that in the former case we speak of falling *under*, in the latter of falling *within*. His purpose, he tells us, is to preserve the distinction of concept and object "with all its sharpness" or, as I would put it, to increase the ontological distance between them. Taken by itself, the passage may be read as merely a plea for pervasive type distinctions. In context it provides subsidiary evidence for my thesis.

Third. An objector might argue as follows: "True, Frege does not specify conditions of identity for functions. But, then, neither does he specify such conditions or criteria for senses. (I follow you in using 'sense' for propositions (thoughts) as well as for what is expressed by nonsentential saturated expressions such as 'the Morning Star'.) Yet senses are objects. This greatly weakens your argument." Wells (*W* 544) shrewdly anticipates part of the answer. Frege, he reminds us, had an additional reason, which does not, or at least not directly, apply to functions, for not specifying criteria for the identity of senses. To grasp this reason, remember that one of Frege's intellectual motives was to solve the problems of intentional contexts. In this enterprise the reification of senses is merely a first step. The decisive second step is to specify criteria of identity among senses. This second step Frege never took, simply because (or so I believe) he could not think of any that were acceptable to him and did the job. In any case, he examined and rejected two. By one of them, two expressions have (express) the same sense if and only if they are analytically equivalent. This criterion he recognized as too broad. By the other, two expressions have the same sense if and only if they are different tokens of the same type. If we accepted this criterion, logic, he thinks (F 46), "would simply be crippled," if only because "all definitions would then have to be rejected as false." [13] However that may be, Frege had an additional reason for not specifying a criterion of identity for senses. This is part of the answer I would give to the objector. For the rest, I would remind him of what was pointed out at the beginning of this section, namely, that its main argument is completely independent of what does or does not hold for senses.

Fourth. Frege, who started from mapping, was forced to reify classes. Does the realist who starts from exemplification find himself similarly compelled? If the answer were no, it would greatly add to the poignancy of my theme. The answer, I believe, is no. However, this is not the place to go into the reasons for that belief. So I shall merely hint at what is rather familiar. Our realist may so explicate the philosophical use of 'exist' that only what undefined terms stand for exists in this very peculiar sense. (This is an issue I promised to keep out of the main argument.) When Russell supported his contention that classes do not exist by defining the expressions standing for them in terms of predicative expressions, he was at least implicitly guided by this explication of 'exist.' [14] A realist who accepts Russell's analysis of the class notion together with the explication of 'exist' it implies or at least suggests need not therefore, like the Fregean nominalist, reify classes. The contrast adds depth to that between mapping and exemplification.

---

[13] I do not subscribe to the dogma. This, though, is another story. See "Intentionality," in *Semantica* (Archivio di Filosofia, 1955), 177-216; "Elementarism," l.c.; and "Concepts," *Phil. Studies,* VII (1957), 19-27 (jointly with H. Hochberg). Reprinted in *Meaning and Existence.*

[14] See "Particularity and the New Nominalism," *Methodos,* VI (1954), 131-148. Reprinted in *Meaning and Existence.*

IV

Consider the phrase 'the concept blond' and the sentence 'The concept blond is a concept'. As Wells points out (*W* 550), one would think that the latter is not only true but truistic. Frege, as he must, disagrees. Like every saturated expression beginning with 'the', the phrase is a name. A name denotes an object (existent). These two principles, we saw, Frege never questions. But a concept is not an object (existent). Hence, the supposed truism is false. Perhaps it is even non-sensical. That leaves two alternatives. One is to declare the sentence expendable. The other is to create a new kind of odd objects. Frege chose the second. The new objects are the *concept correlates*. A concept correlate "represents" its concept. Or it is obtained by "converting" the concept into an object. These are Frege's words. Nor must the correlate of a concept be confused with its extension. Starting with one entity, the concept, which as I argue does not exist, Frege thus ends up with two more which indubitably do exist, namely, the concept's correlate and its extension.

The need for the creation of this further kind of odd object is, to my mind, the most obvious intrinsic flaw of the system *as it stands*. By calling it intrinsic I indicate, as before, that I do not on this occasion wish to challenge the odd kinds merely because to some of us they seem odd. Nor do I call it a flaw merely because this particular reification is patently *ad hoc*. For so is that of the two truth values. My point is that, once the new kind, the concept correlate, has been introduced, one cannot escape answering the question in what relation, or connection—use any word you wish—it stands to the other two, the concept itself and its extension. Yet there is no answer. This is the flaw I have in mind. It is as obvious as it is serious. One cue to its being a flaw is the opacity of the two metaphors, representation and conversion. This is not to say that I blame Frege just for speaking meta-phorically. Many philosophers sometimes do, and sometimes it helps. I merely wish to say that these two metaphors do not help me in the least. Nothing comes through.

The way I presented the matter leaves no doubt that the need for concept correlates is a consequence of what I claim is the implicit nominalism of the system. In this respect there is no difference between concept correlates and classes (extensions). But there is in another. Notice that I spoke of the system "as it stands." In the case of concept correlates, though not of classes, a very slight emendation eliminates the need for their reification as a further kind of objects. I shall next use this circumstance to argue that the nominalism which, if it were explicitly present in the system, would necessitate the reification, actually is present in it, at least implicitly.

Take (α) 'Peter', (β) 'Peter is blond', (γ) 'blond'. They exemplify Frege's three basic grammatical categories. Let the Greek letters stand for these categories. Every α and β expression has a reference and a sense. It denotes the former, expresses the latter. The reference of a β expression is a truth value, its sense a proposition (thought). Senses are objects. Hence they can be named. In the case of the paradigm, their names are 'the sense Peter'[15] and 'the proposition Peter is blond'[16] respectively. Being a name, each of these two expressions has in turn a sense. We have entered upon an infinite regress. Within the system, though, that is no difficulty. Nor does it disturb the lucidity of the pattern. The difficulty is, rather, that the pattern does not apply to the unsaturated expressions γ. There (I limit myself to concepts) it is disturbed by that dangling third entity, the concept correlate.

Assume now that concepts are existents. If so, they can be named and the pattern can be extended as follows. A γ expression, say, 'blond', denotes its extension and expresses its sense, which is the concept itself, which in turn is denoted

---

[15] Or, as one says rather, *the concept Peter*. It is obvious why I avoid that locution.

[16] Or, in intentional contexts, *that Peter is blond*.

by 'the concept blond.' With this emendation the same pattern applies to all three categories. Moreover, the need for concept correlates has disappeared.

The emendation is in substance the one Church proposed. With all the respect due to him, it does not seem very far-fetched, at least by hindsight. Nor is it overdoing the respect we owe to Frege's ingenuity to believe that it was not, even by foresight, beyond his grasp. Why, then, one must ask, did he not take this almost obvious step? The answer I propose will not come as a surprise. He balked at the one assumption which as I have shown the step implies, namely, that concepts, though not objects, are yet full-fledged existents. This concludes the main argument of the section. I proceed to two comments.

First. Wells reports (*W* 546) Church to have argued as early as 1939, in a paper not generally accessible, that Frege's concepts are full-fledged existents. In other words, he disagreed sharply with my thesis. I am neither surprised nor disturbed. *As emended* by Church, the system is indeed no longer nominalistic in structure. That merely proves that Church is not a nominalist. It proves nothing about the system *as it stands.* I also grant and even insist that the emendation is nearly obvious. That explains why Church did not want to charge his master with what he must have considered a flaw. But it does not explain why Frege himself put up with an obvious and serious flaw rather than take Church's nearly obvious step. My thesis does explain that.

Second. What can the realist do about Frege's problem? To answer, I first state the problem in the way it impressed itself upon Frege. Consider 'Fido is *a* dog'. If 'dog' and 'the concept dog' stood for the same entity, they would have to be interchangeable *salva veritate.* This is another principle Frege never questioned. Yet, 'Fido is *the* concept dog' is nonsense. (Frege, everyone knows, was tremendously and of course quite rightly impressed with the contrast between the definite and the indefinite article. That is why I changed the paradigm.)

The concept correlates are an obvious way out of the difficulty. The realist does not need them. Admitting, for the sake of the argument, that 'dog' and 'the concept dog' stand for the same entity, he need not therefore abandon the principle. He merely adds the proviso, which I introduced in Section II, that whenever such a substitution is made, 'exemplifies' must, in the nature of things, be substituted for 'is'. In this way he obtains, quite smoothly, 'Fido exemplifies the concept dog'. The reason the realist finds this answer is that, unlike Frege who starts from mapping, he can do justice to that fundamental feature of our world from which he starts. Thus we are once more led back to the contrast between mapping and exemplification.

V

Consider 'This is red'. Frege and the realist agree that the demonstrative denotes an existent. By the realist's account, so does the adjective. Frege, we saw, disagrees, at least implicitly. The root of the matter, we also saw, is that he starts from mapping. The inspiration for this alternative to exemplification is mathematical. In this his nominalism is unique. All other varieties I know of—I am tempted to call them the ordinary varieties—operate with the doctrine of *common names*. Or, as I would rather say, there are really only two kinds of nominalism, Frege's and the doctrine of common names. The difference between the two is by no means negligible. Both kinds, though, in addition to being nominalisms, which to my mind is a weakness, share still another weakness. Neither does justice to the predicative 'is', which stands for exemplification. Both, therefore, more or less covertly take identity to be the fundamental meaning of 'is'. In Section II I showed this for Frege. In this section I shall show it for the doctrine of common names, first generally, then by analyzing an essay of Quine's.[17]

---

[17] "Identity, Ostension, and Hypostasis," reprinted in *From a Logical Point of View* (Cambridge, Mass., 1953). References to this volume are by page number, preceded by the letter *Q*.

Assume that when I said 'This is red' I pointed at an individual, say, a red apple. The demonstrative and the adjective are both names of the apple. The only difference is that while the former is (serves as) a "proper name," the latter is a "common name." A proper name is a label arbitrarily attached to one and only one individual. A common name applies indifferently to each of several individuals, namely, all those sharing a character. This is the doctrine of common names. It runs into an objection and a difficulty.

A common name applies to an individual if and only if that individual has a certain character. Hence it is not an arbitrary label, in the sense in which a proper name is one, unless it be, as the realist insists and the nominalist denies, the name or label of the character itself. What, then, the realist asks the defender of the doctrine, is there "objectively" in or about each of the several individuals by virtue of which the common name is properly applied to each of them? Some nominalists answer (Q 68) that upon hearing and seeing a common name applied, we learn to apply it ourselves "by induction." The realist retorts that for such learning to occur, there must be a clue common to all individuals to which the learner hears and sees the common name applied. That leaves the issue where it was before. The doctrine of common names has no answer to this objection. Frege answered it, after a fashion, by insisting that functions, though not objects (existents), are yet "objective." That is why his nominalism is so superior to the other kind and, being superior, can remain "hidden." That much for the objection. The difficulty relates to what I am about.

Assume that an individual has two names, say 'Napoleon' and 'Bonaparte'. Consider 'Napoleon is Bonaparte'. In this sentence 'is' stands for identity. Generally, if an individual has two names, what way is there of combining them into a sentence except by the 'is' of identity? This suggests that proponents of the doctrine may be tempted to assimilate the predicative 'is' to that of identity. Notice that I just spoke of names, without distinction between common and proper ones. I did this because I do not really understand what it means for a word to be a common name. Or, to say the same thing differently, a name, in the only use of the term I understand, is a word attached as a label to one and only one entity. Or, still differently, in the manner of speaking I wish to discourage, every name, whatever it may name, is a proper name. Notice, second, that I spoke of suggestion. In other words, not every proponent of the doctrine asserts that in 'This is red' the copula stands for identity. To claim anything of the sort would be unreasonable indeed. For is it not the very purpose of the doctrine of common names to prevent this collapse of the two uses of 'is'? Only its proponents still somehow think of "common names" as "names." Therein, I claim, lies a temptation, or a suggestion, or perhaps even a compulsion in the direction of that collapse. This claim is not at all unreasonable. To substantiate it, I shall present two series of comments, the first about classical (Aristotelian) logic, the second about the essay by Quine.

1. For Aristotle, there is an important difference between 'This is green' and 'Socrates is a man'. For my purpose the difference does not matter. Even so, consider the second sentence, if only because everyone knows that classical logic cannot cope with it except by the device of subsuming it, rather artificially, under the A-sentence. To do that is to construe the predicative 'is' as the 'is' (or 'are') of the A-, E-, I-, and O-sentences. For Aristotle, this third use of 'is' is the fundamental one. It is, if I may so put it, the only one for which he can account. (Frege and the realist both construe it as a combination of two predicative uses with a quantifier.) Be that as it may, formally or logically the device does the trick. But it does not even touch the heart of the difficulty, which is ontological rather than logical. Within the hylomorphic scheme, the problem of individuation is insoluble.[18] One

---

[18] This is by now at least a respectable opinion. See, for all this, "Some Remarks on the Ontology of Ockham," *Philos. Rev.*, LIII (1954),

may of course abandon individuals. That is the way Scotus took. But it can be argued that in taking it he also abandoned hylomorphism. The original terminists did not wish to go that far. Yet they faced up to the Parmenidean illusion, which is one of the roots, if not perhaps the root, of the classical difficulty, that every occurrence of the copula indicates an identity. Moreover, they insisted, like Frege, that any two names of an individual must be substitutable for each other *salva veritate* in all contexts; and they noticed that, say, 'this' and 'red' are not so substitutable. Thus they were led to the distinction which is the core of their doctrine of signification. *Connotatively*, they held, the adjective signifies indifferently each of the several red things; *denotatively* it, or, rather, its abstractum 'redness', signifies the character itself. Deny now that characters are existents. Then there is nothing for the adjective (or its abstractum) to signify denotatively and you arrive at the doctrine of common names. This is the step Ockham took.

2. An apple is, in a familiar sense, spatio-temporally extended. Its color and shape, as the realist conceives them, are not. For Quine, to be an existent and to be spatio-temporally extended, or, as for brevity's sake I shall say, to be extended or an extension, are one and the same thing. This is the guiding idea of his ontology. It has an important corollary. The *sum* of any number of extensions is itself extended. Roughly, sum here means set-theoretical sum. Precisely, it is the function axiomatized in the so-called meromorphic calculus. This subtlety we can safely ignore. Notice, though, that the notion of a function, in the Fregean sense of the term, is needed to state the intuitive core of this ontology.

Assume now once more that, pointing at an apple, I say

560-571; "Russell's Examination of Leibniz Examined," *Philosophy of Science*, XXIII (1956), 175-203; "Some Remarks on the Philosophy of Malebranche," *Rev. Metaphys.*, X (1956), 207-226. Reprinted in *Meaning and Existence*. Leibniz, it is true, manages to accommodate both kinds of existent. But he pays the price of having to maintain that in a sense every predication is analytic *(Predicatum inest subjecto)*.

'This is red'. Or for that matter, assume that, pointing at a certain volume of water, I say 'This is the Iowa River'. Quine holds (Q 69) that there is in principle no difference between the two "ostensions." Just as the Iowa River is the sum of certain watery extensions, so the color may be thought of as the sum of all red ones. Which extensions we are meant to sum we learn in either case "by induction" from watching what is being pointed at (Q 68). Pointing, however, is ambiguous (Q 67). Taking advantage of the ambiguity, Quine says that one who speaks and points as by assumption I do "identifies" for the purposes of the discourse what he points at with the sum in question (Q 71). Notice how subtle it all is. Quine does not tell us that the copula in 'This is red' stands for identity. Of course he doesn't. As a logician, he knows better than that. Yet he says obliquely, by means of the opaque metaphor of "identification," that what I really point at is the sum. If this were so and if the color could be conceived as the sum in question, then 'This is red' would indeed state an identity.

Quine is convinced that nobody in his right mind would "hypostatize" characters as the realist does. So he must explain why such hypostasis ever seemed plausible. The explanation takes the form of an anthropological fable. Its hero is misled by a faulty analogy (Q 73). As it happens, some adjectives may be thought of as standing for a sum of extensions. So he is led to hope that this is so for all adjectives. Quine constructs a simple universe in which the sum of all triangles coincides with the sum of all squares (Q 72). Negatively, this frustrates that hope. Positively, we are told (Q 75) that "in ostensively explaining 'square' . . . we say each time 'This is square' *without* imputing identity of indicated object from one occasion to the next." Again the metaphor is opaque. I do not really know what it means to impute identity. I do know, though, that we are left with two alternatives. Either 'square' stands for a character as the realist conceives it; or, even though there is no such character, we learn "inductively" how to use the common name. Quine rejects the first alternative, chooses the second (Q 75). Thus he lays himself open to the classical objection which I rehearsed earlier.

Quine's nominalism is clearly a doctrine of common names. That makes it very different from Frege's. Yet there are also two points of contact. The first is that, sums being functions, the Fregean notion of function is an ingredient of the intuitive core of the doctrine. The other point of contact seems at first rather verbal. Quine is fond of the formula that while sentences are either true or false, a predicate is either true or false *of* something. For Frege, we remember, the predicative 'is' is merely a clumsily disguised 'of'. Ofness, if I may coin a word, thus plays a crucial role in both systems. One may wonder whether this similarity is merely a chance product of the idiom.

3

Professor Bergmann and Frege's "Hidden Nominalism"

E. D. KLEMKE

In a recent paper,[1] Professor Gustav Bergmann maintains that Frege's ontology is that of a hidden or implicit nominalism. Its root, according to Bergmann, is the contrast between exemplification and mapping. That is, whereas the realist construes functions in terms of characters (concepts), Frege construes concepts as a kind of function. "In this way, the nominalism I have shown to be implicit in any analysis that starts from mapping spreads to concepts (characters)."[2]

In spite of the fact that I agree with Bergmann that Frege starts from mapping rather than from exemplification in his discussion of characters or concepts, I should like to question Bergmann's thesis that Frege is a nominalist, even an implicit one, in either a strict or loose sense. For I believe that he makes his case only by omitting a vast range of considerations which must be taken into account and which make the issue much more complex than he shows it to be. First, therefore, I shall characterize Frege's ontology as Bergmann sees

Reprinted with the kind permission of the editor from *The Philosophical Review*, LXVIII (1959), 507-514.

[1] "Frege's Hidden Nominalism," *The Philosophical Review*, LXVII (1958), 437-459.

[2] *Ibid.*, p. 445.

it. Second, I shall adduce evidence which Bergmann's account omits and which suggests other alternatives. Third, I shall select one of these alternatives and present what I take to be the structure of Frege's ontology. (I shall limit the discussion to characters, particularly nonrelational universals, following Bergmann's procedure.)

Bergmann recognizes that, for Frege, every *entity* is either an *object* or a *function*.[3] Oddly enough, he by-passes the consequences which this view entails (except in so far as he makes the loose-strict dichotomy). He is impressed, rather, by the sharp distinction between the two kinds of entities. For one thing, objects are existents; functions are not. For another, objects are saturated, complete; functions are not. And so on. If one were to schematize Bergmann's view of Frege's ontology, the result would be as follows:

"ENTITIES"

Objects (existents):
 Individuals
 Numbers
 Truth values
 Extensions
  (classes, value-ranges)
 Senses
 Thoughts (propositions)
 Concept correlates

Functions (objective but not
  objects and not existents):
 Mathematical functions
 Characters:
  Concepts
  Relations

Bergmann's thesis depends partly upon his formulation of what he holds nominalism (in the strict sense) to be. It is the view that "no characters are existents." With this "definition" of nominalism, and with the limitation that only objects are existents, it would clearly follow that Frege is a nominalist, for all characters (in Frege's view) come under the heading of functions, not objects. Hence, no characters would be existents for him. As far as I can determine, Frege nowhere uses the term equivalent of "existent." Where he

<hr>

[3] "Entity" is not Frege's term, but there are good reasons for employing some general ontological term, as I shall show below.

does speak of *existence*, there is no clear separation in which existence is attributed only to objects. Hence I prefer to drop the term. Bergmann recognizes that Frege does not use "existent" but he nevertheless holds that Frege "would have agreed that everything he calls an object is an existent."[4] No evidence is given for this belief and I cannot find any evidence in Frege's writings. Hence, nothing can be proved one way or another by arguing at this level. If Frege is a nominalist, this has to be shown by some other way than by (1) defining nominalism to mean that no characters are existents and (2) then formulating a hunch that, for Frege, no characters are existents. Frege makes only this much clear: no characters (or functions in general) are *objects* (not existents!). Functions and objects are two separate kinds of things but both are *things*. As Frege says, "An object is anything that is not a function" (p. 32).[5] This need not imply that functions do not exist or that they are less real than objects.

Hence we must get at the matter in another way; Bergmann saw the road to the solution but by-passed it. He spoke of two clusters of words which are used philosophically in ontological discourse.[6] The first cluster contains "thing," "object," "entity," "existent." The second contains "naming," "denoting," "designating," "referring." Bergmann tried to make his case by concentrating upon the first cluster.[7] I suggest that one ought to emphasize the second; hence I shall. In so doing, however, I must point out that not all of the terms in the second cluster have the same use for Frege. Specifically, "naming" is less general than "referring." Naming is a special kind of referring, as when a proper name refers

---

[4] Bergmann, *op. cit.*, pp. 438-439.

[5] All page references are to the volume, *Translations from the Philosophical Writings of Gottlob Frege* (tr. by Black and Geach). Oxford, 1952.

[6] Bergmann, *op. cit.*, p. 437.

[7] Frege does not group these words together. If one insists upon holding them together, this would "load the dice" in a case for nominalism.

to an object. And this is important since there are for Frege other kinds of referring. Not only do proper names refer (designate, stand for, and so forth), but sentences do, too. Furthermore, *concept-expressions* (that is, concept-words, predicate-terms, and so forth) *also refer*. Or, as Frege puts it, just as a proper name has a reference, namely, the individual for which it stands, and a sentence has a reference (a truth value), so a predicate-term has a reference, namely, the *concept* for which it stands. Hence, the concept is an ontological entity and a basic one, a simple. I suggest that following through on the matter of reference is the way by which to determine whether Frege was a nominalist or a realist. I find that one can make a convincing case for the latter (and not merely in a loose sense).

Now Bergmann might hold that Frege was speaking carelessly when he spoke of the references [8] of predicate-terms. I can only say that there are too many passages in which he speaks this way. One would have to attribute extreme sloppiness or forgetfulness to Frege in order to make such a case plausible.

I turn now to some of the passages I have in mind.

1. "The concept . . . is predicative. It is, in fact, the reference of a grammatical predicate" (p. 43).

2. "Something [i.e., an object] falls under a concept, and the grammatical predicate stands for this concept" (p. 44).

3. Speaking of the expression *"no other than Venus,"* Frege says, "These words stand for a concept" (p. 44).

4. "A concept is the reference of a predicate" (pp. 47-48).

5. Speaking of the two expressions, "the concept *square root of 4*" (a proper name) and "square root of 4" (a predicate-expression), Frege says, "The references of the two phrases are essentially different" (p. 50).

6. "There is no direct designation either of an extension or of a collective, but only of a concept" (p. 82).

---

[8] Where we would perhaps say "referent" Geach and Black say "reference."

7. "The so-called common name—which would be better named 'concept-word'— . . . stands for a concept. Under this concept objects may fall; but it may also be empty, and this does not stop the concept-word from standing for something" (p. 83).

8. " 'Round square' . . . is not an empty name, but a name of an empty concept, and thus one not devoid of reference in sentences like " 'There is no round square' or 'The moon is not a round square' " (p. 105).

9. Frege opposes the view that a function is an expression or a combination of signs. It is, rather, "what the combination designates" (p. 152).

10. "Every function-name must have a reference" (p. 170).

11. In numerous places, Frege distinguishes concept-words and concepts, the latter being the references of the former (e.g., pp. 44, 45, 48, 50, 105).

I take it that this is enough. To me, this one fact that, for Frege, concepts are references of concept-terms, is impressive. It would make me think twice before calling him a nominalist (in any sense). For it may be seen that Frege follows the same pattern as he does with respect to names and sentences, and he gives ontological status to concepts. For this notion of *reference* and *not* that of *object* (or existent) is, I believe, what indicates ontological status to Frege. This may be seen by the following. For Frege, there are three types of expressions. Using Bergmann's examples, we get (α) "Peter," (β) "Peter is blond," and (γ) "blond," as instances of each. "Peter" is a proper name. It expresses a sense and stands for reference—the object Peter. "Peter is blond" is a sentence. It expresses a thought (sense) and has a reference—a truth value. This much Bergmann has noted. But being impressed by the fact that (for Frege) both individuals and truth-values (the references of the first two kinds of expressions) are *objects*, he overlooks the fact that expressions of the third type have references, too (although they are not objects). Thus, "blond" stands for a reference—a *concept*. Does it express a sense, too? Frege doesn't say. I see no reason why he should deny that it does. At any rate, it has the reference. Also, a new ontological category, in addition to the concept, enters in here and differentiates concepts from individuals and truth-values. Concepts are common properties (p. 103) and hence have *extensions*, too. The extensions are often called classes. Incidentally, this notion of properties further substantiates my case that, for Frege, concepts are basic ontological entities. He says, "I call the concepts under which an object falls its properties" (p. 51). In other words, an object has properties. Hence, if the object has the right to be called an existent, then surely its properties are existents, too. Both objects and concepts are ontological entities. They are different *kinds* of entities, to be sure. Nevertheless, both kinds have being, as some would say. Neither is more real or more basic than the other, even though one kind (objects) is saturated while the other is not, and even though *some* objects (for example, numbers) can stand alone.

There are two ways by which one might try to continue to insist that Frege is a nominalist, but I believe that both are in error. (1) One might suggest that for Frege, in so far as concepts are references, they are extensions of concepts (that is, that concepts have no ontological status in themselves but only as exemplified by the individuals of a given class). Frege clearly expressed himself on this point. "The extension of a concept is constituted in being, not by the individuals, but by the concept itself; that is, by what is asserted of an object when it is brought under a concept" (p. 102). "The concept is logically prior to its extension; and I regard as futile the attempt to take the extension of a concept as a class, and make it rest, not on the concept, but on single things" (p. 106). "The extension of a concept does not consist of objects falling under a concept, in the way, e.g., that a wood consists of trees; it attaches to the concept and to this alone. The concept thus takes logical precedence of its extension" (p. 106). These passages reveal even more than the purpose for which

I cite them, but they do show this much (among other things): that, for Frege, concepts have ontological status in themselves and not merely as characters of individuals and hence are distinct from classes of objects.

(2) A second way by which one might still try to insist that Frege is a nominalist is to hold that (for Frege) concept and sense are identical in this context. I can find no passages where Frege either explicitly affirms or denies this. But for at least two reasons I should say that Frege would deny that the concept is the sense. (a) He always insists that a term *expresses* its sense and *stands for* (refers to, designates) its reference. He never says that a concept is what is expressed by a predicate-term. He always insists that predicate-terms refer to (stand for, and so forth) a concept. (b) It is entirely conceivable that if a proper name or a sentence expresses a sense, then a predicate-term does also, and that the sense would be different from the reference. Consider the points where Frege presses his sense-reference distinction. It is those cases in which two terms have the same reference but express different senses. For example, the two proper names "Morning star" and "Evening star" stand for the same reference (an object here) but express different senses. Similarly, "$2^4 = 4^2$" and "$4 \cdot 4 = 4^2$" stand for the same reference (the True) but express different senses. I see no difficulty in holding that two predicate terms might refer to the same concept but express different senses. Suppose that we had two color-terms which were used with respect to exactly the same shade of color. They would stand for the same reference (a concept) but express different senses.

Frege's discussion of classes—see (1), above—adds to the antinominalism thesis. For Frege, classes are not collections of individuals; they are collections of *common properties*. In his criticism of Schröder, Frege says that Schröder wanted to found logic "not on the content of concepts but on the extension, and he thought he could here leave it undecided how the delimitation of classes came about. This led him to the domain-calculus, the view that classes consist of single things, are collections of individuals; for what else is there to constitute a class, if we ignore the concepts, the common properties!" (p. 103; see also p. 104). Hence classes are not mere groupings of *objects*; they are collections of characters which objects may or may not possess (see pp. 104-105). In fact, concepts (characters) can have being even though no individuals exemplify them (p. 83). How much more of a (strict) realist can one become?

If I were now to schematize Frege's ontology, I would do it something like this:

ONTOLOGICAL ENTITIES

References:
  Objects
    Individuals
    Numbers
    Truth-values
    Extensions (?)
    Concept correlates
  Functions:
    Mathematical functions
    Characters:
      Concepts
      Relations

Non-references:
  Senses
  Thoughts

I have placed a question mark after "Extensions" for, although Frege sometimes says that they are objects, he also says that they are not direct references.

In summary, just as individuals, numbers, and so forth, are references, so are concepts or characters (and relations). Since references certainly are basic ontological entities, concepts are. Hence Frege appears to be not merely a loose realist but a realist in the strict sense. He *does* succeed in securing full ontological status for concepts as well as for objects. While he preserves the distinction between objects and concepts, he does not "increase the ontological distance between them" to the point of denying the basic reality of the latter.

I must hasten to add that when I say that Frege appears to

be a realist in the strict sense, I do not mean that he was a *traditional* realist, any more than Bergmann is. That is, one need not interpret him as holding that universals exist in some "Platonic heaven." In many of his writings Frege, like Bergmann, appears to be a reconstructionist. In his own way, he explicated what philosophical propositions like "Universals exist" can be taken to mean by talking about the features of an ideal language. Frege's ideal language includes predicate-terms as well as proper names among the undefined descriptive constants. To be sure, the predicate terms look rather peculiar by *our* standards. This is because of the unsaturation feature. This does not allow us, however, to make the unjustifiable leap to asserting that characters are somehow less real, that they are not full ontological simples. On the contrary, both characters and objects are ontological entities, but they are different kinds of such entities. Or, linguistically, proper names differ from predicate-terms but both have ontological significance. Both stand for (designate, and so forth) references.

4

Frege's Ontology

HOWARD JACKSON

In a recent reply[1] to Professor Gustav Bergmann's article[2] dealing with Frege's ontological commitments Mr. E. D. Klemke raises a point to which I would like to add comment.

Klemke asks whether a concept (*Begriff*) could not be the sense (*Sinn*) of a class name. He claims that though he was unable to find a definite rejection of this identification in Frege's writings, such a rejection would be reasonable on the following grounds: (1) Frege ". . . insists that a term *expresses* its sense and *stands for* (refers to, designates) its reference. He never says that a concept is what is expressed by a predicate-term." (2) Since predicate expressions do have reference for Frege, there is no reason to identify their sense and reference, nor to deny them a sense. (2) is argued on the ground that it is a more consistent rendering of Frege with regard to his distinction between the sense and reference of an expression.

The question here considered can be definitely answered. Through the kind permission of Dr. G. Hasenjaeger of the

Reprinted with the kind permission of the author and the editor from *The Philosophical Review*, LXIX (1960), 394-395.

[1] "Professor Bergmann and Frege's 'Hidden Nominalism,'" *The Philosophical Review*, LXVIII (1959), 507-514.

[2] "Frege's Hidden Nominalism," *The Philosophical Review*, LXVII (1958), 437-459.

Institut für mathematische Logik und Grundlagenforschung in Münster, Germany, I was permitted to study yet unpublished papers by Frege. In a paper of 1891-1892 Frege argues that the sense of an expression *is an object*, and since, for Frege, objects and concepts are in every case to be distinguished (a distinction made consistently throughout his writings), the sense of an expression is never to be confused with a concept.

While this answers the question, it also suggests that Klemke's statement (1) is misleading. For if the sense of an expression is an object, it is reasonable to suppose that it could be the reference of a grammatical subject. Certainly this is the case, as a reading of "über Sinn und Bedeutung" will confirm. Expressions occurring in indirect discourse have as their reference their ordinary (*gewöhnlichen*) sense. Frege writes that in those cases where an expression occurs in indirect discourse, ". . . ist es nicht erlaubt . . . einen Ausdruck durch einen anderen zu ersetzen, der dieselbe gewöhnliche Bedeutung hat, sondern nur durch einen solchen, welcher dieselbe ungerade Bedeutung, d.h., denselben gewöhnlichen Sinn hat."[3] Whereas we do not have in natural languages a name for the sense of an expression—which might be regarded as a defect—we may refer to the sense of an expression through the simple expedient of such expressions as "the sense of *x*," where "*x*" takes expressions as values.

Klemke provides a table of ontological entities, dichotomized into those which can be referred to and those which cannot. In the former list appear objects and functions, in the latter senses and thoughts. As we have just noted that the sense of an expression is an object for Frege and can be referred to, we are forced to reject Klemke's dichotomy.

---

[3] "Über Sinn und Bedeutung," *Zeitschrift für Philosophie und philosophische Kritik*, C (1892), 25-50.

5

Frege's Ontology

REINHARDT GROSSMANN

Frege's system has two rather puzzling parts: (1) he insists on the sense-denotation distinction for names but makes no such distinction for concept words; (2) he describes concepts and concept words as being unsaturated. (1) raises the problem whether concept words either denote or express concepts. This problem has been discussed by W. Marshall and M. Dummet.[1] (2) raises a number of different problems, for it led Frege to introduce so-called value ranges and concept correlates. These problems have been discussed by Peter Geach, R. S. Wells, and Gustav Bergmann.[2] Since both kinds of problems arise from Frege's notion of concept, it is plausible, as Bergmann tries to show, that they have their roots in a hidden nominalism. E. D. Klemke, however, has recently

Reprinted with the kind permission of the author and the editor from *The Philosophical Review*, LXX (1961), 23-40.

[1] W. Marshall, "Frege's Theory of Functions and Objects," *Philosophical Review*, LXII (1953), 374-390; and M. Dummett, "Frege on Functions, a Reply," *ibid.*, LXIV (1955), 96-107.

[2] P. T. Geach, "Class and Concept," *Philosophical Review*, LXIV (1955), 561-570; R. S. Wells, "Frege's Ontology," *Review of Metaphysics*, IV (1951), 537-573; and G. Bergmann, "Frege's Hidden Nominalism," *Philosophical Review*, LXVII (1958), 437-459 (reprinted in Bergmann's *Meaning and Existence*, Madison, Wis., 1960).

argued against Bergmann that Frege was clearly not a nominalist.[3]

In this paper I shall first suggest the structural reasons for Frege's insistence on (1) and (2). Then I shall make some comments about the issue whether or not Frege was a nominalist. But of course a complete discussion of Frege's philosophy must not be expected in this paper.

I

I begin by describing some features of Bolzano's *Wissenschaftslehre*, for much of what I shall have to say about Frege can best be understood against the background of Bolzano's view.[4] According to Bolzano, all things are of one of three kinds:

First, there are different kinds of *mental states* (*subjective Vorstellungen*), namely, (a) individual ideas (*subjective Einzelvorstellungen*), (b) general ideas (*subjective Allgemeinvorstellungen*), and (c) thoughts (*gedachte Saetze*). Things of these three kinds are supposed to exist in individual minds; in this respect they are "subjective" rather than "objective."[5]

Second, there are so-called *objects*₁ (*Gegenstaende*), namely, (a) individual things and (b) properties (*Beschaffenheiten* and *Relationen*). These things are not in any individual mind, but exist independently of minds and are therefore "objective" rather then "subjective."[6]

Third, there are *senses* (*objective Vorstellungen*), namely, (a) individual concepts (*objective Einzelvorstellungen*), (b) general concepts (*objective Allgemeinvorstellungen*), and

---

[3] E. D. Klemke, "Professor Bergmann and Frege's 'Hidden Nominalism,'" *Philosophical Review*, LXVIII (1959), 507-514.

[4] B. Bolzano, *Wissenschaftslehre* (new ed., 4 vols.; Leipzig, 1929). Compare also Y. Bar-Hillel, "Bolzano's Definition of Analytic Propositions," *Methodos*, II (1950), 32-55; and H. R. Smart, "Bolzano's Logic," *Philosophical Review*, LIII (1944), 513-533.

[5] *Wissenschaftslehre*, I, 77, 99, 219.

[6] *Ibid.*, pp. 219-222, 331, 378-387.

(c) propositions (*Saetze an sich*). These things differ from mental states in that they are as "objective" as objects$_1$. But they also differ from the latter. One important difference is that they are more closely connected with mental states than are objects$_1$. Assume, for instance, that I think that this tree is green. According to Bolzano, there occurs then a thought in my mind. This thought is a mental (subjective) state. By means of it, I am said to think *of* the proposition that this tree is green. In brief, *in* thinking a thought, one is said to think *of* a proposition. Similarly, in thinking (having) an idea, one "connects" directly with a concept (individual or general) and only indirectly, through the concept, with an object$_1$.[7]

The general reason for the introduction of senses is a "logical" one and can be stated as follows. The things properly studied by logic are agreed to be concepts and propositions. But they could not possibly be mental states; for "subjective" mental states are studied by psychology, and logic must be sharply separated from psychology. While the things studied by logic must be very much like ideas and thoughts, they cannot be "subjective." Rather, they are the "objective" counterparts of ideas and thoughts. In short, they are "objective" senses.[8]

One specific reason for the introduction of senses consists in the following consideration. Assume that two persons think, as one says, of the same mathematical theorem. This presumably raises the question whether or not the two thoughts are the "same." Some philosophers hold that there are in this case most certainly two thoughts, but they do not explain what is expressed by saying that the two thoughts are of the same theorem. Other philosophers, impressed by the latter fact, are tempted to say that the two thoughts are the "same." But this is equally unsatisfactory; for there are obviously two thoughts and not just one. According to Bolzano, the

[7] *Ibid.*, pp. 216-218.
[8] *Ibid.*, pp. 61-67.

correct analysis of our example has two steps. He holds, first, that there are indeed two thoughts, that is, two "subjective" mental states and not just one. He claims, second, that these two thoughts are of one and the same objective thing, namely, of the mathematical proposition. This analysis, it is evident, introduces senses as objective entities.[9]

According to Bolzano, mental states and objects$_1$ on the one hand and senses on the other exist in different ways. In one sense of the term, what exists exists at a certain place and for a certain length of time. Mental states and objects$_1$ are existents in this sense. Senses, however, do not exist in this way or manner. Yet they are not nothing; they are there. What in this manner is there can fall under a concept or, in other words, can be the object$_2$ of a concept.[10] This distinction explains my use of the subscripts attached to the word "object." By means of these subscripts, I wish to distinguish between two meanings of the word "object." The use of "object$_1$" signifies an ontological kind. Objects$_1$ must be distinguished from senses; for only the former exist in the sense just explained. However, "object" may also be used to refer to whatever may fall under a concept. In particular, a sense itself may fall under a concept. I indicate this use by writing "object$_2$." According to this distinction, every object$_1$ is an object$_2$ but not every object$_2$ is an object$_1$.[11]

I mentioned that there are two kinds of senses, namely, propositions on the one hand and concepts (individual or general) on the other. Now in regard to these two kinds, we must note the following important points.

Propositions. (1) Bolzano distinguishes between judgments (*Urteile*) and propositions (*Saetze an sich*). Every judgment contains a proposition, but the mere thought of a proposition

---

[9] *Ibid.*, pp. 84, 113-114, 216-218, 428-429.

[10] *Ibid.*, pp. 78, 112, 144-145, 154-155, 216-218, 426-427; II, 52-54.

[11] This distinction applies also to Frege's ontology. However, in regard to Frege, one must note the further distinction between objects$_2$ (proper) and concepts. See below.

is not a judgment.[12] Moreover, judgments are said to exist in the minds of persons that make them, while propositions, as we just saw, do not exist in this way.[13] (2) A sentence, that is, a string of spoken or written words, is said to *express* a proposition.[14] (3) Every proposition consists of a number of concepts in the manner in which a whole consists of its parts. A singular proposition, for instance, consists of an individual concept (*Subject-vorstellung*), the concept expressed by "has" ("is"), and the concept expressed by the predicate (*Praedicat-vorstellung*).[15] (4) The *sum* of these concepts is called the *content* of a proposition. All that matters for the determination of a content are the respective concepts but not the manner in which they are conjoined.[16] For instance, the two propositions expressed by "John loves Mary" and "Mary is loved by John" have the same content.[17] However, Bolzano also insists that they are not the same proposition; these two sentences express different senses although they have the same content.[18]

Concepts. (1) Bolzano distinguishes between the content (*Inhalt*) and the extension (*Umfang*) of a concept.[19] The content of a "complex" concept, individual or general, consists of the sum of its "simple" constituents.[20] The content of a simple concept is the concept itself. The extension of a concept consists of the objects$_2$ that fall under it.[21] An individual concept, for instance, has as its extension one and only one object$_2$. A general concept, on the other hand, can either be empty or have more than one thing as its extension. (2) Concepts are never identical, although they may have either the

---

[12] *Wissenschaftslehre*, I, 154-155.
[13] *Ibid.*, pp. 154-155.   [14] *Ibid.*, p. 121.
[15] *Ibid.*, pp. 99, 216-218; II, 8-10, 16, 18.
[16] *Ibid.*, pp. 113-114, 243-244, 353-354, 434.
[17] I think Bolzano would also say that the propositions expressed by "John loves Mary" and "Mary loves John" have the same content. See *Wissenschaftslehre*, I, 243-244.
[18] *Ibid.*, pp. 428-429, 434, 436-438, 445-447.
[19] *Ibid.*, pp. 297-300, 353-354.
[20] *Ibid.*, pp. 243-244.   [21] *Ibid.*, pp. 297-300.

same content (in which case neither one can be simple) or the same extension, or both.[22] This means that two different expressions always express different concepts.[23]

This concludes my description of Bolzano's system. I turn now to Frege.

II

Frege, in his *Begriffsschrift*, does not outline a comprehensive semantical or philosophical system.[24] Keeping this point in mind, let us review some of his ideas in the light of Bolzano's distinctions.

First, Frege tells us that the most important single notion for what he is about is that of a *conceptual content* (*begrifflicher Inhalt*).[25] In his explanation of this notion he makes the following three points. (1) He distinguishes between contents that can and contents that cannot be judged about.[26] This corresponds to Bolzano's distinction between contents of concepts (individual or general) and contents of propositions. (2) He distinguishes between judgments and mere conjunctions of concepts, the latter being conceived as possible contents of judgments.[27] This corresponds to Bolzano's distinction between judgments and mere contents of propositions. (3) Frege claims that two sentences may have the same conceptual content and yet differ in sense.[28] On this view, for instance, "John loves Mary" and "Mary is loved by John" express different senses but have the same conceptual con-

[22] *Ibid.*, pp. 428-429, 434, 436-437.

[23] *Ibid.*, p. 434. Compare also Frege's point of view: *Translations from the Philosophical Writings,* trans. by P. Geach and M. Black (Oxford, 1952), p. 29 and the footnote on p. 46. For a recent discussion of this view, see, for instance, N. Goodman, "On Likeness of Meaning," *Analysis,* X (1950), 1-7; "On Some Differences about Meaning," *ibid.,* XIII (1953), 90-96; P. D. Wienpahl, "More about Denial of Sameness of Meaning," *ibid.,* XII (1951), 19-23; R. Rudner, "On Sinn as a Combination of Physical Properties," *Mind,* LXI (1952), 82-84; and my "Propositional Attitudes," *Philosophical Quarterly,* X (1960), 301-312.

[24] G. Frege, *Begriffsschrift* (Halle, 1879).

[25] *Ibid.,* p. iv.   [26] *Ibid.,* p. 2.

[27] *Ibid.,* p. 2.   [28] *Ibid.,* p. 3.

tent. This corresponds to Bolzano's view that two propositions cannot be identical, although they may have the some content.

This comparison between Frege's notion of a conceptual content and Bolzano's notion of the content of a proposition shows that there is no significant difference between the two. And this seems to suggest that Frege was well aware of a general sense-denotation distinction at the time when he wrote the *Begriffsschrift*, though, of course, not necessarily of the specific one described in "On Sense and Denotation." [29] For it seems extraordinary to assume that he should not have distinguished between senses (concepts and conceptual contents) and objects₁.[30] But the best way to show that this assumption is unreasonable consists in explaining why Frege, though aware of it, did not explicitly mention a sense-denotation distinction in the *Begriffsschrift*.

I think he had at least three reasons. First, and perhaps of greatest importance, the system of the *Begriffsschrift* centers around the notion of a conceptual content of a sentence. Conceptual contents consist of concepts rather than objects₁. Hence there was no necessity for the purposes of the *Begriffsschrift* to talk about anything but what is expressed rather than denoted by expressions. Second, as far as whole sentences are concerned, there are no objects₁ corresponding to thoughts and propositions, in Bolzano's ontology. To conceive of sentences as names that denote as well as express something, as Frege does in "On Sense and Denotation," required a radically new step, namely, the introduction of the True and the False as denotations of sentences. If one therefore assumes that this step was not yet taken by Frege when he wrote the *Begriffsschrift*, it becomes obvious that he could

---

[29] His "Ueber Sinn und Bedeutung," *Zeitschrift fuer Philosophie und philosophische Kritik*, C (1892), 25-50 (*Translations*, pp. 56-78).

[30] This does not mean, however, that Frege held in the *Begriffsschrift* that sentences are names denoting the True or the False. I think that he took this specific step much later (at the time of "Ueber Sinn und Bedeutung").

not possibly have talked about the denotation (in addition to the sense) of a sentence. Third, upon Frege's analysis of identity (equality) as outlined in the *Begriffsschrift*, identity statements assert that two expressions have the same conceptual content rather than the same denotation, as he later holds. I shall not explain his earlier view, but remind the reader that it involves Frege's intention to account for the "synthetic nature" of some identity statements.[31]

Second, if Frege's *Begriffsschrift*, as I have tried to show, resembles Bolzano's system in several important respects — if, in particular, Frege should have been fully aware of a sense-denotation distinction before he wrote "On Sense and Denotation" — then it must also not be overlooked that there are at least two important differences between Frege's and Bolzano's treatment of senses. First, Frege introduced so-called second-level concepts.[32] Second, he replaced Bolzano's subject-predicate analysis by a function-argument analysis.[33] This step is obviously suggested to him by the logistic treatment of mathematics. But it is also in direct accord with his (and Bolzano's) notion of a conceptual content. To see this clearly one must remember that conceptual contents are conceived of as sums of concepts. This means that as far as conceptual contents are concerned, the subject and predicate places of sentences are of no importance whatsoever. All parts of a proposition are of equal status, irrespective of their positions in a proposition. However, Frege seems to have noticed, soon after the appearance of the *Begriffsschrift*, that the very notion of a proposition requires a distinction between concepts and objects$_2$.

III

He mentions this matter briefly in the *Grundlagen*.[34] A full

---

[31] *Begriffsschrift*, pp. 13-15, and "Ueber Sinn und Bedeutung" (*Translations*, pp. 56-57).

[32] *Begriffsschrift*, p. 17.

[33] *Ibid.*, p. vii.

[34] *Die Grundlagen der Arithmetik* (Breslau, 1884); *The Foundations*

account is given in Frege's answer to some remarks by B. Kerry.[35] Kerry had pointed out, basing his statements on Bolzano's view, that a concept itself is an object$_2$. Consider, for example, the sentence "The concept 'horse' is a concept easily attained." Kerry claims that this sentence says that the concept "horse" falls under the concept "a concept easily attained," and is thus an object$_2$ of the latter. Frege, on the other hand, defends the view that the phrase "the concept 'horse' " does not refer to a concept, but rather to an object$_2$ as distinguished from a concept.[36] He holds that a concept is always predicative in character and that it can never occur as the subject of a sentence. So much for the two opposing views. I wish to show that Frege's treatment of concepts can be considered a direct consequence of his earlier and also of Bolzano's view.

Bolzano and the Frege of the *Begriffsschrift* hold that all propositions consist of concepts in analogy to a whole's consisting of parts. Frege now seems to have raised the following question: how can three concepts, taken as things of the same kind and standing side by side, yield the kind of unity a proposition is supposed to have?[37] In other words, how can an individual concept, a general concept, and the relational concept of falling under a concept, when taken as things of the same kind, yield a proposition rather than a conceptual content, that is, a sum of concepts? Frege, I think, discovered here a very genuine problem. How important it is can perhaps best be seen if we look at it from a different point of view.

According to some philosophers, "this tree is green" (if

---

of Arithmetic, trans. by J. L. Austin (New York, 1950), p. x.

[35] B. Kerry, "Ueber Anschauung und ihre psychische Verarbeitung," *Vierteljahrsschrift fuer wissenschaftliche Philosophie,* IX (1885), 433-493; X (1886), 419-467; XI (1887), 53-116, 249-307; XIII (1889), 71-124, 392-419; XIV (1890), 317-353; XV (1891), 127-167.

[36] Frege's "Ueber Begriff und Gegenstand," *Vierteljahrsschrift fuer wissenschaftliche Philosophie,* XVI (1892), 192-205 (*Translations,* pp. 42-55).

[37] See, for instance, *Translations,* pp. 54-55.

true) describes the fact that a certain individual exemplifies a certain property. In order to speak about facts, they must therefore speak about the relation of exemplification. One can now formulate Frege's question in terms of exemplification: how can three things — an individual, a property, and the relation of exemplification, standing side by side — yield a fact? Facts just do not consist of three things standing side by side like chairs. The problem is usually solved by a distinction between two kinds of "things": things like individuals and properties on the one hand and the "thing" exemplification on the other. One adds that the relation of exemplification is a very special "thing," unlike all other things including ordinary relations.[38] Notice, though, that in saying this one introduces a new kind of thing, an "unsaturated" thing if you wish. But this, as we know, is precisely Frege's own solution. However, while some philosophers make the nexus of exemplification into a special unsaturated thing and hence introduce a new kind of entity in addition to individuals and properties, Frege solves the problem on a different level by making concepts themselves into unsaturated things.[39] This allows him to dispense with the relational concept of falling under (a concept). He needs therefore no "tie" at all between objects$_2$ and concepts. In this respect his solution is extremely ingenious.[40] One wonders why later students

[38] See, for instance, G. Bergmann, *Meaning and Existence*, pp. 208 and 210.

[39] See, for instance, Frege's "Ueber Begriff und Gegenstand" and his "On the Foundations of Geometry," *Philosophical Review*, LXIX (1960), 3-17.

[40] It should be noted, though, that Frege's solution requires one further distinction and one more explanation. The distinction is this. According to Frege, concepts can fall under higher concepts. In this case, since concepts are unsaturated, we have as it were two unsaturated things standing side by side. Frege consistently holds that two concepts "hold together" in a different way from a concept and an object$_2$. Thus he solves a problem which I think is peculiar to his system. His solution can be expressed either by saying that an object$_2$ falls *under* a concept, while a concept falls *within* a concept of higher level; or by saying that a concept of second level is a radically different thing from a con-

thought it false at worst and curious at best.[41]

The point I wish to make, however, has nothing to do with whether one accepts or rejects Frege's solution. It is that Frege's object-concept distinction must be regarded as "syntactical" rather than "ontological." It must be viewed as a distinction between objects$_2$ and concepts rather than between objects$_1$ and concepts. At least two considerations speak for this interpretation.

First, Frege's distinction can be made in a purely "syntactical" way, that is, without reference to criteria of existence. So formulated it reads as follows. There are expressions that can appear only in the subject places of well-formed (singular) sentences; there are also expressions that can occur only in the predicate places of sentences; no expression can occur in both the subject and the predicate places of sentences. Expressions that occur in subject places denote objects; expressions that occur in predicate places denote concepts.[42]

Second, one can easily show that senses other than concepts are objects$_2$, though of course not objects$_1$. In the sentence "John believes that the earth is round," the phrase "the earth is round" appears, according to Frege, as a name.[43] This name, when standing alone, denotes the True and expresses a sense. Let us call its denotation (the True) its ordinary denotation; its sense, the ordinary sense. In belief contexts, Frege holds, this sentence no longer denotes its ordinary de-

---

cept of first level in that than can "hold together," although they are both unsaturated. (See "Ueber Begriff und Gegenstand," p. 201; *Translations,* p. 51.) The explanation concerns such sentences as "green is a color." As far as I know, Frege does not explain how he would analyze such sentences. One might suggest, however, that they be rewritten in the form "the concept green is a color-concept." Upon this kind of analysis, they would say that a certain concept correlate (an object$_2$) falls under a certain concept.

[41] Compare, however, M. Black, "Language and Reality," *Proceedings and Addresses of The American Philosophical Association,* XXXII (1959), 5-17.

[42] I assume here that concept words *denote* concepts; see below.

[43] "Ueber Sinn und Bedeutung," p. 39 (*Translations,* p. 68).

notation, but rather its ordinary sense. The subordinate clause in "John believes that the earth is round" thus denotes the sense of "the earth is round." In other words, in belief contexts, "the earth is round" is a *name* of the ordinary sense of this sentence. What is denoted by a name, according to Frege's object$_2$-concept distinction, must be an object$_2$. Hence senses (other than concepts) must be objects$_2$.

To sum up: so far I have tried to show that something like the sense-denotation distinction, namely, a sense-object$_1$ distinction, must have been known to Frege before he introduced it (in a specific form) in his paper "On Sense and Denotation." I emphasized that this distinction was ontological in kind. Then I explained how the two notions of a proposition and a conceptual content led to Frege's distinction between concepts and objects$_2$. I stressed that this further distinction was a syntactical rather than ontological one. If this account is correct, it follows that the ontological status of concepts will be determined by the sense-object$_1$ rather than the concept-object$_2$ dichotomy. It would follow, at any rate, that the two must be sharply distinguished in a discussion of the question whether or not Frege was a nominalist. Before we can enter into this discussion, however, we must clear up one more point, namely, Frege's use of the terms "concept" and "property."

IV

Bolzano distinguishes between (general) concepts and properties. This is an ontological distinction; for only properties, not concepts, are objects$_1$. Frege, on the other hand, makes no such distinction. He holds that to say that F is a property of x means the same as to say that x falls under the concept F.[44] "Property" and "concept" are used by him interchangeably. Usually he speaks of concepts; occasionally, though, when German grammar makes the use of "concept" rather clumsy, he also uses the word "property." In most accounts of Frege's

---

[44] "Ueber Begriff und Gegenstand," p. 201 (*Translations*, p. 51).

view, no significance is attached to this fact. Frege's interchangeable use of "property" and "concept" is apparently thought to be merely a terminological matter.[45] I shall show that it is more than that, that it signifies an important feature of Frege's philosophy.

It must first be observed that Frege assimilates properties to concepts and not conversely. He explains his notion of concept and states then that the word "property" may be used to refer to concepts. Assume now that Frege's concepts and hence his properties are senses in Bolzano's use of the term. It follows, of course, that they could not possibly be Bolzano's properties. Nor, I think, could they possibly be the things one ordinarily calls properties. And this means that Frege does not speak about "ordinary" properties when he uses the words "concept" and "property."[46] This is indeed the conclusion we must draw if we take the similarity between Frege's and Bolzano's systems seriously. But has Frege really banished "ordinary" properties? I think that he has. However, my view may appear so extraordinary that I shall have to prove it independently of the contention that Frege's concepts are senses rather than objects₁ in Bolzano's sense.

Frege explains that *concepts belong to the realm of logic; they are not sensible.* A concept word may be accompanied by mental states, that is, for instance, by sense impressions, *but these sense impressions are not the referent of a concept word.*[47] A concept, I take it, is thus not the kind of thing that "comes through the senses," but rather something that is "grasped by the mental eye."[48] It is clear that this use of "concept" and hence "property" does not agree with what one ordinarily means when talking about properties.

At another place Frege tells us that *there are no concepts*

---

[45] See, for instance, Klemke, *op. cit.*

[46] I realize, of course, that the phrase "ordinary property" needs explanation. But I think that it will become sufficiently clear from the following paragraphs.

[47] *Foundations*, p. 37, footnote.

[48] Frege's *Grundgesetze der Arithmetik*, I (Jena, 1893), xxiv.

in the outside world.[49] Taking "concept" to be synonymous with "property," he asserts here that there are no properties in the outside world. Surely this use of "property" differs considerably from the ordinary use of the word. At still another place Frege asserts that concepts are objective but not *real* (*wirklich*). He denies that they are real because they do not act, mediately or immediately, on our senses.[50]

These and other contexts show that Frege's concepts are not properties in the ordinary sense. Still, someone may refuse to accept the conclusion that Frege omitted properties from his onotology. The only thing I can do at this point is to explain how the omission fits well into the wider frame of his philosophy, that it makes sense, and that it is therefore not unreasonable to attribute it to Frege.

Now, according to Frege, there are so-called *"subjective Vorstellungen"* (mental states). In particular, all sense impressions are such mental states. Hence, if one sees a blue spot, then one has a *"subjective Vorsetellung."* This sense impression, however, is not the referent of the concept word "blue." Moreover, whatever one can communicate about the blue spot is not of the same kind as a sense impression but is rather a conceptual kind. *"Subjective Vorstellungen"* in general are not communicable.[51] Hence there is no room for words referring to them in the clarified language proposed by Frege. What then do we mean by the concept word "blue"? We always mean, according to Frege, an objective concept, something that does not come through the senses but is grasped by the mind. Of course, sense impressions may in some sense be necessary for our intellectual life; without them, as Frege puts it, we might be as dumb as a board.[52] But this must by no means obscure the truth that concept words refer to things that have nothing whatsoever to do with our senses.

Upon this explication of "concept" and "property" what

---

[49] *Foundations*, p. 99.
[51] *Foundations*, p. 35.

[50] *Grundgesetze*, p. xviii.
[52] *Ibid.*, p. 115, footnote.

can be said about the question whether concept words denote
or express concepts? Frege says that concept words denote
(*bedeuten*) concepts. I take it, therefore, that he thinks of
them as denoting rather than expressing concepts. I take it
for granted also that he does not make the sense-denotation
distinction for concept words, at least not explicitly. These
two things seem reasonably certain. What is so puzzling
about them is the fact that one sees no obstacle to extending
the sense-denotation distinction to cover concept words in
addition to names. What is puzzling, in other words, is that
one has no answer to the question why Frege did not make
the distinction for concept words after he had introduced it
for names. I think that his reasons can now be easily seen.
Consider two of the most obvious proposals to extend the
distinction of concept words.

First, a concept word could not possibly denote a property
(an object$_1$) as distinguished from a concept; for there are
no such properties in Frege's system. He could therefore not
possibly hold that concept words denote properties and express concepts.

Second, a concept word could not possibly denote a class
(value range), and this for at least two reasons. First, classes
are objects$_2$ for Frege.[53] Hence if a class were the denotation
of a concept word in a sentence, we would have the case
where two objects$_2$, the object$_2$ denoted by the subject expression and the object$_2$ (the class) denoted by the predicate expression, stand side by side without yielding a whole. Second,
a concept could not be the sense of the name of the corresponding class, because the denotation of, say, "green" must
be different from the denotation of "the sense of 'the class
of green things.' " That it must be different follows directly
from Frege's (and Bolzano's) view; for when one thinks the
subjective idea "green," one thinks of a different thing from

---

[53] See "Function and Concept," *Translations*, p. 32. I note in passing
that this view eventually leads to the Russell paradox; see W. V.
Quine, "On Frege's Way Out," *Mind*, LXIV (1955), 145-159.

what one thinks of when one thinks the idea "the class of green things." This means that Frege could not hold that concept words denote classes and express concepts.

But although it is now clear that concept words could not denote anything but concepts, in accordance with Frege's use there is the possibility that they could express so-called concept correlates. Frege could have said that "green," for instance, denotes a concept and expresses the concept correlate denoted by "the concept green"; for even though he insists that "the concept green" denotes an object$_2$ (rather than a concept), he does not claim that it denotes an object$_1$ rather than a sense. In other words, although he holds that it denotes a saturated rather than an unsaturated thing, he does not hold that it denotes something other than a sense. Assuming that it does denote a sense, one could complete Frege's system in such a fashion that concept words are said to denote concepts and to express concept correlates. This, I think, is the only possibility within Frege's system of introducing the sense-denotation dichotomy for concept words.[54]

V

The question whether or not Frege was a nominalist makes little sense if one does not specify what one means by "nominalism," or, alternatively, what one's criterion for existence is. I shall consider three possible specifications.

First, Frege himself distinguishes between two meanings of "there is." Let me call them exist$_1$ and exist$_2$. He says that one must keep apart two wholly different cases in which one speaks of existence. In the one case the question is whether a proper name denotes something; in the other it is whether a concept comprehends objects under itself.[55] Frege argues in

---

[54] Compare in this respect Frege's system with the one outlined by A. Church in his "A Formulation of the Logic of Sense and Denotation," in *Structure, Method and Meaning: Essays in Honor of Henry M. Sheffer* (New York, 1951), pp. 3-24.

[55] *Translations*, pp. 104-105.

this context against the following view. Construing the thing denoted by a proper name as the extension of this name, and holding that a concept word refers to its extension, one may mistakenly think that since a proper name without denotation is illegitimate, a concept word without extension must be equally illegitimate. Against this view Frege asserts that a concept word does not denote an extension but a concept. A concept word may well have a denotation, that is, it may denote a concept, even though nothing falls under the concept. For instance, the concept word "round square" denotes, according to Frege, a concept. It has therefore a denotation. But since nothing is a round square, nothing falls under the concept. It is implied here, I think, that a certain concept exists even if nothing falls under it as long as there is a concept word that refers to it. One must therefore distinguish between the following two kinds of existence statements: (1) "α exists." This I write "α exists$_1$" and take to mean "'α' denotes something." Eisenhower exists$_1$. Clearly, every object$_2$ exists$_1$. Moreover, if concept words do name concepts, then (1) is true in case either "tree" or "round square" is substituted for "α," irrespective of the fact that while there are trees, there are no round squares. (2) "An F exists." This I write "F exists$_2$" and take to mean "There is an F." Trees exist$_2$; round squares do not.

It is clear, of course, that in Frege's ontology objects$_2$ exist$_1$. But it is also obvious that concepts exist$_1$ in the same way; for concept words denote concepts. Hence there is no distinction between the manner in which objects$_2$ and the manner in which concepts exist. Klemke seems to take Frege's exist$_1$ as his criterion.[56] He concludes therefore that Frege is not a nominalist. Upon his criterion this is undoubtedly so. But to accept it as the only relevant one means to overlook some important features of Frege's ontology.

Second, according to Bolzano, concepts do not exist like

[56] Klemke, *op. cit.*

objects$_1$. Since objects$_1$ comprise properties, one must conclude that concepts do not exist like properties. This suggests the following consideration. One may hold that properties do not exist in space and time. They do not exemplify spatial and temporal relations; only individuals do. In a schema like that of *Principia Mathematica*, this is brought out by the fact that properties and spatial and temporal relations are of the same type-level.[57] In this sense, then, properties are not in space and time. They are not, as I shall say for short, localized$_1$. However, Bolzano asserts that properties are in space and time while concepts are not and this leads him to say that the latter do not exist like the former. What he seems to have in mind is this. Although agreeing that properties are not localized$_1$, he wishes to say that they are nevertheless localized (localized$_2$) in the sense that they are exemplified by individuals which are localized$_1$. For example, the property blue may be said to be localized$_2$ here and now by being exemplified here and now a certain individual. Another way of saying the same thing is to insist that although properties do not exemplify spatial and temporal relations, their being exemplified by individuals takes place in space and time. Upon this distinction between what is localized$_1$ and what is localized$_2$, it is easily seen that concepts do not exist like properties. For properties, though not localized$_1$, are at least localized$_2$; concepts, on the other hand, are neither localized$_1$ nor localized$_2$. This is to say, we are never acquainted with an individual's exemplifying a concept but only with its exemplifying a property.

Consider in the light of this Frege's view of concepts. We remember that he does not distinguish between concepts and properties. In his philosophy there are only concepts. We also remember that concepts are not got through the senses but grasped by the mind. It would seem that what can only be so grasped must be unlocalized$_2$. Frege's concepts, I therefore

---

[57] See, for instance, G. Bergmann, *Meaning and Existence*, pp. 124-131.

think, not only do not exemplify spatial and temporal relations; they are not even exemplified in space and time. There are no concepts, as he says, in the outside world, in the totality of space.[58]

If, therefore, one understands by "nominalism" the view that properties are not even localized$_2$ in space and time, then Frege was most certainly a nominalist. This conclusion agrees well with some of the things a realist may say to defend his position that properties exist. For though he admits that properties are not localized$_1$ in space and time, he also insists that they are localized$_2$. In other words, even though the realist acknowledges that properties do not exemplify spatial and temporal relations, he nevertheless asserts that they are exemplified in space and time by individuals. That they are in this manner exemplified, and that he can therefore be acquainted with them by being acquainted with individuals, is the realist's reason for holding that properties exist. From his point of view a nominalist is one who denies that he is ever acquainted with properties in this way. From this point of view Frege is a nominalist. But notice that his is a very peculiar kind of nominalism. For though he denies that properties (concepts) are localized$_2$, he steadfastly asserts that they exist. In what further sense may concepts be held to exist?

Third, Frege's answer, I submit, would take the following form. There are things which are localized$_1$ in space and time. There are also things which are not so localized. All senses in general and all concepts in particular are of the latter kind. That these things exist, even though they are not localized in any sense, is shown by the fact that they can be apprehended by minds. What exists in this sense is what can interact with minds.[59] We may reasonably infer from this criterion (1) that Frege could agree that concepts do not exist

[58] *Foundations*, p. 99.
[59] Frege's "The Thought: A Logical Inquiry," *Mind*, LXV (1956), 309-311.

in terms of being localized (in any sense) and that he could be considered a nominalist for this reason; and (2) that he holds concepts to be real because they can be apprehended by minds and that he must therefore be called a realist.

6

An Apparent Difficulty
in Frege's Ontology

CHARLES E. CATON

Frege's ontology is erected on the distinction between objects and functions. According to Frege, everything is either an object or a function, and nothing is both an object and a function. The essential difference between objects and functions he describes in three different but synonymous ways: functions are said to be unsaturated (*ungesättigt*), incomplete (*unvollständig*), or in need of supplementation (*ergänzungsbedürftig*), while objects are said to to be saturated, complete, or not in need of supplementation.[1] Frege's semantics is erected on the distinction between the sense and the reference of a linguistic expression. Since everything is either an object or a function, it follows that any given sense or reference must also be either an object or a function. And, in combining these two basic distinctions, Frege held that the sense of an expression is an object. Yet he describes the senses of certain expressions as unsaturated. That is, he held three

Reprinted with the kind permission of the author and the editor from *The Philosophical Review*, LXXI (1962), 462-475.
[1] I use throughout the translations of P. T. Geach and Max Black's *Translations from the Philosophical Writings of Gottlob Frege* (2d ed.; Oxford, 1960). Page references to Frege's writings are to this volume unless otherwise noted.

doctrines which may be expressed as an apparently inconsistent triad:

(I) The sense of an expression is an object;
(II) The senses of some expressions are unsaturated;
(III) No object is unsaturated.

Clearly if the terms involved in these three doctrines were used always in the same sense, the three doctrines would be incompatible. If these terms were used unambiguously and if, further, Frege held these three doctrines or held things that entailed them, there would be a difficulty in his ontology of senses: there would be a contradiction. In this paper I will show that Frege in fact held three doctrines which may be expressed in his terminology as above, that, given his basic ontology, there are very good reasons why he held these doctrines, but that the three are not really incompatible. The resolution of the apparent incompatibility leads to further consideration of the notion of unsaturatedness.

I

First, Frege did in fact hold three such doctrines. Concerning Doctrine I, that the sense of an expression is always an object, Howard Jackson, in his note "Frege's Ontology,"[2] reports that Frege, in an unpublished paper from 1891-1892, actually argues that the sense of an expression is always an object. This doctrine, Jackson says, leads one to suppose that the sense of an expression can be the reference of a grammatical subject, which he notes is confirmed by a reading of "On Sense and Reference." He then remarks: "Whereas we do not have in natural languages a name for the sense of an expression . . . we may refer to the sense of an expression through the simple expedient of such expressions as 'the sense of x,' where 'x' takes expressions as values."[3] Jackson here

[2] *Philosophical Review*, LXIX (1960), 394-395. Jackson's paper is a comment on E. D. Klemke, "Professor Bergmann and Frege's 'Hidden Nominalism,'" *ibid.*, LXVIII (1959), 507-514.

[3] *Loc. cit.*, p. 395.

follows Frege himself: Frege says, "In order to speak of the sense of an expression 'A' one may simply use the phrase 'the sense of the expression "A."' " [4] If this is so, then it follows from what Frege says in "On Concept and Object" that the sense of an expression is, in every case, an object.[5] For Frege there offers what he calls a "criterion" of objects: "The three words 'the concept *horse*' do designate an object, but on that very account they do not designate a concept, as I am using the word. This is in full accord with the criterion I gave — that the singular definite article always indicates an object, whereas the indefinite article accompanies a concept-word." [6] Since, according to Frege himself, the sense of an expression can be referred to by means of an expression of the form 'the sense of the expression "...,"' it follows from the fact that such an expression involves the singular definite article that the sense of any expression is an object.[7]

---

[4] "On Sense and Reference," p. 59. Frege does not indicate any exceptions and in the immediate context is speaking quite generally of the sense and reference of "words" in indirect discourse.

[5] And hence, as Jackson argues (*loc. cit.*, p. 394) that it can never be a concept.

[6] Page 45. I take it that the exceptions Frege goes on to notice ("The Turk besieged Vienna" and "The horse is a four-legged animal"— actually only the latter, apparently) are not relevant to the present point. Frege attaches a footnote to the last sentence in the quotation above, indicating that the previous statements of the criterion are in the *Grundlagen der Arithmetik*, secs. 51, 60 n., 68 n., p. 80.

[7] It may be noted that from this criterion it also follows that a phrase of the form 'the reference of "..."' always has as its (customary) reference an object—even when the expression in double quotes is an expression for a function. I do not know whether Frege held this, but it would cause him no difficulty, since he has already postulated what Rulon Wells has called function-correlates, which are objects, as the references of expressions of the form 'the function $\varphi(\xi)$' and '$\varphi(\xi)$.' (See below and "On Concept and Object" and the *Grundgesetze*, I, sec. 4, last note—p. 156, note * in Geach and Black, *op. cit.*) And he could identify these references with reference of 'the reference of "..."' in the cases where the blank was filled with an expression for a function. As Frege notes (p. 58), the normal way of referring to the (customary) reference of 'E' is, of course, just to use 'E' (in direct discourse).

Doctrine II, that the senses of some expressions are unsaturated, is explicitly stated in a number of places by Frege. For example, in "On Concept and Object" he says:

Not all the parts of a thought can be complete; at least one must be 'unsaturated' or predicative; otherwise they would not hold together. For example, the sense of the phrase 'the number 2' does not hold together with that of the expression 'the concept *prime number*' without a link. We apply such a link in the sentence 'the number 2 falls under the concept *prime number*'; it is contained in the words 'falls under,' which need to be completed in two ways— by a subject and an accusative; and only because their sense is thus 'unsaturated' are they capable of serving as a link. Only when they have been supplemented in this twofold respect do we get a complete sense, a thought.[8]

Note that here Frege is speaking generally and using "falls under" merely as an example of an expression the sense of which is unsaturated, and that part of the point of the passage is precisely that it must hold in general that at least one part of a thought is unsaturated. The rest of the point of the passage (which I will discuss below) is that the same is true of the *references* of such expressions, i.e., of concepts and relations.

The following example, also showing that according to Frege some senses are unsaturated, taken from his "Negation," is typical of his treatment of logical connectives:

If one thought contradicts another, then from a sentence whose sense is the one it is easy to construct a sentence expressing the other. Consequently the thought that contradicts another thought appears as made up of that thought and negation. (I do not mean by this, the act of denial.) But the words 'made up of,' 'consists of,' 'component,' 'part' may lead to our looking at it the wrong way. If we choose to speak of parts in this connexion, all the same these parts are not mutually independent in the way that we are elsewhere used to find when we have parts of a whole. The thought does not, by its make-up, stand in any need of completion; it is self-sufficient. Negation on the other hand needs to be completed by a thought. The two components, if we choose to employ this expression, are quite different in kind and contribute quite differently toward the formation of the whole. One completes, the other is com-

---

[8] Page 54.

pleted. To bring out in language the need for completion, we may write 'the negation of . . .,' where the blank after 'of' indicates where the completing expression is to be inserted. For the relation of completing, in the realm of thoughts and their parts, has something similar corresponding to it in the realm of sentences and their parts.[9]

Frege then gives an example and remarks that in the example "we can see how the thought is made up of a part that needs completion and a part that completes it."

Finally, I take an example from Frege's "Gedankengefüge," in which he explains that the sense in which a sign is unsaturated is derivative from that in which its sense is unsaturated:

The 'and' which is thus more precisely defined in its use appears doubly unsaturated. It requires for its completion a sentence which precedes and a sentence which follows. Moreover what corresponds to 'and' in the realm of senses must be doubly unsaturated. When it becomes saturated with thoughts, it unites these thoughts. As a mere thing the group of letters 'and' is of course as little unsaturated as any other thing. In respect to its use as a sign that is to express a sense, one can call it unsaturated, in that here it can have the intended sense only in the position between two sentences. Its purpose as a sign requires completion by a preceding and a following sentence. Strictly speaking, unsaturatedness occurs in the realm of senses and is transferred from there to the sign.[10]

Doctrine III, that no objects are unsaturated, is of course familiar from the passages in which Frege expounds his ontology.[11]

It is clear, then, that Frege in fact held three doctrines which can, in his own terminology, be expressed as the apparently inconsistent triad above.

II

It is no accident that Frege held Doctrines I and II: given his basic ontology (including Doctrine III), there are good,

[9] Pages 131-132.
[10] *Beiträge zur Philosophie des deutschen Idealismus,* III (1923), No. 1, 36-51. The passage translated above is from p. 39.
[11] Cf. pp. 24, 47 (including note †), 115, 152-154, 166.

perhaps compelling, reasons for his holding such doctrines.

Why did Frege hold Doctrine II, that the senses of some expressions (viz., as we have seen, expressions for functions) are unsaturated? It is, I think, clear from the end of his essay "On Concept and Object" that his reason for holding this is that he thought one had to hold it in order to understand how there could be thoughts (the customary senses of declarative sentences) at all. I quote the entire relevant passage:

> Somebody may think that this is an artificially created difficulty; that there is no need at all to take account of such an unmanageable thing as what I call a concept; that one might, like [Benno] Kerry, regard an object's falling under a concept as a relation, in which the same thing could occur now as object, now as concept. The words 'object' and 'concept' would then serve only to indicate the different positions in the relation. This may be done; but anybody who thinks the difficulty is avoided in this way is very much mistaken; it is only shifted.

So far Frege is discussing a difficulty that arises in ontology, that of seeing how objects and functions fit together, a difficulty at least akin to the traditional problem of the relation between a universal and the particulars that exemplify it. But now (in the passage already quoted) Frege turns to senses and what they must be like in order to fit together into thoughts:

> For not all the parts of a thought can be complete; at least one must be 'unsaturated' or predicative; otherwise they would not hold together. For example, the sense of the phrase 'the number 2' does not hold together with that of the expression 'the concept *prime number*' without a link. We apply such a link in the sentence 'the number 2 falls under the concept *prime number*'; it is contained in the words 'falls under,' which need to be completed in two ways — by a subject and an accusative; and only because their sense is thus 'unsaturated' are they capable of serving as a link. Only when they have been supplemented in this twofold respect do we get a complete sense, a thought.

Frege now turns to the same kind of difficulty as it involves the references of the expressions in question:

> I say that such words or phrases stand for a relation. We now get the same difficulty for the relation that we were trying to avoid

for the concept. For the words 'the relation of an object to the concepts it falls under' designate not a relation but an object; and the three proper names 'the number 2,' 'the concept *prime number,*' 'the relation of an object to a concept it falls under,' hold aloof from one another just as much as the first two do by themselves; however we put them together, we get no sentence.

And finally Frege returns to thoughts: "It is thus easy for us to see that the difficulty arising from the 'unsaturatedness' of one part of the thought can indeed be shifted, but not avoided." [12]

Here Frege seems hardly to have distinguished the question how a function can fit together with an object or objects so as to yield another object from the question how senses can fit together so as to yield a thought. [13] And his solution to the problem in the case of senses and in the case of functions and objects was to regard senses of two kinds, saturated and unsaturated, as he regarded entities generally as of two kinds, saturated and unsaturated. Thus the reason, or at least one of the reasons, Frege held Doctrine II, that the senses of some expressions are unsaturated, is that in the realm of senses a problem arose which was precisely analogous to a problem arising in the realm of entities; and his solution to the problem concerning senses was precisely analogous.

That these two problems are, from the standpoint of Frege's ontology, *different* problems is clear. A thought is not a truth-value, although both are objects. Functions whose values are truth-values, when completed (saturated) by appropriate arguments, yield truth-values. The truth-value which is the value of such a function for an appropriate argument is not

---

[12] The entire passage quoted is from "On Concept and Object," pp. 54-55. Cf. "On the Foundations of Geometry," *Philosophical Review,* LXIX (1960), 12-13, where the analogous point is made in terms of references.

[13] William Marshall, in his "Sense and Reference: A Reply" (*Philosophical Review,* LXV [1956], 342-361) regards this passage as showing that a concept or relation "may be called" either the sense or the reference of a predicate. But since none of Marshall's evidence for the fact that they may be called the sense is convincing, the better interpretation seems to be to take the passage above as it stands.

the set whose only members are the function and its argument. Nevertheless, the problem for senses is precisely analogous: two (or more) senses are just so many objects. A thought, however, is a complex of senses which fit together in a way analogous to (though not the same as) the way a function and its argument fit together. What a declarative sentence expresses is not a set of senses (which might be listed), any more than what it stands for is a set of objects. For example, in the thoughts that $3 > 2$ and that $2 > 3$, the senses of "3," "2," and ">" are fitted together differently, just as the function and its arguments are so as to yield as values the True in the one case and the False in the other. And if the notion of something's being unsaturated is required to explain how the latter is possible, it might well be thought that it, or something like it, is required in order to explain how the former is possible.

But now, since according to Frege's ontology everything that there is is either a function or an object, senses must be either all functions or all objects or some of them functions and the rest objects; that is, the problem arises of how the function-object and the sense-reference distinctions are related. It might be thought that from Doctrine II, together with his doctrine that all and only functions are unsaturated, it followed that some senses are objects (viz., the saturated senses) and that some senses are functions (viz., the unsaturated senses). Nevertheless, as we have seen above, Frege held that all senses are objects. What I now wish to show is, then, that, given his ontology, there is a good reason why Frege held this doctrine.

The reason is the following. Frege says that he cannot give a proper definition of what an object is:

When we have thus admitted objects without restriction as arguments and values of functions, the question arises what it is that we are here calling an object. I regard a regular definition as impossible, since we have here something too simple to admit of logical analysis. It is only possible to indicate [*hindeuten*] what is meant. Here I can only say briefly: An object is anything that is not a function, so that an expression for it does not contain any empty place.[14]

Since everything that there is is either an object or a function, an object can of course be defined as anything that is not a function, and vice versa; but such a definition would be of little use unless there were some way of telling or at least some clue as to whether something was an object which did not require knowing that it was not a function, and vice versa. But Frege did provide such a way or clue in his "criterion" of objects: "the singular definite article always indicates an object, whereas the indefinite article accompanies a concept-word" or, as above, that an expression for an object "does not contain any empty place." Neither does Frege give any better explanation of what a function is, and in connection with functions he uses the corresponding grammatical test.

That this criterion of objects is important in Frege's system is clear from his well-known doctrine that the concept *horse* is not a concept. It cannot be, according to Frege, since the phrase "the concept *horse*" involves the singular definite article and hence stands for an object rather than a concept.[15] Here Frege takes his criterion of objects so seriously that he postulates a new type of object, what Rulon Wells has called "concept-correlates," rather than give it up. But given the criterion and given that one can refer to the sense of any expression '. . .' by means of the phrase 'the sense of the expression ". . .," ' Doctrine I follows; i.e., it follows that the sense of any expression is an object.

Thus Frege's basic ontology gives him good, perhaps compelling reasons for holding Doctrines I and II.

III

Clearly the question of what Frege meant by saying that functions are unsaturated and that objects are saturated is

---

[14] "What Is a Function?" p. 32.

[15] Cf. "On Concept and Object," pp. 45 ff.; the *Grundgesetze*, p. 56 of Geach and Black, *op. cit.*, note *.

relevant here. I will, however, not attempt to explain this.[16] Frege himself characterized these locutions as figures of speech [17] and, as far as I know, never undertook to explain in more nearly literal terms what he meant. But nevertheless the ontology that Frege states in terms of unsaturatedness clearly requires certain things of that notion itself. According to the ontology, whatever unsaturatedness is it must be either an object or a function. But it seems quite clear, e.g., from the fact that many different functions are unsaturated, that unsaturatedness is a function and indeed a function whose values are truth-values.

What I wish now to suggest is that, given Frege's ontology of functions, there must be infinitely many different functions, all of which, because of their similarity, might be called unsaturatedness, rather than just one which applies to all functions. Clearly to show this it would suffice to show (a) that, according to Frege, there are infinitely many different kinds of function and (b) that, according to Frege, a function (in our case, unsaturatedness) that takes a function of one of these kinds as an argument cannot take a function of another of these kinds as an argument. These two, together with his doctrine that all functions are unsaturated, would clearly involve an infinite number of different functions any of which might be called unsaturatedness. Now Frege states (b) for at least two different ways in which functions may be separated into kinds and held what at least appears to entail (a). This can be seen from a consideration of his ontology of functions.

Frege distinguished what he called different *levels* of func-

---

[16] This question—or rather what Frege could have meant—has been considered by William Marshall, "Frege's Theory of Functions and Objects," *Philosophical Review*, LXII (1953), 374-390; Michael Dummett, "Frege on Functions: A Reply," *ibid.*, LXIV (1955), 96-107, and "Note: Frege on Functions," *ibid.*, LXV (1956), 229-230; and Max Black, "Frege on Functions," in *Problems of Analysis* (Ithaca, 1954), pp. 229-254.

[17] Cf. "On Concept and Object," p. 55; "The Foundations of Geometry," *loc. cit.*, p. 12.

tions: "Now just as functions are fundamentally different from objects, so also functions whose arguments are and must be functions are fundamentally different from functions whose arguments are objects and cannot be anything else. I call the latter first-level, the former second-level functions." [18] Frege regarded difference of level as such a fundamental difference that nonsense would result from ignoring it:

I do not want to say it is false to assert about an object what is asserted here about a concept [viz., in the particular case he is discussing, that there is at least one thing realizing it]; I want to say it is impossible, senseless, to do so. . . .

What has been shown here in one example holds good generally; the behavior of the concept is essentially predicative, even where something is being asserted about it; consequently it can be replaced there only by another concept, never by an object. Thus the assertion that is made about a concept does not suit an object. Second-level concepts, which concepts fall under, are essentially different from first-level concepts, which objects fall under. The relation of an object to a first-level concept that it falls under is different from the (admittedly similar) relation of a first-level to a second-level concept.[19]

From Frege's remarks on the relation of falling-under here, it looks as though he would want to, and in consistency have to, say the same thing of unsaturatedness (assuming it to be a function), viz., that the unsaturatedness predicable of first-level functions was different from the unsaturatedness predicable of second-level functions. If so, then there must be an infinity of unsaturatedness functions of different levels, since unsaturatedness at any level n is itself a function and hence must fall under an unsaturatedness function of level $n + 1$, if (as Frege holds) all functions are unsaturated.

This reasoning applies equally well to any infinite regress of functions of successively higher levels. Although I do not know of any place where Frege explicitly recognizes such a hierarchy, it seems clear that he held what entails that there should be one. For example, he regards the universal and

[18] "On Function and Concept," p. 38.
[19] "On Concept and Object," p. 50.

existential generalization of a propositional function as involving a function of the next higher level. And if from the fact that something falls under a function of a given level it follows that there is a function of that level, then an infinity of such generalization functions of different levels will obviously result. For each of these latter to be unsaturated an infinity of unsaturatedness functions of different levels would be required.[20]

Actually, an infinity of such functions is, I think, already involved as a consequence of another part of Frege's ontology of functions. Among first-level functions, Frege distinguished functions of one and two arguments, and among second-level functions between those whose argument (a first-level function) was a function of one argument and those whose argument was a function of two arguments:

In regard to second-level functions with one argument, we must make a distinction, according as the role of this argument can be played by a function of one or of two arguments; for a function of one argument is essentially so different from one with two arguments that the one function cannot occur as an argument in the same place as the other.[21]

Similarly, from the *Grundgesetze:*

Functions of two arguments are as fundamentally different from functions of one argument as these are from objects. For while the latter are entirely saturated, functions of two arguments are less saturated than those of one argument, which are already *unsaturated.*

Thus in $\neg\!\!\frown\!\!\frown\!\!\phi(a)$ we have an expression in which we can replace the name of the function $\varphi(\xi)$ with the name of a function of one argument, but neither by the name of an object nor by the name of a function of two arguments.[22]

From the doctrine here stated it would follow that even at the first level a function of one argument and one of two

---

[20] The directions for constructing *bedeutungsvoll* names, including function names, out of other names given in the *Grundgesetze*, sec. 30, would allow the construction to go on indefinitely.

[21] "On Function and Concept," p. 40.

[22] *Op. cit.*, I, sec. 21, p. 37 (my translation). The formula means "there is at least one object which is φ."

arguments would fall under different second-level unsaturatedness functions; for the former could not be an argument to *any* function of which the latter could be an argument, and vice versa. Thus an infinity of second-level unsaturatedness functions would be involved, provided only that there were an infinity of first-level functions which differed in that they were functions of different numbers of arguments. For example, iteration of the implication function, adding a new argument each time, would yield an infinity of second-level unsaturatedness functions.

Let me be clear here about what I am basing my reasoning on. I know of no place where Frege explicitly says that there are an infinite number of functions differing in level or that there are an infinite number of relations differing in their number of arguments. I base my reasoning rather (i) on the fact that the radical differences which (as above) Frege finds between first- and second-level functions and between functions of one and two arguments seem, in the first case not to depend on the functions being of the *first* as opposed to the *second* level but rather merely on their being of *different* levels and, in the second case, not on the functions being of *one* as opposed to *two* arguments but rather merely on their taking *different* numbers of arguments, and (ii) on that fact that Frege sets no limit to the number of levels or to the degree of a relation. But even if these assumptions are erroneous, if unsaturatedness is a function, Frege would, on his principles, require four different unsaturatedness functions even to deal with the basic functions of the *Grundgesetze* (cf. sec. 31).

It is now clear that Doctrine III of the triad with which I began, viz., the doctrine that no object is unsaturated, can only mean something like:

(III') No object is an appropriate argument of any unsaturatedness function of which a function is an appropriate argument.

The reason for this would, of course, be that any unsaturatedness which is truly or even meaningfully predicable of a function must itself be of at least the second level, and to predicate a second-level function of an object is, according to Frege, nonsense. That is, III' is just a consequence of Frege's distinction between levels of functions. Furthermore, it seems clear that when Frege says that objects are *saturated*, he again must mean something like III'.

Now, of course, it becomes evident that the triad of doctrines which I have shown that Frege held are not incompatible at all, at least not in the way it might *prima facie* have seemed that they are. For Doctrine III is now seen to mean something like III'. And if Doctrine I is true, i.e., if all senses are objects, then for II (some senses are unsaturated) not to be nonsense, the unsaturatedness referred to in II must be a function of the first level, i.e., a function of objects. But none of the infinitely many unsaturatedness functions covered by III' is a first-level function.[23]

Thus it appears that a more precise statement of Frege's ontology would involve infinitely many functions all called unsaturatedness: two of the first level (one for linguistic expressions, one for senses) and infinitely many others: for an unsaturatedness function taking a function of a given level as an argument cannot take a function of another level as an argument; and even within a given level, an unsaturatedness function taking a function of a certain number of arguments as an argument cannot take a function of a different number of arguments as an argument.[24]

[23] As far as I know, Frege explicitly distinguished only the sense applying to linguistic expressions from that applying to senses, never remarking a difference between the latter and the sense or senses applying to functions.

[24] Frege held that one could deal with second-level functions in terms of first-level functions (cf. the *Grundgesetze*, sec. 34), but he also held that "this does not banish from the world the difference between first-level and second-level functions" ("On Function and Concept," p. 41, where Frege also makes a similar remark about functions of one and two arguments). It may be noted that similar remarks apply to the functions we now call universal and existential generalization, as Frege himself points out.

7

Ontological Alternatives

GUSTAV BERGMANN

In a recent essay[1] Dr. Egidi, stating what she takes to be
Frege's ontology, starts from and uses throughout as a foil
what in another essay[2] I have said about Frege. She holds
that Frege is an idealist, takes me to hold that he is a nominalist. As I use 'nominalism', Frege is not a nominalist. Nor
did I ever say that he was one. I merely tried to show that
there is in the very structure of his ontology a tendency toward nominalism. That makes the title of my essay, "Frege's
Hidden Nominalism," suggestive rather than accurate. In
spite of what Dr. Egidi says, I still believe that the nominalistic tendency is unmistakably there. Nor has she convinced
me that Frege is an idealist. She has, however, shown very
convincingly what I, for one, had not seen as clearly as she
does, namely, that there is also an unmistakable structural
tendency toward idealism in Frege's ontology. Thus, if I were

This is the English original of "Alternative Ontologiche Riposta
alla Dotoressa Egidi," which appeared in *Giornale Critico della Filosofia Italiana*, XVII (1963). Reprinted with the kind permission of the
author and the editor.

[1] "La Consistenza Filosofica della Logica di Frege," *Giornale Critico
della Filosofia Italiana*, 16, 1962, 194-208. See also her "Matematica,
logica e filosofia nell' opera di Gottlob Frege," *Physis*, 4, 1962, 5-32.
The essays will be cited as CFLF and MLFF, respectively.

[2] "Frege's Hidden Nominalism," *Philosophical Review*, 67, 1958, 437-
59. See also "Propositional Functions," *Analysis*, 17, 1956, 43-48.

asked to choose for her essay a title as suggestive and as exaggerated as mine, I would call it "Frege's Hidden Idealism."

Those who are merely clever sometimes discover tendencies which are not there. Those who discern hidden tendencies which are there think structurally and, sometimes, profoundly. In my judgment Dr. Egidi's essay is of a profundity that deserves high praise. Yet I also judge much of what she says to be radically mistaken. Because of these mistakes she makes an idealist out of Frege. Her mistakes reflect the idealistic ambience that has nourished her. So she should not be blamed for them too severely. Those who know how difficult metaphysics is also know that, since its core is dialectical, there is nothing paradoxical about judging an essay in metaphysics to be both profound and profoundly mistaken.

Dr. Egidi, I just said, makes an idealist out of Frege. This is not quite accurate and the inaccuracy is of a sort to which one as committed as she is to accurate intellectual biography might well object. Explicitly she merely claims that Frege's renovation of logic and, inseparably from it, his analysis of the simple clause '*a* is *F*' is implicitly idealistic, i.e., that it fits with or perhaps even suggests an idealistic ontology, just as in her opinion Aristotle's logic and philosophical grammar fit only with the realistic ontology he actually propounds. If you wish, replace "fits and perhaps even suggests" by "inspires and perhaps even is inspired by." The idea is clear. I express it by calling a claim of this sort structural. Structurally, Dr. Egidi claims, the philosophical grammar of the *Begriffsschrift* is idealistic.

My own concern is exclusively structural. That determines what I shall say as well as the order in which I shall say it. In Section One I shall state and unravel the relevant part of the fundamental ontological dialectic. Section Two is about Frege. In Section Three some of Dr. Egidi's arguments will be examined. In Section One, which must be most succinct, the main issues will be stressed at the expense of all the de-

tails which may be found elsewhere.[3] Since in Section Two it
will be taken for granted that Frege's ontology is realistic, I
refer to a recent essay by Reinhardt Grossmann[4] in which
this appraisal, which as it happens is also the traditional one,
has been freshly examined and impressively documented,
structurally as well as biographically.

I

Mind is One; the world is Many. This is but an aphorism.
Aphorisms must be unpacked. Yet they remain suggestive
even after they have been unpacked. Also, they allow us to
express our sense of debt to and continuity with the tradition.
That is why I shall try to expose the deepest roots of the
idealism-realism issue by unpacking this particular aphorism.
Nor, since they are so deep, are they the roots of just this
one issue. But I shall focus on it.

To exist or to be an *entity* is one and the same. Your or my
now or at some other time perceiving or remembering or imagining that Peter is blond is called an *act.* Peter's being
blond is the single *intention* of these several acts. Acts are
mental entities. Peter's being blond is a *nonmental* entity. The
intentions of some acts are mental; those of some others, nonmental. Restating these bits of common sense shows how,
commonsensically, 'entity', 'act', 'intention', 'mental' and 'nonmental' will be used. Idealism holds that all entities are mental; materialism, that they are all nonmental. Only realism$_2$
sides with common sense, asserts that (1) some entities are
mental, some nonmental. Materialism we may safely dismiss
as absurd. (1) by itself is an empty husk. Realists$_2$[5] also

[3] See in particular the first four essays of my *Logic and Reality.*
[4] "Frege's Ontology," *Philosophical Review,* 70, 1961, 23-40; see also
his "Conceptualism," *Review of Metaphysics,* 14, 1960, 243-54.
[5] The meaning of 'realism' in 'realism-nominalism' is radically different from that in 'realism-idealism'. The first dichotomy, being one
of general ontology, lies deeper than the second. The choice of subscripts reflects this difference.

must assert and justify that (2) minds can know what is non-mental. To justify (2) is to present and to defend against all dialectical attacks an ontological assay of acts and their intentions that fulfills two conditions. (a) When I believe what is false, the act is there, its intention is not. The assay must account for such acts. (b) The assay must provide a "connection" between an act and its intention which is so "close" that it justifies (2), irrespective of whether the intention is (α) mental or (β) nonmental. (α) leads to the dialectic of the Cartesian *Cogito;* (β), to that of (2). An example will help. According to the Aristotelian-Thomistic account of perception, when I perceive a tree, two substances, mine and the tree's, exemplify one universal. Clearly, this "connection" is sufficiently "close." The dialectical difficulties of (a) and (b) are notorious. So I need not and shall not here consider them except as they impinge upon that particular piece of the dialectic I propose to unravel.

(What has been said in the last paragraph suffices to unpack the aphorism that *epistemology is merely the ontology of the knowing situation.* This use of 'knowing' is of course generic, comprehending the several *species* of perceiving, remembering, believing, imagining, doubting, entertaining, and so on. Henceforth 'species' will be used only for these kinds of "knowing.")

Yesterday I perceived that Peter is blond. The act that would have occurred if instead of perceiving this fact I had remembered it is different from the one that actually occurred. This no philosopher has ever questioned. That shows that they all take two things for granted, namely, first, that an act and its species are both mental entities, and, second, that the latter is a constituent of the former. If instead of perceiving that Peter is blond I had perceived that Mary is tall, is the act that would have occurred different from the one that actually occurred? Their intentions are different, but they are both nonmental. *Prima facie* that provides an ontological alternative. One may hold that the "two" acts are one and not two. Or one may hold that each act has a constituent such that in two acts this constituent is the same if and only if they have the same intention. Call a constituent of this sort a *thought*. As one ordinarily speaks, 'thought' is used in two ways. Once the word stands for the act itself; once for a constituent of it which varies with its intention. That makes our use of 'thought' in this essay technical, although only in the very limited sense that we shall employ the word in only one of the two ways in which we employ it when speaking as we ordinarily do. (Some philosophers use 'thought', technically, as I use 'intention'. The dangers and inconveniences of this use are obvious.) Thoughts, as we use the word, are constituents of acts. Hence, *if* there are thoughts, they are mental entities. If there are none, then what I am about to assert of them holds of acts, i.e., of those mental entities which, speaking as we ordinarily do, we sometimes also call thoughts. That is why I need not as yet commit myself as to whether or not there are thoughts.

An ontology is an inventory of what exists (is there). In his own peculiar way and for his own peculiar purposes, an ontologist, therefore, describes the world. His description is inadequate unless it accounts by what is for what is (phenomenologically) presented to us. I shall next call attention to two striking features of what is so presented. *No* ontology, therefore, is adequate unless it accounts for both of them. That is why I shall not make any specific ontological commitment until these two features have been stated and the dialectics which because of them *every* ontology must face has been exhibited.

Call a thought unitary if and only if it has no constituent which is itself a thought. All thoughts are unitary. This is one of the two striking features. Call it the *unity of thought*. Replace 'unity' by 'One', 'thought' by 'mind' and you will see that the first half of the aphorism is already unpacked.

Some hold that awareness is propositional, i.e., that there are no thoughts whose intentions are not represented by sen-

tences. If so, then all thoughts whose intentions are represented by simple clauses are unitary. Take the thought whose
intention is represented by 'Peter is blond'. The only thoughts
that could be constituents of it are those of Peter, of is, and
of blond. If awareness is propositional then there are no such
thoughts and the unity thesis asserts something new or further
only for those thoughts whose intentions are represented by
compound sentences. As it happens, though, the arguments for
such thoughts being unitary are the same as those for all
thoughts being unitary. Thus, once more, we need not commit
ourselves.

If the unity of thought is a striking (phenomenological)
feature, what need is there for arguments to support it, what
point in arguing against it? The question is reasonable indeed.
The reasonable answer is that the arguments in support
merely clear up the misunderstandings which have been caused
by the (phenomenologically) inaccurate way in which many
philosophers and psychologists have described what is called
introspection or introspective analysis. Introspection presumably "decomposes" thoughts into their constituents. What actually occurs when one introspects a thought is a series of
further thoughts that fulfills certain conditions. Two such
conditions are, first, that the intention of each member of the
series is a constituent of the intention of the thought that is
being "decomposed," and, second, that the intentions of all
members of the series are all the constituents of the intention
of that thought. A thought's being unitary (a) and its intention having no constituents (b) are two propositions and not
one. The invalid inference from (a) to (b) is one of the pivots
of the traditional dialectic. Of that more presently. The invalid inference from the negation of (b) to the negation of
(a) is the main source of the misunderstandings that may
weaken one's grasp of the unity of thought. The premiss as
well as the alleged conclusion of an invalid inference may be
either true or false. (a) is true. How about (b)? One's answer
depends on his grasp of the second feature.

Unless some intentions were mental, we could not know that there are minds, just as we could not know that there are nonmental entities unless some intentions were nonmental. The difference between the mental and the nonmental is itself (phenomenologically) presented to us. Call the part of the world which is nonmental the truncated world. The idealists claim that the truncated world does not exist. The second feature strikes us most forcefully in nonmental intentions. As to whether it is also a feature of minds we need not as yet commit ourselves. I shall therefore call attention to it by attending to some nonmental entities *as they are (phenomenologically) presented to us*. And I shall save words by omitting the italicized phrase. That the omission does not prejudge anything will soon be clear beyond doubt.

Take a spot which is red and round. The spot is an entity; its shape (round) and its color (red) are two others. The latter (red, round) are *constituents* of, or as I shall also say, they are "in" the former (the spot). An entity which has constituents is *complex* or a complex. If you challenge any of this, I answer that the example shows how in ontology I use 'constituent' and 'complex' and that therefore there is nothing to be challenged.

Take two spots; one red and round, the other green and square. Red and round are "tied" together. So are green and square. Red and square are not. Nor are green and round. That is why there are two spots and not four and why these two are what they are. That shows two things. *First*. There is a sort of entities which are constituents of others and yet so "independent" that a complex is more than, as one says, the sum or class of them. Entities of this sort I here call *things*. This is of course a very special use of the word. *Second*. The something more, the "tie" which makes a complex out of the class, must have an ontological ground. Everything except sameness and diversity must have an ontological ground. One who does not understand that does not understand the task and nature of ontology. The entity or entities which are the ground of the "tie" I call *subsistents*.

In the *truncated* world *as it is* (*phenomenologically*) *presented to us* there are many things. This is the second striking feature. If it were not for the italicized word and the italicized phrase, we would already have unpacked the second half of the aphorism: The world is Many. It will be better if before finishing this job I interrupt for four comments which, although they are badly in need of expansion, may yet help to avoid puzzlement.

1. Not all subsistents are "ties," but they are all "dependent" in the sense in which things are "independent." Since the distinction corresponds to the traditional one between *categorematic* and *syncategorematic*, I shall also use these two words even though the traditional distinction is among words rather than, like mine, among the entities which I hold these words represent. That is not to say that there are two (or more) modes of exist*ing*. 'Exist' is univocal indeed. Otherwise I, for one, do not know what it means to exist. But there are several kinds of exist*ents* and the differences among the highest kinds or *modes* are very great indeed. Categorematic and syncategorematic are two modes.

2. A thing that has no constituent which is a thing (except, as the mathematicians speak, trivially itself) is called *simple* or a simple. What has been said so far does not at all depend on whether or not there are simples. Among subsistents the distinction simple-complex does not even make sense. Nor do syncategorematic entities need further ones to connect them with the categorematic entities they connect. (Thus Bradley's paradox is avoided.)

3. Complexes are constituents of other complexes. They are also "independent" in the sense in which I just used this ambiguous word. As I proposed to use 'thing', that makes complexes things, which is rather awkward, since the most interesting complexes are of the kind one would rather call facts, in ontology as well as when speaking as we ordinarily do. The cause of the awkwardness is that any classification of complexes, e.g., in "facts" and "complex things," requires

some of those specific ontological commitments which I as yet wish to avoid. In an ontology that admits simples, for instance, one could reserve 'thing' for simples and divide all "independent" entities into two kinds, things and complexes.

4. Minds are in the world, of course. Are they, too, Many? Less aphoristically, are acts complex? I have not as yet committed myself. But we understand already why, *if* acts are complex, this feature imposes itself forcefully in their case. Thoughts are unitary, i.e., they have no constituents which are thoughts. That is not the same as being things and being simple. Yet the ideas are close. Nor is there any doubt that even if its thought is merely one among the constituents of an act, it imposes itself so forcefully that the others are easily overlooked.

The task of ontology is to account for what is (phenomenologically) presented to us. If one holds that awareness is propositional, he must also hold that all (nonmental) intentions are complexes. Everyone agrees that some are. Every ontologist must account for this manifold (complexity). The realist$_2$ accounts for it by a corresponding manifold in the truncated world of which, unlike the idealist, he claims that it exists. At least, that is for him structurally the obvious way to account for the second striking feature. Nor do I know of any articulate realistic$_2$ ontologist who has found another way. That fully unpacks the second half of the aphorism. The world is Many.

The basic dialectic that controls the realism-idealism issue has *three centers*. The interactions among these centers determine the ontological alternatives which are or seem available to us.

Most ontologies, whether realistic$_2$ or idealistic, recognize that there are things, be they mental or nonmental or either. Very few recognize the ontological status of the subsistents, i.e., they do not recognize that the syncategorematic *terms* represent *entities*. The only two recent exceptions from this almost universal neglect are Frege and the early Husserl, i.e.,

the author of the *Logische Untersuchungen*. That is indeed
one very major reason for my admiration of these two thinkers. Characteristically they are both realists$_2$. Ontologies
which do not recognize the syncategorematic entities I call
reistic. For an ontology to be realistic$_2$ is one thing; to be
reistic is quite another thing. A reistic ontology, we know,
cannot be adequate. It cannot even account for the truncated
world. This impossibility is the *first center*. The unity of
thought must be adequately accounted for. That task is the
second center. To spot the third, remember the old idea of
adequation, *adequatio rei et intellectus*. If mind (thought) is
One and the (truncated) world is Many, how can a unitary
thought be adequate to a complex intention? This difficulty,
or apparent difficulty, of reconciling the One and the Many
in the knowledge situation is the *third center*.

A realistic$_2$ ontology cannot be adequate unless it fulfills
three conditions. It must not be reistic. It must account for the
unity of thought. It must resolve the difficulty of adequation.
Or, to hark back to what has been said earlier, the realist$_2$
must show that in his world the "connection" between a unitary thought and the complex it intends is so "close" that he
can defend against all dialectical attacks the propostition
which he must hold lest his realism$_2$ remain an empty husk,
namely, that minds may know what is nonmental. That unpacks and thereby gets rid of that old phrase, *adequatio rei
et intellectus*. (Let me point out, in parenthesis, since at this
point I neither need nor wish to make any specific ontological
commitment, that as far as the third center is concerned it
makes no dialectical difference whether the complex intention
is mental or nonmental. That is why I am convinced that
the crucial task is an adequate ontological assay of the act
and that the realism-idealism issue *as such* is rather shallow,
or, at least, that it does not lie as deep as it was thought to
lie during the last three hundred years or so, ever since the
structral drift toward idealism which has still to be stopped
got its start for reasons that will be touched briefly at the
very end of this essay.)

Let us look at the alternatives open to one who does not know how to meet all three conditions. An ontology which is reistic as, alas, almost all are, cannot even adequately account for the truncated world. This inadequacy and its source need not be clearly seen in order to be more or less strongly felt as a difficulty. Its source, we know, is the second feature, which, as we also know, imposes itself more forcefully in the truncated world. That shows how one may be tempted to choose the idealistic alternative.

If one shrinks away from the absurdity of idealism he still has two alternatives left. He may relieve the pressure from the third center by opting for materialism. If one also shrinks away from the absurdity of materialism he has only one alternative left. He may relieve the pressure from the second center by doing violence to the feature that is its source, making thought complex. That also removes the pressure from the third center (adequation). Thus, if he remains insensitive to the subtler pressure from the first center (inadequacy of all reistic ontologies), he may be content. This is the choice or, at least, it is the tendency as well as the basic weakness of the British succession from Locke to Russell. In Locke and Berkeley it remains a tendency; they at least still recognize the act. Hume makes the choice. For him, all mental entities are mosaics of sense data. Literally, the phenomenalism which so frequently also appears in this succession is of course a kind of idealism. Structurally, though, as well as in flavor, it is more often than not materialistic. Russell oscillated between these two equally unattractive alternatives, phenomenalism and materialism, all through his career.[6]

---

[6] The concern here is only with intellectual *reasons,* not with personal or cultural *motives. Of course* there are such motives. They may and often do affect the choice. For *many* they are indeed its only determiners. The absurd doctrine that these motives are the only determiners, or the only important or perhaps even the only valid ones for *all* is not, alas, limited to Italy, but I notice of late a certain recrudescence of that doctrine in the neo-Croceans of both extremes. If these gentlemen were right, then there wouldn't be any history of philosophy for them to write about. Nor, if it were not for the *few* who are sensitive to dialectical pressures, would there be alternatives for the many

I am ready to state my own ontological commitments and to show that they meet the three conditions every adequate realistic₂ ontology must meet. But it will be better if first I say what in ontology I mean (and what I believe most philosophers have meant) by 'universal' and 'individual', and, also, how I use the two labels 'realism₁' and 'nominalism'.

Take two spots of exactly the same color, say, red. An ontologist may account for their both being red by a single entity which is "in" both of them. Such an entity is a *universal*. Ontologists who hold that there are universals may differ in what they hold about them.

Assume that two spots agree exactly not only in color but in all (nonrelational) properties. (I ignore in this essay relational universals as well as those of higher types. Relations, however, are not "in" any of the several entities they relate.) Every ontology must solve the problem of individuation, i.e., in the example, it must account for there being two spots and not just one. On way of solving the problem is by two entities, one "in" each spot. Such an entity is an *individual*. All ontologists who accept individuals make them *things*, not subsistents. There is also always more or less clearly the idea that an individual is a *simple*. I say more or less clearly because the conflict between this idea and some others which philosophers also have had about individuals is notorious.

(The expressions referring to) individuals cannot be predicated of anything. All ontologies recognize this obvious difference between individuals and universals. Some ontologists introduce another. Universals, they hold, differ qualitatively; individuals are merely numerically different. In the Anglo-Saxon tradition such individuals are called *bare particulars*. Ontologists who accept bare particulars implicitly recognize that sameness and diversity are primary, i.e., that they and they alone need no ontological ground. An ontologist who ex-

---

to choose from according to those motives. One need not reject what makes sense in either Marx or Croce to avoid such intemperate extremes.

plicitly recognizes that faces squarely the striking feature Aristotle first faced when he introduced his notion of matter. The difficulties of that notion are notorious. Yet, every adequate ontology must come to terms with the feature.

Bare particulars are one extreme, individual substances are the other. In most classical ontologies, particularly those of the Aristotelian-Thomistic variety, individuals are substances. Substances and universals are both things, i.e., they are both "independent" (as I used this ambiguous word), but there is nevertheless an ontological difference between them which (in another sense of the word) makes the former "more independent" than the latter. Clearly that depresses the ontological status of universals as compared with individuals.

Few ontologists have completely ignored the problem of accounting for "sameness in diversity" in such cases as that of the two spots of exactly the same color. Quite a few, though, took the problem rather lightly. Perhaps they were too concerned with epistemology, not enough concerned with ontology. Some of these tell psychological stories which may or may not be more or less true but are completely irrelevant to the ontological problem. To call only such patently inadequate assays nominalistic seems to me a waste of a good word. I rather speak in such cases of dead-end nominalism.

I call an ontology *realistic*₁ if and only if its individuals and its universals are both things and there are only two fundamental ontological differences between them; one, the obvious one; the other, that individuals are only numerically different (bare).[7] To call all other ontologies *nominalistic* may seem and, as things now stand, probably is idiosyncratic. But it is anything but idiosyncratic to insist, as I do, that any ontology which depresses the ontological status of universals as compared with individuals is *nominalistic in tendency*. Every one familiar with the *structural* history of the dialectic

---

[7] There is the *prima facie* possibility of realistic₁ ontologies in which the only difference is the obvious one. But they encounter structural difficulties that lead quickly to catastrophe.

will appreciate that. In ontologies which make universals syncategorematic entities the nominalistic tendency is as pronounced as it can be, stops just one step short of the dead end.

In my world there are individuals and universals (characters). All individuals are simple and bare. A character is either simple or complex. In all other respects, except for the obvious difference, individuals and characters are alike. That makes me a realist$_1$. In my world there are also subsistents. Not being reistic, my ontology fulfills the second of the three conditions every adequate realistic$_2$ ontology must fulfill. Its fundamental tie is *exemplification*. In 'Peter is blond' it is represented by 'is'. Peter's being blond is a complex of the kind called a *fact*. (The other kind are the complex characters. Their ontological status, though, is merely derivative. Thus we can safely ignore them in this essay.) "In" the fact represented by 'Peter is blond and Mary is tall' there are two others, Peter's being blond and Mary's being tall, as well as the subsistent, represented by 'and', which ties them together. And so on. The idea is clear, I trust. My world is not "atomistic"; it is not just a class or collection of disjoined entities. Rather, it is *completely structured*.

(A *Begriffsschrift* or ideal schema (language) reveals the explicit or implicit ontology of its author. Although I shall presently introduce a few abbreviations, I shall not in this essay use a schema of my own. But it will help to bring out an important point if we consider what in such a schema the transcription of 'This spot is red and round' would be. If 'a', 'red', and 'round' are made to represent the individual and the two characters "in" the spot, respectively, then the transcription reads 'a is red and a is round'. Thus it looks very much like the sentence which it transcribes even though 'a' does not represent the spot but, rather, the individual "in" it. The spot itself, in this world, is the fact represented by the sentence! That is the point which the schema helps to bring out.)

In my world acts are very similar to spots. Take a case of

my perceiving the fact P, namely, that Peter is blond. In my world there are thoughts, e.g., the-thought-that-Peter-is-blond ($\ulcorner P \urcorner$). An act is an individual exemplifying two simple characters; one is a species (perceiving, believing, remembering, and so on); the other is the thought "in" the act. The act in question, for instance, is the fact which (in my schema) is represented by 'b is perceiving and b is $\ulcorner P \urcorner$', with b representing the individual "in" it.[8] Such (mental) individuals I call awarenesses. $\ulcorner P \urcorner$ is simple. *All thoughts are simple characters.* Thus I account for the unity of thought, meet the first condition every adequate realistic ontology must meet. Notice, too, that since thoughts are universals, you and I may literally have the same thought although a thought is a mental entity and although of the two individuals which exemplify it when you and I both have it one is in my mind and one is in yours.[9]

In my world there is a subsistent, M, such that $\ulcorner P \urcorner MP$ is a formal fact. 'M' transcribes the word 'means' as we sometimes use it in such sentences as 'the-thought-that-Peter-is-blond means (intends, is about) Peter is blond'. A fact is formal or a fact of (in) the world's form if and only if the sentence representing it is analytic.[10] Through the thoughts

---

[8] 'b is perceiving' is not very idiomatic. We would rather say 'b is *a* perceiving' and 'b is *a* thought-that-Peter-is-blond', just as we say 'Peter is *a* man' rather than 'Peter is man' even though we also say 'Peter is blond'. If perceiving, the-thought-that-P, man, and blond are four characters, as in my world they are, then such idiomatic strain or awkwardness is irrelevant. Nor could a schema be what it is supposed to be if it conformed in *all* contexts to the idioms of this or that language.

[9] Frege tried very hard to account for this piece of "realistic" common sense. That is indeed a major intellectual motive for his inventing those nonmental entities he calls senses (*Sinn*) and which therefore, revealingly even though most misleadingly, he also calls thoughts.

[10] This is merely a convenient hint. Lest it be misleading, I add that the basic idea (the world's form) is ontological, not logical (analyticity). *A* world's form is what it is because its subsistents are what they are. Our notion of analyticity is grounded in the form of the only world we know.

"in" them, acts are by the subsistent I call M "connected" with their intentions. That immediately raises three questions.

First. Is the "connection" sufficiently "close" to fulfill the third of the three conditions? One only has to consider such complex facts as P-and-Q and P-or-Q in order to realize that some subsistents establish connections which are very loose indeed. (If they were closer, fewer ontologies would be reistic.) Thus the question is very reasonable. All I can say here is that the required closeness is accounted for by $\ulcorner P \urcorner$ MP being a fact in the world's forum.

Second. The-thought-that-Caesar-was-murdered and the-thought-that-Calpurnia's-husband-was-murdered are two, not one. Yet they *seem* to mean (M) the "same" fact. Can two thoughts mean a single fact? The affirmative answer bogs down in difficulties which are insuperable. This is the logical problem of intentionality; or, rather, it is the logical aspect of the problem of intentionality.[11] Since it can be kept out, I shall keep it out of this essay, merely drop a hint that will come in handy soon. The key to the solution is the recognition that the subsistents exist. For, if they exist, then two facts (complexes) are literally the same, i.e., one and not two if and only if (1) the simples in them are the "same" and (2) these simples are "tied" to each other in the same way. Upon this strict use of 'same', P and Q may therefore be two facts and not literally one even if P-if-and-only-if-Q is a fact in the world's form (i.e., if 'P if and only if Q' is analytic).

---

[11] It is a measure of Frege's greatness that he was (as far as I know) not only the first who clearly saw the logical problem of intentionality but that he also realized its ontological import. That provided *another* major intellectual motive for his eventually hypostatizing senses (thoughts) as nonmental entities. That he missed the solution, in spite of this hypostatization and even though he recognized that some subsistents exist, is a measure of his failure. His fear was that he would have to give up all definitions. How typically a mathematician's fear! See also *Meaning and Existence,* p. 217, and the crucial passage from "Begriff und Gegenstand" which is there quoted (p. 46 of the Black-Geach translation). Structurally the deepest root of this failure is that in his world there are no facts (complexes). See below.

Third. What if *P* does not exist? More precisely, how can ⌜P⌝ *MP* be a fact if there is no fact for ⌜P⌝ to intend?[12] Once more, the answer depends on *M* being a subsistent. For *P-or-Q* to be a fact it suffices that either *P* exists or *Q* exists. This could not be so if *or* were not a subsistent but a relational universal, such as, say, being to the left of, which is a thing. This book being to the left of something else, for instance, is a fact only if that something else exists. Not so, we just saw, for *or*. As for *or*, so for *M*. (In my world a fact that isn't there yet exists, though only in the *mode of possibility*, which is of course the lowest ontological status of all. I call such "nonexistent" facts *p*-facts.[12] Nor is that an *ad hoc* construction. But I cannot here pursue this matter.)

Succinct as it is, almost desperately so, this sketch of an ontology will do as a foil for what must be said about Frege before I can intelligently attend to what Dr. Egidi says about him, except that the sketch could not even serve this purpose without some indications as to the ontological assays of judgment and of truth which it implies.

A judgment is an act. It will keep out issues that can be kept out of this essay without prejudging anything that will have to be said if we take it for granted that the species "in" an act of judgment is believing. That makes for a threefold distinction:

$$(\alpha) \qquad P \qquad\qquad ⌜P⌝ \qquad\qquad G(P).$$

P is the fact intended. ⌜P⌝ is the thought "in" the judgment. *G(P)* is the judgment itself. *P* is never a constituent of *G(P)*. If *P* is nonmental, which is the only case we need consider, that is obvious. ⌜P⌝ is merely one constituent of *G(P)*. The other two are the species believing and the awareness which "individuates" the act, e.g., my judgment now that *P*, yours tomorrow, mine yesterday. 'Truth', or, rather, 'true' has (at

---

[12] *P* obviously exists or doesn't exist depending on whether the sentence '*P*' is true or false. It is by now equally obvious, I trust, why at this point I avoid 'true' and 'false'. The root of all matters philosophical, including logic, is ontology.

least) four uses; one is primary; the second derives from the first; the third from the second; the fourth from the third.

In the *primary* use, 'true' and 'false' are predicated of thoughts, which are characters. A character is true if and only if there is an entity such that the character means (M) it and it is a fact. A character is false if and only if there is an entity such that the character means it and its negation [13] is a fact. This assay has two consequences. First. *True and false, as represented by the primary use of 'true' and 'false', are subsistents.* More specifically, they are subsistents of the kind some call defined logical characters.[14] Other entities of this kind are the integers, integer itself, transitivity, reflexivity, and so on. *Subsistents are neither mental nor nonmental.* Second. (1) $\ulcorner P \urcorner$ being true and (2) P itself are two facts, not one. That is again obvious, if only because (1) does while (2) does not contain the constituent $\ulcorner P \urcorner$. Nor is it a source of difficulties that the sentence '$\ulcorner P \urcorner$ is true if and only if P' is analytic. Just remember the hint of which it was said a moment ago that it would come in handy soon.

In their *secondary* use, 'true' and 'false' are predicated of judgments. A judgment is true (false) if and only if the thought "in" it is true (false).

An assertion is a kind of linguistic gesture. Typically, it involves the utterance of a sentence. Typically, it communicates a judgment of the one who makes the assertion. In their *tertiary* use, 'true' and 'false' are predicated of assertions. An assertion is true (false) if and only if the judgment it communicates is true (false).

The sentence involved in an assertion represents the fact the judgment communicated intends. What a sentence of a natural language represents depends on the context in which

---

[13] Negation being a subsistent, 'P' and 'not-P' both represent entities, one a fact, one a p-fact.

[14] 'Defined' suggests complexity. If one holds, as I do, that among subsistents the dichotomy simple-complex makes no sense, then the word is misleading. So, since characters are things, is 'character'.

it is uttered. This is not so for the schemata called ideal languages. The fact represented by a sentence of an ideal language (*Begriffsschrift*) is completely determined by the sentence itself.[15] In their *fourth* use, 'true' and 'false' are predicated of the sentences of ideal languages. Such a sentence is true (false) if and only if what it represents is a fact (*p*-fact).

II

Some of the terms Frege chose are very awkward. Probably he sought for words to serve him as weapons in his life-long struggle against psychologism. For instance, he calls "thoughts" entities which he himself strenuously insists are nonmental and which one would therefore much rather call the (potential) intentions of thoughts (or of judgments, or of acts in general). Under the circumstances I shall continue to use my own words with the meanings I have given to them, make a special point of avoiding his use of 'thought'. It will be convenient, though, occasionally to replace 'mental-nonmental' by 'subjective-objective', which is the dichotomy he happened to prefer, probably because he felt that it stressed his opposition to psychologism.

Begriffsschrift appeared shortly before 1880, *Function und Begriff, Ueber Sinn und Bedeutung*, and *Ueber Begriff und Gegenstand* shortly after 1890. The three later essays present an explicit and rather detailed ontology of the objective (truncated) world. About minds as such they tell us nothing. They merely specify the objective entities which are the (potential) intentions of subjective acts. Nor does the earlier

---

[15] To realize the dependence of natural languages on context, consider (1) 'It is cold today' and (2) 'I am cold'. What (1) represents depends on when and where it is asserted; what (2) represents, on when and by whom it is asserted. The independence, in this sense, of schemata called ideal languages is one of the radical differences between them and natural languages. Because of this difference, those schemata could not even in principle be used for communication. Also, this difference unpacks part of the metaphor that an ideal language is, or purports to be, a picture of the world.

essay contain an ontology of mind. Yet it makes in §2 an important contribution to the ontology of judgment. To this contribution, as far as I know, none of Frege's later writings adds anything. Some even blur it. Perhaps that is why that early contribution has been somewhat neglected. It is a great merit of Dr. Egidi to have called attention to it. I shall next describe this partial ontology of judgment, then the eventual ontology of the objective world.

The heart of §2 is a distinction among three entities, represented by

(β) P,   ——P, |——P,

respectively. If you compare (β) with (α) above, you will be able to guess what I take to be the natural reading of the paragraph. |——P is the judgment, the entity I call $G(P)$; ——P is the entity I call ⌜P⌝, i.e., the thought "in" the judgment; P is its intention, or, as Frege here calls it, its "content." A string of six comments will support this reading and prepare the ground for what follows.

1. Frege here says nothing about whether P is simple or complex. Nor does anything he says depend on that. This is not to deny, though, that in his eventual ontology (of the objective world) all (potential) intentions are simple. 2. ——P is called a "complex of ideas" (F2).[16] That shows three things. (a) ——P is a mental entity. (b) Frege has not yet hypostatized thoughts into objective entities to serve as the intentions of judgments. (c) Verbally at least, he was still not completely free from the tradition that makes thoughts complex. 3. ——P is not the judgment itself but, rather, that constituent of it which also occurs in an act of merely entertaining P without either believing or disbelieving it. That shows that ——P is ⌜P⌝. 4. Of the horizontal stroke in ——P it is said that it "combines the symbols following into a whole" (F2). Literally that does not make sense. For one, the sym-

---

[16] "F2" refers to page 2 of the Black-Geach translation. But I have the German text of *Begriffsschrift* before me. 'Complex of ideas' stands for '*Ideenverbindung*'.

bols of a well-formed sentence are a whole. Thus the stroke
would be redundant. For another, this whole is a nonmental
entity. The only way of making sense out of the passage is
to read it, with Dr. Egidi, as an assertion of the unity of
thought. So read, it far outweighs the evidence to the contrary from 2(c). Or so at least it seems to me. One must not
forget after all how very difficult it was in 1879 to speak about
these things accurately. Nor is it very easy today. 5. Even
though Frege insists that ——P is not the whole of |——P,
he does not tell us what else there is "in" |——P. *At this place
he leaves a blank. Eventually the blank will become a blur.*
6. P and ——P are two entities, not one. Nor is there anything
to indicate that P is "in" ——P. That shows that *the contribution is realistic*$_2$, or, at least, that it is compatible with
realism$_2$.

In the eventual ontology (of the objective world) each
entity is of one of two kinds. It is either a *Gegenstand* or a
Function. The former are "independent" in exactly the same
sense in which (in my world) things are. That makes them
things. Frege's notion of function is mathematical. A function
projects or maps one thing (or an ordered pair of things, etc.)
on another thing. That makes a function "dependent" on the
things mapped and mapped upon in exactly the same sense
in which (in my world) the subsistents called ties are "dependent" on the things (and facts) they tie into complexes.
Nor does a function need a further tie to tie it to what it
maps and maps upon. That makes functions *syncategorematic
entities*.

Things are of three kinds. The only members of the *first
kind* are the two truth values, the thing True (T) and the
thing False (F). The things of the *second kind* are all "senses,"
e.g., the sense-*that*-Peter-is-blond, the sense-*of*-Caesar, the
sense-*of*-Calpurnia's-husband. Judgment is propositional, of
course. Hence, only the senses whose names contain 'that' are
the (potential) intentions of judgments. But Frege is not (as
far as I know) committed to the view (which happens to be

mine) that all awareness is propositional. Thus the senses whose names contain 'of' could be and probably are in his world the (potential) intentions of other acts, e.g., of perception. *All possible senses exist.*[17] The things of the *third kind* are either ordinary "things" such as Peter or Mary or a colored spot; or they are integers, classes, and so on. For our purposes it will be safe to ignore all but the "ordinary" members of this kind. (The quotation marks around 'things' are a reminder that in my world a colored spot is a fact, just as numbers are subsistents of the kind some call defined logical characters.)

Functions are of two kinds. One is exemplified by blond, tall, and so on.[18] Frege calls them concepts (*Begriffe*), but we can do without this word. The other kind is exemplified by the connectives, i.e., by the entities represented by 'and', 'or', 'if-then', and so on. The connectives map (ordered pairs of) truth values on truth values. The other kind of function maps ordinary things (or ordered pairs of such, etc.) on truth values. Blond, for instance, maps the thing Peter on either the thing T or the thing F depending on whether Peter is or is not blond.

Blond and tall being universals, this is the proper place for saying what little needs to be said about Frege's "hidden nominalism." Since his universals have ontological status in the objective world, he is not a dead-end nominalist. On the other hand, since his universals are functions and functions are "merely" subsistents (syncategorematic entities), his nominalistic tendency is as pronounced as it could be, stops just one step short of the dead end. A comment may add perspec-

---

[17] I.e., if the dots in 'sense-that- . . .' are replaced by a well-formed sentence, the resulting expression is the name of a thing that exists. Similarly for 'sense-of- . . .'. 'Sense' stands of course for Frege's *'Sinn'*.

[18] Or, more accurately and in the spirit of the system, being-blond, being-tall. But I permit myself this simplification, just as I ignore, safely for the purposes of this essay, the problem of the appropriate ranges (domain and counterdomain) of functions, which is of such crucial importance in the foundations of arithmetic.

ONTOLOGICAL ALTERNATIVES   **135**

tive. The ontological status of the connectives is very "weak,"
so weak indeed that the reists either overlooked it or quite
explicitly insisted that they had none. Frege recognized that
they have some. That is one of his glories. On the other hand,
he depressed the ontological status of universals by lumping
them with the connectives. That is one of his fatal errors.

Are Frege's things all simple or are some of them complex?
We are not told; as far as I know, he ignores this fundamental
dichotomy. Structurally, that is perhaps the most striking
feature of his ontology. As far as I know, his is indeed the
only articulate ontology of this kind. The only way, therefore, of arriving at an answer is to infer it from the structure
of what we are told. Presently I shall propose an answer.
Frege's things are all simple. First, though, I shall explain
why the dichotomy is so fundamental that one cannot thoroughly discuss his ontology without answering the question.

Remember what was said earlier. The world is not just a
class or collection of disjoined entities; it is completely structured. I say and mean the world as a whole. But we may once
more focus on the objective world. To account for the world's
structure is an obvious task or problem every adequate ontology must solve. Recognizing a task and tackling it in a
certain way or style is one thing. The adequacy of a solution
proposed is another thing. Consider a world (ontology) all
whose things are simples and all whose complexes are facts.
That merely brushes aside details. In such a world one may
try to solve the task by making things (simples) constituents
of facts (complexes) which are in turn constituents of other
(more complex) facts. This is *a* style. As it happens, it is *the*
style of virtually all articulate ontologies. The key to it is the
dichotomy simple-complex. That shows why the dichotomy
is so fundamental. This is one thing. That a reistic ontologist
cannot in this style arrive at an adequate solution is another
thing.

Let us check how the prevailing style works in my world.
Assume for the sake of the argument that Peter and blond

are simples. Consider Peter's being blond. Four entities are involved: (1) the simple thing (individual) Peter, (2) the simple thing (character) blond, (3) the subsistent called exemplification, (4) the fact of Peter's being blond. (4) is the complex which exists because (3) "connects" (1) and (2); thus making (1), (2), and (3) constituents of (4). The world of my ontology is completely structured.

There are two reasons for holding that Frege's things are all simple. One of them I am not yet ready to state. The other is as follows. Frege recognized the need for subsistents. That makes it more than plausible that he also recognized that there cannot be complexes unless there are some subsistent ties which make complexes out of simples. Yet none of his subsistents is a tie; they are all functions; and a function, rather than making a complex out of, say, two things, maps one of them upon the other.

I take it, then, that Frege's things are all simple. It does not follow that his (objective) world is completely unstructured. His functions do establish "connections." Not to recognize that is to miss the very point of their having ontological status. On the other hand, since functions do not make complexes, these "connections" are not, as I use the word, facts. *In Frege's world there are no facts.* It may help, though, if occasionally we speak and think of his "connections" as "facts." (This is a recognition of, as well as an attempt to overcome, the difficulty of speaking without distortion about a style radically different from one's own.)

In Frege's world Peter's being blond involves at least four entities; (1) the thing Peter; (2) the thing T; or, if Peter is not blond, the thing F, but the difference makes no difference for what we are about; (3) the function blond; (4) the thing sense-that-Peter-is-blond. (3) maps (1) on (2). That is the "fact" in the case, which itself is not an entity. (1) and (2) are nevertheless objectively "connected" by (3). There is, however, no objective "connection" whatsoever between (4) on the one hand and (1), (2), (3), on the other. That shows that *Frege's world is not completely structured.*

One may try to remedy the defect by bringing in two more things, namely, (5) the sense-of-Peter and (6) the sense-of-(being)-blond. (6) is the sense of a function. Are there in Frege's world such senses? Whatever expedients either he himself or his disciples may have resorted to, structurally, I believe, the answer is No. But we need not insist, may even for the sake of the argument assume that there are such senses. If so, then (4) will be "connected" with (1), (2), (3) if and only if the following two conditions (a) and (b) are fulfilled. (a) (5) and (6) are constituents of (4). (b) (5) and (6) are "connected" with (1) and (3), respectively. (a) makes (4) a complex. Hence, if all things are simple, the attempt at remedying the defect fails on this ground alone. But let us waive that argument, look at the first half of (b), i.e., at the two things Peter and sense-of-Peter. There is no objective "connection" whatsoever between them. To appreciate the gravity of the point, introduce two more things, Mary and the sense-of-Mary. There is no "connection" between any two of these four things. What, then one must ask, is the objective "fact" that makes the sense-of-Peter the sense of Peter rather than that of Mary and conversely? I conclude that the things Frege calls *senses are totally disjoined from all other entities of his objective world.* Nor is that surprising. Senses, after all, are merely the (objective) hypostatizations of (subjective) thoughts.[19]

Assume next, for the sake of the argument, that there is an objective "connection" between (4) on the one hand and at least one of the entities (1), (2), (3) on the other. The only likely candidate is (2), the thing T. Assume, then, contrary to fact, that there is an objective "connection" between (4) and (2), i.e., between the sense-that-Peter-is-blond and T. If this were so, since (1), (2), (3) are "connected," (4) would over (2) also be connected with (1) and (3) and this world would in

---

[19] The two major dialectical motives for this hypostatization are Frege's antipsychologism and his awareness of the logical problem of intentionality. See fns. 9 and 11.

its own peculiar way be completely structured. To appreciate how peculiar that way would be, consider that, if Mary is tall, the "connection" among the three entities Peter, blond, and the sense-that-Peter-is-blond would be exactly the same as that between the three entities Peter, blond, and the sense-that-Mary-is-tall. One could argue that such a "connection" is worse than none. That shows the absurdity of hypostatizing the two subsistents true and false into the two things T and F.

Virtually all studies of Frege start from and are dominated by his *semantics*. I deliberately stated his ontology without any reference to his semantics. This is not to deny the crucial importance of the linguistic turn or even of ideal languages. Their importance, though, is methodological. Once one has either by this or by any other method enucleated an ontology, either his own or another's, he will be well advised to check his result by trying to state it without even mentioning words. Otherwise he will be in danger of mistaking for ontology what is merely semantics. In Frege's case, he may mistake for objective a "connection" which is merely semantical and therefore in the relevant sense subjective even though words as such and the ways we use them are of course "objective" facts of the world "as a whole." Or is it not obvious that an objective "connection" between objective things does not depend on whether or how we or any one else talks about them? What if there is no one at all to talk about them or, for that matter, about anything else? Isn't that just another bit of realistic$_2$ common sense?

In Frege's semantics 'Peter' and 'Peter is blond' are expressions of the kind he calls saturated. Every saturated expression has a double semantical tie, one to the thing called its sense (*Sinn*), one to the thing called its reference (*Bedeutung*). The sense and the reference of 'Peter' are the sense-of-Peter and Peter; those of 'Peter is blond' the sense-that-Peter-is-blond and the thing T, respectively. In this way the two things Peter and sense-of-Peter are linked semantically. So are the two things T and the sense-that-Peter-is-blond.

Thus, if a semantical link were what of course it is not, namely, an objective "connection," Frege's objective world would be completely structured.

Words are objective (nonmental); judgments are subjective (mental). Yet the former are used to express the latter. There is a cue here. Following it, we shall discover that there is in Frege's world as a whole a mental "connection" between such nonmental things as, say, T and the sense-that-P even though in his objective world these two things remain totally disjoined.

Sinn und Bedeutung contains two crucial passages [20] (F65, F78) to the effect that *a judgment is the "advance" from a sense-that to "its" truth value*. I do not quote the passages only because I continue to use my own words. 'Advance' and 'its', though, are Frege's. They leave no doubt that the advance is held to provide a mental link between such nonmental things as, say, T and the sense-that-P. Thus, the "connection" established is at best subjective. Unfortunately, though, the very idea of this advance is irremediably confused. Frege himself was not wholly at ease. Otherwise he would not have warned (F65) against mistaking the italicized formula for a definition. The formula is nevertheless the heart of his irremediably confused eventual ontology of judgment. *The blank of the early contribution has become a blur.* I shall remove the blur by stating the only clear idea of an "advance" in this context.

Suppose that three acts occur successively in my mind. The species of the first is entertaining (without either believing or disbelieving); the species of the second is perceiving; that of the third, believing. The intention of all three is the same, P. The thought "in" all three is the same, $'P'$. That is merely a schema of course, but it will serve. One starts by entertaining P; one ends by judging that P (believing that

---

[20] Characteristically, they are also crucial for the problem, from which the whole essay is developed, of how, if 'a' and 'b' are both "names," '$a = a$' and '$a = b$' can differ in "cognitive value." See also below.

P). Or is there any other way of "advancing" toward a judgment? In the schema, the "advance" is from an entertaining through a perceiving to a believing; the thoughts and the intentions of the three acts happen to be the same. I say happen partly because not all "advances" are that simple; partly because I want to repeat that even if there were such objective things as the sense-that-P and T and even if these two things were the intentions of the first and the third act, respectively, the "connection" which the "advance" establishes between these two objective things would still be subjective. Nor, alas, is that all. T is a thing. Thus it could not in Frege's world be the intention of a judgment. That alone shows that the confusion is irremediable. Notice, too, that unless a judgment has actually occurred, there is no actual but at most a possible "connection."

Since some of its things are totally disjoined from all others, Frege's truncated world is not completely structured. If, however, one follows him in adding to the (nonmental) "connections" available in this world some others which are mental and therefore not available at all unless there are minds, then, after a fashion at least, his truncated world becomes completely structured. (I say after a fashion because of the blur.) This is the diagnosis at which we have arrived. It suffices to identify the idealistic tendency in Frege's ontology. But it will be better if we postpone this job, turn first to some comments that will support and round out what has been said so far.

The early contribution to the ontology of judgment, although sound, was yet fragmentary. Eventually the blank became a blur. Can one so fill this blank that Frege's world as a whole becomes completely structured? Since he tells us but very little about minds as such, the question is rather moot. Yet the answer may, and I believe does, yield some dialectical insight. My answer has two parts. 1. As we just saw, one would have to make truth values intentions and admit merely possible "connections." But both emendations are antistructural. (This is but another way of saying that the confusion requiring them is irremediable.) 2. Remember the problem of false belief. Since the intentions of *some* acts do not exist, the "connection" between *any* act and its intention cannot be a relation. In my world the difficulty is solved by making it a subsistent (M). Frege has no difficulty. All possible senses exist. Thus one could fill the blank by making minds things which are "connected" with their intentions by relations. Or, to say the same thing in Frege's style, one could add to his world things which are minds and an appropriate class of binary functions. The modified Frege-world which is the result of this addition and of the counterstructural emendation is indeed completely structured. Yet it has three peculiar features. (a) Certain "connections" among objective things remain as subjective as before. (b) If I judge that P then, irrespectively of whether my belief is true or false, the believing-function maps my mind and the thing T on T. That makes it embarrassingly clear that the judgment as such is completely disjoined from the sense, even though one may have "advanced" to the former from entertaining the latter. 3. If acts are relational, then the mental entity the early Frege called ——P has no place in the system. Thus a further emendation is required. We must abandon a most valuable part of the early contribution.[21]

In Frege's semantics all sentences and all definite descriptions are *names*. 'Peter is blond', for instance, is a name of

---

[21] All this is further evidence that senses are but hypostatized thoughts. But there is here a striking dialectical connection with representative realism in the style of, say, Locke, which has been pointed out to me by E. B. Allaire. In those ontologies a mind is "connected" to that wholly mythical entity called a percept by a relation which corresponds structurally to one of the binary functions I added to Frege's world. The only difference is that while all Fregean intentions are nonmental, percepts are meant to be mental entities. The more striking it is that in spite of this difference the two worlds suffer from the same structural weakness. Just as the representative realist cannot bridge the gap between the subjective percept and the objective entity of which it is the percept, so the "connection" between a sense and what it is the sense of remains even in the modified Fregean world subjective.

T or F, depending on whether Peter is or is not blond. 'Cal-
purina's husband' is another name of Caesar.[22] This is the
second structural reason for holding that in Frege's ontology
all things are simple. Since it is semantical and since, for a
reason that has since been explained, I did not want to introduce Frege's semantics before having stated his ontology, I
did not state this second reason when stating the first. Now
I am ready.

Speaking as we ordinarily do, we use 'name' very broadly.
In this century the philosophers who were most influenced by
Frege used the word very technically. Their use, which is
very narrow, carries more or less clearly three connotations.
(1) A name represents a simple thing. (2) A name tells nothing
about the entity it represents.[23] (3) In a well-constructed
Begriffsschrift (ideal language) a name does not occur unless
the entity it purports to represent exists. Had Frege himself
always and clearly used 'name' with all these connotations, I
would in view of (2) have made my point. I do not make so
extreme a claim concerning Frege's use of the word. I merely
claim that all these connotations are more or less clearly implicit in the way he uses it. Just remember how it puzzled
him that '$a = b$', where 'a' and 'b' are names, can convey any
information.[24] Nor is it just chance that in the post-Fregean
debate these connotations became ever more clear and explicit.

In my world, you will remember, P and $\ulcorner P \urcorner$ being true are
two facts, not one. In Frege's world there are no facts. Literally, therefore, he cannot either agree or disagree. But he
comes as close to disagreeing as he can by asserting (F64)

---

[22] According to Frege, a description that fails names the arithmetical
thing Zero. In *Meaning and Necessity* Carnap, prone as always to mistake a mathematical construction for a philosophical idea, recently
revived this infelicitous "stipulation."

[23] Except, by its shape, about the ontological kind (individual or
character) to which it belongs. This, though, is another detail we may
safely ignore.

[24] See fn. 20.

that the sense-that-P and the sense-that-P-is-true are one thing, not two. We ought to be able to understand how he came to assert that. Let us see.

In his world there is only one kind of "fact." Something maps something on something else. Blond mapping Peter on T is such a "fact." Call it α. 'P' does not really state α; it is merely a name of T. Let us express this by saying that 'P' corresponds to α. The sentence corresponding to $[P]$ being true is '$P = T$', with '$=$' representing an identity function,[25] i.e., a binary function projecting two things on T if and only if the "two" are one. The identity function projecting P and T on T is a "fact." Call it β. Are α and β two or one? I am prepared to argue that by the logic of "facts" they are two. If you disagree I shall take your disagreement to show how very difficult it is to think and talk about a world without facts (not: "facts"!) particularly when one is committed to a schema whose sentences do not even state "facts" but are merely names of T or F. Fortunately we need not argue. For I also believe that Frege agreed with you, held α and β to be one. Thus, whether or not you agree with me that they are two, we can agree that he wanted to assert their being one. Moreover, it is obvious that he could not possibly assert that by asserting that 'P' and '$P = T$' both name T. For, that would imply that the two "facts" by virtue of which Peter is blond and Mary is tall also are one. So he asserts instead that the sense-that-P and the sense-that-P-is-true are one. That leads to two further observations.

First. If 'P' is false, then it is a name of F while '$P = F$' names T. Hence 'P' and '$P = F$' do not have the same sense. That shows that the symmetrical treatment of T and F is mere sham. Nor is that surprising, since T (but not F) does the job which in my world is done by exemplification and

---

[25] In *Begriffsschrift* identity holds between names, which makes even identity subjective. Eventually Frege introduces an objective identity function. Grossmann argues convincingly that this change occurred at the approximate time of the three great essays.

exemplification produces entities which are not merely in the mode of possibility.

Second. Consider the infinite series

$$(P = T), \quad (P = T) = T, \quad [(P = T) = T] = T, \ldots,$$

all of whose members are well-formed, compare it with the familiar classical regress

I know *P*,   I know that I know *P*,

I know that I know that I know *P*, . . . ;

notice that in my schema the mark for the subsistent true cannot be iterated without adding corners

⌐*P* is¬ true,   ⌐⌐*P*¬ is true¬ is true,

⌐⌐⌐*P*¬ is true¬ is true¬ is true, . . . ;

and you will see that T also does the job of that mental character which I call the species "in" an act of judgment. Or are we to infer that only a true judgment is ontologically a judgment, only a true belief a belief?

These observations show the absurdity of hypostatizing true and false into two objective things. The next paragraph is not strictly necessary in the context of this essay. Yet it is short and it at least states the answers to some questions that must have arisen in the mind of the reader. So I shall indulge in the digression.

In a schema that reflects a world like mine no compound expression is a name. A name is a primitive symbol that represents a simple thing. No simple thing has more than one name. Sameness and diversity themselves are not represented but merely "show themselves" by the sameness and diversity of (types of) expressions. (That shows, once more, that ideal languages are not really languages. Also, it unpacks part of the metaphor that they are pictures of their worlds.) Two things are identical and not one, or, as one says, the same, if and only if whatever can be said about the one also can *salva veritate* be said about the other (Leibnizian identity of indiscernibles). Identity is represented in the schema (Leibniz-Russell definition of identity). It is, however, a categorial feature of the *truncated* world that no two simples are identical. Two awarenesses, it seems, can be two and yet identical (discernibility of identicals). All this unpacks part of the aphorism that sameness and identity are primary. Notice, finally, that in Frege's case I spoke of an identity function, not of a sameness function. A sameness function would be a monadic function mapping every thing on itself.

Subjective idealists hold that only minds exist. Upon the commonsensical use of 'mental' and 'nonmental', which I shall not abandon, some things are mental, some are nonmental. That makes subjective idealism absurd. Objective idealists hold that all nonmental things are, in a very special sense of the word, "mental." The only way to find out what this very special sense is, is to state commonsensically those features or alleged features of the nonmental which are held to make it "mental." Thus one can discover the dialectical core of objective idealism. Its proponents may or may not add that the nonmental (the truncated world) is literally a Mind of which our own minds are "moments." That is merely speculation. So I merely ignore it. But I reject any ontology, with or without speculative accretions, whose dialectical core is absurd. *The dialectical core of objective idealism is the proposition that minds contribute (create) the structure of the nonmental.* That is absurd.

Frege's truncated world is not "mental." Nor does he claim that it is. That makes him a realist$_2$. He is indeed one of the very few realists$_2$ whose truncated world is at least partly structured. That makes his realism sturdier than most others. For the inadequacy of reism creates a very strong pull toward idealism. That we saw when we discussed the interaction between the three centers of the basic dialectic. On the other hand, according to the diagnosis at which we arrived some time ago, *part* of the structure of his truncated world is contributed by mind. That makes his ontology idealistic in tendency.

Frege also hypostatized mental things (thoughts) into

nonmental ones (senses). Does that make his ontology materialistic in tendency? A materialist either denies that there are mental things, which is absurd, or, which is equally absurd, he "identifies" them with "ordinary" nonmental things. Frege's T and F and his senses are, alas, most "extraordinary" nonmental things. That is why they do not make him a materialist. Rather, they testify to the tenacity with which he clung to his realism₂ under dialectical pressures to which no one before him had been as sensitive as he was.

III

Dr. Egidi is exquisitely sensitive to the pressures from the three centers of the basic dialectic. Her strongest and clearest commitment is to the unity of thought. In her own way she insists on the inadequacy of reism. She is aware of the problem of adequation. This is her profundity. She sees no realistic₂ way of resolving the basic dialectic. That is why, under the pressure of her strongest commitment, she opts for objective idealism. But she not only makes a choice, she also makes a claim. Structurally, she claims, Frege is an objective idealist. Not surprisingly, the argument or reasons by which she supports her claim depend on those by which she supports her choice. That is why before examining the former I shall examine the latter. The conclusion at which I shall arrive is that none of her arguments, either for the choice or for the claim, is a good argument.[26]

Dr. Egidi believes, with one qualification, that one must choose between Aristotelianism and objective idealism. The qualification concerns those who see through the inadequacy of Aristotelianism, yet persist in rejecting objective idealism. These, she believes, are forced to withdraw into the desert of dead-end nominalism. Since she also seems to believe that

---

[26] Notice once more the heavy emphasis on the dialectic. I need not and do not claim that her ontology is "false" or that her reading of Frege is "mistaken." I merely claim that the reasons or arguments she gives for them are not good reasons. This is just one of the many lessons I have learned from G. E. Moore.

I am among the dwellers in this desert, I shall try to convince her that I am not by showing first of all what is or ought to be obvious, namely, that dead-end nominalism is not a way out of the impasse of reism.

Realists$_1$ hold that "in" Peter's being blond there are two things, Peter and blond. Reistic realism$_1$ fails because it cannot "connect" the two. Dead-end nominalists find "in" this fact only one thing, namely, Peter. Hence, if they could otherwise solve the problem of universals, i.e., if they could assign an ontological ground to Peter's and Mary's both being blond, they would not at this point have to face the problem no reist can solve. Yet they would be up against it at the very next step. What "connects" the several facts of their world? Since they are all reists, any two facts (or should I say things?) remain disjoined. That shows that the only way out of the impasse of reism is not dead-end nominalism but, rather, the recognition of the ontological status of a class of subsistents sufficient not only to make realism$_1$ viable but also to account for a world that is completely structured.

Aristotle's individuals are substances; his characters, attributes.[27] The former "create" or "produce" the latter, the latter "inhere" in the former. The traditional words ('create', 'produce', 'inhere') suggest a characteristic feature. Attributes "depend" on substances in a sense in which the latter do not "depend" on the former. That spots a nominalistic tendency. On the other hand, Aristotle's substances and attributes are both things. Any one who does not use the word as narrowly as I sometimes do will therefore call him a "realist$_1$." Nor is it fair to call him a reist. "Inherence" or, conversely, "creation" is a sort of tie. The trouble is that closer analysis reveals it to be irremediably anthropomorphic. This is the fatal flaw not just of Aristotelianism, but of all substantialist ontologies.[28]

---

[27] For our purposes it is safe to ignore the distinction between attributes and accidents.

[28] This shows how the issue of bare particulars versus substances ties into the basic dialetic.

Dr. Egidi identifies Aristotelianism (substantialism) not only with realism₁ but also with reism. More fatally still, since Aristotle is of course a realist₂ and since she sees in him the only alternative to either objective idealism or the nominalist desert, she identifies realism₁ and realism₂. Thus she fails to distinguish between any two of four things as different from each other as Aristotelianism (substantialism), realism₁, realism₂, and reism. This is her *first major mistake*. It vitiates all her arguments.

Aristotle, like Frege, was not only an ontologist but also a logician. That makes it convenient to introduce next some distinctions Dr. Egidi misses in the area of logic, even though this second failure affects the arguments for her claim more than those for her choice. First, though, I must delineate a subarea of this area on which we completely agree.

Logic without ontology is merely a calculus. A calculus acquires philosophical import only if its author claims that it is an ideal language (*Begriffsschrift*), i.e., that it perspicuously reflects an adequate ontology. I shall mark this distinction by consistently so using the two words that 'calculus' stands for what is merely a calculus, 'logic' for a calculus to which that claim has been attached. Ordinary grammar or language, although we cannot but start from it, is not a reliable guide to logic. Our (Indogermanic) languages are all of the subject-predicate form. Aristotle's logic more or less perspicuously reflects his ontology. His calculus is an *exaggerated subject-predicate calculus*, i.e., it hugs the subject-predicate form of ordinary grammar so closely that it reflects (rather perspicuously) certain specific inadequacies of his ontology. The subject of 'Peter loves Mary' is 'Peter'; that of 'Mary is loved by Peter' is 'Mary'. In an exaggerated subject-predicate calculus that is an important difference. Yet there is an important sense of 'same' in which both sentences represent the same fact.[29] 'Loves Mary' in 'Peter loves Mary' is

---

[29] 'Peter loves Mary if and only if Mary is loved by Peter' is analytic. But we need not at this point commit ourselves as to whether the-

construed as is 'is red' in 'This is red'. That reflects an inadequate ontological assay of relations. The transcription of 'All dogs are mammals' into the calculus preserves the subject-predicate form. That reflects an inadequate ontological assay of generality. And so on. (Ordinary language is not an exaggerated subject-predicate calculus simply because it is not a calculus. That is why on the one hand it is flexible enough to represent everything while, on the other, there is much which it does not represent perspicuously.)

It is a great merit of Dr. Egidi to have seen all this very clearly, more clearly indeed than many in whose ambience these insights are more widely spread than in hers. As far as I know, she is also right in insisting that Frege was the first who saw all this; and I share her admiration for his momentous achievement. There, though, our agreement ends.

A calculus may be a *moderate subject-predicate calculus,* i.e., it may be of the subject-predicate form without hugging this form so closely that any ontology it perspicuously reflects must suffer from those specific inadequacies with respect to relations, generality, and so on, which mar Aristotle's. I am not sure that Dr. Egidi disagrees. But I am very sure, alas, that she believes any such calculus to be inadequate in an even more radical sense. According to her, any ontology perspicuously reflected by a moderate subject-predicate calculus must be reistic. This is her *second major mistake.* Four comments will show how bad a mistake it is and at the same time prepare the ground for the third major criticism.

1. *Principia Mathematica* (PM) is a moderate subject-predicate calculus. Yet it can be used and in fact has been used for the correction of those specific inadequacies of the Aristotelian ontology. 2. Notice the condition of perspicuous reflection. To unpack this label is a very major job. Also, the matter is very technical. If one understands it completely, then he sees that a calculus which perspicuously reflects a

---

thought-that-Peter-loves-Mary   and   the-thought-that-Mary-is-loved-by-Peter are two things or one.

(non-reistic!) world whose fundamental tie is exemplification must be a moderate subject-predicate calculus and conversely. This is not to say that all philosophers who propounded a PM-type logic realized that the syncategorematic entities exist. But, then, neither did they fully understand those very technical matters. (3. Presently we shall see that in all calculational respects Frege's logic is a moderate subject-predicate calculus. Its perspicuity is a different matter. That we have seen already.) 4. I believe, first, that the logic of the truncated world is of the PM-type. I believe, second, that the logic of our world as a whole, that is, including minds, is not of this type. Or, to say the same thing in a way that suits our purpose, while such a calculus can be used to represent perspicuously all nonmental intentions, it contains no means for so representing either the subsistent I call M or the simple characters I call thoughts ⌜P⌝ or the facts called acts and, in particular, judgments $(G(P))$. (This fits nicely with the materialistic (behavioristic) tendencies of most "PM-philosophers.")

Peter's being blond (P) is *one* fact. Your or his or my judging that Peter is blond $(G(P))$ is an*other* fact.[30] Dr. Egidi would not put it this way, yet she would agree. She also holds that a calculus may perspicuously represent one of the two facts, namely, P, without so representing the other, namely, $G(P)$. With this I agree. This is indeed the very point of what I just said. A PM-type calculus can be used to represent perspicuously every nonmental intention but contains no means for so representing $G(P)$. There, though, our agreement ends.

Dr. Egidi holds that no calculus can perspicuously repre-

----

[30] If the first fact is represented by 'P', then the second is in my world represented by 'a is believing and a is ⌜P⌝', where ⌜P⌝ is a simple character and a the individual "in" the act. Thus, the first fact is not upon this assay a constituent of the second, the "connection" between the two being accounted for by the analyticity of '⌜P⌝MP'. Of the third, formal fact represented by the latter sentence both P and ⌜P⌝ are constituents.

sent the act of judging. Any logic for which this claim is made (as I make it for mine) she calls "formalistic." The idea is that no formalistic logic can perspicuously represent an adequate ontology. This is her *third major mistake*. Some of my reasons for judging it to be a mistake may be merely implicit in Sections One and Two. Most of these reasons, though, are quite explicit in what has been said so far. Repetition is tedious on any occasion. Complete explicitness is not practical on this occasion. So I shall next show that the intellectual motive behind the mistake is structural idealism.

Dr. Egidi's ontological assay of judgment is idealistic. According to such an assay, the mind first "posits" what, after having posited it, it judges. To posit something, in this sense of the word, is to create or produce it; or, at least, to "contribute" to the "product" something without which it would not be what it is. That makes the idealistic assay of judgment the structural heart of idealism. Thus, if she will permit me to say so, Dr. Egidi shows even in some of her mistakes the flair of those who can think structurally. Rightly or wrongly, she goes to the heart of the matter.

To connect this diagnosis with what she actually says, turn to CLFC 203-205. Rather than quote, I shall express her ideas in my own words. Without the unitary act, she holds, there would not be that manifold which is such a striking feature of its (nonmental) intention. Logic (language) can only represent the manifold which is, wholly or in part, the product. It cannot represent the producing. Or, to say the same thing differently, language (logic) can only represent what we know. It cannot represent the "ideal conditions" which make it "possible" for us to know what we know.[31] That shows beyond doubt that the intellectual motive behind Dr. Egidi's third major mistake is the structural core of idealism.

That much for her choice. I now turn to her claim.

---

[31] I am of course aware of the Kantian flavor of this 'possible'. Dr. Egidi would not, I think, repudiate the structural connection thus hinted at.

Her claim stands or falls with her contention that Frege's ontology of judgment is structurally idealistic, i.e., that implicitly at least it agrees with hers. The main evidence she has so far produced for this contention is what is said about judgment in *Begriffsschrift*, particularly in §2. Let me once more draw a clear line between agreement and disagreement. She gives Frege credit for distinguishing between |——P and ——P, i.e., between a judgment and what I call the thought "in" it. If you recall what has been said about that early contribution in Section Two, then you will see that I agreed. She takes what Frege says in §2 to be an assertion of the unity of thought. I agreed that he may plausibly be credited with this fundamental insight. There, though, our agreement ends. For I also believe to have shown three things which are incompatible with her contention. First. The natural reading of §2 is realistic₂. Second. This early contribution to the ontology of judgment is fragmentary; it leaves a blank. Third. Eventually the blank becomes a blur. Frege's idea of judgment as an "advance" from a sense to a truth value is irremediably blurred.

Dr. Egidi takes advantage of the blur by filling the blank with her own idealistic ontology of judgment. In this she shows once more her keen sense of structure. For the blur is indeed the seat of the idealistic tendency of the system. If you want to verify this diagnosis, turn to MLFF 19, where she says perhaps most bluntly what more subtly she intimates again and again, namely, that a Fregean "advance" is really a Fichtean "posit." [32] It does not follow, alas, that her claim is sound. Frege's T and F and his senses are most "extraordinary" things indeed. So are his functions, even though to a mathematician bent above all on refuting psychologism that

---

[32] Idealistic ideas are not easily explicated by means of a calculus; not, alas, because Dr. Egidi is right but, rather, because they are so vague and elusive. If I were to try, though, I would say that according to Dr. Egidi the mind in its advance "posits" the identity (|——P) $= T$. I merely add that while '|——($P = T$)' is at least well-formed, '(|——$P = T$' is ill-formed in the Fregean calculus!

may not have been as obvious as it really is. Yet all these entities are clearly nonmental. For one, Frege himself, as far as I know, has never claimed them to be either mental or "mental." For another, irrespective of what he himself may or may not have said or believed, they all are structurally nonmental. That is indeed the argument of Section Two. So I shall without repeating myself conclude this examination by attending to two of Dr. Egidi's arguments for her claim, both of which I find rather disappointing.

Are functions and ordinary things, say, blond and Peter, "determinate" entities "independent" of the acts which posit them? The two words between double quotes are hers, not mine. Yet there is no doubt what the question means. Are these entities objective or nonmental in my (and, if I am right, Frege's) sense? Dr. Egidi consistently denies that they are. Functions in particular she calls "ideal" entities in the sense that they make "experience" possible. She also calls them "objective." But then it transpires (CLLF 207) that all she means by that is that the experience they make "possible" is independent of its linguistic representation in exactly the same sense in which a certain fact that was mentioned earlier is independent of its being represented by either 'Peter loves Mary' or 'Mary is loved by Peter'. This I find disappointing.

Frege, like his successor Russell and like Russell's successors, writes '$f(x)$', '$r(x, y)$', and so on. The only difference is in the semantics. For Russell, the substitution instances of '$f(x)$' represent facts or possible facts; for Frege, they are names of either T or F. And so on. That makes it obvious that *in all calculational respects* Frege's logic is a moderate subject-predicate calculus. But it will help if before turning to the second argument I state the two qualifications which are covered by the italicized phrase. (a) On the one hand, the assertion sign ('|——') and the horizontal stroke ('——') do not fit into a moderate subject-predicate calculus. On the other hand, Frege himself makes no real calculational use of them. That is why the later logicians were puzzled by them and eventually dropped them, which in turn fits well with what Dr. Egidi and I agree upon, namely, that Frege in §2 introduced the two signs in order to make by means of them a point in the ontology of judgment. (b) 'T' and 'F' do not fit into a moderate subject-predicate calculus. More precisely, if they are taken to represent things, then '$P = $ T' and '$P = $ F' are in such a calculus ill-formed. But then, as far as I know, neither Frege nor, with the possible exception of Alonzo Church, any of his followers have paid any attention to these two expressions. Rather, it was I, who, for a purpose of my own, insisted that they are, or, at least, that they ought to be considered as well-formed. My purpose, or, rather, the use to which I put them in Section Two, was to expose by means of them some of the perplexities of Frege's ontology as well as the lack of perspicuity with which it is reflected by his calculus.

Dr. Egidi makes much of the fact that in dealing with the sentential calculus the Frege of the *Begriffsschrift* uses sentential variables, writing 'p' instead of, say, '$f(x)$'. This she takes to be *his* assertion of the unity of thought, upon which she foists *her* ontology of judgment. The truth of the matter is that no mathematician of even the most moderate skill who had either conceived or been told the idea of the sentential calculus would in constructing it use any but sentential variables. Sentential logic is the most fundamental part of logic. To have recognized that is without doubt one of Frege's major achievements. But it is disappointing to see Dr. Egidi build so much of her argument on the trivial fact that he writes the sentential calculus in sentential notation. Besides, if it were the job of the single variable to express the unity of thought, may I ask how she would explain what she also asserts, namely, that the same job is also done by the horizontal stroke?

The indictment I have drawn up against Dr. Egidi is severe. Yet I do not want to end on a note of disappointment. So I shall change sides, from the prosecution to the defense, as it were, and conclude with some remarks which will add perspective in a way that amounts to a plea of attenuating circumstances.

The basic dialectic of the realism-idealism issue lurks in the things themselves. The trend toward idealism began only about three hundred years ago, that is, roughly, at the time of the Cartesian revolution. Why did this trend start at just that time? The gist of what I believe to be the right answer can be stated very briefly.[33] The Aristotelian-Thomistic account of perception, which was dominant until then, is realistic$_2$ in structure. A single substantial form informs the mind of the perceiver and the thing perceived. This account was supported by and is compatible with the idea that a mind can only know what is "in" it. The revolution overthrew the old account of perception. The idea continued to be taken for granted. That suffices to account for the rise of the trend.

The lure of idealism continues undiminished. The structure of Deweyan instrumentalism is idealistic.[34] The same is true of the present misery, at Oxford and elsewhere, which goes by the name of ordinary-language philosophy. If the temptation of a philosophy so absurd continues so strong for so long, it stands to reason that, for all its absurdity and even though at a prohibitive price, it accounts more adequately than its competitors for at least one striking feature of the world. The thing to do, therefore, is to identify this feature and try to do justice to it in a realistic$_2$ ontology. Then and only then will the temptation cease.

The role of minds in the world is unique. This is the feature. The idealists' way of safeguarding it is to insist, with or without some attenuation, that minds "create" their intentions, which is absurd. My way of safeguarding it is different.

---

[33] For a more detailed statement see essay XII of my *Logic and Reality*.

[34] See May Brodbeck, "La filosofia di John Dewey," *Rivista di Filosofia*, 50, 1959, 391-422.

Consider (1) 'P and Q', (2) 'not-(not-P or not-Q)', (3) 'P and Q if and only if not-(not-P or not-Q)'. Call the facts represented by (1) and (2) F_1 and F_2, respectively. Are F_1 and F_2 two or one (the same)? There is an important meaning of 'same' upon which they are the same. This meaning I explicate by the analyticity of (3). Since the subsistents exist, there is also a stricter meaning of 'same', such that two facts are the same if and only if the same simples are in the same way connected by the same subsistents. With this meaning of 'same', F_1 and F_2 are two and not one. The subsistents and the truths which depend only on them are "the world's form." The ontological ground of F_1 and F_2 being two and not one thus lies not in the world's things but wholly in its form. Yet there are in my world two things, namely, the-thought-that-P-and-Q and the-thought-that-not-(not-P-or-not-Q) which are two and not one for the sole reason that if the world's form is taken into account the facts they represent are two and not one. There is thus a kind of things, namely, thoughts, which are unique in that they and they alone among the world's things reflect its form.[35] This, I submit, is an adequate realistic$_2$ account of the feature.

I shall of course not convince Dr. Egidi. To expect that would be merely presumptuous. But I do nourish a more modest hope. I may convince her that there are realists$_2$ who in *their* way try to resolve the dialectical tensions to which she so keenly responds. If this hope is justified, then I am confident she will eventually find *her* way of rejecting idealism.

---

[35] This is also the deepest structural reason for so explicating 'analytic' that '$\ulcorner P \urcorner MP$' becomes analytic or, synonymously, that it becomes a truth in the world's form. There are also quite a few logical (calculational) reasons for this step. Philosophically, though, such reasons do not carry conviction unless they support and are supported by a structural reason that lies rather deep.

8

Frege's Ontology: Realism

E. D. KLEMKE

Some time ago, Professor Gustav Bergmann maintained that Frege's ontology is that of a hidden nominalism.[1] In a critical discussion I argued that Frege was a strict realist, though not necessarily a Platonist.[2] Reinhardt Grossmann then replied and maintained that, in effect, we were both right: since the term 'realism' may mean different things, in one sense Frege may be a realist, whereas in another important sense, he is not.[3] Howard Jackson and Charles E. Caton have brought up points which are related to the discussion,[4] and in a later, excellent paper, "Ontological Alternatives," Professor Bergmann again took up the theme (along with others) and held that Frege is not a "dead-end nominalist," but "his nominalistic tendency is as pronounced as it could be."[5] After

[1] G. Bergmann, "Frege's Hidden Nominalism," *The Philosophical Review*, LXVII (1958), 437-496. Reprinted in *Meaning and Existence* (Madison: University of Wisconsin Press, 1960), pp. 205-224.

[2] E. D. Klemke, "Professor Bergmann and Frege's 'Hidden Nominalism'," *The Philosophical Review*, LXVIII (1959), 507-514.

[3] R. Grossmann, "Frege's Ontology," *The Philosophical Review*, LXX (1961), 23-40. Reprinted in Allaire *et al.*, *Essays in Ontology* (Iowa City: University of Iowa, and the Hague: Martinus Nijhoff, 1963), pp. 106-120. I have profited greatly from this paper.

[4] H. Jackson, "Frege's Ontology," *The Philosophical Review*, LXIX (1960), 394-395. C. E. Caton, "An Apparent Difficulty in Frege's Ontology," *The Philosophical Review*, LXXI (1962), 462-475.

[5] G. Bergmann, "Ontological Alternatives," in *Logic and Reality*

much further effort to make sense of Frege's ontological position, I now wish to argue that, in a most basic meaning of the term, and in the strict sense, Frege is a realist. Indeed, I am prepared to agree with Quine that Frege is a Platonist.[6]

I must make clear at the start that I am not interested in engaging in any kind of polemic with my friend and teacher, Professor Bergmann. His paper, referred to above, is a challenging one. But I am convinced that various aspects of Frege's thought lend themselves to various interpretations. In this respect, most of the material that has been written about Frege has been terribly one-sided. One writer affirms categorically that Frege says so and so. The next writer denies it. Let us face it; the totality of statements written by Frege simply do not cohere with one another. Thus any interpreter must engage in selection, but I believe that the selecting should be done in a way which tries to make sense of Frege's views, even if this means pointing out that here and there Frege simply was wrong or made a bad mistake. I occasionally shall do this in my remarks. I also try to support various points with arguments which Frege, to my knowledge, did not put forth. Perhaps I should not then say that Frege clearly and without doubt is a strict realist. Very well, I shall be happy to say that he is at least implicitly a strict realist.

I

Clearly, the question as to whether or not Frege is a realist boils down to this: Are (Fregean) *concepts* (and other functions) *Entities*? By Entities I mean: objective, fundamental,

---

(Madison: University of Wisconsin Press, 1964), pp. 124-157. This paper is the English original of "Alternative Ontologiche: Riposta alla Dotoressa Egidi," which appeared in *Giornale Critico della Filosofia Italiana*, XVII (1963). The above quotation is from the former volume, p. 140. In many places Prof. Bergmann seems to acknowledge that Frege's Ontology is realistic, but holds that it is an inadequate realism.

[6] W. V. Quine, *From a Logical Point of View* (Cambridge, Mass.: Harvard University Press, 1964), p. 76. In maintaining this, I go further than I did in my earlier article.

irreducible, ultimate ontological "units."[7] I believe that everyone would agree that for Frege objects are clearly Entities. The best arguments in favor of the thesis that concepts and all other functions are Entities are these: (1) Concepts are *references* (pp. 43, 44, 45, 47-48, 50, 82, 105, 152, 170).[8] It seems clear that Frege takes references to be Entities. A reference is what an expression (word, sign, etc.) designates, stands for, or refers to. So, since concepts are references, and references are Entities, concepts must be Entities. Similarly for other functions. (2) The expressions that refer to (designate, stand for) concepts and other functions are *names* (pp. 105, 140, 153, 157, 170-171). Now a principle which is held in common by many ontologists is: "To be a name and to be an expression standing for an existent is one and the same thing."[9] It seems that Frege agreed with this principle. Hence, since he holds that expressions which stand for concepts and other functions are names, it follows that the references of these names are ultimate ontological Entities. (3) Frege refers to concepts as properties (pp. 51, 103). Now properties are certainly real. They are Entities. Hence concepts are Entities. However, as we shall see shortly, for this argument to have force, it depends upon what is meant by 'property'. (4) Concepts, like objects, *have* properties. That is, concepts fall under, or within, second-level concepts (pp. 38 f., 142). One might argue: Can something have a property without being real? (I assume, along with Frege, that we are excluding fictional contexts from the discussion.) (5) Concepts *are*, independently of all human minds (p. 85). They are objective, even though they are not objects. We discover concepts; we do not invent them or construct them or define them into being. I maintain that the above arguments provide an affirm-

---

[7] I capitalize the term to indicate this special meaning. When I use the term in a more neutral sense, I write 'entity'.

[8] Unless otherwise noted, all references to Frege are to the volume edited by Geach and Black: *Translations from the Philosophical Writings of Gottlob Frege*, revised edition (Oxford: Blackwell, 1966).

[9] Bergmann, "Frege's Hidden Nominalism," p. 215.

ative answer to the question 'Are concepts (and other functions) ontological Entities?'

It will be noticed that I have continually spoken of concepts *and other functions* in the above paragraph. There are two reasons for my having done so. First, Frege's 'concept' is not equivalent to such terms as 'character' or 'property'. Frege limits the use of the term 'concept' to designate the reference of monadic predicate expressions. But where at least two objects are involved, as in the reference of, say, 'is greater than', Frege speaks of *relations*. Furthermore, there are yet other functions that are neither concepts nor relations. I would maintain that, for Frege, these functions are also Entities (as defined above). This would mean that Frege's realism is not only strict but complete. However, in this paper I shall follow Professor Bergmann's lead and emphasize primarily concepts and, analogously, relations.

II

Now if we grant that concepts are Entities, the next question must be: 'What is the ontological *status* of concepts (and other functions)?' As I noted above, Frege says that concepts are *properties* (pp. 51, 103). The term 'property' may be used in at least two senses, which I shall for convenience call the 'concrete' and the 'abstract'. We may get at the difference by considering four statements which Frege holds to be equivalent (pp. 47, 51). These are:

  (A) Socrates is a man.
  (B) To be a man is a property of Socrates.
        (Or perhaps: Being a man is a property of Socrates).
  (C) Socrates has the property man..
  (D) Socrates falls under the concept *man*.

When Frege speaks of the property man or the property of being a man, does 'man' here designate the concrete, existent character that Socrates has or the abstract property manhood? I shall argue that Frege means the second of these alternatives. In all four of the above statements, since all are equivalent, 'Socrates' designates a spatiotemporal (at least in part) concrete individual *with* his particular specific and concrete properties, and 'man' designates an abstract entity which might be referred to by some term such as 'manhood'— or just 'man' as long as the latter is differentiated from 'a man' and from 'men'. My arguments in support of this thesis are:

(1) Frege says that objects are definite and particular (pp. 33, 110). Traditionally, the contrast to a particular is a *universal*. This suggests that Frege's properties are universals. And since concepts are properties, for Frege, it follows that concepts are universals. More of this shortly.

(2) Frege says that objects are complete: they stand alone. Whereas concepts are unsaturated, objects are saturated (p. 32), etc. Now a bare particular, an unpropertied individual, could not be complete. And all the particulars we encounter in the world are propertied. Thus, since objects are complete and are particulars, then an object must consist of both an individual (the thing) and its concrete characters—characters that are instances of universals. But if an object consists of the individual with its concrete characters, then, since a concept is not an object, nor presumably part of one, a concept must be an abstract property. (I am not maintaining that every sentence in this paragraph is explicitly found in Frege, but it seems reasonable to believe that he would agree.)

(3) Frege holds that different individual objects can fall under the *same* concept. We may say, e.g., 'Socrates falls under the concept *man*' and also 'Plato falls under the concept *man*'. 'Man' here has the same reference in both cases. But then 'man' cannot refer to, say, Socrates' particular character of being a man. Surely the concrete property being a man which Socrates possesses is not also possessed by Plato. Therefore the property which they do have in common is *not* the empirical, specific property which either of them has.

(4) Frege holds that there can be concepts under which *no* objects fall (pp. 82-83). Let us take a case of a concept under which no objects fall—say, *unicorn*. Now if there can be such concepts even though no objects fall under them, then concepts cannot be the specific, concrete properties possessed by any individual objects, for in this case, there are no such objects, and hence no such properties.

(5) Frege says that a concept word "has nothing to do with objects directly, but stands for a concept" (p. 83). That is, the reference of a proper name is an object. But the reference of a concept word (or concept expression) is not the individuals which fall under the concept, nor the collection of them. Rather, the reference is the concept itself. Thus, take a proposition such as 'All men are mortal'. Frege says that this proposition relates two concepts. Therefore it is not about particular men. "When anyone uses the sentence 'All men are mortal' he does not want to assert something about some Chief Akpanya, of whom perhaps he has never heard" (p. 83). But if it is not about particular men, then it is not about particular instances of being a man. And therefore it must be about the abstract property manhood.

(6) Frege holds that objects fall under first-level concepts and that first-level concepts fall under, or within, second-level concepts (pp. 50-51). Now objects cannot fall under second-level concepts. But objects do have properties—concrete characters. Therefore it cannot be the concrete characters which objects possess that do the falling under, or within, second-level concepts. Therefore it must be some other kind of property which does the falling under or within. And therefore there must be such properties, and since they are not concrete characters, they must be abstract entities.

(7) Frege distinguishes between two domains: (a) the domain of the actual, and (b) the domain of what is objective yet *not* actual. The entities of the latter domain have a status which is independent of the judging subject, even though they are not actual. To say of anything, x, that it is actual is to

say, for Frege, that x is capable of acting directly or indirectly on the senses. Concepts are objective, but not actual. For "psychological logicians" this would mean that they must be ideas. But Frege denies this. Ideas are subjective, and private to each person. But concepts are not; we can all grasp them in common. By grasping, Frege here means: grasping by the mind. Just as a pencil exists independently of my physically grasping it, the same holds for "that which we grasp with the mind"—it exists independently of the activity of grasping. Since concepts are among the things which must be grasped by the mind, and since concepts are called properties, it follows that Fregean properties must be abstract rather than concrete.[10]

III

I conclude from these arguments that when Frege says that concepts are properties, he means properties in the abstract sense. Concepts are, then, universals. It is clear that Frege holds that there really *are* such things as concepts. Their reality is no less than that of objects, even though they are not objects. Just as a proper name has as its reference an object, so a concept word or predicative expression has as its reference a concept. Surely, in the most basic sense of the term, this means that Frege is a realist. Indeed, it suggests that he is also a Platonic realist. This is suggested all the more strongly if we next turn to another question.

Which are ontologically prior—concepts or objects? It is clear that Frege's answer must be concepts. (1) There can be concepts even though, at any given time, there are no objects which fall under them (pp. 82, 104-5). And (2) to say that objects are prior entails that concepts must be reached or formed by some sort of process of abstraction. At least, this is commonly held by those who emphasize the objects. But

---

[10] G. Frege, *Grundgesetze der Arithmetik, I*. Partial English translation by M. Furth (Berkeley & Los Angeles: University of California Press, 1964), pp. xviii-xix, xxiv, 3-4.

this would mean that *we* determine which objects fall under which concepts, depending upon what properties we happen to emphasize or which our attention is focused on. Frege denies this: "On my view, bringing an object under a concept is just recognition of a relation [falling under] that was *there already*" (p. 85, my italics). Is any more evidence for my thesis needed?

But why, then, would anyone think that Frege might be a nominalist? Before answering that question, I must deal with an objection that might be posed in connection with the above arguments.

Someone might object: But is there any such distinction as that which you draw between concrete properties and abstract properties? There surely must be such a distinction. Even ordinary language suggests that there is. For example, 'round' and 'cat' might be called general, concrete terms. They apply to individual objects—this coin or Waldo the cat. But 'roundness' and 'felinity' are singular abstract terms. They do not apply to various individual objects. For example, you can say 'Waldo is a cat' or 'Waldo is feline', but not 'Waldo is felinity'. What you can say is that Waldo exemplifies felinity. But it is precisely by so doing that he is feline—i.e., that he has the concrete property which he has. Similarly, it would be appropriate to say 'Socrates is just', 'Plato is just', etc., but not 'Socrates is justice'. 'Just' can apply to Socrates, Plato, Aristotle, etc., but 'justice' designates—if anything—a single abstract entity.

One might object further that all this is making too much out of a syntactical matter. Granted that universals (and Frege's concepts) are abstract entities, why must there *be* both abstract and concrete properties? Why not just say that *all* properties are abstract? Socrates simply has the abstract property *man* and no other? There are two arguments for holding both that there are two kinds of properties and that Frege would hold that there are both kinds. (1) Socrates is an object, for Frege, and hence complete. If there were only abstract properties, then Socrates would be incomplete too, for he would be a bare, unqualitied particular. Since, for Frege, objects are complete, they must consist of an individual plus its concrete qualities. (2) Suppose that at 2:34 P.M., on a certain day long ago, Hume's physician had uttered the sentence 'Hume is dead'. Surely 'is dead' here must refer to the actual state of this dead person. Doubtless this is what the physician meant when he uttered the sentence. 'Is dead' refers to the actual, concrete property possessed by Hume at 2:34, a state which is different from that which existed at 6:00 A.M. that morning. But then the abstract property *death*—or Frege's concept of death—cannot be identified with the actual, concrete state of Hume's body. Concepts—abstract properties—are not, then, the same as concrete properties. Yet surely there *are* such things as concrete properties. Hence we must admit that there are both, and it seems evident that Frege would have to say that there are both.

(Incidentally, it seems that Frege was wrong, then, in saying that (A) 'Socrates is a man' and (B) 'Socrates falls under the concept *Man*' are always equivalent. For there are certain contexts in which (A) could be used to mean something other than (although, of course, related to) what is meant by (B).)

Lest anyone be puzzled by my insistence on two kinds of properties, I might point out that the distinction seems to be an old one.

Shall we . . . affirm that there is such a thing as equality, not of one piece of wood or stone with another, but that, over and above this, there is absolute equality? . . . Then these (so-called) equals are not the same with the idea of equality?

Are these essences . . . each of them always what they are? . . . And what would you say of the many beautiful . . . which are named by the same names and may be called equal or beautiful.

I cannot help thinking, if there be anything beautiful other than absolute beauty should there be such, that it can be beautiful only in so far as it partakes of absolute beauty. . . . Nothing makes a thing beautiful but the presence and participation of beauty . . . I stoutly contend that by beauty all beautiful things become beautiful.[11]

I believe that the arguments above must lead one to hold that Frege is a realist in the strict sense, and perhaps even a Platonist.

IV

But why would anyone think that Frege might be a nominalist—or that his position is even that of a hidden nominalism? I suggest that such a characterization stems from an undue stress on *objects* as the ultimate ontological Entities. It is true that one of Frege's basic principles is "Never to lose sight of the distinction between concept and object." [12] But on the basis of the above arguments, we surely must hold that this is a distinction within ontological ultimates, not a way of distinguishing ontological ultimates from nonultimates. Why might one take it to be the latter? Perhaps because Frege constantly speaks of objects as being complete, whereas concepts are incomplete (unsaturated, etc.). But surely 'incomplete' is not a synonym for 'less real', or 'unreal'. Something can be incomplete yet fully real. To be incomplete is the nature of a concept. This does not in any way lessen the ontological status of concepts. So we must reject the notion that the distinction between concept and object provides a proper way by which to decide whether Frege is a realist or a nominalist. A distinction between objects and functions (including concepts) is a distinction within the realm of Entities. And there is no basis for taking Entities of either of the two categories to be more real than those of the other.

Furthermore, the sense-reference distinction cannot be reduced to the concept-object distinction. The reason is: the concept-object distinction is a distinction *within* the realm of *references*. However, this means that it is simply not true

---

[11] Plato, *Phaedo.*
[12] G. Frege, *The Foundations of Arithmetic,* trans. J. L. Austin (New York: Harper, 1960), xxii.

that "An object is anything that is not a function" (p. 33).
When Frege made this statement (in his "Function and Concept") he was dealing only with the two categories of function and object and attempting to "define" one via the other.
It is clear in the paper that the distinction is meant to be one
of two main kinds of *references*. On the other hand, Frege's
statement in "On Concept and Object" (p. 44) is more accurate. He holds there that it is "very important" to recognize a distinction between "what can occur *only* as an object,
and everything else" (my italics). Here there is no restriction
that the class of nonobjects is limited to functions. But it is
possible that there could be Entities which are nonreferences.
And even in "Function and Concept" Frege suggests that
senses might be nonreferences and also nonobjects. He
writes: "We must distinguish between sense and reference"
(p. 29). Since objects are clearly references, it follows that
if we were to take senses to be objects, we would be also
taking them to be references; but then we would *not* be distinguishing between senses and references, as Frege says we
must.

It seems then, that the two distinctions of sense-reference
and object-concept must somehow both be held without merg-
ing the two or reducing one to the other. The only way in
which we may retain both is by placing one pair within one
of the members of the other pair. (Simply setting them one
alongside of the other would not relate them adequately.) The
theoretical possibilities are:

(1) Entities
   A. Senses
      1. Objects
      2. Concepts
   B. References

(2) Entities
   A. Senses
   B. References
      1. Objects
      2. Concepts

(3) Entities
   A. Objects
      1. Senses
      2. References
   B. Concepts

(4) Entities
   A. Objects
   B. Concepts
      1. Senses
      2. References

Of these alternatives, only (2) is plausible. (1) fails because objects and concepts are *references* of grammatical predicates or concept-words. (3) and (4) fail because *both* objects and concepts are references.

Thus, in my earlier article I schematized Frege's ontology in this way: [13]

ONTOLOGICAL ENTITIES

References:	Functions:
Objects:	Mathematical functions
Individuals	Characters (Properties)
Numbers	Concepts
Truth-values	Relations
Extensions (and other ranges)	Nonreferences:
Concept correlates	Senses
	Thoughts

V

I am still inclined to adhere to this table as being more significant than that which I attributed to Professor Bergmann or that of Professor Wells.[14] However, Howard Jackson has pointed out that a certain view of Frege's poses a problem for such a dichotomy.[15] Indeed, in his view it forces one to reject the dichotomy. In answering the question, 'What is the ontological status of senses?' Mr. Jackson says that there is a definite answer; in an unpublished paper of 1891-92, "Frege argues that the sense of an expression is an object."[16] Mr. Jackson has given no hint at the argument Frege presents. And I have not had access to the paper. However, I am inclined to argue that, even within his own system, Frege is *not* justified in saying that senses are objects. Here is my argument.

---

[13] Klemke, *op. cit.*, p. 513. The table is not complete. For example, various other objects must be added: places, time-spans, etc.

[14] R. S. Wells, "Frege's Ontology," *Review of Metaphysics*, IV (1951), 537-573.

[15] H. Jackson, "Frege's Ontology," *The Philosophical Review*, LXIX (1960), 394-395.

[16] *Ibid.*, p. 394.

First, an object is the *reference of a proper name*—or any expression which (for Frege) is transformable into or equivalent to a proper name—e.g., a definite description. A sense is always characterized as being different from a reference. Frege says: "A proper name (word, sign, combination, expression) *expresses* its sense, *stands for* or designates its reference" (p. 61). Indeed, Frege indicates that senses, references, and ideas are all different from one another. "The reference of a proper name is the object itself which we designate by its means; the idea . . . is wholly subjective; in between lies the sense, which is indeed no longer subjective like the idea, but is yet not the object itself" (p. 60). By saying that the sense lies *between* the idea and the reference, Frege strongly suggests that it is a third sort of entity. Indeed, in "The Thought," Frege explicitly refers to a "third realm." "A third realm must be recognized. What belongs to this corresponds with ideas, in that it cannot be perceived by the senses, but with things, in that it needs no bearer to the contents of whose consciousness to belong."[17] And in "On Sense and Reference," he says: "The thought, accordingly, cannot be the reference of the sentence, but must rather be considered as the sense" (p. 62). It is true that he here speaks explicitly only of thoughts, but I see no reason why the same would not hold of senses which are not thoughts (especially since thoughts are made up of such senses). In other passages Frege suggests that, since objects, senses, and ideas are all different, a sense can never be a reference—although it can be an indirect reference. (More of this shortly.) For example, in "On Sense and Reference," Frege writes: "The regular connexion between a sign, its sense, and its reference is of such a kind that to the sign there corresponds a definite sense, and to that in turn a definite reference" (p. 58). If the reference corresponds to the sense, and the sense to the sign, this certainly means that the reference and the sense

---

[17] G. Frege, "The Thought," trans. by A. M. and M. Quinton, in *Mind*, LXV (1956), 302.

are different, and that a sense cannot be a reference. Now if a sense cannot be a reference, then it cannot be what a proper name stands for or refers to, and therefore a sense cannot be an object. Nor, of course, can it be a concept.

Someone might object: But Frege gives a "criterion" of objects.[18] "The singular definite article always indicates an object, whereas the indefinite article accompanies a concept-word" (p. 45). Now Frege allows us to speak of the sense of an expression; e.g., I can use the words 'the sense of (the expression) "Socrates"'. This whole expression—'the sense of "Socrates"'—is a definite description employing the singular definite article and therefore it is a proper name, for Frege. But then it names an object, one might say, and so senses are objects after all.

I reply: Remember the case of the concept horse, that is, of all expressions of the form 'the concept X'. We recall that Frege himself maintained that the reference of 'the concept horse' is not a concept but an object. "The three words 'the concept horse' do designate an object. . . . This is in full accord with the criterion I gave—that the singular definite article always accompanies an object" (p. 45). And thus Frege had to introduce a new kind of entity into his ontology, those objects which are now commonly referred to as concept-correlates. (I believe the term stems from R. S. Wells.) Note that although Frege says, oddly, that a concept is "converted into an object, or, speaking more precisely, represented by an object" (p. 46), strictly speaking concepts cannot *become* objects when referred to by expressions such as 'the concept horse'. No, concept-correlates are different from concepts, for concept-correlates are objects, but concepts are never objects. Something similar occurs here with regard to expressions such as 'the sense of "Socrates"'. Frege should have said that the reference of such an expression is not a sense, for senses are not references. If any expression such as 'the sense of

[18] C. E. Caton, "An Apparent Difficulty in Frege's Ontology," *The Philosophical Review*, LXXI (1962), 463-464.

"Socrates" ' must have a reference, then its reference would have to be something like a sense-correlate, but never a sense. And here we would have another kind of entity.

Now it is generally acknowledged that Frege was wrong in thinking that there were such things as concept-correlates. Even the most ardent Fregean would, I think, try to avoid concept-correlates as a kind of object, or as any fundamental Entity at all. Similarly, one would want to avoid sense-correlates or anything of this sort. But any successful way of avoiding concept-correlates must meet this condition: it must not allow concepts to be objects. Similarly, I would argue that any successful way of avoiding sense-correlates would have to meet this condition: it must not let senses be objects, since objects are among the class of references, and senses are never references (although they may be indirect references, which, however, are never references). I conclude: even though Frege may have once said that senses are objects, he must have been mistaken. Even in his own system, senses cannot be objects, and therefore they cannot be references. Hence we may keep the schematization of Frege's ontology which appears in the above table. One might argue, however, that ideas should be listed as nonreferences, even though Frege may suggest at times that they are objects. The argument would follow closely to the above one for senses. One might also argue that although senses (and thoughts) are not references, they are entities. (See Section VII.)

In the event that anyone is not convinced by the above argument, here is one which, I think, is conclusive to show that senses cannot be objects. Frege holds the following two theses:

(1) An expression may have sense but lack reference.

(2) No expression can have reference but lack sense.

Frege also holds:

(3) Objects are references.

Now suppose that Frege held that

(4) Senses are objects.

Then it would follow that

(5) Senses are references.

But if (5) were true, then (1) would be false. For by having a sense, any expression would thereby have a reference. But (1) is *not* false, according to Frege. Therefore (5) cannot be true. And therefore it is false that senses are references. But all references are either objects or functions. Therefore senses can be neither functions nor objects.

VI

Someone might hold that there is at least one main problem with the above way of characterizing Frege's ontology. Frege speaks of indirect references. "The indirect reference of a word is . . . its customary sense" (p. 59). Now the above characterization makes a sharp distinction between references and senses. But if indirect references are a type of reference, then senses could be a type of object. To this objection I reply: It is true that, in a way, *everything* could be considered a sort of object, and thereby a sort of reference, just by virtue of the fact that it is possible to mention it— to make any reference to it at all, whether direct or oblique. One might say, that if you can talk about something, then no matter what that something is, it functions as a sort of object. And this would obviously be true even if one were to talk about a concept—in spite of Frege's protests to the contrary. Now, of course, this is a very broad and generous use of the term 'object'. In this sense of 'object', not only material objects, but ideas, images, concepts and relations are objects. But there is another sense of the term—in its philosophical use—in which 'object' signifies *a* basic ontological category. I shall use a capital letter to distinguish this sense and refer to the entities which fall into this category as Objects. One of the main distinctions which Frege was concerned to make (*within* the realm of Entities) is that between functions and Objects. And most of the things which he calls 'objects' are Objects and not merely objects. This would be the case for physical objects, persons, and, in Frege's view, numbers, truth-values, value-ranges, etc. Many would say that Frege was definitely wrong in thinking that the class of Objects must include such objects as concept-correlates. What I am suggesting is that if Frege were to hold that, because senses can function as indirect references, they thereby are Objects, then he would be equally wrong. Senses, of course, can be objects, but never Objects.

I believe that the above approach is a better way of solving the apparent difficulty in Frege's ontology which is referred to by C. E. Caton. Professor Caton points out that if Frege held a certain group of three propositions and if he used his terms unambiguously, then he would be holding a contradictory position, for the three statements constitute an inconsistent triad. The three propositions are:

(I) The sense of an expression is an object;
(II) The sense of some expressions are unsaturated;
(III) No object is unsaturated.[19]

Frege apparently did (mistakenly, I have argued) hold (I), according to Jackson.[20] However, (I) does not entail (I') 'The sense of an expression is an Object'. I believe that Caton is correct in saying that Frege held (II). He is quite explicit in "On Concept and Object":

Not all the parts of a thought can be complete; at least one must be 'unsaturated' or predicative; otherwise they would not hold together. For example, the sense of the phrase 'the number 2' does not hold together with that of the expression 'the concept *prime number*' without a link. We apply such a link in the sentence 'the number 2 falls under the concept *prime number*'; it is contained in the words 'falls under', which need to be completed in two ways — by a subject and an accusative; and only because their sense is thus 'unsaturated' are they capable of serving as a link. Only when they have been supplemented in this twofold respect do we get a complete sense, a thought [p. 54].[21]

---

[19] C. E. Caton, *op. cit.*, p. 462.
[20] See footnote 4.
[21] I believe, then, that Grossmann is wrong in saying that Frege "in-

However, if I am right in the above remarks, then Frege does not hold (III) but instead maintains an assertion that might be confused with it, namely (III') 'No *Object* is unsaturated'. (But some objects are unsaturated.) It would follow that Caton is incorrect in saying (A) According to Frege, "everything is either an object or a function, and nothing is both an object and a function."[22] Rather, according to Frege, (B) every *reference* is either an Object or a function, and no reference is both an Object and a function.

VII

At this point, the suggestion might occur that since (A) and (B) are not equivalent, we can therefore answer the question as to what kinds of things are Entities (for Frege) on the basis of which of them are references—Objects and functions. Is this the case? Does Frege actually hold that every Entity is either an Object or a function? The answer to this question, of course, depends upon the status of senses (including thoughts). I believe that strong arguments can be put forth for holding that, for Frege, senses (including thoughts) *are Entities*. Frege especially stresses the *reality* of thoughts, but since he holds that thoughts are made up of parts—at least one of which is incomplete—it seems reasonable to believe that he holds the same view regarding those senses which are not complete thoughts. In "Negation" he constantly speaks of the *being* of thoughts (p. 117 ff.). He says that in judging, "the act of judging did not make the thought or set its parts in order; for the thought was already there" (p. 127). And in "The Thought" he writes: "When one apprehends or thinks a thought, one does not create it, but only comes to stand in a certain relation . . . to what has already existed beforehand."[23] Later he explicitly raises the

sists on the sense-denotation distinction for names but makes no such distinction for concept words." R. Grossmann, p. 106; cf. p. 116.

[22] C. E. Caton, *op. cit.*, p. 462.

[23] G. Frege, "The Thought: A Logical Inquiry," *Mind*, LXV (1956), 307.

question as to whether or not thoughts are real. He ends this discussion by saying:

Thoughts are by no means unreal but their reality is of a quite different kind from that of things. And their effect is brought about by an act of the thinker without which they would be ineffective, at least as far as we can see. And yet the thinker does not create them but must take them as they are. They can be true without being apprehended by a thinker and are not wholly unreal even then, at least if they could be apprehended and by this means brought into operation.[24]

I submit, then, that Frege holds that thoughts and other senses are Entities and that *these* Entities are neither functions nor objects. Hence our *major* ontological division will have to follow the lines I indicated in my earlier paper:

ENTITIES

references		nonreferences
Objects	functions	senses, including thoughts

VIII

The main points for which I have argued so far are: (1) (Fregean) concepts are Entities. (2) They are abstract properties or universals (which must be distinguished from concrete properties). (3) Concepts are ontologically prior to Objects. (4) The concept-Object distinction is one *within* the realm of Entities, not a basis for distinguishing Entities from non-Entities. (5) The sense-reference distinction cannot be reduced to the concept-object distinction. (6) Senses cannot be objects. (7) The problem of indirect references can be answered by distinguishing between objects and Objects. (8) The distinction between references and nonreferences is not a basis for the distinction between Entities and non-Entities, for senses are also Entities.

It will be noted that I have denied that the question as to what sort of ontology Frege has can be taken to be reducible to the question as to what sorts of things Frege takes

[24] *Ibid.*, p. 311.

as Objects or to the question as to what sorts of things he takes as references. How then can we answer the question? I believe that the best way to answer the question is to read Frege without pressing some of his distinctions beyond their proper limits and in such a way as to relate the various distinctions. I believe that such a reading gives strong support for the thesis that, for Frege, among the main kinds of Entities, there are both Objects and functions (including concepts and relations) and very likely senses. Thus the distinction of Objects and functions—important as it is—is not a distinction between what sorts of things are ontological ultimates and what sorts of things are not. Rather it is a distinction within the realm of Entities—more specifically within the realm of references. It may, indeed, be the case that we should think of Frege's distinction between Objects and concepts as a distinction between *things* and *kinds of things*.[25] Socrates is a thing (an individual with his concrete properties). Man (or a man) is a kind of a thing. Frege's dictum that concepts are not Objects would then simply come to this: a kind of a thing is not a thing. But this approach, I think, tends to deontologize Frege too much. And further this still leaves open the question as to what is to be included in the category of things (or Objects). I believe that my arguments for (1)-(8) lead overwhelmingly to part of my conclusion that (9) Frege is a strict realist, at least implicitly.

What about the other part of the conclusion, that (10) Frege may even be a Platonist? There are many things Frege says that lend strong support to this thesis. (a) Again, he holds that a concept word "has nothing to do with objects directly, but stands for a concept" (p. 83). (b) He points out that even if no objects fall under a given concept, "this does not stop the concept word from standing for something" (p. 83). (c) He maintains that "the concept is logically prior to its

[25] As suggested by P. T. Geach, in Anscombe and Geach, *Three Philosophers* (Oxford: Blackwell, 1961), p. 156.

extension" (p. 106). (d) Finally, Frege says: "On my view, bringing an object under a concept is just recognition of a relation that was there already" (p. 85). How much more of a realist can one be? Indeed, how Platonic this is!

9

Frege, Concepts, and Ontology

M. S. GRAM

Philosophical discussions of concepts usually suffer from two
fatal defects. The first defect is that few philosophers have
undertaken to offer an analysis of "concept." The notion is
usually introduced by means of synonyms. Thus we are told
that concepts are meanings, that they are second intentions,
or that they are logical intensions. But we will be none the
wiser about what a concept is if we take these synonyms as
analyses. For we shall be unable to grasp what a concept is
until we have grasped the meaning of the expression with
which it is said to be synonymous. And since synonyms are
identical in meaning, we will be unable to grasp the meaning
of the expression synonymous with "concept" until we have
first grasped the meaning of "concept"—all of which shows
that synonyms are useless as an analysis.

The second defect vitiating much of the discussion about
concepts is that virtually none of the participants in the discussion bother to offer demonstrations that there are really
things which are denominated by the word "concept." That
there are concepts cannot be assumed. For a concept—at least
as it figures in philosophical argument—is a problematic entity. Philosophers use concepts as explanatory devices. And
as long as there can be a dispute about the adequacy of a
philosophical explanation, any of the devices used in that

explanation can be questioned. The existence of concepts is no exception to this.

Frege's theory of concepts escapes both of the defects besetting traditional accounts. He does not give an analysis of "concept," but he does offer a description of the notion and supplements this description with arguments purporting to show that there are things answering to it. Here I want to state these arguments, go on to ask whether they are sound, and conclude by exposing what I consider to be a fatal defect in Frege's theory. In order to bring the issues into sharper focus, I shall contrast the theory which I find in Frege with a theory I believe to be more adequate than Frege's.

1. Frege's Arguments for the Existence of Concepts

Frege introduces concepts in two ways, and they must be kept strictly separate. According to the first way, a concept is a kind of function. Thus Frege says that a concept is a function which, when completed, yields the name of a truth-value.[1] Frege's characterization of a function is familiar: it is dependent, unsaturated, and incomplete.[2] And what distinguishes a concept from a function is that a concept, in addition to having all of the characteristics of a function, has the further characteristic of being a predicate. Consider, for example, the expression $(\ )^2 + (\ )^3$. No value that can be given to the gaps in the expression will yield a truth-value. And the reason is that a function of this sort is not a predicate, while a concept is.

What is important about this way of introducing concepts is that they are used to account for predication. But whatever the merits of this account of predication, the arguments governing the introduction of concepts here are different from

---

[1] Gottlob Frege, "Function and Concept," in *Translations from the Philosophical Writings of Frege,* ed. Peter Geach and Max Black (Oxford: Blackwell, 1966), p. 30.

[2] *Ibid.,* p. 31.

those which Frege uses to explain such epistemic phenomena as the ability of several people to entertain the same thing in thought, the existence of a common perceptual world, or our ability to classify perceptual objects. Frege finds the notion of a concept indispensable to the explanation of these phenomena. But the arguments he gives here are not merely independent arguments for the existence of concepts as predicates. For you can hold a theory of concepts adequate to these epistemic phenomena and still be unable to account for the relation of subject and predicate in judgment or to describe the kinds of entities which can function as subjects and predicates. I do not say that Frege understands the notion of a concept differently when he discusses predication than when he discusses the epistemic problems I have mentioned. The fact is that he does not. All I am concerned to do here is to point out that this is an accident of his position and, accordingly, that the arguments drawn from the problem of predication do not necessarily commit him to the same theory of concepts as the arguments from these epistemic phenomena. I shall thus ignore the issue of predication in this paper and consider only the epistemic arguments for concepts.

I distinguish three different arguments by which Frege tries to show that concepts exist. All of these arguments are embedded in his discussion of complete thoughts. But the arguments he gives for the existence of thoughts can be deployed *mutatis mutandis* to show that concepts exist: since concepts are logical constituents of complete thoughts, any argument proving that thoughts exist will also prove that concepts exist. The arguments for the existence of concepts can be designated as follows: the argument from cognitive identity; the argument from cognitive objectivity; and the argument from recognition. Let us take them in turn.

A. *The Argument from Cognitive Identity.* Two people can conceive, say, the Pythagorean theorem.[3] If they both

---

[3] Gottlob Frege, "The Thought: A Logical Inquiry," trans. in *Mind* (July, 1956), pp. 289-311.

correctly conceive that theorem, we say that they are contemplating the same thing. For they do not contemplate something different merely because more than one person con-
templates the theorem.[4] Frege seeks to explain this fact by
arguing that there exists a concept which is before the mind
of every person who correctly conceives the Pythagorean
theorem. And this entity is numerically the same through
various acts of conceiving it.

The structure of Frege's argument, then, is this. He takes
it as a fact that several people can contemplate the same
thing. Confronted with this fact, we can say that what they
conceive is either numerically the same in all cases or that
it is not. If we hold that the conception several people have
of a thing when they are conceiving the same thing is not
numerically identical despite the different acts of conception,
then we will not be able to explain how several people can
contemplate the same thing. And this generates the consequence that no two people can conceive the same thing. Frege's
alternative is to hold that there is a numerically identical
entity which two people have before their minds when they
conceive the same thing. And this is what he calls a concept.

B. *The Argument from Cognitive Objectivity.* There are
two different versions of this argument, the first of which runs
as follows. Consider equiangularity. For anything to be equi-
angular is for it to have all of its interior angles equal. And
that this is what constitutes equiangularity is, according to
Frege, independent of the way in which we happen to think
about it. Let us, however, assume the opposite: That what
constitutes equiangularity is really dependent upon my conception of it and does not exist apart from my conception. If
this were so, Frege argues, then it would follow that I could
falsify any claim about equiangularity by simply thinking
about equiangularity in a different way. This is an obviously
absurd consequence; hence, we must assume the existence of
entities which exist independently of our conception of them

---

[4] *Ibid.*

in order to explain how we can genuinely misconceive what things are. Thus the fact that we can misconceive what things are is taken by Frege to imply the existence of entities—which he calls concepts—that are independent of our conception of them. It is impossible to misconceive something which owes its existence to the way in which we choose to think about it. To conceive of something incorrectly assumes a distinction between our conception and what it is about. When that distinction collapses, then the notion of error collapses with it. So in order to preserve that distinction, we must recognize the existence of concepts.

The source of the argument which I have just paraphrased is Frege's discussion of the Pythagorean theorem, where he argues this way:

> If the thought I express in the Pythagorean theorem can be recognized by others just as much as by me then it does not belong to the content of my consciousness. I am not its bearer; yet I can, nevertheless, recognize it to be true. However, if it is not the same thought at all which is taken to be the content of the Pythagorean theorem by me and by another person, one should not really say "the Pythagorean theorem" but "my Pythagorean theorem", "his Pythagorean theorem" and these would be different. . . . Therefore the words "true" and "false", as I understand them, could also be applicable only in the sphere of my consciousness, if they were not supposed to be concerned with something of which I was not the bearer, but were somehow appointed to characterize the content of my consciousness.[5]

The argument here is cast in terms of complete thoughts. Yet, since concepts are logical parts of complete thoughts, a demonstration that complete thoughts exist is an *a fortiori* demonstration that concepts exist. Frege argues here as follows. To say that the Pythagorean theorem is dependent upon me for its existence implies that every person conceiving that theorem has something before his mind which is different from that which everybody else has before his mind. This implies that there is no Pythagorean theorem. And this, in turn, implies

---

[5] *Ibid.*, p. 301.

that it is logically impossible to misconceive that theorem.[6] Hence, there is no standard in terms of which we can apply the notions of correct and incorrect. And this is why concepts must exist; if they did not, we could not explain how we misconceive what we plainly do misconceive.

But this is not the only version of the argument from cognitive objectivity. Frege argues to the same conclusion from the ability we have to discover whether we are entertaining the same concept. This is possible, according to Frege, only if it is possible for us to share something in common. Either we share our ideas, sense impressions, moods, and feelings in common or we must share concepts in common. Consider the former class of things first. Frege holds that we cannot share any member of this class in common. For all of these exist "only because of me, I am [their] bearer."[7] Or, again, he says that "every idea has only one bearer; no two men have the same idea."[8] From this he concludes that ideas are not communicable. If every idea has only one bearer, then I cannot compare your idea and mine to see if they are the same.

There is an exegetical problem about Frege's claim that ideas are incommunicable, for there are two ways of interpreting that claim. Frege could be holding that it is logically impossible for an idea to be shared by two people because he has *defined* an idea as that which "exists only because of me."[9] Hence it would be self-contradictory to say of anyone

[6] *Ibid.*, pp. 301-302; cf. the parallel argument in *The Basic Laws of Arithmetic*, trans. Montgomery Furth (Berkeley: University of California Press, 1964), pp. xvii-xix.

[7] "The Thought," p. 299.

[8] *Ibid.*, p. 300.

[9] *Ibid.* There appears to be an argument for this conclusion in "The Thought"; but it is not clear that it is being put forward as such or that, if it is, it has anything to do with the issue. Thus we are asked ("The Thought," p. 300) to consider the referent of the expression "that lime tree." We are told that there are two possibilities: (1) If the lime tree exists, the thought "That lime tree is my idea" is false; (2) If the lime tree does not exist, then neither the thought "That lime tree is my idea" nor the thought "That lime tree is not my idea" is true. This does not, however, prove that every idea has only one

that he had the idea of another person. On this interpretation, Frege would have established his claim; but he would have established it by fiat, which will give him the conclusion he wants on pain of circularity. But there is a second interpretation of which his claim admits: he could be holding, not that it is definitionally impossible for two people to share the same idea, but rather that we cannot know when two people do share the same idea. He appears to be taking this view of incommunicability when he says outright that you cannot find out whether the idea you presumably share with another is the same in both cases.[10] Here Frege grants by implication that it is logically possible for two people to share the same idea and points out only that there is no criterion for discovering any actual occurrence of such identity.

Which of these interpretations is an accurate account of what Frege is claiming? He is, I think, holding that it is logically impossible for two people to share the same idea. But he is asserting this as the conclusion of an argument, although the character of that argument is obscure in Frege's text. The argument I find there which can support the claim that it is logically impossible for two people to share the same idea proceeds by showing that we cannot know when two people share the same idea. The strategy which I am attributing to Frege, then, is this: By drawing out the consequences of saying that it is impossible to discover when two people share the same idea, he can derive the conclusion that it is logically impossible for them to share the same idea. It does, of course, seem that these two claims are mutually exclusive: To say that it is logically impossible for two people to share the same idea excludes the claim that we cannot know when two people share the same idea. The latter claim presupposes the logical possibility of sharing ideas—which is

---

bearer. It proves, rather, that the definite description "that lime tree" must be fulfilled as a condition for assigning the thought in which it figures a truth-value. This conclusion leaves it an open question whether ideas do have only one bearer.

[10] *Ibid.*

just what the former claim denies. But this reading of Frege's strategy would be a mistake. Just why this reading is a mistake will emerge from a consideration of Frege's argument.

The argument, as I reconstruct it, is this. We grant for the sake of argument, as Frege himself does, that an idea can wander from consciousness to consciousness. This is an admission that it is logically possible for two people to share numerically the same idea as a content of consciousness. But even if your idea and mine are numerically the same, it does not follow that we can ever know this. In fact, on my interpretation, what Frege is claiming is that we can never know whether your idea and mine are the same. And this results from a logical impossibility. In order to discover whether you and I have the same idea, I must be able to compare your awareness of that idea with my own awareness. I must be able to hold them together in one act of consciousness and compare them. And this I can do only on pain of contradiction, for it is logically impossible for your act of awareness to be mine. Hence, it is logically impossible for two people to share the same idea in the sense that it is logically impossible for one person's act of awareness to be another's.

Ideas, then, are incommunicable. Yet we do share something in common when we talk about the Pythagorean theorem or equiangularity. For we can know that two people think of these things in the same way. Identity of ideas cannot explain this. So Frege infers that there must exist an entity called a concept, which exists independently of the mental contents of persons apprehending it. A concept can, accordingly, be communicable. For it can be present to more than one consciousness; and this explains how it is possible for us to know when two people conceive of things in the same way. The second version of the argument from cognitive objectivity comes, then, to this. Starting from the fact that we can discover when we are conceiving of things in the same way, Frege sees two ways of explaining this fact. Either we must share ideas in common or we must share entities in common which are independent of acts of consciousness. We cannot share ideas; therefore, we must share entities whose existence does not depend upon the minds which apprehend them. And these entities are concepts.

C. *The Argument from Recognition.* When we are aware of something that is perceptually given to us, we are aware of it as being of a certain kind. This is a commonplace of perceptual awareness. And it presupposes, according to Frege, the kind of entity which he calls a concept. Thus for Frege "having visual impressions is certainly necessary for seeing things but not sufficient. What must still be added is non-sensible; and yet this is just what opens up the outer world for us; for without this non-sensible something everyone would remain shut up in his inner world." [11]

This argument is difficult to reconstruct. It appears that Frege is merely drawing the distinction once more between what is essentially private to the perceiver and what is public and capable of being shared by all perceivers. And this distinction would appear to be irrelevant to the problem of explaining how we can recognize items in our experience as being of a certain kind. Indeed, the problem of recognition would seem to apply indifferently to both the public and the private items of our experience. We can, for example, ask how we can classify our sensations just as readily as we can ask how we can classify those items which are available to more than one perceiver.

All of this is true, but irrelevant. Frege begins with a perceptual object. And he wants to know how he can see it as an object of a certain kind. One of the conditions of seeing such an object is that we have sense impressions. But we do not see a perceptual object by merely apprehending the impressions we have of it. For the impressions we have are not what we are trying to see. Now it is just this distinction between having a sense impression and seeing a perceptual object that, according to Frege, demands the existence of concepts.

---

[11] *Ibid.*, p. 309; cf. p. 308 of the same essay.

To see a perceptual object is to classify it as being an object of a certain kind. This ability presupposes that we share a common stock of concepts in virtue of which we sort out objects, which are public, from ideas, which are private. Without an acquaintance with entities that exist independently of the acts by which we are conscious of them, we cannot see perceptual objects. We could, at best, entertain sense impressions. But we manifestly can see perceptual objects; so concepts must exist.

This argument contains a premise that is crucial to the soundness of the argument but for which Frege nowhere directly argues. The possibility of distinguishing between the having of impressions and the perception of objects is held to imply the existence of concepts. But this assumes that we cannot apply concepts to the impressions we have. And Frege does not argue for this assumption. Unless the assumption is true, however, the argument Frege gives for concepts here will not show that concepts exist. For while it might show that any act of classification of items in our experience implies the existence of concepts, it would not show, as Frege insists, that the distinction between sensation and perception alone implies the existence of concepts.

But an argument can be constructed for this crucial assumption on Fregean principles. It is this. When we apply a concept to a perceptual object as opposed to a sense impression, we can always raise the question of whether we have correctly applied that concept. You cannot, however, raise that question with regard to the contents of your own consciousness. What Frege said earlier about the consciousness of two different people holds with equal cogency for the content of one's own consciousness at different times. Just as two people cannot share the same idea, one person cannot have the same idea at two different times. This contention can be used to show why Frege would deny that you can apply concepts to sense impressions. Any idea I might have is perishable. For this reason an idea that I have at one time cannot be compared with an idea that I have at another time: I cannot bring together these two ideas in one act of consciousness. But the only way that I might be able to make sure that I had classified an idea correctly is to compare the idea I sought to classify with an idea I have in the present. Yet this is precisely what I cannot do: I cannot hold a past idea together with a present idea. For the only thing that I can compare with my present idea is, not the past idea itself, but only a memory of the past idea. But I cannot discover whether I have correctly classified the past idea until I have first discovered that I have correctly classified the memory of that idea. And this is a hopeless task just because I cannot compare my memory with the idea of which it is a memory. From this it follows that I cannot check any classification of an idea in order to discover that the classification is correct. And if I cannot discover this, then I cannot apply concepts to my ideas. For my ability to apply concepts to anything implies the further ability of discovering whether the application is correct or not.

This concludes the battery of arguments by which Frege tries to show that concepts exist. The following description of a concept emerges from the foregoing discussion. Frege concludes that concepts are "neither things of the outer world nor ideas." [12] That a concept cannot be mental follows from Frege's contention that what is mental cannot be shared, while concepts can be shared. That a concept is not a thing of the outer world is not, however, a direct consequence of any of the foregoing arguments. Sometimes Frege merely lays it down that concepts are not physical, as when he says that they are not in space and time or when he says that we grasp them through the eye of the mind and not through the senses. [13] At other times, however, what he says about concepts yields an argument for this conclusion, as when he says

---

[12] *Ibid.*, p. 301.
[13] *Ibid.*, p. 310; cf. Gottlob Frege, *Foundations of Arithmetic*, trans. J. L. Austin (Harper Torchbooks, 1960), p. 99.

that the characteristic marks of a concept are to be distinguished from the properties of a concept.[14] Thus the *concept* "square" is not a rectangle, which is nonetheless one of the characteristic marks of that concept. The objects falling under that concept, however, are rectangles; hence, rectangularity is said to be one of the properties of the concept. To say, then, that a concept is physical would imply for Frege that the concept had assumed the properties of things falling under it. And since this consequence is absurd, it follows that concepts are not physical.

2. Are There Any Fregean Concepts?

Consider once again what I have called the argument from cognitive identity. The problem here was to explain how it is possible for two people to think the same thing. Frege's solution is to say that, when two people are thinking the same thing, they are contemplating a concept which is present before both their minds. What is wrong with this solution, however, is just that it is another way of expressing the original problem. The entity which is introduced to explain how two people can conceive the same thing has just that characteristic in virtue of which an explanation was demanded in the first place. We want to know how two people can conceive of something without destroying the numerical identity of the thing which is conceived. And we are told that two people entertain a concept which is numerically identical despite the plurality of people entertaining it. But if the problem disappears as a result of this explanation, why should it not have disappeared as soon as it was stated? The concept which is said to be numerically identical through various acts of contemplation is just a duplication of the entity whose numerical identity must be explained. And it will do no good to object here that the numerical identity of the concept is not just postulated by Frege but is explained by the fact that

---

[14] Cf. Frege, *The Basic Laws of Arithmetic*, p. xiv.

a concept is not a part of the mental act of any of the people contemplating it. This will not show that Fregean concepts exist. For the numerical identity of the thing in the world falling under the concept would then be enough to explain how two people could think of the same thing. And concepts would not be required at all. I conclude that the argument from cognitive identity fails to establish the existence of Fregean concepts.

But what about the argument from cognitive objectivity? Does it not alone suffice to prove the existence of concepts? The first version of the argument demanded the existence of concepts to explain how we can make mistakes about the analysis of what it is to be something of a certain kind. The second version moved to the same conclusion as a way of explaining our ability to find out that we are talking about the same thing. Neither of these versions of the argument under consideration justifies the inference to the existence of concepts. Take these versions in turn. You can account for our ability to make mistakes in analysis by holding that the adequacy of any analysis must be measured against the way things are as distinct from the concepts we have of these things. So the first version of the argument does not prove the existence of concepts. What it establishes is the quite different conclusion that we must recognize the existence of either common properties or concepts. And this is compatible with the nonexistence of concepts.

Now it may not be at once clear that this is a genuine objection to Frege's theory. Someone might object that I succeed in refuting Frege only by bestowing a different name on what Frege calls a concept. Thus what I have called a property Frege calls a concept.[15] But the objection which I am making rests on more than a verbal difference. No property can ever be a Fregean concept, for Frege distinguishes the characteristic marks from the properties of a concept.[16]

---

[15] Frege, *Translations*, p. 51.
[16] Frege, *The Basic Laws of Arithmetic*, p. xiv.

It is a characteristic mark of the concept of a triangle, for example, that the sum of the angles of any triangle is equal to 180 degrees. The *concept* of a triangle, however, does not have this property, which applies only to the objects falling under the concept. It follows from this distinction, accordingly, that properties cannot be concepts. Hence the objection stands: the existence of Fregean concepts is not a necessary conclusion of Frege's argument here.

But worse is to come. The second version of the argument will not do either. Here Frege argues from the possibility of discovering that we conceive of things in like ways to the conclusion that what we are conceiving are concepts. But this is not an adequate solution to the problem. Frege rejects any reliance upon sensations to discover that two people share common conceptions. But he allows concepts to account for this ability. Yet there is nothing about a Fregean concept that prevents us from raising the same question about it that Frege raises about sensations. We cannot share sensations because, even though we might have numerically the same sensation as a content of consciousness, it is logically impossible for one person to compare his act of awareness with that of another in order to discover this. And this is so because nobody can hold together in one act of consciousness two acts of awareness. This is why Frege falls back upon the numerical sameness of concepts in order to explain how we can discover that two people are thinking the same thing. Two people are said to be aware of the same concept. Yet how do they know that they are being presented with numerically the same concept? To use simple apprehension or awareness here as an explanation does not distinguish this situation from the situation in which two people are said to be aware of the same sensation. For the same reason two people cannot be said to know whether they apprehend the same concept by simple inspection. For it is logically impossible for one person to compare his act of apprehension with that of another person.

And this is just the reason why Frege denied that we can share sensations.

The last of Frege's arguments for the existence of concepts moves from our ability to classify perceptual objects to the conclusion that we must be acquainted with the concepts under which we subsume these objects. For it is only by grasping a concept that we can, according to Frege, see a perceptual object. But this no more justifies the conclusion drawn from it than the arguments which have gone before. To show this, let us suppose that acquaintance with a concept is a condition of recognizing things which fall under it. Now Frege does not say much about the epistemic character of this kind of acquaintance. He says only that a concept is grasped by "the mental eye." [17] I understand him to mean by this that the epistemic relation involved here is that of simple apprehension. And if this is an accurate account of what Frege means by that relation, then the account he offers of our ability to see perceptual objects merely duplicates the problem it was intended to solve. How, for example, do I distinguish between a veridical and an erroneous apprehension of a concept? Frege is silent about this. But there are only two ways in which he could seek to answer this question. He could say that the question does not arise and insist that every act of simple apprehension is self-certifying. Or he could say that acts of simple apprehension are not self-certifying and that every such act is certified as correct or incorrect only by other acts which take previous acts of apprehension as their object.

It should be clear that the first way of answering the question will not do. To say that simple apprehension is self-certifying is fatal to the explanatory power of Frege's theory. The theory was constructed to account for our ability correctly to distinguish perceptual objects from one another. And the theory will not do this if it reproduces this epistemic

[17] *Ibid.*

situation at another level. The initial problem was to account for our classification of perceptual objects. But in order to do this we must, according to Frege, be able to distinguish one concept from another. And this, in turn, involved classification all over again. And so, if simple apprehension is enough to recognize concepts for what they are, there is no reason why it is not enough to recognize perceptual objects for what they are. The problem is the same on both levels: any act of classification demands an explanation, whether what is classified is a perceptual object or a concept. Either simple apprehension is enough to explain recognition or it isn't. If it is, then concepts are rendered superfluous. If it is not, concepts give you the same problem that you had with perceptual objects. Either way, then, the theory cannot account for recognitional capacities.

But there is a second way of explaining how we are to distinguish between veridical and erroneous apprehension of concepts. With the failure of simple apprehension as an account of our grasping concepts, Frege could hold that all that is required to explain our ability to recognize concepts is a further concept of higher order. Thus what is being claimed is that the recognition of concepts does require an explanation just as much as the recognition of objects. And the explanation tendered is that we can form concepts of concepts in virtue of which we recognize a concept serving as the object of a concept of higher order.

But this way of answering the question about the recognition of concepts is as hopeless as its predecessor. The reason it will not do is that it merely postpones and does not eliminate the failure of Frege's theory. That theory seeks to explain recognition by the simple apprehension of a concept. And once this is denied, the theory is left without any way of explaining just how we do grasp concepts. So Frege's theory is committed to this view of what it is to grasp a concept. And the commitment is not removed merely by distinguishing between higher- and lower-order concepts. For somewhere in the order of concepts Frege must either invoke simple apprehension or leave the grasping of concepts without even the pretense of an explanation. So the difficulty which forced the abandonment of simple apprehension at one level arises all over again for concepts of higher order.

My conclusion is that the argument from recognition does not show that Fregean concepts exist. The main defect of the argument is that the justification for our belief in such concepts is drawn from their alleged capacity to account for the fact of perceptual recognition. But Frege's concepts do not so much account for this fact as repeat it. And this is enough to remove the grounds we would otherwise have for believing in their existence.

3. Concepts: An Alternative Approach

In the remaining part of this paper I shall contrast a theory of concepts with Frege's theory and try to show that the alternative theory, unlike the one Frege holds, can account for the phenomena for which Frege wants an explanation. The alternative theory treats a concept as a rule. As it stands, however, this claim merely replaces one mysterious locution by another. And I cannot here state and defend an analysis of "rule." I shall rather single out a characteristic I believe belongs to a large class of rules and show that it supports the claim that concepts are rules. The relevent characteristic is that a rule expresses a criterion in virtue of which an action is assessed as correct or incorrect. Thus many of the definitions in Euclidean geometry which define a term by means of a procedure of construction would count as rules. The action which is called correct or incorrect in terms of such a definition is the application of a word to a construction. Most rules are, in fact, statements of criteria for the application of words. There are others, however, which assess nonverbal actions like swimming or dancing as correct or incorrect. On the characterization I have given of a rule, there is no restriction in principle on the kinds of action which a rule can govern.

Given this notion of a concept, incomplete as it obviously is, let us apply it to the phenomena for which Frege demands an account. There is, first of all, our ability to conceive the same thing. What vitiated Frege's theory here was that the entity he introduced to account for this ability recapitulated the problem. But can a regulist theory succeed in accounting for this phenomenon? I believe that it can. A regulist would hold that for two people to conceive of, say, triangularity is for them to conceive of a rule which expresses the criterion for correct application of the word "triangle." And the identity of the concept entertained by two people would, accordingly, be the identity of the rule.

The regulist solution is faced, however, with two immediate objections. According to the first objection, what the theory claims is a falsification of the phenomenon to be explained. When we conceive of anything, the objection runs, what we are conceiving is different from a rule prescribing a criterion. To conceive of a triangle is not the same thing as conceiving of a rule for applying a word to triangles. I can describe a triangle without including as part of that description a reference to a rule for the correct application of the word for a triangle. And since this is so, it follows that I can conceive of the referent of the former description without conceiving of the referent of the latter.

What is wrong with this objection is that it leaves its crucial premise undefended. The premise is that the description of the concept of anything must never include a description of anything that does not belong to the object of that concept. Thus it is assumed that, since something like a triangle can be described without reference to rules, the concept of a triangle cannot be so described. But there is no reason to believe that this follows. For you can admit that it is possible to describe the object of a concept without referring to rules and still hold that you cannot describe the *concept* of that object without specifying rules.

The second objection to the regulist solution is this. It might be claimed that the regulist theory has the same defect as Frege's theory. In order to explain how two people can conceive of the same thing, the regulist holds that they are conceiving of the same rule. And this merely reproduces the problem. For the identity of a rule appears to be just another case of the identity of conception which we are trying to explain.

What was wrong with Frege's solution was that it supplied us with an entity which was allegedly numerically identical through various acts of awareness in order to explain how another entity could be numerically identical through various acts of awareness. But the regulist solution does not recapitulate the problem in this way. When two people conceive the same thing, what they have before their minds is the same rule. But a rule is not the kind of thing that can be numerically identical; it can be only qualitatively identical through various acts of conception. Thus the criterion of sameness for a rule is that the two people contemplating it can give exactly similar descriptions of the rule they have before their minds. But this does not permit us to infer that they are giving descriptions of something that is numerically identical. For the notion of numerical identity does not apply to concepts. This can be shown as follows. If two people give exactly similar descriptions of the concept they have, we cannot ask how many things answer to that description. But if two people give exactly similar descriptions of objects which fall under concepts, it is always significant to ask how many objects answer to the description. Thus the notion of numerical identity does not apply to concepts. And this is why the regulist solution differs from Frege's. A regulist seeks to explain how it is possible for two people to conceive the same thing by saying that they conceive qualitatively the same rule. And the rule they conceive, unlike a Fregean concept, does not have the same kind of identity as the object to which it applies.

What about cognitive objectivity? Here there are two questions for which Frege wants an answer: (1) What are the conditions of our ability to correct mistaken analyses? (2) What are the conditions of our ability to discover when we share the same concepts? Frege's answer to (1) is that such an ability requires the existence of entities which exist independently of our conception of them. But this conclusion does not necessarily follow from such an ability. That we can decide between rival analyses can, I have argued, be explained equally well on the assumption that there exist properties in things as distinct from concepts. Thus (1) is not a question which a theory of concepts is required to answer.

The second question does, however, raise an issue in the theory of concepts. We might, for example, succeed in proving that there are properties which exist apart from our conception of them and still not be able to account for our ability to discover that we share concepts in common. Moving from the argument that we cannot share ideas, Frege seeks to account for our ability to discover that we share concepts in common by introducing numerically identical entities called concepts with which we can be immediately acquainted. I have already argued that such a solution merely duplicates the problem: How can we know that our acquaintance with concepts is any different from our acquaintance with ideas?

But can the regulist offer a better account? I think he can. Two people discover that they possess the same concept when they discover that the descriptions they give are exactly similar. And finding this out does not demand that one person compare his act of awareness with that of another. It requires only a knowledge of the rules and conventions of language—all of which are public. So the exact similarity of the descriptions can be discovered without any reference to the acts of awareness of either person. This is what distinguishes our possession of concepts from the acquaintance we have with ideas. The latter presupposes a reference to an act of awareness which must be compared with another act of awareness if we are ever to find out that our experience of an idea is qualitatively the same as that of another person's experience. The former has no such presupposition. For this reason we can discover that we share a concept with another person.

What remains is to ask whether the regulist can account, as Frege could not, for our ability to see perceptual objects. Frege's account has two levels. That we can perceive perceptual objects is for Frege the result of our ability to classify certain items in our experience as veridical and nonveridical. This ability is explained by saying that we subsume these items under concepts. The second level of the explanation requires that we apply the same distinction to concepts. And Frege's account provides only that we grasp concepts by simple apprehension, with regard to which the problem of veridical and nonveridical apprehension arises all over again.

Can the regulist avoid the consequence, deducible from Frege's theory, that our epistemic relation to concepts duplicates the epistemic relation it was meant to explain? The answer to this question is given once it is seen that the regulist is committed to deny the crucial premise of Frege's account; the premise, namely, that we grasp concepts by simple apprehension. There are two ways in which we grasp rules; and neither of them presupposes the epistemic relation of simple apprehension. Consider, first of all, the kind of rule involved in perception in virtue of which veridical and nonveridical apprehension can be distinguished. The rule here states the relations obtaining in a sequence of possible presentations of a perceptual object. To perceive a perceptual object is, accordingly, to relate the present perception we have with future possible perception and the present actual perception of other observers. What counts as a veridical perception is a presentation that has been correctly related to the family of perceptions which constitute a perceptual object of a certain kind.

I cannot defend this account of perceptual rules here. All I wish to do is to show the kind of theory that a regulist view of concepts would involve and to show, further, that it does not entail the consequence that besets Frege's theory. We can grasp a rule of perception by demonstrating our ability to connect the presentations of perceptual objects; we can, that is, predict future possible experience and the present actual experience of others. But this kind of grasping of a concept does not entail that we have a simple perception of a rule. To grasp the rule is not to stand in a relation of simple apprehension to any entity but rather to demonstrate a kind of ability. And even the explicit grasp of the rules involved in perception does not entail a case of simple apprehension. To grasp any rule explicitly is to exercise another ability. In this case, the ability we demonstrate is the capacity to formulate the rule. And here, again, this does not entail that we stand in the epistemic relation of simple apprehension to a rule which we formulate. So the regulist solution does not duplicate the problem it was supposed to solve. We are not given a relation to concepts that is just a repetition of the relation in which we stand to perceptual objects.

PART TWO

Frege's Semantics

10

Frege's Sinn und Bedeutung

PAUL D. WIENPAHL

Reference to Frege's *Sinn und Bedeutung* is frequent in the literature on meaning. Writers apparently take for granted that Frege: (*a*) proved the necessity for distinguishing between the sense of a word and its referent, and (*b*) clarified the distinction by specifying a meaning for 'sense' required by the proof.[1] Examination of his famous argument is therefore in order.

This is particularly the case since the argument proves only that a distinction between *something* to be called sense and referent is necessary. The argument does not specify a meaning for 'sense', although it does, as stated by Frege, make possible an inference to a meaning of 'sense' which is unsatisfactory because it requires that the sense of a word be a subsistent entity. Careful examination of the argument reveals

---

Reprinted with the kind permission of the author and the editor from *Mind*, LIX (1950), 483-494.

[1] In this discussion I use the terms 'sign', 'sense', 'referent', 'mode of designation', and 'mode of presentation' as they occur in the English translation of Frege's paper made by Max Black in the *Philosophical Review*, Vol. LVII, No. 3, May, 1948. The particular argument to which I refer occurs on pp. 209-210 in the English translation and pp. 25-27 in the original which was published in *Zeitschrift für Philosophie und Philosophische Kritik*, Vol. 100, pp. 25-50, 1892. Quotations are followed by page references in parentheses. These references are to both editions of the article and are given in the order English-German.

an oversight which requires this unsatisfactory meaning of 'sense'. Correction of this oversight makes possible a conception of sense which is satisfactory in the respects that it fits the data in Frege's discussion and does not make the sense of a word a subsistent entity.

This examination is divided into two parts: (A) a statement and analysis of Frege's argument, and (B) specification and justification of a meaning of 'sense' which fits the data of Frege's discussion and does not make sense a subsistent entity. The specification probably applies generally, however, because of the generality of Frege's demonstration and because of advantages this specification has which will be listed.

I

Frege's argument for the need for distinguishing sense from referent runs as follows. Brackets are used to enclose statements which are mine and not Frege's.

'$a = b$' differs in cognitive value from '$a = a$' because '$a = a$' is analytic and because '$a = b$' is synthetic, as we see from such discoveries as that the rising sun is the same every morning. If the relation of identity asserted in '$a = b$' holds between that which 'a' and 'b' name, '$a = b$' does not differ cognitively from '$a = a$', provided that '$a = b$' is true. [For, if 'a' and 'b' as signs (forgetting their physical properties) have only a single property, that of referring to an object, then, when that object is the same for both 'a' and 'b', '$a = a$' and '$a = b$' would say the same or be cognitively equal.] Furthermore, the relation in this case would be one a thing holds to itself. But in '$a = b$' it seems we want to assert the relation between 'a' and 'b'; i.e., to say that 'a' and 'b' refer to the same thing. Therefore, the relation of identity is asserted in '$a = b$' to hold between the signs and not that of which they are signs.

However, if the relation (identity) holds between 'a' and 'b' in so far as they are signs, that is, refer to something, then '$a = b$' would "express no proper knowledge"; because the

connexion of a sign with that of which it is a sign is arbitrary.
(P. 209, p. 26.) Any arbitrarily producible event or object can
be a sign. Thus '$a = b$' would no longer refer to the subject
matter but only its mode of designation; *i.e.*, express no proper
knowledge. "If the sign 'a' is distinguished from the sign 'b'
only as object (here, by means of its shape), not as sign (*i.e.*,
not by the manner in which it designates something), the
cognitive value of '$a = a$' becomes essentially equal to that
of '$a = b$', provided that '$a = b$' is true." (P. 209, p. 26.)

Hence, '$a = b$' can differ cognitively from '$a = a$' only if
there is some other difference between 'a' and 'b' as signs [than
mode of designation, or having a referent]. This difference lies
in the mode of presentation. The latter is exemplified by the
difference between 'Point of intersection of a and b' and 'Point
of intersection of b and c', where a, b, and c are lines connecting the vertices of a triangle with the midpoints of the opposite sides. Therefore, signs have a *sense* (wherein the mode of
presentation is contained) as well as a *referent*.

Preliminary to examining the meaning of 'sense' we observe
the following about Frege's argument. We must assume that
the argument as stated is incomplete, for it must be inferred
that Frege changed his mind about the terms between which
the relation of identity is asserted to hold in '$a = b$'. The view
that identity does *not* hold between that to which 'a' and 'b'
refer must be rejected. We infer that Frege concludes that
identity holds between that to which 'a' and 'b' refer when we
say that $a = b$. Otherwise, since he has *explicitly* shown reason why the relation of identity cannot hold between that to
which 'a' and 'b' refer, nor the modes of designation of 'a' and
'b', it would have to hold between their modes of presentation.
But since the modes of presentation of 'a' and 'b' are by hypothesis *different*, this would mean 'identity' was given a use
contradictory with that which it has in 'the rising sun is the
same (identical) every morning'. In this case Frege's argument is fallacious. Or, if we allowed the modes of presentation
of 'a' and 'b' to be the same, despite the hypothesis, then
'$a = b$' would not differ cognitively from '$a = a$'.

Furthermore, it will be noticed that the argument is difficult to follow as Frege gives it because he did not employ the useful notion of metalanguage. It seemed to him that '$a = b$' and ' 'a' and 'b' refer to the same object' were equivalent statements, and that, therefore, '$a = b$' says something about 'a' and 'b' instead of a and b. Were this the case, however (Frege perceived correctly), '$a = b$' would express no proper knowledge. Whenever we want '$a = b$' to express proper knowledge, it cannot be equivalent to ' 'a' and 'b' refer to the same object'. Hence, as we can say to-day, '$a = b$' is not a statement in the metalanguage and ' $=$ ' not a sign in the metalanguage.

Finally, the term 'mode of designation' as Frege uses it is superfluous for it can always be replaced by the term 'referent' without changing the meaning of the sentence in which it occurs.

In the light of these observations it is useful to restate Frege's argument briefly as follows. Signs must have a sense as well as a referent otherwise we cannot account for the cognitive difference between '$a = a$' and '$a = b$'. For between what terms is the relation of identity asserted to hold in '$a = b$'? If between the objects to which 'a' and 'b' refer, then '$a = b$' has the same cognitive value as '$a = a$' provided '$a = b$' is true. If between the signs 'a' and 'b' then '$a = b$' is a statement in the metalanguage (or, as Frege says, would be about the signs and, therefore, "express no proper knowledge"). If, however, 'a' and 'b' have something besides referents, even if their referents are the same (as they are asserted to be in '$a = b$'), '$a = b$' can have a different cognitive value from '$a = a$'. This difference is that of sense illustrated as follows: the difference between 'Point of intersection of a and b' and 'Point of intersection of b and c', where a, b, and c are lines connecting the vertices of a triangle with the midpoints of the opposite sides.

This argument clearly proves that we must talk of something besides the referent of a sign. Frege calls this something 'sense'. The proof follows from the requirements which the use of 'identity' forces upon us. As the argument and Frege's discussion stand, however, what is the sense of a sign?

Consider one of the examples Frege employs. 'Point of intersection of a and b' and 'Point of intersection of b and c' have the same referent and different senses. The only *observable* differences between these signs are: (i) the physical differences of shape, etc., and (ii) the differences of referents of their component parts, specifically of 'a', 'b', and 'c'. Since not all signs have component parts which are themselves signs, we may discount the importance of (ii). However, Frege also discounts the importance of (i), or at least he implies that difference of sense has nothing to do with differences of shape and other physical properties of signs. For he says: "If the sign 'a' is distinguished from the sign 'b' only as object (here, by means of its shape), not as sign (*i.e.*, not by the manner in which it designates something), the cognitive value of '$a = a$' becomes essentially equal to that of '$a = b$', provided that '$a = b$' is true." (P. 209, p. 26.)

Elsewhere in the article Frege distinguishes sense from referent and other elements in sign usage, but these distinctions do not tell us what sense is. For example, we are told that a sign may have a sense without a referent, as in 'the least rapidly convergent series'. (P. 211, p. 28.) We are also told that the referent and sense of a sign are to be distinguished from the associated conception. "If the referent of a sign is an object perceivable by the senses, my conception of it is an internal image, arising from memories of sense impressions which I have had and activities, both internal and external, which I have performed. . . . The conception is subjective. . . . This constitutes an essential difference between the conception and the sign's sense, which may be the common property of many and therefore is not a part or mode of the individual mind." (P. 212, p. 29.) "The referent is the object itself which we designate by its (the sign's) means; the conception, which we thereby have, is wholly subjective; in between lies the sense, which is indeed no longer subjective like the conception, but is yet not the object itself." (P. 213, p. 30.)

Frege's discussion leaves us with the distinction between sense and referent, and with a clear meaning for the latter but none for the former. Since the sense of a sign is distinguishable from the objective elements (referent) and the subjective elements (conception, in Frege's usage) connected with its employment, *and* since we do not know clearly what sense is, it has been regarded as a subsistent entity. This is unsatisfactory on two counts: it multiplies entities, and it prevents us from verifying *that* there is sense, since verification depends on controlled observation. That is to say, this makes the sense of a sense an "entity" like whiteness or chairness, "things" which can be thought but not observed. Proof that such "things" exist cannot be given in the ordinary way we prove that things exist, namely by observing them. Usually when someone maintains there are fairies and we cannot observe them, we say that he is mad or that this is just a manner of speaking. Sense which is neither subjective nor the object is similar to fairies which no one can see and yet about which everyone can talk when they are willing to tell tales or speak metaphorically.

II

Frege correctly observes that there is a cognitive difference between '$a = a$' and '$a = b$'. He demonstrates that the properties of identity require a distinction of sense and referent to account for this difference. Under the conditions set by this demonstration and accepting Frege's concept of the referent, the sense of a sign (and, therefore, the cognitive difference between, say, '$a = a$' and '$a = b$') can be accounted for as follows. I wish to stress that the following specification of the meaning of 'sense' is given in connexion with Frege's reasons for speaking of sense which are the most explicit grounds for distinguishing something besides the referent of a sign. There has been a tendency to talk of the sense of a sign before investigating the reasons necessitating the distinction of sense at all.

There is a most important difference between '*a* = *a*' and '*a* = *b*' which Frege discounts but which can, nonetheless, explain the difference in cognitive value between '*a* = *a*' and '*a* = *b*'. This is the difference between '*a*' and '*b*' *as objects* whether they function as signs or not, but particularly in the case that they do. This difference explains why '*a* = *b*' can "express . . . proper knowledge" and '*a* = *a*' is analytic.

'*a* = *b*' expresses proper knowledge because you can use '*a*' and '*b*' without knowing that their referents are the same (*i.e.*, identical; or, that *a* = *b*). That is, you must look at something besides '*a*' and '*b*' to know that *a* = *b*. On the other hand you do not have to look at anything except '*a*' and '*a*' to know that *a* = *a*. '*a* = *a*' is analytic precisely because examination of the signs as objects and *not as signs* reveal its truth. This is another way of saying that pure logic is a game; or, that the "signs" in pure logic have no referents, are not properly speaking signs (to use Frege's term). Sometimes we say that they are uninterpreted signs. Put otherwise and more precisely it can be said that the truth of '*a* = *a*' can be established simply on the basis of the semantical rules of our language without reference to empirical (non-linguistic) facts; whereas we have to employ something besides and in addition to semantical rules to prove that '*a* = *b*' is true, namely *a* and *b*. Therefore, one difference in cognitive value between '*a* = *a*' and '*a* = *b*' is due to the differences between the physical properties of '*a*' and '*b*'. As far as Frege's proof that signs must have a sense as well as a referent is concerned this difference is sufficient to account for the difference in cognitive value between '*a* = *a*' and '*a* = *b*'. We conclude that the *sense of a sign is the combination of its physical properties* in so far as it is an object which functions as a sign.

Regarding the sense of a sign as the combination of its physical properties is compatible with all subsequent statements Frege makes about sense in the article "Sinn und Bedeutung." For example: 'morning star' and 'evening star' have the same referent but different senses. 'The least rapidly convergent series' has a sense but no referent. It will be noted that in the case of complex signs (*i.e.*, signs composed of signs) the cognitive value of a sign depends not only on its sense but also on the referents of its component parts. Where there is no referent and never has been a referent in the case of a simple sign, it is *not* a sign and we would not speak of sense in such cases. Furthermore, as Frege observes, the sense of a sign is objective. It is objective on our interpretation in the respect that it can be common to many minds, in the same way that any physical object can be common to many observers.

It may be supposed that Frege and others have discounted the importance of the physical differences between signs in the problem of sense because they have been too impressed with the arbitrary character of signs. Although it is true that any arbitrarily producible event or object can function as a sign, it is false that once it does its relation to its referent is arbitrary. The relation is then necessary in the respect that without it the event or object is not a sign (or, in particular *the* sign it is). This is one reason why to say that $a = b$ requires that you be talking about that to which 'a' and 'b' refer, that is, talking about a and b.

As long as we suppose that any other object can be arbitrarily substituted for 'a' *and* that this is all there is to it, the physical properties of 'a' considered simply as an object are indeed unimportant. The cognitive value of any statement in which 'a' occurs does not seem to depend at all on these properties of 'a'. But this overlooks the fact that because any object will serve as a sign we *cannot* infer that *no object* to serve as a sign is required, which is what paying no attention to the physical properties of signs amounts to. Sign behaviour can occur without any *given* sign but we cannot infer from this that the physical properties of any given sign once it is used are unessential in accounting for the ways in which signs function, such as referring, having sense, etc.

Another reason why the importance of the difference we are stressing has been overlooked and, hence, another possible objection to the view advanced here is the influence of the phrase 'thinking of'. Thus, it may be argued, to say one of the cognitive differences between '*a*' and '*b*' (or difference of sense) is simply their differences as physical objects is to make these objects of our utterances or writings of them our cognitions or thoughts. But when I am thinking, say, that $a = b$, I am *thinking of* something. The signs '*a*', etc., are the means by which I think *of* this something. (G. E. Moore employs this argument in "The Conception of Reality." See his *Philosophical Studies*, 1922, p. 215.)

Nothing can gainsay this argument if we persist in employing the distorted way it uses words or in employing the inference it makes from linguistic use. But if we reflect that there is no difference in ordinary usage between 'I am thinking that $a = b$', 'I am thinking of $a = b$', *and* 'I am thinking $a = b$', we see that the superfluous (in this case) preposition 'of' has made us look for something which we have no *other* reason to suspect is there; namely, a thought, a sense, a signification, etc. It is a little like hearing that Wienpahl [2] has left town under a cloud and looking for the cloud. Although we use 'think of' like 'have of' (in 'have of this') and 'box of' (in 'box of this'), there is no reason to suppose in the case of 'think of' that the 'of' must have an object. To do this is to be misled by a grammatical form *which can be eliminated* without using a forced expression, although that form cannot be eliminated in the other cases without distorting ordinary usage.

On the other hand, in one respect the construction 'think of'

---

[2] This example is from "The Secret Life of James Thurber," James Thurber, in *The Thurber Carnival*, 4th ed., Harper & Bros., New York, 1945.

need not lead to difficulties; say, in 'I am thinking of *a*'. The object of the preposition 'of' is '*a*', that is, the sign. It is only when we overlook the essential characteristic of signs (that they have referents and can function as signs when the referents are not present in the situation in which they are used), that it seems absurd to say I am thinking of a sign. In one way of looking at it I *am*. And to say that I am is trivial only if we regard the sign as being *merely* a physical object and forget what kind of a physical object it is; namely, a sign. 'I am thinking of' may in other words be regarded as a part of a pseudo-object statement. As such the phrase is actually in the metalanguage. Due, however, to the common confusion of words and things its metalingual character has been overlooked, leading to a search for something besides the sign and referent to which it refers when actually it refers to the sign.

It may be further objected that we can have: (*a*) *different* senses for the *same* sign, or (*b*) the *same* sense for *different* signs. To this the reply is as follows. In the first place, if the sense of a sign is the combination of its physical properties as an object, neither of these possibilities is cogent. I do not intend here, by the way, to impugn the familiar assertion that words in different languages can mean the same thing. In one sense of 'mean' they can, namely 'refer to'. In another sense of 'mean' they cannot, namely when 'mean' is used as equivalent to 'sense' (Frege's term with whatever explication we give it).

In the second place, consider (*a*) (different senses for the same sign). Under the conditions which Frege gives for requiring that a distinction be made between sense and referent at all the possibility suggested cannot be stated significantly. Suppose we argue that 'tear' is a word having two different senses ('tear (drop)' and 'tear (rent)') and yet in either case we write 'tear'. Note, first, that the most obvious difference between 'tear' as 'tear (drop)' and 'tear' as 'tear (rent)' is that they have different referents. However, it may be urged, 'tear' also has different senses. It has but *only in a most peculiar way*. Take Frege's argument which runs: if the relation of identity asserted in '$a = b$' holds between that which 'a' and 'b' name, '$a = b$' does not differ cognitively from '$a = a$', provided that '$a = b$' is true (for, if 'a' and 'b' as signs (forgetting their physical properties) have only a single property, that of referring to an object, then, when that object is the same for both 'a' and 'b', '$a = b$' and '$a = a$' would say the same or be cognitively equal). '$tear = tear$' corresponds to '$a = a$', but you cannot construct the equivalent of '$a = b$' without adding more letters to each 'tear'. In other words, you cannot state the conditions for arguing that a sign must have a sense as well as a referent at all. For the case for 'tear' equivalent to '$a = b$' is 'tear (drop) = tear (rent)'. Here there is a difference of sense, but there is also a physical difference between the signs.

Note also that Frege's argument requires that '$a = a$' is cognitively equal to '$a = b$' *provided* that '$a = b$' is true. In cases such as 'tear', 'tear (drop) = tear (rent)' will always be *false*. That is, where it is urged that the same sign can have different senses we find that the signs in question have different *referents* (of necessity, otherwise you do not have different cases). This is why '$a = b$' is false in such cases, thus violating another condition of Frege's argument.

Although this reasoning goes contrary to what we *expect*, it appears nonetheless correct (and should serve to set us straight in some matters). Nevertheless it may be argued that 'tear' and 'tear' do in some situations have different senses without adding more letters to them. To this may only be replied that you cannot say or write this without *saying to yourself* " 'tear (rent)' and 'tear (drop)'." 'Tear' for 'tear (rent)' or 'tear (drop)' can only be used without these additions when the context of usage makes it clear whether 'tear (rent)' or 'tear (drop)' is being used. And a different context of usage is equivalent to adding more letters. It seems, therefore, that strictly speaking the same word (considered as a physical object) *cannot* have different senses. We say that it can, but do so uncritically, loosely. When the question of sense arises this loose manner of speaking is dangerous. Therefore, the objection that there can be different senses for the same sign does not hold.

Consider (b), different words with the same sense; say, 'chat' and 'cat'. In this case you cannot construct the equivalent of '$a = a$' in that portion of Frege's argument which runs: if the relation of identity asserted in '$a = b$' holds between that which 'a' and 'b' name, '$a = b$' does not differ cognitively from '$a = a$', provided that '$a = b$' is true. In the second place, where the supposed equivalent of '$a = b$' can be constructed, 'chat = cat', the statement is in the metalanguage and therefore does not correspond to '$a = b$' in Frege's argument. Therefore, the objection that we can have different words with the same sense does not hold under the conditions required for talking about sense. Considerations similar to those for signs which are written the same apply to those which sound the same, *e.g.*, 'rain' and 'reign'.

Finally I wish to call attention to some sentences in this paper which, by the way in which terms are used in them illuminate the theory of 'sense' explicated here. Consider first: "This makes the sense of a sign an "entity" like whiteness or chairness, "things" which can be thought but not observed." (P. 5.) This sentence is illuminating because it suggests that the reason why we can think whiteness, chairness, sense, etc., is due to 'whiteness', 'chairness', and 'sense'. Nobody ever suggests that we can *observe* them because in one way people are thoroughly aware of the difference between 'dog' and dog, the word and the thing. But in another way it has seemed plausible to claim we can think of whiteness because it is also easy to forget the distinction between word and thing, or idea and object. That it is easy is evidenced by the conviction carried by the ontological argument for God's existence. 'Whiteness' has "sense" because it is a word that can "run through our minds," and because of its similarity to 'white' which does have a referent and hence also sense (since it is a sign, which 'whiteness' is not when it is used to "name" the universal). We would not claim that 'gobbledegoop', although it can "run through our minds," has sense because it does not resemble some legitimate sign which, being a sign, does have sense; and because 'gobbledegoop' is not a sign. Sense is a property of physical objects which are signs, not any physical object whatsoever. And, of course, we can talk about sense even when we treat it as a subsistent entity because we can talk 'sense', that is, utter the word 'sense'.

In a way we are thinking when we do this just as in a way a child playing with *toy* guns is fighting a battle. In another way he is not because the gun is a toy gun not, as we say, a real gun. In this way, too, to talk about sense as a subsistent entity is not really thinking because in this case 'sense' is like the toy gun: it is not a real sign, that is, it is not a sign.

Consider next: "This difference (between '$a = a$' and '$a = b$') lies in the mode of presentation; *e.g.*, between 'morning star' and 'evening star'." When we say the modes of presentation (senses) of 'morning star' and 'evening star' are different is this not like saying "the ways 'evening star' and 'morning star' present their object (the star) are different"? And is this not like saying " 'morning star' and 'evening star' are different"? But what are 'morning star' and 'evening star' if they are not physical objects serving as signs? Saying they are different is like saying that Joe's bed is different from Joe's coat. The difference in both cases is the same in that it is a difference of physical properties. We have seen that the term 'mode of designation' is superfluous, that the only term we need is 'referent'. Similarly, either 'sense' or 'mode of presentation' is superfluous. 'Sense' may have been preferred because it is a familiar word, but 'mode of presentation' is more illuminating when we are concerned with the problem of the meaning of 'sense' or what sense is. 'Mode of presentation' suggests simply that the referent of 'sense' or 'mode of presentation' is the sign itself as a physical object. The way of presenting the evening star is 'evening star'. 'The evening star is the same as the morning star' differs cognitively from 'the evening star is the same as the evening star' because 'evening star' differs from 'morning star'.

Consider finally: "I do not intend here, by the way, to impugn the familiar assertion that words in different languages can mean the same thing. In one sense of 'mean' they can, namely 'refer to'. In another sense of 'mean' they cannot, namely when 'mean' is used as equivalent to 'sense' (Frege's term)" (p. 9). These sentences are illuminating because we might have written: "according to one meaning of 'mean', they can namely 'refer to'"; or, "in one way that 'mean' is used, namely as 'refer to'" instead of "In one sense of 'mean'. . . ." The term 'sense' in other words is employed equivocally in English in such fashion as to make it seem that the same word can have more than one sense. Whenever this claim is made we see that what is claimed is that the same word can have two different *referents*. The sentences quoted are also illuminating because 'mean' is employed with a similar equivocation.

Suppose that in the sentence 'In one sense of 'mean' they can, namely 'refer to'' the 'sense' used is Frege's; that is, the name for that property of signs which differs from their property of referring to something or naming. This supposition is contrary to the fact of the usage of 'sense' which actually occurs in 'In one sense of 'mean' they can . . .' as we see from the preceding remarks, but let us make the assumption anyhow. The sense (Frege's term) of a word as distinguished from its referent is then intuitively seen to be its physical shape, etc. For when we want to speak of a different sense of 'mean' we have to use a different word. 'Mean' apparently has only one sense. If we want to employ a different sense we must use a different word.

Off hand, it looks as though the phrase 'a different sense of 'mean'' contradicts the observation we are making. This is because the phrase is legitimate when the 'sense' occurring in it is equivalent to 'referent'. When the 'sense' has the usage

Frege introduced, the phrase is illegitimate in the same way
that the sentence 'God exists' is illegitimate according to Russell's theory of descriptions. Thus we can speak of different
senses (Frege's term) but not different senses *of a word*. To ask
for a different sense is to ask for a different mode of presentation, a different way of referring to the same objects; that is,
for different words. The phrase 'a different sense of 'mean' ' is
seen to be legitimate in one way (when we are asking for a
different referent) and illegitimate in another (when we are
asking for a different sense, Frege's term). Or the phrase may
be regarded as a loose way of simply asking for a different
sense; a request which amounts to: 'can't you put it differently' or 'can't you say it differently' which are requests for
different terminology.

In conclusion, by supposing that the cognitive difference
between '$a = a$' and '$a = b$' depends on the difference between
'a' and 'b' as objects in so far as they function as signs, there
are the following advantages. We do not have to believe in
a subsistent entity, the sense of the word. We have to speak
only of signs, their referents and our responses to and uses
of the signs. We do not overlook the characteristic feature of
a sign, that it has or had a referent. We clear up the puzzle
caused by phrases like 'think of'. Finally, by regarding the
sense of a word in this way, 'sense' is interpreted in a fashion
which relates its interpretation to the theory that language
and thinking are inextricably connected. It used to be supposed that man developed language to communicate thoughts
he already had. The analysis of language given by men such
as Locke, Wundt, and Sapir was based on this false theory
of language, that words are expressions of thoughts or ideas.
For various reasons it has been necessary to develop a new
theory of language according to which thought is not possible without speech. The interpretation of 'sense' given here
not only accords with Frege's reasons for speaking of sense
but agrees with the current theory of language. For, according
to this interpretation the sense of a word is the "thought" we

have when using the word, but the word is an integral and major portion of the "thought."

As far as Frege's discussion is concerned the explication or 'sense' given here suffices. However, further explication is clearly necessary for adequate description of sense. For example, in speaking of the physical properties of signs, say the spoken word 'dog', there is the problem of where the line is to be drawn between the sound 'dog' and the physiological, anatomical, etc., processes involved in producing and hearing the sound before we can say that this or that is the sign. However, if this account is correct we do not have to worry about the sense of a sign being something different from words or the acts of producing them.

11

On Sinn *as a Combination of Physical Properties*

RICHARD RUDNER

In a recent article [1] Dr. Paul D. Wienpahl proposes an explication for Frege's notion of sense that, he believes, "fits the data of Frege's discussion and does not make sense a subsistent entity" (p. 483). Wienpahl's proposal is that "the *sense of a sign is the combination of its physical properties*" (p. 488). But in the face of the requirements which he has set himself, there seem to be three considerations which lead to the conclusion that his proposal is defective.

I

Wienpahl's attribution of physical properties to linguistic signs indicates that he is taking expressions of the kind '*a* = *a*' and '*a*' to be physical tokens. Now, although Frege undoubtedly had some conception of a symbol-token dichotomy, it has never seemed wholly obvious to the writer whether the entities to which he attributed sense are to be taken to be tokens or to be symbols. I think a strong case can be made

Reprinted with the kind permission of the author and the editor from *Mind*, LXI (1952), 82-84.

[1] "Frege's *Sinn und Bedeutung*," *Mind*, vol. lix, no. 236 (1950), pp. 483-494.

to substantiate the hypothesis that the latter is his intention. However, this point need not be debated here, for Wienpahl's proposal seems to fail on grounds independent of fitting "the data of Frege's discussion" on this particular issue.

Since symbols (*i.e.*, classes of similar tokens) are not physical things, Wienpahl's assertion, that the sense of a sign is the combination of its physical properties, shows *prima facie* that the entities to which *he* believes sense may be ascribed are tokens. But one of the conditions of Frege's discussion which Wienpahl explicitly attempts to meet[2] is that in expressions (for Wienpahl, inscriptions) like

$$a = a$$

the sign to the left of the identity sign has the same sense as the sign to the right of the identity sign. Actually, the condition is the stronger one that every occurrence of a token of a given symbol has the same sense as every other occurrence of a token of that symbol. Clearly, however, no two tokens have the same physical properties and hence if the sense of a token is the combination of its physical properties, no two tokens have the same sense. In particular, in inscriptions like

$$a = a$$

the token on the right may not be said by Wienpahl to have the same sense as the token on the left.

II

If Wienpahl has not meant to ascribe senses to tokens but rather to symbols, his proposal is still not tenable for reasons already patent in the foregoing remarks. Since *classes* of tokens do not have physical properties, the proposal thus interpreted would amount to the denial that a linguistic sign has a sense; and this is surely contrary to the data of Frege's discussion; and really not seriously to be entertained as Wienpahl's intention either.

---

[2] *Vide ibid.*, pp. 490-491.

III

There is, however, a third possibility. Although classes do not have physical properties, they do have certain *physical-like* properties. Among these, for example, is the property of order in, *e.g.*, an ordered class of classes. We can speak cogently of 1 as preceding 2 in the series of positive integers and of the first symbol as preceding in order the second in the ordered class of classes which might constitute the (symbol) statement 'A rose is a rose'.[3] It may be the case then that Wienpahl intended to identify senses not with the combination of physical properties of a token, but with the combination of *physical-like* properties of a symbol. If this is the case, however, one becomes even less sure that Wienpahl has met the second requirement he has set himself; namely that of dispensing with subsistent entities.

But even if we were to concede that the proposal thus liberally interpreted does no violence to the second requirement, it yet turns out to be unacceptable. Since among the *physical-like* properties of the first symbol in the series of symbols constituted by the symbol-statement '$a = a$' is the property of being first in occurrence in that series, the combination of *physical-like* properties of the first of the symbols will not be the same as the combination of properties of the last of the symbols and hence, according to the proposal, they will not have the same sense.

Although this third possibility is an interesting one, for the reasons mentioned under I, it is unlikely that it is the one intended by Wienpahl. And it seems to the present writer that Wienpahl's difficulties, insofar as he is interpreted as dealing with physical properties of physical inscriptions, stem from his attempt to meet a condition of Frege's which is simply

---

[3] *Cf.* my "A Note on Likeness of Meaning," *Analysis*, vol. x, no. 5 (1950), p. 117.

too strong; namely that in expressions like

$$a = a$$

the two 'a' 's have the *same* meaning.

What is the *raison d'être* for such a demand? If the fact that they denote the same entity is brought forward as justification for demanding sameness of meaning, then clearly the argument is infirm; for so do the expressions 'the morning star' and 'the evening star'. On the other hand, if the argument is based on the assumption of the identity of the expressions, such an assumption is obviously false insofar as the expressions are regarded as physical inscriptions and in any event, quite begs the question.[4] And why should a meeting of the demand be attempted at all? Surely any of the syndrome of problems in discourse which might be handled by the assumption that two expressions have the *same* meaning could be handled with perhaps greater precision by the much weaker assumption that the expressions have a certain degree of similiarity of meaning.[5]

Aside from the difficulties which arise out of this attempt to meet Frege's too severe demand, Wienpahl's analysis seems successfully as does Goodman's [6] to dispense with the dubious subsistent entities he seeks to eliminate. Moreover, he has further illuminated the entire problem by arguing effectively for the conclusion (the converse of Goodman's thesis), that there must be difference in signs where there is difference in meaning.

---

[4] Currently being discussed in *Analysis*, vol. x, nos. 1 and 5, and vol. xi, nos. 2 and 3, by N. Goodman, C. D. Rollins, R. Rudner, and A. Smullyan.

[5] See, *e.g.*, Nelson Goodman's "On Likeness of Meaning," *Analysis*, vol. x, no. 1, pp. 1-7.

[6] *Ibid.*

12

Frege on Functions

MAX BLACK

The argument does not belong with the function, but goes together
with the function to make up a complete whole; for the function
by itself must be called incomplete, in need of supplementation, or
'unsaturated.' And in this respect functions differ fundamentally
from numbers.[1]

1. Frege thought he was here formulating the basis of a distinction between a function and an "object" (*Gegenstand*)
that he regarded as "of the highest importance" (p. 54); yet
no passage in his writings is harder to understand. By a "function" Frege understood not only a function in the mathematical sense but also any property or relation. So his contention
that all functions are incomplete would lead one to suppose
that he was making each of the following claims: that the
sine function is incomplete, the property of solubility in water
is incomplete, the relation of parenthood is incomplete. In
fact, however, Frege intended not a single one of these assertions to follow from his claim that functions are incomplete.[2]

[1] *Translations from the Philosophical Writings of Gottlob Frege*, by
Peter Geach and Max Black (Oxford, 1952), p. 24. In subsequent references to this work, only the page number will be cited.

[2] In order to infer "The sine function is incomplete" from "All functions are incomplete," we should need the further premise "The sine

At first sight, this seems to be inconsistent with the customary conventions for the meaning of a sentence of the form "All *A* are *B*"; and even the most sympathetic student of Frege's work may be hard put to it to explain Frege's contention.

There is scarcely another instance where Frege's meaning is in doubt. Here, however, he explains that "complete" and "unsaturated" are mere "figures of speech" (p. 55) and asks the reader to meet him "half-way" in interpreting these "metaphorical expressions" (p. 115). "All that I wish or am able to do here is to give hints," he says (p. 55). We shall see later that on Frege's view it is logically impossible to express his thought literally and explicitly. If this is so, we seem to be committed to the quixotic task of trying to understand the ineffable. We must not be too hasty in assuming that this is what Frege required of his readers.

How shall we take advantage of the "hints" that Frege has supplied? The most obvious thing to do is to unravel the analogies suggested by his use of the word "incomplete."[3] The sense we make of Frege's claim that functions are incomplete will depend upon our success in transferring to this unusual context the meanings that "incomplete" would have in its *literal* uses. By considering the relevant features of such ordinary uses of "incomplete," as I shall do in the next section, it should become possible to see how much of the literal meaning can be preserved in the metaphorical use. Our purpose is to discover the extent to which Frege's metaphorical use of "incomplete" requires us to attach an extraordinary meaning to that word.

2. In nonphilosophical conversation or writing, the word "incomplete" can often be replaced, without substantial change of meaning, by the word "unfinished." Now if it makes sense

---

function is a function." We shall see (section 9 below) that Frege holds this additional premise to be false.

[3] The same might be done for Frege's word "unsaturated" (*ungesättigt*), which he uses as an alternative to "incomplete" (*unvollständig, ergänzungsbedürftig*). I do not think this would substantially affect my argument.

to say of something that it is unfinished, it must make sense
to say of that thing, however falsely, that it is finished. Again,
we apply the word "finished" only to something that *takes
time*—time to do, time to make, or time to happen. It is sensible to speak of finishing a speech, a painting, or a war; but it
is logically absurd to talk of finishing a mountain, the number seven, or the boiling point of water. In none of these last
cases can there be any sensible question of the time needed. It
would be the height of absurdity to ask, "How long did this
mountain take?" or "Has the number seven lasted longer
than the number five?" or "When was the boiling point of
water finished?"

There is, therefore, a simple test for the applicability of
the word "incomplete" in any sense in which it is roughly synonymous with "unfinished." If we are in doubt whether the
word applies to some particular thing, we have only to ask
whether any sense can be made of the question "How long
does that thing take to do (or to make, or to happen)?" Only
if this question makes sense will it be sensible (whether true
or false) to call that thing unfinished; only then can we speak
without absurdity of that thing being incomplete *because* it
is unfinished.

Something that takes time to do, to make, or to happen—
let us say "a process," for short—may be of such a character
that it results in the existence of a relatively permanent thing.
When the storm has ended, nothing remains; but when the
chef has finished his work, he has a cake to show for his pains.
In such a case, let us say the process has resulted in a "product," and if that product is the work of man or animal let
us call it an "artifact." Since the production of a product takes
time, there will be what we might call "preliminary stages" in
the coming into existence of the thing in question. Very well:
the word "unfinished" is often applied, not to the process, but
rather to a preliminary stage of a corresponding product.

Not to any kind of product, however. If the reader will
make a list of things that come most readily to mind as in-

stances of the "unfinished" or "incomplete," he is likely to hit upon such things as *The Mystery of Edwin Drood*, or Cologne Cathedral, or Schubert's *Unfinished Symphony*—all of which are artifacts. In each of these cases, the process finishes when a certain goal has been reached: it "comes to completion," as we say, and does not merely cease or end. We have only to take instead some examples of processes that do not involve an active agent working toward some goal, to see the absurdity of using "incomplete" in such cases. There is no sense in speaking of an "incomplete gale" or an "incomplete earthquake." We do sometimes speak of "incomplete oxidation" or "incomplete fertilization"; but then it is we, the speakers, who set the goal and judge the natural process by its distance from that goal.

At this point, Frege might interrupt to protest that all this talk of "time needed," of "process," "artifact," and "goal," has nothing to do with what he wanted to say. Precisely. We can attach no sense to such sentences as "the sine function has lasted a thousand years," or "the property of solubility in water has taken a long time" or "the relation of parenthood is swift"—all of which would have been as repugnant to Frege as they are to us. But just because there can be no question of time in connection with functions in Frege's sense, there can be no question of a metaphorical transfer of the common senses of "incomplete" in which it can be equated with "unfinished." We can no more speak of functions being incomplete in these senses that we can of four o'clock being venomous.

There does remain another set of senses of "incomplete" in ordinary talk in which it is roughly equivalent to "having a part missing." This chess set is incomplete, because the king is not in the box; this specimen of *Gentiana crinita* is incomplete, because the stamens have become detached; this copy of the *First Folio* is incomplete, because the frontispiece has been lost. Even in these cases the thing most naturally called incomplete is still an artifact, judged to be incomplete or defective because it fails to meet a standard set either by its maker or by the speaker.

But let us try to exclude any such teleological considerations and suppose that Frege meant by "incomplete" simply "having a part missing," no matter if the thing in question could not sensibly be regarded as requiring human agency or resulting from a process. Even then, we must notice, the question "Is this incomplete?" needs further elaboration before it can have a determinate sense. To know whether a given thing is incomplete, in the sense of having a part missing, we must know with what kind of thing it is being compared: an incomplete chisel can be a complete handle, an incomplete sentence a complete clause, and so on. The question "Is this incomplete?" no more admits of an answer in the absence of further specification than does the question "Is this an ingredient?" We have to reply with further questions: "Ingredient of *what?*" and "Incomplete *what?*" Of course, the context itself often makes this unnecessary. If I am asked whether "this essay" is complete, I understand that the question is whether it is a complete essay—not a complete book or something else.

Too much philosophical lexicography becomes boring, so I will merely add two further features of the ordinary uses of "incomplete." (a) A cup without a handle is still a cup, but an incomplete sentence may be only a clause, not a sentence at all. But in both cases, the incomplete thing is the *same kind of thing* as the complete thing with which it is contrasted. Remove the handle and you still have a cup; remove the end of a sentence and you still have a set of words. On the other hand, it would be absurd to say that the redness of a red flag was incomplete with respect to that flag. For redness is not a flag, nor is it the same kind of thing as a flag. (b) When we say Schubert's symphony is incomplete, we mean something is actually missing: if the missing part were supplied, the symphony would cease to be unfinished. And so in general: A complete door is not composed of an incomplete door plus a handle—when the handle is added, the door *ceases* to be incomplete.

Let us now apply these considerations to Frege's claim that functions are incomplete.

3. Frege's reason for saying that a function is incomplete is a parallel contention about "function signs," i.e., the symbols or words by means of which we talk about functions. "The expression of a function," he says, *"needs completion, is 'unsaturated.'* The letter '*x*' only serves to keep places open for a numerical sign to be put in and complete the expression; and thus it enables us to recognize the special kind of need for completion that constitutes the peculiar nature of the function . . ." (152).[4] This is why he concludes that the function itself must be incomplete. "The peculiarity of function signs, which we here call 'unsaturatedness,' *naturally has something answering to it in the functions themselves.* They too may be called 'unsaturated,' and in this way we mark them out as fundamentally different from numbers" (p. 115, italics inserted).

The line of thought that led Frege to regard the function sign as incomplete or "unsaturated" is substantially the following: In speaking of the sine function, say, a mathematician uses the symbol "sin *x*." Here, however, the "*x*" merely serves the purpose of holding a place open for the insertion of a numeral. Thus the symbol is essentially "sin( )" where the empty place is shown without the use of a letter. Hence the function is incomplete (cf. p. 25).

I shall examine this argument later (section 6). For the time being, let us simply apply what we learned about the literal uses of the word "incomplete" to the assertion that the function sign is incomplete. We may begin by asking our old question, "Incomplete *what?*" The answer cannot be "Incomplete function sign," for Frege held that *every* function sign was "unsaturated"; if completed, it ceases to be a function sign.

---

[4] A similar statement is this: "The sign for a function is 'unsaturated' (*ungesättigt*); it needs to be completed with a numeral, which we then call the argument-sign" (p. 113). Frege returned many times to these themes, using almost the same words each time.

Whenever a function sign is completed by the insertion of a name in the empty place we always get what Frege called an "*Eigenname*" or, literally, a "proper name." We might accordingly suppose Frege to be asserting that a function sign is an incomplete proper name. But this, as it stands, is misleading, for reasons that must now be explained.

4. To understand what Frege meant by "*Eigenname*," we must turn to a crucial passage in his essay, "On Sense and Reference":

It is clear from the context that by 'sign' and 'name' I have here understood any designation representing a proper name, which thus has as its reference a definite object (this word taken in the widest range), but not a concept or a relation. . . . The designation of a single object can also consist of several words or other signs. *For brevity, let every such designation be called a proper name* (*Eigenname*) [p. 57, italics inserted].

By an "*Eigenname*," he means, accordingly, either a name or a definite description, provided however that it does not stand for either a concept or a relation (or, more generally, a function). The need for brevity hardly excuses the use of "proper name" in this most unusual sense; it would surely have been better, if an abbreviation was needed, to use the word "designation" (*Bezeichnung*). In what follows, I shall myself use the word "designation," to mean the same as "name or definite description," but with the important difference that, unlike Frege, I shall not stipulate that a function cannot have a designation.

Frege's view that a function sign is an incomplete designation is complicated by his view that declarative sentences are designations—either of "the True" or of "the False" (see pp. 62-63). The following argument seems to me to be a sufficient refutation of Frege's view that sentences are designations of truth values.

We may assume that if A and B are designations of the same thing the substitution of one for the other in any declarative sentence will never result in nonsense. This assumption would not have been questioned by Frege. Let A be the

sentence "Three is a prime" and B the expression "the True."
Now "If three is a prime then three has no factors" is a sensible declarative sentence; substitute B for A and we get the
nonsense "If the True then three has no factors." The last
form of words has no more use than "If seven then three has
no factors" or "If the third smallest prime number then three
has no factors" or indeed any form of words containing an
expression of the form "If X then . . ." where "X" is replaced
by a designation. Hence, according to our assumption, A and
B are not designations of the same thing—which is what we
set out to prove. By the "truth value of a sentence," Frege
said, he understood "the circumstance that it is true or false"
(p. 63) and added: "There are no further truth values. For
brevity I call the one the True, the other the False" (*ibid.*).
He failed to notice that he had given a use for the expression
"the True" only in conjunction with a given sentence (the "*it*"
in his statement) and not in other uses.

5. In the light of our own conclusion that sentences are not
designations, we must now distinguish two interpretations
of Frege's claim about function signs, depending upon whether
we take him to be saying that function signs are incomplete
designations or incomplete sentences. Fortunately, we can accept both contentions. It matters little whether we take the
function sign to be "sin x" or "sin( )" or just "sin" (and
Frege vacillates on this point): we can, if we choose, look
upon each of them as a stage in the construction of "sin 1,"
or similar numerical designations. It can hardly ever happen
that in order to get "sin 2" a mathematician first writes down
"sin x," then erases the "x," and only then writes down the
"2." No matter—it could be done. A man might fill a mug
of beer by first getting a mugful of sand, then emptying the
sand, and finally inserting the beer; and looked at in this way,
the mugful of sand would be a preliminary stage in the production of a mug of beer. Of course, if we start with "sin( )"
or simply "sin," it is easier to look upon the function sign as
an unfinished numerical designation. Similarly, we can look

upon the predicate "is a parent of" as a preliminary stage in the construction of a sentence like "Tom is the parent of Dick." We are certainly entitled to say, and without a trace of metaphor, that a function sign is a designation with a part missing—or, from another standpoint, that a function sign is a sentence with a part missing.

This interpretation is useless for Frege, however. For parallel assertions hold for designations. A name can be a part of a function sign, as in "$x + 2$"; and many sentences contain a name or other designation as a part. We have as much justification, so far, for saying that a designation is an incomplete function sign as for saying that a function sign is an incomplete designation; we have as much right to say that a designation is a sentence with a part missing as for saying the same about a function sign. Thus Frege's intention, to mark "a distinction of the highest importance" (p. 54) seems to have been unfulfilled and we must be on the wrong track.

6. Consider, next, how the ellipsis could be removed from Frege's assertion that the function itself, rather than the sign by which it is represented, is incomplete. To the question "Incomplete *what?*" the only answer now must be the paradoxical "Incomplete *object* (*Gegenstand*)."

The following statement is typical of several to be found in Frege's philosophical writings:

> The function is completed by the argument; I call what it becomes on completion the *value* of the function for that argument. We thus get a name of the value of a function for an argument when we fill the argument-places in the name of the function with the name of the argument. Thus, for example, '$(2 + 3.1^2)1$' is a name of the number 5, composed of the function-name '$(2 + 3.\xi^2)\xi$' and '1' [p. 153].

The "completed" thing with which the function is here contrasted is the number 5; so if the function is to be an incomplete anything, we must be prepared to say it is an incomplete number. Every function whose values are numbers will have to be called an incomplete number.

However, nobody has yet given any good sense, metaphorical or literal, to the expression "incomplete number" in its application to functions. There can be no question here of the creation of numbers, a process requiring time, or a resulting artifact. And to think of a function as a number with a part missing is to strain ordinary language beyond endurance. Of course, the words "part" and "whole" are commonly used in all sorts of ways, and so an ingenious man might perhaps give the expression "incomplete number" a plausible meaning. But the locution would be so unusual that it would have to be explained. We can not be expected to meet a writer half way if we do not know in which direction to move.

Frege seems to agree:

> . . . I have here used the word 'part' in a special sense. I have in fact transferred the relation between the parts and the whole of the sentence to the reference by calling the reference of a word part of the reference of the sentence, if the word itself is a part of the sentence. This way of speaking can certainly be attacked. . . . A special term would need to be invented [p. 65].

But to introduce a technical term will merely provide an unfamiliar word to stand for a mysterious idea; what we need is some explanation of what "part" can mean when used in Frege's extraordinary fashion. It is no help to be told that the term is used figuratively when the ground of the figure of speech is completely hidden.

We can be sure at least of this, that the expression "incomplete number" is a misnomer if it suggests that an incomplete number is a *kind* of number: a function is not a number at all. A door with a missing handle is still a door, but an incomplete object, in Frege's sense of "object," is not an object at all. This is most obvious in the case of truth values: it is perfectly absurd to think of "the True" or "the False" as being incomplete, or having a part missing, in any senses of "incomplete" and "part" suggested by the ordinary uses of those words.

I conclude that the ideas that the word "incomplete" is likely to suggest to us on the basis of its literal uses will mislead us as to Frege's intention. Let us, then, make a fresh start by examining in detail the argument by means of which Frege thought he had established that the function sign must be "incomplete." For whatever the argument proves will be presumably what Frege wanted to say.

7. I have already summarized the argument by means of which Frege tries to show that a function sign is incomplete. Here is the argument in his own words:

It is precisely by the notation that uses 'x' to indicate [a number] indefinitely [e.g. '$2.x^3 + x$'] that we are led to the right conception [of a function]. People call x the argument and recognize the same function in

$$\text{'2.1}^3 + 1\text{'}$$
$$\text{'2.4}^3 + 4\text{'}$$
$$\text{'2.5}^3 + 5\text{'}$$

only with different arguments, namely 1, 4, and 5. From this we may discern that it is the common element of these expressions that constitutes the essential peculiarity of a function; i.e. what is present in

$$\text{'2.}x^3 + x\text{'}$$

over and above the letter 'x'. We could write this somewhat as follows:

$$\text{'2.( )}^3 + ( )\text{' [p. 24].}$$

If I say 'the function $2.x^3 + x$', x must not be considered as belonging to the function; this letter only serves to indicate the kind of supplementation that is needed; it enables one to recognize the places where the sign for the argument must go in [p. 25].

The expression for a function must always show one or more places that are intended to be filled up with the sign of the argument [p. 25].

From the third of these quotations, in conjunction with Frege's remarks elsewhere, we can arrive at the following interpretation of the claim that the function sign is "incomplete": A function sign, unlike a designation (*Eigenname*) must have gaps—places intended to be filled by designations; it is logically impossible to refer to a function except by means of a sign having such gaps or hiatuses.

This claim seems to contradict the possibility of using the

traditional symbolism of free variables ("x," "y," and so on) which does not literally contain spaces to be subsequently filled. As the second quotation shows, Frege holds that the free variables are simply used to mark the gaps. He is thinking of the function sign as a kind of container—something, as he often says, that can be "filled up." From this standpoint, the function sign is like a frame without a picture, a glove without a hand, or an empty mold; and the free variable is like a lay figure, a mere dummy used to draw attention to the way in which the gap might be filled. Perhaps the etymology of *"vollständig"* or its Romance equivalents, *"complet"* and "complete," encourages a tendency to think of anything incomplete as an empty container or mold, intended to be completed by being "filled up."

Now is it really necessary for the function sign to include some indication of empty spaces that are intended to be filled up? We must notice, first, that the use of such a sign can be demanded only when the function sign is used separately, and is not attached to a designation to form a complex designation of an object. As Frege said, his notation of gaps is needed "only for the exceptional case where we want to symbolize a function in isolation" (p. 114, *fn.*). The case is so exceptional in the formal development of a deductive system of calculus as never to arise; there is constant need for it, however, in Frege's remarks *about* symbolism and the world. Only in examples like "The function $\xi^2 = 4$ can have only two values" (p. 154), and "The function $x^2 + y^2$ has numbers as values" (p. 39), where we want to talk about the function itself, can there be any question of the function sign necessarily containing hiatuses. It would be too farfetched to regard an expression like "log 2" as containing a gap or space in addition to the signs "log" and "2." This would be like saying that a bottle of wine consists of the empty bottle, the wine, and the space filled by the wine.

Suppose now that it should be logically impossible to refer to functions in isolation. In that case, it would be impossible to use Frege's notation of "spaces," and instead of saying that a function sign must contain a hiatus, we should have to say a function sign can never have a hiatus. If this were so, our present question—whether there must be gaps in a function sign used in isolation to refer to a function—would simply not arise. If there cannot be empty rivers, the question of whether an empty river must contain a space fails to arise; if there can be no reference to a function, the question whether a sign referring to a function must have gaps fails to arise. We shall see there is serious reason to suppose that on Frege's view this is indeed the situation (see sections 9 and 10 below).

For the time being, however, let us suppose there is no objection to the use of such sentences as "Log x is continuous," in which there seems to be reference to the function itself and not to one of its values. To find out whether it is essential for an empty space to be indicated, we need only consider what information is actually conveyed by the use of the free variable or an equivalent device in such contexts. When we have a clear idea of the work done by the free variable or the hiatus, it will not be too hard to decide what "*must*" be the case for this work to be done.

In the statement "Log x is continuous," the free variable "x" is used to convey the following information: (a) We are reminded that the preceding word "Log" stands for a function. (b) The fact that "x" occurs, rather than "(x,y)," say, tells us that a function of only a single variable is in question. (c) The design of the symbol "Log x" may remind us that values of the function will be log 1, log 4, log 5, etc. In more complex statements, a free variable may also be used to "identify variables"—as in "$F(x, x)$"—but we shall not need to refer to this.

Can these three items of information be conveyed by Frege's gap notation? In "log( )" the work of indicating that "log" is a function sign is performed by the brackets: I doubt that Frege would have been happy to say that the function sign "*must*" be accompanied by brackets whose presence shows something about the "essential peculiarity" of functions; functions are not *that* peculiar. If the hiatus is to show that we have to do with a function of one variable, it will have to do so in virtue of the absence of a comma, such as we have in "$F(\ ,\ )$." What a remarkable empty space, as Frege might have said. The fact is that the gap symbolism effectively draws attention to *one* feature of such a symbol as "Log"— the possibility of combining it with numerals to get numerical designations. But we are certainly not compelled to use a gap to remind us that a function has values; nor are we compelled to use letters from the end of the alphabet to communicate the information conveyed by the traditional symbolism of free variables. That a symbol is a function sign can be shown in all sorts of ways—by the use of special type, numerical subscripts, and so on; and the same is true of information about the number of variables involved. As for being reminded that the function has values, this may be, and usually will be, quite irrelevant to the assertion we are making with the aid of the function sign. To use the sign "log" correctly, we must of course know its "logical grammar," that is to say, the rules governing its correct use. But the demand that this grammar shall always be explicitly symbolized in the case of every sign used obviously leads to an infinite regress. If it is legitimate to omit explicit symbolization of, say, restrictions upon admissible values of the function (an important feature of the grammar of the corresponding sign), why should it not be equally admissible to omit explicit indication of the relation of the function to its values?

Alternatively, if it is held that the logarithmic function must be symbolized by "log x" or "log ( )" because it is part of the essential nature of a function to have values, we might reply that it is just as much a part of the essential nature of objects that they can combine with functions. This line of thought might lead us to insist, with no less justification than Frege did in the case of function signs, that all designations shall be accompanied by brackets and gaps. To understand the use of numerals in higher mathematics is to know, *inter alia*, how they may be substituted for variables and otherwise used in combinations. Neither designations nor function signs have any use in isolation, and to know how to use them is to know how to combine them with their associates. When it comes to demanding that logical "grammar" be explicitly indicated, all signs are on an equal footing. To be vividly reminded of part of the grammar of a sign may be useful— or it may be a paper-wasting nuisance; we shall certainly go astray if we try to draw philosophical inferences from such purely practical considerations.

There is, indeed, something absurd in trying to base inferences about the logical structure of reality upon any physical characteristics of the signs we use. Yet Frege comes near to doing so. At times he seems to think of the sign "log( )" almost as literally containing a hole, and one which is preserved in every symbol by which it could be faithfully translated. But the physical gap between the brackets is of no ontological interest: exactly the same information might be conveyed by allowing the brackets to approach, overlap, or disappear. All that is "essential" to the function sign is that we recognize it correctly, without confusing it with other signs: a particular pattern of ink traces may help us in this, but no design can guarantee understanding, nor does " the nature of things" (p. 41) impose any restrictions whatsoever upon the character of the signs that we can successfully use. Once we see that there is no necessity for the function sign to be regarded as an empty container, it is to be hoped that the metaphor of the function itself as a kind of container will lose whatever appeal it might have had.

8. Yet another metaphorical basis for the contention that functions are incomplete is expressed in the following passage:

Not all the parts of a thought can be complete; at least one must be 'unsaturated,'[5] or predicative; otherwise they would not

---

[5] Notice that here a "part" of an existing whole is called "unsaturated." We have seen above that if a *B* is actually a part of some inclusive

hold together. For example, the sense of the phrase 'the number 2' does not hold together with that of the expression 'the concept *prime number*' without a link. We supply such a link in the sentence 'the number 2 falls under the concept *prime number*'; it is contained in the words 'falls under,' which need to be completed in two ways—by a subject and an accusative; and only because their sense is thus 'unsaturated' are they capable of serving as a link (*Bindemittel*) [p. 54].

This can be paraphrased as follows: "No series of designations constitutes a sentence. So they must be united in order to form a whole. This can only be done by having an 'incomplete' sign with 'spaces' or 'holes' which the designations can 'fill up.'" Then the train of thought is carried over to what the signs signify: the sense of the sentence could not "hold together" unless something "unsaturated," a function, were to complete the sense of the designations.

Here the picture is that of a "bond" or "link" holding the parts together. The following is a crude physical analogue of the way in which Frege was here thinking of the relation of subject to predicate in a sentence: Two men side by side do not make up a whole—they "hold aloof from another" (p. 55); but this can be remedied by a pair of handcuffs. Just because the handcuffs have a pair of empty spaces that can be filled up, they can unite the two men into a single unified whole. (The very crudity of this picture will help us to see better the logical blunder involved.)

The picture has only to be taken seriously in order to appear inept. Even as a paradigm of physical connection, the image of the separate objects that need a "link" immediately proves inadequate. The fact that more handcuffs are not needed to join the handcuffs themselves to the men is enough to show that some physical bodies "hold together" without benefit of intermediaries. The string around a parcel does not have to be attached by string; nor does glue need an in-

---

whole, an *A*, it is improper to speak of the *B* as an incomplete *A*. This is another instance of how Frege plays fast and loose with the underlying metaphors.

visible superglue in order to be effective. (If we had superglue, what purpose would be served by the ordinary stuff?) As soon as we realize this, however, the archetypal image loses its attraction. If a hand and a glove can "hold together" without assistance from a third object, why should we not be content to say that a designation and a function sign may combine to form a sentence, without either being "unsaturated" or incomplete?

Of course a sentence is not a mere series of designations; but neither is it a chain with links. Consider the following analogy. A chessboard with pieces standing on its squares is what chess players call a "position." Now a philosopher might be inclined to say that a chess position is not merely a board *plus* the pieces; the position, he might say, "has a kind of unity." But in fact nothing is needed to "bind" the board and the pieces together. The fact that they stand upon the board is enough to make them a "position," and if they have been so placed in the course of a game, they constitute a "real" or "actual" position. If the chessboard had grooves into which the pieces had to fit, one might be tempted to call the chessboard "incomplete"; but what would be gained by this?

Similarly for language. What gives the series of sounds used in a genuine assertion its "unity" is simply the fact that they are used by a speaker in accordance with the rules for correct speech of the language in question. To put it another way, the series of sounds "I am going for a walk now" is what we call a sentence according to the correct use of English (and parallel remarks apply to German or any other language). As Frege saw, no link or copula between the words is needed. Names, predicates, and other expressions are abstractions from sentences: the question "How do they hold together?" has no more sense than the question "How do the bricks and mortar of a wall hold together?" When bricks and mortar are put together under certain conditions, it is simply a fact that they adhere. When an English speaker says the four words "I am going home" (in that order, with appropriate intonation, in the right circumstances, and so on) it is simply a fact that he makes himself understood and does not leave his audience waiting for more information. If we imagine the continuous band of sound dissected into segments that are then separated from one another, we may be able to puzzle ourselves with the question "How do they hold together?" But to answer "Because one of them has an empty space waiting to be filled" is to practice self deception. We are saying, in effect, "Because one of them has the power of combining with the others." There is no good use for the idea of the function as a kind of ghostly grappling hook.

9. There remains one final interpretation of Frege's thought, suggested by the following remarks:

> It is clear that a concept cannot be represented independently as an object can but that it can occur only in combination (*in Verbindung*). One can say that a concept can be distinguished (*unterschieden*) in a combination but not separated (*abgeschieden*) out of it. All apparent contradictions which one can come upon here result from treating a concept as an object, contrary to its incomplete nature ["Über die Grundlagen der Geometrie," *Jahresbericht der Deutschen Mathematiker-Vereinigung,* 12 (1903): 372, *fn.*].

This interesting statement suggests one perfectly clear and quite unmetaphorical meaning for the contention that functions are incomplete. It might be taken simply to mean that it is logically impossible to make a function the subject of an assertion. This view was once held by Russell and was very clearly stated by him:

> The essence of a substance, from the symbolic point of view, is that it can only be named—in old fashioned language, it never occurs in a proposition except as the subject or as one of the terms of a relation. . . . Attributes and relations, though they may not be susceptible of analysis, differ from substances by the fact that they suggest a structure, and that there can be no significant symbol which symbolizes them in isolation. All propositions in which an attribute or a relation *seems* to be the subject are only significant if they can be brought into a form in which the attribute attributes or the relation relates. If this were not the case, there would be significant propositions in which an attribute or

a relation would occupy a position appropriate to a substance, which would be contrary to the doctrine of types and would produce contradictions ["Logical Atomism," in *Contemporary British Philosophy; Personal Statements,* First Series (London, 1924), pp. 375-376].

I do not think that all Frege meant by saying that functions are incomplete was that functions cannot be designated; but he was at least implying this. Yet he still wants to use expressions of the form "the function *F*," and therefore tries to show that such expressions are not really designations of functions at all. This, as we shall soon see, is the crux of his theory.

Frege's argument is, briefly, (a) that functions (including "concepts" as a special case) can never be referred to by a name or definite description (i.e., cannot be designated), (b) that nevertheless we often need to make assertions about functions, (c) that consequently the grammatical subjects of such assertions do not really stand for functions, as they seem to do, but refer to objects representing those functions.

The three words 'the concept "horse"' do designate an object, but on that very account they do not designate a concept, as I am using that word [p. 45].

In logical discussions one quite often needs to assert something about a concept and to express this in the form usual for such assertions—*viz.,* to make what is asserted of the concept into the content of the grammatical predicate. Consequently, one would expect that the reference of the grammatical subject would be the concept; but the concept as such cannot play this part, in view of its predicative nature; it must first be converted into an object, or, speaking more precisely, represented by an object. We designate this object by prefixing the words 'the concept'; e.g.:

'The concept *man* is not empty.'

Here the first three words are to be regarded as a proper name, which can no more be used predicatively than 'Berlin' or 'Vesuvius' [pp. 46-47].

It must indeed be recognised that here we are confronted by an awkwardness of language, which I admit cannot be avoided, if we say that the concept *horse* is not a concept, whereas e.g. the city of Berlin is a city and the volcano Vesuvius is a volcano [p. 46].

By a kind of necessity of language, my expressions taken literally sometimes miss my thought; I mention an object, when what I intend is a concept [p. 54].

Over the question what it is that is called a function in Analysis, we come up against the same obstacle; and on thorough investigation it will be found that the obstacle is essential, and founded on the nature of our language; that we cannot avoid a certain inappropriateness of linguistic expression; and that there is nothing for it but to realize this and always take it into account [p. 55].

It would be most unsatisfying if a theory about symbolism and its connection with reality had to culminate in lamentations about the inescapable inadequacy of language. Frege does not notice the disastrous consequences for his own formulation of the view that it is logically impossible to refer to a function. If the expression "refer to a function" is nonsense, as it needs to be on his view, then the sentence containing that expression "It is logically impossible to refer to a function" is also nonsense: if Frege's view implies that the very formulation of that view is nonsensical, no further refutation is needed. Of course, it would remain open for him to say, simply, "The expression 'refer to a function' is without sense," but this is not what he intended.

The view that expressions that seem to refer to functions are not nonsensical, because they really refer to objects, escapes the objection just made, but is open to equally serious criticism. Consider, for example, the statement "Log x is incomplete." If the grammatical subject of the sentence is taken to designate some object (*Gegenstand*) the statement becomes not false, but nonsensical. Frege said it was "impossible, senseless" (p. 50) to assert of an object what could be asserted of a concept—or, more generally, of a function. "What . . . is asserted about a concept can never be asserted about an object" (p. 50), and "The assertion that is made about a concept does not suit an object" (p. 50). Now the statement "Log x is incomplete" is intended to suit a function, and hence the predicate, "is incomplete," does not "suit" an object. On the other hand, if "Log x" really stands for some object, as Frege suggests, then the predicate cannot mean what it seems to mean; it must express some other sense appropriate to an *object*. (Perhaps it is for that reason that Frege says "functions are incomplete," but not "log *x* is incomplete.")

The position would then be that in trying to say of functions that they are incomplete we should succeed only in saying something else about objects [6] that in some unexplained way managed to go proxy for the functions. Frege's own assertion about the incompleteness of functions would have to consist in the attribution of unknown characters to unidentified objects. Could mystification go further?

Even if the assertion "Functions are incomplete" had a sense on this farfetched construction, Frege would have succeeded only in recognizing some character of *objects*—and would have failed to make the desired distinction between *functions* and objects. Suppose that in saying, "Functions are incomplete," we are really predicating some character *K* of certain objects. Some objects, but not all, will then have the character *K*. So, in saying that functions are incomplete, we are really distinguishing between two kinds of objects, those that have and those that do not have *K*; we fail utterly to explain or characterize the difference between objects and nonobjects (functions). The reason is plain enough: we cannot say anything about functions without talking about them, and if we insist that we are talking about something else we shall at best succeed in saying something that we hadn't intended.[7]

---

[6] The only object uniquely associated with a given function in Frege's system is the corresponding value-range (*Werthverlauf*). Now the value-range is never defined, and is introduced solely for the purpose of making possible what Frege's doctrine about functions forbids, viz., reference to and quantification upon functions. No wonder that Frege regarded the existence of value-ranges as "indemonstrable" (p. 26)—or recognized this as a weak point in his system (p. 234).

[7] I think Frege's general position on sense and reference could have been made consistent with the view that "the concept *C*" does refer to a concept, and "the function *F*" does refer to a function. Why not say (a) in a statement like "Bucephalus is a horse" the words "is a horse" *express* the property of being a horse, so that that property is the sense (*Sinn*) of the predicate; but (b) in the statement "The concept *is a*

10. The proper course for Frege to have taken was to forbid the use of expressions of the form "the function F" except in statements which, as Russell put it in the quotation used above, "can be brought into a form in which the attribute attributes or the relation relates." For instance, in the statement *"The property of being a man is exemplified,"* we can treat the whole italicized part as synonymous with "Something is," so that the sentence is taken to mean the same as "Something is a man." [8] On this construction, the expression "a man" occurs predicatively, and we need not suppose that the grammatical subject of the original sentence (i.e., the expression "the property of being a man") stands for anything at all.

Now this way of handling sentences containing the expression "the function F" will work only when "F" has no free variable attached: in order that "F" shall be used predicatively there must be either a designation or a quantifier attached to the function sign. But we have already seen that the only cases which Frege had in mind when he claimed that functions are incomplete were those in which the function sign occurs "by itself," as he said, i.e., without attached designation or quantifier. If one insists that function signs shall be

---

horse is often realized" the expression "The concept *is a horse*" *refers* to the property (has that property as its reference or *Bedeutung*)? The expression "is a horse" would, in the latter case, occur in what Frege calls "indirect reference" (p. 59)—which would incidentally explain why, as Frege pointed out (p. 46), one naturally italicizes or puts quotation marks around the expression. This way of looking at the matter would have the merit of removing some of the mystery from Frege's notion of *Sinn*. Frege allows that a *Sinn* may be referred to, in indirect reference; hence the *Sinn* cannot be a function. But what other kind of object recognized by him would serve instead?

[8] The example is taken from P. T. Geach, "Subject and Predicate," *Mind*, 59 (1950): 472-473. Geach differs from Frege in not regarding "the property of being a man" as designating anything at all. He does not observe that this makes it impossible to construe most of his own interesting remarks about properties, functions, and so on. Expressions like "the property of being a man" can usefully be treated as mere circumlocutions for predicative uses of the predicates contained within them only so long as one is content not to generalize about properties, relations, and functions.

used only predicatively, all such locutions become nonsensical.

This policy would put a gag upon any attempt to generalize about properties, relations, or functions. We would have to count as nonsensical such characteristic statements of Frege himself as "What a name expresses is its sense" (p. 154), "An object is anything that is not a function" (p. 32), "Relations are functions" (p. 142), and so on. Even the main contention of the theory itself, "A function is incomplete," would have to be regarded as nonsensical. For this contention has the form "(x) (If x is a function, x is incomplete)." Now nothing can be properly substituted for the "x" in "x is a function": the name of a function cannot be substituted, since functions, according to Frege, cannot be designated; and if we substitute the name of an object we get a statement that is "impossible, senseless." Hence the functional expression "x is a function," is ill formed and any attempt to generalize by binding the free variable is absurd. The same, of course, applies to the second clause, "x is incomplete." Now a doctrine that reduces philosophy to silence might conceivably be correct; but nobody can reasonably be expected to accept a theory which, on its own showing, is trying to say what cannot be said.[9]

11. Let us end by considering what reasons Frege had to offer for the paradoxical view, from which so many unwelcome consequences flow, that an expression of the form "the function F" cannot designate a function. In order to designate, the expression would have to be what Frege called an *Eigenname* ("proper name"). Now if the reader will refer back to Frege's definition of "*Eigenname*" (section 4 above) he will find that functions are expressly excluded from being referred to by an *Eigenname*. To put the matter in another way, Frege so *defines* "designation," "object," and "function" that it is impossible for a function to be designated. But this tells us

---

[9] One may be reminded of Wittgenstein's position in the *Tractatus*. He was showing, however, that his own metaphysical statements were senseless. Frege had no such intention.

only how he has chosen to use these words. It by no means follows that it is wrong to begin a sentence with an expression of the form "the function F"; nor does it in the least follow, as Frege mistakenly supposed, that the definite description must then stand for what he called an object.

Nothing that I have said in this essay is intended to deny the validity of the distinction that Frege points out between names (and expressions that can be substituted for names), on the one hand, and predicates or functional expressions, on the other. That these two classes of expressions have different "logical grammars," i.e., are controlled by different rules of meaningful usage, is obvious upon the most cursory inspection. But this can be understood without recourse to mystifying and misleading metaphors about the "incompleteness" or "lack of saturation" of what the functional expressions are confusedly supposed to stand for. In fact, the muddle arises, I suggest, because Frege, in spite of this clear distinction in the uses of the two types of expressions, still wants to think of the functional expressions as *names* for functions (cf. his use of the term *"Functionname"* and his tendency to say that function names and function expressions "stand for" something). Of course, if one intends to use the term "name" in such a way that "objects" can, but functions cannot, have names, and yet thinks of the functional expression as after all still, somehow, naming a function, confusion will be bound to result; one will try to speak of functions as if they were and at the same time were not "objects." The use of the figurative expressions *"unvollständig"* and *"ungesättigt"* is an attempt, but an unsuccessful one, to have the matter both ways—to call functions objects, albeit peculiar, "unsaturated," ones. As to the question whether "the function *log x*" *really* refers to a function, I do not see how this is to be answered in the absence of any criterion for "really" referring to anything. I would suppose that we have uses for expressions like "the function *log x*" and that if they were banned much of what we now succeed in saying in mathematics, logic, and philosophy would become impossible of utterance. If a reader desires a more profound justification than this, I cannot help him, and he must look elsewhere for satisfaction.

12. *Summary and conclusions.* I have tried in this essay to understand Frege's contention that functions are incomplete and the considerations that led him to make it. In its literal uses, "incomplete" is usually a synonym for "unfinished" or "having a part missing"; only the second set of uses can provide a plausible basis for Frege's metaphors, since the first involves reference to a temporal process or a resulting product. In ordinary usage, "this *B* is incomplete" is always an ellipsis for "this *B* is an incomplete *A*" where either *A* is identical with *B*, or *A* and *B* are species of a common genus. Frege's assertion that a function *sign* is incomplete might accordingly be taken to mean that a function sign is an incomplete *Eigenname* ("proper name"). Since I found reason to reject Frege's view that a sentence is an *Eigenname*, I had to consider separately the assertion that a function sign is an incomplete designation and the assertion that it is an incomplete sentence. Both assertions can be taken to be *literally* true, but only in trivial senses which do not serve to distinguish function signs from designations. On the other hand, the suggestion that the function itself might be considered as an incomplete object (*Gegenstand*) had to be rejected as absurd. The metaphors of the function sign as container or link were examined and found wanting. Nor could I find any good reason to agree that the function sign "must" show empty places. Frege's theory finally breaks down in its implication that "the function *F*" cannot refer to a function. This seems to imply the impossibility of generalizing about functions and thus the impossibility of formulating the theory itself.

The major difficulties of the theory seem to have arisen from incompatible inclinations to count function signs both as being and not being designations and this, in turn, may have something to do with Frege's relative neglect of all symbols that are not "names" or parts of names. If Frege had not been so impressed by the importance of "names," he might have avoided the whole imbroglio.

13

Frege's Theory of Functions and Objects[1]

WILLIAM MARSHALL

I

The purpose of this paper is to discuss Frege's distinction between functions (in particular, concepts and relations) and objects. Besides being of historical interest, a discussion of this type will, I think, illuminate several well-known philosophical views, such as: (1) There are some things which can exist alone or apart and others which cannot; (2) There exist logically complete wholes or unities, some of the parts of which, being essentially adhesive in character, link the other parts together; and (3) Relations are internal.

Since Frege's distinction seems not to be widely known, I shall compare it briefly to the familiar distinctions, universal-particular and substance-attribute, to which it is related.

Classes, traditionally, have been considered as universals, but under Frege's classification they are objects. Furthermore, Frege classifies as functions certain things—e.g., the mean-

Reprinted with the kind permission of the author and the editor from *The Philosophical Review*, LXII (1953), 374-390.

[1] I am very much indebted to Professor Max Black for many of the ideas expressed in this paper. It should not, of course, be assumed that he would agree with the whole or any part of what I say here.

ing [2] of "the capital of," occurring in the expression "the capital of Germany"—which have not traditionally been classified as universals, nor, for that matter, classified at all.

According to some versions of the substance-attribute view, an attribute or property is part of any substance possessing the property. Frege, in contrast, asserts that a property, which for him is a special kind of function, is not part of the object possessing it, but instead, forms together with the object a "complete whole," having as constituents the object and property.[3]

Thus "function" is a more general term than "attribute." Furthermore, a function, even when a property, does not bear the same relation to an object possessing it as an attribute supposedly bears to a substance. Functions, however, cannot exist apart,[4] Frege holds, and in this respect they resemble attributes; while objects, like substances, are independent or self-sufficient.

As I indicated above, concepts (or properties)[5] and relations are special kinds of functions. A concept, roughly, is the meaning of a grammatical predicate.[6] In the sentence "Bismark is dead," the expression "is dead,"[7] occurring as part, designates[8] a concept.[9] If a sentence contains two proper

---

[2] The German word is *Bedeutung*. In contexts like the one above, this word does not, I think, have the technical meaning of denotation or reference, given it in the essay "Ueber Sinn und Bedeutung." For one thing, *Bedeutung* is not here opposed to *Sinn* (sense), because function-expressions do not have a sense. Secondly, it appears that only proper names, i.e., names of objects, have a denotation in the technical use of the word.

[3] Cf. *Function und Begriff* (Jena, 1891), p. 6.

[4] Cf. "Ueber die Grundlagen der Geometrie," *Jahresbericht der deutschen Mathematiker-Vereinigung*, XII (1903), p. 372, footnote.

[5] To be accurate, a property is a special kind of concept, but as the distinction is unimportant for my purpose, I shall not elaborate it.

[6] Cf. "Ueber Begriff und Gegenstand," *Vierteljahrsschrift für wissenschaftliche Philosophie*, XVI (1892), p. 198.

[7] Sometimes the copula is ignored.

[8] The usual German word is *bezeichnet*, although *bedeutet* is also used.

[9] That is, a concept of the first level. Frege has a hierarchy of concepts (indeed of all functions), resembling a simple theory of types for functions.

names or more, the part of the sentence lying outside any two of the names designates a relation.[10] The expression "is north of," for example, occurring in "Canada is north of Mexico," designates a relation.

Frege has no special name for functions which are neither concepts nor relations. One such function, the meaning of "the capital of" in "the capital of Germany," has been given already. The meaning of "+ 3," occurring in the numerical expression "2 + 3," is another instance of a function of this type.

In the examples above, an expression designating a function was used in conjunction with proper names to form sentences, descriptions, and complex numerical expressions. Frequently, however, Frege wishes to designate functions "in isolation,"[11] and to do so, uses free variables, considered by him as analogous to brackets. Thus to speak in isolation of the function designated by the predicate of "Bismark is dead," Frege would usually replace "Bismark" by a letter, e.g., "x," acquiring "x is dead." In Frege's technical terminology, "Bismark" designates an argument to the function, while "Bismark is dead" designates the value of the function for the argument Bismark. The value of a function is always an object, but an argument to a function may, depending on the kind of function, be either an object or a function.

The distinction between designating a function in isolation and designating it by means of an expression occurring as part of a larger expression, which stands for the value of the function, has been mentioned because it is closely related to several of the issues I wish to discuss—for example, whether functions can exist apart from objects or not.

I have given a provisional explanation of the term "func-

[10] By a relation, Frege always understands a two-termed relation. However, I shall frequently use the term to refer to relations having any number of terms.

[11] Cf. "Was ist eine Function?," *Festschrift Ludwig Boltzmann gewidmet zum sechzigsten Geburtstage 20. Februar 1904* (Leipzig, 1904), p. 664.

tion" by indicating the kinds of expressions which stand for functions. Following an analogous procedure for "object," an object is anything designated by a proper name (in the ordinary sense), numeral, definite description, or true or false sentence.[12] Thus the author of *Waverley* is an object. Frege would describe this object, Scott, as a "complete whole" made up of two logical parts, *Waverley* and the function designated by "the author of." If an object is made up of logical parts, in Frege's sense, I shall call it a complex object. Otherwise it will be called a simple object.[13] A complex object, therefore, is an object which is a value of some function; a simple object is an object which is a value of no function.

Having given a provisional account of the difference between functions and objects, I wish now to present the distinction in detail.

(1) Functions are described as "unsaturated," "in need of supplementation," "incomplete" (*ungesättigt, ergänzungsbedürftig, unvollständig*); objects, in contrast, as "saturated," "supplemented," "complete wholes" (*gesättigt, ergänzt, vollständige Ganzen*).[14]

(2) Functions are logical bonds (*Bindemittel*), without which the parts of complex objects could not adhere. Objects lack this peculiar adhesive property.[15]

(3) Functions, unlike objects, "can occur only in combination." They can be "distinguished within" objects but not "separated from" objects.[16]

(4) No function can be a logical subject, a place reserved

---

[12] Frege holds that sentences refer to truth-values, the true and the false. Cf. "Ueber Sinn und Bedeutung," *Zeitschrift für Philosophie und philosophische Kritik*, n.s. C (1892), pp. 34-35.

[13] Simple objects are never explicitly discussed by Frege.

[14] Cf. "Was ist eine Function?," p. 664; *Function und Begriff*, p. 6; "Ueber die Grundlagen der Geometrie," pp. 371-374; *Grundgesetze der Arithmetik* (Jena, 1893), Vol. I, pp. 5-7.

[15] Cf. "Ueber Begriff und Gegenstand," p. 205; "Ueber die Grundlagen der Geometrie," p. 372.

[16] Cf. "Ueber die Grundlagen der Geometrie," p. 372, footnote.

for objects alone, and no object can be a logical predicate.[17] It follows from this, as I shall show later, that a function cannot be designated "in isolation," a point on which Frege wavers somewhat.

These four characterizations of functions and objects are by no means distinct and independent. The second and third are really elaborations of the first, and both are related to the fourth in a somewhat intricate manner.

II

The terms "complete" and "incomplete" and their cognates, by means of which Frege distinguishes functions from objects and indicates the "essential nature" of each, are admittedly metaphorical. The difficulty is to find the ground of the metaphor. One might naturally think that a function, being incomplete, has a missing part, like a house with no roof or a book with a chapter still to be written. Nevertheless, a function has no missing part, and so in the ordinary sense is perfectly complete just as it is. The only thing that could qualify as a missing part is an argument to the function, but Frege says "the argument does not belong to the function, but rather forms together with the function a complete whole." [18]

The argument, Frege says, completes the function,[19] but what is here called completing the function is more appropriately described as converting the function into an object. If a function is completed, in Frege's sense, it becomes not a completed function—for that, like the round square, is a logical absurdity—but an object. Ordinary people complete a house and the result is a house. Frege completes a house and finds he has constructed the moon.

I have considered, so far, only the pair of terms "complete," and "incomplete," but Frege's use of the other pairs of meta-

---

[17] Cf. "Ueber Begriff und Gegenstand," pp. 193, 195.
[18] *Function und Begriff*, p. 6.
[19] Cf. *Grundgesetze der Arithmetik*, Vol. I, p. 6.

phors, "saturated" and "unsaturated," etc., is similar. A function, it is said, is saturated by the argument. The result, however, of saturating a function is not a saturated function but an object. This is like saying a man saturates a sponge and then has the leviathan on his hands.

One might, then, say that a function is incomplete in the sense of being merely a part or fragment of a complex object. Perhaps we might call a function an incomplete object. But if so, objects, contrary to Frege's view, would also be incomplete, since objects too may be parts of complex objects. The object, England, for example, is part of the complex object, the capital of England, i.e., London.[20]

A clue, perhaps, to the interpretation of Frege's metaphors is the fact that a function is apparently conceived as something with a hole in it. We can, he says, indicate the unsaturated nature of functions by using brackets in function-signs, as in "( ) + ( )²" or "( ) is a man."[21] These expressions are called incomplete or unsaturated, and their incompleteness is said to correspond to an analogous property in what they stand for.[22] A function, therefore, seems to be a kind of logical frame or rack. This interpretation is reinforced by the following considerations. First, an argument to a function is not, according to Frege, part of the function; and it is also the case that whatever is placed in a frame or rack is not part of the rack. A gun, for example, standing in a rack, is not part of the rack. Secondly, racks, like functions, serve to hold things together.

It now appears that the terms "complete" and "incomplete" cannot be clarified except by means of "part" and "whole."

---

[20] Functions, too, may be made up of parts. The function, *x likes Bismark,* contains Bismark as part (cf. *Die Grundlagen der Arithmetik,* Oxford, 1950, p. 77). Since, however, functions are said to be timeless, it is difficult to see what sense can be given to "part" here; for Bismark, who changes, has a beginning and end, etc., is clearly not timeless. The part here seems to make no difference to the whole.

[21] Cf. "Was ist eine Function?," p. 664.

[22] *Ibid.,* p. 665; "Ueber die Grundlagen der Geometrie," p. 371.

By saying functions are incomplete, Frege seems to mean they are those parts of "complete wholes" which, being perforated, bind the other parts together. Objects, being complete, lack this property to generate such wholes.

An explanation of this type is hardly satisfactory, however, because the terms "part" and "whole," among others, are, like the terms to be explained, also metaphors.[23] It is no doubt admissible to say that a whole is part of itself, but to say, as Frege is required to do, that a whole may be a part of one of its parts is to use "part" and "whole" somewhat mysteriously. The value of the function *not-x* for the argument not-P is, on Frege's view, the complete whole, not-not-P, i.e., P. Here P is part of not-P, which, in turn, is part of P. The value of the function, *the worst enemy of x,* for the argument denoted by "the state governed by Hitler," might be said to be Hitler himself. Yet the argument is "part" of the "whole" and the "whole" is "part" of the argument.

Ordinarily we have a complete whole whenever all the parts are present and together in the right form. An expression such as "the father of Adam," however, not standing for anything, does not stand for a complete whole. Nevertheless, the parts are all present and are presumably together in the right form, since the parts expressed by the similar expression, "the father of Bismark," are so united as to give a complete whole. Frege, it is true, says that when an expression lacks an ordinary reference, we may give it an arbitrary one, e.g., zero.[24] But then whether or not we have a complete whole does not depend upon whether the parts are present or absent. The discovery of the golden mountain would then be a complete whole, although here a part is surely missing.

Finally, Frege says that expressions like "is the same as b" or "x + b," or, more generally, those of the form "xFb," stand for functions that are completed by an argument *a*. But when *a* is the same as *b*, it is not easy to see how *a* can complete the

---

[23] Frege is aware of this. Cf. "Sinn und Bedeutung," pp. 35-36.
[24] Cf. "Sinn und Bedeutung," p. 41, footnote.

function. The expressions xFb and aFb have precisely the same parts, provided *a* equals *b*. Nevertheless, Frege says that aFb is a complete whole, while xFb is not, and this sounds as if one could construct a complete whole by doing nothing.

Thus the attempt to clarify "complete" and "incomplete," and also "function" and "object," by the use of "part" and "whole," owing to the obscurity of the last pair of terms, has been unsatisfactory.

One might, next, suppose that the figure of a function as something with a hole in it is not to be taken seriously, and that Frege, by his use of "complete" and "incomplete," primarily intended to point out that functions "can occur only in combinations," whereas objects are self-subsistent or independent. A function, he holds, is like a coat and "cannot stand upright by itself; in order to do that, it must be wrapped about somebody." [25] This, I suppose, is a way of saying that a function cannot exist by itself. If there is a function, there is also, necessarily, an argument to the function (and hence a value of the function).

The interpretation here suggested of "complete" and "incomplete," though perhaps plausible, is not, I think, an adequate one. First, it seems to ignore the adhesive character of functions, surely according to Frege, one of their most important properties, and therefore it does not present the whole meaning of "complete" and "incomplete." (There is, however, a close and peculiar relationship, which I shall point out below, between the insubstantial and the adhesive characteristics of functions.) Secondly, unless we use the notions of part and whole, we cannot distinguish functions from objects by saying that functions cannot exist alone but objects can.

Suppose we say: If there is a function *F*, then there is an object *a* and either a function *G* (distinct from *F*) [26] or an

---

[25] "Die Verneinung," *Beiträge zur Philosophie des deutschen Idealismus*, I (1919), p. 157.

[26] Frege's functions do not take themselves as arguments.

object b (b may be a), such that a $= \mathrm{F}(\mathrm{G})$ or a $= \mathrm{F}(\mathrm{b})$. This condition, which states that there is no function without an argument and value, guarantees that no function exists alone.

It is easy to show, however, that in this sense of "exists alone," no complex object can exist alone either. For, by definition, if b is a complex object, there is a function F and an argument a, such that b $= \mathrm{F}(\mathrm{a})$.[27]

The sense of "exists alone" which I have used is, I think, quite like the one we employ in saying there could be no husbands unless there were also wives; and it is pretty obvious that this is not the sort of use which Frege would have in mind. For one thing, husbands, being objects, are not incomplete.

Suppose, therefore, that we try to distinguish functions from objects by saying that an object could exist if nothing other than its parts existed, assuming it has parts, and that a function could not exist except as part of some object. Frege, it appears, would agree that this is one way of distinguishing functions from objects, for he says concepts, unlike objects, "can occur only in combination" and that, although they can be "distinguished within" a combination, they cannot be "separated from" it.[28]

Again, however, the distinction drawn is unsatisfactory, since there cannot be just one *simple* object. Let a be the object which is the only simple object. Then a is the value of the function, *the object which is x,* for the argument denoted by "the simple object." Consequently, a, being the value of some function, cannot be simple.[29]

---

[27] Section 34 of *Grundgesetze der Arithmetik,* Vol. I, involving the occurrence of function-variables in quantifiers, is worth noting in this connection.

[28] Cf. "Ueber die Grundlagen der Geometrie," p. 372, footnote.

[29] Roughly, a simple object is one that cannot be described (in Russell's sense). It is also doubtful if it can be referred to at all, given Frege's theory of names. He holds that every name has a sense, which is apparently a uniquely determining property of an object. But if a simple object had such a property, it could be described and so could not be simple.

The above argument depends upon the fact that Frege's functions are one-valued, and while the assumption that there is but one simple object implies that this object cannot be simple, the assumption that there are two or more simple objects does not have an analogous consequence. What I have shown is that if there is one simple object, there are at least two. Consequently, we cannot say, as I said above, that objects can exist even if nothing else exists (aside from their parts, if they have any). For a simple object cannot exist unless another object also exists, and of course this second object cannot be part of the simple object.

Apparently, then, Frege's view that objects are self-subsistent or independent means simply that objects can exist without being parts of other objects or wholes; and the view that functions are not self-subsistent means simply that functions cannot exist without being part of some whole.

In this section I have tried to show that Frege seems to mean two things by describing objects as complete and functions as incomplete. First, functions, in contrast to objects, have a peculiar capacity to link together the parts of complete wholes. Secondly, functions, unlike objects, can exist only as parts of complete wholes. Neither of these explanations is satisfactory, because we do not understand "part" and "whole," as Frege uses them.

In the next section I shall consider Frege's reasons for distinguishing functions and objects. He holds that the distinction must be made, but that since it is so very fundamental, he can only give hints as to what he means by it.[30] Perhaps if we can see the reasons why the distinction must be made, then the distinction itself will become intuitively clear.

III

Frege, after describing an object as complete and a concept as incomplete, remarks:

---

[30] Cf. "Ueber die Grundlagen der Geometrie," pp. 371-372; "Ueber Begriff und Gegenstand," pp. 204-205.

I am well aware that expressions like "complete" and "incomplete" are metaphorical. . . . Nevertheless, it can, perhaps, be explained why the two parts must be distinct. [The two parts here referred to are the logical subject and logical predicate, i.e., concept.] An object —e.g. the number 2—cannot logically adhere to another object—e.g. Julius Caesar—without a link, which, however, cannot be an object but must be incomplete. A logical combination which gives rise to a whole can take place only when an incomplete part is completed or saturated by one or several parts. We have something similar when we complete "the capital of" by means of "Germany" or "Sweden"; or when we complete "the half of" by means of "6".[31]

Frege, in the passage above, says that objects will not cling together without a link. What he means can be illustrated by considering the meaning of certain types of complex expressions. The expression "Bismark hates Napoleon" or "2 + 3" contains parts which stand for objects, and yet the meaning of the whole expression has a unity which an expression like "Bismark, Frederick, Napoleon" lacks. An expression of the latter type, though it might be used in making an enumeration or in calling a roll, does not, as a whole, stand for anything at all. Frege tries to account for the unity associated with "Bismark hates Napoleon" by saying that "hates," the sign for a relation, refers to a logical bond that links Napoleon and Bismark together. In the case of "Bismark, Frederick, Napoleon," such a bond is missing, so that we do not have a complete whole.

Let signs like "Bismark hates Napoleon" and "2 + 3" be called logically complex signs.[32] Then a logically complex sign will be a sign that (1) contains parts which stand for things and (2) stands, as a whole, for one thing only.

An expression for the value of a function is a logically complex sign. If $F(a)$ is such an expression, F is a sign for the function, a for the argument, and $F(a)$ for the complete whole made up of the function and argument. Such a sign might be compared, not only to signs used in enumerating,

---

[31] "Ueber die Grundlagen der Geometrie," p. 372; cf. also "Ueber Begriff und Gegenstand," p. 205.
[32] Cf. *Grundgesetze der Arithmetik* (Jena, 1903), Vol. II, p. 255.

but also to grammatically but not logically complex signs like "Pringle-Pattison" or "New York." Frege would say that "with respect to the contents" of the latter signs, "there is no combination at all." [33]

Now a peculiarity of the meaning of a logically complex sign is that, although it contains parts, the parts cannot be enumerated or listed, a point of some importance for understanding the view that functions must always be parts of wholes. The meaning of "Bismark is different from Napoleon" cannot be analyzed into the parts: Bismark, the relation of being different from, and Napoleon; for, according to Frege, the relation of being different from is no relation. [34]

One reason offered for this conclusion, that the relation of being different from is no relation, is that the expressions "Bismark," "the relation of being different from," and "Napoleon" can be seen to "hold themselves aloof from each other," so that "however we combine them, we get no sentence." [35] I doubt, however, whether Frege attaches much importance to this argument, since he holds, as a general rule, that linguistic considerations "are unreliable on logical questions." [36] Offhand, the argument seems rather weak. It may plausibly be said that "is different from," occurring in "Bismark is different from Napoleon," and "the relation of being different from" each stand for the same relation, and that although "the relation of being different from" will not combine with "Bismark" and "Napoleon" to form a sentence, this fact is the result of a linguistic accident. [37] Indeed, one

[33] *Ibid.*

[34] Cf. *Grundgesetze der Arithmetik*, Vol. I, p. 8, footnote; "Ueber Begriff und Gegenstand," pp. 195-198. Frege holds, in general, that the function $F(x)$ is no function. This sounds like a contradiction, but is really, I think, more like a kind of mild pun. It is like saying, with reference to the *Chicago Tribune*, that the world's greatest newspaper is not the world's greatest newspaper.

[35] "Ueber Begriff und Gegenstand," p. 205.

[36] "Die Verneinung," p. 150.

[37] Cf., in this connection, Russell, *Principles of Mathematics*, 2d ed. (London, 1937), pp. 45-46.

might "analyze" the meaning of "Bismark is different from Napoleon" by writing "Bismark, is different from, Napoleon." Surely the parts would then combine to form sentences.

In that case, however, I am sure Frege would say that the expression "is different from" is ambiguous. When occurring in the sentence "Bismark is different from Napoleon," it designates a relation, but when occurring in "Bismark, is different from, Napoleon," it designates an object. The reason is that a relation cannot exist apart, and therefore cannot be designated in isolation.[38] The main reason why Frege holds that relations cannot exist apart is, I think, the extreme difficulty, given his view that logically complex signs stand for complete wholes, of distinguishing the meaning of "Bismark is different from Napoleon" from that of "Bismark, the relation of being different from, Napoleon."

If we "analyze" the meaning [39] of "Bismark is different from Napoleon"—i.e., if we enumerate its parts—the result, of course, is Bismark, the relation of difference, Napoleon; all the parts, it appears, but no unity. Yet if the meaning of "Bismark is different from Napoleon" and that of "Bismark, the relation of difference, Napoleon" contain the same parts, they would, it seems, be the same. The difference between the two arises, Frege holds, because the relation of difference is no relation. It is not indentured and cannot hold the parts

[38] Frege's views as to whether or not a function can be designated "in isolation"—i.e., by an expression which is not part of an expression for a value of the function—do not seem consistent. (Cf., for example, "Was ist eine Function?," p. 664, footnote, and "Ueber die Grundlagen der Geometrie," p. 372, footnote.) He does consistently hold, however, that only an object can be a logical subject. Assume, then, that an expression "F(x)," occurring in isolation, designates a function. It seems an obvious principle that if an expression designates something in a given manner, then what is designated is designated in the given manner. Hence F(x) would be a function designated in isolation. But this is false, because F(x), being a logical subject, is no function. Consequently a function cannot be designated in isolation.

[39] For the present discussion, it makes no difference in principle whether a sentence is taken as referring to a truth-value, a proposition, a fact, or a judgment.

together. Frege's logical chains, by being disconnected from objects, lose their essence.

Russell once tried to account for the kind of difference seen in "Bismark is different from Napoleon" and "Bismark, the relation of difference, Napoleon" by saying that in the first case the relation actually relates, thereby generating a unity, and in the other case it does not.[40] Obviously this will not do in general. The relation expressed in the false sentence "Aachen is larger than Berlin" does not, in any ordinary sense, relate the terms, since the relation does not hold between the terms. Nevertheless, the meaning of "Aachen is larger than Berlin" is as much a unity as that of "Aachen is smaller than Berlin," a sentence expressing a relation which does relate the terms.

One might, however, appeal to a physical analogy and elaborate Russell's view by saying that the difference between a logical unity and the collection of its parts is that in the first case a certain relationship holds between the parts. A house and a pile of bricks may contain the same parts, but they are different because the parts are arranged differently. This type of solution is not open to Frege (nor to Russell either), however, because the relationship between the parts of a logical whole or unity is itself a part. Consequently, if *Bismark is different from Napoleon* and Bismark, the relation of difference, Napoleon contain the same parts, the difference between them cannot be a result of a relationship between the parts. Frege, therefore, is required to say that they do not contain the same parts, and so says that the relation of difference is no relation.

An alternative, perhaps, to the paradoxical view that the relation R is no relation is the view that the meaning of "Bismark is different from Napoleon" contains an unexpressed relation, absent in the case of "Bismark, the relation of difference, Napoleon." Aside, however, from the difficulty of

---

[40] Cf. *Principles of Mathematics,* pp. 49-50.

saying what this unexpressed relation might be,[41] other difficulties, of the sort pointed out by Bradley, stand in the way
of such a view.

If the relation of difference is a relation and yet does not,
as in "Bismark, the relation of difference, Napoleon," give
rise to a logical unity, it is difficult to see how we could ever
have such a unity, no matter how many relations are added
to the collection. If the relation of difference requires to be
connected to the parts, so does any additional relation, and
the parts will always "hold themselves aloof from each other."

Consider this analogy. There is a bundle of sticks tied up
by a piece of string. Someone dissolves the bundle by cutting
the string, so that we have sticks and a piece of string, all in
a pile. Suppose a man asks: "Why do we not have a bundle?
The thing that holds sticks together, the string, is present in
the pile." If the man believes that any relation which the
string might bear to the sticks is itself, like the string and the
sticks, a part of the collection, then it is futile to reply that
the string is not tied round the sticks. He will no doubt say:
"Being tied round the sticks is either a string or a stick. If
it is a stick, it obviously will not make the pile a bundle,
and if it is a string, the same is true. If the first string will
not give us a bundle, throwing other strings on the pile will
be futile."

The result is an infinite regress but no bundle. Frege avoids
this by saying that if the string is not tied round the sticks,
it is not really a string, thereby adopting the paradoxical view
that the relation R is no relation. The alternative, however,
is apparently the view that logical unities are not possible.

Bradley thought the view that all relations are external is
incompatible with the existence of logical unities.[42] An external relation is opposed to an internal one, and by an internal relation, Bradley means one which "essentially pene-

---

[41] Cf., in this connection, Russell, *op. cit.*, p. 51.
[42] Cf. Bradley, "On Appearance, Error, and Contradiction," *Mind*, n.s.
XIX (1910), p. 179.

trates the being of its terms."[43] It seems to connect the terms in an organic sense, by growing into them, somewhat as the neck connects the head and body of a man. No part of a whole so connected can be torn away without destruction.

An external relation is one which is not part of its terms, as in Frege's conception, and Bradley does not see how such relations can give rise to complete wholes. If it does not form part of the terms, it can, without destruction, be taken from the whole, as in "analysis," and the above sort of infinite regress seems to arise.[44] Frege, of course, like Bradley, refuses to let a whole be "analyzed," and as a consequence Bradley's organic imagery seems more appropriate here than Frege's jigsaw picture.

Bradley also thought that any relation is really an appearance, the reason being that we cannot explain how it ever connects anything together. We might say that aRb is a unity or complete whole, the parts of which are linked together by R. But how is this possible? If a and b are to be linked by R, they require to be linked to R. Hence we need two more relations—and so on.[45] The parts of a logical unity will always rattle.

Frege seems to hold that a and b do not need to be linked to R by other links, because R is indentured. I doubt whether this image would satisfy Bradley. He would no doubt ask what keeps the terms in the slots—and so another infinite regress.

I wish to say that Bradley and Frege have erroneously assimilated logical parts and wholes to physical parts and wholes, and as a consequence, have asked questions about the former which apply only to the latter. Physical links, chains,

---

[43] *Appearance and Reality* (Oxford, 1893), p. 392.

[44] Bradley says, "If relations are facts that exist *between* facts, then what comes *between* the relations and the other facts? The real truth is that the units on one side, and on the other side the relation existing between them, are nothing actual. . . . Relations exist only in and through a whole which cannot in the end be resolved into relations and terms" (*Principles of Logic*, 2d ed. [London, 1922], p. 96).

[45] Cf. *Appearance and Reality*, chap. iii.

racks, etc. no doubt belong to the wholes whose parts they hold together, but a relation between the parts of a whole is never itself a part of the whole. A mechanic who lists the parts of a car does not attach the blueprint. Frege's use of "part" and "whole" hardly resembles the ordinary use of the terms more than it does the use of any two terms chosen at random. Hence the question as to what holds the parts of a logical whole together does not arise. There are no parts and there are no wholes.

It is now easy to see one reason why Frege should think that a relation is insubstantial. If a relation between the parts is itself a part of the whole, then of course a whole cannot be taken apart or "analyzed." The relation will always be missing.

The image of logical parts and wholes, though extremely misleading, arises quite naturally for anyone who, like Frege, is caught in the grip of the name-relation. If we take the grammatical subject as a name and the grammatical predicate as a name, it is natural to say that the two things referred to are united into a whole, which is named by the sentence. Once this view is adopted, Frege's distinction between logical subjects and predicates follows as a matter of course. We can easily feel the difference between a substantive and a predicate. If both are taken as names, this difference will be expressed by saying substantives and predicates stand for entirely different sorts of things. A collection of names does not have the sort of unity we associate with a sentence. Yet if a predicate is a name, how does "Bismark is a man" differ from a collection of names? One is almost compelled, in order to make the distinction, to say that the predicate stands for something which has to grasp on to the subject for support. It is like a coat, which will not stand upright by itself.

We can now, I think, see why Frege found a close relationship between the insubstantiality of functions and their incapacity of being designated in isolation and by grammatical subjects. The predicate of "Bismark is a man" is taken as a name of a concept. But to refer to this concept as a logical subject, we should ordinarily write "the concept *man*" or "manhood," an expression which cannot replace "is a man." No unity can be associated with "Bismark the concept *man*," a fact which Frege can explain only by saying that the concept *man* is not something incomplete and hence is no concept at all.

IV

To completely dissolve the image of logical parts and wholes, it would be necessary to show in detail various important logical differences between substantives and predicates, adjectives, verbs, and the other expressions which Frege calls function-names. I cannot do this here. However, I can indicate some of the differences. Indeed, Frege, in trying to establish his view that functions can never be objects, points out several such differences.

For Frege there is no difference in principle between calling a roll and making an assertion about something. In either case we simply utter a series of names. The difference between these two uses of language lies, according to Frege, in the things named. In the second case, we must refer to at least one function; in the other case, we talk only of objects. The difference, for example, between saying "Bismark is a man" and "Bismark, the concept *man*" is found in the difference between what is referred to.

Now to speak in this way implies that proper names and descriptions are very much more like predicates and adjectives than in fact they are. One characteristic of names (including here descriptions) seems to be this: If a and b are names, a can be interchanged with b in a sentence and the result is a sentence. Hence if "is a man" in "Bismark is a man" is a name, then "Bismark the concept *man*" ought to be a sentence. More generally, if a and b are names, a can be interchanged with b without resulting in a jumble of nonsense. Hence if "the author of," occurring in "the author of *Waver-*

ley," is a name, then the result of replacing it by the descriptive phrase "the author of (x)" ought not be nonsense. Nevertheless, "the author of (x) *Waverley*" is a jumble of nonsense.[46]

Expressions for functions, Frege says, do not occur alone on either side of an identity sign.[47] Frege should conclude from this that the nature of functions is so peculiar that we cannot in principle state their identity conditions. I think it shows that in order to identify something, we must use a name, not a predicate, or adjective, or in general, a function-sign. We say both "That is Venus" and "That is a planet," but as Frege points out, there is a great difference between identifying something and saying it "falls under a concept."[48]

We should not say, as Frege does, that a predicate is a name, but a name of a peculiar sort of thing. Frege has taken a linguistic difference to be a rift in nature.

---

[46] Cf., in this connection, *Grundgesetze der Arithmetik*, Vol. I, p. 8, footnote; "Ueber Begriff und Gegenstand," pp. 200-202.

[47] "Was ist eine Function?," p. 663.

[48] "Ueber Begriff und Gegenstand," p. 194.

14

Frege on Functions: A Reply

MICHAEL DUMMETT

Most of the details of Frege's theory of functions can be put
in the form of rules laying down which combinations of the
expressions of a correctly constructed language are to be regarded as sense and which as nonsense. This part of Frege's
theory is of the greatest interest; it constitutes a justification
on grounds of philosophical necessity (rather than, say, of
ease of manipulation) of the structure of the logic which Frege
invented and which, under the title "mathematical logic," is
now everywhere accepted.[1] This part of the theory is also
highly disputable; but Mr. William Marshall, in his interesting article on the subject in the *Philosophical Review* for
July, 1953, directs his attack solely toward the other feature
of Frege's theory, namely the fact that he expresses it not in
terms of the putting together of certain kinds of linguistic
expression—proper names, predicates, and so on—but of the
things these expressions stand for—objects, concepts, functions and the rest. Mr. Marshall's conclusion is that "Frege
has taken a linguistic difference to be a rift in nature" (more
accurate would be: "linguistic differences"). This conclusion

---

Reprinted with the kind permission of the author and the editor from
The Philosophical Review, LXIV (1955), 96-107.
[1] It should be noted here that there are in Frege's logical system distinctions of level which amount to the simple theory of types for functions but not for classes.

is surprising after so long and intricate an argument, for it is a natural first reaction to Frege's theory; the point can be made without elaborate analysis. The difficulties which Frege unsuccessfully tried to overcome in *Über Begriff und Gegenstand*, and which threaten to destroy his whole theory, could have been avoided simply by adopting (to use the well-worn jargon) the formal instead of the material mode of speech. Most people would admit that Frege made clearer than anyone had done before him the radical difference in logical rôle of what he called proper names, concept-words, second-level concept-words,[2] and so on (roughly speaking, in more familiar terminology, denoting expressions, predicates and quantifiers); Mr. Marshall would perhaps concede this, although by failing to preserve in his article more than a trace of Frege's distinction between first- and second-level functions, he obscures this part of Frege's achievement and gives a misleading picture of Frege's theory. Now if Frege had confined himself to talking about these various types of *expression*, instead of that for which they stood, the appearance of paradox, the awkwardnesses of phrasing, the resort to metaphor, which pervade his writing, would all have been avoided. Frege was quite wrong in pretending[3] that the same ills affect the formal mode of speech. There is no more paradox in the fact that the expression "the grammatical predicate 'is red' " is not a grammatical predicate than there is in the fact that the phrase "the city of Berlin" is not a city. In the material mode of speech Frege was forced into such at least superficially contradictory expressions as "The concept *horse* is not a concept," "The function x^2 is not a function"; but when we are talking about expressions, then we have no motive for denying the obvious fact that the predicate "is a horse" is a predicate, nor for affirming the obvious falsehood that the phrase "the predicate 'is a horse' " is a predicate.

---

[2] This phrase is not Frege's; it is formed by analogy with Frege's term "second-level concept."

[3] *Über Begriff und Gegenstand*, p. 196, second footnote.

A plausible case can therefore be made out for Mr. Marshall's final conclusion without any of his ingenious dialectic. One would, however, have expected him to discuss Frege's reasons for talking not only about concept-words but also about concepts, not only about functional expressions but about functions. Yet he has in fact precluded himself from doing this. In *Über Sinn und Bedeutung* Frege argues (as against Mill and Russell) that proper names [4] must be conceded to have a *sense*; of course, it needs no argument that they also sometimes have *Bedeutung*, in Frege's use of this term. Conversely, no one has ever doubted that such expressions as predicates have *Sinn*; but a justification is required for asserting them to have *Bedeutung*. As Mr. Marshall notes, Frege explained the meaning of his term "concept" by saying that a concept is the *Bedeutung* of a predicate; a concept is what a predicate stands for. The crucial question therefore is why Frege should have ascribed *Bedeutung* to words and phrases other than "proper names": we cannot understand why Frege did not adopt the solution of his difficulties which Mr. Marshall recommends, if we do not try to see why he thought that predicates and functional expressions could be said to stand for something.

Mr. Marshall therefore makes a very serious mistake when, on his first page (note 2), he rules out the possibility of tackling the problem from this angle, by wrongly asserting that Frege did not ascribe *Sinn* to functional expressions such as predicates, and assuming that it is possible in connection with functional expressions to translate the word "*Bedeutung*," without uttering a caution, quite simply as "meaning." If, then, concepts are the meanings of predicates, in no special sense of "meaning," there can appear no satisfactory reason why we need have anything to do with them; we can get on quite well, it seems, with the predicates themselves, with occasional recourse to phrases like "means the same as." The use

---

[4] In the ordinary, as well as in Frege's grossly extended, use of "proper name."

of the term "meaning" here, without further warning, calls up
in the reader's mind vague memories of innumerable polemics
against the hypostatisation of the meanings of words, and it
becomes a foregone conclusion that we shall dismiss Frege as
simply one more philosopher unwilling to use Occam's razor,
and misled into trying to say about the world what should
really have been applied to forms of speech.

Mr. Marshall has been led astray by the fact that the rôle
of the *Sinn-Bedeutung* terminology is quite different in its
application to predicates from its rôle when it is applied to
denoting expressions ("proper names," in Frege's language).
In the latter case the point is the *distinction* between their
Sinn and their *Bedeutung*: Frege was concerned that we
should recognize that a proper name *has* a *Sinn* as well as a
Bedeutung, and that we should not mistake the *Sinn* of a
sentence for its *Bedeutung*; a sentence stands, not for a proposition (a "thought"), but for a truth-value. With predicates
and other functional expressions it is quite different; Frege
was not exercised to point out the *distinction* here. What was
important for him here was that he should have the right to
talk about the *Bedeutung* of such an expression at all. Mr.
Marshall of course does not take the absurd view that predicates do not have sense; he thinks rather that Frege used the
word *"Bedeutung"* to mean in connection with predicates what
he used the word *"Sinn"* to mean in connection with proper
names. This is quite wrong: Frege used the word *"Bedeutung"*
in the same way in both contexts; but whereas his task, with
proper names, was to argue that they have *Sinn*, in the case
of predicates the whole interest lies in their having *Bedeutung*.[5]

It is true that Frege nowhere explicitly *argued* in favour
of the view that functional expressions have *Bedeutung*;

---

[5] It is difficult to give exact references to justify my statement: it was
seldom to Frege's purpose to discuss the sense of functional expressions,
nor did he regard it as necessary to argue that they had sense. But a
careful reading of *Über Sinn und Bedeutung* will make it plain that
Frege had no idea of ascribing *Sinn* only to denoting expressions and
sentences, as will *Grundgesetze der Arithmetik*, vol. I, pars. 2, 29.

rather, he wrote as though it could simply be assumed. Nevertheless, a study of his writings shows what powerful arguments he could have used to justify saying that there is something for which a predicate or a relational expression stands, if this part of his theory had ever been attacked. One of the questions which Frege asked was, "What, when we make a statement of number, are we asserting something *about*?" The general answer to this question, according to him, was "A concept"—the word "concept" being taken to mean, not anything psychological, but rather what is more usually called a property. This question can also be put in the form, "What, in general, is a number the number *of*?" It is not obvious offhand that either of these questions is senseless, or that a better answer can be given than Frege's. But the most important argument for talking of the things for which functional expressions stand is that which has been stated so often and forcibly by Quine—namely that we want to quantify over them. We cannot get on in formal logic without some device similar to that which we employ in ordinary speech when we say such things as "He is something which you are not," or "John was to James what Peter was to Andrew"; for example, for Frege's famous definition of "just as many . . . as," it is essential to use the expression, "There is a relation R such that. . . ." Quine holds that when we introduce variables of a certain kind into quantifiers, we thereby recognize as standing for something that type of expression which could replace a free variable of the kind in question; in the example, we are recognizing all relational expressions as standing for something, or, in Quine's language, we are admitting relations into our ontology. We are talking about the existence of a *relation*; it would be impossible to explain this kind of quantification in terms of the existence of relational *expressions*.[6]

---

[6] Quine uses this argument to justify the introduction of classes: he does not allow that an expression can stand for anything but an *object*, and he therefore wants to pass straight from elementary quantification theory to class theory (see *Methods of Logic*, pt. iv). He would, however, argue that anyone who recognized the intermediate stage of ad-

Mr. Marshall is thus rendered by his misunderstanding incapable of attacking Frege's doctrine relevantly. He aims at arriving at the conclusion that Frege fell into error by trying to say in the material mode of speech what he should have said in the formal mode. If this conclusion is correct, then Frege was wrong to suppose that predicates and other functional expressions have *Bedeutung* at all—that we can with sense speak of concepts and relations and functions. The next step would be to examine Frege's reasons for making this mistake, and see where he went wrong: one would have to show the senselessness of the apparently legitimate question, "What is a number the number of?" and to find the flaw in the at least plausible argument about quantification advanced by Quine. But because he misconstrues Frege's use of the verb *"bedeuten"* in connection with predicates, Mr. Marshall has precluded himself from making any such inquiry. Thinking as he does that Frege meant by "relation" or "concept" the meaning, in a straightforward sense, of a relational or predicative expression, he cannot say that such expressions do not have *Bedeutung*, that there are no such things as relations or concepts in Frege's sense: he merely makes Frege's attempted expression of his doctrine in the material mode look ludicrous. Whereas it is at least intelligible to say that in making a statement of number we are asserting something about a property, about a certain *kind* of thing, it is obvious nonsense to say that we are asserting something about what a word means.

Mr. Marshall says that Frege ought to have stated his theory in terms of linguistic expressions: but until the reader

---

mitting predicate-variables into quantifiers would be committed to "countenancing as entities" concepts and relations, i.e., to regarding one- and two-place predicates as having *Bedeutung*. Frege held that this intermediate stage was essential: the notion of a class cannot, he thought, be understood save via that of a concept.

Frege never actually used Quine's argument explicitly, but he did think that one could replace by variables only those expressions which had *Bedeutung* (see, e.g., *Grundgesetze*, vol. II, app., p. 255).

reaches this remark, he would not have been led by Mr.
Marshall to suppose that anything useful would survive the
translation into the formal mode. It is because Mr. Marshall's
misunderstanding of the term *"Bedeutung"* turns the ma-
terial-mode version into such plain rubbish, that he fails to
make clear how powerful that part of the theory is which
can be put in the form of rules for combining linguistic expressions. For this reason also Mr. Marshall commits a serious
error when he says (p. 389): "For Frege there is no difference in principle between calling a roll and making an assertion about something. In either case we simply utter a series
of names. The difference between these two uses of language
lies, according to Frege, in the things named." It is difficult
to see how, if this were so, the argument, which Mr. Marshall
discusses, that the phrase "the relation of love" cannot stand
for a relation, because "Othello the relation of love Desde-
mona" forms no sentence, but only a string of names, could
have seemed so compelling to Frege. It is utterly wrong to
say that for Frege making an assertion about something was
merely uttering a name, or worse, a series of names. Frege
regarded an assertion as a totally different activity from that
of giving the name of something or of uttering a name. In
the sentence, "The Moon is a satellite of the Earth," there
are two proper names and a part which stands for a relation,
but this does not mean that when I utter the sentence, I am
necessarily doing anything analogous to saying, "Brutus,
Cassius, Cinna." The constituent parts of the sentence stand
for two objects and for a relation, and the sentence as a whole
for a truth-value (in this case, the True), whatever I may
choose to do with the sentence—say, use it to practice my
typing. But if I use it to make an assertion, I am not merely
naming the True, or expressing the thought that the Moon is
a satellite of the Earth; still less am I merely naming two
members of the solar system and a relation. What else I am
doing can be expressed in two ways: I am asserting something; I am saying that the truth-value which the sentence

stands for *is* the True. The first description is correct: assertion is *sui generis*, save perhaps in so far as it can be compared with other linguistic activities like asking a question:
of the assertion sign it is meaningless to ask what its sense
is or what it stands for. The second description is helpful—
the distinction is drawn between merely naming the True
(more strictly, uttering a name of the True), and saying that
what I am naming *is* in fact the True. I should be uttering a
name of the True if I were using the sentence as a subordinate
clause, or to practice my typing, or while acting on the stage,
or considering what logical inferences could be drawn from it
if it *did* stand for the True. But this description is also misleading, in that it would be wrong to assimilate the verbal
phrase "it is true that" to the assertion sign. An actor can
utter a sentence starting, "It is true that . . . ," but he is no
more asserting anything thereby than when he says "The air
bites shrewdly; it is very cold." Again, "it is true that" can,
unlike the assertion sign, occur within a subordinate clause.
We have no assertion sign in ordinary speech; we are left to
grasp from the context whether or not the speaker intends to
make an assertion.

In the *Grundgesetze*, Frege uses the term "name" in a very
extended sense—namely, to apply to any expression which has
Bedeutung; "proper name" he uses to apply to expressions
which stand for objects, as opposed to functions. In Part IV of
his article, Mr. Marshall appears to have become fascinated
by this unusual terminology. Not only has he been led by it
to neglect something on which Frege insisted again and again,
and say that there was no difference for Frege between making
an assertion about something and uttering a series of names;
but he actually offers as a criticism of Frege the fact that the
name of a function cannot with sense replace the name of
an object, whereas just this is one of the principal doctrines
in Frege's whole theory.[7] Of course, Mr. Marshall is perplexed

---

[7] I have failed altogether to understand what Mr. Marshall means by
what he says about "the author of (x)."

by the *Grundgesetze* use of the word "name," because, thinking that the *Bedeutung* of a predicate is its meaning, he cannot recognize the *Grundgesetze* terminology for what it is, a mere variant on the more usual terminology.

Mr. Marshall's arguments against Frege's theory as expressed as a theory of *functions* (concepts, relations, etc.) are based upon a consideration of the various metaphorical expressions which Frege uses to contrast functions and objects. He reaches the conclusion that Frege's use of these expressions no more resembles their ordinary use than that of "any two terms chosen at random." The arguments depend on trying to follow out the metaphors in detail; in all cases, when subjected to this treatment, they break down. Mr. Marshall's comment on this is unexpected: he says that Frege, like Bradley, asked questions about logical parts and wholes which it is sense to ask only about physical parts and wholes. One would have anticipated such an accusation rather to have been directed against Mr. Marshall by someone who wished to defend Frege; for it is after all Mr. Marshall who has asked the inappropriate questions.

Mr. Marshall points out that in calling a function "incomplete" Frege does not mean to imply that one could complete it and thereby get a complete function: a function is as such incomplete; complete it, and you get, not a function, but an object. But it is not enough to say merely that in calling a function "incomplete" Frege meant that it was a part of something else; for objects, too, can be (logical) parts of other objects. Mr. Marshall now suggests that we are intended to think of functions as something like racks. For a full explanation, he says, we have to turn to the other metaphor, that of part and whole. This, however, he finds puzzling for various reasons. First, there is the fact that a whole may be part of one of its parts, which is certainly not true of ordinary parts and wholes. Then, it does not seem to follow, as it ordinarily does, that when all the parts are present and put together correctly, we necessarily have a whole—for example, the function *father of* x and Adam do not combine to yield an object whose parts they would be. Finally, one could have a complete whole, say $2 + 2$, and an incomplete function, $x + 2$, which nevertheless consisted of the same parts, namely the object 2 and the function $x + y$: this does not happen with normal parts and wholes. Mr. Marshall next turns to the possibility that Frege meant simply that a function cannot exist by itself: there must also be objects. But, he says, this applies to other things too, e.g., husbands: for, that there may be husbands, there must also be wives. He then tries a refinement, namely that objects could exist if nothing other than their parts existed, whereas functions can exist only as parts of objects. But he finds this unsatisfactory too, since he has an argument to show that there cannot be just *one* object that is not the value of any function, hence an object could not after all exist if nothing other than its parts existed.

If Frege's metaphors break down, as Mr. Marshall claims, this is no very serious matter; the important question is whether Frege has a right to talk of functions (and not just functional expressions) at all. If he has such a right, it is still only to be expected that any metaphor used to describe their general features will at some point prove unsatisfactory; that, after all, is what a metaphor is. If there are such things as functions at all, then if we want to say things which are true of them in general, we shall be unable to avoid the use of metaphors which after a certain way go lame. Either the metaphor is drawn from something which is not itself a function, and then it will be in some ways inappropriate; or it is drawn from a particular kind of function, and then it will seem to presuppose what it is trying to explain. It is just the same when we want to make general observations about time: either we represent time on the analogy of something which is not a process at all, and then we seem to have left out what is essential to time—change; or we represent time on the analogy of a particular process, and then we notice that time appears in the model not only under the guise of this process, but also in its own right, and we are then tempted down an infinite regress.

Even if we accept Mr. Marshall's challenge to defend Frege's metaphors, we find flaws in his dialectic. Consider the argument that, while it is true that (first-level) functions cannot exist without objects to be their arguments and their values, objects which are the values of functions similarly cannot exist without functions for them to be the values of, that is, they could not be objects which were the values of functions unless there were functions, just as husbands could not be husbands unless there were wives for them to be the husbands of. But as far as functions are concerned, it is not a matter of their not being *functions*, but something else, if there were no objects, but rather of its not making sense to speak of their existence at all. President Eisenhower could not be a husband if there were not a Mrs. Eisenhower, but he could exist; whereas if there were no such things as numbers, we should not say that the function *square of* was not a function—we should attach no sense to speaking of it at all. We cannot know what we mean by "the function $f(x)$" unless we have a principle whereby we may determine what the value of the function is for any argument we choose; whereas we may know whom we mean by "President Eisenhower" without knowing that he has a wife. It is, I think, true, as Mr. Marshall suggests (n. 29), that Frege would have said that there could be no object which was not the value of *some* function; but while we cannot know what it is that we are referring to when we refer to a function if we cannot in principle assign it a value for every possible argument, we can know what we are referring to when we refer to an object without being able to cite every function of which it is a value.

Again, Mr. Marshall argues that the father of Adam is not a complete whole, although its parts seem to be put together correctly. He concedes that Frege says we may give an arbitrary reference to an expression which has not ordinarily got one, but argues against this that in this case it is irrelevant to the question whether we have a complete whole, whether the parts exist or not. For example, he says, the discovery of the golden mountain would then be a complete whole, although one of the parts would be missing—i.e., there is no such thing as the golden mountain. This is a straightforward mistake. If we gave a reference to every definite description, even those that would ordinarily be said not to have one, then if we used the phrase "the golden mountain," we should have given a reference to *this* expression too; and in this case it would be false to say that there was no such thing as the golden mountain or that a part was missing in the discovery of the golden mountain. Mr. Marshall also ignores the fact that Frege elsewhere says that we *must* give a reference to every definite description, otherwise our functions will not be genuine functions nor our concepts genuine concepts; the demand was for him more than a convenience for logical symbolism. If this admittedly paradoxical demand were met, the problem about the father of Adam naturally could not arise.

Looked at in this light, Mr. Marshall's argument here seems to savor of cheating. Frege said that a function served, in conjunction with one or two objects, to make up another object. It could not stand on its own, but could be used only in order to pass from one or more objects to another. Two objects together could not form a new whole; they had to be joined together by a function. It does not seem at first sight to follow from this doctrine that every function must make up, together with the requisite number of objects, however chosen, a new object: it does not seem to follow from the fact that a function cannot exist alone, but only joined on to one or two objects, that a function can be joined on to *any* object or pair of objects that you like to take. This was however precisely the conclusion which, surprisingly, Frege drew: that a function must have a value for every possible object (or pair of objects) that could be mentioned as argument(s). So it is all the more surprising that just what Mr. Marshall takes Frege to task for is failing to draw this conclusion.

Mr. Marshall's puzzlement over Frege's use of the part-whole metaphor is due largely to the fact that he wrongly imagines that for Frege the relation of the parts is itself one of the parts (p. 385). Whatever may have been the case with Bradley, Frege recognized that it is not merely a question of what parts (object or objects and function) make up the whole, but also of how they are put together, i.e., in what positions in the function the objects stand (if there is more than one).[8] For this reason Mr. Marshall is wrong in saying that it is an objection to Frege that $2 + 2$ and $x + 2$ are different although made up of the same parts: Frege was not debarred from saying that the parts were put together differently.

Mr. Marshall finally gives an account of Frege's reasons for not regarding "the relation of difference" as standing for a relation. In Part III of his article, Mr. Marshall says that Frege makes the same mistake as a man who cannot understand why the mere compresence of sticks and a piece of string does not constitute a bundle of sticks; this man makes this mistake because he supposes that the relation which, he is told, the string has to bear to the sticks in order that there may be a bundle, namely that of being tied round the sticks, must itself be either a stick or a piece of string, and he therefore does not see how that would get him any further. Similarly, Frege does not think that what "Bismarck is different from Napoleon" stands for can be analyzed into Bismarck, the relation of difference, and Napoleon, because when the analysis has been made we no longer have any unity, and no further supply of relations of the same kind as the relation of difference can make the matter any better. For this reason, Mr. Marshall thinks, Frege came out with the paradoxical

---

[8] See in particular *Gedankengefüge* (*Beiträge zur Philosophie des deutschen Idealismus*, 1923), with the caution that in his late works Frege expressed his notion of the incompleteness of functions in terms of the incompleteness of their sense rather than of the incompleteness of what they stood for.

view that the relation of difference is not a relation, and it is for this reason also that Frege's account of relations and other functions is so obscure.[9] This is to associate with Frege's thought the familiar idealist objection to analysis, that it destroys what it professes to analyze. So far as I know, no trace of this idea is present in Frege's work.

Although somewhat obliquely, Mr. Marshall is here driving at Frege's actual reason for not regarding the phrase "the relation of difference" as standing for a relation. His account suffers, however, from the misconception to which I alluded above. If we could state correctly the results of the analysis into its parts of what "3 is greater than 2" stands for, we should not, by thus listing the parts, any longer be referring to a unity made up out of these parts. Given the three parts, it is not uniquely determined what whole these parts make up. One of the parts (the relation) has two holes in it, into both of which each of the other two parts fits; thus the three parts, arranged in different ways, make up *two* unities—the True and the False. Frege would therefore not have thought that by listing the parts we even determined which unity they composed; a fortiori, it would be for him no objection to the correctness of the analysis that by listing the parts we were no longer *referring* to (giving the name of) a unity. Frege's difficulty was a different one: just because one of the parts is essentially incomplete, we cannot state correctly which the three parts are. We cannot refer to the relation by using a definite description like "the relation of being greater," because a definite description must stand for something complete, i.e., an object, and thus cannot stand for anything incomplete like a relation; this is so by the definitions of "object" and "relation."

<hr/>

[9] Mr. Marshall's footnote 34, in which he defends Frege's statement, "the function $x + 5$ is not a function," to what would have been Frege's great satisfaction, as no more than "a kind of mild pun," and not a real contradiction, is very perplexing here in view of the fact that he is just about to attach great significance—to my mind, rightly—to Frege's saying this kind of thing.

If, on the other hand, we try to refer to the relation by means of an incomplete expression, an expression with two gaps in it, then we still do not succeed in stating what the part other than the numbers 3 and 2 is, for we have not got a complete sentence.

This difficulty is seen under examination to be a real one, and not to be brushed aside, as Frege tried to brush it aside, as a trifling inconvenience of our language. Nor can it be solved as easily as Mr. Marshall suggests (p. 384), by saying that "the relation of difference" stands for the same thing as ". . . is different from . . ." stands for. We cannot say this, because we come by the notion of a relation via the distinction between relational expressions and others, and "the relation of difference" is not a relational expression. A relation, that is, is *explained* as being that for which a relational expression stands, and hence if we allow that an expression of a different kind can stand for a relation, the whole explanation of what a relation is falls to the ground. To put this in another way, if we are going to talk about relations at all, we shall do so because we find it necessary to quantify over them; and, in order to see clearly what kind of quantification this is, we have to construe it on the model of "There is something which John was to James which Peter was not to Paul," rather than on that of "There is a relation which John had to James which Peter did not have to Paul."

In his Part II, because of his misunderstanding about Frege's use of *"Bedeutung"* and his failure to see the point of saying that predicative, relational, and functional expressions stand for something, Mr. Marshall's criticisms of Frege are for the most part either trifling or beside the mark. In his Part III, despite the partial error that I have mentioned, which lies in his account of why Frege said that the relation of difference was not a relation, he has put his finger on the weakest spot in the whole theory. This (at first sight trivial) difficulty shows conclusively that the two parts of Frege's theory—the method of classifying expressions into "proper names," first- and second-level concept-words, etc., and the doctrine that each of these kinds of expression stands for something—will not hang together; some modification is called for. But because Mr. Marshall does not ever really appreciate the case for Frege's denial that "the relation of difference" stands for a relation, he cannot really tackle this problem either.

15

Class and Concept

PETER T. GEACH

A good many philosophers, following Carnap, take both the Fregean distinction between sense and reference, and that between a concept and its extension, to be pretty much the same as the traditional distinction between intension and extension. This interpretation can, I think, be decisively refuted. First, Frege held a purely extensional view of concepts. He adopted the mathematician's attitude toward definitions—that it does not much matter which definition you choose, so long as the same objects come under it; and he expressly says that, though proper identity holds only between objects, the analogue of identity for concepts holds if and only if concepts are coextensive, i.e., have the same objects falling under them.[1] Secondly, the Fregean distinction of sense and reference is founded on quite a different feature of language from that used in old-fashioned discussions about intension and extension (as also by Carnap), viz., the contrasting pairs of concrete and abstract nouns. Thus, "humanity" is related to "men" as abstract to concrete; one would refer to an intension as "the property (of) humanity" and to the corresponding ex-

---

Reprinted with the kind permission of the author and the editor from *The Philosophical Review*, LXIV (1955), 561-570.

[1] *Philosophical Writings of Gottlob Frege*, ed. and trans. by P. Geach and M. Black (Oxford, Blackwell, 1952), p. 80. The original sources and paginations are stated in this edition.

tension as "the class of men." Frege, on the other hand, says that the sense of a name like "the class of men" is itself referred to (not by an abstract noun like "humanity" but) either by the use of that very name in an indirect-speech construction ("Aristotle thought that the class of men had no first member")[2] or, in non-oblique contexts, by an expression of the form "the sense of 'A' "—e.g., "the sense of 'the class of men.' "[3] And so, thirdly, we can show that a concept is not, for Frege, the sense of the name of the corresponding class. For a concept is the reference of a predicate, e.g., of the predicate ". . . is a man"[4]; and plainly this has quite a different reference from "the sense of 'the class of men,' " since the two expressions are never interchangeable *salva veritate* (Frege's test for identity of reference).

Why then distinguish between a concept extensionally regarded and a class or extension? Frege says that extensions are objects and concepts are not.[5] But what then makes concepts not to be objects? Frege replies: *Ungesättigtheit*—unsaturatedness. But I shall not try to explain and defend this part of his doctrine, sound as I believe it to be; we should be led too far, over an obscure and debated territory.

Let us try again with another of his explanations—that a concept is the reference of a predicate, what a predicate stands for. We may well be tempted to ask what are the relations expressed by "reference of" and "stands for" and how they differ from other semantical relations; if we yield, we shall lose ourselves in the wilderness of modern "rigorous" semantics. But we can go another way from here: If A and B are both red, then *there is something*, referred to by the common predicate, *that A and $B* both are. Here the important thing is not the words "referred to" but the existential quantification contained in "there is something that . . ."; as Quine has often urged, what commits one to making predicates stand for con-

---

[2] *Ibid.*, pp. 59, 67.   [3] *Ibid.*, p. 59.
[4] *Ibid.*, p. 43, footnote.   [5] *Ibid.*, p. 32.

cepts, to holding that *there are* concepts, is this replacement of predicates by existential quantification.

"But if you say the predicate 'red' stands for something, and call what it stands for a concept, then you are treating it as if it were a proper name; you cannot escape this by using the verb 'stand for' instead of 'name,' or by saying 'red' is an incomplete, *ungesättigt*, expression. Like Frege, you are blurring out again the distinction he rightly made between a concept word and a name; concept words are after all names, naming a queer sort of entities. This is just like saying that 'some man' stands for some man, only not for any definite man but for an indefinite man. No wonder we find in Frege such tangles about the *Ungesättigtheit* of concepts!"

This criticism breaks down because when we recognize a common predicate, replaceable by an existential quantifier, there need not be even the appearance of our wrongly making out something to be a name. "Smith cut Smith's throat" and "Jones cut Jones' throat" have a recognizable common predicate, and we can say that there is something that Smith and Jones and Castlereagh all are. (Of course "that [they] all *did*" would be a more idiomatic expression; but this is just because "did" is more natural than "are" as grammatical proxy for a predicate formed with a verb in the past tense rather than with "is" followed by a noun or adjective.) But this in no way looks like taking some word or phrase in the two sentences as a proper name of a concept. Similarly, the common predicate in "*A* is red" and "*B* is red" is not just "red" or "is red" but consists in the two sentences' both being formed by writing "is red" after a proper name.

Now if we allow every predicate of objects to stand for a concept, we have to go on and make a sharp distinction between concept and object. For let us suppose that a concept is an object, and can accordingly be given a proper name. From the proper names of concepts we can now form predicates in the following uniform way: That an object falls under the concept whose proper name is "*D*" is to be expressed by writing the name of that object in brackets after "D." We may speak of the predicate "$D(\ )$," remembering, in accordance with what we saw just now, that the occurrence of this predicate in a sentence does not consist merely in there being a "$D($" followed after an interval by a "$)$" but also requires that there shall come between the brackets a proper name or a proxy for one. Now in the statements "not $D(D)$," "not $P(P)$," etc., we can recognize, besides the predicates "$D(\ )$," "$P(\ )$," etc., just introduced, a common predicate as well; for clearly "not $D(D)$" is the same predication about the concept D as "not $P(P)$" is about the concept P. If every common predicate stands for a concept, this one will; and on our present supposition we may give this concept a proper name, "W." From this again we may construct a predicate "$W(\ )$" as above explained. Thus "$W(\ )$" will mean the same as the common predicate in "not $D(D)$" and "not $P(P)$," so that "$W(D)$," "$W(P)$," mean the same as "not $D(D)$," "not $P(P)$." But if so, what will "$W(W)$" mean? The same as "not $W(W)$," which is absurd. To escape this absurdity, we must deny that any concept is an object or can have a proper name; and the two sorts of quantification that answer to proper names and to predicates must be strictly distinguished.

This requirement is not hard to fulfill in a symbolic language; and observe that if we use two styles of quantifier, as Frege did in his *Grundgesetze*, we are not thereby obliged to accept an unending hierarchy of types like Russell's. But it is easy to be misled by phrases like "the concept Man" in philosophical language. Frege himself held that such phrases are proper names, and on that very account stand not for concepts but for objects.[6] I think he went wrong here. Just as "some man" would have to stand for some man if it had any reference at all, so "the concept Man" would have to stand for a concept if it had reference. But "some man" cannot stand for some man, since the question "which man?"

---

[6] *Ibid.*, pp. 45, 46, 49, 50, 54-55.

cannot be answered; and "the concept Man" cannot stand for a concept, for then a concept would have a proper name. We must treat these expressions as just not forming logical units in the sentences where they occur—no more than "Napoleon was a great general" occurs as a logical unit in "The man who finally defeated Napoleon was a great general." "Some man is wise" is an instance not of the simple predicate ". . . is wise," but of a derivative predicate "some . . . is wise," whose contradictory is "no . . . is wise"; and similarly in "The concept Man applies to Socrates" what goes together in "The concept . . . applies to Socrates," which just means "Socrates is (a). . . ." Sentences from which "the concept Man" cannot be thus eliminated, like "the concept Man is an abstract entity," may well be treated as meaningless; *vile damnum*. *General* remarks about concepts, on the other hand, answer to the use of a *quantifier* relating to concepts in a symbolic language.

We had to bring out the necessity in logic for the distinction between concept and object before introducing classes as objects. If there are two predicates neither of which is true of any object that the other is not true of, it seems natural to say that there is an extension common to them both, regarding this as an object; predicates that are true of different things will have differing extensions. (In particular, all predicates true of nothing at all have the same extension.) Thus two predicates that stand for the same concept always determine the same extension, regardless of their wording or sense; it is the concept itself that determines their extension, and we may speak, as Frege does, of the extension *of* a concept. In specifying a particular extension we may accordingly mention a concept whose extension it is, using a predicate to stand for this concept; I shall use as a name for the extension determined (say) by the predicate ". . . cut . . .'s throat" the phrase "the range of x for which x cut x's throat." We have here a paradigm for constructing a name of an extension from any predicate. ("Range" is not meant as a translation of Frege's "*Wertverlauf*.")

Why use a newfangled phrase instead of the Fregean expression "the extension of the concept: x cut x's throat" or the familiar expression "the class (set) of all x's such that x cut x's throat"? The Fregean way of speaking makes use of the pseudo-name "the concept: x cut x's throat"; such pseudonames are to be avoided whenever possible, lest we forget that a concept cannot have a proper name. In my way of speaking, we refer to the concept by using a predicate, and there is nothing that looks like a proper name of the concept.

The familiar way of speaking about classes is even more misleading; it has the look of describing a class by its relation to its members—"that class of which an object is a member if and only if . . ."; the concept comes in only secondarily, because we happen to specify the members as falling under it, and would not have to be mentioned at all if we could list the members by name. Now if a class is constituted as having certain members, how can we arrive at one with no members, such as the extension of an empty concept must be? The null class was introduced into logic by Boole and Schroeder with false identity papers, as the class we are referring to when we use the word "nothing"; and modern logic books too often get over the difficulty with a mixture of sophistry and bluff. If we use "class" and "member" in their ordinary senses, there can be no null class devoid of members. My logic class has as its members the undergraduates whom I teach logic; I could not justifiably enter on my timetable a Hegel class at 9 A.M. every weekday, on the score that the class of people to whom I explain Hegel's philosophy is the same as the class of people I teach at 9 A.M. every weekday, namely the null class.

In point of fact, the familiar senses of "class" and "member" are of no logical importance. The extension of a predicate must be an object correlated with that predicate and with just such other predicates as are true of the same objects; but it is altogether indifferent for logic which object this is. You may think you know which object is called "Geach's logic class of October 1952" and what sort of object this is;

but your supposed knowledge is quite useless in set theory, and there is no reason in that theory to identify the range of x for which x is an undergraduate taught logic by Geach in October 1952 with this object that you think you know, rather than with Geach himself or the moon. (This has a bearing on the view that physical objects can be analyzed away by treating them as classes of more fundamental entities. Given that we know what sense-data are, we can treat the extension of a predicate that is true only of certain sense-data as identical with a certain physical object. But this does not reduce the physical object to a logical construction out of the sense-data; no more than I am reduced to a logical construction out of certain undergraduates, if the object that is the extension of a predicate applying to the undergraduates is taken to be myself.)

We may define "x belongs to y" as meaning: "for some F, y is the range of z for which $F(z)$, and $F(x)$." We can show that if x belongs to y, and y is the range of z for which $G(z)$, then $G(x)$. For if y is both the range of z for which $F(z)$ and the range of z for which $G(z)$, then we have, for any z, $F(z)$ if and only if $G(z)$; otherwise the predicates "$F(\ )$" and "$G(\ )$" would have the same extension y although they were not true of just the same objects, which goes against the meaning of "extension." Now if x belongs to y and y is the range of z for which $G(z)$, then we have by the definition of "belongs to":

For some F, y is both the range of z for which $G(z)$ and that for which $F(z)$, and $F(x)$.

And from this there follows, by our previous result:

For some F, $F(x)$, and, for any z, $F(z)$ if and only if $G(z)$; from which in turn we get: $G(x)$.   Q.e.d.

We thus see that, if there is such an object as the range of z for which $F(z)$, then x will belong to that range if and only if $F(x)$.

The question whether a range or extension belongs to itself

can thus have a perfectly good sense. For, e.g., the range of x for which x is an undergraduate taught logic by Geach in October 1952 may quite well be a human being; and the question whether that range belongs to itself will then be answered by finding out whether that human being was taught logic as an undergraduate by Geach in October 1952. Some logicians who claim to know that it *cannot* make sense to ask whether an extension belongs to itself are making two assumptions: first, that given the objects belonging to A, we can (at least in simple cases) discern an object that is the class of them all, and must identify A with this; secondly, that no predicate can be used without equivocation both for a class so understood and for its members, and that therefore the predicate "member of the class A" cannot be used without equivocation for the class A itself. Even the second assumption is very doubtful; may I not say alike of my logic class taken collectively and of its several members that they were in my room at a certain time? Perhaps I shall be called naïve, and regaled with scholastic subtleties to make me see that the predication is here not univocal. But since I reject the first assumption as well, I shall not be interested.

Since the predicate ". . . is an extension not belonging to itself" makes good sense, it is natural to ask what *its* extension is. But now we find that no object can be its extension—be the range of z for which z is an extension not belonging to itself. For if x were this range, x would belong to x, and thus be an extension belonging to itself, if and only if x were an extension not belonging to itself: Russell's paradox. If we always assign the same extension to coextensive predicates, and different extensions to predicates that are not coextensive, then to certain specifiable predicates we cannot assign any objects as their extensions. There are not enough objects to go round.

The best that we can hope for is to find a certain set of predicates that can all have extensions assigned to them without inconsistency. I would suggest as a basis for set theory the assumption that a predicate has an extension whenever (1) it is expressed wholly by means of truth-functional connectives, quantification over objects, and the symbol for "belongs to"; (2) it is what Quine in *Mathematical Logic* calls "stratified." We need no such restriction on the predicates that are to be taken as standing for concepts.

The theory here sketched is strictly equipollent to Quine's *Mathematical Logic*; quantification over concepts answers to his quantification over Classes, and quantification over objects or extensions answers to his quantification over Elements. (I use capitals to distinguish words given a special sense in Quine's system.) The Members of a Class are what we should call the objects falling under a concept; the Members of an Element are the objects belonging to an extension. Every predicate determines a Class whose Members are (a concept under which there fall) just those Elements (objects) of which the predicate is true. A predicate determines an Element whose Members are just those Elements (a range to which belong just those objects) of which it is true, if it is stratified and Normal, i.e., has all quantifications restricted to Elements (objects); this requirement is a mere different wording of ours. There is an apparent divergence between the two systems in that we sharply distinguish objects and concepts, whereas for Quine every Element is identical with a Class. But an Element's being Identical with a Class means just that they have the same Members; for every Element x there is a Class F such that any Element z is a Member of x if and only if it is a Member of F. This means in our terminology: For every extension x there is an F such that any object z belongs to x if and only if $F(z)$; which is unexceptionable. (It is assumed here tacitly, and explicitly by Quine, that all the objects or Elements over which we quantify are extensions. This leads to no difficulty; for our trouble is that at best there are not enough objects to serve as extensions, not that some objects are unemployed.)

Our system, then, is essentially just a reformulation of

Quine's, and can benefit by the same (relative) consistency proofs. On points of interpretation we of course differ from Quine, since he thinks the distinction between concept and object is unnecessary in logic. I hold with Frege that this distinction is founded in the nature of things, and that a logical system will either express it somehow or turn out inconsistent. In Quine's system the apparently artificial distinction between Class and Element is just the Fregean distinction under a new and misleading guise.

One last point arises about "having enough objects to go round" as extensions. If our set theory is not to be completely trivial, there must be an infinity (at least denumerable) of objects to serve as extensions. But how are we to get this infinity? To prove that if predicates formed according to a certain rule all have extensions, then these extensions will all be distinct, does not yet *give* us all those distinct objects. And I think it is cheating to assume the necessary infinity without proving that *any* infinity in fact exists. But how prove that there is an infinity except by means of a set theory?

I think this difficulty can be overcome. I hold that we can and must recognize numbers as objects apart from any treatment of extensions in general; we have to bring concepts into our account of numbers, but not their extensions. If so, and we can legitimately use numbers to count numbers, we have an infinity independent of any special set theory; for the number of numbers from 0 up to a natural number n is $n + 1$, and the number of natural numbers is greater than any natural number. We can then dismiss our suspicion that our chosen set theory must be wrong somewhere because it brings in infinity; and within the theory we can identify the numbers as the extensions of certain predicates. But this would have been quite illegitimate if we had not got the numbers already; this identification is not a recognition of what the numbers, which we could so far only name, really are, but is a conferment of new titles on old friends, whom we already know by sight.

(And which number we identify with which extension is arbitrary.) Frege was not misled in this matter; he recognized that identifying numbers with certain extensions was both open to question and, as regards the nature of number, of altogether secondary importance.[7] The lure others have felt toward regarding numbers as classes of classes arises from an idea that you can start with concrete objects, out of these build groups, and out of like-numbered groups build those super-groups which are numbers—at no point bringing in anything mysterious and nonphysical. But the view that an extension can be built up out of the objects belonging to it is a crude error that I have already exposed; those objects are related to the extension only indirectly, as falling under the concept whose extension it is.

Note

There is an important difference between the paradox developed on p. 287 and Russell's paradox as expanded on pp. 291-92. In Russell's paradox we have a predicate "$W(\ )$" such that "W[the range of x for which $W(x)$]" would have the same *truth-value* as "not W[the range of x for which $W(x)$]"; the paradox is to be resolved not by rejecting the predicate as senseless, but by denying that it has an extension that can be called "the range of x for which $W(x)$." In the other paradox we *seem* to have a predicate "$W(\ )$" such that "$W(W)$" and "not $W(W)$" would have the same *sense*, not just the same *truth-value*; this apparent predicate must therefore really be senseless.

---

[7] *Grundlagen der Arithmetik*, p. 117.

16

Note: Frege on Functions

MICHAEL DUMMETT

By the great kindness of Professor Heinrich Scholz, of the University of Münster (Westphalia), I have been able to see a number of unpublished manuscripts of Frege's which are in Professor Scholz's care. Among several points of general interest which are made clear by these writings of Frege's, the following two are of particular relevance to the controversy between Mr. William Marshall and myself over the interpretation of Frege's doctrine of functions (*Philosophical Review* for July, 1953, and January, 1955).

(1) In a manuscript of 1906, Frege does for once *argue* that those parts of a sentence which are left when one or more "proper names" are removed have a *Bedeutung*. Such an argument would be quite superfluous if, as Marshall holds, by the "*Bedeutung*" of such an expression Frege meant its "meaning" in the ordinary sense. Frege says, e.g., "It is altogether improbable that a proper name should be so different from the remaining part of a singular sentence that it should be important for it alone to have a *Bedeutung*. . . . It is unthinkable that there could be a *Bedeutung* only in the case of proper names, and not in the remaining part of the sentence." For example, Frege argues, when we make a relational state-

Reprinted with the kind permission of the author and the editor from *The Philosophical Review*, LXV (1956), 229-230.

ment we are saying that the "relation obtains between the *Bedeutungen* of the proper names" which we are using; this relation, he continues, "must therefore itself belong to the realm of *Bedeutungen*"—and not, that is, to the realm of sense.

(2) In his article Marshall attacked as incomprehensible the metaphors which Frege used in speaking about functions; in particular Marshall attacked Frege's use of the metaphor of whole and part. This metaphor I defended in my reply to Marshall; but another unpublished manuscript of Frege's shows that he himself in the end abandoned it. One has to say, I think, not so much that it is an error to regard, e.g., the argument of a function as a part of the value of the function for that argument, as that it is a singularly unhappy metaphor. It has the same disadvantages as if, in discussing the relative architectural merits of two houses, one were to say that one was not in the same street as the other. That is, in many cases, there is an obvious non-metaphorical application of the expressions "part" and "whole." Frege uses as an example the phrase "the capital of Denmark"; one cannot, he says, say that Denmark is a part of the reference of the whole expression, namely Copenhagen. This, rather than Marshall's arguments, is in my view the real objection to the part-whole metaphor. Frege concludes that while the sense of part of an expression is a part of the sense of the whole, we have to deny that the reference of part of an expression is part of the reference of the whole. In view of this retraction of Frege's, it would I think be better if those who discuss Frege's theory of functions concentrated not on the part-whole terminology, but rather on his saying of a function that it is *unselbständig*—that it cannot stand on its own.

The metaphor which is really important, as it seems to me, is that whereby Frege speaks of concepts (properties) and relations in analogy with mathematical functions: it is by the appropriateness or inappropriateness of this analogy that Frege's account stands or falls. Admittedly Frege thought that this was no metaphor; since, on his view, sentences stand for objects, concepts and relations are just particular cases of functions of one and two arguments respectively. But if anyone rejects Frege's view of sentences as standing for truth-values, then it is only an analogy; but to my mind it is the correct analogy, without which we cannot understand the nature of general terms, or even begin to discuss with sense the fundamental question, whether there is in the world any non-linguistic correlate of the meaning of such a term—in Frege's terminology, whether general expressions have *Bedeutung*.

17

Sense and Reference: A Reply

WILLIAM MARSHALL

I

The intended scope of Frege's distinction between the sense
and the reference of names (a technical term that includes
predicates, sentences, and other expressions not ordinarily
called names) is not easy to determine, despite the unusual
clarity of his work. Did he mean that it should be extended
to every kind of name, including predicates, or restricted to
proper names alone? Certainly he speaks both of a predicate's
sense and its reference, but whether this implies a distinction
and, in particular, whether these terms are unambiguous, having the same meaning for both proper names and predicates,
are questions to which conflicting answers are given.

Mr. Michael Dummett, in his discussion of my article
"Frege's Theory of Functions and Objects" (*Philosophical
Review*, LXII [1953], 374-390), answers these questions in
the orthodox way.[1] He believes that Frege did mean to extend his distinction between sense and reference to each kind
of name. Frege, he says, certainly did use "reference" the
same way in each context and certainly did mean to ascribe

Reprinted with the kind permission of the author and the editor from
The Philosophical Review, LXV (1956), 342-361.

[1] M. Dummett, "Frege on Functions: A Reply," *Philosophical Review*, LXIV (1955), 96-107.

a sense (i.e., in his technical use of the word) to predicates (p. 98).

As Dummett himself remarks, however, it is not easy to cite passages in support of this answer. For although Frege is careful to distinguish the sense and reference of proper names, he is reluctant to ascribe a sense to predicates, and when he does, he usually identifies it with the reference.

Dummett tries to explain Frege's reluctance to ascribe a sense to predicates by supposing he justifiably took the sense for granted and concentrated on explaining the nature of the reference (p. 98). But would Frege also take it for granted that a predicate sometimes *expresses* its sense and sometimes *refers* to it? His notion of a name's sense is, after all, a technical one. Nobody would ever deny that a normal man has ideas in his mind, colloquially speaking, but whether he has ideas as John Locke, for example, used the word is undoubtedly controversial and ought not be taken for granted. Similarly, nobody would deny that predicates have a meaning, but that does not obviously imply, and may not imply, that they also have a sense as that word is explained in Frege's "Ueber Sinn und Bedeutung."

Besides, Frege could, in a way, take it for granted that sentences have a sense, but that did not keep him from explaining what the sense is, nor how it differs from the reference. No doubt he would have done the same for predicates had he seen how that were possible. But given his analysis of predicates, he could not apply the sense-reference distinction to them without essentially modifying it. To do so he would have had to abandon his most basic view, the "incompleteness" of predicates and concepts—together with all that it implies: in particular, that a concept is the reference of a predicate.

Usually Frege does not distinguish between a predicate's sense and its reference but identifies both with the concept (*Begriff*). This is not linguistic carelessness; rather, the logic of predicates forces him to do this. The notion of a predicate's reference has to have important features in common with that of a proper name's sense. The explanation of why this is true has important bearing upon two puzzling questions—namely, abstract existence and the logical paradoxes.

II

There is only one place, so far as I know, paragraph 32, Volume I of the *Grundgesetze,* where Frege ascribes to predicates a sense distinct from the reference; and there he distinguishes the sense and the reference of names in general. In the other places (e.g., in "Ueber Begriff und Gegenstand") where he speaks both of a predicate's sense and its reference, the two are not distinct, and the words, in fact, mean the same thing.

Moreover, in the passage I mentioned, where Frege, contrary to his usual practice, does distinguish the sense and the reference of each kind of name, he writes mostly about sentences—saying the sense is a thought and the reference a truth value—and does not explain how we should apply the distinction to other names (a sentence being for him the name of a truth value). He explains this for proper names, in "Ueber Sinn und Bedeutung," and in many places says that a predicate's reference is a concept, but in no place does he ever clearly say how we should think of a predicate's sense (i.e., insofar as it does not mean the reference). Is a concept also a predicate's sense, or is something else the sense? Is a predicate's sense always different from the reference, or do they sometimes coincide? Can a predicate have a sense but no reference? Does a predicate, like a proper name, have an indirect sense as well as a customary one?

In the passage I mentioned, Frege says that the sense of a constituent name within a sentence is its contribution to the sense of the sentence, the thought, and that it is part of the thought; but this does not contain an answer to the above questions. Yet he does not discuss the sense of predicates in any other place, not even in "Ueber Sinn und Bedeutung,"

for the discussion there of sense and reference, although by
far the most detailed that he ever gives, is carefully restricted
to proper names—i.e., names of objects. For a discussion of
concepts and relations, which are functions rather than objects,[2] and of their names, too, apparently, he refers us to
a forthcoming work, doubtless "Ueber Begriff und Gegenstand."

He explains in the former article that a proper name, for
brevity called simply a name, has a sense but not necessarily
a reference; that a name regularly has both a customary and
an indirect sense and reference; that the sense of a name is
understood by anyone sufficiently familiar with the language
to which it belongs, but "in grasping a sense, one is not certainly assured of a reference" (p. 58); and that the sense
"serves to illuminate only a single aspect of the reference,
supposing it to exist. Comprehensive knowledge of the reference would require us to be able to say immediately whether
every given sense belongs to it. To such knowledge we never
attain" (p. 58). (We can evidently have a complete understanding of the sense but never a complete knowledge of the
reference.)

Some consequences, more or less immediate, though not
actually drawn by Frege, are the following: (a) The sense of
a name is always distinct from the reference. (b) The sense
determines what object the reference is, so that one who has
grasped the sense can decide whether any given object is the
reference, provided he has sufficient knowledge of it. (The
sense of, e.g., "the teacher of Alexander the Great" seems to
be a property belonging to Aristotle alone, who is thus the
name's reference. That the sense is a property [or concept]
conflicts, however, with Frege's view that properties must be
"incomplete," and so he never says it is.) (c) By a definition

---

[2] They are functions "whose value is always a truth value" (p. 155).
The reference, here and elsewhere, is to *Translations from the Philo-
sophical Writings of Gottlob Frege*, by Max Black and Peter Geach
(Oxford, 1952).

we can explain the sense and even endow the name with a
new sense; but a well-defined and well-understood name—
such as "the man over forty feet high," for example—may
nevertheless lack a reference.

Of these various features which belong to Frege's distinction between the sense and the reference of proper names, few
if any can be extended without conflict to the case of predicates, as he understands them. For example, anyone who
understands a predicate is assured of its reference, as I shall
show later on. Hence it is not altogether surprising that in the
article to which he refers us, "Ueber Begriff und Gegenstand,"
where concepts and their names, i.e., predicates, are discussed
at length, Frege barely mentions the sense-reference distinction, and then only in relation to proper names. Moreover,
he uses the words interchangeably, as if believing his technical distinction would not fit the new subject matter; so that
his use of terms here is, for example, like that of a naturalist
who makes a technical distinction between two kinds of birds
and then later, seeing a bird similar to both, calls it by the
name of either.

Frege's main purpose in the article, to explain what he
understands by a concept, requires that he tell us how to
recognize one, and he does so in two ways, appealing each
time to grammatical predicates. He says at first that a concept is the reference (*Bedeutung*) of a grammatical predicate
(p. 43). It therefore has a predicative nature—this being just
a special case of the "incompleteness" or "unsaturatedness"
that is the essential feature of all functions—and hence must
be sharply distinguished from the reference of any expression
that can serve as a grammatical subject. The reference of
such an expression as "the concept *horse*" is, therefore, not
really a concept, in spite of appearances; since the expression
may serve as a subject, its reference is "complete," hence is
an object. The reference of a predicate, on the other hand,
being "incomplete," is a function, and in particular, a concept.

Later on, however, he describes concepts in a different way, saying predicates have an "unsaturated" or "incomplete" sense and identifying this with the concept:

Not all the parts of a thought can be complete; at least one must be unsaturated or predicative; otherwise they would not hold together. For example, the sense of the phrase "the number 2" does not hold together with that of the expression "the concept *prime number*" without a link. We apply such a link in the sentence "The number 2 falls under the concept *prime number*"; it is contained in the words "falls under," which need to be completed in two ways—by a subject and an accusative; and only because their sense is thus unsaturated are they capable of serving as a link [p. 54].

A concept, therefore, may be called in Frege's system either the sense or the reference of a predicate; for he calls it both. Relations are described analogously. The phrase "falls under," he says, has an unsaturated sense and "such words or phrases stand for (*bedeuten*) a relation" (p. 54).

Such an account of concepts (and relations) is not peculiar to "Ueber Begriff und Gegenstand," for in the *Grundgesetze* and also in the late writings,[3] Frege sometimes thinks of a concept as the sense of a predicate (though he would rather think of it as the reference). He says in paragraph 56, Volume II, of the *Grundgesetze*:

Any object Δ that you choose to take either falls under the concept ϕ or does not fall under it; *tertium non datur*. E.g., would the sentence "Any square root of 9 is odd" have a comprehensible sense at all if *square root of 9* were not a concept with sharp boundaries? Has the question "Are we still Christians?" really got a sense if it is indeterminate whom the predicate "Christian" can truly be asserted of and who must be refused it?

The sentence "We are still Christians," he says in substance, using a rhetorical question, has no sense if *Christians* is not a well-defined concept. From this it follows, as a matter of course, that the concept, as he thinks of it here, is the predicate's sense. If it were merely the reference, its being defective could have no effect upon the sense of the sentence. As he says in "Ueber Sinn und Bedeutung," "If it were a ques-

---

[3] In "Gedankengefüge" (*Beiträge zur Philosophie des deutschen Idealismus* [1923]), and others, according to Dummett, *op. cit.*, p. 105.

tion only of the sense of the sentence, the thought, it would be unnecessary to bother with the reference of a part of the sentence; only the sense, not the reference of the part is relevant to the sense of the whole sentence" (p. 63).

Frege, then, often does think of a concept as both the sense and the reference of a predicate, in spite of what he says in the *Grundgesetze*, Volume I, paragraph 32, about the two being distinct. Dummett thinks (p. 105) this is an aberration of Frege's late writings, whereas actually it occurs in the earlier works as well, as we have seen.

Someone who—like Dummett—thinks Frege intended without qualification to apply the sense-reference distinction to predicates might wish to say that sense and reference are sometimes identical but never synonymous. Just as one and the same person can be both father and employer of some man, so one and the same concept can be both sense and reference of some expression. For proper names sense and reference are always different, for predicates not, but the terms themselves are used the same way for each.

Whether Frege would have accepted this explanation is doubtful. In "Ueber Sinn und Bedeutung" the sense and the reference of a name are held to be distinct, and if he intended an exception for predicates, no doubt he would have said so in some place or other. The truth is, he probably knew that if "sense" and "reference" were to be used in the same way for both proper names and predicates, then they could not possibly coincide for the latter. Hence the fact that he usually lets them coincide for predicates shows he probably did not intend, on the whole, to extend the distinction to predicates.

(i) The sense of a proper name, as we have already seen, determines what the reference is, if there is one. The sense of, for example, "the teacher of Alexander the Great" belongs to Aristotle, who is thus the name's reference, determined by the sense. Now if the sense of a predicate, for example "man," were a concept (or property), the reference it determined would be what fell under the concept (or that to which the property belonged). But then the sense and reference of the predicate could never coincide, because a concept, on Frege's type theory, can never fall under itself. On his analysis, the sentence "The concept *man* is a man," besides expressing what is false, is not even about a concept. Hence the reference determined by a concept, supposing it were a predicate's sense, could never be that concept itself. To say that sense and reference coincide for predicates would require us, therefore, to abandon the stipulation that the sense determines what the reference is (i.e., if the reference is a concept, as Frege holds).

(ii) Frege says in "Ueber Sinn und Bedeutung" that if we replace one word of a sentence by another having the same reference, this can have no bearing upon the reference of the sentence; and that in indirect discourse, words do not have their customary reference but refer to what is customarily their sense. If this is so—and certainly it partially describes what is meant by the sense and reference of proper names— then again the sense and reference of predicates cannot coincide.

This can be shown in the following way. The sentence

> The square root of 9 is odd   (1)

refers, on Frege's analysis, to a truth value and, moreover, continues to do so as the grammatical subject varies, so long as the latter has a reference. Consequently the sentence

> The sense of "the square root of 9" is odd   (2)

also refers to a truth value—evidently to the False, as he calls it. On the other hand, according to his analysis of indirect discourse, the sentence (1), when occurring as part of the sentence

> A said the square root of 9 is odd

refers to a thought, not a truth value. This could not be the case, however, if the concept *odd* were the predicate's sense. For according to the doctrine of indirect discourse, the parts of (1) would then refer, as do the parts of (2), to the sense of "the square root of 9" and to the concept odd. The reference of the whole being a function of the reference of each part and each part of (1) having the same reference as the corresponding part of (2), the sentence (1) as a whole would in this context have the same reference as (2), namely, the False.

By the same argument, the sentence (1) also refers to a truth value when occurring as part of the expression

The thought that the square root of 9 is odd,

supposing again that the sense of the predicate is a concept. We might say, using Frege's language, that the function "the thought that x" would then have a truth value as its argument; namely, the value of the concept "x is odd" for the argument, the sense of "the square root of 9." Since a thought is not a truth value, the thought that *the square root of 9 is odd* would then be as paradoxical as the concept *horse* that is no concept, discussed in "Ueber Begriff und Gegenstand."

Actually, the argument above does not depend upon the assumption that sense and reference coincide for predicates but upon the assumption that a concept is the customary sense of a predicate.[4] No matter what the customary reference might be, if the sense were a concept and were *referred to* in indirect discourse by the predicate, the relation of the concept to the logical subject would, according to Frege's principles of substitution, be that of a function to its argument. Then, since a concept is a function "whose value is always a truth value," the indirect reference of a sentence would be a truth value instead of a thought. Whether this would also be true if a predicate did not refer in indirect discourse to its customary sense would depend upon what it did refer to, if to anything; but in any case, the notion of a name's sense would have been changed. As for Frege's own view of the indirect reference of a predicate, it is not known;

---

[4] We should not infer from this, however, that a concept is therefore the customary reference of a predicate. Frege did not extend his theory of indirect discourse to predicates.

he never says to what a predicate in indirect discourse refers. For him the important thing about a predicate is the associated concept, sometimes called the sense, sometimes the reference, since—as I shall show later—it is similar to both, as these are explained for proper names.

Dummett thinks that when Frege says a concept is the sense of a predicate, he does not mean it (p. 105); and probably this would be true had he meant to extend to predicates the sense-reference distinction. Then a predicate's sense— which might perhaps be some other function than a concept —would be relevant for determining the reference, and an understanding of the predicate would not imply a reference. But as it is, a predicate's reference, which is a concept, does not have to be determined by something else, any more than does the sense of a proper name; and, moreover, an understanding of the predicate implies a reference, as the understanding of a proper name implies a sense.

The simplest way to extend to predicates the sense-reference distinction as it is explained in "Ueber Sinn und Bedeutung" is to let the sense be a function whose value, unlike that of a concept, is not a truth value,[5] and to let the reference be the class the sense determines, or if not the class, then the *Wertverlauf* (which itself, however, is a type of class).

To each argument of a function $F(x)$ there is correlated the value of the function for that argument (as in plotting a graph in analytical geometry). Thus

$$F(a) \; : \; a$$
$$F(b) \; : \; b$$
$$F(c) \; : \; c$$
.
.
.
$$F(n) \; : \; n$$

The class of all these pairs of objects is the *Wertverlauf* determined by the function.

---

[5] Or we might simply abandon the stipulation that a concept be a function whose value is a truth value and say its value is a thought.

In this way of applying the sense-reference distinction to predicates, which is essentially that of Alonzo Church,[6] the reference is determined by the sense, and the nature of the sense is not in conflict with the doctrine of indirect discourse. Frege himself, however, did not make such an application, probably because he thought a "logical whole" had to contain one or more "incomplete" parts, a view he would have had to give up if a predicate referred to a class or a *Wertverlauf*, since these, being objects rather than functions, are not "incomplete." His reasons for thinking a predicate must refer to something "incomplete," insofar as these concern an analysis of language, will be given later. Here, as in almost every other case, his reasons are excellent.

Church's method of applying the sense-reference distinction to predicates is perhaps not the only one possible; but whether it is or not, the doctrine of "incompleteness" requires that predicates have a sense and a reference—if at all—in a way different from proper names.

(i) One of its consequences is that the reference of a predicate, i.e., the concept, cannot be specified, for (P being a predicate) any assertion of the form "P refers to x" must be false. The predicate "horse," for example, does not refer to anything we can name, not even to the concept *horse*, because the latter, Frege says, is really an object in spite of its name. Since this is not true for proper names—e.g., "Aristotle" refers to Aristotle—they and predicates cannot have a reference in the same way.

Let N be a proper name and P a predicate. Then whereas the assertion

N has a reference

implies

$(\exists x)\,(N$ refers to $x)$,

the assertion

---

[6] Cf. his review of W. V. Quine's "Notes on Existence and Necessity" in the *Journal of Symbolic Logic*, VIII (1943), 45-47.

P has a reference

does not correspondingly imply

($\exists x$) (P refers to x).

That is, whereas N, if it has a reference, satisfies the condition

($\exists x$) (y refers to x),

P, on the contrary, does not, even if it has a reference. Since "P refers to x" is false for any x, existential generalization with respect to x is never valid.

Suppose that although no one whom we could possibly name ever did any work for Mr. B, people who knew this nevertheless said, "B has an employee"—meaning, "For anyone at all, it is determinate whether he would apply to B for a job." Such an employee would be like a predicate's reference, in Frege's sense of the word, for to say a predicate has a reference is to say that for any object, it is determinate whether the predicate applies to it.[7] Just as "B has an employee" does not imply "There is someone whom B employs," so "P has a reference" does not imply "There is something to which P refers."

(ii) A second consequence of the doctrine of "incompleteness" is that a predicate is always to be defined by defining its contexts, and a concept by specifying what properties something must have in order to fall under it. If we say "x is a square" means "x is a rectangle in which the adjacent sides are equal," we must think of the "x" as indicating some unspecified object. The definition explains the predicate "square" for such contexts as "a is a square," "b is a square," and so on, but not for contexts where its "empty space"[8] is not filled—e.g., "x is a square is a concept"; that is, not for contexts where "square" is not used as a predicate. As an alternative definition, we might say: "A square is a rectangle in which the adjacent sides are equal." Frege calls this a

---

[7] Cf. *Grundgesetze*, vol. I, par. 29, where this is implied.

[8] *Ibid.*, par. 21.

definition of the concept *square*,[9] i.e., of the concept to which "square" refers.

From this it is clear that a predicate has a reference if it is adequately defined. Consequently, the only kind of condition that Frege could lay down for predicates' having a reference is the kind he lays down in paragraph 29, Volume I, of the *Grundgesetze*; namely, that a predicate has a reference if the sentence formed of it and a proper name always has a reference (i.e., a truth value) whenever the name has. For predicates of ordinary speech, which are not defined as precisely nor for so wide a range of objects as the predicates of the *Begriffsschrift* he had in mind, this condition is too strict and would have to be relaxed somewhat. Whether certain objects are, for example, red or not, is probably indeterminate, but it is nevertheless obvious that Frege would not care to say that such predicates as "red" are without a reference, for he often speaks of their reference.

Thus a predicate's reference is very much like a proper name's sense. Whereas a definition endows a proper name with a sense (though not with a reference), it endows a predicate with a reference. Frege says that in grasping the sense of a proper name, one is not certainly assured of a reference. This is not true for predicates. Anyone who understands the sense of a predicate knows whether to assert it of various kinds of objects, provided he has the relevant facts about them at hand. A person who could not say whether Indians are red would not have grasped the sense of that predicate— perhaps through lack of familiarity with English; but if he has grasped its sense, he should know it has a reference. Indeed, there is no difference between them.

We can now see why Frege is indifferent about calling a concept both the sense and the reference of a predicate. For if by a definition predicates are endowed with a reference, then the distinction between their sense and reference has been obliterated.

---

[9] *Ibid.*, p. xiv.

We can also see why Frege's view of concepts is extensional.[10] To describe a given concept, we say that if an object has such and such characteristics, it falls under the concept. This is like describing a man by stating what properties someone has to have in order to be a relative of him. Imagine that someone said: "I cannot describe my coat directly, but I can give you the measurements of everyone whom it would fit (or a list of everyone whom it would fit)." This would give us some information about the coat's size, but not about its other features. Still, if that were all we could say about coats, and if we required a criterion of identity, then we should have to say that coats fitting the same people were the same coat.

In my article discussed by Dummett, I took the position that the peculiarities ascribed by Frege to concepts are really an appearance, caused by looking at their names—or rather at what are taken to be their names—from a certain standpoint. If this position is correct, predicates cannot have a reference in the way proper names have. Dummett is wrong, however, when he says (p. 98) that on my interpretation of Frege, a concept is the sense, not the reference, of a predicate. My interpretation is, as I have already explained, that a concept may be called either the sense or the reference of a predicate. Moreover, I think, as I shall explain later, that Frege had a good reason to say that predicates have a reference. Certainly I do not object to Frege's—or to anyone else's—calling a predicate a name, though a peculiar kind of name, so long as this does not obscure important logical differences between predicates and proper names. It sometimes causes us to think, however, that, for example, the predicate "master" and the proper name "Aristotle" are more alike than they actually are. I believe this is one reason that Frege tried to explain the seemingly peculiar "incompleteness" of predicates by attributing a corresponding peculiarity to concepts. But that we need something so peculiar as the

---

[10] Cf. p. 80.

"Ungesättigtheit der Begriffe" to account for the logical differences between predicates and proper names hardly seems
necessary. The doctrine does not explain what it is supposed
to, anyway. Essentially, it means that concepts cannot exist
apart from their arguments; but that fails to explain why
concepts cannot be named apart from their arguments. To
name something is not to remove it from its setting.

Mr. Peter Geach, in his article "Class and Concept," [11] says
he holds with Frege that the distinction between concepts and
objects is founded in the nature of things, and he argues that
if we try to blur it by treating a concept as an object, we
involve ourselves in a paradox. His argument is substantially
the following:

Grant that every predicate refers to a concept; and suppose
that a concept is an object and can accordingly be given
a proper name. If *"D"* is the proper name of some concept,
the expression *"D(x)"* means "*x* falls under *D*." Now since
every predicate refers to a concept, so, in particular, does
"*x* falls under *x*" and hence "not-(*x* falls under *x*)." Call the
concept to which the latter refers by the proper name *"W."*
Then "*x* falls under *W*," or *"W(x)*," will mean "not-(*x* falls
under *x*)." Consequently, *"W* falls under *W*" will mean
"not-(*W* falls under *W*)," which is an absurdity, Geach says.

Suppose that a shopkeeper sells two kinds of jewelry—
namely, *A*'s and *B*'s. The *B*'s are marked with a price and are
sold either by themselves or attached to an *A*. The *A*'s are not
marked with a price and are not sold alone. To find the price
of an *AB,* the merchant uses the rule: multiply the price of
the *B* by two. But what if he attaches an *A* to itself and tries
to compute its price by the old rule? He might reason: An
AA is simply an *A*; so by my rule, the price of an *AA* is
always twice what it actually is, which is absurd. What
should the merchant say?—"I should not have done what I
did. I have gone against the nature of things. The true state
of affairs has now asserted itself"?

<hr/>

[11] *Philosophical Review,* LXIV (1955), 561-570.

In this example we see the kind of circularity that Russell takes to be the essence of many paradoxes. To compute the monetary value of certain objects, using the given rule, we should have to know it already. But if we do know it already, the rule is unnecessary, and if we do not know it, the rule is useless. Indeed, the rule could be used only if the notion of monetary value were, so to speak, ambiguous. If using a rule R we compute one value for the object, and then using a second rule R' we make use of the first value to compute a second, we get conflicting values; but that should not be surprising.

Geach—and others, of course, who derive Russell's paradox for properties—introduces an apparent relational predicate, "falls under" (or some logically similar phrase such as "satisfies" or "belongs to"), and an apparent name of the form "the concept F"; and uses them in such a way that "x falls under the concept F" means simply "$F(x)$." The sentences "Socrates is a man" and "Socrates falls under the concept *man*," for example, both make the same assertion about Socrates. We should expect, therefore, to find that "is a man" and "the concept *man*" are logically different, for otherwise "falls under" would have no function. If the former refers to a concept, then the latter, it seems, does not—or a least not to the same concept; and the question arises, to what does it refer?

Geach, unless I have misunderstood him, would say it does not refer to anything, for it is an incomplete symbol; and I think this is correct. If so, the phrase "falls under" does not refer to a relation after all. We cannot separate out "falls under" from predicates such as "falls under the concept *man*" and "falls under the concept *horse*" and treat it as a predicate in its own right. Nor can we ask whether a concept falls under itself.

To take a particular case, suppose we ask: Is "the concept *man* is a man" (or using Frege's notation, "*is a man* is a man") true or false? The phrase "the concept *man*," which is ordinarily the accusative of its sentence, is here the subject and so cannot be got rid of. What it means is, therefore, not at all clear. One might suppose that we could explain it by explaining the predicate "man," but this is not true. A predicate is explained by explaining what values it expresses for the various possible arguments, but it is not explained for cases where it occurs without an argument—i.e., with its "empty spaces" unfilled.

Nevertheless, what we want is that "the concept *man*" refer to the concept expressed by the predicate of the sentence "The concept *man* is a man"; and it seems as if we could explain the phrase in that way. But the trouble with such an explanation is that since concepts with different extensions are different concepts, we cannot determine (i.e., if we accept the explanation) to which concept the predicate refers until we first determine to which concept "the concept *man*" refers, and this kind of circularity conflicts with the nature of predicates. Does "the concept *man*" refer to the concept containing the reference of that expression within its extension, or not? To answer the question, we should have to know the reference of "the concept *man*," and we have not yet said what it is. The reference varies, depending upon which answer we give to the question whether the concept *man* falls under itself.

If someone asks, "Is cow *A* black or not?", we should like to know which cow *A* he has in mind before we try to answer. If he said, "Answer the question first, and then you shall know," his question would be similar to the one above. But this shows that "the concept *man*" cannot refer to a concept—i.e., that it cannot function as predicates do. Jesus Christ may or may not have been a man, but how we answer the question has no bearing upon the sense (or reference) of the predicate "man." In general, the definition of a predicate is logically prior to the question whether it applies to any given thing; and consequently its sense is not affected by how the question is to be answered. As Russell says, "A function is not a well-defined function unless all its values are already well-defined." [12] (A predicate is a special case of a function, as Russell uses the word.)

To say that a predicate refers to a concept is merely to say that the predicate's values for a certain class of arguments is determinate, and this presupposes that the predicate be used as a predicate. (Its essential characteristic, Russell says, is ambiguity.) [13] If we use the predicate as a subject, it cannot in that context refer to a concept, and what it does refer to is not known, because we have not given it a meaning. On the other hand, in expressions such as "x falls under the concept *man*," the term "man," although not used as a predicate, is nevertheless clear, the reason being that the whole context —which means "x is a man"—is clear.

The expression "falls under" is, therefore, merely a linguistic device for reading an expression of the form "$F(x)$," and whatever the latter means will be what "x falls under F" will mean. If the latter means "not-(x falls under F)," that is what "x falls under F" will mean. If it means nothing, that is what "x falls under F" will mean.

Until we specify what predicate "F" represents, the expression "$F(x)$" does not refer to anything; hence, neither does "x falls under F." To say that "x falls under F" is a predicate is, therefore, like saying "x is a man" is a proposition. It is not itself a proposition, but it becomes a proposition when the "x" is replaced by a name. Similarly, "x falls under F" is not itself a predicate, any more than is "$F(x)$," but it becomes one when "F" is replaced by a predicate. If we wished to call "x falls under F" a predicate, we should have to call it a variable predicate, as $G(x)$—though not log x or sin x—might be called a variable function. In "x hits himself," we can think of the predicate as "( ) hits ( )." If we do the same with "x falls under itself," we get "( ) falls under ( )." But "x falls under itself" means "$x(x)$," and should "( )" be called a pred-

[12] *Principia Mathematica*, 2d ed. (Cambridge, 1950), p. 39.
[13] *Loc. cit.*

icate? How would one express it aloud? By saying nothing?

To say that "x falls under itself" is a senseless expression does not, of course, explain the paradox (though it will make its derivation impossible), for many expressions are senseless but do not generate paradoxes. But then we do not try to explain most expressions by their own negations, either. Someone who introduced the expression "$G(x)$" might define it by giving a rule determining the value it expressed for each argument—e.g., to get the value, take the square of the argument. Then $G(x)$ would be the function $y = x^2$. For the expression "$W(x)$," used above in deriving Russell's paradox, the rule is: Take the negation of what results from having the argument x fall under itself. This is obviously circular, since "x falls under W," meaning "$W(x)$," already contains the words "falls under." According to the rule, the value expressed by "$W(W)$" is the same as that expressed by "not-$W(W)$"; so that to find the former, we should have to know it already, and then "$W(x)$" would have a meaning different from the one we tried to give it by stating our rule. Using two different rules, we might get conflicting values for "$W(W)$"; but then $W(W)$ if and only if not-$W(W)$ would be an ambiguity, not a contradiction.

Since the sentences "Socrates is a man" and "Socrates falls under the concept *man*" both make the same assertion about Socrates, it is not surprising that "is a man" and "the concept *man*" are logically different. The consequences of treating them as if they were logically identical are, perhaps, about what we ought to expect—i.e., senselessness and circularity. So when confronted by certain paradoxes, we can say in a way, echoing Frege, "Die Wahre Sachlage hat sich geltend gemacht."

The function of "falls under" in a sentence is, according to Frege, twofold. It links together the grammatical subject and accusative; and it refers to a concept that links together the logical subject and accusative. It is "incomplete" and its sense is "incomplete." It is a peculiar name of a peculiar thing—

like all predicates. Thus Frege's reasons for saying predicates and concepts are "incomplete" are closely related to the logical differences between such expressions as "is a man" and "the concept *man*."

These differences show, however, that there is an incompatibility among the following principles of the name relation, all of which have been, and still are, widely accepted; and this, too, is closely related to the doctrine of "incompleteness."

(i) If one can quantify with respect to an expression, it is a name, i.e., it has a reference. As Quine says, "A word *W* *designates* if and only if existential generalization with respect to *W* is a valid form of inference." [14]

(ii) Two names with the same reference are interchangeable, *salva veritate*.

(iii) What a name refers to can always be described as the so-and-so.

By the first principle, the predicate of "Socrates is a man" must be a name with a reference; for we can infer "There is an f such that f(Socrates)," as we can infer "There is an x such that x is a man." Suppose, then, we ask what the reference is. Frege says, "A concept." To the question "What concept?", the natural answer would be "The concept *man*"; but this, though in accord with the third principle, is in conflict with the second. The result of substitution, "Socrates is the concept *man*," or (taking the predicate in a different way) "Socrates the concept *man*," is, if not senseless, then false. As Frege says, in a similar context, of the expressions "square root of 4" and "the concept *square root of 4*," they "have an essentially different behavior, as regards possible substitutions . . .; i.e., the reference of the two expressions is essentially different" (p. 50).

Indeed, we cannot replace the predicate of the original sentence "Socrates is a man" by even "the reference of 'man' ' "; Socrates is a man, but he is not the reference of the predicate

[14] "Designation and Existence," *Journal of Philosophy*, XXXVI (1939), 706.

"man." And when Frege says the reference of a grammatical predicate is a concept, this, too, is false, by his own principles. The grammatical subject "the reference of a grammatical predicate" is a "complete" expression whose reference is thus an object, not a concept. He seems, however, to have overlooked this.

Frege says, in substance, that predicates are names, but peculiar names, not subject to the third principle. One consequence, as we have seen, is that predicates do not have a reference in the way proper names have. Church and Carnap, on the other hand, would rather give up the second principle, so far as predicates go, and keep the first and third.[15] The predicate of "Chicago is a city," they say, refers to a class, the class of cities—even though "Chicago is the class of cities" does not express a true thought, nor "Chicago the class of cities" any thought.

There is no necessary reason, however, to accept the first principle, with its consequence that a predicate is a name, though a strange one. We are not forced to assimilate quantification over predicates to quantification over proper names. But whatever we do, it will not make predicates any more nor any less like proper names than they already are, and quantification with respect to predicates will continue to be a valid operation.

Frege thought, with the analogy of proper names in mind, that since one can quantify over predicates, they must have a reference, which he called a concept. What is important for his theory of quantification, however, is that the concept be there; and considering how he conceived an expression's sense, he could easily have said that a predicate, though it is not a name and has no reference, can nevertheless be quantified over because it expresses a sense, a concept. An expression's sense, or its reference, as he conceived it, is a thing correlated with a word and has to be, to be either.

---

[15] Cf. R. Carnap, *Meaning and Necessity* (Chicago, 1947), p. 19.

According to the condition (cited above) that Frege lays down, however, a predicate has a sense (or reference) if it is well-defined, and this—which accords with common sense—does not imply that the sense of a predicate is just another kind of object, analogous to the reference of a proper name but perhaps less substantial. If a predicate is defined, we can say, if we wish, that it denotes or expresses a concept and that the concept exists. But to know that a concept exists is merely to know that a predicate is used according to rules. Every time we say something such as "*a* is (or is not) a man," we can infer that there exists a concept, or property, and nothing could be more certain, nor less extraordinary, than the existence of properties; for it involves nothing more remarkable than the fact that we can make up and follow rules of one sort or another—play games, as it were. Therefore, whether we speak a language that "countenances" (to use Quine's word) quantification over predicates or whether we do not is of no concern whatever, at least for ontology. That we can quantify with respect to predicates does not imply that our language contains a regrettable bias in favor of realism.

Frege sometimes compares the concept to Kant's synthetic apperception and says that it gives to things their form and structure: "The concept has a power of collecting together far superior to the unifying power of synthetic apperception. By means of the latter it would not be possible to join the inhabitants of Germany together into a whole; but we can certainly bring them all under the concept 'inhabitant of Germany' and number them" (*The Foundations of Arithmetic* (Oxford, 1950), p. 61e). Now certainly we can understand the predicate "inhabitant of Germany" and can determine whether "*a* inhabits Germany" is true and what the number of such inhabitants is; but if the existence of the concept "inhabitant of Germany" implies anything beyond this, it has not been explained. Even Quine's nominalistic language, not allowing quantification with respect to abstract terms, would require the existence of concepts in the sense above; for it would have to contain the possibility of true and false statements.

18

Nominalism

MICHAEL DUMMETT

In a review which I wrote of Nelson Goodman's *Structure of Appearance*,[1] I said briefly that Goodman's nominalism sprang from his failure to understand Frege's doctrine that only in the context of a sentence does a name stand for anything. This remark of Frege's, quoted by Wittgenstein both in the *Tractatus* (3.3) and in the *Investigations* (sec. 49), is probably the most important philosophical statement Frege ever made; but it is widely misunderstood and in some ways hard to interpret, and I shall therefore begin by discussing it.

The statement "Nur im Zusammenhange eines Satzes bedeutet ein Wort etwas," which I shall refer to as "*A*," occurs in Frege's *Grundlagen der Arithmetik* (secs. 60, 62; cf. Introduction, p. x) and in no other of his writings. It has therefore to be admitted that it is slightly tendentious to translate *bedeuten* in *A* as "stand for," since Frege did not arrive at the *Sinn-Bedeutung* distinction until after the publication of *Grundlagen*. In any case it seems at first sight extremely hard to interpret *A*. Frege deduces from *A* that one must never "inquire after the meaning of a word in isolation." This appears at first to go clean against his later repudiation, in *Grundge-*

Reprinted with the kind permission of the author and the editor from *The Philosophical Review*, LXV (1956), 491-505.

[1] Cambridge, Mass., 1951; hereafter referred to as *SA*.

setze der Arithmetik, of contextual definitions. One might thus naturally propose the view that Frege simply reversed his position on contextual definitions; and I cannot pretend to be able to refute anyone who holds this view. But although Frege does not expressly criticize contextual definitions in *Grundlagen,* it seems to me that the whole structure of the argument of that book is based on the presupposition that only explicit definitions are legitimate: thus the insistence that numbers are *selbstständige Gegenstände* is taken in practice to involve that we have to find explicit definitions of their "proper names": "the number 0," "the number 1," "the number 2," and so on.

If the statement *A* is not intended as a defense of contextual definition, what then does it mean? W. V. Quine says [2] that Frege discovered that the unit of meaning is not the word but the sentence. Likewise grammarians debate whether the word or the sentence is the primary element in meaning. This dispute seems to me empty and Frege's alleged discovery absurd. As Wittgenstein says in the *Tractatus* (4.032; cf. 4.026, 4.027, 4.03), the sentence is necessarily complex. P. F. Strawson's fantasy (in his review of Wittgenstein's *Investigations,* *Mind* [1954]) of a language whose sentences were not divisible into words is at best highly misleading: try to envisage someone expressing in that language the thought that no one knows whether there is an odd perfect number or explaining to a child that the world is round. The idea seems plausible at first sight only because we think of extreme cases of what Frege called "incomplete sentences" (sentences whose truth value varies with the occasion of their utterance), sentences like "Rain" or "Sorry," which lean heavily on the context to convey their sense. Sometimes, too, it is argued that the sentence is primary on the ground that we can learn the meaning of a word only by learning the meaning of the sentences

---

[2] "Two Dogmas of Empiricism," *Philosophical Review* (January, 1951), reprinted in *From a Logical Point of View* (Cambridge, 1953), p. 39.

in which it occurs. But though it is certainly true of *some* words that we can learn their sense only by learning the use of representative sentences containing them, conversely there are some sentences—e.g., "I expect Jones will resign within the next month"—whose sense we could not be taught directly, which we understand only by already knowing the meanings of the constituent words. Any attempt to express clearly the idea that the sentence is *the* unit of meaning, or even the idea that the meaning of sentences is primary, that of words derivative, ends in implicitly denying the obvious fact—which is of the essence of language—that we can understand new sentences which we have never heard before.

As I understand it, Frege's statement *A* can be expressed thus. When I know the sense of all the sentences in which a word is used, then I know the sense of that word; what is then lacking to me if I am to determine its reference is not linguistic knowledge. At this point a number of difficult problems arise which are, however, irrelevant to the appreciation of the point Frege is making. It is clearly too strong a demand that someone should know the sense of *all* the sentences in which the word occurs, for he may fail to understand some of them by reason of his not knowing some of the other words in them; we might express this by saying that all he needs in order to be able to understand any sentence in which the word occurs is an explanation of the use of various other sentences in which the word does not occur. Again, we may raise the question how we recognize that someone has this knowledge, since we can only test his understanding of finitely many sentences. (Here we may feel inclined to have recourse to the notion, notoriously difficult to explain, of a *type* of context: a notion which, it seems to me, plays an important but almost unacknowledged rôle in Wittgenstein's *Investigations*.)

If, however, we simply agree to let these questions stand unanswered for the moment, it appears that if my interpretation of Frege's principle *A* is correct, it reduces to the utmost banality. This charge must stand, if by a banal statement is meant one which, once formulated, is recognized as indisputable. Yet I agree with Frege in thinking that a great number of philosophical mistakes, which it is very natural to us to make, arise from failure to reflect on the consequences of this evident truth.

Someone might object to the statement A that, on Frege's own showing, we recognize that "Odysseus was set ashore at Ithaca" has no truth value only by first recognizing that "Odysseus" has no reference, so that it must be possible to recognize whether or not a word has *Bedeutung* quite independently of any context in which it occurs. But the principle A is meant to have relevance to *philosophical,* not to everyday, discussions of whether a given word has reference. In everyday discussions, we are concerned with a particular word for its own sake: when we ask whether "Odysseus" has a reference, we are wondering whether there was such a person as Odysseus. But in the discussions to which the principle A is relevant, we are interested in the particular case only for the sake of example. We ask whether "the number 28" stands for an object, but we are not concerned with "28" rather than "29." We are not asking whether there is such a number as 28.

But what then *are* we asking? We are on the verge of introducing a philosophical sense of "exists" which is distinct from the ordinary application of "there is. . . ." Admittedly we do not ordinarily say that there is such a number as 28; but we do say that there is a perfect number between 10 and 30 and that that number is 28. But all the same, we want to add, the number 28 does not *exist* (in the philosophical sense). One of the consequences of A is the repudiation of this philosophical existence. If a word functions as a proper name, then it *is* a proper name. If we have fixed the sense of sentences in which it occurs, then we have done all that there is to be done toward fixing the sense of the word. If its syntactical function is that of a proper name,[3] then we have fixed the sense, and with

---

[3] It is important that for Frege whether or not a word is a proper

it the reference, of a proper name. If we can find a true statement of identity in which the identity sign stands between the name and a phrase of the form "the x such that Fx," then we can determine whether the name has a reference by finding out, in the ordinary way, the truth value of the corresponding sentence of the form "There is one and only one x such that Fx." There is no further philosophical question whether the name—i.e., every name of that kind—*really* stands for something or not.

The mistake which makes Frege's view difficult to accept, which makes one feel that "28" does not really stand for anything as "Eisenhower" does, is the idea that proper names are the simplest parts of language, hardly parts of language at all. This rests on imagining that learning the sense of a proper name consists in learning to attach a label to an object *already picked out as such*: whereas of course this is the case only when we already know how to use other names of the same kind, when we, so to speak, all but know the sense of the name.[4]

When we "ask for the *Bedeutung* of a name in isolation," we are asking to be shown the object for which the name stands. But in philosophical contexts we are not interested in the particular name but in all names of that kind. So it is no use identifying the object from among others of its kind. When we ask, "What *is* the number 1?" it is no use to reply, "It is the number whose product with any other number is equal to that number"; when we ask, "What *is* fear?" we do not want to be informed that it is the emotion we feel when

---

name is a syntactical question: the only semantic question is whether or not it has a *Bedeutung*. (The terminology is of course not Frege's.)

[4] Frege's famous argument to show that proper names have sense as distinct from reference, from the difference in general between the cognitive value of "$a = a$" and that of "$a = b$," concerns the difference in sense of two names of the same kind, two names which, so to speak, largely agree in sense. I am suggesting that the principle A, understood in the light of his other doctrines, applies to the case of two names whose sense is wholly different: it is intended to stop us from asking fruitless philosophical questions when confronted by such a case.

we think, but do not know, that something very unpleasant is due to happen to us. But since we have made it impossible that we should be satisfied with any answer that is given to a question of this sort, we can go only two ways: either, as Frege says, we conclude that the name whose reference we are inquiring after stands for some image or sensation; or we conclude, like Goodman, that it is simply unintelligible. Frege on the other hand holds that the only answer that can be given to the general question, what names of a certain kind stand for, is an explanation of the sense of the sentences in which they are used.

I must make it clear here that I am concerned wholly with questions about whether what Frege calls "proper names," i.e., singular terms, have a reference. As is well known, Frege further held that other kinds of expression, what he called "incomplete expressions," could be regarded as having a reference. Except to say that I do not consider it profitable to discuss the general realist-nominalist controversy without making Frege's distinction between complete and incomplete expressions, I shall not be concerned with this part of Frege's doctrine at all: I am interested here in whether we are to say that "the color red" has a reference, not in the separate question whether we are to say that the predicate ". . . is red" has a reference.

Goodman's explanation in *SA* of what it is to be his kind of nominalist at first makes it appear that the issue between nominalism and platonism arises for him only in the context of some formal system: the platonist is he who employs in his formalism the machinery either of set theory or of higher-level quantification; the nominalist is he who dispenses with these and uses at most the calculus of individuals. The nominalist acts in this way because he finds classes (and also properties, functions, and so on) unintelligible. A reader who understood Goodman's nominalism in this way would be surprised later to discover Goodman demanding (quite outside any formal system) that we substitute for such a statement as "The word 'Paris' consists of five letters" such locutions as "Every 'Paris'-inscription consists of five-letter-inscriptions." (This recommendation is very different from those which have often been made to translate statements about wisdom into statements about wise people or ones about the species tiger into ones about individual tigers. In this case philosophers making these recommendations could point to a certain redundance in the language, which they expressed by saying, "There are not wise people *and* wisdom; there are not individual tigers *and* the species tiger." But in the case of words and letters, there is no redundance: Goodman has to invent words for the things to statements about which he wants to reduce statements about letters and words.)

There is a flat contradiction here between Goodman's attitude to words and letters and Frege's principle *A*. The expression "the word 'Paris' " functions as a proper name: there is hence, on Frege's view, no question but that it *is* a proper name. We know how to attach certain predicates to it and say, e.g., "The word 'Paris' has two syllables" or "The word 'Paris' is a proper name"; we can judge the truth of statements of identity like "The word 'Paris' is the third word in line ten on page 252 of my copy of *Oliver Twist*"; we can even point and say, "This is the word 'Paris'." Since we can in this way use this name in sentences, all is logically in order with it: there is no sense to continuing to ask, "But what *is* the word 'Paris'?" and, finding no answer, declaring "the word 'Paris' " unintelligible. Goodman finds it unintelligible only because he has committed the fallacy of "asking for the meaning of a word in isolation."

But what sort of name does Goodman find intelligible? Considering his attitude to "the word 'Paris'," we might suggest that his nominalism is nothing more than materialism of the crudest sort: he finds the notion of an "inscription" (in his sense) intelligible because it can be understood as applying to actual lumps of matter, that of a word unintelligible because it cannot. This diagnosis, I shall maintain, is basically correct: but it at first appears to meet with a telling objection when we examine the formal system presented in *SA*.

This system is, in Goodman's terminology, phenomenalistic and realistic. Phenomenalism certainly does not seem to square with materialism; but realism perhaps even less. By saying that his system is realistic, Goodman means that its basic individuals are "qualia"—such things as colors, times, and places within the visual field, and also presumably kinds of smell, or of noise, and so on; "concrete" sensations (i.e., sensations occurring at a particular time) are then defined in terms of qualia with the help of the calculus of individuals. Since Goodman holds that it is optional whether we choose to regard concrete things as thus built up out of abstract ones or conversely to regard qualities as sums of concrete entities, it seems that his objection to words and letters of the alphabet cannot have rested on a straightforward rejection of abstract entities: his nominalism must, it seems, be something more subtle than materialism.

When he comes to deal in *SA* with the concepts of shape and size, Goodman points out certain features wherein they differ from such concepts as color, place, and time. (1) The parts of a red individual are red, the parts of an individual occurring at a certain moment occur at that moment, and so on, but the parts of a square object are not all square, nor the parts of a large object all large. (2) Size and shape are derivative qualities, in that if one knows what places and times an individual occupies, one thereby knows what its shape and size are, but not conversely. For these reasons, Goodman will admit into his system size and shape *predicates* but not *names* of sizes or shapes.

If we ask why Goodman will not introduce into his system names of sizes or of shapes, the answer is simple: there is no way in his system of defining such names. The question, rather, ought to be: Why does Goodman adopt a system in which names of colors and times, but not of shapes or sizes, can be formulated? When we know the answer to this, we shall understand also why Goodman carries his distrust of shapes *outside* the particular system he has happened to construct (for of course names of letters are names of shapes, and names of words are names of sound shapes). Anyone who starts to try to understand this from the realistic standpoint of *SA* is, I think, bound to fail; so I shall instead use Quine's well-known article, "Identity, Ostension and Hypostasis,"[5] to throw light on Goodman's motives.

The color red, Quine says, can be regarded as something "concrete": as the sum total of red things, "a spatially extended particular on a par with" the river Thames. We can, that is, construe the statement "This is red" as like "This is Socrates" or "This is the river Thames"; the only difference is that the criterion of identity for colors is different from that be parts of squares, and then if we construed "This is square" for all squares might be divided into triangles and all triangles be parts of squares, and if then we construed "This is square" and "This is triangular" in this way, the two statements would have the same meaning. (It is true that it might be that the river Thames, and it alone, was red; but the answer would be that we should then be unable to make a conceptual distinction between red things and the river Thames, whereas if the sum total of squares coincided with the sum total of triangles, we should still be able to distinguish squares from triangles.) We can thus get rid of some universals by interpreting them as spatiotemporally scattered material objects; but we cannot get rid of them all in this way: adjectives of color, but not of shape, can be construed as proper names.

If we do not share this suspicion of "universals," Quine's preference for expressions which can be understood as designating specifiable lumps of matter may seem puzzling. If someone says, "This is red," but his language is too poor for him to understand the question, "This what?" it is senseless to ask whether "red" was a name or a predicate. If he can answer

---

[5] *Journal of Philosophy* (1950), also reprinted in *From a Logical Point of View.*

the question, if he says, e.g., "This flower," "red" was a predicate, but if he says, "This color," it was a name. The use of general nouns like "flower" and "color" (as opposed to adjectives) involves the use of "same" (in the context "same flower" or "same color"). The use of a proper name, like "red" as the name of a color, presupposes an understanding of a general noun such as "color." The use of "red" as a predicate presupposes the use of some noun like "flower." What is used as a criterion for *identity* of color is used as a criterion for the obtaining of the relation of being like-colored between, e.g., flowers. The use of "red" as a name also presupposes the use of predicates like "is a primary color" which can be attached to it; otherwise it would be pointless to have this *name* in the language at all.

Suppose we used "square" as a name as well as a predicate —that we talked of the shape square as we talk of the color red. In order to do this we should need a criterion for identity of shapes: this we have to hand in the criterion we use for two objects' standing in the relation of similarity (in the geometrical sense). To give any point to using "square" as a name, we should have also to know what predicates we may attach to it. Here the use of "square" as a name rather than as a predicate appears quite analogous to the use of "red" as a name rather than as a predicate. We learn in each case what the name stands for both by ostension and by being given a criterion of identity. Why are we in the one case supposed to be "countenancing abstract entities" but in the other case not?

I can point on different occasions at the same object (man, river, letter of the alphabet, shape). Where he can, Quine interprets this as pointing to a *part* of a spatiotemporal object. I could circumscribe the actual lump of matter to which I am pointing, and this would, for Quine, be part of the object which I said I was pointing at. Thus a man A is said to consist of the various molecule-moments x-t such that the molecule x is part of A's body at the moment t, and similarly for the river Thames and the color red. (These are not lumps of matter in the ordinary sense, but, so to speak, lumps of matter-time.) Shapes and letters of the alphabet cannot, however, be treated in this way; they are therefore "abstract entities" suspect to the nominalist in a way that colors and men are not. If an expression of the form "This is *F*" cannot be translated into the form "This circumscribable temporal cross section of matter is part (or the whole) of *Z*," then, Quine says, "*F*" is either irredeemably a predicate or else it purports to be the name of an "abstract entity" or "universal."

Quine comes by this notion, I think, by means of the following steps: When I wish to teach someone what object I refer to as "the color red," I point to some object, say a flower, to which the predicate "red" applies, saying, "This is the color red." I then teach the criterion for saying, "This is the same color as that"; this criterion coincides with that which I might use for saying, "This (flower) matches that one," where "matches" meant "resembles in color," but of course the latter criterion could have been learned before I acquired the word "color." Thus, given an equivalence relation between objects of a certain kind, we can introduce names for objects of a new kind, the criterion of identity for which will be the same as the criterion for the equivalence relation's obtaining. Now we also have criteria of identity for men: i.e., we explain what we mean by "Dr. Goodman" both by pointing and saying, "That is Dr. Goodman" and also by giving the criterion for saying, e.g., "That is the same man as the one you saw yesterday." One may now ask, "What is the criterion of identity for men being applied *to*?" in the sense in which the criterion of identity for colors was applied to such things as flowers; i.e., between things of what kind is it that the criterion for the obtaining of some equivalence relation coincides with the criterion for the identity of men?

Quine's answer is "temporal cross sections of matter." Here we seem to have reached rock bottom: although we must be able to say when two descriptions refer to the same temporal cross section of matter, there is no question of recognizing such cross section as the same *again*. Temporal cross sections of matter can thus be regarded as the *ultimate* constituents: out of them we can construct men and flowers and out of these in turn, sexes and colors. The usual method is to construe men and flowers as classes of molecule-moments and then sexes as classes of men, colors as classes of flowers and other material objects. But since the nominalist rejects classes in favor of sums, and since the relation of part to whole is transitive, this means that sexes and colors can be constructed *directly* out of molecule-moments. But shapes cannot be construed as sums of molecule-moments; hence to talk of shapes (or letters of the alphabet) is to recognize abstract entities; to say that something is of a certain shape is not to say that it is a spatiotemporal part of something else. The nominalist can therefore admit shape words only as predicates. On this basis, the concept of being a man would be of the same abstract character as the concept of being square, although the concept of being Dr. Goodman would not, since the sum total of molecule-moments which are parts of men coincides with the sum total of those which are parts of living human cells. The concept of being a color would be abstract, since the sum total of colors coincides with the sum total of places; though the concept of being red would not. By contrast, we should normally say that the use of the name "Dr. Goodman" presupposed the use of "man" as a general noun; the use of "red" as a *name*, that of "color"; the use of "Times Square," that of "place."

This account, however, is still back to front. It is not because they reject classes and accept sums that Goodman and the earlier Quine "countenance" colors and refuse to countenance shapes: it is the other way round. The rejection of classes is the general case of the rejection of shapes. I said earlier that Frege, confronted with the philosophical question "What does 'the color red' stand for?" held that an explanation of the sense of sentences (including statements of identity) in which "the color red" occurred was a sufficient an-

swer. It might be objected that this is an incorrect account of
Frege's procedure: in *Grundlagen* he *first* gives an account of
the sense of certain sentences containing "the number 1" and
then goes on to *use* this account to frame an explicit definition.
Likewise, in Frege's own example, a general account of the
sense of some sentences containing the phrase "the direction
of" is later used in constructing an explicit definition of this
expression. But these explicit definitions are given in terms
of classes ("extensions of concepts"), about which Frege remarks merely that he presumes that everyone knows what
they are. If someone does not know what a class is, then it
appears that Frege's explicit definition of "the number 1" is
no use to him. Elsewhere Frege explains that the notion of a
class is not to be equated with that of a whole made up of
parts, an organization, system, collection, or any like notion:
it is, he says, a notion peculiar to logic. But this cannot be
allowed. Nothing can be peculiar to logic: what is part of logic
is part of everything. The only way in which someone who
does not already know what a class is can achieve an understanding of Frege's meaning, then, is to take Frege's example
not as one in which "direction" is explained by means of the
already understood notions of a class and of the relation of
being parallel, but rather as an illustration, which presupposes that we understand "direction," of the rôle which the
notion of a class is to play. That is, we are already familiar with the transition from talking about one kind of
object—lines—to talking about another kind of object—
directions—by using the criterion for the obtaining of an
equivalence relation between objects of the former kind as the
criterion of identity for objects of the new kind: the notion of
a class is thus intended to represent the general form of this
familiar kind of transition. (When we speak of the class of x's
such that Fx, the equivalence relation involved is that which
holds between x and y when Fx if and only if Fy.) We do not
need to ask any further than this what the nature of a class is:
what we have learned from the paradoxes is that while we

can introduce such transitions piecemeal, it is impossible consistently to introduce every possible such transition simultaneously. Thus it is only in a formal sense that Frege supplies a definition of "the number 1" or of "number." The definition of numbers in terms of classes adds nothing to the description of the sense of sentences containing number words; anyone who insists on asking after the meaning of these words in isolation, on asking for more than the description of their use in sentences, ought to be equally dissatisfied with the definition in terms of classes. All that has been achieved is the concentration of all his questions into the one big question, "But what *is* a class?"

Thus it is incorrect to say that Quine rejects shapes because he rejects classes and classes are indispensable to the definition of shapes from material objects; rather, his rejection of classes is the general case of which the rejection of shapes is a particular instance. And the reason he wants to repudiate names of shapes is that he "asks for the reference of a name in isolation." To the philosophical question "What *is* the color red?" Quine has an answer—the sum total of the molecule-moments to which we apply the predicate "red"; but to the analogous question, "What *is* the shape square?" (or "What *is* the letter '*A*'?"), no such answer can be returned. The best we can do is to do, in a more systematic way, what we should do if we encountered someone who *genuinely* did not understand the use of the phrase "the shape of . . ." (or of "letter of the alphabet"): namely, to give an account of the sense of the sentences in which these expressions occur; and this, for Quine and Goodman, is not enough.

I have discussed this in terms of Quine's article rather than Goodman's book, because in his article Quine expressly adopts a materialist standpoint; for him the basic entities are molecule-moments. Although Goodman's system is realistic, I think that it is the possibility of a particularistic system admitting colors as entities that makes a realistic system seem unobjectionable to Goodman and the impossibility (without classes) of admitting shapes into a particularistic system which leads him to set up the system of *SA* in the way he does. Goodman starts off by "admitting into his ontology" only what can be construed as a sum of molecule-moments, such as colors, places, and times, and refusing admittance to shapes and letters of the alphabet, which cannot. Since colors and so forth *can* be construed in this way, Goodman has no qualms about constructing a system in which these things are basic individuals, even though their respectability is not guaranteed in *this* system by their being constructed out of irreproachably concrete entities. But a system in which it would be possible to frame names of shapes, directions, or sizes would presumably be inadmissible for Goodman. I do not think that Goodman's plea that he has no prejudice in favor of any special kind of entity as constituting the basic individuals of a system is to be taken at its face value. Particularistic systems are not for him the only possible ones, but they constitute a justification for any other kind of system.

My claim that Goodman's nominalism amounts to no more than simple materialism is thus in essence correct, if we read "particularism" for "materialism": what would correspond on the phenomenal plane to molecule-moments would be concrete, unrepeatable presentations. That this claim is correct is very hard to see from *SA*, especially if one takes seriously Goodman's protest that he has no philosophical predilection for any special type of basic individual. But until one recognizes the correctness of the claim, one cannot understand Goodman's finding classes or letters of the alphabet "unintelligible" as other than a psychological quirk peculiar to Goodman. Once we see the justice of the claim, we see that Goodman's distribution of marks for intelligibility is based on a very crude principle, well hidden from the reader by the subtlety of the maneuvers occasioned by it. Material objects, i.e., sums of molecule-moments, whether continuous or scattered, are regarded as intelligible presumably because they are thought of as par excellence what may be pointed at; we can hold them, or bits of them, in our hands. I suppose that the phenomenal equivalents, sums of presentations, are likewise thought of as the end terms of a kind of mental pointing. The failure to understand what purport to be names, but cannot be construed as names of entities of the above kinds, rests on the other hand on setting an impossibly high standard for explanations, on posing the question "What *are* these entities?" and rejecting any answer which does not state the reference of the name in isolation. These tendencies are the obverse and reverse of the belief Wittgenstein attacks throughout the *Investigations,* the idea that an ostensive definition can contain within itself the *whole* explanation of the use of a name.

In speaking of "concrete particulars," I do not mean to suggest that I attach, as Goodman does, any absolute sense to this expression. (Goodman nowhere offers any explanation of his application of "concrete" or "particular" *outside* any given system.) By a "particular" I understand an object of a kind such that we do not speak of objects of any kind such that the criterion for the obtaining of some equivalence relation between objects of this latter kind coincides with the criterion of identity for objects of the former kind. Whether or not objects of a given kind are particulars is relative to the language in question: I hold that there is no kind of objects such that they must be particulars relative to every possible language. How Goodman would explain "particular" I do not know; but I hope it is intuitively clear what sort of thing he would count as a particular, and further that I have established that his philosophical attitude and that of his kind of nominalist in general can be understood only on the assumption that there is for them a sense in which these particulars are "epistemologically" (or metaphysically) "prior."

19

Russell's Objections to Frege's Theory of Sense and Reference

It is commonly supposed that Russell adopted the Theory of Descriptions in preference to Frege's Theory of Sense and Reference entirely because of puzzles about the truth value of propositions like "The King of France is bald." In fact Russell's objections to Frege's theory were much more extreme. In an obscurely written passage in "On Denoting"[1] he argues that the theory is an "inextricable tangle" and "wrongly conceived." I shall try to reproduce Russell's arguments in a way which will preserve their strength while discarding their unclarity and then I shall criticize them.

Russell's argument proceeds from two explicit assumptions:

(1) When we wish to refer to the sense of a referring expression we do so by enclosing the expression in inverted commas.[2]

Reprinted with the kind permission of the author, publisher, and editor from *Analysis*, XVIII (1957-58), 137-143.

[1] *Mind*, 1905, pp. 485-88; reprinted in Feigl and Sellars, pp. 108-110; also, Russell, *Logic and Knowledge*, pp. 48-51.

[2] Russell uses the expressions 'meaning' and 'denotation' respectively for Frege's 'Sinn' and 'Bedeutung'. I have adopted the more modern translation 'sense' and 'reference' or 'referent' and substituted them for Russell's terms throughout. Cf. *Translations from the Philosophical Writings of Gottlob Frege*, trans. Geach and Black, pp. 56 ff.

(2) The sense of a referring expression refers to the referent.

Russell takes (2) to be Frege's thesis on the relation of sense and reference, and it is this which he tries to reduce to absurdity. An immediate consequence of it for Russell is the corollary

(2a) Whenever the sense of an expression *occurs in* a proposition, the proposition refers to the referent of that sense.

The *reductio ad absurdum* which Russell attempts to draw from Frege's theory takes the form of a dilemma for the theory: either the relation between sense and reference is a logical relation, as expressed by (2), or it is not a logical relation. But in the former case it becomes impossible to refer to *the sense* of a referring expression, and in the latter case, though we might claim to be able to refer to the sense of a referring expression, the relation between the sense and reference of an expression remains "wholly mysterious" and the theory has no explanatory value. Thus if the theory is explanatory it breaks down and if not explanatory it is philosophically worthless.

The crucial proposition then which Russell must prove is that on the assumption that (2) is true it becomes impossible to refer to the sense of a referring expression. He proves this by means of examples, and (1) is used as an aid in presenting the examples. As such an aid however it suffers from two serious defects; first it is false and therefore its bald assertion is confusing to the reader and produces confusion in what follows. A systematic account of the use of inverted commas is difficult to give because of the wide variety of uses to which they are put in ordinary speech, but it does not seem to me that there are any contexts at all in ordinary speech where enclosing an expression in inverted commas is by itself sufficient to indicate that the resultant expression is being used to refer to its customary sense; rather, as Frege said, do we

use the expression "the sense of the expression '. . . . .' "
to refer to the sense of an expression. And secondly even if
(1) were true, or were taken by the reader to be true, or
were treated by the reader as an arbitrary ruling introduced
by Russell to aid him in presenting his argument, its subsequent employment is confusing, for Russell uses inverted
commas in at least three different ways: as indicating that
expressions are being presented and spoken of rather than
used in their customary way; as "scare quotes"; and as a
means of referring to the sense of expressions.[3] Furthermore
on some occasions Russell does not use quotes where the
context indicates that they should be included. Thus in order
to give a clear exegesis of Russell's argument I shall adopt a
variation of (1) as an arbitrary convention to be employed
for purposes of the argument. I shall rewrite (1) to read

(1) Whenever an expression occurs surrounded by the
squiggle signs thus $\int$ . . . . . $\int$, the resultant expression is to be
taken as referring to the sense of the original expression. In
other words, for any expression, say "the dog," the sense of
the expression "the dog" $= \int$ the dog $\int$.

We are now in a position to restate Russell's arguments for
the conclusion that on Frege's theory it becomes impossible to
refer to the sense of a referring expression. Russell's method
here is to exhaust the possibilities by showing that each locution one could propose will fail of its purpose. Let us suppose that we wish to refer to the sense of some expression,
e.g. "the dog." Now if we wish to refer to its sense we cannot
use the expression "The sense of the dog," for to do so would
be to refer to the sense of some dog, which being an animal
and not a symbol, does not have a sense, and even if it did as
part of some *tableau vivant*, that would not be the sense we

---

[3] Church supposes that Russell's carelessness with quotes is sufficient
to vitiate his argument; see his review of Carnap, *Philosophical Review*,
1943 (Vol. LII), p. 302. Russell's argument however can be stated independently of these ambiguities, as was first suggested to me by Miss
G. E. M. Anscombe and Mr. M. E. Dummett.

intended. It seems we must use the expression "the sense of
'the dog'" which by (1) is the same as "ʃ the dog ʃ." But,
and this is the crucial point, these expressions won't do either,
for *if the sense in question were genuinely referred to it would
then become a constituent of the proposition, it would occur
in the proposition, and by (2a) if the sense occurs in a proposition reference is then made to the referent of that sense,
viz. the dog,* and we have not succeeded in referring to the
sense we wanted. In Russell's words, "the moment we put a
denoting complex [i.e. sense] in a proposition the proposition
is about the denotation (of that complex)."

Nor will it solve our problem to use any of the phrases,
(a) "the reference of the dog," (b) "the reference of 'the
dog'" or (c) "the reference of ʃ the dog ʃ" for (a) refers to
nothing since the dog being an animal does not have a reference, (b) refers to the dog, and by (2a), so does (c) unless
it is the same as (a) and has no reference. In any case we
have exhausted all the possibilities without having succeeded
in referring to what we wanted.

To put it briefly take any referring expression, say "X,"
then its sense will be called "ʃ X ʃ," but paradoxically
enough whenever "ʃ X ʃ" occurs without inverted commas
it must refer to X and not to the sense of the expression we
wanted it to refer to.

Thus to speak of the sense, our subject must not be "ʃ X ʃ"
but something which refers to the sense which we wanted
"ʃ X ʃ" to refer to. Let us *ad hoc* introduce an expression to
do this job, say "Y." But now what is the relation between
"Y" and its reference? "ʃ X ʃ" cannot be a constituent of
any definition we could give of "Y," for we saw that whenever "ʃ X ʃ" appeared without inverted commas, it was the
reference of the sense and not the sense that was referred to.
And of course we cannot argue backwards from the reference
to the sense, since there are an indefinite number of senses
attaching to any reference. Thus if "Y" really does succeed
in referring to a sense, the relation of sense and reference

cannot be a logical one, for if it were, reference would drop straight through the sense to the reference of that sense without stopping. But if it is not logical, then the relation of "Y" to its reference remains wholly mysterious. Either Frege's house of cards collapses or we can only pretend to ourselves that it has not collapsed by succumbing to mysticism. Thus Russell's argument.

Two remarks should be made about where my exegesis differs from the original. First, the explanation in the text suffers from a pragmatic paradox in that Russell has to refer to what his argument claims cannot be referred to in order to specify what cannot be referred to. I try to avoid this by a freer use of the formal mode. Secondly, the original suffers from a slipshod use of the phrase "denoting complex." Russell introduces the phrase in a way which indicates that a denoting complex is identical with a sense, thus "denoting complex" just provides an alternative way of speaking, but he then goes on to speak as though a denoting complex *had* a sense—a view which is inconsistent with his explanation of the phrase. I adopt his original view and ignore any phrases of the argument which depend on the other use as they seem to be nonsensical. Furthermore, no such phrase can be found in Frege: either a denoting complex is a sense, in which case the phrase is superfluous, or it is not a sense, in which case it is totally unclear and apparently irrelevant to Frege's argument.

Perhaps it will help us to understand the drift of Russell's argument if we can state it in more graphic terms. Imagine a game where marbles are dropped into bowls through pipes. This act is called referring. Pipes (senses) lead to bowls (references). It is a rule of the game that anything can be referred to. The difficulty is though that we cannot live up to this rule because we cannot refer to a pipe. Every time a marble drops into a pipe it goes through to the corresponding bowl. And it's no use saying we can construct a second pipe leading to the first for if the second pipe really leads into the first the marble will drop through to the bowl. And if it is not connected with the first, then how can it be used to refer to the first in accordance with the rules of the game? And of course we cannot get to the pipe by going to the bowl first for every bowl has an infinite number of pipes. "There is no backward road from denotations [references] to meanings [senses]." The way we have set up the rules of the game involves an absurdity. We must invent a new game (descriptions) that will eliminate referring.

Russell has a second argument emerging from the first. Not only, he says, does the reference of an expression occur in a proposition, but the sense as well. This is proved by example: "Scott is Scott" expresses a different proposition from "Scott is the author of *Waverley*," for the latter proposition possesses a property not possessed by the former, namely that George IV wanted to know if it was true. Yet on Frege's view (or rather Russell's version of Frege's view) only the reference of an expression occurs in a proposition. Hence on Frege's view the two propositions would have to be the same. But they are not the same, therefore Frege's view must be false since it entails a false proposition.

Russell's arguments suffer from unclarity and minor inconsistencies throughout and I have tried to restate them in a way which avoids these. But even in their restated form, they are faulty. Their faults spring from an initial mis-statement of Frege's position, combined with a persistent confusion between the notions of *occurring as a part of a proposition* (being a constituent of a proposition) and *being referred to by a proposition*. The combination of these two leads to what is in fact a denial of the very distinction Frege is trying to draw and it is only from this denial, not from the original thesis, that Russell's conclusions can be drawn. Let me explain.

Russell expresses Frege's principle by saying that the sense of a referring expression refers to the reference. Now strictly speaking this is not what Frege says. According to Frege,[4] not the sense, but the *sign* refers and it refers in virtue of its sense, the sense provides the *mode of presentation* of the referent. A sign *expresses* its sense and *refers* to its referent. Russell's way of putting it might seem a pardonable metonymy on Frege, were it not for the fact that Russell adds to it the *inexplicit* assumption that if an object is referred to by a proposition then that object occurs *as part* of that proposition. The crucial stage of the argument, you recall, was that when "∫ X ∫" is used in asserting a proposition then a sense is referred to by a proposition, but if a sense is referred to then it occurs in a proposition, but if it occurs in a proposition then its referent is referred to by the proposition (by (2a)), hence "∫ X ∫" does not after all succeed in referring to a sense. Furthermore if its referent occurs as part of the proposition then it and only it occurs as part of the proposition, the sense being relegated to some higher limbo outside the proposition altogether. All this rests, I suggest, on an equivocation between the notions of *referring,* and *occurring in a proposition.* Once these are clearly distinguished, the argument collapses. It is not easy at first sight to understand what might be meant by *occurring in a proposition,* except perhaps that words occur as part of a sentence used to assert a proposition. I think though that a plausible account can be given of this expression: it is equivalent to Frege's notion of what is *expressed* in a proposition. To say that a sense occurs in a proposition is to say that that sense is expressed in the proposition. This explanation is of course far from clear—it is no clearer than is Frege's explanation of the notion of *expressing*—but whatever its unclarity it is certainly different from the notion of *referring.* It is hard to find any conceivable sense in which a referent occurs as a part, or a constituent of a proposition. The tenth King of France is not a constituent of propositions about him the way his elbow is a constituent of his arm or he

---

[4] Op. cit., pp. 57 and 61.

a constituent of a French wrestling team. Any view that makes the objects referred to by a proposition literally parts of that proposition is bound to be nonsensical. And even if we could assign some arbitrary rule that "occurring in" was to be treated as equivalent to "referred to," this sense of *occurring in* is quite different from the one which is equivalent to "expressed by," hence any arguments which rest on equating them are guilty of sheer equivocation. *In other words, Russell's argument which purports to develop Frege's thesis in fact develops the negation of that thesis,* for Russell's assumption that *occurring in a proposition* is the same as *being referred to by that proposition* is an *equation of sense and reference,* and the whole point of Frege's theory is to assert a *distinction between sense and reference.*

Once Frege's intentions are kept clearly in mind, the puzzles about referring to the sense of an expression dissolve. The sense of any expression can be referred to by such a phrase as "the sense of the expression 'E' " and the sense in question does not *occur as part* of the proposition in which this phrase is used, rather it is *referred to* by the phrase in virtue of the sense of the phrase, viz. the sense of the phrase "the sense of the expression 'E'." In short, the sense of an expression *occurs in* (to use Russell's expression) a proposition, and in virtue of that sense the proposition refers to the referent. The referent *does not occur in* the proposition. Thus when a sense is referred to, the sense does not occur as part of the proposition, only the sense in virtue of which it is referred to occurs, thus the referent of the first sense is not referred to at all by the proposition.

Similarly Russell's second conclusion, that Frege is unable to account for the difference between "Scott is Scott" and "Scott is the author of *Waverley*," collapses. It only seemed a valid conclusion because of the equation of "occur in" and "refer to." Once these are distinguished—and it is the whole point of Frege's theory to distinguish them—it is easy to see how the two sentences express different propositions: they contain expressions with different senses.

Conclusion: Russell does not succeed in performing a *reductio ad absurdum* of Frege's distinction but only of the conjunction of the distinction and its negation.

20

The 'Fregean' Annahme

G. E. M. ANSCOMBE

It has sometimes perplexed readers of Wittgenstein that he refers, both in the *Tractatus* (4.063), and in *Philosophical Investigations,* to "the Fregean *Annahme*," as if '*Annahme*' (assumption) had been a technical term in Frege, as it was in Meinong. His reference is to a passage in *Function and Concept,* and it is evident that his attention was especially fixed on it by a passage in Russell's account of Frege in the *Principles of Mathematics,* Appendix A, § 477. Russell says: "There are, we are told, three elements in judgment: (1) the recognition of truth, (2) the *Gedanke* (the thought), (3) the truth-value. Here the *Gedanke* is what I have called an unasserted proposition—or rather, what I have called by this name covers both the *Gedanke* alone and the *Gedanke* together with its truth-value. It will be well to have names for these two distinct notions; I shall call the *Gedanke* alone a *propositional concept*; the truth-value of a *Gedanke* I shall call an *assumption*." And here Russell has a footnote referring to the passage in *Function and Concept,* and saying: "Frege, like Meinong, calls this an Annahme." "Formally, at least," he goes on, "an assumption does not require that its

Reprinted with the kind permission of the author and the publisher from *An Introduction to Wittgenstein's Tractatus* (London: Hutchinson, 1959), 105-106.

content should be a propositional concept; whatever x may be, 'the truth of x' is a definite notion. This means the true if x is true, and if x is false or not a proposition it means the false."

What Russell refers to as "the truth of x" is of course Frege's function ——x. Frege introduces a second function

$$\overline{}_{_\shortmid} x$$

whose value is the false for just those arguments for which the value of ——x is the true. Thus, as Russell says, we do not have assertions and negations—there is not a negation sign, corresponding to the assertion sign—but we have assertions of the truth and falsity of "thoughts," or, as Russell calls them, "propositional concepts."

It is a peculiarity of Russell's account that he takes

$$\text{——} 5 > 4$$

to be something different from

$$5 > 4$$

and calls '5 > 4' the "thought" and '——5 > 4' the "assumption" thus turning Frege's quite innocent and untechnical expression "a mere assumption" into a technicality.

What Russell failed to notice was that if a proposition is substituted for x in '——x' there is no difference at all, for Frege, either in sense or in reference, between the proposition by itself, and the proposition with the horizontal stroke attached; moreover a 'thought' is not a proposition, not even an unasserted proposition, but is the sense of a proposition, and hence there is the same *Gedanke* when we have a proposition and when we have a proposition with the stroke attached. It is only when we substitute the designation of something *other* than a truth-value for 'x' in '——x' that there is any difference, either in sense or in reference, between the designation by itself and the designation with the stroke attached. In that case, the designation designates whatever it does designate—the Moon or the number 3 for example; and the designation with the stroke attached designates a truth-value, in these cases the false.

Russell's remarks, which mistakenly give special prominence to Frege's use of the word 'assumption', must be the source of Wittgenstein's references to it. Further, it appears that Wittgenstein actually accepted Russell's interpretation; for his comment on Frege at the end of 4.063 is not otherwise intelligible: "The proposition does not stand for any object (truth-value) whose properties are called 'true' or 'false'; the verb of the proposition is not 'is true' or 'is false'—as Frege thought—but what 'is true' must already contain the verb." Although in *Begriffsschrift* Frege said that the verb of the proposition was 'is true'—a view which he rejected in *Sense and Reference*—he never thought this of 'is false'. But if we were to adopt Russell's interpretation of the passage in *Function and Concept*, we should say that according to Frege there are three stages

(1) x

(2) the truth of x

or: the falsehood of x

and then (3) the final stage of assertion, which we might think of as a tick put against whichever is right, the truth of x or the falsehood of x; and *such* a view might easily be rendered as a view that the real verb in the proposition that gets asserted—i.e., in the 'assumption'—is 'is true' or 'is false'.

21

Naming and Predicating

PETER T. GEACH

As used in this work, the terms "subject" and "predicate" will always be linguistic terms; I shall never call a man a logical subject, but only the name of a man—the name "Peter," not the Apostle, is the subject of "Peter was an Apostle," and not the property of being an Apostle but its verbal expression is a predicate. I shall say, however, that what the predicate in "Peter was an Apostle" is predicated of is Peter, not his name; for it is Peter, not his name, that is being said to have been an Apostle. In saying that something is predicated of Peter, I do not mean that this predicate is true of or applies to Peter, but only that in some significant sentence, true or false, it is predicated of Peter. I shall say that a predicate is *attached* to a subject, is *predicated of* what the subject stands for, and *applies to* or is *true of* this if the statement so formed is true.

The stipulations in the last paragraph are of course arbitrary; but it is convenient to make some such stipulations and adhere to them. For lack of this, logicians as distinguished as Aristotle and Russell have fallen into almost inextricable confusions, so that you just cannot tell whether a predicate is something within language or something represented by means of language.

Reprinted (with slight revisions) by the permission of the author and the publisher from sections of P. T. Geach, *Reference and Generality* (Ithaca: Cornell University Press, 1962).

Let us now try to get provisional explanations of the terms "subject" and "predicate." (These are *not* to be taken as proper definitions.) A *predicate* is an expression that gives us an assertion about something if we attach it to another expression that stands for what we are making the assertion about. A *subject* of a sentence *S* is an expression standing for something that *S* is about, *S* itself being formed by attaching a predicate to that expression.

There is a divergence between these explanations: "subject" is defined as "subject of a sentence," but "predicate" is not defined as "predicate in a sentence." This divergence is deliberate. It would be very inconvenient not to recognize the same predicate in "Jim broke the bank at Monte Carlo" and in "The man who broke the bank at Monte Carlo died in misery"; but in the latter sentence the predicate in question is attached not to the name of somebody to whom the predicate allegedly applies, but to the relative pronoun "who," which is not anybody's name. What makes this predicate to be a predicate is that it can be attached to a person's name to make an assertion about him, not that it actually is so attached whenever it is used.

There are, however, also inconveniences about not having "subject" and "predicate" as correlatives. We can remove these by taking the explanation just given as an explanation not of "predicate" but of "predicable"; the older use of the noun "predicable" is too little current in recent philosophical literature to stop me from staking out my own claim to the term. Thus in "Jim broke the bank . . ." and "The man who broke the bank . . . died in misery" we have two occurrences of the same *predicable,* but only in the first sentence is it actually a *predicate* attached to the subject "Jim."

A further difficulty arises over the expression "assertion about something." Round this and similar expressions there is piled a secular accumulation of logical error; we have here a suggestion that "*P*" is predicated of *S* only if it is actually asserted, affirmed, that *S* is *P*. A moment's consideration ought to have shown that this will not do: *"P"* may be predicated of *S* in an *if* or a *then* clause, or in a clause of a disjunction, without the speaker's being in the least committed to affirming that *S* is *P*. Yet it took the genius of the young Frege to dissolve the monstrous and unholy union that previous logicians had made between the import of a predicate and the assertoric force of a sentence. Even when a sentence has assertoric force, this attaches to the sentence as a whole, not specially to the subject, or to the predicate, or to any part of the sentence.

Frege's lesson still has to be learned by many philosophers. A philosophical theory of certain predicables may win popularity, when it is not even plausible if we consider occurrences of them as predicates in hypothetical or disjunctive clauses. I have even read an author maintaining that "if . . . then . . ." itself means something different in an asserted hypothetical from what it means in a hypothetical that itself occurs as a subclause in a longer hypothetical. Would he say "and" meant something different in an asserted conjunctive proposition? Probably he would say in that case that the assertoric force attached not to "and" but to the clauses it joined. Such a position, however, is clearly arbitrary.

To avoid these absurdities, we had best reword our explanation of "predicable," using some term less objectionable than "assertion." "Statement" will hardly do; a statement is something we state, as an assertion is something we assert, and by both terms assertoric force is equally suggested. (How misleading is the fashionable talk about sentences being true or false only qua 'used to make statements'! Can we then not assign any truth values to the clauses of a disjunction?) "Proposition" is much better; a proposition is something we propound or put forward—it may or may not be asserted. Unfortunately, though the traditional use of "proposition" makes a proposition something linguistic, there is a prevalent use of the term to mean a supposed kind of nonlinguistic entities, signified by what I call propositions. But we can avoid ambiguity very simply: in discussing the philosophers who introduce these nonlinguistic entities, I shall dignify "Proposition" with an initial capital. Thus our explanation of "predicable" and "predicate" will be: A *predicable* is an expression that gives us a proposition about something if we attach it to another expression that stands for what we are forming the proposition about; the predicable then becomes a *predicate,* and the other expression becomes its *subject*; I call such a proposition a *predication.*

How are we to apply this definition of "subject"? How can we tell that an expression within a proposition is being used to stand for something that the proposition is about? If Frege and Wittgenstein were right in supposing that a name stands for something only in the context of a proposition, then this question would be formidably difficult: but I think they were clearly wrong. A name may be used outside the context of a sentence simply to call something by name—to acknowledge the presence of the thing named. Such an act of naming is of course no proposition, and, while we may call it correct or incorrect, we cannot properly call it true or false. It does, however, as grammarians say concerning sentences, express a complete thought; it is not like the use of "Napoleon" to answer the question "Who won the Battle of Hastings?" where we have to take the single word as short for the complete sentence "Napoleon won the Battle of Hastings."

I call this use of names "independent"; but I do not mean that it is independent of the language system to which the names belong or of the physical context that makes their use appropriate; I mean that names so used do not require any immediate context of words, uttered or understood—it is quite a different case when names are used to answer spoken or unspoken questions of the form "Who . . . ?" or "Which one . . .?" Nouns in the vocative case used as greetings illustrate this independent use of names; we get a very similar use when name-labels are stuck on things or worn at conferences.

I have said by implication that the use of proper nouns **is** dependent on the language system to which they belong; perhaps, therefore, it will be as well to mention the odd view that proper names are not exactly words and do not quite belong to the language in which they are embedded, because you would hardly look for proper names in a dictionary. On the contrary: it is part of the job of a lexicographer to tell us that "Warsaw" is the English word for "Warszawa"; and a grammarian would say that "Warszawa" is a Polish word— a feminine noun declined like "mowa." And what is wrong with this way of speaking?

In many propositions we can pick out a part functioning as a name of something that the proposition is about; such an expression could always be used, outside the context of a sentence, for a simple act of calling by name, and it always makes sense to ask whether these two kinds of use fit together —whether an expression stands for the same object in a given use of a sentence as it does in a given act of calling by name, so that we have a proposition about the object then and there named. For example, if my friend points to a man and says "Smith!" I may ask him *sotto voce* "Is that the Smith you were telling me nearly went to prison?"; and if my friend assents, he is linking up his present use of "Smith" in an act of naming with his past use of it in "Smith nearly went to prison." Whenever an expression in a sentence could thus be linked up with an act of calling by name, the expression is a name, and the sentence will have the role of a proposition about the bearer of the name. The cases most easily recognized are certain uses of proper names (what Quine calls the 'purely referential' uses). Any proposition in which we can thus recognize the name of something the proposition is about may rightly be regarded as a predication, with that name as its logical subject.

We must be aware of supposing that a proposition admits of only one subject-predicate analysis. "Peter struck Malchus" is at once a predication about Peter and a (different) predication about Malchus; either "Peter" or "Malchus" may be taken as a logical subject—as Aristotle observed long ago, a logical subject need not be in the nominative case.[1] A traditionalist might protest that only "Peter" can be treated as the subject, and some modern logicians might say we have here a relational proposition, not admitting of subject-predicate analysis; both would be making the mistake of treating an analysis of a proposition as the only analysis. Logic would be hopelessly crippled if the same proposition could never be analyzed in several different ways. Some people hold that it is a matter of which name is emphasized, "Peter" being the subject of "*Peter* struck Malchus" and "Malchus" the subject of "Peter struck *Malchus*." I reply that for logic these are not different propositions; they have, on the contrary, just the same logical content—either implying and implied by just the same propositions as the other.

The object named by a name may be called its bearer. No reference to time is involved in the questions whether a proper name in a given use (e.g., "Peter" in the Gospels, "Cerberus" in Greek theology, "Vulcan" in astronomy) has a bearer, and whether such-and-such an object is that bearer. Thus, the proper noun "Augustus" as used in Roman history books has Octavian for its bearer; this is true without temporal qualifications, even though Octavian lived for years before being called by that name; it would be absurd to object to the question "When was Augustus born?" because the name was not conferred on him then. Again, after a woman has married, it may be a social solecism to call her by her maiden name; but this is not the sort of linguistic fault to make a sentence containing the name to be no longer a proposition with a sense and a truth-value.

Nor yet does it cease to be true that so-and-so is the bearer of a name because so-and-so is no more. Otherwise—if I may adopt the style of a Stoic logician—"Dion is dead" could not possibly be true, because if the person so called is not dead

---

[1] *Analytica priora*, I. 36.

"Dion is dead" would be false and not true, and if the person so called is dead "Dion" would stand for nothing, and so "Dion is dead" would be no longer a proposition and again would not be true. There are, one would normally wish to say, things that can hold good of Dion even if Dion is no more—e.g., that Dion is loved and admired by Plato. Naturally, formal logic cannot sort out what can and what cannot be true of a man who is no more; that is no job for formal logic; it would be silly to cut the knot by saying that nothing at all is true of the dead. It suffices, for a name to have a bearer, that it could have been used to name that bearer in a simple act of naming; it does not matter if such use is not at present possible, because the bearer is too remote from the speaker, or has even ceased to be.

If we remove a proper name from a proposition, the whole of the rest of the proposition supplies what is being propounded concerning the bearer of the name, and is thus, by our explanation, the predicate attached to that name as subject. In "Peter struck Malchus" the predicate is "——— struck Malchus" if we take "Peter" as the subject and "Peter struck ———" if we take "Malchus." As I said before, either choice of subject is legitimate. The proposition relates both to Peter and to Malchus; what is propounded concerning Peter is that he *struck Malchus,* and what is propounded concerning Malchus is that *Peter struck* him.

We may get the very same proposition by attaching different predicates to the same subject. The predicates "——— shaved Peter" and "Peter shaved ———" are quite different, and when attached to the subject "John" yield different propositions, but when attached to the subject "Peter" they yield the very same proposition "Peter shaved Peter." This simple example shows that the sense of a predicate cannot be determined, so to say, by subtracting the sense of the subject from that of the whole proposition. We need rather to consider a way of forming propositions; "——— shaved Peter" and "Peter shaved ———" represent two different ways of forming propositions, and this is what makes them two different predicates even in "Peter shaved Peter."

We may in some instances recognize a common predicate in two propositions even though this predicate is not an identifiable expression that can be picked out; for example, "John shaved John" propounds the very same thing concerning John as "Peter shaved Peter" does concerning Peter, and thus we may regard the two as containing a common predicate, but this is by no means identifiable with the mere word "shaved" occurring in both. We could, of course, replace the second occurrences of the proper names in these propositions by the reflexive pronoun "himself," and then treat "——shaved himself" as a predicable which can occur even where it is not attached to a logical subject—as in "Nobody who shaved himself was shaved by the barber." But this is not what makes it legitimate to treat "John shaved John" and "Peter shaved Peter" as having a common predicate; it is the other way round—because these propositions have a common predicate, it is legitimate to rewrite them so that the common predicate takes the shape of an explicit predicable that can be extracted from each of them.

Given my explanations of "subject" and "predicate," it follows that a name can occur in a proposition only as a logical subject; if the same expression appears to be used now predicatively, now as a name, that is a misleading feature of our language. Thus names and predicables are absolutely different. A name has a complete sense, and can stand by itself in a simple act of naming; a predicable, on the other hand, is a potential predicate, and a predicate never has a complete sense, since it does not show what the predication is about; it is what is left of a proposition when the subject is removed, and thus essentially contains an empty place to be filled by a subject. And though a predicable may occur in a proposition otherwise than as a predicate attached to a subject, it does not then lose its predicative, incomplete character; it has sense only as contributing toward the sense of a proposition, not all by itself.

A predicable applies to or is true of things; for example, "Peter struck ——" applies to Malchus (whether it is actually predicated of Malchus or not). This relation must be sharply distinguished from the relation of name to bearer, which is confounded with it in the 'Aristotelian' tradition under the term "denoting." A predicable never names what it is true of, and "Peter struck ——" does not even look like a name of Malchus.

Again, when a proposition is negated, the negation may be taken as going with the predicate in a way in which it cannot be taken to go with the subject. For predicables always occur in contradictory pairs; and by attaching such a pair to a common subject we get a contradictory pair of propositions. But we never have a pair of names so related that by attaching the same predicates to both we always get a pair of contradictory propositions.

It is easy to prove this formally. The conjunction of a pair of predicables when attached to a name "x" signifies the same as the conjunction of the propositions that we get by attaching each predicable separately to "x"; this is precisely what conjunction means when applied to predicables rather than propositions. Now suppose we had a pair of names "x" and "y" such that by attaching the same predicate to both we always got a pair of contradictory propositions. Thus we have:

"$(P \& Q)x$" is contradictory to "$(P \& Q)y$."

Hence, in view of what the conjunction of predicables, "$P \& Q$," has to mean:

"$Px \& Qx$" is contradictory to "$Py \& Qy$."

But, by our supposition about "x" and "y," "Px" and "Py" are contradictories, and so are "Qx" and "Qy." We may thus infer:

"$Px \& Qx$" is contradictory to "not $(Px) \&$ not (Qx)."

And from this it is easily proved, by way of the truth-functional tautology:

$$(\sim(p \& q) \equiv (\sim p \& \sim q)) \equiv (p \equiv q)$$

that for this name "x" arbitrary predications "Px" and "Qx," assuming they can be significantly formed into one predication, must always have the same truth-value—which is absurd. Thus no names come in contradictory pairs; but all predicables come in contradictory pairs; therefore no name is a predicable.

Again, puzzling as tenses are, we can at least see that they attach to predicables; we may say not only of the proposition "Peter struck Malchus," but also of the predicables "Peter struck ——" and "—— struck Malchus," that they are in the past tense. But names are tenseless, as Aristotle observed; [2] the reference of a name to its bearer admits of no time-qualification. On the other hand, we may quite well say that since "—— struck Malchus" *does* apply to Peter, "—— is striking Malchus" *did* apply to Peter; and thus the relation of a predicable to what it applies to does admit of time-qualification.

We must thus make an absolute distinction between names and predicables; if a name and a predicable have the same external form, that is a defect of language, just as it is a defect in a language if it fails to distinguish the uses of "Peter" to talk about the man Peter and about the name "Peter."

A term, as conceived in Aristotelian logic, is supposed capable of being a subject in one proposition and a predicate in another; since only names, not predicables, can be logical subjects, this notion of terms has no application whatsoever. This initial confusion has led to a multitude: *pessima in principiis corruptio.*

One center of confusion is the copula. Should a proposition be analyzed into subject and predicate, or into subject, predicate, and copula? Aristotle had little interest in the copula;

----

[2] *De interpretatione,* c. 3.

he remarks casually at the beginning of the *Analytica priora* that a proposition is analyzable into a pair of terms, with or without the verb "to be." This was natural, because the Greek for "Socrates is a man" might be (literally rendered) either "Man the Socrates" or "Man is the Socrates." Frege repeatedly says that the bare copula has no special content; this is the view I shall defend.

If terms are thought of as (at least potential) names, then a natural idea is that the truth of a categorical consists in its putting together two names of the same thing. In fact, a categorical is true if its predicate is a predicable applying to that which its subject is a name of; the two-name theory of predication is derivable from this principle if one confounds the relation *being a predicable applying to* with the relation *being a name of*. Hobbes, who held the two-name theory of predication, held also that the copula was superfluous; but we might very well object that on the contrary it is necessary, because a pair of names is not a proposition but the beginning of a list and a redundant list at that if the two names do name the same thing. (If I am listing the things in my room, I do not need to enter both a cat and Jemima.)

The two-name theory breaks down in any event—whether we have a copula or not. Of a name it always makes sense to ask what it names, but it is clearly nonsense to ask which cat "cat" stands for in "Jemima is a cat," or which dog "dog" stands for in "Jemima isn't a dog." I suppose somebody might try saying that in "Jemima is a cat" "cat" stands for Jemima, because the proposition is true. But what the names in a proposition stand for cannot be determined by whether the proposition is true or false: on the contrary, we can determine whether the proposition is true only when we know what it is about, and thus what the names contained in it do stand for.

Again, consider propositions like "Socrates became a philosopher." "Philosopher" clearly has the same sort of predicative use as "cat" and "dog" did in the examples last discussed; in Polish, a language sensitive to the distinction of subject and predicate, all three nouns would take the predicative (instrumental) inflection. Now if Socrates did become a philosopher, he certainly did not become Socrates, nor did he become any other philosopher, say Plato; so "philosopher" does not stand for a philosopher—it does not serve to name a philosopher.

Even here, a resolute champion of the two-name theory will not give up. Ockham for example regards propositions like "Socrates became a philosopher" as exponible, somehow like this: "First of all Socrates was not a philosopher and then Socrates was a philosopher"; the first half of this would be true in virtue of the predicate-term's referring to all the people (Anaxagoras, Parmenides, etc.) who were philosophers when Socrates was not one, and the second half would be true in virtue of the predicate-term's referring to the philosopher that Socrates eventually was—viz. Socrates.[3] But this ought not to satisfy us. It is clear that a two-name theory, though it starts off simple, is ultimately going to let us in for more and more futile subtleties, just as, if you insist on describing planetary motions in terms of uniform circular motions, you need an immense number of cycles and epicycles.

Our distinction between names and predicables enables us to clear up the confusion, going right back to Aristotle, as to whether there are genuine negative terms: predicables come in contradictory pairs, but names do not, and if names and predicables are both called "terms" there will be a natural hesitation over the question "Are there negative terms?"

If the two-name theory is rejected but the terms are still thought of as names, people will naturally come to regard the copula as expressing a relation. As I said, two names by themselves cannot form a proposition; but this can be done if we join two names with a word for a relation, as in "Smith excels Robinson." It will then be a problem whether the relation

---

[3] Ockham, *Summa logicae, pars prima*, ed. Philotheus Boehner, O.F.M. (St. Bonaventure, N.Y.: Franciscan Institute, 1951), c. 75.

expressed by the copula is always the same; logicians of our time commonly suppose that the copula may express either class membership or class inclusion, and some make even further distinctions. But it is quite wrong to say that "is" means different relations in "Socrates is an animal" and in "Every man is an animal"; there is the same unambiguous expression "is an animal" in both, and the propositions differ in just the same way as "Socrates can laugh" and "Every man can laugh," where there is no copula to be ambiguous.

Admittedly, if "animal" stood for the class of animals and "every man" stood for the class of men, then "is an" would have to mean different things in "Socrates is an animal" and "Every man is an animal"; but the supposition is plainly false, at least about "every man" (being in this case, I suppose, a hangover from the muddled fusion of the doctrine of distribution with class logic). Frege has sometimes been credited with distinguishing these two brands of copula; in criticism of Schroeder, Frege actually pointed out that if we turn "Every mammal is a vertebrate" into "The class of mammals is included in the class of vertebrates," the predicate is now not "vertebrate" but "included in the class of vertebrates," and "is included in" is not the copula but the copula plus a bit of the predicate.[4]

By my explanation of "predicable," there is a single predicable occurring in "Socrates is an animal" and in "Every man is an animal," viz. "is an animal"; the grammatical copula is thus part of this predicable. This does not settle the problem of the copula, but just determines how we state it. In a predicable like "is an animal," has the "is" any definite content? I can see no reason for saying so. Naturally, if a tensed proposition contains a copula, the tense will attach to the copula just because the copula is grammatically a verb; but a tensed proposition need not contain a copula, and anyhow tense is something utterly different from the copula's supposed

[4] G. Frege, *Philosophical Writings*, ed. P. T. Geach and Max Black (Oxford: Blackwell, 1952), pp. 90-91.

role of linking two terms. The traditional logic drilled pupils in twisting propositions into a form where they had a predicable beginning "is" or "are," and preferably one consisting of that prefixed to a noun(-phrase); this was a pernicious training, which might well disable the pupils for recognizing predicables that had not this special form.

A proper name 'used predicatively' ceases to be a proper name, as in "He is a Napoleon of finance" or (Frege's example) "Trieste is no Vienna"; in such cases the word alludes to certain attributes of the object customarily designated by the proper name. On the other hand, we may certainly say that in statements of identity the copula joining two proper names has a special role. I shall not here discuss the difficult question whether "Tully is Cicero" exemplifies the classical uses of "Tully" and "Cicero" as names, or whether we should rather regard it as a proposition about these names in this use; that is, whether its analysis is something like "Tully is the same man as Cicero," the names being used just as they might be in making historical statements, or rather something like "In history books the names 'Tully' and 'Cicero' are commonly used for the same man." But in any event the copula is no longer the trivial bit of grammatical form that it is in "Socrates is a man." On that very account, however, our absolute distinction of names and predicables is inviolate; for the predicable (say) "—— is the same man as Cicero" is totally different from the name "Cicero."

A further difference between names and predicables is this: there is nothing to stop a predicable from being logically complex; but a name cannot be logically complex—any complexity it has is accidental. A name cannot be dissected by a definition.[5] A name relates directly to what it names; a complex sign cannot bear a direct relation to the thing signified—the relation must be mediated by the constituent signs of the

---

[5] L. Wittgenstein, *Tractatus Logico-philosophicus* (London: Routledge and Kegan Paul, 1960), 3.26.

complex. So a name, as Aristotle already said, must have no parts that signify separately;[6] and equally, a name cannot be an abbreviation for a complex expression, for then also it would be related to the thing signified only via the signs in the complex expression.[7]

We can always turn a proposition ostensibly of the form "f(the A that is P)," one where the definite description seems to take the place of a proper name, into the form "just one A is P, and f(that same A)." The change of form is great only under the aspect of surface grammar; logically, all that we have done is to expand the portmanteau word "that" into the connective "and" and the relative pronoun "that same."

Predicative occurrences of definite descriptions are not instances of the schema "f(the A that is P)." The predicable "—— is *the* A that is P" is analyzable as "—— is *an* A that is P and only —— is an A that is P." Here "is an A that is P" is in turn analyzable as "both is an A and is P."

A proper name can never be an abbreviation for a definite description; though we may of course introduce a proper name as a name for the object described by such a description. A natural way of effecting such an introduction would be to enunciate a proposition with the proper name as subject and the definite description as predicate: "Neptune is the planet of the Solar System next out from Uranus." If we have no other way of identifying the object named than is supplied by the definite description, it may be natural to think of the proper name as short for the description; but this would be wrong.

Here as elsewhere, we must remember that if a term in a proposition has reference there must be some way to specify this reference regardless of that proposition's truth-value. To be sure, "Smith" has as its reference the man who broke the bank at Monte Carlo iff "Smith is the man who broke the bank

---

[6] *De interpretatione*, 16a 20-21.
[7] Cf. Wittgenstein, *op. cit.*, 3.261.

at Monte Carlo" is true; but the reference of "Smith" must be specifiable in some other way that does not depend on whether this proposition is true. For "Smith" must already have a reference before the question "Is Smith the man who broke the bank at Monte Carlo?" can be asked; and its reference in this question cannot depend on which answer is right.

Frege's view on the definability of proper names is of some interest in this connection. On the one hand, he insisted that the *definiendum* must be simple, and that for a sign like "2" we must supply one elucidation, not a number of elucidations of its use in different contexts; on the other hand, he regarded a simple proper name as short for a complex sign (which also would be for him an *Eigenname*, i.e., a proper name). Now there is no reason at all why an abbreviation should be syntactically simple; and if several abbreviations all contain the mark "2," there need not be one single rule for expanding them into an unabbreviated form (though no doubt it is neater, more elegant, to have a single rule); all that is logically requisite for an abbreviation is that one shall be able to construct the unabbreviated expression from it in a unique way. On the view I have been advocating, "2" must be syntactically simple if it is a name, and a name must be introduced once for all by an elucidation that warrants our using it in all available contexts; and so far this agrees with what Frege says: on the other hand, no name can on this view be an abbreviation for anything. We should observe here that the definitional equation by which Frege introduced a simple *Eigenname* always has the role of a substantive proposition in which the name is used for the first time. Frege makes no such distinction as we find in *Principia Mathematica* between "=" and "=Df"; on the contrary, he says that the sign of equality, just because it is used in all definitions, cannot itself be defined.[8]

After considering the relation between names and definite

---

[8] *Philosophical Writings*, p. 80.

descriptions, it will be proper to consider in a general way the relation between names and referring phrases (to use a handy though somewhat misleading term). A referring phrase consists of a general term combined with what Johnson called an *applicative*: i.e., an expression such as "a," "the," "some," "any," "no," "every," "only," "just one," "all but two," "most," and the like.[9]

It is always possible to substitute an applicative-plus-general-term for a proper name without destroying the syntax of the proposition: e.g., starting from "Some boy loves Mary" we can form "Some boy loves every girl," "Some boy loves only pretty girls," "Some boy loves just one girl," and so on.

I shall count an applicative-plus-general-term phrase as a referring phrase only when it stands in a context where a proper name might have stood. Thus, when "a man," or "the man who broke the bank at Monte Carlo," occurs predicatively after "is," I shall not recognize it as a referring phrase; for in such places a proper name used referentially can stand only by reason of a change in the force of "is," so that it means (say) "is the same man as." Many logicians, I am aware, have taken the "is" or "was" in a proposition like "Louis XV was the King of France at that time," or "Smith is (was) the man who broke the bank at Monte Carlo," to be a copula of identity as in "Tully is (was) Cicero" or "The Thames is the Isis." I think this is quite wrong: the definite description is in such cases used predicatively or attributively, and in Polish it would bear a predicative inflection (even in sentences where the definite description comes first, like "The King of France at that time was Louis XV"). Predicative uses of definite descriptions have just been discussed.

It will be convenient for our purposes to introduce a little symbolism at this point. I shall use signs like "*" and "†" to go proxy for applicatives; the letters "$A, B, C \ldots$" for gen-

---

[9] W. E. Johnson, *Logic*, Pt. I (Cambridge University Press, 1921), p. 97.

eral terms; and the letters "$a, b, c \ldots$" for proper names. I shall use "$f(\ )$," "$g(\ )$," "$h(\ )$," and so forth to represent contexts into whose empty place we may insert either a proper name or an applicative-*plus*-general-term phrase.

In discussing the subject-predicate relation, I argued that in any proposition in which a 'purely referential' proper name occurs, we may treat that name as a logical subject to which the rest of the proposition is attached as a predicate. Now for such an occurrence of a proper name a referring phrase can always be substituted without further disturbance of the syntax. So, if we use "$f(a)$" to represent a predicate "$f(\ )$" attached to a subject "a," it seems appropriate to say that in "$f(*A)$" we have the same predicable attached to a *quasi subject*, to the referring phrase "$*A$." Similarly in chemistry a complex molecule may have a place that can be occupied either by a single atom or by a radical, e.g., either by the sodium atom Na or by the ammonium radical NH_4, or again by the chlorine atom Cl or by the cyanide radical CN.

Why should I use the grudging term "quasi subject"? Let us use "$f(\ )$" and "$f'(\ )$" to represent contradictory predicables; then, when attached to any proper name "a" as subject, they will give us contradictory predications; but if "$*A$" takes the place of "a," the propositions "$f(*A)$ and $f'(*A)$" will in general not be contradictories—both may be true or both false. "Some men can laugh" and "Some men cannot laugh" are both true; "Jemima can lick any dog in town" and "Jemima cannot lick any dog in town" are both false if Jemima can lick one dog but not another; and yet "——— can laugh," "——— cannot laugh" and "Jemima can lick ———," "Jemima cannot lick ———" are contradictory predicables. Thus we cannot regard "some men" or "any dog in town" as genuine subjects, to which contradictory predicates are attachable to get contradictory propositions. To be sure, "Every man is P" and "Every man is not P" may readily be taken as contradictory forms; but only because the latter form would be commonly read as meaning "Not every man is P," in which there is not even the appearance of attaching "——— is not P" to "every man" as subject.

These facts about contradictories led Frege to deny that a referring phrase is an expression at all from a logical point of view. On his view, we should regard "every," for example, as logically going with the grammatical predicate; "Every ——— can laugh" and "Not every ——— can laugh" will be contradictory predicables, which yield contradictory predications when the blanks are filled with a general term like "man." "Every man" will no more occur in the proposition as a logical unit than "Plato was bald" occurs as a logical unit in "The philosopher whose most eminent pupil was Plato was bald"; the question what it refers to will thus not arise, and attempts to answer it reveal according to Frege a "superficial, mechanical or quantitative" way of regarding the matter.

Frege's analysis is both legitimate and important; but on his own principles the possibility of one analysis does not show that none other is possible,[10] and indeed an alternative analysis could easily be fitted into Frege's general view. Let us use the term "first-level predicable" for the sort of predicable that can be attached to a proper name to form a proposition about what is named. On Frege's view any such first-level predicable, if well-defined, itself stands for something —for a concept (*Begriff*); and a pair of propositions "Every man is P," "Not every man is P" would be contradictory predications about the concept for which the predicable "——— is P" stood. It thus seems natural to regard "every man ———" and "not every man ———" as being likewise predicables—a contradictory pair of *second*-level predicables, by means of which we make contradictory predications about a concept.

Referring phrases are examples of quantification restricted to some 'universe' marked out by a general term like "man"; an account of unrestricted quantification must, I think, take

[10] *Ibid.*, p. 46.

a different form. A proposition beginning with a quantifier "For some ——" is true iff the proposition minus this quantifier could be read as a true proposition by taking the occurrence(s) of the letter 'bound to' the quantifier as if these were occurrence(s) of an actual expression belonging to the appropriate category. I do not mean here that the language we are using must already contain an actual expression of the appropriate category, which, if substituted for the bound variable in the proposition minus the quantifier, would give us a true proposition; it is sufficient that we could coherently add such an expression to our language. For example, the truth value of:

For some x, x is a pebble on the beach at Brighton

does not depend on anybody's having given a proper name to such a pebble; it is enough that we could coherently add to our language a proper name of such a pebble.

To find out what expressions could coherently be added to a language we need not rely on vague intuitions, or plunge into a labyrinth of modal logic; we can appeal to the proof procedures that work in a given language. It would, for example, be entirely useless for Quine to protest that, since he uses a symbolic language from which all proper names are eliminable, the "x" in a proposition of the form "For some x, $F(x)$" is not a proper-name variable; for this symbolic language contains methods of proof in which a conclusion is treated as inferable from a premise "For some x, $F(x)$" because it is inferable from a line "$F(x)$," and here "x" is handled as an *ad hoc* proper name. Moreover, Quine frequently refers to interpretations of letters like "x" and "y," and surely assigning an object to a letter as its interpretation differs only nominally from treating the letter *pro hac vice* as a proper name of the object.[11] Indeed, in the first of the passages just cited, when speaking of assigning an object to a letter as its interpretation, Quine uses the actual expression:

---

[11] *Methods of Logic*, pp. 90f., 97f., 100, 143f., 150, 152.

" 'x' is reinterpreted as a name of that object." In the circumstances, Quine's thesis that names are theoretically dispensable is pretty well empty.

What are we to say of Quine's slogan: "To be is to be the value of a variable"? Verbally at least, Quine's slogan involves what Frege would have called a confusion between concepts of different level and would have regarded as almost the grossest that could be committed.[12] "There is a square root of 4" is true iff, for a suitable language L, "a square root of 4 is a value of a variable in L" is true. But although "a square root of 4" is the grammatical subject of both the sentences just quoted, its logical roles differ. Of the number 2, which is a square root of 4, we may truly say: "2 is a value of a variable in L." But we cannot say "There is 2"; the gap in "There is ——" used this way (in the sense of French "il y a" and German "es gibt") can be filled only by a predicable expression, not by a proper name. "Is a value of a variable in L" is predicable of objects, "there is" is not; it is easy to see how these expressions should come to be thought coextensive predicables, but almost equally easy to see that it is wrong to think so.

I am afraid that there is a genuine confusion in Quine's doctrine, not merely an inaccuracy for the sake of rhetorical effect. For in discussing the problem of existential propositions, Quine nowhere tries to draw a sharp distinction between propositions of the types "There is (not) such a thing as a winged horse" and "There is (not) such a thing as Pegasus." On the contrary, he wishes to assimilate "Pegasus" to general terms. Keeping this example, I should follow Frege in holding that "There is such a thing as a winged horse" is true iff "(—— is a) winged horse" is truly predicable of something or other; whereas "There is such a thing as Pegasus" relates to (and does not exemplify) a certain use of "Pegasus" as a proper name, its purport being that "Pegasus" in that use does indeed name something.

---

[12] Frege, *Philosophical Writings*, p. 146.

With Frege, I believe that there is no place for empty proper names in scientific discourse, or in any discourse aimed simply at conveying the truth. When an astronomer discovered that he had failed to identify an intra-Mercurian planet under the style "Vulcan," he dropped "Vulcan" from his vocabulary; when the university authorities discover that a name on their records answers only to a fraudulent pretense on the part of an undergraduate clique that there is a person so named, they erase the name. On the other hand, there is no call to erase a description from our language because we conclude that nothing answers to it.

This view of vacuous proper names raises a difficulty over the occurrence of proper names in oblique contexts, such as the following:

(1) The heathen believed that Jupiter dethroned his father.
(2) The examiners believe that Joe Doakes is worthy of an A grade.

We may suppose (1) to be asserted by a Christian, and (2) by one to another of the undergraduate clique through whose concerted action a fictitious undergraduate named "Joe Doakes" has got put on the university's records. If we adopt Frege's rule that when a proper name is empty, clauses containing it are no longer propositions with a truth-value, then it should seem that (1) and (2) could not be consistently asserted in the supposed circumstances.

Frege's own solution, as is well known, is that "Jupiter" and "Joe Doakes" and other proper names each have an oblique or indirect reference (whether or not they also have an ordinary reference, i.e., actually do name something or other) and that this is what propositions like (1) and (2) are about. But we need not go so far; as Aquinas is wont to say about the more dubious utterances of the Fathers, (1) and (2) ought to be charitably interpreted rather than imitated.

One way of charitably construing (1) and (2) would be:

(3) The heathen intended to use "Jupiter" as a name for a god who dethroned his father

(4) The examiners believe that there is an undergraduate named "Joe Doakes" who is worthy of an A grade

(3) being so read that all the words following "The heathen intended" fall within an indirect-speech construction. In some instances it may be disputable whether an indirect-speech construction really gives us a fair report of what was said, thought, meant, and so forth; however, these ways of expounding (1) and (2) fall well within the limits of fair reporting. For although the heathen, or the examiners, would no doubt normally use "Jupiter" or "Joe Doakes," as (if it were) a proper name, the truth of (1) or (2) implies that they would reply affirmatively to a suitable question in which the name was not used as a name but quoted, a question such as the following:

(5) Do you use "Jupiter" as a name for a god who dethroned his father?

(6) Is there an undergraduate named "Joe Doakes" who deserves an A grade?

And if we replace (1) by (3) or (2) by (4), we no longer have a proposition that even seems to commit those asserting it to the use of a proper name which they themselves would regard as naming nothing.

This technique of interpretation is called for only in cases where an ostensible proper name is used in indirect speech to report the words or attitudes of people who regard it as a name of something, whereas the reporter does not so regard it. No such technique is called for in dealing with propositions like:

(7) Jenkins is a man, and Johnson disbelieves that Ralph de Vere is a shopkeeper and does not disbelieve that Jenkins is a shopkeeper, and Jenkins is the same man as Ralph de Vere.

For somebody who asserted (7) would be committed, no less

than Johnson himself whose beliefs are reported, to using both "Jenkins" and "Ralph de Vere" as names; so the problems raised by (7) are quite different from those raised by (1) and (2).

The set-up I have in mind for example (7) is as follows: Let us suppose that Johnson is acquainted with a social figure, Ralph de Vere, and a shopkeeper, Jenkins; unknown to Johnson, Ralph de Vere and Jenkins are one and the same man. (Perhaps Ralph de Vere is an impostor; or perhaps he has a taste for keeping a shop, which he can indulge only in secret; or what you will.) Now Johnson may be quite incredulous when told that Ralph de Vere is a shopkeeper. In that case, we can find an interpretation of "x" in the category of proper names such that the formula:

(8) x is a man, and Johnson disbelieves that Ralph de Vere is a shopkeeper and does not disbelieve that x is a shopkeeper, and x is the same man as Ralph de Vere

becomes a true proposition when "x" is read thus. On our hypothesis this is obviously the case; for (8) will come out true if we read "x" as "Jenkins." Accordingly, the following proposition will also be true:

(9) For some x, x is a man, and Johnson disbelieves that Ralph de Vere is a shopkeeper and does not disbelieve that x is a shopkeeper, and x is the same man as Ralph de Vere.

Quine, as is well known, would reject propositions like (9) as ill formed. His reason for doing this is as follows. If (9) were well formed, (9) would be validly inferred from (7). Quine would admit (7) to be well formed. On the other hand, he would say, (9) is equivalent to:

(10) For some man x, Johnson disbelieves that Ralph de Vere is a shopkeeper and does not disbelieve that x is a shopkeeper, and x is the same man as Ralph de Vere.

And obviously in the case supposed there could be no man x

such as to make (10) true. Only Ralph de Vere is the same man as Ralph de Vere; and it is not the case that Johnson both disbelieves that Ralph de Vere is a shopkeeper and does not disbelieve this. But if (9) is well formed, (9) and therefore (10) must be true propositions if (7) is true. Since in fact (7) could be true whereas (10) could not, (9) and (10) cannot be well-formed propositions: a quantifier outside an *oratio obliqua* clause cannot bind a variable within the clause.

Quine refuses to explore such escape routes as Carnap's— making "Ralph de Vere" and "Jenkins" relate to different intentional[13] objects but nevertheless to the same man. Carnap's idea is to assume different modes of reference, so that, whereas the intentional objects referred to in the one mode are different, the man referred to in the other mode is one and the same. The objection I should bring, however (one that Quine would share), is that "intentional object" simply fails to supply any criterion of identity whatsover; there is no saying what is the same intentional object.[14]

For all that, I think Quine's rejection of (9) is misconceived. On my specification as to the use of "for some x," the question "For which entity x?" will not arise at all. For unrestricted quantifiers construed as I suggest, there will be no question which entities they 'refer to' or 'range over'; such questions seem appropriate only because we wrongly assimilate the use of quantifiers now under discussion to the use of quantifiers when they are tacitly restricted to some 'universe'.

---

[13] This is the etymologically correct spelling: the adjective in this use refers to the intention of a term, i.e., what we intend by it. The spelling "intension(al)" came in from a characteristic muddle of Sir William Hamilton, who thought the intention of a term was a sort of intensive magnitude, the Scholastic *intensio*; the spelling of "extension" has no doubt been influential too. Hamilton's neologism has ousted "intention" from its application to terms, except when preceded by "first" or "second"; the spelling of the adjective or adverb "intentional(ly)" and of "intentionality" in current philosophical literature is merely chaotic.

[14] See W. Van O. Quine, *From a Logical Point of View* (Cambridge, Mass.: Harvard University Press, 1953), pp. 153f.

I do not want to say that all the troubles of indirect-speech constructions and quantifications that reach into them can now be lightly dismissed. For example, if we regard (9) as a well-formed proposition, we can nevertheless not take it to be of the form "For some x, $F(x)$," where "$F(\ )$" represents an ordinary one-place predicable. Although the context:

(11) —— is a man, and Johnson disbelieves that Ralph de Vere is a shopkeeper and does not disbelieve that —— is a shopkeeper, and —— is the same man as Ralph de Vere

always yields a proposition when we insert the same proper name in all three blanks, we cannot take it as an ordinary one-place predicable; for then it would have to be a predicable that applied to Jenkins but not to Ralph de Vere, which is *ex hypothesi* ruled out. However these complications may have to be unraveled, (9) is certainly, on our interpretation, a well-formed proposition. We have specified its truth-conditions, and therefore its sense; its sense, as Frege would say, is the sense of: Such-and-such conditions are fulfilled.

We may say that (11) is not a *Shakespearean* predicable; that is, not one which is true of whatever it *is* true of by any other name, as "smells sweet" is true of a rose. For this reason, although (9), the result of 'existentially' quantifying (11), is clearly interpretable, we may not take the truth-condition of (9) to be that (11) shall be true of something or other.

In most of this work we have been wholly concerned with Shakespearean predicables. In the present connection the schematic letter "F" will be used to represent an arbitrary Shakespearean predicable.

With this restriction, we may assert that "For some x, x is F" has exactly the same truth-condition as "Something or other is F" or as "There is something that is F"—namely, that the predicable represented by "F" should be true of something or other. For "For some x, x is F" will be true iff

"x is F" is true for some interpretation of "x" as a proper name; and since "F" is a Shakespearean predicable, this will be the case iff "F" is true of an object namable by some proper name.

It makes absolutely no logical difference whether we say "There is something that is F" or "There exists something that is F"; "exists" is merely a shade more formal than "is." It ought not to be necessary to say this; but it is necessary, in view of what certain Oxford philosophers say about "exists." Some of their dicta—e.g., that "exist" does not occur often in ordinary language, that it is a word of philosophical provenance—besides happening to be false, could not possibly be philosophically relevant. As for the idea that "There exists an even prime" commits us to an objectionably metaphysical assertion that the number 2, which is an even prime, *exists*—this is again Frege's "grossest of all possible confusions." The purport of the quoted proposition is that "is an even prime" is true of something, not that "exists" is true of something. Russell has repeatedly pointed this out; but the Oxford philosophers in question despise Russell and do not read him.

22

Frege on Sense-Functions

HOWARD JACKSON

In this note I wish to point out an extension of Frege's distinction between the *sense* and *denotation* of a name.[1] I shall argue that Frege countenanced entities in the realm of sense corresponding to his notion of a *Funktion* as something *ungesättigt*; that these entities are likewise *Funktionen*; and that this extension of the distinction is (more or less) advanced by A. Church in his article, "A formulation of the logic of sense and denotation" (in *Structure, Method and Meaning—Essays in honor of Henry M. Sheffer*, New York (1951)).

Dummett has argued convincingly[2] that the expression remaining after the deletion of one or more names from a declarative sentence denotes, according to Frege, a *Funktion*. In the case of a sentence the resulting *Funktionsname* denotes what Frege called a *Begriff* (where two or more names are removed, a *Beziehung*), that is, a *Funktion* which for any argument determines a truth-value. In the second paper mentioned in footnote 2 Dummett mentions an unpublished paper

Reprinted with the kind permission of the author, editor, and publisher from *Analysis*, XXIII (1962-63), 84-87, Basil Blackwell & Mott Ltd., publisher.

[1] The idea that Frege's theory requires extension in the manner described below was suggested to me by P. T. Geach.

[2] See "Frege on Functions: A Reply," *The Philosophical Review*, LXVII (1955), 96-107; and "Note: Frege on Functions," *ibid.*, LXVIII (1956), 229-230.

from 1906 wherein Frege argues explicitly for *Begriffe* as the denotation of such "unsaturated" sentence-parts. In a passage from that paper Frege writes: [3] "Wie der Gedanke Sinn des ganzen Satzes ist, ist ein Teil des Gedankens Sinn eines Satzteils. Nun ist die Frage, ob nicht auch dem ungesättigten Teil des Gedankens, der als Sinn des entsprechenden Satzteils anzusehen ist, etwas entspricht, was als Bedeutung dieses Satzteils aufzufassen ist." As Dummett has pointed out, Frege identifies that *Bedeutung* with a *Begriff* (or *Beziehung*). What is curious in this passage is the mention of "the unsaturated part of the thought" which corresponds to a part of the sentence. The corresponding sentence-part is the *Begriffsname*, and consistent with Frege's distinction between the sense and denotation of a name it is natural that this name also have a sense. In the same paper from 1906 Frege writes: "Wenn wir einen Satz zerlegen in einen Eigennamen und den übrigen Teil, so hat dieser übrige Teil als Sinn einen ungesättigten Gedankenteil."

If we are to admit "unsaturated thought-parts" into Frege's zoo of abstract beings, it is reasonable to inquire further concerning their properties. In another unpublished paper from 1925, where he is considering the trigonometric functions (sine, cosine) as examples of *Funktionen*, Frege writes: ". . . 'sin α' ist also ein ergänzungsbedürftiges Zeichen und unterscheidet sich dadurch von den Eigennamen. Dementsprechend ist auch sein Inhalt ergänzungsbedürftig und unterscheidet sich dadurch von jedem Gegenstande. . . ." It will be recalled that Frege consistently, and often, in his writings cites this *Ergänzungsbedürftigkeit* as the defining characteristic of *Funktionen*. (In fact, in one place Frege argues that this property applies more properly to the sense than to the denotation of a *Funktionsname*. In a paper from 1891-92 he writes: "Die Wörter 'ungesättigt' und 'prädikativ'

---

[3] I am indebted to the *Institut für mathematische Logik und Grundlagenforschung* in Münster, Germany, for granting me access to Frege's *Nachlass*.

scheinen besser auf den sinn als die Bedeutung zu passen; aber es muss dem (*sic*) doch auch etwas bei der Bedeutung entsprechen; und ich weiss keine besseren Wörter.") If we agree that 'Inhalt' may be translated by 'sense' in this context, it follows that the sense of such *Funktionsnamen* are indeed *Funktionen*.[4] To clinch the matter I offer one final quotation from the same paper: ". . . man kann aber dem Zeichen 'cos' nicht jeden Inhalt absprechen. Wenn man jedoch mit dem bestimmten Artikel sagen wollte, "*der* Inhalt des Zeichens 'cos' ", gäbe man damit der falschen Meinung Ausdruck, dass ein Gegenstand Inhalt des Zeichens 'cos' wäre." An acquaintance with Frege's writings produces the feeling that all this sounds very familiar. Certainly it should, for Frege uses the same argument with 'Inhalt' replaced by 'Bedeutung' in demonstrating the consquences of the "unsaturated" nature of *Funktionen*.

My discussion rests solely upon unpublished material, and though there is evidence for my interpretation in Frege's published works, he is nowhere as clear on this issue as he is in the papers cited above. I shall not give here a detailed account of this point as it occurs in published articles but rather indicate one passage where the interpretation I have advanced is requisite, I feel, to a proper understanding of Frege.

In *Über Begriff und Gegenstand* Frege writes that the words 'fällt unter' in the expression 'die Zahl 2 fällt unter den Begriff P r i m z a h l' have an "unsaturated sense" which is doubly in need of completion. A complete sense (or *Gedanke* in this case) results just in case this incomplete sense

---

[4] It is not always accurate in translating Frege to render 'Inhalt' by 'sense', that is, 'Inhalt' and 'Sinn' are not always synonymous for Frege. *Inhalt* is a broader notion in most cases than *Sinn*, and "includes" what Frege sometimes called the "poetischer Duft" of an expression as well as its sense. That there is no non-metaphorical means of expressing this relationship between the *Inhalt* and the *Sinn* of a name—though perhaps uninteresting in itself—suggests that these notions are not without difficulties (as has often been pointed out).

is doubly completed. For the pair of arguments, the sense of 'die Zahl 2' and the sense of 'der Begriff P r i m z a h l' the *Funktion*, which we have identified with the sense of 'fällt unter', yields as value the proposition expressed by 'die Zahl 2 fällt unter den Begriff P r i m z a h l'.

Similar passages are to be found in *Die Verneinung* and *Gedankengefüge*, and it is left to the reader to accept (or reject) my interpretation as it applies to such expressions as 'Die Verneinung des Gedankens, dass 3 grösser als 5 ist'.

I would now like to show that Professor Church in his tentative formulation of Frege's intensional logic (the above-mentioned article) proposes the admission of certain functions which correspond rather well with those *Funktionen* we have been considering. There are, however, two points where care should be taken in drawing parallels between Church's work and Frege's. First, Church introduces the notion of a *concept* of an object (not to be confused with Frege's *Begriff*) which corresponds to Frege's *Sinn*, yet is independent of language. That is, Church admits the possibility of a concept for which there is no expression in a given language having that concept as its sense. Further, a given object may be determined by many concepts, but a given concept determines at most one object. In Fregean terms this amounts to saying that a given object may have many names with different senses, but each sense determines one object and no other. Secondly, Church abandons Frege's notion of a *Funktion* as something *ungesättigt*, and treats the names of functions on a par with the names of other (*gesättigte*) entities. These discrepancies to the contrary, it is still worthwhile, I feel, to point out the parallel. I ignore all reference to type here, though Church's use of the simple theory of types is very essential to his formulation.

In Frege's terms, Church proposes the following: Where F is a name of the function ϕ, there exists a function ϕ' determined by the rule that the value of ϕ' for an argument μ is the sense of F(a), where the sense of a is μ. It remains to identify ϕ' with the sense of F; and I claim that ϕ' closely resembles Frege's *ungesättigter Inhalt*.

Church goes on to add that though this proposal is not to be found in Frege's writings, there is nothing in it which seems inconsistent with what he says. I agree that there is indeed no inconsistency, and that Frege himself proposed something very similar.

The preceding discussion should settle a point raised by R. Grossmann (in "Frege's Ontology," *The Philosophical Review*, vol. LXX no. 1 (1961), pp. 23-40), who writes: "Frege's system has two rather puzzling parts: (1) he insists on the sense-denotation distinction for names but makes no such distinction for concept words. . . ." Mr. Grossmann later goes on to say (p. 35) that this is puzzling, "for one sees no obstacle to extending the sense-denotation distinction to cover concept words in addition to names." I have argued that it is not puzzling because it is not true.

Grossmann is not alone in failing to find this extension of the sense-denotation distinction in Frege's writings. W. Marshall in a review (*The Journal of Symbolic Logic*, vol. 18 no. 1 (1953), pp. 90-91) writes: "Since Frege applies the sense-denotation distinction only to proper names, that is, names of *objects* (*Gegenstände*, as opposed to *Funktionen*), it would seem that functions are neither senses nor denotations. . . ." (Incidentally, this last clause contains, at least tacitly, a common confusion regarding sense and denotation. Whereas we may speak of *the sense of A*, and of *the denotation of A*, and these two entities must be distinct (on Frege's theory), it is not correct to speak of sense on the one hand and denotations on the other as though these two classes of things were disjoint. They are not. Geach's paper "Class and Concept" (*The Philosophical Review*, vol. LXIV no. 4 (1955), pp. 561-570, goes a long way toward dispelling a tendency to this and related confusions.)

Finally, I would like to point out that Mr. Grossmann does propose an extension of Frege's much-discussed distinction along the lines that Frege himself in fact proposed. It is also significant that Grossmann refers to the paper by Church mentioned above, though it is not clear precisely what feature of that work he had in mind. With charity for all, I take it to be the passage just discussed.

23

A Paradox
in Frege's Semantics

MILTON FISK

I

In his "On Concept and Object" Frege writes: "we are confronted by an awkwardness of language, which I admit cannot be avoided, if we say that the concept *horse* is not a concept."[1] This awkwardness cannot be avoided, because "expressions like 'the concept *F*' designate not concepts but objects."[2] For 'the concept *F*' is a "proper name," and thus "has as its reference a definite object . . . but not a concept."[3] On the other hand, "a concept is the reference of a predicate," and "an object is something that can never be the whole reference of a predicate."[4] I wish to show that these principles, which constrain Frege to deny that the concept *horse* is a concept, lead to a contradiction. I shall interpret this contradiction as indicating the impossibility of drawing a distinction between the reference of a proper name and

Reprinted with the kind permission of the editor and the author from *Philosophical Studies*, XIV (1963), 56-63.

[1] *The Philosophical Writings of Gottlob Frege*, translated by P. Geach and M. Black (Oxford: Blackwell, 1952), p. 46.

[2] *Ibid.*, p. 48.

[3] *Ibid.*, p. 57.

[4] *Ibid.*, p. 48.

that of a predicate in terms of Frege's object-concept duality. The contradiction can be avoided by adopting either of two alternative object-concept dualities which are distinctively non-Fregean in that in each the "predicative nature of the concept"[5] is rejected.

II

However Frege would explicitly draw the proper-name-predicate distinction, it is clear that he would accept the following:

(1) 'the concept *horse*' is a proper name.

(2) 'is a horse' is a predicate.[6]

Moreover, he would accept the three following semantical assertions:

(3) If 'the concept *horse*' is a proper name, the concept *horse* is an object.[7]

(4) If 'is a horse' is a predicate, 'is a horse' refers to the concept *horse*.[8]

(5) If 'is a horse' is a predicate, 'is a horse' does not refer to an object.[9]

Now from (2) and (5) we derive the following:

(6) 'is a horse' does not refer to an object.

And from (1) and (3), and (2) and (4), respectively, we derive the following:

(7) The concept *horse* is an object.

(8) 'is a horse' refers to the concept *horse*.

Since arguments of the form 'Gx and Fyx, therefore there is

---

[5] *Ibid.*, p. 47, n. 2.

[6] *Ibid.*, pp. 44 and 46, n. 2.

[7] "One would expect that the reference of the grammatical subject [in an assertion about a concept] would be the concept; but the concept as such cannot play this part, in view of its predicative nature; it must first be converted into an object, or, speaking more precisely, represented by an object" (*ibid.*, p. 46).

[8] "A concept is the reference of a predicate" (*ibid.*, p. 48).

[9] "An object is something that can never be the whole reference of a predicate" (*ibid.*).

a z such that Gz and Fyz' are valid, (7) and (8) yield:

(9) 'is a horse' refers to an object.

But (9) contradicts (6). Let it be agreed that for the predicate-realist predicates refer to objects, and that for the predicate-nominalist predicates do not refer to objects since they either refer to non-objects or do not refer at all. Then one can say that Frege is inconsistent in that he is both a predicate-realist and a predicate-nominalist.

III

The inference from (7) and (8) to (9), i.e., to 'There is a z such that z is an object and "is a horse" refers to z,' can be challenged if the following claims can be established. (a) In (8), 'the concept *horse*' does not have its "customary" reference but only its "indirect" reference.[10] (b) In a context where an expression has only its indirect reference, i.e., in an "oblique" context, it cannot, on pain of obtaining a "meaningless" result, be replaced by a variable referring to a quantifier whose scope is the entire context.[11] From (a) and (b) it would follow that (9) is meaningless, even though (7) and (8) are meaningful. There would then be no inference and inconsistency would be averted.

One might think that (8) is an oblique context, since (8) becomes false when 'the concept *creature like-in-species to Citation*' replaces 'the concept *horse*.' It should be noted, however, that while

The extension of the concept *horse* = the extension of the concept *creature like-in-species to Citation*

is true, we can hardly claim that the following is true:

The concept *horse* = the concept *creature like-in-species to Citation*.

Though the extensions are identical the concepts themselves

---

[10] *Ibid.*, p. 59.

[11] Cf. Quine, *From a Logical Point of View* (Cambridge, Mass.: Harvard University Press, 1953), pp. 147-50.

would not seem to be. Unless the concepts named are identical, failure of interchange of concept names to preserve truth is no indication that (8) is oblique. Moreover, it would seem that concept identity is a sufficient condition for the preservation of the truth of (8) under interchange of concept names. Synonymy of concept names is not required. Since

The concept *horse* = the concept used as an example in II

is true, it would be plausible to suppose that

(8′) 'is a horse' refers to the concept used as an example in II,

which results from (8) by interchange, is true. Yet, it seems clear that the following is false:

The sense of 'the concept *horse*' = the sense of 'the concept used as an example in II.'

If interchange of concept names could be trusted to preserve the truth of (8) only when the names interchanged had the same sense, then (8) would indeed be oblique. Since concept identity does not entail the synonymy of concept names [12] and since concept identity is a sufficient condition for a truth-preserving interchange in (8), (8) is not oblique and (a) cannot be established.

Even if Frege had held (a), he is faced with a dilemma in regard to (b). If he had held (a) and if quantification into oblique contexts is *admissible*, then the inference from (7) and (8) to (9) cannot be objected to on the above grounds. In this case the charge of inconsistency would still apply. If he had held (a) and if quantification into oblique contexts is *inadmissible*, then he would have been committed to holding that (5), as well as (9), is meaningless. The consequent of (5) expands into 'it is not the case that there is a *z* such

---

[12] The question as to whether property identity entails the synonymy of property names has been discussed by Wolterstorff, "Are Properties Meanings?" *Journal of Philosophy*, 57:277-81 (1960). In this regard it is to be noted that, for Frege, the concepts under which an object falls are its properties (p. 51). On the question as to whether Frege could or did specify conditions for concept identity, see Bergmann, "Frege's Hidden Nominalism," *Philosophical Review*, 67:448-49 (1958).

that z is an object and "is a horse" refers to z.' One of Frege's own principles would then be meaningless. Either the move to (9) is sanctioned, or it is impossible to raise the general question whether predicates do or do not refer to objects.

IV

Frege speaks both of proper names and of predicates as referring. In respect to the schema 'A refers to x,' replacements for 'x' are, as objects of the preposition 'to,' proper names, both when replacements for 'A' are quoted proper names and when they are quoted predicates. One cannot replace 'x' both by proper names and by predicates in order to express a difference between the references of proper names and those of predicates. Frege abides by this restriction when he chooses, among the available substantival alternatives, expressions of the form 'the concept F' as replacements for 'x' in the schema for predicate-referring. We shall attempt to avoid the contradiction developed in II without abandoning Frege's thesis, expressed by (4), that predicates refer to concepts. While holding to (4), the contradiction can be avoided by abandoning either (3) or (5). In devising a replacement for (3) or for (5) we must be guided by the fact that, in saying what the reference of a predicate is, a proper name must be used to mention that reference.

i. One might abandon (3), while retaining (5), in view of accepting the following terminological restrictions. Proper names are to be divided into two groups. Those of the first can be used in stating what the reference of a predicate is, what the reference of a function is, what the sense of a proper name is, or what the sense of a sentence is. Thus, 'the concept *horse*,' 'the function x^2-4x,' 'the sense of "Aristotle," ' and 'the thought that Caesar conquered Gaul' belong to the first group. Proper names which cannot be so used are included in the second group. Among those of the second group are 'Aristotle,' 'the president of the Confederacy,' 'the extension of the concept *wise*,' '$3^2 - 4 \cdot 3$,' and 'the True.' It shall be agreed that, in non-oblique contexts, proper names of the first group are used to refer to "concepts" and that those of the second are used to refer to "objects." Since some proper names refer to objects and others refer to concepts, we must replace (3) by the following:

(3') If 'the concept *horse*' is a proper name, the concept *horse* is an object or a concept.

Statement (7) cannot be inferred from (1) together with (3'). Clearly, under the present restrictions on 'concept' and 'object,' *concept* is not a species of *object*. Rather, using the term 'individual' for the comprehensive category of references of proper names, conceptual and objective individuals form mutually exclusive classes. Moreover, both 'is a horse' and 'the concept *horse*' can be used to refer to the concept *horse*. All predicates and some proper names refer to conceptual individuals. 'The concept *horse* is a concept' is true, while 'The concept *horse* is an object' is false.

ii. One might abandon (5), while retaining (3), in view of accepting the following terminological restrictions, which differ from those of (i). Proper names are to be divided into the same groups as were mentioned under (i), but those groups are to be labeled differently. Proper names which can be used to mention the references of predicates, the references of functions, the senses of proper names, or the senses of sentences will be said to be proper names of "conceptual objects." Those which cannot be so used will be said to be proper names of "nonconceptual objects." Here the categorial term 'object' does the work assigned to 'individual' under (i). All proper names refer to objects. All predicates, but only some proper names, refer to conceptual objects. Thus, in place of (5), one would have the following:

(5') If 'is a horse' is a predicate, then 'is a horse' does not refer to a nonconceptual object.

Statement (6) cannot be inferred from (2) and (5′). In this context, both 'The concept *horse* is a concept' and 'The concept *horse* is an object' are true.

Whether (i) or (ii) be taken as the more promising resolution of the contradiction, the concept loses what Frege called its predicative nature. For, under either resolution, the concept, i.e., the conceptual individual of (i) or the conceptual object of (ii), can be the reference of a proper name as well as of a predicate.[13]

V

Since the concept loses its predicative nature under either (i) or (ii) of IV, we are led to suspect that Frege's undoing was his insistence that the concept is predicative.

When Frege says that the concept is predicative he does not mean just that it can be the reference of a predicate. He means, in addition, that the concept cannot be the reference of a proper name.[14] Now let us assume that we are in possession of a language in which it is possible to frame meaningful sentences of the form 'A refers to x.' In the context of this assumption the claims that the concept can be the reference of a predicate and that it cannot be the reference of a proper name are, when taken together, inconsistent. This can be seen as follows.

On the one hand, suppose that concepts can be the references of predicates. Now the grammatical objects of 'refers to,' like those of 'corresponds to,' 'mirrors,' and 'means,' are proper

---

[13] In abandoning the idiom 'the concept of wisdom' in favor of the less usual 'the concept *wise*' Frege in no way strengthens the claim that concepts are predicative. Grammar demands that some device, such as italics, be employed in order to render 'wise' substantival so that it can follow 'the concept.' The merits of Frege's 'the concept *wise*' lie in (a) its avoidance of the suggestion that there must be an impalpable something which the concept is *of*, and (b) its greater flexibility in allowing a distinction to be drawn between the concept *wise* and the concept *wisdom* which cannot be drawn in terms of the 'concept of'-without-italics idiom.

[14] Cf. footnote 7 above.

names. In saying that a given predicate refers to a certain
concept a proper name is used to refer to that concept. Thus
concepts can be the references of proper names.

It might be claimed that in arriving at this conclusion I am
overlooking Frege's distinction between the concept as reference of a predicate (the concept "proper") and the concept
as reference of a proper name (the concept "correlate").[15]
For, it will be said, when I say ' "is a horse" refers to the
concept *horse*' I am using 'the concept *horse*' to refer to
the concept correlate and not to the concept proper. Thus one
can say that a given predicate refers to a certain concept
proper only if a proper name is used to refer to the appropriate concept correlate, rather than to the concept proper.
But this leads to a result which, from Frege's point of view,
is equally unacceptable. If the reference of a predicate is indicated by a proper name referring to a concept correlate, then
it follows that the reference of the predicate is a concept correlate.[16] And this is contrary to Frege's thesis that predicates
refer only to concepts proper. In a context, like (8), in which
the concept is both referred to by a proper name and said to
be the reference of a predicate, we can no longer distinguish
concept proper from concept correlate. For here the reference
of the proper name and that of the predicate must be the
same, if the predicate referential statement is to be true.

On the other hand, suppose that concepts cannot be the references of proper names. Once again, it is possible to say that
a certain entity is the reference of a given linguistic unit only
by using a proper name to refer to that entity. To say that
a certain concept is the reference of a given linguistic unit, a

---

[15] Cf. Frege, p. 46; and Wells, "Frege's Ontology," *Review of Metaphysics*, 4:550 (1951).

[16] Making explicit the reasoning, in terms of an example, we have:
(i) 'is a horse' refers to the concept *horse*. (ii) The proper name 'the
concept *horse*' refers to a concept correlate. (iii) If the proper name
'the concept *horse*' refers to a concept correlate, the concept *horse* is a
concept correlate. (iv) ∴ The concept *horse* is a concept correlate.
(v) ∴ 'is a horse' refers to a concept correlate.

proper name must be used to refer to that concept. But our supposition is that concepts cannot be the references of proper names. We cannot, then, frame a single meaningful sentence of the form 'A refers to x' in which the replacement for 'A' is a predicate in quotes. Thus concepts cannot be the references of predicates.

The claim that the concept is predicative leads both to the conclusion that concept can be the reference of a proper name and to the conclusion that the concept cannot be the reference of a predicate. Each of these conclusions, in its turn, contradicts a part of the claim that the concept is predicative. Hence Frege's notion of the predicativity of the concept is inconsistent. If we wish to retain the thesis that the concept can be the reference of a predicate, we must abandon the thesis that it cannot be the reference of a proper name. Further, if, while retaining this thesis, we deem it desirable to say that the concept is "predicative," or that it is "unsaturated,"[17] in a sense still related to Frege's, then we must understand by this only that the concept can be the reference of a predicate.[18]

---

[17] Cf. Frege, p. 47, n. 2.

[18] This point is not at odds with Strawson's claim (*Individuals* (London: Methuen, 1959), p. 188) to have found an "additional depth in Frege's metaphor of the saturated and the unsaturated constituent." For he has shown, at most, a deeper significance in saying that the predicate is unsaturated. For him, the predicate, unlike the subject, does not present a fact while introducing a term, which in the case of the predicate is a universal, into a proposition. But there is no indication that this circumstance, which contributes to the unsaturatedness of the predicate, is transferred to the universal, thereby giving it a non-linguistic unsaturatedness.

24

*Is Frege's Concept of a Function Valid?**

RULON S. WELLS

1. Thesis of the paper. The criticism I have to make of Frege can be expressed in various ways. Our current ways of talking about concepts are so confused and unsettled that I find several modes of expression at hand, with no difference of meaning between them or at least none that is relevant at present.

The most exact expression, in my opinion, is to say that, although Frege purported, or claimed, to have a certain set of concepts—it is customary to pick out function as the central one of these—which served to unify philosophy with mathematics (logic being the mediator), this claim is mistaken. According to this mode of expression, Frege doesn't have a valid concept of function. But inasmuch as, still according to this mode of expression, validity is a transcendental property —to be a concept at all is to be a valid concept—it follows that to speak of a valid concept is redundant, and we need only say that Frege doesn't have a concept of function. The

Reprinted with the kind permission of the author and the editor from *The Journal of Philosophy*, LX (1963), 719-730.

* Presented in a symposium on "Frege" at the sixtieth annual meeting of the American Philosophical Association, Eastern Division, December 28, 1963.

disadvantage of this mode of expression lies in its suggesting that then the word 'function' in his writings is simply meaningless, a *flatus vocis,* which is not what I contend.

But if the word is not simply meaningless, then it must express something—therefore some concept; if that is so, the most severe criticism we could possibly make would be that, although Frege has a concept of function, it isn't a valid one, or doesn't do what he thinks it does, or the like. That is the way of speaking that I adopt in this paper.

A more exact statement of my critique is that the alleged *general* concept of function is pointless. What it does can be done on the technical side by other concepts (one of which would be *'propositional* function'), and what it claims to do on the philosophical side cannot be done at all.

In order to keep this a paper about Frege and save it from being primarily a paper about concepts, I will not attempt to draw any distinction between concepts and conceptual schemes, or frameworks, or systems; nor, consequently, between concepts and propositions of any kind, including definitions, postulates, stipulations, axioms, and principles.

2. What did Frege discover? It is part of Frege's realism to believe that the mathematician discovers, he does not invent; or rather, that his inventions and creations are not only invented for the sake of expressing his discoveries, but in their very possibility rest on discoveries. Fundamentally, the mathematician is a Magellan or a Cook, not a Leonardo or an Edison.

Casting Frege himself in his chosen type of role, we would best regard him as a Columbus. Discover he did, but he didn't discover what he thought he did.

What Frege hoped to discover was the uniquely best system of philosophy that would found the uniquely best system of logic on which in turn the uniquely best system of mathematics could be constructed. This he did not accomplish. What he did accomplish was to discover a system of logic, which at every turn suggests alternative systems and which, though as it stands it is untenable, is no more untenable than any other system of equal power. Moreover, this system admits of an interpretation that has certain philosophical merits. It also has some philosophical liabilities (implausibility, for one) which Frege recognized but slighted, and moreover the formal system proper admits of quite divergent philosophical interpretations, a fact of which Frege shows no awareness.

Thus Frege hoped for something, but didn't discover it; and discovered something, but didn't appreciate it. The reason for this two-sided failure is that he mistook a compatibility for a necessity. His technical system is determined in part by technical and in part by philosophical considerations; the two kinds of considerations agree in the sense of not contradicting each other, but (contrary to what he seems to suppose) they don't agree in the stronger sense of independently giving the same determinate result.

Error in general cannot be explained; a given individual error can be explained, but only as the consequence of some other error. I suggest an explanation of this kind for Frege's mistaking weak for strong agreement. His initial error, according to this suggestion, is a mistake about realism: he thought that, if the mathematician can discover a real world, he can discover the best way of describing it. This is not necessarily wrong, but what Frege overlooked was that the best description may consist in saying, at some second level, that at the first level there are various tenable descriptions no one of which is the best. To restate his oversight, instead of assuming, more generally, that at some level there is a best description, he assumed, more specially, that at the very first level there is a best description. I put in these terms the initial mistake that I ascribe to him, in order to point up its nature: Frege, who advocated generalization as a major method, failed here to generalize. Now although in his hands the method is not properly controlled, it is not totally invalid; a corrected, more cautious version could be given, and

even that corrected version would enjoin the present generalization about the level of the best description; and it can be
put down as a mere lapse that Frege didn't follow the injunc-
tion. When the lapse is corrected, there results a tenable view
in keeping with his own principles.

3. Frege's uncontrolled method of discovery. Frege thought
he had a method for making conceptual discoveries: the
method of generalization. In believing in this method, Frege
was a child of his time. The method was enunciated in the
seventeenth century, rather neglected in the eighteenth,
and energetically revived in the nineteenth, when ever so
many successes seemed to justify it pragmatically. In the
twentieth century, after mathematicians had again become
disenchanted with it, it had great influence on philosophers—
an embarrassing instance of "cultural lag." The reason why
it lost popularity with mathematicians was that its limita-
tions became clear. It was *too* productive: it yielded some
products one would sooner not have had, and was incapable
of discriminating between the good and the bad. It was a
method, therefore, whose net usefulness would be greatly
enhanced by a supplementary method that would do the
work of discrimination. The philosophers who belatedly imitated the method—Peirce, Dewey, and Whitehead are conspicuous examples—failed to imitate and failed to devise any
such supplement, to the fundamental detriment of their work.
The same is true of Frege in his philosophizing, which is our
present concern.

A brief survey of Frege's other aims and methods will fur-
nish a context and background for our discussion of function. His central concern is to give a two-layer foundation
for arithmetic: immediately, a logic; this logic, in turn, to be
founded on a sound philosophy. His concern for philosophy
is limited to those matters which concern the logic; though it
may happen (as with his account of indirect discourse) that
there are wider implications. The two foundations are visibly

distinguished by being stated in different languages: the logic proper in a formalized language of his own creation, the bottom-layer philosophy in ordinary natural language (accidentally, German).

The formalized language is meant to be not only perspicuous, but exact (or an aid to exactness) in two ways. It is meant to aid exactness (a) of reference, (b) of demonstration. Exactness of reference is achieved not only by the distinction of use and mention, and of sense and denotation, but also by Frege's account of variables and by the ways in which he uses them. Exactness of demonstration is achieved by means which are not original with Frege and which he applies better than his contemporaries but not as well as his successors.

Frege wants his formalized language to be not only perspicuous and capable of exact use, but also regular. Regularity of the system is achieved by generalizing in various ways. For example, before Frege it would have been said that some but not all things that have a meaning additional to their sense have a denotation. Names (noun phrases) have denotation but not truth; propositions have truth but not denotation. By generalizing the concept of denotation to subsume truth as a variety, Frege makes exceptionless, and therefore completely regular, the proposition 'All objective meaning other than sense is denotation'.

The ideals of simplicity, economy, parsimony have little weight for Frege, except so far as they are already included in the above-stated aims; and the aim of plausibility has for him still less weight. He is not indifferent to it, but explains (*Grundgesetze* 1.x-xi) that he has been forced to sacrifice it in favor of higher-ranking aims.

Regularity is an aim; generalization is a method of achieving it. The nineteenth-century watchword "Generalize!" led a number of mathematicians to mathematical discoveries. It does not lead Frege to any discovery in mathematics, but it does lead him to a philosophy of mathematics. In particular, it is sometimes supposed that the generalizing method leads him to a successful and fruitful concept of function. And since the concept to which he applies his method is itself the result of generalization by predecessors, the supposition would mean that Frege succeeded in carrying further a generalization that others had already carried far. Mr. Bartlett, in his fine monograph[1] on Frege, adopts this view. Frege, following hints of Lotze, extends the concept of function from mathematics to philosophy. (I might add another historical remark: that the basic attempt would then be the same as that attempted several decades later by Cassirer in his 'functionalism'.) The only major threat to the success of this generalization would be the threat presented by the logical antinomies.

I see the matter quite differently.

4. The requirement of unity. Mathematicians, and people influenced by them, speak of generalizing various things: concepts, systems, proofs, theorems. Let us limit our attention to generalization of concepts. It may be that the other kinds, or applications, of generalization can be reduced without artificiality to this kind. A stock example is successive generalizations of the concept of number. The generalized concept is regarded as a genus; if the Greeks said that One was not a number but the principle of number, this shows that they lacked the general (generic) concept of number.

Imagine that some anti-Greek had said: "All right, we won't quarrel about words. We may suppose that there is *some* class comprising (*a*) all the numbers—2, 3, etc.—and (*b*) 1. Call this the class of Arithmeticals. Then (i) 1 is an Arithmetical, and (ii) the concept of Arithmetical is a generalization of the concept of Number." No doubt the Greeks would have replied that there is *not* such a class as the supposer supposes. They would have argued that if such a supposition is to be allowed, then we can make up any class we

[1] James M. Bartlett, *Funktion und Gegenstand* (dissertation, München, 1961).

please. Given any assemblage of things, however random, we can form, or suppose, a class to which all and only those things belong.

The modern rejoinder to the Greeks would be to agree that this follows, and to see it as a harmless and perfectly acceptable consequence.

So simple an example is enough to show a great difference in view between ancients and moderns. The modern generalization of number depends on disjunction—not in every case, perhaps, but in some, and many, cases. A concept determines a class, and for the modern there is no question whether, given two classes, their logical sum exists, and hence no question but that there is some concept determining this class; such questions as the modern may wish to raise would have to be questions not of the existence of the concept, but of its unity, or its fruitfulness, or something like that.

The question of *unity*—the question of whether an alleged concept is unified, or unitary—does not attract the attention that it used to attract. I see two main reasons for this, namely that the question involves two others, attempts to answer which have broken down. These are the questions of intensionalism and of linguistic relativism.

If disjunctive concepts are allowed, then there is no question of unity. A disjunctive concept is as unified as any concept can be; and the existence of such a concept is "trivial"—meaning, approximately, that it is (a) an a priori necessity, and (b) that its demonstration is very easy. To give a further, better account of what the mathematician's term 'trivial' means is one of the tasks turned over by our past to our future.

The question of linguistic relativism is involved because the obvious way to tell whether a concept is simple (atomic) or disjunctive is to see how it is expressed: by a simple word, or by a disjunctive phrase. The question of intensionalism is involved because of such questions as whether Parent (apparently simple) and Mother-or-Father (apparently disjunctive) are the same concept or different but logically equivalent concepts. If we say that they are the same concept, then the form (simplicity or disjunctiveness) of the expression tells nothing of the form of the concept; if different concepts, then there is nothing to stop a man from instituting a simple term and saying that it expresses a concept different from but equivalent to some given disjunctive expression. And what linguistic relativism makes us realize is that our linguistic test for unity has no validity or force beyond the language in which the test is conducted.

5. The requirement of fruitfulness. A more popular criterion today than unity is fruitfulness. It is often proposed to judge concepts by their fruitfulness. Granting that a given word expresses a concept, one raises the question whether the concept it expresses is fruitful.

Evidently, this criterion depends on viewing concepts as hypotheses. As a property of hypotheses, fruitfulness has been discussed for some time and is fairly widely understood. And the warrant for conceiving concepts as hypotheses would seem to be this: that, like hypotheses, they are tested by a certain reverse process. A fruitful concept will enable one to describe things better (does this mean more fruitfully?) than an unfruitful one. We might, on reflection, want to limit hypothesis to explanations and conception to descriptions, but on the other hand the contrast between explanations and descriptions is itself viewed with widespread suspicion. We might end up making no distinction at all between concepts and other hypotheses.

The conception of concepts as hypotheses would seem to be particularly attractive for *fundamental* concepts, such as Frege claims his concept of function to be. A fundamental concept, by its fundamentality, cannot be defined; something like an inverse to definition must be used on it, in order to make it clear or do whatever is needed.

Let us remember—what Frege forgot, and what many people today forget—that, so far as a concept is like a hypothesis, its verification must necessarily involve comparison. To show that it "works," or is fruitful, is not enough; we must further show that it works better, or at least no worse, than any other concept. If a concept is analogous to a hypothesis, it must pass something analogous to a crucial test.

Another thing to keep in mind, when exploiting the resemblance, is that hypotheses belong to systems. Concepts likewise, then, will be embedded in systems, or frameworks. If this is correct, it will be wrong—misleading, at least—to single out any one concept as central. In Frege's conceptual system, for instance, it would be groundless to single out function as the central concept.

The question is, then, whether Frege's system taken as a whole uses, or employs, fruitful concepts. It surely does so in some indirect way, for the system was worth putting forward in order that we might study it. But that it does so in a direct way is an estimation that can only be defended with severe qualifications. Critical scrutiny shows that his system falls apart into a technical component and a philosophical component and the appearance that the two components are united is an illusion.

Certain first signs of this cleavage may be found in the following well-known features of Frege's system: (i) his unformalized metalanguage is stronger than his formalized object language; (ii) his object language, though relatively weak, is strong enough to fall into Russell's antinomy; (iii) his metalanguage, though relatively strong, is inherently inadequate to express what he wants to express about functions, because such statements as 'Functions are not objects' do not mention functions.

As for the relative strength of his metalanguage, it is not to be presumed as obvious that it is essentially richer, in Tarski's sense, than his object language. This metalanguage does not simply incorporate his object language; rather, translation is required, and the two languages are not isomorphic. Consider, for example, such a metalinguistic statement as 'Functions are not objects', which give rise to difficulty (iii). It is not a translation of any statement in his object language. Even if we replaced it by this paraphrase within the metalanguage, 'For every x, if x is a function then x is not an object', the paraphrase would not be a translation of any object-language sentence, because no object-language statement would contain a variable that ranges without restriction.

Evidently Frege's metalanguage is richer than his object language in this regard, whether or not it is richer in every regard. Now is this greater richness put to use? In raising the question of use we offer the beginning of a criterion for fruitfulness. We envision the possibility of a needlessly wide generalization, and may propose to say that it is no more fruitful than some less wide generalization. Now Frege in his metalinguistic statements generalizes his concept of function needlessly, I submit; we can see this from at least two considerations. One is that he doesn't need an endless series of levels of functions. The other is that, even within the lower levels, he fails largely to bring his function variables and his function constants into close relation.

The first consideration is tentative and conditional. To the best of my knowledge no one has worked out a modification of Frege's formal system in which his antinomous Axiom V (principle of abstraction) is replaced by something about which we can secure the usual assurances that it is not antinomous. And what further modifications would be needed to give a system that would yield not only arithmetic but also analysis and other parts of mathematics, has likewise not been investigated in any detail.

The second consideration can be presented with more definiteness.

One of Frege's most famous doctrines is his treatment of the True and the False as objects, and so as denotable. And he is sometimes given credit for the notion of truth function. Actually, by the usual current definition (modified by speaking of the True and the False rather than of Truth and False-hood), he has no truth functions, for, by that definition, a truth function is a function all of whose arguments and all of whose values are either the True or the False. In Frege's system such functions as negation and conditionality have only the True and the False as values, but other objects besides the True and the False as arguments. But this is not an important point. What is important is that his formal system admits of a generalization that, though possible, is useless.

In ordinary mathematics one of the situations in which we say that a generalization has taken place is in the introduction of a variable that ranges over certain substituends. These substituends denote that which was generalized *from*. Thus we may generalize from particular powers to the nth power. Now in Frege's system, verity is a function (*Grundgesetze* 1.9 §5; the informal name for it is my own—Frege always denotes it by his formal expression, a horizontal line), and negation is a function; it would, then, be permissible to institute a second-level function that would include among its arguments verity and falsity. Such a function would be the nearest counterpart in Frege's mathematical system to the ordinary mathematician's practice of introducing, not once and for all but just for the duration of his discussion, a free variable whose range is stipulated (in this case the range would be the set {verity, falsity}). It would be permissible to do this, but apparently it would be quite pointless, and presumably that is why Frege doesn't do it.

The situation then is this: that Frege provides certain function constants that he does not in fact treat as substituends of function variables, and sets up some function variables that in fact he never instantiates.

I shall consider two possible defenses of this practice.

i. "It is not customary in systems of mathematical logic to restrict the use of variables to uses where the variables are in fact sometimes replaced by constants. For example, the development in *Principia Mathematica* of higher arithmetic and of analysis is carried out in a language that has no elementary constants except the 'logical constants' that are not treated as functions."

Reply: There is no objection to the customary mathematical practice unless the variables are interpreted as generalizations. We ought to distinguish generality from generalization. Variables signify generality, and we may even say that they signify a possible generalization from some previous particularity; but they do not always signify an actual generalization. Therefore the generality of Frege's function variables does not guarantee generalization.

ii. "Frege's generalization of the function concept is shown in quite a different way. It is shown by his considering things as functions that had not before him been so considered."

What is the evidence that he considered them functions? Two things: (*a*) that he *called* them functions, and (*b*) that he specified their value-courses. To specify the value-course (*Wertverlauf*) of an *n*adic function is to specify a certain set of ordered $(n + 1)$-ads, each $(n + 1)$-ad consisting of n arguments followed by one value. Now what if someone does *a* but not *b*, or *b* but not *a*? And just what will count as specifying a value-course? Consider concepts, i.e., those functions which have as their values only the True, or the False, or both. Perhaps no one before Frege had said that no matter what name be put in place of both occurrences of '*x*', the result of putting such a name in place of both '*x*'s in '$x = x$' is a name of the True. And perhaps no one had taken the view that, if we take a name of a function and replace the variables in it by names of arguments, we get a name of some value of the function. If value-courses can only be specified in terms of three kinds of names, then Frege may well have been the first to do that. But in that case Frege was the first to specify value-courses for *any* function and, thus (since *a* and *b* are both required for considering anything to be a function), the first to treat *anything* as a function—a reflection that shows us that we have gone too far. We must, to remain plausible, retreat and say that specification in terms of three kinds of names is one way, but not the only way, to specify a value-course. And then we are free to say that anyone who discussed truth conditions of proportions virtually specified a value-course for every concept and, thus, virtually treated concepts as functions; the only new thing Frege added was to make the virtual treatment explicit; in other words, to come right out and *call* concepts "functions."

With that conclusion we are back in linguistic relativism. When Frege calls concepts functions, is he a discoverer or an inventor? Is he declaring a resemblance he has noticed, or is he stipulating a new use for an old word? A discussion of this question would be aside from my present concern, which is only to remark that Frege has no method for discussing such a question. And as long as the possibility of mere stipulation is open, the possibility is open that the purported union of mathematics with philosophy, via the general concept of function, is merely verbal achievement.

6. Place of semantics in Frege's function theory. It was noted two paragraphs above that Frege characterizes value-courses in terms of three kinds of names, which is to say that he characterizes them semantically. There is a further point to be made, which is that a value-course must be combinatorially exhaustive. Frege, without using any such word as 'category', sets up categories of things: objects, one-place first-level functions, and so on. Now a value-course is a set of $(n + 1)$-ads, the last term of each being a value and all the preceding terms being arguments. If, in one such $(n + 1)$-ad, the ith term $(1 \leq i \leq n)$ belongs to a certain category, then every member of that category must occur in at least one $(n + 1)$-ad belonging to the set; moreover, each combination of terms that must occur must also occur. Usually, a value-course is not described by describing each set individually but by grouping the sets into cases, ordinarily some very small number of cases. Now Frege's requirements of combinatorial

exhaustiveness serves his aim of regularity and at the same time illustrates his comparative indifference to plausibility. This may be seen in his treatment of the singular description. He would have agreed with Quine (*Mathematical Logic*, 147) that "the truth or falsehood of statements must indeed wait . . . upon inquiries . . . ; but the *meaningfulness* of an expression . . . is a matter over which we can profitably maintain control." Not having Russell's technique of contextual definition at hand, his way of maintaining control is to assign a value to the function for every possible argument, even for those cases where there is not one and only one thing answering to the description. This achieves combinatorial exhaustiveness, in the interest of regularity and at the expense of plausible conformity to ordinary usage.

7. Technical versus philosophical fruitfulness. Combinatorial exhaustiveness serves a very important technical purpose in Frege's formal system: It enables him to present a consistency proof.

Bartlett in his monograph (45-47, 68) calls attention to this consistency proof and emphasizes its role. I regard this as a very important contribution to our understanding of Frege. In seeing the need for such a proof, and a concrete way of carrying it out, Frege once again showed himself to be a genius. Let me take this occasion to say that none of my severe criticisms of Frege's system are to be understood as criticisms of Frege the man. Although in his desire for rigor and for generalization he was a child of his time and in his less than central concern with the problems of the infinite he was not (in his middle and later years) abreast of his time, he was in many features ahead of his time. Not that I agree with all the "firsts" that are commonly credited to him, nor with all the opinions that Peirce, Whitehead, Russell, etc. in this or that way relapsed, or failed to profit from his insights; I am not, for example, convinced that Russell's position on propositional functions is to be viewed, as most logicians of today view it, as simply a confusion, simply a failure to distinguish steadfastly between the symbol and what is symbolized. But I do agree that Frege moved logic into a new phase beyond the Boole–De Morgan phase. But, to come back to my initial metaphor, he did this by being a Columbus: by seeing certain things *and by being blind to certain things.* Frege was just blind to the leading idea of the English development, namely, the idea of giving alternative interpretations to the same syntactical calculus; this idea had to be rediscovered after Frege. I connect this blindness with his general insensitivity to alternatives and with his belief (a belief that I ascribe to him partly on the basis of his practice) that a best alternative could always be found.

This simultaneous vision and blindness is exhibited in Frege's consistency proof. Let us at once come to terms with the fact that he made a mistake in his proof. He was particularly astonished when Russell in June, 1902, called his attention to the antinomy in his system, because he not merely had been unaware of any antinomy, but had, as he thought, expressly proved that there was none. But there was a mistake in his proof.

Bartlett locates the mistake precisely. A constructive proof calls for a review of all possible cases, and at one point Frege fails to subdivide cases minutely enough, thinking he has dealt with a case when he has only dealt with a subcase. The subcase he overlooks is, precisely, a subcase dealing with impredicative expressions.

The mistake is a mere lapse, in the sense that all would agree, without any dispute, once the matter is called to their attention, that the subcase requires to be dealt with. But it is no lapse in the sense that it is easily corrected; the subcase cannot be dealt with in Frege's system. What Frege overlooks, then, is not just that his purported proof has a flaw, but that it has an irremediable flaw.

What to do about impredicative expressions is not the concern of the present paper. I am concerned only to accept Bartlett's emphasis on the consistency proof and to offer an interpretation of its significance. Frege's leading idea is to prove that, if every primitive expression is a name, then every derivative composite expression is a name. To prove this would be to prove more than consistency, but a consistency proof would be included. For a name is a name of only one thing; therefore every proposition that names the True does not name the False, and therefore the system is consistent.

Disregard the fact that Frege does not prove this. The point I am concerned to make is that, even if he did prove this, it would not thereby confirm his semantics of sense and denotation, and his requirement of combinatorial exhaustiveness, and his concept of function. For the constructive consistency proof would offer a certain model; Frege with his concepts of categories and function and sentences as names would be giving us the model *plus* a certain interpretation. That a model is needed is what he sees; that no more than a model is needed is what he is blind to. The need for a model is a technical need; the need for an interpretation of it is a philosophical need. Frege offers us as a unit, an atom, what should be regarded as a package or bundle. If a system of concepts achieves a certain technical purpose, such as consistency, this is a kind of fruitfulness, and a minimal validity; if, furthermore, no other system achieves the purpose, then by default the system has maximal validity. My present criticism of Frege's concept of function—or of his whole system of concepts—can be put in this way: he attempts (though unsuccessfully) to establish its minimal validity, but he does not even raise the question of maximal validity.

25

On Questioning
the Validity of Frege's
Concept of Function*

JAMES BARTLETT

A basic exception must be taken to Professor Wells' paper in that it ascribes to Frege goals which he in fact did not pursue. It was Frege's actual pursuit of a better (nota bene, not *best*) language for mathematics that led—secondarily—to his development of the function concept. This same pursuit, however, had first led to a specific language which, despite the deficiencies that extended versions of it later proved to display, was certainly a singular improvement over those available at the time (and as such constituted a considerable discovery). It was to justify this linguistic system—the predicate logic—that Frege embarked on a philosophical explication of the function concept. He did not do this out of any predilection for, or even

Reprinted with the kind permission of the author and the editor from *The Journal of Philosophy*, LXI (1964), 203.

* Abstract of a paper presented in a symposium on "Frege" at the sixtieth annual meeting of the American Philosophical Association, Eastern Division, Dec. 28, 1963; commenting on Rulon Wells, "Is Frege's Concept of Function Valid?," *The Journal of Philosophy*, LX (1963), 719-730.

experience with, the traditional concept juggling of philosophers. He did it out of his adherence to the methodological principle that in proposing a linguistic system to incorporate logic and mathematics, one must give the undefined concepts underlying the system an explanation which is rational and consistent with the system.

Frege's explanation of his underlying concept of function always had a number of awkward elements from the standpoint of rationality and, indeed, was not entirely consistent with his later extended system. Wells has made note of many of these insufficiencies. In so doing, he has rejected one explication of the concept underlying Frege's system. This explication, however, was not for Frege the absolute Wells would have it, but was relative to the system being explained. To contest the validity of the very concept underlying the system would be a more ambitious endeavor since it would call into question predicate logic itself. Here then is fruitful grounds for questioning the validity of Frege's concept of function—but a necessary prerequisite to discussion would be the proposal of an adequate alternative.

PART THREE

Frege's Logic and Philosophy of Mathematics

26

The Logical and Arithmetical Doctrines of Frege

BERTRAND RUSSELL

LIST OF ABBREVIATIONS

Bs.   *Begriffsschrift.* Eine der arithmetischen nachgebildete Formelsprache des reinen Denkens. Halle a/S, 1879.

Gl.   *Grundlagen der Arithmetik.* Eine logisch-mathematische Untersuchung über den Begriff der Zahl. Breslau, 1884.

FT.   *Ueber formale Theorien der Arithmetik.* Sitzungsberichte der Jenaischen Gesellschaft für Medicin und Naturwissenschaft, 1885.

FuB.   *Funktion und Begriff.* Vortrag gehalten in der Sitzung vom 9. Januar, 1891, der Jenaischen Gesellschaft für Medicin und Naturwissenschaft. Jena, 1891.

BuG.   *Ueber Begriff und Gegenstand.* Vierteljahrschrift für wiss. Phil., xvi 2 (1892).

SuB.   *Ueber Sinn und Bedeutung.* Zeitschrift für Phil. und phil. Kritik, Vol. c (1892).

KB.   *Kritische Beleuchtung einiger Punkte in E. Schröder's Vorlesungen über die Algebra der Logik.* Archiv für syst. Phil., Vol. i (1895).

BP.   *Ueber die Begriffsschrift des Herrn Peano und meine eigene.* Berichte der math.-physischen Classe der Königl. Sächs. Gesellschaft der Wissenschaften zu Leipzig (1896).

Gg.   *Grundgesetze der Arithmetik.* Begriffsschriftlich abgeleitet. Vol. i, Jena, 1893. Vol. ii, 1903.

Reprinted with the kind permission of George Allen & Unwin Ltd. and W. W. Norton & Company, Inc. from *The Principles of Mathematics* (1938), Appendix A.

475. The work of Frege, which appears to be far less known than it deserves, contains many of the doctrines set forth in Parts I and II of the present work, and where it differs from the views which I have advocated, the differences demand discussion. Frege's work abounds in subtle distinctions, and avoids all the usual fallacies which beset writers on logic. His symbolism, though unfortunately so cumbrous as to be very difficult to employ in practice, is based upon an analysis of logical notions much more profound than Peano's, and is philosophically very superior to its more convenient rival. In what follows, I shall try briefly to expound Frege's theories on the most important points, and to explain my grounds for differing where I do differ. But the points of disagreement are very few and slight compared to those of agreement. They all result from difference on three points: (1) Frege does not think that there is a contradiction in the notion of concepts which cannot be made logical subjects (see § 49 *supra*); (2) he thinks that, if a term a occurs in a proposition, the proposition can always be analysed into a and an assertion about a (see Chapter VII); (3) he is not aware of the contradiction discussed in Chapter X. These are very fundamental matters, and it will be well here to discuss them afresh, since the previous discussion was written in almost complete ignorance of Frege's work.

Frege is compelled, as I have been, to employ common words in technical senses which depart more or less from usage. As his departures are frequently different from mine, a difficulty arises as regards the translation of his terms. Some of these, to avoid confusion, I shall leave untranslated, since every English equivalent that I can think of has been already employed by me in a slightly different sense.

The principal heads under which Frege's doctrines may be discussed are the following: (1) meaning and indication; (2) truth-values and judgment; (3) *Begriff* and *Gegenstand*; (4) classes; (5) implication and *symbolic logic*; (6) the definition of integers and the principle of abstraction; (7) mathematical induction and the theory of progressions. I shall deal successively with these topics.

476. *Meaning and Indication.* The distinction between meaning (*Sinn*) and indication (*Bedeutung*)[1] is roughly, though not exactly, equivalent to my distinction between a concept as such and what the concept denotes (§ 96). Frege did not possess this distinction in the first two of the works under consideration (the *Begriffsschrift* and the *Grundlagen der Arithmetik*); it appears first in BuG. (cf. p. 198), and is specially dealt with in SuB. Before making the distinction, he thought that identity has to do with the names of objects (Bs. p. 13): "A is identical with B" means, he says, that the sign A and the sign B have the same signification (Bs. p. 15) —a definition which, verbally at least, suffers from circularity. But later he explains identity in much the same way as it was explained in § 64. "Identity," he says, "calls for reflection owing to questions which attach to it and are not quite easy to answer. Is it a relation? A relation between *Gegenstände*? or between names or signs of *Gegenstände*?" (SuB. p. 25). We must distinguish, he says, the meaning, in which is contained the way of being given, from what is indicated (from the *Bedeutung*). Thus "the evening star" and "the morning star" have the same indication, but not the same meaning. A word ordinarily stands for its indication; if we wish to speak of its meaning, we must use inverted commas or some such device (pp. 27-8). The indication of a proper name is the object which it indicates; the presentation which goes with it is quite subjective; between the two lies the meaning, which is not subjective and yet is not the object (p. 30). A proper name *expresses* its meaning, and *indicates* its indication (p. 31).

This theory of indication is more sweeping and general than mine, as appears from the fact that *every* proper name is

---

[1] I do not translate *Bedeutung* by *denotation*, because this word has a technical meaning different from Frege's, and also because *bedeuten*, for him, is not quite the same as *denoting* for me.

supposed to have the two sides. It seems to me that only such proper names as are derived from concepts by means of *the* can be said to have meaning, and that such words as *John* merely indicate without meaning. If one allows, as I do, that concepts can be objects and have proper names, it seems fairly evident that their proper names, as a rule, will indicate them without having any distinct meaning; but the opposite view, though it leads to an endless regress, does not appear to be logically impossible. The further discussion of this point must be postponed until we come to Frege's theory of *Begriffe*.

477. *Truth-values and Judgment.* The problem to be discussed under this head is the same as the one raised in § 52,[2] concerning the difference between asserted and unasserted propositions. But Frege's position on this question is more subtle than mine, and involves a more radical analysis of judgment. His *Begriffsschrift*, owing to the absence of the distinction between meaning and indication, has a simpler theory than his later works. I shall therefore omit it from the discussions.

There are, we are told (Gg. p. x), three elements in judgment: (1) the recognition of truth, (2) the *Gedanke*, (3) the truth-value (*Wahrheitswerth*). Here the *Gedanke* is what I have called an unasserted proposition—or rather, what I called by this name covers both the *Gedanke* alone and the *Gedanke* together with its truth-value. It will be well to have names for these two distinct notions; I shall call the *Gedanke* alone a *propositional concept*; the truth-value of a *Gedanke* I shall call an *assumption*.[3] Formally at least, an assumption does not require that its content should be a propositional concept: whatever x may be, "the truth of x" is a definite notion.

---

[2] This is the logical side of the problem of *Annahmen,* raised by Meinong in his able work on the subject, Leipzig, 1902. The logical, though not the psychological, part of Meinong's work appears to have been completely anticipated by Frege.

[3] Frege, like Meinong, calls this an *Annahme*: FuB. p. 21.

This means the true if x is true, and if x is false or not a proposition it means the false. (FuB. p. 21). In like manner, according to Frege, there is "the falsehood of x"; these are not assertions and negations of propositions, but only assertions of truth or of falsity, *i.e.* negation belongs to what is asserted, and is not the opposite of assertion.[4] Thus we have first a propositional concept, next its truth or falsity as the case may be, and finally the assertion of its truth or falsity. Thus in a hypothetical judgment, we have a relation, not of two judgments, but of two propositional concepts (SuB. p. 43).

This theory is connected in a very curious way with the theory of meaning and indication. It is held that every assumption indicates the true or the false (which are called truth-values), while it means the corresponding propositional concept. The assumption "$2^2 = 4$" indicates the true, we are told, just as "2^2" indicates 4[5] (FuB. p. 13; SuB. p. 32). In a dependent clause, or where a name occurs (such as Odysseus) which indicates nothing, a sentence may have no indication. But when a sentence has a truth-value, this is its indication. Thus every assertive sentence (*Behauptungssatz*) is a proper name, which indicates the true or the false (SuB. pp. 32-4; Gg. p. 7). The sign of judgment (*Urtheilstrich*) does not combine with other signs to denote an object; a judgment indicates nothing, but asserts something. Frege has a special symbol for judgment, which is something distinct from and additional to the truth-value of a propositional concept (Gg. pp. 9-10).

478. There are some difficulties in the above theory which it will be well to discuss. In the first place, it seems doubtful whether the introduction of truth-values marks any real analysis. If we consider, say, "Caesar died," it would seem that what is asserted is the propositional concept "the death of

---

[4] Gg. p. 10. Cf. also Bs. p. 4.

[5] When a term which indicates is itself to be spoken of, as opposed to what it indicates, Frege uses inverted commas. Cf. § 56.

Caesar," not "the truth of the death of Caesar." This latter seems to be merely another propositional concept, asserted in "the death of Caesar is true," which is not, I think, the same proposition as "Caesar died." There is great difficulty in avoiding psychological elements here, and it would seem that Frege has allowed them to intrude in describing judgment as the recognition of truth (Gg. p. x). The difficulty is due to the fact that there is a psychological sense of assertion, which is what is lacking to Meinong's *Annahmen*, and that this does not run parallel with the logical sense. Psychologically, any proposition, whether true or false, may be merely thought of, or may be actually asserted: but for this possibility, error would be impossible. But logically, true propositions only are asserted, though they may occur in an unasserted form as parts of other propositions. In "p implies q," either or both of the propositions p, q may be true, yet each, in this proposition, is unasserted in a logical, and not merely in a psychological sense. Thus assertion has a definite place among logical notions, though there is a psychological notion of assertion to which nothing logical corresponds. But assertion does not seem to be a constituent of an asserted proposition, although it is, in some sense, contained in an asserted proposition. If p is a proposition, "p's truth" is a concept which has being even if p is false, and thus "p's truth" is not the same as p asserted. Thus no concept can be found which is equivalent to p asserted, and therefore assertion is not a constituent in p asserted. Yet assertion is not a term to which p, when asserted, has an external relation; for any such relation would need to be itself asserted in order to yield what we want. Also a difficulty arises owing to the apparent fact, which may however be doubted, that an asserted proposition can never be part of another proposition: thus, if this be a fact, where any statement is made about p asserted, it is not really about p asserted, but only about the assertion of p. This difficulty becomes serious in the case of Frege's one and only principle of inference (Bs. p. 9): "p is true and p implies q; therefore

q is true." [6] Here it is quite essential that there should be three actual assertions, otherwise the assertion of propositions deduced from asserted premisses would be impossible; yet the three assertions together form one proposition, whose unity is shown by the word *therefore*, without which q would not have been deduced, but would have been asserted as a fresh premiss.

It is also almost impossible, at least to me, to divorce assertion from truth, as Frege does. An asserted proposition, it would seem, must be the same as a true proposition. We may allow that negation belongs to the content of a proposition (Bs. p. 4), and regard every assertion as asserting something to be true. We shall then correlate p and not-p as unasserted propositions, and regard "p is false" as meaning "not-p is true." But to divorce assertion from truth seems only possible by taking assertion in a psychological sense.

479. Frege's theory that assumptions are proper names for the true or the false, as the case may be, appears to me also untenable. Direct inspection seems to show that the relation of a proposition to the true or the false is quite different from that of (say), "the present king of England" to Edward VII. Moreover, if Frege's view were correct on this point, we should have to hold that in an asserted proposition it is the meaning, not the indication, that is asserted, for otherwise, all asserted propositions would assert the very same thing, namely the true (for false propositions are not asserted). Thus asserted propositions would not differ from one another in any way, but would be all strictly and simply identical. Asserted propositions have no indication (FuB. p. 21), and can only differ, if at all, in some way analogous to meaning. Thus the meaning of the unasserted proposition together with its truth-value must be what is asserted, if the meaning simply is rejected. But there seems no purpose in introducing the truth-value here: it seems quite sufficient to say that an

---

[6] Cf. *supra*, § 18, (4) and § 38.

asserted proposition is one whose meaning is true, and that to say the meaning is true is the same as to say the meaning is asserted. We might then conclude that true propositions, even when they occur as parts of others, are always and essentially asserted, while false propositions are always unasserted, thus escaping the difficulty about *therefore* discussed above. It may also be objected to Frege that "the true" and "the false," as opposed to truth and falsehood, do not denote single definite things, but rather the classes of true and false propositions respectively. This objection, however, would be met by his theory of ranges, which correspond approximately to my classes; these, he says, are things, and the true and the false are ranges (*v. inf.*).

480. *Begriff and Gegenstand. Functions.* I come now to a point in which Frege's work is very important, and requires careful examination. His use of the word *Begriff* does not correspond exactly to any notion in my vocabulary, though it comes very near to the notion of an assertion as defined in § 43, and discussed in Chapter VII. On the other hand, his *Gegenstand* seems to correspond exactly to what I have called a *thing* (§ 48). I shall therefore translate *Gegenstand* by *thing*. The meaning of *proper name* seems to be the same for him as for me, but he regards the range of proper names as confined to things, because they alone, in his opinion, can be logical subjects.

Frege's theory of functions and *Begriffe* is set forth simply in FuB. and defended against the criticisms of Kerry[7] in BuG. He regards functions—and in this I agree with him—as more fundamental than predicates and relations; but he adopts concerning functions the theory of subject and assertion which we discussed and rejected in Chapter VII. The acceptance of this view gives a simplicity to his exposition which I have been unable to attain; but I do not find any-

---

[7] Vierteljahrschrift für wiss. Phil., vol. XI, pp. 249-307.

thing in his work to persuade me of the legitimacy of his analysis.

An arithmetical function, *e.g.*, $2x^3 + x$, does not denote, Frege says, the result of an arithmetical operation, for that is merely a number, which would be nothing new (FuB. p. 5). The essence of a function is what is left when the x is taken away, *i.e.*, in the above instance, $2(\ )^3 + (\ )$. The argument x does not belong to the function, but the two together make a whole (*ib*. p. 6). A function may be a proposition for every value of the variable; its value is then always a truth-value (p. 13). A proposition may be divided into two parts, as "Caesar" and "conquered Gaul." The former Frege calls the *argument*, the latter the *function*. Anything whatever is a possible argument for a function (p. 17). (This division of propositions corresponds exactly to my *subject* and *assertion* as explained in § 43, but Frege does not restrict this method of analysis as I do in Chapter VII.) A thing is anything which is not a function, *i.e.*, whose expression leaves no empty place. The two following accounts of the nature of a function are quoted from the earliest and one of the latest of Frege's works respectively.

(1) "If in an expression, whose content need not be propositional (*beurtheilbar*), a simple or composite sign occurs in one or more places, and we regard it as replaceable, in one or more of these places, by something else, but by the same everywhere, then we call the part of the expression which remains invariable in this process a *function*, and the replaceable part we call its argument" (Bs. p. 16).

(2) "If from a proper name we exclude a proper name, which is part or the whole of the first, in some or all of the places where it occurs, but in such a way that these places remain recognizable as to be filled by one and the same arbitrary proper name (as argument positions of the first kind), I call what we thereby obtain the name of a function of the first order with one argument. Such a name, together with a

proper name which fills the argument-places, forms a proper name" (Gg. p. 44.)

The latter definition may become plainer by the help of some examples. "The present king of England" is, according to Frege, a proper name, and "England" is a proper name which is part of it. Thus here we may regard England as the argument, and "the present king of" as function. Thus we are led to "the present king of x." This expression will always have a meaning, but it will not have an indication except for those values of x which at present are monarchies. The above function is not propositional. But "Caesar conquered Gaul" leads to "x conquered Gaul"; here we have a propositional function. There is here a minor point to be noticed: the *asserted* proposition is not a proper name, but only the assumption is a proper name for the true or the false (*v. supra*); thus it is not "Caesar conquered Gaul" as asserted, but only the corresponding assumption, that is involved in the genesis of a propositional function. This is indeed sufficiently obvious, since we wish x to be able to be anything in "x conquered Gaul," whereas there is no such asserted proposition except when x did actually perform this feat. Again consider "Socrates is a man implies Socrates is a mortal." This (unasserted) is, according to Frege, a proper name for the true. By varying the proper name "Socrates," we can obtain three propositional functions, namely "x is a man implies Socrates is a mortal," "Socrates is a man implies x is a mortal," "x is a man implies x is a mortal." Of these the first and third are true for all values of x, the second is true when and only when x is a mortal.

By suppressing in like manner a proper name in the name of a function of the first order with one argument, we obtain the name of a function of the first order with two arguments (Gg. p. 44). Thus *e.g.* starting from "$1<2$," we get first "$x<2$," which is the name of a function of the first order with one argument, and thence "$x<y$," which is the name of a function of the first order with two arguments. By suppressing a func-

tion in like manner, Frege says, we obtain the name of a function of the second order (Gg. p. 44). Thus *e.g.* the assertion of existence in the mathematical sense is a function of the second order: "There is at least one value of x satisfying ϕx" is not a function of x, but may be regarded as a function of ϕ. Here ϕ must on no account be a thing, but may be any function. Thus this proposition, considered as a function of ϕ, is quite different from functions of the first order, by the fact that the possible arguments are different. Thus given any proposition, say $f(a)$, we may consider either $f(x)$, the function of the first order resulting from varying a and keeping f constant, or $\phi(a)$, the function of the second order got by varying f and keeping a fixed; or, finally, we may consider $\phi(x)$, in which both f and a are separately varied. (It is to be observed that such notions as $\phi(a)$, in which we consider any proposition concerning a, are involved in the identity of indiscernibles as stated in § 43.) Functions of the first order with two variables. Frege points out, express relations (Bs. p. 17); the referent and the relatum are both subjects in a relational proposition (Gl. p. 82). Relations, just as much as predicates, belong, Frege rightly says, to pure logic (*ib.* p. 83).

481. The word *Begriff* is used by Frege to mean nearly the same thing as *propositional function* (*e.g.* FuB. p. 28); [8] when there are two variables, the *Begriff* is a relation. A thing is anything not a function, *i.e.* anything whose expression leaves no empty place (*ib.* p. 18). To Frege's theory of the essential cleavage between things and *Begriffe*, Kerry objects (*loc. cit.* p. 272 ff.) that *Begriffe* also can occur as subjects. To this Frege makes two replies. In the first place, it is, he says, an important distinction that some terms can only occur as subjects, while others can occur also as concepts, even if *Begriffe* can also occur as subjects (BuG. p. 195). In this I agree with him entirely; the distinction is the one employed in §§ 48, 49.

---

[8] "We have here a function whose value is always a truth-value. Such functions with one argument we have called Begriffe; with two, we call them relations." Cf. Gl. pp. 82-3.

But he goes on to a second point which appears to me mistaken. We can, he says, have a concept falling under a higher one (as Socrates falls under man, he means, not as Greek falls under man); but in such cases, it is not the concept itself, but its name, that is in question (BuG. p. 195). "The concept horse," he says, is not a concept, but a thing; the peculiar use is indicated by inverted commas (*ib*. p. 196). But a few pages later he makes statements which seem to involve a different view. A concept, he says, is essentially predicative even when something is asserted of it: an assertion which can be made of a concept does not fit an object. When a thing is said to fall under a concept, and when a concept is said to fall under a higher concept, the two relations involved, though similar, are not the same (*ib*. p. 201). It is difficult to me to reconcile these remarks with those of p. 195; but I shall return to this point shortly.

Frege recognizes the unity of a proposition: of the parts of a propositional concept, he says, not all can be complete, but one at least must be incomplete (*ungesättigt*) or predicative, otherwise the parts would not cohere (*ib*. p. 205). He recognizes also, though he does not discuss, the oddities resulting from *any* and *every* and such words: thus he remarks that every positive integer is the sum of four squares, but "every positive integer" is not a possible value of x in "x is the sum of four squares." The meaning of "every positive integer," he says, depends upon the context (Bs. p. 17)—a remark which is doubtless correct, but does not exhaust the subject. Self-contradictory notions are admitted as concepts: F is a concept if "a falls under the concept F" is a proposition whatever thing a may be (Gl. p. 87). A concept is the indication of a predicate; a thing is what can never be the whole indication of a predicate, though it may be that of a subject (BuG. p. 198).

482. The above theory, in spite of close resemblance, differs in some important points from the theory set forth in Part I

above. Before examining the differences, I shall briefly re-capitulate my own theory.

Given any propositional concept, or any unity (see § 136), which may in the limit be simple, its constituents are in general of two sorts: (1) those which may be replaced by anything else whatever without destroying the unity of the whole; (2) those which have not this property. Thus in "the death of Caesar," anything else may be substituted for Caesar, but a proper name must not be substituted for *death*, and hardly anything can be substituted for *of*. Of the unity in question, the former class of constituents will be called *terms*, the latter *concepts*. We have then, in regard to any unity, to consider the following objects:

(1) What remains of the said unity when one of its terms is simply removed, or, if the term occurs several times, when it is removed from one or more of the places in which it occurs, or, if the unity has more than one term, when two or more of its terms are removed from some or all of the places where they occur. This is what Frege calls a function.

(2) The class of unities differing from the said unity, if at all, only by the fact that one of its terms has been replaced, in one or more of the places where it occurs, by some other terms, or by the fact that two or more of its terms have been thus replaced by other terms.

(3) Any member of the class (2).

(4) The assertion that every member of the class (2) is true.

(5) The assertion that some member of the class (2) is true.

(6) The relation of a member of the class (2) to the value which the variable has in that member.

The fundamental case is that where our unity is a propositional concept. From this is derived the usual mathematical notion of function, which might at first seem simpler. If $f(x)$ is not a propositional function, its value for a given value of x ($f(x)$ being assumed to be one-valued) is the term y satisfying the propositional function $y = f(x)$, *i.e.* satisfying, for the given value of x, some relational proposition; this relational proposition is involved in the definition of $f(x)$, and some such propositional function is required in the definition of any function which is not propositional.

As regards (1), confining ourselves to one variable, it was maintained in Chapter VII that, except where the proposition from which we start is predicative or else asserts a fixed relation to a fixed term, there is no such entity: the analysis into argument and assertion cannot be performed in the manner required. Thus what Frege calls a function, if our conclusion was sound, is in general a non-entity. Another point of difference from Frege, in which, however, he appears to be in the right, lies in the fact that I place no restriction upon the variation of the variable, whereas Frege, according to the nature of the function, confines the variable to things, functions of the first order with one variable, functions of the first order with two variables, functions of the second order with one variable, and so on. There are thus for him an infinite number of different kinds of variability. This arises from the fact that he regards as distinct the concept occurring as such and the concept occurring as term, which I (§ 49) have identified. For me, the functions, which cannot be values of variables in functions of the first order, are non-entities and false abstractions. Instead of the rump of a proposition considered in (1), I substitute (2) or (3) or (4) according to circumstances. The ground for regarding the analysis into argument and function as not always possible is that, when one term is removed from a propositional concept, the remainder is apt to have no sort of unity, but to fall apart into a set of disjointed terms. Thus what is fundamental in such a case is (2). Frege's general definition of a function, which is intended to cover also functions which are not propositional, may be shown to be inadequate by considering what may be called the identical function, *i.e.* x as a function of x. If we follow Frege's advice, and remove x in hopes of having the function left, we find that nothing is left at all; yet nothing is not the meaning of the identical function. Frege wishes to have the empty places where the argument is to be inserted indicated in some way; thus he says that in $2x^3 + x$ the function is $2(\ )^3 + (\ )$. But here his requirement that the two empty places are to be filled by the same letter cannot be indicated: there is no way of distinguishing what we mean from the function involved in $2x^3 + y$. The fact seems to be that we want the notion of any term of a certain class, and that this is what our empty places really stand for. The function, as a single entity, is the relation (6) above; we can then consider any relatum of this relation, or the assertion of all or some of the relata, and any relation can be expressed in terms of the corresponding referent, as "Socrates is a man" is expressed in terms of Socrates. But the usual formal apparatus of the calculus of relations cannot be employed, because it presupposes propositional functions. We may say that a propositional function is a many-one relation which has all terms for the class of its referents, and has its relata contained among propositions: [9] or, if we prefer, we may call the class of relata of such a relation a propositional function. But the air of formal definition about these statements is fallacious, since propositional functions are presupposed in defining the class of referents and relata of a relation.

Thus by means of propositional functions, propositions are collected into classes. (These classes are not mutually exclusive.) But we may also collect them into classes by the terms which occur in them: all propositions containing a given term a will form a class. In this way we obtain propositions concerning variable propositional functions. In the notation $\phi(x)$, the ϕ is essentially variable; if we wish it not to be so, we must take some particular proposition about x, such as "x is a class" or "x implies x." Thus $\phi(x)$ essentially contains two variables. But, if we have decided that ϕ is not a

---

[9] Not all relations having this property are propositional functions; v. inf.

separable entity, we cannot regard ϕ itself as the second variable. It will be necessary to take as our variable either the relation of x to $\phi(x)$, or else the class of propositions $\phi(y)$ for different values of y but for constant ϕ. This does not matter formally, but it is important for logic to be clear as to the meaning of what appears as the variation of ϕ. We obtain in this way another division of propositions into classes, but again these classes are not mutually exclusive.

In the above manner, it would seem, we can make use of propositional functions without having to introduce the objects which Frege calls functions. It is to be observed, however, that the kind of relation by which propositional functions are defined is less general than the class of many-one relations having their domain coextensive with terms and their converse domain contained in propositions. For in this way any proposition would, for a suitable relation, be relatum to any term, whereas the term which is referent must, for a propositional function, be a constituent of the proposition which is its relatum.[10] This point illustrates again that the class of relations involved is fundamental and incapable of definition. But it would seem also to show that Frege's different kinds of variability are unavoidable, for in considering (say) $\phi(2)$, where ϕ is variable, the variable would have to have as its range the above class of relations, which we may call *propositional relations*. Otherwise, $\phi(2)$ is not a proposition, and is indeed meaningless, for we are dealing with an indefinable, which demands that $\phi(2)$ should be the relatum of 2 with regard to some propositional relation. The contradiction discussed in Chapter X seems to show that some mystery lurks in the variation of propositional functions; but for the present, Frege's theory of different kinds of variables must, I think, be accepted.

483. It remains to discuss afresh the question whether concepts can be made into logical subjects without change of

---

[10] The notion of a constituent of a proposition appears to be a logical indefinable.

meaning. Frege's theory, that when this appears to be done it is really the name of the concept that is involved, will not, I think, bear investigation. In the first place, the mere assertion "not the concept, but its name, is involved," has already made the concept a subject. In the second place, it seems always legitimate to ask: "what is it that is named by this name?" If there were no answer, the name could not be a name; but if there is an answer, the concept, as opposed to its name, can be made a subject. (Frege, it may be observed, does not seem to have clearly disentangled the logical and linguistic elements of naming: the former depend upon denoting, and have, I think, a much more restricted range than Frege allows them.) It is true that we found difficulties in the doctrine that everything can be a logical subject: as regards "any *a*," for example, and also as regards plurals. But in the case of "any *a*," there is ambiguity, which introduces a new class of problems; and as regards plurals, there are propositions in which the many behave like a logical subject in every respect except that they are many subjects and not one only (see §§ 127, 128). In the case of concepts, however, no such escapes are possible. The case of asserted propositions is difficult, but is met, I think, by holding that an asserted proposition is merely a true proposition, and is therefore asserted wherever it occurs, even when grammar would lead to the opposite conclusion. Thus, on the whole, the doctrine of concepts which cannot be made subjects seems untenable.

484. *Classes.* Frege's theory of classes is very difficult, and I am not sure that I have thoroughly understood it. He gives the name *Wertverlauf* [11] to an entity which appears to be nearly the same as what I call the class as one. The concept of the class, and the class as many, do not appear in his exposition. He differs from the theory set forth in Chapter VI chiefly by the fact that he adopts a more intensional view of classes than I have done, being led thereto mainly by the

---

[11] I shall translate this as *range*.

desirability of admitting the null-class and of distinguishing a term from a class whose only member it is. I agree entirely that these two objects cannot be attained by an extensional theory, though I have tried to show how to satisfy the requirements of formalism (§§ 69, 73).

The extension of a *Begriff*, Frege says, is the range of a function whose value for every argument is a truth-value (FuB. p. 16). Ranges are things, whereas functions are not (*ib.* p. 19). There would be no null-class, if classes were taken in extension; for the null-class is only possible if a class is not a collection of terms (KB. pp. 436-7). If x be a term, we cannot identify x, as the extensional view requires, with the class whose only member is x; for suppose x to be a class having more than one member, and let y, z be two different members of x; then if x is identical with the class whose only member is x, y and z will both be members of this class, and will therefore be identical with x and with each other, contrary to the hypothesis.[12] The extension of a *Begriff* has its being in the *Begriff* itself, not in the individuals falling under the *Begriff* (*ib.* p. 451). When I say something about all men, I say nothing about some wretch in the centre of Africa, who is in no way indicated, and does not belong to the indication of *man* (p. 454). *Begriffe* are prior to their extension, and it is a mistake to attempt, as Schröder does, to base extension on individuals; this leads to the calculus of regions (*Gebiete*), and not logic (p. 455).

What Frege understands by a range, and in what way it is to be conceived without reference to objects, he endeavours to explain in his *Grundgesetze der Arithmetik*. He begins by deciding that two propositional functions are to have the same range when they have the same value for every value of x, *i.e.* for every value of x both are true or both false (pp. 7, 14). This is laid down as a primitive proposition. But this only

---

[12] *Ib.* p. 444. Cf. § 74 *supra*.

determines the equality of ranges, not what they are in themselves. If $X(\xi)$ be a function which never has the same value for different values of ξ and if we denote by ϕ' the range of ϕx, we shall have $X(\phi') = X(\psi')$ when and only when ϕ' and ψ' are equal, *i.e.* when and only when ϕx and ψx always have the same value. Thus the conditions for the equality of ranges do not of themselves decide what ranges are to be (p. 16). Let us decide arbitrarily—since the notion of a range is not yet fixed—that the true is to be the range of the function "x is true" (as an assumption, not an asserted proposition), and the false is to be the range of the function "$x =$ not every term is identical with itself." It follows that the range of ϕx is the true when and only when the true and nothing else falls under the *Begriff* ϕx; the range of ϕx is the false when and only when the false and nothing else falls under the *Begriff* ϕx; in other cases, the range is neither the true nor the false (pp. 17-18). If only one thing falls under a concept, this one thing is distinct from the range of the concept in question (p. 18, note)— the reason is the same as that mentioned above.

There is an argument (p. 49) to prove that the name of the range of a function always has an indication, *i.e.* that the symbol employed for it is never meaningless. In view of the contradiction discussed in Chapter X, I should be inclined to deny a meaning to a range when we have a proposition of the form $\phi[f(\phi)]$, where f is constant and ϕ variable, or of the form $f_x(x)$, where x is variable and f_x is a propositional function which is determinate when x is given, but varies from one value of x to another—provided, when f_x is analyzed into things and concepts, the part dependent on x does not consist only of things, but contains also at least one concept. This is a very complicated case, in which, I should say, there is no class as one, my only reason for saying so being that we can thus escape the contradiction.

485. By means of variable propositional functions, Frege

obtains a definition of the relation which Peano calls ϵ namely the relation of a term to a class of which it is a member.[13] The definition is as follows: "$a\epsilon u$" is to mean the term (or the range of terms if there be none or many) x such that there is a propositional function ϕ which is such that u is the range of ϕ and ϕa is identical with x (p. 53). It is observed that this defines $a\epsilon u$ whatever things a and u may be. In the first place, suppose u to be a range. Then there is at least one ϕ whose range is u, and any two whose range is u are regarded by Frege as identical. Thus we may speak of *the* function ϕ whose range is u. In this case, $a\epsilon u$ is the proposition ϕa, which is true when a is a member of u, and is false otherwise. If, in the second place, u is not a range, then there is no such propositional function as ϕ, and therefore $a\epsilon u$ is the range of a propositional function which is always false, *i.e.* the null-range. Thus $a\epsilon u$ indicates the true when u is a range and a is a member of u; $a\epsilon u$ indicates the false when u is a range and a is not a member of u; in other cases, $a\epsilon u$ indicates the null-range.

It is to be observed that from the equivalence of $x\epsilon u$ and $x\epsilon v$ for all values of x we can only infer the identity of u and v when u and v are ranges. When they are not ranges, the equivalence will always hold, since $x\epsilon u$ and $x\epsilon v$ are the null-range for all values of x; thus if we allowed the inference in this case, any two objects which are not ranges would be identical, which is absurd. One might be tempted to doubt whether u and v must be identical even when they are ranges: with an intensional view of classes, this becomes open to question.

Frege proceeds (p. 55) to an analogous definition of the propositional function of three variables which I have symbolised as $x \, R \, y$, and here again he gives a definition which does not place any restrictions on the the variability of R. This is done by introducing a *double range*, defined by a propositional function of two variables; we may regard this

[13] Cf. §§ 21, 76 *supra*.

as a class of couples with sense.[14] If then R is such a class of couples, and if $(x; y)$ is a member of this class, $x R y$ is to hold; in other cases it is to be false or null as before. On this basis, Frege successfully erects as much of the logic of relations as is required by his arithmetic; and he is free from the restrictions on the variability of R which arise from the intensional view of relations adopted in the present work (cf. § 83).

486. The chief difficulty which arises in the above theory of classes is as to the kind of entity that a range is to be. The reason which led me, against my inclination, to adopt an extensional view of classes, was the necessity of discovering some entity determinate for a given propositional function, and the same for any equivalent propositional function. Thus "x is a man" is equivalent (we will suppose) to "x is a featherless biped," and we wish to discover some one entity which is determined in the same way by both these propositional functions. The only single entity I have been able to discover is the class as one—except the derivative class (also as one) of propositional functions equivalent to either of the given propositional functions. This latter class is plainly a more complex notion, which will not enable us to dispense with the general notion of *class*; but this more complex notion (so we agreed in § 73) must be substituted for the class of terms in the symbolic treatment, if there is to be any null-class and if the class whose only member is a given term is to be distinguished from that term. It would certainly be a very great simplification to admit, as Frege does, a range which is something other than the whole composed of the terms satisfying the propositional function in question; but for my part, inspection reveals to me no such entity. On this ground, and also on account of the contradiction, I feel compelled to adhere to the extensional theory of classes, though not quite as set forth in Chapter VI.

---

[14] Neglecting, for the present, our doubts as to there being any such entity as a couple with sense, cf. § 98.

487. That some modification in that doctrine is necessary, is proved by the argument of KB. p. 444. This argument appears capable of proving that a class, even as one, cannot be identified with the class of which it is the only member. In § 74, I contended that the argument was met by the distinction between the class as one and the class as many, but this contention now appears to me mistaken. For this reason, it is necessary to re-examine the whole doctrine of classes.

Frege's argument is as follows. If a is a class of more than one term, and if a is identical with the class whose only term is a, then to be a term of a is the same thing as to be a term of the class whose only term is a, whence a is the only term of a. This argument *appears* to prove not merely that the extensional view of classes is inadequate, but rather that it is wholly inadmissible. For suppose a to be a collection, and suppose that a collection of one term is identical with that one term. Then, if a can be regarded as one collection, the above argument proves that a is the only term of a. We cannot escape by saying that ϵ is to be a relation to the class-concept or the concept of the class or the class as many, for if there is any such entity as the class as one, there will be a relation, which we may call ϵ, between terms and their classes as one. Thus the above argument leads to the conclusion that either (α) a collection of more than one term is not identical with the collection whose only term it is, or (β) there is no collection as one term at all in the case of a collection of many terms, but the collection is strictly and only many. One or other of these must be admitted in virtue of the above argument.

488. (α) To either of these views there are grave objections. The former is the view of Frege and Peano. To realize the paradoxical nature of this view, it must be clearly grasped that it is not only the collection as many, but the collection as one, that is distinct from the collection whose only term it is. (I speak of collections, because it is important to examine the bearing of Frege's argument upon the possibility of an

extensional standpoint.) This view, in spite of its paradox, is certainly the one which seems to be required by the symbolism. It is quite essential that we should be able to regard a class as a single object, that there should be a null-class, and that a term should not (in general, at any rate) be identical with the class of which it is the only member. It is subject to these conditions that the *symbolic* meaning of *class* has to be interpreted. Frege's notion of a range may be identified with the collection as one, and all will then go well. But it is very hard to see any entity such as Frege's range, and the argument that there must be such an entity gives us little help. Moreover, in virtue of the contradiction, there certainly are cases where we have a collection as many, but no collection as one (§ 104). Let us then examine (β), and see whether this offers a better solution.

(β) Let us suppose that a collection of one term is that one term, and that a collection of many terms is (or rather are) those many terms, so that there is not a single term at all which is the collection of the many terms in question. In this view there is, at first sight at any rate, nothing paradoxical, and it has the merit of admitting universally what the contradiction shows to be sometimes the case. In this case, unless we abandon one of our fundamental dogmas, ϵ will have to be a relation of a term to its class-concept, not to its class; if a is a class-concept, what appears symbolically as the class whose only term is a will (one might suppose) be the class-concept under which falls only the concept a, which is of course (in general, if not always) different from a. We shall maintain, on account of the contradiction, that there is not always a class-concept for a given propositional function ϕx, *i.e.* that there is not always, for every ϕ, some class-concept a such that $x\epsilon a$ is equivalent to ϕx for all values of x; and the cases where there is no such class-concept will be cases in which ϕ is a quadratic form.

So far, all goes well. But now we no longer have one definite entity which is determined equally by any one of a set of equivalent propositional functions, *i.e.* there is, it might be urged, no meaning of *class* left which is determined by the extension alone. Thus, to take a case where this leads to confusion, if a and b be different class-concepts such that $x \epsilon a$ and $x \epsilon b$ are equivalent for all values of x, the class-concept under which a falls and nothing else will not be identical with that under which falls b and nothing else. Thus we cannot get any way of denoting what should symbolically correspond to the class as one. Or again, if u and v be similar but different classes, "similar to u" is a different concept from "similar to v"; thus, unless we can find some extensional meaning for *class*, we shall not be able to say that the number of u is the same as that of v. And all the usual elementary problems as to combinations (*i.e.* as to the number of classes of specified kinds contained in a given class) will have become impossible and even meaningless. For these various reasons, an objector might contend, something like the class as one must be maintained; and Frege's range fulfils the conditions required. It would seem necessary therefore to accept ranges by an act of faith, without waiting to see whether there are such things.

Nevertheless, the non-identification of the class with the class as one, whether in my form or in the form of Frege's range, appears unavoidable, and by a process of exclusion the class as many is left as the only object which can play the part of a class. By a modification of the logic hitherto advocated in the present work, we shall, I think, be able at once to satisfy the requirements of the contradiction and to keep in harmony with common sense.[15]

489. Let us begin by recapitulating the possible theories of classes which have presented themselves. A class may be identified with (α) the predicate, (β) the class concept, (γ) the concept of the class, (δ) Frege's range, (ϵ) the numerical

---

[15] The doctrine to be advocated in what follows is the direct denial of the dogma stated in § 70, note.

conjunction of the terms of the class, (ζ) the whole composed of the terms of the class.

Of these theories, the first three, which are intensional, have the defect that they do not render a class determinate when its terms are given. The other three do not have this defect, but they have others. (δ) suffers from a doubt as to there being such an entity, and also from the fact that, if ranges are terms, the contradiction is inevitable. (ϵ) is logically unobjectionable, but is not a single entity, except when the class has only one member. (ζ) cannot always exist as a term, for the same reason as applies against (δ); also it cannot be identified with the class on account of Frege's argument.[16]

Nevertheless, without a single object[17] to represent an extension, mathematics crumbles. Two propositional functions which are equivalent for all values of the variable may not be identical, but it is necessary that there should be some object determined by both. Any object that may be proposed, however, presupposes the notion of *class*. We may define *class* optatively as follows: A class is an object uniquely determined by a propositional function, and determined equally by any equivalent propositional function. Now we cannot take as this object (as in other cases of symmetrical transitive relations) the class of propositional functions equivalent to a given propositional function, unless we already have the notion of *class*. Again, equivalent relations, considered intensionally, may be distinct: we want therefore to find some one object determined equally by any one of a set of equivalent relations. But the only objects that suggest themselves are the class of relations or the class of couples forming their common range; and these both presuppose *class*. And without the notion of class, elementary problems, such as "how many combinations can be formed of m objects n at a time?" be-

---

[16] Archiv I, p. 444.

[17] For the use of the word *object* in the following discussion, see § 58, note.

come meaningless. Moreover, it appears immediately evident that there is some sense in saying that two class-concepts have the *same* extension, and this requires that there should be some object which can be called the extension of a class-concept. But it is exceedingly difficult to discover any such object, and the contradiction proves conclusively that, even if there be such an object sometimes, there are propositional functions for which the extension is not one term.

The class as many, which we numbered (ϵ) in the above enumeration, is unobjectionable, but is many and not one. We may, if we choose, represent this by a single symbol: thus $x\epsilon u$ will mean "x is one of the u's." This must not be taken as a relation of two terms, x and u, because u as the numerical conjunction is not a single term, and we wish to have a meaning for $x\epsilon u$ which would be the same if for u we substituted an equal class v, which prevents us from interpreting u intensionally. Thus we may regard "x is one of the u's" as expressing a relation of x to many terms, among which x is included. The main objection to this view, if only single terms can be subjects, is that, if u is a symbol standing essentially for many terms, we cannot make u a logical subject without risk of error. We can no longer speak, one might suppose, of a class of classes; for what should be the terms of such a class are not single terms, but are each many terms.[18] We cannot assert a predicate of many, one would suppose, except in the sense of asserting it of each of the many; but what is required here is the assertion of a predicate concerning the many as many, not concerning each nor yet concerning the whole (if any) which all compose. Thus a class of classes will be many many's; its constituents will each be only many, and cannot therefore in any sense, one might suppose, be single constituents. Now I find myself forced to maintain, in spite of the apparent logical difficulty, that this is precisely what is re-

---

[18] Wherever the context requires it, the reader is to add "provided the class in question (or all the classes in question) do not consist of a single term."

quired for the assertion of number. If we have a class of classes, each of whose members has two terms, it is necessary that the members should each be genuinely two-fold, and should not be each one. Or again, "Brown and Jones are two" requires that we should not combine Brown and Jones into a single whole, and yet it has the form of a subject-predicate proposition. But now a difficulty arises as to the number of members of a class of classes. In what sense can we speak of two couples? This seems to require that each couple should be a single entity; yet if it were, we should have two units, not two couples. We require a sense for diversity of collections, meaning thereby, apparently, if u and v are the collections in question, that $x\epsilon u$ and $x\epsilon v$ are not equivalent for all values of x.

490. The logical doctrine which is thus forced upon us is this: The subject of a proposition may be not a single term, but essentially many terms; this is the case with all propositions asserting numbers other than 0 and 1. But the predicates or class-concepts or relations which can occur in propositions having plural subjects are different (with some exceptions) from those that can occur in propositions having single terms as subjects. Although a class is many and not one, yet there is identity and diversity among classes, and thus classes can be counted as though each were a genuine unity; and in this sense we can speak of *one* class and of the classes which are members of a class of classes. *One* must be held, however, to be somewhat different when asserted of a class from what it is when asserted of a term; that is, there is a meaning of *one* which is applicable in speaking of *one term*, and another which is applicable in speaking of *one class*, but there is also a general meaning applicable to both cases. The fundamental doctrine upon which all rests is the doctrine that the subject of a proposition may be plural, and that such plural subjects are what is meant by classes which have more than one term.[19]

---

[19] Cf. §§ 128, 132 *supra*.

It will now be necessary to distinguish (1) terms, (2) classes, (3) classes of classes, and so on *ad infinitum*; we shall have to hold that no member of one set is a member of any other set, and that $x\epsilon u$ requires that x should be of a set of a degree lower by one than the set to which u belongs. Thus $x\epsilon x$ will become a meaningless proposition; and in this way the contradiction is avoided.

491. But we must now consider the problem of classes which have one member or none. The case of the null-class might be met by a bare denial—this is only inconvenient, not self-contradictory. But in the case of classes having only one term, it is still necessary to distinguish them from their sole members. This results from Frege's argument, which we may repeat as follows. Let u be a class having more than one term; let ιu be the class of classes whose only member is u. Then ιu has one member, u has many; hence u and ιu are not identical. It may be doubted, at first sight, whether this argument is valid. The relation of x to u expressed by $x\epsilon u$ is a relation of a single term to many terms; the relation of u to ιu expressed by $u\epsilon\iota u$ is a relation of many terms (as subject) to many terms (as predicate).[20] This is, so an objector might contend, a different relation from the previous one; and thus the argument breaks down. It is in different senses that x is a member of u and that u is a member of ιu; thus u and ιu may be identical in spite of the argument.

This attempt, however, to escape from Frege's argument, is capable of refutation. For all the purposes of arithmetic, to begin with, and for many of the purposes of logic, it is necessary to have a meaning for ϵ which is equally applicable to the relation of a term to a class, of a class to a class of classes, and so on. But the chief point is that, if every single term is a class, the proposition $x\epsilon x$, which gives rise to the contradiction, must be admissible. It is only by distinguishing x and ιx, and insisting that in $x\epsilon u$ the u must always be

---

[20] The word *predicate* is here used loosely, not in the precise sense defined in § 48.

of a type higher by one than x, that the contradiction can be avoided. Thus, although we may identify the class with the numerical conjunction of its terms, wherever there are many terms, yet where there is only one term we shall have to accept Frege's range as an object distinct from its only term. And having done this, we may of course also admit a range in the case of a null propositional function. We shall differ from Frege only in regarding a range as in no case a term, but an object of a different logical type, in the sense that a propositional function $\phi(x)$, in which x may be any term, is in general meaningless if for x we substitute a range; and if x may be any range of terms, $\phi(x)$ will in general be meaningless if for x we substitute either a term or a range of ranges of terms. Ranges, finally, are what are properly to be called *classes*, and it is of them that cardinal numbers are asserted.

492. According to the view here advocated, it will be necessary, with every variable, to indicate whether its field of significance is terms, classes, classes of classes, or so on.[21] A variable will not be able, except in special cases, to extend from one of these sets into another; and in $x\epsilon u$, the x and the u must always belong to different types; ϵ will not be a relation between objects of the same type, but $\acute{\epsilon}$ or $\epsilon R\acute{\epsilon}$ [22] will be, provided R is so. We shall have to distinguish also among relations according to the types to which their domains and converse domains belong; also variables whose fields include relations, these being understood as classes of couples, will not as a rule include anything else, and relations between relations will be different in type from relations between terms. This seems to give the truth—though in a thoroughly extensional form—underlying Frege's distinction between terms and the various kinds of functions. Moreover the opinion here advocated seems to adhere very closely indeed to common sense.

Thus the final conclusion is, that the correct theory of

---

[21] See Appendix B.
[22] On this notation, see §§ 28, 97.

classes is even more extensional than that of Chapter VI; that the class as many is the only object always defined by a propositional function, and that this is adequate for formal purposes; that the class as one, or the whole composed of the terms of the class, is probably a genuine entity except where the class is defined by a quadratic function (see § 103), but that in these cases, and in other cases possibly, the class as many is the only object uniquely defined.

The theory that there are different kinds of variables demands a reform in the doctrine of formal implication. In a formal implication, the variable does not, in general, take all the values of which variables are susceptible, but only all those that make the propositional function in question a proposition. For other values of the variable, it must be held that any given propositional function becomes meaningless. Thus in $x\epsilon u$, u must be a class, or a class of classes, or etc., and x must be a term if u is a class, a class if u is a class of classes, and so on; in every propositional function there will be some range permissible to the variable, but in general there will be possible values for other variables which are not admissible in the given case. This fact will require a certain modification of the principles of symbolic logic; but it remains true that, in a formal implication, all propositions belonging to a given propositional function are asserted.

With this we come to the end of the more philosophical part of Frege's work. It remains to deal briefly with his symbolic logic and arithmetic; but here I find myself in such complete agreement with him that it is hardly necessary to do more than acknowledge his discovery of propositions which, when I wrote, I believed to have been new.

493. *Implication and Symbolic Logic.* The relation which Frege employs as fundamental in the logic of propositions is not exactly the same as what I have called implication: it is a relation which holds between p and q whenever q is true or p is not true, whereas the relation which I employ holds whenever p and q are propositions, and q is true or p is false.

That is to say, Frege's relation holds when p is not a proposition at all, whatever q may be; mine does not hold unless p and q are propositions. His definition has the formal advantage that it avoids the necessity for hypotheses of the form "p and q are propositions"; but it has the disadvantage that it does not lead to a definition of *proposition* and of negation. In fact, negation is taken by Frege as indefinable; *proposition* is introduced by means of the indefinable notion of a truth-value. Whatever x may be, "the truth-value of x" is to indicate the true if x is true, and the false in all other cases. Frege's notation has certain advantages over Peano's, in spite of the fact that it is exceedingly cumbrous and difficult to use. He invariably defines expressions for all values of the variable, whereas Peano's definitions are often preceded by a hypothesis. He has a special symbol for assertion, and he is able to assert for all values of x a propositional function not stating an implication, which Peano's symbolism will not do. He also distinguishes, by the use of Latin and German letters respectively, between *any* proposition of a certain propositional function and *all* such propositions. By always using implications, Frege avoids the logical product of two propositions, and therefore has no axioms corresponding to Importation and Exportation.[23] Thus the joint assertion of p and q is the denial of "p implies not-q."

494. *Arithmetic.* Frege gives exactly the same definition of cardinal numbers as I have given, at least if we identify his *range* with my *class*.[24] But following his intensional theory of classes, he regards the number as a property of the class-concept, not of the class in extension. If u be a range, the number of u is the range of the concept "range similar to u." In the *Grundlagen der Arithmetik*, other possible theories of number are discussed and dismissed. Numbers cannot be asserted of objects, because the same set of objects may have different numbers assigned to them (Gl. p. 29); for example,

[23] See § 18, (7), (8).
[24] See Gl. pp. 79, 85; Gg. p. 57, Df. Z.

one army is so many regiments and such another number of soldiers. This view seems to me to involve too physical a view of objects: I do not consider the army to be the same object as the regiments. A stronger argument for the same view is that 0 will not apply to objects, but only to concepts (p. 59). This argument is, I think, conclusive up to a certain point; but it is satisfied by the view of the symbolic meaning of classes set forth in § 73. Numbers themselves, like other ranges, are things (p. 67). For defining numbers as ranges, Frege gives the same general ground as I have given, namely what I call the principle of abstraction.[25] In the *Grundgesetze der Arithmetik,* various theorems in the foundations of cardinal arithmetic are proved with great elaboration, so great that it is often very difficult to discover the difference between successive steps in a demonstration. In view of the contradiction of Chapter X, it is plain that some emendation is required in Frege's principles; but it is hard to believe that it can do more than introduce some general limitation which leaves the details unaffected.

495. In addition to his work on cardinal numbers, Frege has, already in the *Begriffsschrift,* a very admirable theory of progressions, or rather of all series that can be generated by many-one relations. Frege does not confine himself to one-one relations: as long as we move in only one direction, a many-one relation also will generate a series. In some parts of his theory, he even deals with general relations. He begins by considering, for any relation $f(x, y)$, functions F which are such that, if $f(x, y)$ holds, then $F(x)$ implies $F(y)$. If this condition holds, Frege says that the property F is inherited in the f-series (Bs. pp. 55-8). From this he goes on to define, without the use of numbers, a relation which is equivalent to "some positive power of the given relation." This is defined as follows. The relation in question holds between x and y if every property F, which is inherited in the f-series and is such that $f(x, z)$ implies $F(z)$ for all values

[25] Gl. p. 79; cf. § 111 *supra.*

of z, belongs to y (Bs. p. 60). On this basis, a non-numerical theory of series is very successfully erected, and is applied in Gg. to the proof of propositions concerning the number of finite numbers and kindred topics. This is, so far as I know, the best method of treating such questions, and Frege's definition just quoted gives, apparently, the best form of mathematical induction. But as no controversy is involved, I shall not pursue this subject any further.

Frege's works contain much admirable criticism of the psychological standpoint in logic, and also of the formalist theory of mathematics, which believes that the actual symbols are the subject-matter dealt with, and that their properties can be arbitrarily assigned by definition. In both these points, I find myself in complete agreement with him.

496. Kerry (*loc. cit.*) has criticized Frege very severely, and professes to have proved that a purely logical theory of arithmetic is impossible (p. 304). On the question whether concepts can be made logical subjects, I find myself in agreement with his criticisms; on other points, they seem to rest on mere misunderstandings. As these are such as would naturally occur to any one unfamiliar with symbolic logic, I shall briefly discuss them.

The definition of numbers as classes is, Kerry asserts, a ὕστερον πρότερον. We must know that every concept has only *one* extension, and we must know what *one* object is; Frege's numbers, in fact, are merely convenient symbols for what are commonly called numbers (p. 277). It must be admitted, I think, that the notion of *a term* is indefinable (cf. § 132 *supra*), and is presupposed in the definition of the number 1. But Frege argues—and his argument at least deserves discussion—that *one* is not a predicate, attaching to every imaginable term, but has a less general meaning, and attaches to concepts (Gl. p. 40). Thus *a term* is not to be analyzed into *one* and *term*, and does not presuppose the notion of *one* (cf. § 72 *supra*). As to the assumption that every concept has only one extension, it is not necessary to be able to state this in language which employs the number 1: all we need is, that if ϕx and ψx are equivalent propositions for all values of x, then they have the same extension—a primitive proposition whose symbolic expression in no way presupposes the number 1. From this it follows that if a and b are both extensions of ϕx, a and b are identical, which again does not formally involve the number 1. In like manner, other objections to Frege's definition can be met.

Kerry is misled by a certain passage (Gl. p. 80, note) into the belief that Frege identifies a concept with its extension. The passage in question appears to assert that the number of u might be defined as the concept "similar to u" and not as the range of this concept; but it does not say that the two definitions are equivalent.

There is a long criticism of Frege's proof that 0 is a number, which reveals fundamental errors as to the existential import of universal propositions. The point is to prove that, if u and v are null-classes, they are similar. Frege defines similarity to mean that there is a one-one relation R such that "x is a u" implies "there is a v to which x stands in the relation R," and vice versa. (I have altered the expressions into conformity with my usual language.) This, he says, is equivalent to "there is a one-one relation R such that 'x is a u' and 'there is no term of v to which x stands in the relation R' cannot both be true, whatever value x may have, and vice versa"; and this proposition is true if "x is a u" and "y is a v" are always false. This strikes Kerry as absurd (pp. 287-9). Similarity of classes, he thinks, implies that they have terms. He affirms that Frege's assertion above is contradicted by a later one (Gl. p. 89): "If a is a u, and nothing is a v, then 'a is a u' and 'no term is a v which has the relation R to a' are both true for all values of R." I do not quite know where Kerry finds the contradiction; but he evidently does not realize that false propositions imply all propositions and that universal propositions have no existential import, so that "all a is b" and "no a is b" will both be true if a is the null-class.

Kerry objects (p. 290, note) to the generality of Frege's notion of relation. Frege asserts that any proposition containing a and b affirms a relation between a and b (Gl. p. 83); hence Kerry (rightly) concludes that it is self-contradictory to deny that a and b are related. So general a notion, he says, can have neither sense nor purpose. As for sense, that a and b should both be constituents of one proposition seems a perfectly intelligible sense; as for purpose, the whole logic of relations, indeed the whole of mathematics, may be adduced in answer. There is, however, what seems at first sight to be a formal disproof of Frege's view. Consider the propositional function "R and S are relations which are identical, and the relation R does not hold between R and S." This contains two variables, R and S; let us suppose that it is equivalent to "R has the relation T to S." Then substituting T for both R and S, we find, since T is identical with T, that "T does not have the relation T to T" is equivalent to "T has the relation T to T." This is a contradiction, showing that there is no such relation as T. Frege might object to this instance, on the ground that it treats relations as terms; but his double ranges, which, like single ranges, he holds to be things, will bring out the same result. The point involved is closely analogous to that involved in the contradiction: it was there shown that some propositional functions with one variable are not equivalent to any propositional function asserting membership of a fixed class, while here it is shown that some containing two variables are not equivalent to the assertion of any fixed relation. But the refutation is the same in the case of relations as it was in the previous case. There is a hierarchy of relations according to the type of objects constituting their fields. Thus relations between terms are distinct from those between classes, and these again are distinct from relations between relations. Thus no relation can have itself both as referent and as relatum, for if it be of the same order as the one, it must be of a higher order than the other; the proposed propositional function is therefore meaningless for all values of the variables R and S.

It is affirmed (p. 291) that only the concepts of 0 and 1, not the objects themselves, are defined by Frege. But if we allow that the range of a *Begriff* is an object, this cannot be maintained; for the assigning of a concept will carry with it the assigning of its range. Kerry does not perceive that the uniqueness of 1 has been proved (*ib.*): he thinks that, with Frege's definition, there might be several 1's. I do not understand how this can be supposed: the proof of uniqueness is precise and formal.

The definition of immediate sequence in the series of natural numbers is also severely criticized (p. 292 ff.). This depends upon the general theory of series set forth in Bs. Kerry objects that Frege has defined "F is inherited in the f-series," but has not defined "the f-series" nor "F is inherited." The latter essentially ought not to be defined, having no precise sense; the former is easily defined, if necessary, as the field of the relation f. This objection is therefore trivial. Again, there is an attack on the definition: "y follows x in the f-series if y has all the properties inherited in the f-series and belonging to all terms to which x has the relation f."[26] This criterion, we are told, is of doubtful value, because no catalogue of such properties exists, and further because, as Frege himself proves, following x is itself one of these properties, whence a vicious circle. This argument, to my mind, radically misconceives the nature of deduction. In deduction, a proposition is proved to hold concerning *every* member of a class, and may then be asserted of a particular member: but the proposition concerning *every* does not necessarily result from enumeration of the entries in a catalogue. Kerry's position involves acceptance of Mill's objection to Barbara, that the mortality of Socrates is a necessary premiss for the mortality of all men. The fact is, of course, that general propositions can often be established where no means exist of cataloguing

[26] Kerry omits the last clause, wrongly; for not all properties inherited in the f-series belong to all its terms; for example, the property of being greater than 100 is inherited in the number-series.

the terms of the class for which they hold; and even, as we have abundantly seen, general propositions fully stated hold of *all* terms, or, as in the above case, of *all* functions, of which no catalogue can be conceived. Kerry's argument, therefore, is answered by a correct theory of deduction; and the logical theory of Arithmetic is vindicated against its critics.

Note. The second volume of Gg., which appeared too late to be noticed in the Appendix, contains an interesting discussion of the contradiction (pp. 253-65), suggesting that the solution is to be found by denying that two propositional functions which determine equal classes must be equivalent. As it seems very likely that this is the true solution, the reader is strongly recommended to examine Frege's argument on the point.

27

Frege's Logic

H. R. SMART

In view of the recognition generally accorded Frege as a pioneer in the field of symbolic or mathematical logic, it is a surprising fact that no systematic survey of his work as a whole has as yet been undertaken. Perhaps the nearest approach to such a study is a very interesting and full exposition and discussion of certain of Frege's basic doctrines in an Appendix to Bertrand Russell's *Principles of Mathematics*; but this, like the other discussions extant, does not pretend to present a clear general account of just what Frege was trying to do, or a critical estimate of how near he came to accomplishing it. The following article represents an attempt partly to fill this gap in the recent history of logic.

The principal works of Gottlob Frege (1848-1925) include the *Begriffsschrift, eine arithmetische nachgebildete Formalsprache des reinen Denkens* (1879; later partly repudiated), *Die Grundlagen der Arithmetik* (1884, reprinted 1934), *Funktion und Begriff* (1891), and the *Grundgesetze der Arithmetik* (2 vols. 1893-1903), together with supplementary articles in various periodicals. An English translation of a small portion of the last mentioned work, by Johann Stachelroth and P. E. B. Jourdain, appeared in *The Monist* (Vols. XXV (1925), XXVI (1926), and XXVII (1927)).

Reprinted with the kind permission of the author and the editor from *The Philosophical Review*, LIV (1945), 489-505.

According to Frege's great admirer, Bertrand Russell, the *Grundlagen* marks the beginning of "the logical theory of arithmetic." The first step, therefore, towards acquiring an understanding of the import of Frege's work for logic and mathematics must be to determine as precisely as possible the meaning of this phrase. As the title of the book indicates clearly enough, its author is explicitly concerned with the logic of mathematics, just as other scientists, before and since, have been concerned, among other things, with the logic of physics or biology, as the case may be. But in Frege's case this concern led in a certain direction, and issued in results of considerable significance for the future of logic, and more especially of symbolic logic itself, as well as for the special science in question.

The starting-point of his studies was his interest in the demand which had steadily been growing stronger for some time, for more rigorous proofs of mathematical propositions, and a more precise determination of the limits of their validity. The obvious need for accurate definitions in this context had led to new conceptions of functions, of infinity, and of negative and irrational numbers. And it led finally, in the work of Cantor, Dedekind, and Frege himself, to a radical attempt to define even the simple whole numbers themselves, and to prove the simplest laws binding these numbers together in a system.

And with Frege at any rate, the urge to go further yet, to search out and wherever possible to come to some definitive conclusions about the philosophical and methodological presuppositions of his science was insistent and dominant over all other motives.

Taking first the problem of definition, Frege finds that previous attempts at a definition of number have presupposed erroneous theories concerning what kind of object it is to which number can properly be ascribed, and that the resultant definitions have naturally enough failed of their purpose. Upon examination it will be found, according to this authority, that these theories fall into two groups, namely that number is to be ascribed to physical objects (Cantor, Schroeder, and especially Mill), or to psychological ones (Berkeley, Dedekind, *et al.*).

But physical entities may be regarded either as one or as many—*two* boots or *one* pair, thousands of leaves or *the* foliage of a tree, etc. Therefore Frege argues that it is impossible to predicate unambiguous numbers of such objects, or to define the numbers themselves unequivocally. Neither is the view that number is an object of psychology, or the resultant of psychical processes, at all tenable. Whoever determines the area of the North Sea as so many square miles, or the number of petals of a rose, is plainly not referring to a psychical state or process, but is stating a fact as objective as the saltiness of the sea or the color of the rose. What in fact is common to number and saltiness, or to number and color, for example, is not that they are both sensibly perceptible in external things, but that they are both objective. In fine, number is neither spatial and physical, nor subjective and mental, but non-sensible and objective, like the earth's axis or the center of the solar system (*Grundlagen*, sec. 26). Thinking, it seems plain to Frege, creates none of these 'objectives'; rather, they are eternally 'there', metaphorically speaking, to be thought about. Hence any attempt either to determine the nature of number genetically, or to trace the historical development of the number-concept, and in this wise to inquire into its possible derivation from more elementary but less precise ideas, Frege rules out *ab initio* as beside the mark. Like Bolzano's ideas-in-themselves, which Frege's 'objectives' quite closely resemble, mathematical entities are thus assigned to a special, sacrosanct realm of being, not subject to the vicissitudes of this earth, which the fortunate spectator may discover and contemplate, and, if constituted like Bertrand Russell's "free man," worship from afar.

So far, then, the position has been reached that number is a predicate, neither of physical things nor of psychological ideas, but of objective concepts. In 'The earth has one satellite', 'one' may properly be ascribed, not to the moon itself (which may just as well be regarded as 'many' molecules), but to the concept or general term 'earth's satellite'. Still more clearly, in 'Venus has 0 satellites', '0' is a property, not of a physical object (for to what physical object could the number 0 apply?) but of the concept 'satellite of Venus'.

Here, incidentally, Frege points out that it is important to distinguish between the proper name of a thing, *e.g.*, 'Venus', and words signifying concepts; and especially is this so where only one object "falls under" the concept. Obviously it is nonsense to ask what objects fall under a proper name. 'The moon' is the proper name of the object falling under the concept designated by the words 'satellite of the earth' (*Grundlagen*, secs. 45-54).

Now it seems to be Frege's contention, though this is nowhere expressed with anything like the desirable clarity or convincing argumentation, that concepts, 'objectives', being neither mental nor physical, can therefore only be described as purely logical entities. It follows at once from such considerations, that number, as predicable of, or applicable to concepts, is also to be included within the general sphere of logic. Or, to put it in another way, since the subject matter of both logic and mathematics belongs to the same realm, they are to all intents and purposes inseparable, if not identical sciences.

Since at all events number is applicable to concepts, and since concepts possess objective existence, in the sense elucidated above, existence and number may be said to have a certain something in common. In fact, "the affirmation of existence (presumably in the logical and mathematical sense of the word) is nothing other than the denial of the number zero (*Nullzahl*)" (*Grundlagen*, sec. 53)! Further consideration of the way in which numbers occur in statements shows, so Frege contends, that the copula 'is' of such statements is really an abbreviation for 'is equal to', or 'is the same as'. 'Jupiter has four moons' means 'The number of moons of Jupiter is four'; and this means, in turn, that the phrase 'the number of Jupiter's moons' designates the same 'object' as the word 'four' (sec. 57). Numbers, then, Frege concludes, designate "independent objects" (*selbstaendige Gegenstaende*).

Now it happens to be the case, however, that one genus of propositions is that which gives expression to a re-cognition (*Wiedererkennen*) of something previously cognized. Hence if 'a' is to designate an 'independent object' unambiguously, there must be a criterion which will enable one to decide whether 'b' designates the same object or not. That is to say, in order to define numbers "we must clarify the meaning of the proposition, 'the number (*Zahl*) which applies to the concept F is the same as that which applies to the concept C'; *i.e.*, we must reproduce the content of this proposition in another manner, without using the expression, 'the number (*Anzahl*) which applies to the concept F'" (sec. 62). According to Frege it will be found that this clarification will further yield a general criterion for determining the equality of numbers, for grasping a determinate number as such, and for bestowing a proper name upon it.

But to be able to assert the proposition just formulated is tantamount to being able to answer the question: When do the concepts (*e.g.*, F and C above) applicable to two collections of objects (*e.g.*, those 'falling under' concepts F and C) have the same number of terms—or, as would ordinarily be said, the same extension? And the answer is: When there obtains a one-to-one relation between all the terms of the one collection and all the terms of the other, taken severally (such as that which holds, for example, of the collections 'husbands' and 'wives' in monogamous countries). Finally this "similarity" of two such collections—to use Russellian language—leads to the definition of the number of a given collection (extension of a given concept) as the class of all collections that are similar (stand in a one-one relation) to it; or, more precisely, 'the number of terms in a given class' is defined as the equivalent of 'the class of all classes that are similar to a given class'. Thus 'two' is 'the class of all couples'; 'three', 'the class of all triads', and so forth. Frege contends that this extensional definition follows from, and confirms, his view that numbers are to be predicated of concepts, that it yields the usual arithmetical properties of numbers, finite and infinite alike, and that it applies to '0' and '1', which are often treated as special cases, in the same manner as to all other numbers (cf. *Grundlagen*, sec. 62 ff.).

A rather obvious criticism of this definition, namely that it is circular, in that it presupposes the very terms it professes to define—although this circularity may be concealed by an elaborate technical circumlocution—has been advanced by various students of the logic of mathematics (*e.g.*, Kerry, Cassirer, Poincaré); but Frege and Russell have both rather abruptly brushed this criticism aside as based on a misunderstanding, and there, to all intents and purposes, the matter rests at the present time. Nevertheless, a feeling that all of the issues here in question have not yet been met as squarely as could be desired is bound to linger in the minds of students both of logic and of mathematics. And from many authorities —Husserl, Fraenkel, Brunschvicg, Spaier, Meyerson, to mention only a few—have come criticisms directed against various aspects of this whole extremely abstruse line of thought.

Why, for example, should it be *assumed*, without argument, that number must be a 'property'—to use the Frege-Russell terminology—or intrinsically 'applicable to', 'predicable of' anything at all? In fact do not the very considerations adduced by Frege himself all but positively declare that number is essentially an extrinsic or relational determination of the phenomenal objects of experience, and not 'predicable of' them either ambiguously or unambiguously, for that very reason? The leaves of a tree are possessed of various properties *qua* leaves, or intrinsically; but they are not numerable *qua* leaves, but rather only because and in so far as they are phenomenal objects qualitatively or intrinsically distinguishable from all other such objects, and at the same time only extrinsically or quantitatively distinguishable from, and related to, each other. Unfortunately Frege debars himself from any such simple alternative account of the matter, by his deliberate refusal to consider the relevant history of the number concept, which certainly strongly supports this suggestion. And in holding instead that number is 'predicable of' concepts—*e.g.*, presumably of the concept 'leaf', among others —he is simply trying to assert, in unsuitable and not merely awkward language, what he has forbidden himself to assert in suitable terms, with the result that both concepts and numbers come to be hypostatized, and the latter, at least, are thus miraculously transported across the borderline separating logic from the special sciences.

In other words, according to a most plausible alternative which Frege fails to consider, the scientific formulation of the concept of number involves a process of ideal selection and abstraction from the 'data of experience', whereby the notion of a whole (the number system) composed of related elements or 'units' ideally homogeneous with each other, and with the whole they constitute, is finally arrived at, and made an object of scientific—*i.e.*, mathematical—investigation on its own account. What renders this alternative especially attractive, not to say compelling, from the point of view of the logic of science, is that it alone squares perfectly with the generally accepted account of the way in which, *mutatis mutandis*, basic concepts of the other sciences have been logically formulated and developed. Sense perception provides the data, the raw material, for all of the natural sciences, and it is to essentially the same process of ideal selection and abstraction, differing however in the degree and extent to which it is carried out, that each of the several sciences owes its fundamental concepts. On this view numbers constitute the simplest, most elementary, and most abstract system of relationships pertaining to the phenomenal order. On the contrary, to accept the account of the Frege-Russell school of thought of the way in which the number concept is arrived at, is arbitrarily to cut mathematics off from its undeniably intimate connections with the other sciences, and is to attempt to link it instead with logic, in an unholy alliance which actually raises more problems than it solves.

And there is one more important point worth mentioning in this connection. From the point of view of mathematics as a science, and that means as a progressively developing body of knowledge, the very attempt to formulate a definitive definition of number is basically mistaken. No definition of any scientific concept can be more than provisional and temporary, and no scientific definition can have more than pragmatic sanction as a working instrumentality of the science at any given stage of its development.

So much by way of exposition and criticism of the first phase of Frege's endeavor to provide an absolutely impeccable basis for mathematical reasoning.

The second methodological and philosophical problem, that of establishing criteria for absolutely rigorous proofs, may next be approached. The best brief account of Frege's teaching on this subject is also to be found in the *Grundlagen*.

Practising mathematicians are usually satisfied if the truth of the propositions composing their science is subject to no serious doubt, without being troubled too much by the problem of establishing the strict interdependence of truths with each other, and without searching too closely into the question as to what constitutes logical rigor in demonstration. But precisely these questions weigh most heavily upon Frege's mind, and will give him no peace until he has come to some definitive conclusion about them.

The ideal of a strictly scientific method in mathematics Frege describes in the following terms. Recognizing the utter impossibility of proving all propositions, the only alternative that he can envisage is to reduce to a minimum the number of unproved propositions, and to recognize and formulate these in the most explicit manner possible. This will insure clear knowledge of the fundamental premises of the science. And secondly all methods of proof must be specified definitely in advance, for otherwise the question of the validity of any given or proposed proof cannot be settled definitively and by general agreement. If arithmetic is to make good its claim to be only a more highly developed logic, no transitions from one proposition to another not vouched for by acknowledged and absolutely incontestable logical laws can be allowed.

In this connection Frege adopts the Kantian terminology of analytic and synthetic, *a priori* and *a posteriori* judgments, but construes these terms in his own, decidedly non-Kantian manner (*Grundlagen*, sec. 3, 87ff.). For one thing, Frege finds that Kant's classification is not exhaustive. For example, the distinction between analytic and synthetic is made to turn upon whether the predicate-concept is or is not contained in the subject-concept. But how about cases in which the subject is a single object, or those in which the judgment is existential? In neither of these species of judgment, argues Frege, is there any question of a subject-concept at all.[1] Moreover, Kant seems to think of the concept as determined by its adjunct marks or properties only, but according to his critic this is only one of the least fruitful ways of constructing a concept. Frege holds that scarcely one of the definitions formulated in the *Grundlagen* is of concepts composed in this fashion. Or consider the definition of the continuity of a function. There is here no series of adjunct properties, but rather an organic unity of determinations. And what can be deduced from such a definition is not to be discovered beforehand, so that propositions embodying these consequences are according to Kant synthetic; yet (according to Frege) they can be demonstrated by pure logic, and are hence also analytic. Furthermore, more than one definition is often required for the proof of a proposition, so that it cannot be said that the conclusion follows from any one alone, and yet it may

---

[1] This criticism of course overlooks Kant's contention that concepts without percepts are empty and percepts without concepts are blind.

follow in purely logical fashion from the several definitions conjointly. Very often, indeed, says Frege, one first acquires the content of a proposition, and is then confronted with the difficult problem of finding a rigorous proof for the proposition. Hence it is essential to differentiate these two features of propositions from each other.

These considerations lead Kant's critic to the conclusion that the distinction between *a priori* and *a posteriori*, between analytic and synthetic, properly apply, not to the content, but to the means of justification of the judgment. From this point of view, "to call a proposition *a posteriori*, or analytic, is not to pass judgment upon the psychological, physiological, and physical conditions which have made it possible to form the content of the proposition in consciousness, nor about how another person has happened—perhaps in an erroneous manner—to maintain its truth (is Frege charging Kant with proceeding on these lines?), but upon the ultimate grounds of the justification for the maintenance of its truth." In this way the question is removed from the domain of psychology, and referred to the domain of mathematics. Thus it becomes a matter of finding the proof for the proposition, and of following this proof back to the basic truths upon which all that follows rests. If these basic truths turn out to be general logical laws, and definitions, then the proposition in question is analytic *a priori*. But if, on the contrary, it is not possible to carry out the proof without using truths referable to a particular domain of knowledge, then the proposition is synthetic. And if the proof involves appeal to matters of fact it is *a posteriori*. According to Frege it can be shown that the propositions of arithmetic are in this sense analytic *a priori*, while those of geometry are synthetic. But if the criticisms advanced above have any validity, then this contention is highly questionable.

At all events, the two complementary contentions which have emerged so far from this study of Frege's work on the foundations of mathematics are: (1) that the basic concepts of arithmetic can be reduced, by the process of definition, to concepts of pure logic; and (2) that the basic propositions of arithmetic may be derived, by the process of proof, from purely logical premises. The *Grundgesetze der Arithmetik* undertakes to justify this thesis by actually establishing the science in the manner proposed. As a means to this end the author devised a symbolism which almost succeeds in literally picturing the interconnection of the successive steps in his demonstrations. Unfortunately, however, this symbolism is so cumbersome and inflexible that it is well-nigh unworkable, and has generally been discarded by later students of symbolic logic. For this reason, no attempt will be made to introduce it, or the specific demonstrations clothed in it, into this account. Attention will be concentrated, instead, upon the logical foundations of the work as a whole.[2]

These foundations are, to say the least, very peculiar. There is no doubt that they are rather difficult to comprehend, and this fact may lead some students to suppose that they are unusually profound; but such is by no means the case. The difficulties spring, rather, from Frege's odd terminology, and from his use of familiar terms in unfamiliar and even very strange and ambiguous senses. Even so staunch an admirer as Russell himself (in his *Principles of Mathematics:* Appendix A) finds some of Frege's doctrines very curious, some untenable, and some the result of a simple confusion of psychology with logic. Russell nevertheless declares—whatever such a declaration can possibly mean in the light of these criticisms—that Frege's work "avoids all the usual fallacies which beset writers on logic"!

In an article entitled "Ueber Sinn und Bedeutung" in Volume 100 of the *Zeitschrift für Philosophie und philosophische Kritik* (1892, pp. 25-52), Frege first sets forth some conceptions that are all-important for a proper understanding of

---

[2] Any reader who is interested in studying Frege's symbolic calculus in detail may be referred to Vol. I of Jørgen Jørgenson's *Treatise of Formal Logic*.

his later work. Taking 'signs' and 'names' to include any sort of notation for proper names, he in turn construes the *Bedeutung* of the latter as the definite objects (*Gegenstaende*) to which they apply. Thus 'evening star' and 'morning star' may be proper names for the same object, and in such circumstances their *Bedeutung*, their indication (to adopt Russell's translation), will be the same, but they will nevertheless differ in meaning (*Sinn*). For in the meaning is contained the mode or "way of being given"; while the indication of a proper name is the object it indicates. "A proper name (word, sign, combination of signs, expression) expresses its meaning, and indicates or designates its indication" (p. 31). Finally, it should be specially noted, proper names, so construed, cannot apply to concepts or relations; separate consideration of their logical rôle will come later.

But now comes an application or extension of this doctrine which is little short of astounding. Frege observes that it is also permissible and necessary to speak of the meaning and indication of an entire assertive sentence. Some sentences, however, for example those poetic assertions which have as subjects proper names, such as 'Odysseus', which indicate no real object, seem *ipso facto* to have as a whole no indication but only a meaning (say, as part of a poem). And in this case the sentence has no value, when the question of its truth or falsity, as distinct from its meaning, arises. Thus it can be said that "it is the search for truth that inspires us to press on from the meaning to the indication" (p. 33). And conversely, to ask for the truth-value of a sentence is to seek its indication, and hence the indication of its proper parts. From this line of reasoning Frege concludes that he is compelled to recognize the truth-value of a sentence—*i.e.*, the fact that it may be either true or false—as its indication. And thus every assertive sentence is to be taken as a quasi-proper name, whose indication, if it have one, is either the true or the false. Of this doctrine Frege himself observes that this implicit denomination of truth-values as objects (*Gegen-*

staende) may appear to be merely an arbitrary edict or verbal jugglery, from which no important results are to be anticipated. Yet he insists that in every judgment—*i.e.*, in every assertion or recognition of the truth of a thought content— a transition has already implicitly been made from subjective ideas to objective indications. For "a truth-value can no more be part of a thought content than can the sun, which is not a meaning but an object" (p. 35). Furthermore, it is obvious on this view that all true propositions have the same indication, as do also all false propositions, however much they may differ in meaning; and this dichotomous division of propositions will turn out to be an important consideration from the point of view of logical demonstration as Frege conceives it.

Frege nevertheless also states that to say, 'the thought, that 5 is a prime number, is true', is to say no more and no other than '5 is a prime number' (p. 34). But on this point Russell sharply (and rightly) disagrees. "There is great difficulty in avoiding psychological elements here, (he says) and it would seem that Frege has allowed them to intrude in describing judgment as the recognition of truth. Psychologically, any proposition, whether true or false, may be merely thought of, or may be actually asserted; but for this possibility, error would be impossible. But logically, true propositions only are asserted . . ." (*Prin. of Math.*, Appendix A).

It is, however, by means of the preceding doctrine that Frege develops his strange conception of functions, to which attention must next be directed. For it is in terms of this conception that he will explain what he means by a 'relation' as distinguished from objects and concepts. Readers who know their calculus are familiar with the mathematical concept of function, involving the idea of one or more independent variables, each capable of assuming all values in a given domain. Thus the quantity y is said to be a function of the independent variable (or argument)—symbolised by $y = f(x)$ —or of the n independent variables (or arguments) $x_1, x_2, x_3, \ldots x_n$, if to every value or set of values which the independent variable or variables may assume, there corresponds a value of y. For example, the distance traveled by a moving body is a function of several independent variables, such as the time during which the motion takes place, the initial velocity, the accelerative force, or forces, and the resistance. And the dependent variable may remain constant while the independent variable varies, as a person's weight at successive intervals of time. But on pain of being badly confused otherwise, such readers had best rid their minds entirely of this ordinary mathematical conception, when attempting to understand Frege's doctrine, though Frege does use some mathematical terms to explain his meaning.

Russell quotes the two following statements from Frege as to the nature of a function: (1) If in an expression, whose content need not be propositional (*beurtheilbar*), a simple or composite sign occurs in one or more places, and we regard it as replaceable, in one or more of these places, by something else, but by the same everywhere, then we call the part of the expression which remains invariable in this process a *function*, and the replaceable part we call its argument. (2) If from a proper name we exclude a proper name which is part or the whole of the first, in some or all of the places where it occurs, but in such a way that these places remain recognizable as to be filled by one and the same arbitrary proper name (as argument positions of the first kind), I call what we thereby obtain the name of a function of the first order with one argument. Such a name, together with a proper name which fills the argument-places, forms a proper name (cf. *Grundgesetze*, p. 43).

As Frege remarks, this way of regarding functions extends the circle of functional values far beyond the range of numbers; and, as he does not make sufficiently clear, also alters entirely the meaning of the term. For example, taking 'the present President of the United States' as a proper name, 'United States' is the argument and 'the present President of' is the function, in Frege's terminology. Similarly, '$x > y$' is a first order function with two arguments; and by carrying the procedure a step further a second order function may be obtained: 'There is at least one value of x satisfying ϕx' is a function of ϕ, which is itself a function. Functions of the first order with two variables, it should now be carefully observed, *express relations*. This illustrates the way in which relations are to be construed generally in Frege's logical calculus. And finally, the value of the function '$x^2 = 4$' is either the truth-value of the true or the false; and '$2^2 = 4$' and '$3 > 2$' *indicate* the same truth-value, namely the true. In '$x^2 = 4$', the value is the true for the arguments '2' and '-2', and the false for all other arguments.

The next notion to be introduced is that of a range (*Wertverlauf*). The extension of a concept Frege defines as the range of a function whose value for every argument is a truth-value (*Grundgesetze*, p. 8). In this sense the intensional aspect of concepts is logically prior to their extensional aspect, and hence he holds that Schroeder was badly mistaken in taking the opposite view. Two functions are said to have the same range when they have the same value for every value, say of x; when, namely, for every value of x both are true or both are false.

The importance of this doctrine is, that if 'range' be identified—as Russell helpfully suggests—with what Russell calls a 'class', cardinal numbers can hereupon be defined in such a way as seemingly to unify logic and mathematics even more completely than was possible in terms of the earlier and simpler doctrines of the *Grundlagen*. Only, following Frege's intensional view, number will still be a 'property' of class-concepts, not, as for Russell, of classes in extension (and accordingly criticisms similar to those already expressed above also apply here). To quote Russell, "if u be a range, the number of u is the range of the concept 'range similar to u'". On this 'logical' basis, Russell asserts, the *Grundgesetze* proves "various theorems in the foundations of Cardinal Arithmetic . . . with great elaboration, so great that it is often very difficult to discover the difference between successive steps in a demonstration."

To complete this account of this part of Frege's work it only remains to set forth his doctrine of logical implication, which is very simple indeed. According to Frege, the sole mode of drawing conclusions requisite for his demonstrations is a dichotomous relation which holds between p and q whenever 'either q is true or p is not true'—(false)—where p is not necessarily a proposition, and whatever q may be (*Grundgesetze*, pp. 25ff.). *Whatever q may be*, 'the truth-value of q' indicates the true if q is true, and the false otherwise. Negation is indefinable, and belongs to the content of an assertion; and the joint assertion of p and q is the denial of 'p implies not-q'. In the process of 'proof' all *further* definitions are merely nominal, in that they substitute a simple, brief expression for a more complicated one.

The statements just made, however, should not be taken to mean that *all* definitions are nominal. On this point Frege is very explicit, to the effect that mathematics requires definitions (like those of number, given above) which will enable one to decide unambiguously whether for example a given empirical thing 'falls under' a given concept or not; *i.e.*, whether the concept can be predicated unambiguously of the thing or not. And a similar test must be applied in defining relations. A plain implication of this doctrine, namely that concepts can never be subjects of categorical judgments, Frege also always maintains. Ultimate simples, of course, are indefinable, and their nature can only be made clear by some method of 'pointing out'; so that in the end, it would seem, curiously enough, all non-verbal definitions must rest upon a quasi-empirical test of givenness.

Furthermore, in addition to the one law of reasoning formulated above, Frege either implicitly or explicitly recognizes the universal validity of the usual so-called laws of thought— the laws of identity, non-contradiction, and excluded middle. Whether these laws are in some sense ultimate, or derivative from such as are—and if the latter, what these ultimate laws are—is never brought out. But it hardly seems worth while, in the light of subsequent developments in symbolic logic, to pursue a criticism of what is manifestly, in these very important respects, an unfinished piece of work.

But is it not astonishing, to anyone at all familiar with the actual intricacies of even the most rigorous mathematical reasoning, and the richly diverse procedures deemed essential to their work by the greatest mathematicians, to be told that the sole method of demonstration which ideally *ought* to be recognized is that which Frege specifies? How perverse in principle is the demand that human reason, even when occupied with the high abstractions of pure mathematics, deliberately restrict itself beforehand to any one such quasi-mechanical routine! No more than definitions fixed once and for all, would this principle of inference, if so it may be called, really serve the very complex logical requirements of a genuine science. Even the qualifications suggested by Russell in his discussion of Frege's doctrines are not such as to render the principle more adequately representative of modes of reasoning which both mathematicians and logicians recognize as both indispensable and perfectly legitimate for the purposes of even the most rigorous science. Under these circumstances, one is forced to the hard alternative of either accepting Frege's dictation and of throwing out, as a consequence, much of what would otherwise pass as perfectly valid reasoning, or of simply refusing to abide by the severe strictures which Frege would impose. And there can be little doubt as to which alternative will actually prevail in practice.

In the second volume of the *Grundgesetze*, moreover, the author gives much space to a sound criticism of formalist theories of mathematics, which hardly seems quite consistent with all that has gone before. The formalist is one who thinks of his science as closely analogous to a game such as chess, the counters or figures meaning nothing in themselves, but serving merely as tags to which arbitrarily fixed rules may be applied. According to the critic, this view forgets the difference between a theory of the game, and the game itself. "The moves of the game take place, it is true, according to the rules; but these rules are not objects in the game, but constitute the basis of the theory of the game. In other words, while the moves in chess take place according to rules, no position of the chess figures, and no move, expresses a rule; for the status of the figures in a chess game is in general not to express anything, but simply to be moved in accordance with the rules." So in *formal* arithmetic 'a + b = b + a' would have to be regarded, not as an object of the game, but as one of the rules forming the basis of the theory of the game (*Grundgesetze*, II, 114). The actual rules of arithmetic, however, are really based upon the import of the symbols, and this import, according to Frege, is none other than the content of the science. But could you not, indeed must you not go further, and by broad analogy construe logic as theory of reasoning, and mathematics (as well as every other science) as operating *with* certain material, *according* to the laws of logic? Must one not here also, much as in the case of the game, carefully distinguish between laws according to which one reasons, and premises from which one reasons—a basic distinction which it would seem that Frege had implicitly failed to observe in his own case?

At all events Frege insists that mathematics is a genuine science whose aim is truth, and not a mere game played according to arbitrary rules with meaningless counters. One potent consideration that is of itself decisive here is the fact to which Frege calls attention, that mathematics can be applied to all sorts of problems in many fields, whereas a mere game, by its very nature, can be applied to nothing.

Such, then, in brief, are the results attained by a logician and mathematician in struggling with problems which have since been wrestled with by a host of other students of those subjects. Richly suggestive and stimulating though Frege's pioneering endeavors undoubtedly are, it must be admitted that he succeeded rather in raising such problems than in settling any of them in a tolerably satisfactory manner. Not only is his work essentially incomplete, in spite of its considerable voluminousness, but in failing to consider other possible solutions more consonant with the actual developments in mathematics as a going concern, it must be admitted that he seriously misdirected and misguided other thinkers, and that from a philosophical point of view in particular his equipment for the tasks he set himself was obviously far short of being adequate. Neither in formulating his definitions of numbers, functions, and the like, nor in his attempted identification of (objective) truth with truth-values, nor in his theory and practice of mathematical reasoning, does he reveal profound appreciation of the philosophical issues involved, much less succeed in meeting those issues squarely.

28

Frege's Grundlagen[1]

PETER T. GEACH

Frege's "Logicomathematical Enquiry into the Concept of Number," now reissued together with an English translation, is mainly concerned with the sort of number that he calls *Anzahl*—cardinal number. When I speak of a number in this review I shall always mean a cardinal number. (Mr. Austin renders *"Anzahl"* by "Number," *"Zahl"* by "number"; this does a lot towards making the English text run smoothly.)

Frege first gives his reasons, which seem to me decisive, for rejecting Mill's view that numbers are physical properties. These still need to be emphasized, for this sort of view is still put forward. Only recently two eminent logicians proposed to analyze "there are more cats than dogs" as meaning that if you take a bit of every cat you get a bigger physical aggregate than if you take an equal bit of every dog! Such an analysis will not do even for very simple observation statements like "this solid has fewer corners than edges" or "the clock struck more times than I have fingers on my hands." The notion of number is in fact applicable wherever we have things

Reprinted with the kind permission of the author and the editor from *The Philosophical Review*, LX (1951), 535-544.

[1] Gottlob Frege, *The Foundations of Arithmetic: A Logicomathematical Enquiry into the Concept of Number,* translated by J. L. Austin (New York, Philosophical Library, 1950), pp. i-xii, I-XI, 1-119, and parallel pages vi^e-xiii^e, i^e-xi^e, i^e-119^e.

that can be identified, and discriminated from other things in the same field of thought; we can as easily speak of three sounds, three syllogisms, or three numbers, as of three cats or three dogs. If "three" stood for a physical attribute, like "blue," such ways of talking would be nonsense, or at best farfetched metaphors.

Again, a number cannot be uniquely ascribed to a physical object. A pile of playing cards has a definite weight but not a definite number; "how heavy is this?" makes sense as it stands, but "how many is this?" does not make sense without some added word, expressed or understood—"how many *packs*?" or "how many *cards*?" or "how many *suits*?" And the answer will be quite different according to the word supplied; the same physical object is, e.g., two whist packs, eight complete suits, and 104 cards; none of these numbers, then, can be attributed to the physical object *simpliciter*.

Finally, Mill's sort of view altogether breaks down over 0 and 1. The numerals "0" and "1" are allowable answers to the question "how many?" on the same footing as "2", "3", etc. But 0 and 1 certainly are not physical properties; and where the number 0 can rightly be assigned (e.g., when we say "the number of moons of Venus is 0") there is no physical object to *be* noughtish. Perhaps one may feel inclined to compare "0" and "1" as answers to "how many?" with "nobody" as an answer to the question "who?" But this comparison will not do. As Frege pointed out in controversy with Husserl, the use of "0" and "1" in arithmetic according to the same general rules as other numerals does not lead to any such paradoxes as would arise from treating "nobody" as the proper name of a person. We must unequivocally recognize 0 and 1 as numbers; a theory of number that fails to fit them in is hopeless.

Frege fails, however, to see the fact that makes Mill's sort of view attractive. In spite of Frege's denial (Sec. 24, 58), there is a recognizable physical property common to the *four* faces of a die and the four of diamonds and four pennies and the four sides of a square and a plate broken in four; we could learn to use the word "four" whenever we met with this attribute. When a plate breaks in four, a certain sample of china changes from being *in one piece* to being *in four pieces;* the words in italics stand for different species of a certain generic physical property. This generic property must however be sharply distinguished from number; for number is not restricted to what is spatial, as this property is, but applies to everything thinkable. In particular, the number one must be sharply distinguished from the physical property expressed by "in one piece." When we say that the number of the earth's satellites is 1, we are not saying of the Moon that it is all in one piece—an attribute, as Frege says, in which our Moon nowise excels the *four* moons of Jupiter.

A popular rival to Mill's sort of view is the view that we ascribe numbers to things in accordance with subjective associations. Frege dismisses this briefly and with the contempt it deserves. We get a typical expression of this view in William James's explanation of the term "number" as signifying primarily "the strokes of our attention in discriminating things" (*Principles of Psychology,* II, 653). The number of men in a regiment would thus presumably be a lot of strokes of attention performed by the commanding officer at a parade, or by an Army pay clerk.

Frege next gives us a brilliant and devastating criticism of the idea that the addition of numbers is a putting together of units—e.g., that the number 3 consists of 3 units put together. Frege shows that people who talk this way are simply playing fast and loose with the word "unit"—taking it to stand now for the number 1, now for a single countable object. (Mr. Austin is surely wrong in suggesting [p. 39^e,n.] that any peculiarity of the German word *"Einheit"* is here specially important. As Frege's quotations show, the same fallacies are committed just as often over the Greek and English words for a unit, which, unlike the word *"Einheit,"* are not derived from the words for one in the respective languages.) How is it that "one and one" makes sense, unlike "the Moon and the Moon"? This cannot be answered by saying that "one and one" means "one and *another* one"; arithmetic does not allow us to speak of *ones*, but only of *the* number one. It is senseless to ask which of the 1's in the number 3 we mean when we say that $3 - 1 = 2$, or to qualify "$(2 - 1) - 1 = 0$" by the proviso that the 1's mentioned here must be different. "$+$" between numerals does not express any putting together, like putting three eggs with two eggs. Plato expressed this by saying that units are uncombinable; Aristotle's lengthy criticism of this doctrine in the *Metaphysics* is an *ignoratio elenchi*—he cannot see that there are not two ones in the number two. (People who translate ἀσύμβλητοί by "unaddable" commit the very mistake that Plato sought to rule out by using the word —the confusion between adding numbers and putting things together.)

We now come to Frege's positive account of number statements. In "there are n ...," or "the number of ... is n," the blank cannot be filled up with a possible logical subject—with a name of an object, or a list of objects. We can truly say "there is one Pope in 1949" or "there are two Martian moons"; and here "Pope in 1949" is truly predicable just of Pius XII and "Martian moons" just of Deimos and Phobos. But these expressions are not being used to *name* the objects of which they are predicable; if we substitute proper names of the objects, we get the nonsense sentences "there is one Pius XII" and "there are two Deimos and Phobos." We must never confuse a predicate that applies to an object with a name of the object, as the old logic does in speaking of a *term* that *denotes* an object. In "there are n A's" the grammatical subject "A's" is not being used to name certain A's; it is logically predicative. Frege calls such a predicative expression a *concept word* (*Begriffswort*).

A concept word is so called because it stands for a concept (*bedeutet einen Begriff*). A concept, in Frege's sense, is that of which we express our apprehension by using a logical predicate; our apprehension belongs to the subject matter of psychology, but the concept itself does not. "*x* falls under the concept *man*" means simply "*x* is a man" and has no reference to a conceiving mind. In "there are *n* *A*'s," "*A*," being used predicatively, stands for the concept of an *A*; here we are not asserting or denying that certain specified objects are *A*'s or fall under the concept of an *A*, but rather ascribing a property to the concept itself—saying how often it is realized, whether many times or only once or not at all. And the number of times a concept is realized cannot be a mark (*Merkmal*) of the concept itself. The marks of a concept are properties of the objects that fall under it; but unity and plurality cannot be significantly ascribed to any object; it does not make sense to ask concerning an object whether it occurs once or more often, whether there is one or many of it. Unity and plurality can be ascribed only to concepts under which objects fall, i.e., to properties of objects, expressible by predicates. (Aquinas seems to have grasped this; *Summa Theologica*, Ia, q. 13, art. 9, has a strongly Fregian ring.)

To understand what Frege says about the concept, we must read his essay "Ueber Begriff und Gegenstand" ("On Concept and Object"). Frege there asserts that the concept is essentially predicative and incomplete. A logical predicate is in need of completion and can be completed by adding the name of an object (which then becomes a logical subject); Frege holds that *only* expressions with this sort of incompleteness *can* stand for concepts. Even if we want to make an assertion *about* the concept (as opposed to asserting or denying the concept of an object), we cannot have as the logical subject of our assertion an expression for the concept itself. Abstract expressions like "redness" or "the property of being red" or "the concept *red*" certainly seem to be used as logical subjects; but none of these (not even the last) can stand for a concept. The predicates "is red" and "falls under the concept *red*" alike stand for a certain concept; but "the concept *red*" does not stand for this concept—it is not a concept word like the adjective "red." Frege admits the odd look of this result, but holds that some such oddity must arise in any symbolism, because the incomplete nature of the concept must express itself somehow or other. I think Frege is here fundamentally right. It seems to me, indeed, that a phrase like "the redness *of* . . ." can stand for a concept, although it is not a logical predicate; such phrases, however, have the same incompleteness as predicates; "the redness *of* . . ." is completable in just the same way as ". . . is red"—by adding the name of an object.

Abstract expressions like "the property of being red" or "the concept *red*" are to be avoided whenever possible; they are stylistically clumsy and philosophically dangerous. It is unfortunate that Frege so often needlessly resorts to them; as we shall see later, he is thus led to give false analyses. Here are some examples:

"falls under the concept *F*"	instead of: "is an *F*"
"stands in the relation ϕ to"	instead of: "is a ϕ of"
"the Number that applies to the concept *F*"	instead of: "the Number of *F*'s"
"the extension of the concept *F*"	instead of: "the class of all *F*'s"
"the concept *F* is equal-in-number to the concept *G*"	instead of: "there are just as many *F*'s as *G*'s."

(In the last instance Mr. Austin mitigates the clumsiness by using "equal" for the made-up German word "*gleichzahlig*," "equal-in-number"; he can do this because he consistently renders "*gleich*" not as "equal" but as "identical.")

Frege's next point is that in mathematics we speak as if each number were an identifiable object, to which properties can be ascribed, and which can have a definite description: we say, e.g., that the number 2 has the property of primeness, or that 2 is the even prime number. Frege does not see how this way of speaking can be justified unless numbers *are* objects. What he means by an object is by no means made clear in the *Grundlagen*; but light is thrown on the question by his essay "Funktion und Begriff." Here the distinctive feature of objects is said to be that expressions for them lack the incompleteness that belongs, as we saw, to concept words (e.g., ". . . breathes"), and belongs also to expressions for relations (e.g., ". . . loves . . .") and for functions (e.g., "the capital of . . ."); names of objects, like "Caesar," can rather be used to fill the blanks in such incomplete expressions. Now a numeral like "2" seems to behave like a name; compare "2 is prime," "3 is greater than 2," "the square of 2," with: "Caesar is bald," "Brutus is nobler than Caesar," "the father of Caesar." Such appearances are not indeed always to be trusted; "nothing" and "nobody" likewise have a prima facie similarity to names of objects. But there is no decisive proof that we are wrong in assimilating "2" to names of objects; whereas an attempt to treat "nobody" and "nothing" as names would land us in contradictions almost at once. We do indeed get paradoxes if we treat classes as objects; but that is quite a different thing. And nobody has shown how ostensible references to numbers as objects can be analyzed without assuming such objects. Russell claimed to have done so, but his attempt will not bear close examination; his use of the term "propositional function" is hopelessly confused and inconsistent, and at a critical point he uses a symbolism of capped variables (e.g., '$\phi\hat{x}$') without formulating, even vaguely, the rules of formation and inference.

If a number is an object, we shall need a criterion of identity for it. Frege accordingly considers how to analyze "there are just as many F's as G's." (As he points out, this can consistently be transformed into "the same object is both the number of F's and the number of G's" only if we always have: If there are just as many F's and G's, and just as many G's as K's, then there are just as many F's as K's.) As is well known, Frege gives the analysis: "there is one-one correspondence of the F's to the G's." This analysis does not involve that "the F's" or "the G's" refers to a single object—a class. The relation *being a ϕ of* sets up one-one correspondence of the F's to the G's provided that

(i) if any object x is an F, then of some object y that is a G it is true that x is *the* object that is a ϕ of y;

(ii) if any object y is a G, then of some object x that is an F it is true that y is *the* object of which x is a ϕ.

Thus, to use Frege's own example, the waiter knows he has put out just as many knives as plates because

(i) for every plate x there is a knife y that is *the* object directly to the right of x;

(ii) for every knife y there is a plate x which is *the* object that y is directly to the right of.

And there is no mention here of a class of knives or of plates.

We use here the notion of a relation between objects. Such relations, for Frege, are on the same level as concepts under which objects fall; only, whereas a concept word needs only a single name (a logical subject) to complete its sense, the sense of a relation word requires two such names of objects to be supplied. Quantification over relations, as in: "There is a relation that sets up one-one correspondence between F's and G's" is radically different from quantification over objects. If we generalize "Solomon is a son of David, and David a son of Jesse" to "There is something that Solomon is to David and David is to Jesse," it would obviously be senseless to replace "something" by "some object."

I think Frege is wrong in treating identity as a relation between objects. The mistake comes out plainly in Leibniz' definition, which Frege accepts (Sec. 65); for a thing cannot be significantly said to be substitutable for *the same thing*; what are interchangeable are the *names* of a thing. To regard "is identical with Cicero" as standing for a property of Tully is the same sort of mistake as to think donkeys have a property of beginning with D. The predicate "is *the A*" must *not* be analyzed as meaning "has identity with the A," where "the A" is used to name an object (cf. p. 77, n. 2). This comes out most clearly when we say "nothing is the A"; we are then not using "the A" as if it named an object and denying that anything has identity with this object; on the contrary, we are using "the A" predicatively to stand for a concept and denying that anything falls under the concept. Frege practically gives this explanation for "nothing is the greatest proper fraction" (pp. 87-88, n.). Whenever "is *an A*" stands for a well-defined concept, so also does "is *the A*." Admittedly the latter concept cannot have more than one object falling under it and may have none at all; but Frege himself points out that no concept can be disqualified on such grounds. The equation "the A is the B" or "the A = the B" should be taken not as asserting a relation between named objects, but as saying that the concept expressed by "both is *the A*, and is *the B*" has some object falling under it.

Only small changes would be needed in the *Grundlagen* in order to get rid of the alleged relation of identity. For example, we should have to analyze "there are just as many F's as G's" as follows: "Either any given object is an F if and only if it is a G, or there is a relation that sets up a one-one correspondence of the F's to the G's"; for we may not use identity to establish a one-one correspondence of the F's to the F's. But the symbolism of the *Grundgesetze* would need drastic repairs.

Frege generates the infinite series of finite numbers by appealing to the fact that the finite number n is always immediately followed by the number of numbers from 0 to n inclusive. I think this procedure is valid. Difficulties might indeed arise if we regarded the number 2 as a member of pairs which were in their turn members of the number 2; but we are not committed to this by using numbers in order to count numbers. Russell's Axiom of Infinity lies open to his own taunt about the advantages of theft over honest toil; and it is surely incredible that mathematical truths should depend on empirical facts about how many things there are.

The main results we have so far considered seem to me solidly established. We still have to discuss Frege's view that numbers are classes—extensions of concepts. He himself attached only secondary importance to this (Sec. 107); rejection of it would ruin the symbolic structure of his *Grundgesetze*, but not shake the foundations of arithmetic laid down in the *Grundlagen*.

Frege holds, as we saw, that we may pass from "there are just as many A's as B's" to "some object is at once the number of A's and the number of B's" and vice versa. His aim in treating numbers as classes is to reduce this way of recognizing a logical object to a simpler and more general one; he holds that we may pass in general from "any given object is an F if and only if it is a G" to "some object is at once the class of all F's and the class of all G's" and vice versa. The more general assumption, however, involves a difficulty that does not arise for its supposed special case. This may be shown as follows. Let us define "x is a K" to mean: "for some F, x is the number of F's, and x is not an F." Then the number of K's is itself a K; for if it is not, then it is the number of K's and is not a K; consequently, for some F, it is the number of F's and is not an F—i.e., it is after all a K. Therefore, by the definition of "is a K," we have: "For some F, the number of K's is the number of F's and is not an F." Thus the same object is both the number of K's and the number of F's, although some object (viz., *this* object) is a K without being an F. This conclusion is no paradox. But if now we define "x is an M" to mean "for some G, x is the class of all G's, and x is not itself a G" we may prove by precisely similar reasoning that, for some G, the same object is both the class of M's and the class of G's, although some object (viz., *this* object) is an M without being a G. This proof, given by Frege himself in the appendix to Volume II of the *Grundgesetze*, shows that the ordinary idea of a class involves a contradiction and therefore cannot be used to explain what numbers are; in fact, Frege found he must recant.

To see how Frege was led to believe in such objects as classes, we must consider again his essay "Ueber Begriff und Gegenstand" (in conjunction with *Grundlagen*, p. 80, n.). Frege holds not merely that the abstract expression "the concept *man*" does not stand for a concept, but also that it does stand for an object; he is inclined to think that "the extension of the concept *man*" or "the class of all men" stands for the same object. But Frege's inference:

"The concept *man*" does not stand for a concept;

Ergo, the concept *man* is not a concept but an object contains just the same fallacy as the inference:

"Some man" does not stand for any definite man;

Ergo, some man is not any definite man, but is an indefinite man.

In the latter case Frege has himself pointed out the mistake. Sentences with "some man" as their grammatical subject are not assertions about something named by "some man"; otherwise "some man is wise" and "some man is not wise" would be contradictories, since contradictory predicates would relate to the same subject. Logically "some man" is not a unit at all, and it is senseless to ask what it stands for; "some man is wise" logically breaks up into "man" and "some . . . is wise," and this last complex predicate must be replaced by its contradictory "no . . . is wise" if we want to negate the whole sentence. Similarly, "the concept *man*" stands neither for a concept nor for an object; where it is legitimately used, its apparent unity breaks up under logical analysis. For example, "the concept *man* is realized" does not assert of some object that it is realized; an attempt to assert that an object, e.g., Julius Caesar, is realized leads not to a falsehood (as Frege thinks) but to nonsense. Really the sentence splits up into "man" and "the concept . . . is realized"; the latter is simply a circumlocution for "something is a. . . ." Sentences not exponible in some such innocent way (e.g., "the concept *man* is timeless") may be regarded as nonsensical.

Frege rejected the analysis of "*x* is a man" by which "is a" stands for a logical relation between *x* and an object (a class) called "man." With a sound view of concept and object, there is no place for a copula; a concept word no more needs a copula to join it to a logical subject than a relation word needs a pair of copulas to join it to the names of the related objects. But before his recantation Frege did allow the transformation of "*x* is a man" into "*x* falls under the concept *man*" or "belongs to the class *man*" and conversely, and took "falls under" or "belongs to" to express a logical relation between *x* and the object called "the concept *man*" or "the class *man*." Now surely this rule of transformation does not substantially differ from the rule of interpretation that Frege rejects— from taking "is a" to mean "belongs to" and "man" to mean "the class *man*." If we want a sharp distinction between concept and object, we must reject such a rule of transformation.

Frege defines the Number that belongs to the concept *G*, as being the class of everything that is equal (*gleichzahlig*) to the concept *G*. Now this is legitimate only if we may take "the concept *F* is equal to the concept *G*" as asserting that an *object* called "the concept *F*" is equal to the concept *G*; and "the concept *G*" in "the Number that belongs to the concept *G*" will also, on Frege's view, stand for an object. Frege thus slips back into regarding a number as the number of an *object*. In his *Grundgesetze* he expressly defines the symbol answering to "the Number of . . ." so that the blank must be filled with the name of an object; moreover, he there throws off his reluctance to say definitely that the object a number belongs to is a class; "the number of *A*'s" is taken to mean "the number of the class of all *A*'s." As against this we must re-emphasize Frege's own results. In "the number of . . . ," or "how many . . . are there?" the blank can be filled only with a concept word (in the plural), not with a name of an object nor even a list of objects. Moreover, Frege argued in his recantation that the only tenable view of classes as objects would be such that the class of *A*'s may be the same as the class of *B*'s although something is an *A* without being a *B*; and this surely rules out the idea that the number of *A*'s is the number of the *class* of *A*'s, for the number of *B*'s may be different when the class is the same. (Cf. *Grundgesetze*, II, 264, col. 2.)

29

Quine on Classes and Properties

PETER T. GEACH

On page 120 of Quine's *Mathematical Logic* we find the relation between classes and properties stated thus:

Once classes are freed . . . of any deceptive hint of tangibility, there is little reason to distinguish them from *properties*. It matters little whether we read "$x \, \epsilon \, y$" as "x is a member of the class y" or "x has the property y." If there is any difference between classes and properties, it is merely this: classes are the same when their members are the same, whereas it is not universally conceded that properties are the same when possessed by the same objects. . . . But classes may be thought of as properties if the latter notion is so qualified that properties become identical when their instances are identical. Classes may be thought of as properties in abstraction from any differences which are not reflected in differences of instances.

Quine here uses the strange notion of abstraction so often criticized by Frege. How do things or properties *become* identical merely because somebody chooses to *abstract from*, i.e., ignore, the differences between them? His account of how classes stand in relation to properties looks intelligible only because the notion of a class is so familiar. Suppose, however, that I introduced a new term "surman" (plural "surmen") and explained its relation to the term "man" as follows:

There is little reason to distinguish surmen from men; it matters little whether we say 'Smith is a surman' or 'Smith is a man.' If

---

Reprinted with the kind permission of the author and the editor from *The Philosophical Review*, LXII (1953), 409-412.

there is any difference between surmen and men, it is merely this: surmen are the same when their surnames are the same, whereas it is not universally conceded that men are the same when they have the same surname. But surmen may be thought of as men if the latter notion is so qualified that men become identical when their surnames are identical. Surmen may be thought of as men in abstraction from any differences which are not reflected in differences of surname.

Would this in any way serve to explain how the word "surman" is meant to be used? Would it even be justifiable to use the term "surman" at all, if this were the way it had been introduced? I hardly think so. Possibly Quine would object that my term "surman" is not really parallel to his term "class"—that there is a difference as regards *tangibility*. Classes are to be intangible; whereas men are tangible, and presumably remain tangible even when thought of as surmen, i.e., in abstraction from any difference not reflected in difference of surname. But I do not understand the importance Quine seems to attach to tangibility. The notion is indeed used in schoolboy explanations of the difference between concrete and abstract nouns:

> Abstract nouns in -io call
> *Feminina* one and all;
> Masculine will only be
> Things that you can touch or see;

but in logic I do not think it has even expository value.

It may be admitted that the term "property" would have little value if we were so using it that expressions like "redness" or "the property of being red" were uniquely referring names of properties. Properties so regarded would involve all the difficulties that arise over classes; for instance, the property of being a property that does not belong to itself would involve a difficulty parallel to that about Russell's class of all classes that are not members of themselves; and there would be the added problem how properties were related to classes. But if we use "property" (as Frege used *Begriff*) in the sense "what a logical predicate stands for," then these abstract expressions are not names of properties; nor can any paradox like Russell's be generated as regards properties thus understood.

Of course, this notion of a property has difficulties of its own. When I say that a predicate stands for a property, is not this just a euphemism for its *naming* the property? This objection would have force if I regarded a predicate as an actual expression occurring in sentences. But in fact I should rather regard it as a common property of sentences; thus, I should say that "Smith loves Smith" and "Jones loves Jones" were sentences formed from a common predicate by supplying the respective subjects "Smith" and "Jones." In this instance, though we readily discern the common predicate, it is plainly not something that can be extracted from the sentences and displayed between quotes all by itself. The distinction between thing and property comes out in the distinction between name and predicate just because a name is an actual expression whereas a predicate is rather a common property of expressions.

Again, how can one know whether or not two predicates stand for the same property? Here I must admit partial defeat; I can suggest no necessary and sufficient criterion for such identity of reference; I am, however, prepared to state a necessary condition for it. If one predicate applies to an object and another does not, they certainly do not stand for one and the same property; for otherwise this property would both belong to the object and not belong to it. Sameness of application is therefore a necessary condition for two predicates' having the same property as their reference.

This last common-sense consideration is enough to expose Quine's mistake in identifying properties with classes. For Quine's own way of escaping Russell's paradox is to hold that two predicates may have the same class as their extension though they do not apply to the same objects. E.g., the predicates "—— is a class not belonging to itself" and "—— is a class that belongs to some class but not to itself" have the

same class as their extension;[1] but there is a class—viz., this
common extension itself—that satisfies only the first of these
predicates, not the second. I have no objection to this type
of solution; Frege himself sketched one on similar lines in
the Appendix to his *Grundgesetze*. It does however involve a
sharp distinction between class and property; for in this instance we have *ex hypothesi* the same class, and we cannot
have the same property, because the application of the two
predicates differs. (It is remarkable that in the earlier parts
of his *Methods of Logic* Quine is content to assume that two
"open sentences" have the same class for their extension if
and only if they come out true for the same objects; he does
not tell us that the solution of Russell's paradox he is going
to suggest will involve a restriction on this equivalence; nor,
having once propounded that solution, does he indicate how
matters shall be straightened out.) No amount of *abstraction*
will serve to remove the difference.

A further proof of the need for our distinction may be got
by considering numbers. I hold that a question of number is
a question how many things there are of a certain *kind* or
nature; the words "kind" and "nature" here are just variant
expressions for my "property" or Frege's *Begriff*. Now it is
easy to slide from this view into the view that a number
belongs to a class. But the idea of a class as many—the many
having, in Russell's words, "just so much unity as is required

---

[1] This sentence may appear inconsistent with my previous statement
that a predicate cannot be displayed by itself within quotes. In fact
there is no inconsistency; the actual expressions occurring within quotes
after "the predicates" are not themselves predicates, but serve to indicate predicates. To take a simpler predicate as an example: when I say
that "Booth shot Lincoln" and "Booth shot Booth" contain the common predicate "Booth shot ——," I do not mean that the expression
last quoted occurs in both sentences; plainly it does not, for neither
sentence contains a dash! What I mean is that the two sentences have
the common property of being related in the same way to the expression "Booth shot ——"; viz., each of them is obtained by substituting
a uniquely referring name for the dash in this expression; and this
common property *is* the common predicate.

to make them many, and not enough to prevent them from remaining many"[2]—is I think radically incoherent. When we try to attach a number to a class α, we are really attaching it to the property expressed by "—— is a member of α." This is not a trivial point; for when we attach a number to a property, the property is usually not expressed in the above form; and Russell's paradox seems to show that not all properties are expressible in that form.

As regards Quine's *Mathematical Logic* special difficulties arise; we can show that the formulae he takes to express number-statements will not serve that purpose. This does not, of course, mean that they are senseless or lead to contradiction, but only that Quine suggests a wrong way of reading them. An adequate symbolism for number-statements would have the effect that, no matter how "F" were interpreted, the formula read "the number of F's is 0" would be true if and only if there were no F's, and the formula read "the number of F's is 1" would be true if and only if there were something that was *the* F. Let us now interpret "x is an F" as follows:

For any class α, α is a member of x if and only if α is a member of some class and is not a member of α.

It is then easy to prove in Quine's system all of the theorems that may be put in words as follows:

(1) Some class is *the* F. (There is a class α such that any class β is identical with α if and only if β is an F.)

(2) The class of all F's is a member of 0.

(3) The class of all F's is not a member of 1.

As I said, this involves no inconsistency within the system; but it does mean that reading a formula as "the class of all F's is a member of 0" is not always consistent with reading it as "the number of F's is 0," and reading a formula as "the class of all F's is a member of 1" is not always consistent with reading it as "the number of F's is 1." This difficulty, I

---

[2] *Principles of Mathematics,* p. 69.

think, would not be peculiar to Quine's system; I think it is no less absurd to read "the number of F's" as "the number of the class of F's," than to read "the class of F's" as "the class of the class of F's." In both forms of phrase, the plural noun is used predicatively, to express a property; the class and the number alike are specified by mentioning the property. As Frege would say: *sie haben an dem Begriff selbst und nur an diesem ihren Halt.*

30

On Frege's Way Out

W. V. QUINE

In his review [1] of Geach and Black's *Translations from the Philosophical Writings of Gottlob Frege*,[2] Scholz urges that I evaluate the idea which Geach and Black express thus in their Preface:

Special attention should be paid to Frege's discussion of Russell's paradox in the appendix to vol. ii of the *Grundgesetze*. It is discreditable that logical works should repeat the legend of Frege's abandoning his researches in despair when faced with the paradox; in fact he indicates a line of solution, which others (*e.g.* Quine) have followed out farther.

Geach becomes more explicit in a footnote (p. 243):

The way out of Russell's Paradox here suggested by Frege has been followed by several later writers—*e.g.* by Quine in *Mathematical Logic*. Quine's particular form of the solution would be stated as follows in Frege's terminology: The concepts *not a member of itself* and *member of some class but not of itself* have the same class as their extension; but the class in question is not a

---

Reprinted with the kind permission of the author and the editor from *Mind*, LXIV (1955), 145-159. Prof. Quine has requested that this statement be added: "I have omitted an appendix because, as Church showed me, it was wrong."

[1] Heinrich Scholz, in *Zentralblatt für Mathematik*, vol. 48 (1954), pp. 1 f.

[2] Peter Geach and Max Black, editors and translators (Oxford: Blackwell, 1952).

member of *any* class, and thus falls only under the first of these concepts, not under the second. (But the relation of Quine's solution to Frege's is obscured because Quine does not explicitly make Frege's distinction between a concept or property and its extension.)

It is thus that I have been prompted to write the present paper.

Church has described Geach and Black's idea as "farfetched at best," [3] and a paper on the scale of the present one is scarcely needed to bear him out. It has seemed worth while, however, to relate Frege's "line of solution" to the history of set theory and also to show how it leads to contradiction.

1. Frege, Whitehead, and Russell on Attributes

Taking our cue from the concluding parenthesis of the note quoted from Geach, we may begin by reflecting briefly on "concepts or properties." Or, since 'concept' hints of mind and 'property' hints of a distinction between essence and accident, let us say *attributes*. In an appendix I shall show motivation for not admitting such entities, but meanwhile we must bear with them. An open sentence, *e.g.*, '*x* has fins', is supposed to determine both an attribute, that of finnedness, and a class, that of fin bearers (past, present, and future). The class may be called the *extension* of the open sentence; also it may be called the extension of the attribute.

Since Whitehead and Russell's work is nearer home than Frege's, and since occasion will arise anyway for certain comparisons, let us first view the notion of attribute in the context of *Principia Mathematica*. Whitehead and Russell, like Frege, admitted attributes in addition to classes. At the level of primitive notation, indeed, Whitehead and Russell adopted attributes to the exclusion of classes, and then introduced class names and class variables by contextual definition in terms of their theory of attributes; but at any rate their de-

---

[3] Alonzo Church, review in *Journal of Symbolic Logic,* vol. 18 (1953), p. 93.

rived body of theory embraces the attributes and classes in effect side by side. The attributes were called *propositional functions* in *Principia*, and there was confusion between propositional functions in this sense and propositional functions in the sense of open sentences or predicates;[4] but this confusion is now inessential, for we know how to rectify it without upsetting the system.[5] To proceed, then: in *Principia* we find variables 'ϕ', 'ψ', etc. for attributes, and 'α', 'β', etc. for classes. Also we find two ways of using circumflex accents in connexion with open sentences, one for the abstraction of attributes and the other for the abstraction of classes; thus '$\hat{x}$ has fins' names the attribute and '$\hat{x}(x$ has fins)' the class. Formally, the one difference between attributes and classes, for *Principia*, is that the law of extensionality

$$(x)(x \in \alpha . \equiv . x \in \beta) \supset . \alpha = \beta \qquad (1)$$

holds for classes whereas the corresponding law

$$(x)(\phi x \equiv \psi x) \supset . \phi = \psi \qquad (2)$$

is not supposed to hold for attributes. The whole trick of defining class notation contextually in terms of attribute notation, in *Principia*, is indeed a trick of rendering the law of extensionality demonstrable for classes without adopting it for attributes.

The use of distinctive notation for attributes and classes is a feature of Frege's theory as well as of *Principia*. On the other hand there are differences. In *Principia* the realm of attributes can stand intact without benefit of classes—as in-

---

[4] For a treatment of the relevant notion of predicate see my *Methods of Logic* (New York: Holt; London: Kegan Paul, 1950), pp. 131 ff. Predicates in this sense are, like open sentences, notational forms. They are so devised as to expedite technical discussions of substitution. At those points in *Principia* where the "propositional functions" ambiguously so-called can be construed as notational entities at all (rather than as attributes), they are identifiable more aptly with predicates than with open sentences.

[5] *Cf.* pp. 144 ff. of my "Whitehead and the rise of modern logic," in *The Philosophy of Alfred North Whitehead*, edited by P. A. Schilpp (Evanston, Ill.: Library of Living Philosophers, 1941).

deed it explicitly does, from the point of view of primitive notation. For Frege, on the other hand, attributes depended in large part upon classes. Frege treated of attributes of classes without looking upon such discourse as somehow reducible to a more fundamental form treating of attributes of attributes. Thus, whereas he spoke of attributes of attributes as *second-level* attributes, he rated the attributes of classes as of first level; for he took all classes as rock-bottom objects on a par with individuals.[6]

2. In the Jaws of the Press

When most of the second volume (1903) of Frege's *Grundgesetze der Arithmetik* was in type and ready for printing, Russell wrote Frege announcing Russell's paradox and showing that it could be proved in Frege's system. In response Frege wrote an appendix to that second volume. This appendix was a report of the crisis and an essay at surveying the situation after the body of the book was beyond recall. It was to his translation of this appendix that Geach attached the footnote quoted at the beginning of the present paper.

According to Frege's original system, every attribute ϕ had a class $\hat{x}(\phi x)$ as its extension, and

$$\hat{x}(\phi x) = \hat{x}(\psi x). \supset . (x) (\phi x \equiv \psi x). \tag{3}$$

The line he takes in his appendix is that of revoking (3). In so doing he impoverishes, to some degree, his universe of classes. He now allows attributes to have as their extensions the same class even where the attributes differ to the extent of holding and failing of some object.

Readers of *Principia* know that Russell's paradox of classes has a direct analogue in terms of attributes, and that the authors of *Principia* therefore found need to frame their theory of types for attributes as well as for classes. Indeed, the basic form of the theory of types in *Principia* is the theory

---

[6] Frege, *Grundgesetze der Arithmetik,* vol. 1 (Jena, 1893), §§ 23, 24, 35. See also Rudolf Carnap, *The Logical Syntax of Language* (New York: Harcourt Brace; London: Kegan Paul, 1937), p. 138.

of types of attributes, or propositional functions. The type structure is automatically inherited by classes, through the contextual definitions by which the theory of classes is derived in *Principia* from that of attributes. Readers of *Principia* may wonder, therefore, that Frege can leave his own universe of attributes intact, and molest only the classes. Can we not reproduce Russell's paradox in Frege's theory of attributes, without using his classes at all?

We can not. The reason is that Frege had, even before the discovery of Russell's paradox, the theory of levels of attributes hinted at above; an anticipation, to some degree, of the theory of types.[7] If in response to Russell's paradox Frege had elected to regiment his classes in levels corresponding to those of his attributes, his overall solution would have borne considerable resemblance to that in *Principia*.

Actually it is not to be wondered that Frege did not think of this course, or, thinking of it, adopt it. It was by having all his classes at ground level that he was able to avoid the use of high-level attributes, and this he liked to do. He regularly avoided ascent in his hierarchy of attributes by resorting at appropriate points to classes as zero-level proxies of attributes.[8] Thus, though he gives examples of third-level attributes and alludes to a continuation of the hierarchy,[9] in practice he uses no variables for attributes above the first level, nor constants for attributes above the second.

Russell's *Principles of Mathematics*, like the second volume of *Grundgesetze*, appeared in 1903. Russell had written *Principles* in ignorance of Frege's work; but before *Principles* was off the press he discovered Frege's writings and read various,

---

[7] A somewhat clearer anticipation of the theory of types is to be found still earlier, in Ernst Schröder, *Vorlesungen über die Algebra der Logik*, vol. 1 (Leipzig, 1890), pp. 245-249. *Cf.* Alonzo Church, "Schröder's anticipation of the simple theory of types," preprinted for Fifth International Congress for Unity of Science (Cambridge, Mass., 1939) as from *Journal of Unified Science*, vol. 9 (which never appeared).

[8] Frege, op. cit. § 35.

[9] Op. cit. § 24.

including the first volume of *Grundgesetze*. There was time for him to add a long and appreciative appendix to *Principles*; time also, we have seen, for him to write Frege and evoke, in turn, an appendix in the second volume of *Grundgesetze*; and time even for him to see that appendix of Frege's and add still a note to his own appendix to *Principles* (p. 522), as follows:

The second volume of *Gg.*, which appeared too late to be noticed in the Appendix, contains an interesting discussion of the contradiction . . . , suggesting that the solution is to be found by denying that two propositional functions which determine equal classes must be equivalent. As it seems very likely that this is the true solution, the reader is strongly recommended to examine Frege on this point.

3. Frege's Details

Thus far I have described Frege's suggestion only incompletely, *viz.* as the rejection of (3). Russell in the above note describes it likewise, using different terminology. To be told that (3) is no longer to hold, or is no longer to retain its full generality, is to be told merely in what general quarter the revision is to be sought, and not what the revision is to be. Frege went on, however, in that same appendix to *Grundgesetze*, to make his suggestion more definite. Commenting on a step-by-step recapitulation of the argument of Russell's paradox, he writes: [10]

In both cases we see that the exceptional case is constituted by the extension itself, in that it falls under only one of two concepts whose extension it is; and we see that the occurrence of this exception can in no way be avoided. Accordingly the following suggests itself as the criterion for equality in extension: The extension of one concept coincides with that of another when every object that falls under the first concept, except the extension of the first concept, falls under the second concept likewise, and when every object that falls under the second concept, except the extension of the second concept, falls under the first concept likewise.

What Frege calls "concepts" (*Begriffe*) in this passage are of

---

[10] Geach and Black, pp. 242 f. translating *Grundgesetze,* vol. 2 (Jena, 1903), p. 262.

course what I have been calling "attributes." Thus Frege is proposing, contrary to (3), that at least for some attributes ϕ and ψ we take $\hat{x}(\phi x)$ and $\hat{x}(\psi x)$ to be one and the same class even though ' $\phi x \equiv \psi x$ ' be false of one special object x, viz. that class itself.[11]

Classically, the members of $\hat{x}(\phi x)$ are such that

$$(y)\,[y \,\epsilon\, \hat{x}(\phi x). \equiv \phi y]. \tag{4}$$

This implies (3). Frege, in departing from (3), is therefore departing from (4), thus allowing the membership of $\hat{x}(\phi x)$ to deviate somewhat from its classical composition. But he keeps the deviation to a minimum, thus providing [12] that

$$(y)\,[y \,\neq\, \hat{x}(\phi x). \supset \,:\, y \,\epsilon\, \hat{x}(\phi x). \equiv \phi y]. \tag{5}$$

This provision still leaves open the possibility, for any particular ϕ, that $\hat{x}(\phi x)$ either comprise exactly the objects x such that ϕx, or comprise all of them plus $\hat{x}(\phi x)$ itself, or comprise all except $\hat{x}(\phi x)$ itself. Frege implicitly elects this last alternative for all choices of ϕ; [13] thus

$$(y)\,[y \,\epsilon\, \hat{x}(\phi x). \equiv . \, y \,\neq\, \hat{x}(\phi x). \phi y]. \tag{6}$$

Note that even this stipulation does not quite determine $\hat{x}(\phi x)$; to view (6) as a definition of '$\hat{x}(\phi x)$' would involve circularity, because of the recurrence of '$\hat{x}(\phi x)$' on the right. Frege expresses awareness of this lack of specificity, in a remark immediately following the longer passage which I quoted a page back. "Obviously this cannot be taken as *defining* the extension of a concept, but only as specifying the distinctive property of this second-level function."

What we have just been examining would seem to be the "way out of Russell's paradox" which, according to Geach, "has been followed by several later writers—*e.g.* by Quine, in *Mathematical Logic*." But he must have meant to refer only to broader lines of Frege's proposal; for the idea expressed in

---

[11] I am now abandoning Whitehead and Russell's class variables 'α', 'β', etc. (see § 1 above) in favour of the general variables 'x', 'y', etc. This procedure accords with Frege's, and is the appropriate one in the absence of a theory of types.

[12] *Grundgesetze*, vol. 2, p. 264.

[13] *Ibid.*

(5) (let alone (6)) has never been used, so far as I know, by anyone but Frege. This is cause for satisfaction, because the idea leads to contradiction in any universe of more than one member.

4. The New Contradiction

Sobociński reports [14] that Leśniewski proved the inconsistency of Frege's proposal in 1938. Leśniewski's argument, as set forth by Sobociński, is hard to dissociate from special features of Leśniewski's system. But Geach, who lately brought this paper to my attention, has succeeded in reproducing the argument in a Fregean setting, obtaining a contradiction from (6) and

$$(\exists x)(\exists y)(x \neq y). \tag{7}$$

Before hearing of these developments I had derived a contradiction using, in place of (6), the weaker assumption (5). My derivation is as follows. I define 'V', '$\varLambda$', 'ιz', and 'W' as '$\hat{x}(x = x)$', '$\hat{x}(x \neq x)$', '$\hat{x}(x = z)$', and '$\hat{x}(z)(x \,\epsilon\, z . z \,\epsilon\, x . \supset . x = z)$', and make use of four cases of (5):

$$(z)(y)(y \neq \iota z . \supset : y \,\epsilon\, \iota z . \equiv . y = z), \tag{8}$$

$$(y)[y \neq W . \supset : y \,\epsilon\, W . \equiv (z)(y \,\epsilon\, z . z \,\epsilon\, y . \supset . y = z)], \tag{9}$$

and the cases corresponding to 'V' and '$\varLambda$', which reduce quickly to:

$$(y)(y \neq V . \supset . y \,\epsilon\, V), \tag{10}$$

$$(y)(y \,\epsilon\, \varLambda . \supset . y = \varLambda). \tag{11}$$

Two corollaries of (8) are:

$$(y)(y \neq \iota y . \supset . y \,\epsilon\, \iota y), \tag{12}$$

$$(x)(z)[(\exists y)(x \,\epsilon\, y . y \,\epsilon\, \iota z . y \neq \iota z) \supset . x \,\epsilon\, z . z \neq \iota z]. \tag{13}$$

If we change 'ιy' in (12) to '$\varLambda$', then by (11) we can get '$y = \varLambda$'; so

$$(y)(\iota y = \varLambda . \supset . y = \varLambda). \tag{14}$$

---

[14] Boleslaw Sobociński, "L'Analyse de l'antinomie russellienne par Leśniewski," *Methodos,* vol. 1 (1949), pp. 94-107, 220-228, 308-316 (specifically 220 ff.).

If we change 'ιz' to 'z' in (8) and reduce, we get '$y \,\epsilon\, z \,.\, \supset\, .\, y = z$'; so

$$(z)(y)(z = \iota z \,.\, y \,\epsilon\, z \,.\, \supset\, .\, y = z). \tag{15}$$

If we change 'V' to 'Λ' in (10), then by (11) we can get '$(y)(y = \Lambda)$', contrary to (7); so $\mathrm{V} \neq \Lambda$. Hence, by (10) and (14),

$$\Lambda \,\epsilon\, \mathrm{V}, \qquad \iota \mathrm{V} \neq \Lambda, \qquad u \mathrm{V} \neq \Lambda. \tag{16}$$

By (8), $\Lambda \neq u \mathrm{V} \,.\, \supset\, :\, \Lambda \,\epsilon\, u \mathrm{V} \,.\, \equiv\, .\, \Lambda = \iota \mathrm{V}$. Hence, by (16), $\sim (\Lambda \,\epsilon\, u \mathrm{V})$, whereas $\Lambda \,\epsilon\,$ V. So

$$u \mathrm{V} \neq \mathrm{V}. \tag{17}$$

By (15), $\iota y = u y \,.\, y \,\epsilon\, \iota y \,.\, \supset\, .\, y = \iota y$. Hence, by (12),

$$(y)(\iota y = u y \,.\, \supset\, .\, y = \iota y = u y). \tag{18}$$

From (17), by (18), we have '$\iota \mathrm{V} \neq u \mathrm{V}$', and thence by (18) again,

$$u u \mathrm{V} \neq u \mathrm{V}. \tag{19}$$

If $u \mathrm{V} \neq \mathrm{W}$ and $\sim (u \mathrm{V} \,\epsilon\, \mathrm{W})$, then, by (9),

$$(\exists z)(u \mathrm{V} \,\epsilon\, z \,.\, z \,\epsilon\, u \mathrm{V} \,.\, u \mathrm{V} \neq z),$$

whence, by (13), $u \mathrm{V} \,\epsilon\, \iota \mathrm{V}$ and $u \mathrm{V} \neq \iota \mathrm{V}$; but then, by (8), $u \mathrm{V} = \mathrm{V}$, contrary to (17). So

$$u \mathrm{V} = \mathrm{W} \,.\, \mathbf{v} \,.\, u \mathrm{V} \,\epsilon\, \mathrm{W} \,. \tag{20}$$

Suppose $\iota \mathrm{W} = \mathrm{W}$. Then, by (15), $u \mathrm{V} \,\epsilon\, \mathrm{W} \,.\, \supset\, .\, u \mathrm{V} = \mathrm{W}$, and hence, by (20), $u \mathrm{V} = \mathrm{W}$. But then, by (19), $\iota \mathrm{W} \neq \mathrm{W}$. So

$$\iota \mathrm{W} \neq \mathrm{W}. \tag{21}$$

Hence, by (12),

$$\mathrm{W} \,\epsilon\, \iota \mathrm{W}. \tag{22}$$

By (21) and (9),

$$\iota \mathrm{W} \,\epsilon\, \mathrm{W} \,.\, \equiv\, (z)(\iota \mathrm{W} \,\epsilon\, z \,.\, z \,\epsilon\, \iota \mathrm{W} \,.\, \supset\, .\, \iota \mathrm{W} = z). \tag{23}$$

Hence $\iota \mathrm{W} \,\epsilon\, \mathrm{W} \,.\, \supset\, :\, \iota \mathrm{W} \,\epsilon\, \mathrm{W} \,.\, \mathrm{W} \,\epsilon\, \iota \mathrm{W} \,.\, \supset\, .\, \iota \mathrm{W} = \mathrm{W}$. So, by (21) and (22),

$$\sim (\iota \mathrm{W} \,\epsilon\, \mathrm{W}). \tag{24}$$

Then, by (23), $(\exists z)(\iota \mathrm{W} \,\epsilon\, z \,.\, z \,\epsilon\, \iota \mathrm{W} \,.\, \iota \mathrm{W} \neq z)$, whence, by (13), $\iota \mathrm{W} \,\epsilon\, \mathrm{W}$, in contradiction to (24).

5. A Kernel of Truth

It is scarcely to Frege's discredit that the explicitly speculative appendix now under discussion, written against time in
a crisis, should turn out to possess less scientific value than
biographical interest. Over the past half century the piece
has perhaps had dozens of sympathetic readers who, after
a certain amount of tinkering, have dismissed it as the wrong
guess of a man in a hurry. One such reader was probably
Frege himself, sometime in the ensuing 22 years of his life.
Another, presumably, was Russell. We must remember that
Russell's initial favourable reaction, quoted at the end of
§ 2, was a hurried conjecture indeed; five years later we have,
in significant contrast, his theory of types.

In any event, what Russell actually described in that
quoted note was not Frege's full suggestion, but only its
broadest feature: restriction, somehow, of (3). This feature,
though Russell later turned his back on it, is a good one;
and by working out from it we can find what Frege's ill-
starred appendix did contain pertinent to the subsequent
course of logic. That broad feature, and more, can be said
with some plausibility to have "been followed by several
later writers—*e.g.* by Quine, in *Mathematical Logic.*"

In order to implement the ensuing comparisons we must
eliminate Frege's reference to a realm of attributes. This
necessity is remarked, though in an inverted form, in the
concluding parenthesis of Geach's well-thumbed footnote. But
the required elimination is less difficult than that parenthesis
might lead one to expect, thanks to the circumstance that
none of Frege's remarks in this connexion depend on any
principle of individuation of attributes broader than the
principle of individuation (*viz.* sheer sameness of spelling)
of the corresponding open sentences themselves. Where Frege
speaks of classes as extensions of attributes, we can speak
metalogically of classes as determined by open sentences.

This shift requires no rewriting of (3)-(6) and related

formulas. These merely change in status from open sentences, with attribute variables 'ϕ' and 'ψ', to schemata with dummy sentences 'ϕx', 'ψx', and 'ϕy'. The difference, conspicuously immaterial here, would become material in cases where 'ϕ' occurs in a quantifier; such cases would cease to be allowable.[15] But we shall not encounter any of them.

To reject (3), as Frege did, was to allow (3) to be false for some attributes ϕ and ψ. Reconstrued now without reference to attributes, his rejection of (3) comes to consist in allowing (3) to be false under some substitutions of open sentences for 'ϕx' and 'ψx'.

Now it is time to point out an important difficulty in connexion with rejecting (3). The difficulty lurks equally in Frege's account and in Russell's note. It is this: the prefix '$\hat{x}$' has been understood, to begin with, as 'the class of all and only the objects x such that'. If we presume to declare some case of (3) false, thus taking '$\hat{x}(\phi x) = \hat{x}(\psi x)$' as true and '$(x)(\phi x \equiv \psi x)$' as false (for some particular choice of open sentences in place of 'ϕx' and 'ψx'), then surely we have departed from that original reading of '$\hat{x}$', and left no clue as to what the classes $\hat{x}(\phi x)$ and $\hat{x}(\psi x)$ are supposed to be which are talked of in the allegedly true equation '$\hat{x}(\phi x) = \hat{x}(\psi x)$'. Either we must give some supplementary reading of the notation '$\hat{x}$', or we cannot read the presumed counter-instances of (3). Similar difficulties arise over the word 'extension' in Frege's account, and over the word 'determine' in Russell's note.

Earlier we observed that rejection of (3) involves rejection of (4). Let us accordingly concentrate on (4) instead of (3); for it happens that the above difficulty as it affects (4) can be coped with. The reasoning is as follows. In case the open

---

[15] See "Whitehead and the rise of modern logic," pp. 144 ff.; also *Methods of Logic,* pp. 22, 82, 91 f., 129 f., 203-208; also *From a Logical Point of View* (Cambridge, Mass.: Harvard; London: Oxford, 1953), pp. 8-11, 102-116.

sentence represented as 'ϕx' happens to be such that some class z has as members all and only the objects x such that ϕx, certainly $\hat{x}(\phi x)$ is still to be considered as z; it is only in the unfavourable cases that '$\hat{x}$' demands novel interpretation. The question whether to adhere to (4) for all open sentences, or to reject it for some, is thus simply the question whether to adhere to the *abstraction principle*

$$(\exists z)(x)(x \in z \: . \equiv \phi x)$$

for all open sentences or to reject it for some. Instead of talking of rejection of (4), therefore, we can talk of rejection of the abstraction principle. The useful difference between this principle and (4) is that whereas we cannot deny a case of (4) without facing the question what $\hat{x}(\phi x)$ is thenceforward supposed to be, we can deny any case of the abstraction principle without having to recognize the prefix '$\hat{x}$' at all.

All the well-known ways around the paradoxes, except for the theory of types, involve recognizing exceptions to the abstraction principle. This is not to be wondered at, since the abstraction principle yields contradiction by elementary logic as soon as 'ϕx' is taken as the open sentence '$\sim (x \in x)$'. Either you must declare some open sentences to be immune to the abstraction principle or, as is done in the theory of types, you must declare certain harmful forms such as '$\sim (x \in x)$' to be ungrammatical and not sentences at all.

The theories which allow exceptions to the abstraction principle differ from one another, essentially, in where they fix the break between the cases which hold and the cases which fail. Zermelo [16] was perhaps the first to perceive clearly this focal role of the abstraction principle; at any rate, his set theory (1908) was the first that proceeded explicitly by postulation of instances and families of instances of that principle.

---

[16] Ernst Zermelo, "Untersuchungen über die Grundlagen der Mengenlehre," *Mathematische Annalen,* vol. 65 (1908), pp. 261-281.

6. Extension Extended

In turning our attention from (3) and (4) to the abstraction principle as formulated above, we came out where we need no longer worry about novel interpretations of the prefix '$\hat{x}$', and can simply acquiese in the inappropriateness of that prefix in connexion with many open sentences. Some open sentences (those fulfilling the abstraction principle) happen to have extensions; others not. Frege himself touched upon that possibility, in the following words: [17] ". . . we must take into account the possibility that there are concepts with no extension (at any rate, none in the ordinary sense of the word)." However, he promptly and explicitly discarded that alternative, electing rather to require an extension in every case. He thus presented himself squarely with the problem of reconstruing '$\hat{x}(\phi x)$' compatibly with rejection of (3). Actually he cannot, despite the above passage, have hoped to retain extensions generally "in the ordinary sense of the word," since this would mean retaining (4) and so (3). But he wanted there to be, for every case 'ϕx', an extension $\hat{x}(\phi x)$ under some mildly variant reinterpretation of 'extension' and '$x(\phi x)$'. He essayed such a reinterpretation in his final suggestions, as noted above in connexion with (6), but recognized that he had not fixed it uniquely.

Since Frege's full suggestion leads to contradiction, there is no point in trying to devise a unique reinterpretation of '$\hat{x}(\phi x)$' suited to exactly his principles. On the other hand, the general question of devising reinterpretations of '$\hat{x}(\phi x)$' for systems which allow exceptions to the abstraction principle is worth considering. Narrowing the field a little, we might require of a satisfactory reinterpretation that $\hat{x}(\phi x)$ continue to contain only objects x such that ϕx, even if it cannot at the same time exhaust them. Now given this condition, a further imperative becomes evident: $\hat{x}(\phi x)$ must not be a subclass of any further class which contains only objects x such that

---

[17] Geach and Black, p. 239, translating *Grundgesetze*, vol. 2, p. 257.

ϕx. For, if $\hat{x}(\phi x)$ is not to exhaust the objects x such that ϕx, at least we want it to come as near as possible to doing so.

How to reconstrue '$\hat{x}(\phi x)$', conformably with the above requirements, will depend on what cases of the abstraction principle hold; and this is the central point on which set theories differ from one another. The particular distribution of cases for which the principle holds, for a given set theory, can be such as to make any general interpretation of '$\hat{x}(\phi x)$' conformable to the foregoing paragraph impossible. This can happen in either of two ways. It may happen, for some open sentences, that every class whose members all fulfil the sentence is a subclass of a further class whose members all fulfil the sentence, so that there is no final class of the kind. Again it may happen, for some open sentences, that each of several classes qualifies under the requirements of the preceding paragraph, and there is no systematic way of choosing one from among them.

Zermelo's system (1908), von Neumann's (1925),[18] and that of my "New foundations" (1937)[19] are three set theories which differ drastically from one another in point of what cases of the abstraction principle are assumed to hold. Each of the three, however, is such as to render impossible any general interpretation of '$\hat{x}(\phi x)$' within the above requirements. In any such system the sensible course is simply not to call for an extension $\hat{x}(\phi x)$, in any sense, for each open sentence 'ϕx'.[20]

A striking feature of von Neumann's theory is that it, unlike its predecessors, provides for there being some classes

---

[18] J. von Neumann, "Eine Axiomatisierung der Mengenlehre," *Journal für reine und angewandte Mathematik*, vol. 154 (1925), pp. 219-240; vol. 155, p. 128.

[19] "New foundations for mathematical logic," *American Mathematical Monthly*, vol. 44 (1937), pp. 70-80. Reprinted, with emendations and a supplement, in *From a Logical Point of View*.

[20] But one can still apply '$\hat{x}$', in its full classical import, to the particular open sentences for which the abstraction principle holds, defining this usage via singular description. Such is my procedure in "New foundations."

which are not members of any classes at all. Such classes I called *non-elements* when I gratefully carried his idea over into my *Mathematical Logic*. The set theory of *Mathematical Logic*, though depending heavily on the presence of non-elements, differs from von Neumann's system in consequential ways. The cases of the abstraction principle which hold for my system differ from those which hold for von Neumann's,[21] and can be specified in an unusually simple way, as follows: the principle holds except when there are non-elements fulfilling 'ϕx'.[22] Now for this system, unlike von Neumann's, Zermelo's, and that of "New foundations," a general interpretation of '$\hat{x}(\phi x)$' *is* available which conforms to the requirements lately set forth. It turns out to be this: $\hat{x}(\phi x)$ is the class of all *elements* x such that ϕx. Formally stated, $\hat{x}(\phi x)$ is the y such that $(x)[x \, \epsilon \, y \, . \, \equiv \, . \, (\exists z)(x \, \epsilon \, z) \, . \, \phi x]$.

The above description of the system of *Mathematical Logic* does not determine it in full, but applies still to a whole genus of systems.[23] The cases of the abstraction principle which hold for my system may seem just now to have been fully specified, leaving no latitude for further variation; but this is not so, for the above specification appeals to the distinction between element and non-element, and we are still free to draw this line very much as we choose.

7. Frege and the Later Trends

Let us consider, in summary survey, how the suggestions in Frege's appendix relate to set theory from Zermelo onward.

---

[21] See *ibid*. pp. 100 f.

[22] This can be seen by reflecting that in *202 of *Mathematical Logic* the clause of elementhood is dispensable if and only if it is implied by the formula which stands in conjunction with it.

[23] *E.g.* my "Element and number," *Journal of Symbolic Logic,* vol. 6 (1941), pp. 135-149; Hao Wang, "A new theory of element and number," *ibid*. vol. 13 (1948), pp. 129-137. The earliest instance is perhaps the system of the first edition of *Mathematical Logic,* which, however, proved inconsistent. The emendation of the system, used in the revised edition (Cambridge, Mass.: Harvard; London: Oxford, 1951) is due to Wang.

Frege's rejection of (3) implies, we observed, rejecting the universality of the abstraction principle; and this latter departure is a focal point of modern foundations of set theory, from Zermelo onward, aside from the theory of types. But the claim for Frege is weak here. Frege's eyes were on the extension $\hat{x}(\phi x)$, and how to preserve it or a reasonable facsimile in the general case. Zermelo had no such preoccupation, and faced the problem of set-theoretic foundations squarely in terms of the cases of the abstraction principle. Significantly, neither Zermelo's set theory nor von Neumann's nor that of my "New foundations" will accommodate the remotest analogue of an extension operator applicable to open sentences generally. Zermelo, rather than Frege, stands out as the pioneer in the genre of set theories represented by these three. Not but that von Neumann in turn added a drastic innovation, in his admission of non-elementhood. Moreover "New foundations," though like Zermelo's in that it proceeds by selective adoption of cases of the abstraction principle, is in equal measure indebted to Russell's theory of types. The principle determining what cases of the abstraction principle are to hold for "New foundations" is an adaptation of a formal feature of type theory.

If Frege's preoccupation with a generally applicable analogue of the classical extension operator tends to estrange him from the above company, it should count correspondingly in favour of an affinity between his suggestions and my *Mathematical Logic*. For in the latter system there is, we have seen, a generally applicable adaptation of the extension operator. Moreover, to turn to a prominent individual case, the extension $\hat{x} \sim (x \in x)$ fails to be a member of itself, in *Mathematical Logic* as in Frege's plan; this conformity was remarked in Geach's footnote.

Yet the differences are great. Frege's extension operator resisted actual interpretation, but was supposed, in each application, to approximate to the classical extension to within one possible discrepancy of membership. Mine is defined, and admits of infinite discrepancies. Furthermore von Neumann's non-elementhood concept, utterly un-Fregean, is of the essence of *Mathematical Logic*. Incidentally there is the inconsistency of Frege's specific proposal; this is indeed a point of similarity with the first edition of *Mathematical Logic*, but quite possibly a point of contrast with the current edition, thanks to Wang's brilliant repair.

A passing remark, finally, on genesis. We discerned, in the demand for a generally applicable adaptation of the extension operator, a particular resemblance which Frege's proposal bears to the system of *Mathematical Logic* and not to previous set theories such as Zermelo's, von Neumann's, and that of "New foundations." Now this particular resemblance is due not to heredity but to convergence: response to common demands of algorithmic facility. The ancestry of *Mathematical Logic* is an open book; the parents are von Neumann's system and "New foundations," both of whose genealogies were looked into a page back.

All of modern logic owes an incalculable debt to Frege. If anyone can be singled out as the founder of mathematical logic, it is by all odds he. But I have been concerned in these pages, like Geach and Black in the remarks which I quoted from them, only with the hurried appendix to the second volume of *Grundgesetze*.

31

On Frege's Way Out

PETER T. GEACH

In this note I shall give a generalized form of Leśniewski's proof that Frege's way out of Russell's Paradox only generates new contradictions. Frege turns out to have been wrong even in supposing that there was only one 'exceptional case' for each predicate 'F'; for the supposition

$$(y) : y \epsilon \hat{x}(Fx) \; \equiv \; . \; y \ne \mathrm{Ex}\, \hat{x}(Fx) \; . \; Fy \qquad (1)$$

where 'Ex' stands for a specifiable function that has a value for any class as argument, leads to a contradiction, except on the absurd supposition that the universal class $\hat{x}(x = x)$ is a unit class $\hat{x}(x = y)$. (Henceforth I write, as is usual, 'V' for '$\hat{x}(x = x)$' and 'ιy' for '$\hat{x}(x = y)$'.)

From (1) we easily prove that

$$(y) \; . \; y \, \epsilon \, \mathrm{V} \; \mathrm{v} \; y = \mathrm{Ex}\, \mathrm{V} \qquad (2)$$

$$(x) \; (y) : x \, \epsilon \, \iota y \; . \; \equiv \; . \; x \ne \mathrm{Ex}\, \iota y \; . \; x = y \qquad (3)$$

$$(x)(y) : \iota x = \iota y \; . \; \equiv \; . \; x = y \qquad (4)$$

$$(x)(y) : x \, \epsilon \, \iota y \supset . \; x = y \qquad (5)$$

We now define a function θ to satisfy the following conditions:

$$\left. \begin{array}{l} \text{If } \mathrm{Ex}\, x \ne \iota x, \theta x = \iota x. \\ \text{If } \mathrm{Ex}\, x = \iota x \text{ and } x \text{ is a unit class, } \theta x = \mathrm{V}. \\ \text{If } \mathrm{Ex}\, x = \iota x \text{ and } x \text{ is not a unit class, } \theta x = x. \end{array} \right\} \qquad (6)$$

Reprinted with the kind permission of the author and the editor from *Mind,* LXV (1956), 408-409.

On Frege's principles, this function is legitimately introduced, since its value is specified (provided that the value of the Ex-function is) for all possible arguments.

We now easily see, since V cannot be a unit class, that

$$(x) \cdot \theta x \neq \mathrm{Ex}\ x \tag{7}$$

By (7) and (1) we have:

$$\theta \hat{x}(Fx) \ \epsilon \ \hat{x}(Fx) \cdot \equiv \cdot F(\theta \hat{x}(Fx)) \tag{8}$$

Again, we can prove that:

$$(x)(y) : \theta x = \theta y \cdot \theta x \neq \mathrm{V} \cdot \supset x = y \tag{9}$$

For if $\theta x = \theta y$ and is not a unit class and not V, we must have: $\theta x = x$, $\theta y = y$, $x = y$. And if $\theta x = \theta y$ is a unit class, then, since V is not a unit class, we must have $\theta x = \iota x$ and $\theta y = \iota y$, and therefore $\iota x = \iota y$ and $x = y$ by (4).

We now write 'W' for '$\hat{x}(y)(x = \theta y \supset \sim(x \epsilon y))$'. We have, by (8):

$$\theta \mathrm{W} \epsilon \mathrm{W} \equiv (y)(\theta \mathrm{W} = \theta y \supset \sim(\theta \mathrm{W} \epsilon y)) \tag{10}$$

Hence: $\sim(\theta \mathrm{W} \epsilon \mathrm{W}) : (\exists y)(\theta \mathrm{W} = \theta y \cdot \theta \mathrm{W} \epsilon y)$ (11)

By (9), however, unless $\theta \mathrm{W} = \mathrm{V}$, we can never have $\theta \mathrm{W} = \theta y$ and $\mathrm{W} \neq y$. So we have:

$$\theta \mathrm{W} = \mathrm{V} \tag{12}$$

Since $\theta \mathrm{V} \neq \mathrm{Ex V}$, by (7), $\theta \mathrm{V}\ \iota \epsilon\ \mathrm{V}$, by (2). So, since $\sim(\theta \mathrm{W} \epsilon \mathrm{W})$, $\mathrm{W} \neq \mathrm{V}$[1]. But $\theta \mathrm{W} = \mathrm{V}$; so we must have $\mathrm{Ex}\ \mathrm{W} = \iota \mathrm{W}$, and W must be a unit class.

$$\mathrm{Ex}\ \mathrm{W} = \iota \mathrm{W} \cdot (\exists z)(\mathrm{W} = \iota z) \tag{13}$$

From (1), (4), (5), and (13), we easily derive:

$$(x)(x \neq \iota \mathrm{W} \cdot \iota x \neq \mathrm{W} \cdot \supset (\exists y)(x = \theta y \cdot x \epsilon y)) \tag{14}$$

Now put 'ιv' for 'x' in (14) and use (4). This gives:

$$(v)(v \neq \mathrm{W} \cdot \iota \iota v \neq \mathrm{W} \cdot \supset (\exists y)(\iota v = \theta y \cdot \iota v \epsilon y)) \tag{15}$$

But θy is a unit class ιv only if $\theta y = \iota y = \iota v$ and $v = y$. So we have:

---

[1] This simple proof that $\mathrm{W} \neq \mathrm{V}$ was suggested to me by Mr. Michael Dummett.

$$(v) (v \neq W . \iota \iota v \neq W . \supset \iota v \, \epsilon \, v) \tag{16}$$

Now since $V \neq \iota \iota V$, $\sim (\iota \iota V \, \epsilon \, \iota V)$, by (5); so, writing '$\iota V$' for '$v$' in (16), we get:

$$\iota V = W \, \mathsf{v} \, \iota \iota \iota V = W \tag{17}$$

Again, since $\iota V \neq \iota \iota \iota V$, $\sim (\iota \iota \iota V \, \epsilon \, \iota \iota V)$, by (5); so, writing '$\iota \iota V$' for '$v$' in (16), we get:

$$\iota \iota V = W \, \mathsf{v} \, \iota \iota \iota \iota V = W \tag{18}$$

But since V is not a unit class, by (4) the classes ιV, $\iota \iota V$, $\iota \iota \iota V$, $\iota \iota \iota \iota V$ are all distinct; so (17) and (18) cannot both be true.

If, as Frege supposed, Ex x is always x itself, we could reach contradiction more simply by considering the consequences of '$\iota U \epsilon U$', when $U = \hat{x}(y) (x = \iota y \supset \sim (x \epsilon y))$. This was essentially Leśniewski's way.

APPENDICES

Three Essays by Gottlob Frege

The Thought:
A Logical Inquiry

GOTTLOB FREGE

[Translators' Note: This essay was first published in the *Beiträge zur Philosophie des Deutschen Idealismus* for 1918-19, and was the first of three connected essays, the others being 'Die Verneinung,' which has been translated into English by Mr. P. T. Geach, and appears in his and Mr. M. Black's *Translations from the Philosophical Writings of Gottlob Frege*, and 'Gedankengefüge'. A. M. and Marcelle Quinton.]

The word "true" indicates the aim of logic as does "beautiful" that of aesthetics or "good" that of ethics. All sciences have truth as their goal; but logic is also concerned with it in a quite different way from this. It has much the same relation to truth as physics has to weight or heat. To discover truths is the task of all sciences; it falls to logic to discern the laws of truth. The word "law" is used in two senses. When we speak of laws of morals or the state we mean regulations which ought to be obeyed but with which actual happenings are not always in conformity. Laws of nature are the generalization of natural occurrences with which the occurrences are always in accordance. It is rather in this sense that I speak of

Reprinted with the kind permission of M. Quinton and the editor from *Mind*, LXV (1956), 289-311.

laws of truth. This is, to be sure, not a matter of what happens so much as of what is. Rules for asserting, thinking, judging, inferring, follow from the laws of truth. And thus one can very well speak of laws of thought too. But there is an imminent danger here of mixing different things up. Perhaps the expression "law of thought" is interpreted by analogy with "law of nature" and the generalization of thinking as a mental occurrence is meant by it. A law of thought in this sense would be a psychological law. And so one might come to believe that logic deals with the mental process of thinking and the psychological laws in accordance with which it takes place. This would be a misunderstanding of the task of logic, for truth has not been given the place which is its due here. Error and superstition have causes just as much as genuine knowledge. The assertion both of what is false and of what is true takes place in accordance with psychological laws. A derivation from these and an explanation of a mental process that terminates in an assertion can never take the place of a proof of what is asserted. Could not logical laws also have played a part in this mental process? I do not want to dispute this, but when it is a question of truth possibility is not enough. For it is also possible that something not logical played a part in the process and deflected it from the truth. We can only decide this after we have discerned the laws of truth; but then we will probably be able to do without the derivation and explanation of the mental process if it is important to us to decide whether the assertion in which the process terminates is justified. In order to avoid this misunderstanding and to prevent the blurring of the boundary between psychology and logic, I assign to logic the task of discovering the laws of truth, not of assertion or thought. The meaning of the word "true" is explained by the laws of truth.

But first I shall attempt to outline roughly what I want to call true in this connexion. In this way other uses of our word may be excluded. It is not to be used here in the sense of "genuine" or "veracious," nor, as it sometimes occurs in the

treatment of questions of art, when, for example, truth in art
is discussed, when truth is set up as the goal of art, when the
truth of a work of art or true feeling is spoken of. The word
"true" is put in front of another word in order to show that
this word is to be understood in its proper, unadulterated
sense. This use too lies off the path followed here; that kind
of truth is meant whose recognition is the goal of science.

Grammatically the word "true" appears as an adjective.
Hence the desire arises to delimit more closely the sphere in
which truth can be affirmed, in which truth comes into the
question at all. One finds truth affirmed of pictures, ideas,
statements, and thoughts. It is striking that visible and au-
dible things occur here alongside things which cannot be
perceived with the senses. This hints that shifts of meaning
have taken place. Indeed! Is a picture, then, as a mere visible
and tangible thing, really true, and a stone, a leaf, not true?
Obviously one would not call a picture true unless there were
an intention behind it. A picture must represent something.
Furthermore, an idea is not called true in itself but only with
respect to an intention that it should correspond to something.
It might be supposed from this that truth consists in the correspondence of a picture with what it depicts. Correspondence
is a relation. This is contradicted, however, by the use of the
word "true," which is not a relation-word and contains no
reference to anything else to which something must correspond. If I do not know that a picture is meant to represent
Cologne Cathedral then I do not know with what to compare
the picture to decide on its truth. A correspondence, moreover,
can only be perfect if the corresponding things coincide and
are, therefore, not distinct things at all. It is said to be possible to establish the authenticity of a banknote by comparing
it stereoscopically with an authentic one. But it would be
ridiculous to try to compare a gold piece with a twenty-mark
note stereoscopically. It would only be possible to compare
an idea with a thing if the thing were an idea too. And then,
if the first did correspond perfectly with the second, they

would coincide. But this is not at all what is wanted when truth is defined as the correspondence of an idea with something real. For it is absolutely essential that the reality be distinct from the idea. But then there can be no complete correspondence, no complete truth. So nothing at all would be true; for what is only half true is untrue. Truth cannot tolerate a more or less. But yet? Can it not be laid down that truth exists when there is correspondence in a certain respect? But in which? For what would we then have to do to decide whether something were true? We should have to inquire whether it were true that an idea and a reality, perhaps, corresponded in the laid-down respect. And then we should be confronted by a question of the same kind and the game could begin again. So the attempt to explain truth as correspondence collapses. And every other attempt to define truth collapses too. For in a definition certain characteristics would have to be stated. And in application to any particular case the question would always arise whether it were true that the characteristics were present. So one goes round in a circle. Consequently, it is probable that the content of the word "true" is unique and indefinable.

When one ascribes truth to a picture one does not really want to ascribe a property which belongs to this picture altogether independently of other things, but one always has something quite different in mind and one wants to say that that picture corresponds in some way to this thing. "My idea corresponds to Cologne Cathedral" is a sentence and the question now arises of the truth of this sentence. So what is improperly called the truth of pictures and ideas is reduced to the truth of sentences. What does one call a sentence? A series of sounds; but only when it has a sense, by which is not meant that every series of sounds that has sense is a sentence. And when we call a sentence true we really mean its sense is. From which it follows that it is for the sense of a sentence that the question of truth arises in general. Now is the sense of a sentence an idea? In any case being true does not consist in the correspondence of this sense with something else, for otherwise the question of truth would reiterate itself to infinity.

Without wishing to give a definition, I call a thought something for which the question of truth arises. So I ascribe what is false to a thought just as much as what is true.[1] So I can say: the thought is the sense of the sentence without wishing to say as well that the sense of every sentence is a thought. The thought, in itself immaterial, clothes itself in the material garment of a sentence and thereby becomes comprehensible to us. We say a sentence expresses a thought.

A thought is something immaterial and everything material and perceptible is excluded from this sphere of that for which the question of truth arises. Truth is not a quality that corresponds with a particular kind of sense-impression. So it is sharply distinguished from the qualities which we denote by the words "red," "bitter," "lilac-smelling." But do we not see that the sun has risen and do we not then also see that this is true? That the sun has risen is not an object which emits rays that reach my eyes, it is not a visible thing like the sun itself. That the sun has risen is seen to be true on the basis of sense-impressions. But being true is not a material, perceptible property. For being magnetic is also recognized on the basis of sense-impressions of something, though this property corresponds as little as truth with a particular kind of sense-impressions. So far these properties agree. However, we need sense-impressions in order to recognize a body as mag-

---

[1] In a similar way it has perhaps been said 'a judgment is something which is either true or false'. In fact I use the word 'thought' in approximately the sense which 'judgment' has in the writings of logicians. I hope it will become clear in what follows why I choose 'thought'. Such an explanation has been objected to on the ground that in it a distinction is drawn between true and false judgments which of all possible distinctions among judgments has perhaps the least significance. I cannot see that it is a logical deficiency that a distinction is given with the explanation. As far as significance is concerned, it should not by any means be judged as trifling if, as I have said, the word 'true' indicates the aim of logic.

netic. On the other hand, when I find that it is true that I do not smell anything at this moment, I do not do so on the basis of sense-impressions.

It may nevertheless be thought that we cannot recognize a property of a thing without at the same time realizing the thought that this thing has this property to be true. So with every property of a thing is joined a property of a thought, namely, that of truth. It is also worthy of notice that the sentence "I smell the scent of violets" has just the same content as the sentence "it is true that I smell the scent of violets." So it seems, then, that nothing is added to the thought by my ascribing to it the property of truth. And yet is it not a great result when the scientist, after much hesitation and careful inquiry, can finally say "what I supposed is true"? The meaning of the word "true" seems to be altogether unique. May we not be dealing here with something which cannot, in the ordinary sense, be called a quality at all? In spite of this doubt I want first to express myself in accordance with ordinary usage, as if truth were a quality, until something more to the point is found.

In order to work out more precisely what I want to call thought, I shall distinguish various kinds of sentences.[2] One does not want to deny sense to an imperative sentence, but this sense is not such that the question of truth could arise for it. Therefore I shall not call the sense of an imperative sentence a thought. Sentences expressing desires or requests are ruled out in the same way. Only those sentences in which we communicate or state something come into the question. But I do not count among these exclamations in which one vents one's feelings, groaning, sighing, laughing, unless it has been decided by some agreement that they are to communi-

---

[2] I am not using the word 'sentence' here in a purely grammatical sense where it also includes subordinate clauses. An isolated subordinate clause does not always have a sense about which the question of truth can arise, whereas the complex sentence to which it belongs has such a sense.

cate something. But how about interrogative sentences? In a word-question we utter an incomplete sentence which only obtains a true sense through the completion for which we ask. Word-questions are accordingly left out of consideration here. Sentence-questions are a different matter. We expect to hear "yes" or "no." The answer "yes" means the same as an indicative sentence, for in it the thought that was already completely contained in the interrogative sentence is laid down as true. So a sentence-question can be formed from every indicative sentence. An exclamation cannot be regarded as a communication on this account, since no corresponding sentence-question can be formed. An interrogative sentence and an indicative one contain the same thought; but the indicative contains something else as well, namely, the assertion. The interrogative sentence contains something more too, namely a request. Therefore two things must be distinguished in an indicative sentence: the content, which it has in common with the corresponding sentence-question, and the assertion. The former is the thought, or at least contains the thought. So it is possible to express the thought without laying it down as true. Both are so closely joined in an indicative sentence that it is easy to overlook their separability. Consequently we may distinguish:

(1) the apprehension of a thought—thinking,
(2) the recognition of the truth of a thought—judgment,[3]
(3) the manifestation of this judgment—assertion.

We perform the first act when we form a sentence-question. An advance in science usually takes place in this way; first a

---

[3] It seems to me that thought and judgment have not hitherto been adequately distinguished. Perhaps language is misleading. For we have no particular clause in the indicative sentence which corresponds to the assertion, that something is being asserted lies rather in the form of the indicative. We have the advantage in German that main and subordinate clauses are distinguished by the word-order. In this connexion it is noticeable that a subordinate clause can also contain an assertion and that often neither main nor subordinate clause expresses a complete thought by itself but only the complex sentence does.

thought is apprehended, such as can perhaps be expressed in a sentence-question, and, after appropriate investigations, this thought is finally recognized to be true. We declare the recognition of truth in the form of an indicative sentence. We do not have to use the word "true" for this. And even when we do use it the real assertive force lies not in it but in the form of the indicative sentence, and where this loses its assertive force the word "true" cannot put it back again. This happens when we do not speak seriously. As stage thunder is only apparent thunder and a stage fight only an apparent fight, so stage assertion is only apparent assertion. It is only acting, only fancy. In his part the actor asserts nothing, nor does he lie, even if he says something of whose falsehood he is convinced. In poetry we have the case of thoughts being expressed without being actually put forward as true in spite of the form of the indicative sentence, although it may be suggested to the hearer to make an assenting judgment himself. Therefore it must still always be asked, about what is presented in the form of an indicative sentence, whether it really contains an assertion. And this question must be answered in the negative if the requisite seriousness is lacking. It is irrelevant whether the word "true" is used here. This explains why it is that nothing seems to be added to a thought by attributing to it the property of truth.

An indicative sentence often contains, as well as a thought and the assertion, a third component over which the assertion does not extend. This is often said to act on the feelings, the mood of the hearer, or to arouse his imagination. Words like "alas" and "thank God" belong here. Such constituents of sentences are more noticeably prominent in poetry, but are seldom wholly absent from prose. They occur more rarely in mathematical, physical, or chemical than in historical expositions. What are called the humanities are more closely connected with poetry and are therefore less scientific than the exact sciences which are drier the more exact they are, for exact science is directed toward truth and only the truth.

Therefore all constituents of sentences to which the assertive force does not reach do not belong to scientific exposition but they are sometimes hard to avoid, even for one who sees the danger connected with them. Where the main thing is to approach what cannot be grasped in thought by means of guesswork these components have their justification. The more exactly scientific an exposition is the less will the nationality of its author be discernible and the easier will it be to translate. On the other hand, the constituents of language, to which I want to call attention here, make the translation of poetry very difficult, even make a complete translation almost always impossible, for it is in precisely that in which poetic value largely consists that languages differ most.

It makes no difference to the thought whether I use the word "horse" or "steed" or "cart-horse" or "mare."[4] The assertive force does not extend over that in which these words differ. What is called mood, fragrance, illumination in a poem, what is portrayed by cadence and rhythm, does not belong to the thought.

Much of language serves the purpose of aiding the hearer's understanding, for instance the stressing of part of a sentence by accentuation or word-order. One should remember words like "still" and "already" too. With the sentence "Alfred has still not come" one really says "Alfred has not come" and, at the same time, hints that his arrival is expected, but it is only hinted. It cannot be said that, since Alfred's arrival is not expected, the sense of the sentence is therefore false. The word "but" differs from "and" in that with it one intimates that what follows is in contrast with what would be expected

[4] [Professor Peter T. Geach has brought to my attention a certain problem of translation in connection with this passage. In German, there are four words all of which are synonymous with the English word 'horse.' Since English is, in comparison, somewhat impoverished, the translators resorted to 'steed,' 'carthorse,' and 'mare.' The first of these will pass. But 'carthorse' and 'mare' are not adequate. Professor Geach suggests that perhaps 'nag' might serve. But this would still leave us with a need for a suitable fourth term. Ed.]

from what preceded it. Such suggestions in speech make no difference to the thought. A sentence can be transformed by changing the verb from active to passive and making the object the subject at the same time. In the same way the dative may be changed into the nominative while "give" is replaced by "receive." Naturally such transformations are not indifferent in every respect; but they do not touch the thought, they do not touch what is true or false. If the inadmissibility of such transformations were generally admitted then all deeper logical investigation would be hindered. It is just as important to neglect distinctions that do not touch the heart of the matter as to make distinctions which concern what is essential. But what is essential depends on one's purpose. To a mind concerned with what is beautiful in language what is indifferent to the logician can appear as just what is important.

Thus the contents of a sentence often go beyond the thoughts expressed by it. But the opposite often happens too, that the mere wording, which can be grasped by writing or the gramophone does not suffice for the expression of the thought. The present tense is used in two ways: first, in order to give a date, second, in order to eliminate any temporal restriction where timelessness or eternity is part of the thought. Think, for instance, of the laws of mathematics. Which of the two cases occurs is not expressed but must be guessed. If a time indication is needed by the present tense one must know when the sentence was uttered to apprehend the thought correctly. Therefore the time of utterance is part of the expression of the thought. If someone wants to say the same today as he expressed yesterday using the word "today," he must replace this word with "yesterday." Although the thought is the same its verbal expression must be different so that the sense, which would otherwise be affected by the differing times of utterance, is readjusted. The case is the same with words like "here" and "there." In all such cases the mere wording, as it is given in writing, is not the complete expression of the thought, but the knowledge of certain accompanying conditions of utterance, which are used as means of expressing the thought, are needed for its correct apprehension. The pointing of fingers, hand movements, glances may belong here too. The same utterance containing the word "I" will express different thoughts in the mouths of different men, of which some may be true, others false.

The occurrence of the word "I" in a sentence gives rise to some questions.

Consider the following case. Dr. Gustav Lauben says, "I have been wounded." Leo Peter hears this and remarks some days later, "Dr. Gustav Lauben has been wounded." Does this sentence express the same thought as the one Dr. Lauben uttered himself? Suppose that Rudolph Lingens were present when Dr. Lauben spoke and now hears what is related by Leo Peter. If the same thought is uttered by Dr. Lauben and Leo Peter then Rudolph Lingens, who is fully master of the language and remembers what Dr. Lauben has said in his presence, must now know at once from Leo Peter's report that the same thing is under discussion. But knowledge of the language is a separate thing when it is a matter of proper names. It may well be the case that only a few people associate a particular thought with the sentence "Dr. Lauben has been wounded." In this case one needs for complete understanding a knowledge of the expression "Dr. Lauben." Now if both Leo Peter and Rudolph Lingens understand by "Dr. Lauben" the doctor who lives as the only doctor in a house known to both of them, then they both understand the sentence "Dr. Gustav Lauben has been wounded" in the same way, they associate the same thought with it. But it is also possible that Rudolph Lingens does not know Dr. Lauben personally and does not know that he is the very Dr. Lauben who recently said "I have been wounded." In this case Rudolph Lingens cannot know that the same thing is in question. I say, therefore, in this case: the thought which

Leo Peter expresses is not the same as that which Dr. Lauben uttered.

Suppose further that Herbert Garner knows that Dr. Gustav Lauben was born on 13th September 1875 in N.N. and this is not true of anyone else; against this, suppose that he does not know where Dr. Lauben now lives nor indeed anything about him. On the other hand, suppose Leo Peter does not know that Dr. Lauben was born on 13th September 1875 in N.N. Then as far as the proper name "Dr. Gustav Lauben" is concerned, Herbert Garner and Leo Peter do not speak the same language, since, although they do in fact refer to the same man with this name, they do not know that they do so. Therefore Herbert Garner does not associate the same thought with the sentence "Dr. Gustav Lauben has been wounded" as Leo Peter wants to express with it. To avoid the drawback of Herbert Garner's and Leo Peter's not speaking the same language, I am assuming that Leo Peter uses the proper name "Dr. Lauben" and Herbert Garner, on the other hand, uses the proper name "Gustav Lauben." Now it is possible that Herbert Garner takes the sense of the sentence "Dr. Lauben has been wounded" to be true while, misled by false information, taking the sense of the sentence "Gustav Lauben has been wounded" to be false. Under the assumptions given these thoughts are therefore different.

Accordingly, with a proper name, it depends on how whatever it refers to is presented. This can happen in different ways and every such way corresponds with a particular sense of a sentence containing a proper name. The different thoughts which thus result from the same sentence correspond in their truth-value, of course; that is to say, if one is true then all are true, and if one is false then all are false. Nevertheless their distinctness must be recognized. So it must really be demanded that a single way in which whatever is referred to is presented be associated with every proper name. It is often unimportant that this demand should be fulfilled but not always.

Now everyone is presented to himself in a particular and primitive way, in which he is presented to no-one else. So, when Dr. Lauben thinks that he has been wounded, he will probably take as a basis this primitive way in which he is presented to himself. And only Dr. Lauben himself can grasp thoughts determined in this way. But now he may want to communicate with others. He cannot communicate a thought which he alone can grasp. Therefore, if he now says "I have been wounded," he must use the "I" in a sense which can be grasped by others, perhaps in the sense of "he who is speaking to you at this moment," by doing which he makes the associated conditions of his utterance serve for the expression of his thought.[5]

Yet there is a doubt. Is it at all the same thought which first that man expresses and now this one?

A person who is still untouched by philosophy knows first of all things which he can see and touch, in short, perceive with the senses, such as trees, stones and houses, and he is convinced that another person equally can see and touch the same tree and the same stone which he himself sees and touches. Obviously no thought belongs to these things. Now can he, nevertheless, stand in the same relation to a person as to a tree?

Even an unphilosophical person soon finds it necessary to recognize an inner world distinct from the outer world, a world of sense-impressions, of creations of his imagination, of sensations, of feelings and moods, a world of inclinations, wishes

---

[5] I am not in the happy position here of a mineralogist who shows his hearers a mountain crystal. I cannot put a thought in the hands of my readers with the request that they should minutely examine it from all sides. I have to content myself with presenting the reader with a thought, in itself immaterial, dressed in sensible linguistic form. The metaphorical aspect of language presents difficulties. The sensible always breaks in and makes expression metaphorical and so improper. So a battle with language takes place and I am compelled to occupy myself with language although it is not my proper concern here. I hope I have succeeded in making clear to my readers what I want to call a thought.

and decisions. For brevity I want to collect all these, with the exception of decisions, under the word "idea."

Now do thoughts belong to this inner world? Are they ideas? They are obviously not decisions. How are ideas distinct from the things of the outer world?

First: ideas cannot be seen or touched, cannot be smelled, nor tasted, nor heard.

I go for a walk with a companion. I see a green field, I have a visual impression of the green as well. I have it but I do not see it.

Secondly: ideas are had. One has sensations, feelings, moods, inclinations, wishes. An idea which someone has belongs to the content of his consciousness.

The field and the frogs in it, the sun which shines on them are there no matter whether I look at them or not, but the sense-impression I have of green exists only because of me, I am its bearer. It seems absurd to us that a pain, a mood, a wish should rove about the world without a bearer, independently. An experience is impossible without an experient. The inner world presupposes the person whose inner world it is.

Thirdly: ideas need a bearer. Things of the outer world are however independent.

My companion and I are convinced that we both see the same field; but each of us has a particular sense-impression of green. I notice a strawberry among the green strawberry leaves. My companion does not notice it, he is colour-blind. The colour-impression, which he receives from the strawberry, is not noticeably different from the one he receives from the leaf. Now does my companion see the green leaf as red, or does he see the red berry as green, or does he see both as of one colour with which I am not acquainted at all? These are unanswerable, indeed really nonsensical, questions. For when the word "red" does not state a property of things but is supposed to characterize sense-impressions belonging to my consciousness, it is only applicable within the sphere of my consciousness. For it is impossible to compare my sense-impression with that of someone else. For that it would be necessary to bring together in one consciousness a sense-impression, belonging to one consciousness, with a sense-impression belonging to another consciousness. Now even if it were possible to make an idea disappear from one consciousness and, at the same time, to make an idea appear in another consciousness, the question whether it were the same idea in both would still remain unanswerable. It is so much of the essence of each of my ideas to be the content of my consciousness, that every idea of another person is, just as such, distinct from mine. But might it not be possible that my ideas, the entire content of my consciousness might be at the same time the content of a more embracing, perhaps divine, consciousness? Only if I were myself part of the divine consciousness. But then would they really be my ideas, would I be their bearer? This oversteps the limits of human understanding to such an extent that one must leave its possibility out of account. In any case it is impossible for us as men to compare another person's ideas with our own. I pick the strawberry, I hold it between my fingers. Now my companion sees it too, this very same strawberry; but each of us has his own idea. No other person has my idea but many people can see the same thing. No other person has my pain. Someone can have sympathy for me but still my pain always belongs to me and his sympathy to him. He does not have my pain and I do not have his sympathy.

Fourthly: every idea has only one bearer; no two men have the same idea.

For otherwise it would exist independently of this person and independently of that one. Is that lime-tree my idea? By using the expression "that lime-tree" in this question I have really already anticipated the answer, for with this expression I want to refer to what I see and to what other people can also look at and touch. There are now two possibilities. If my intention is realized when I refer to something with the ex-

pression "that lime-tree" then the thought expressed in the
sentence "that lime-tree is my idea" must obviously be
negated. But if my intention is not realized, if I only think I
see without really seeing, if on that account the designation
"that lime-tree" is empty, then I have gone astray into the
sphere of fiction without knowing it or wanting to. In that
case neither the content of the sentence "that lime-tree is my
idea" nor the content of the sentence "that lime-tree is not
my idea" is true, for in both cases I have a statement which
lacks an object. So then one can only refuse to answer the
question for the reason that the content of the sentence "that
lime-tree is my idea" is a piece of fiction. I have, naturally,
got an idea then, but I am not referring to this with the
words "that lime-tree." Now someone may really want to
refer to one of his ideas with the words "that lime-tree." He
would then be the bearer of that to which he wants to refer
with those words, but then he would not see that lime-tree
and no-one else would see it or be its bearer.

I now return to the question: is a thought an idea? If the
thought I express in the Pythagorean theorem can be recognized by others just as much as by me then it does not belong
to the content of my consciousness, I am not its bearer; yet
I can, nevertheless, recognize it to be true. However, if it is
not the same thought at all which is taken to be the content
of the Pythagorean theorem by me and by another person,
one should not really say "the Pythagorean theorem" but
"my Pythagorean theorem," "his Pythagorean theorem" and
these would be different; for the sense belongs necessarily to
the sentence. Then my thought can be the content of my
consciousness and his thought the content of his. Could the
sense of my Pythagorean theorem be true while that of his
was false? I said that the word "red" was applicable only
in the sphere of my consciousness if it did not state a property of things but was supposed to characterize one of my
sense-impressions. Therefore the words "true" and "false," as
I understand them, could also be applicable only in the sphere

of my consciousness, if they were not supposed to be concerned with something of which I was not the bearer, but were somehow appointed to characterize the content of my consciousness. Then truth would be restricted to the content of my consciousness and it would remain doubtful whether anything at all comparable occurred in the consciousness of others.

If every thought requires a bearer, to the contents of whose consciousness it belongs, then it would be a thought of this bearer only and there would be no science common to many, on which many could work. But I, perhaps, have my science, namely, a whole of thought whose bearer I am, and another person has his. Each of us occupies himself with the contents of his own consciousness. No contradiction between the two sciences would then be possible and it would really be idle to dispute about truth, as idle, indeed almost ludicrous, as it would be for two people to dispute whether a hundred-mark note were genuine, where each meant the one he himself had in his pocket and understood the word "genuine" in his own particular sense. If someone takes thoughts to be ideas, what he then recognizes to be true is, on his own view, the content of his consciousness and does not properly concern other people at all. If he were to hear from me the opinion that a thought is not an idea he could not dispute it, for, indeed, it would not now concern him.

So the result seems to be: thoughts are neither things of the outer world nor ideas.

A third realm must be recognized. What belongs to this corresponds with ideas, in that it cannot be perceived by the senses, but with things, in that it needs no bearer to the contents of whose consciousness to belong. Thus the thought, for example, which we expressed in the Pythagorean theorem is timelessly true, true independently of whether anyone takes it to be true. It needs no bearer. It is not true for the first time when it is discovered, but is like a planet which, already before anyone has seen it, has been in interaction with other planets.[6]

But I think I hear an unusual objection. I have assumed several times that the same thing that I see can also be observed by other people. But how could this be the case, if everything were only a dream? If I only dreamed I was walking in the company of another person, if I only dreamed that my companion saw the green field as I did, if it were all only a play performed on the stage of my consciousness, it would be doubtful whether there were things of the outer world at all. Perhaps the realm of things is empty and I see no things and no men, but have only ideas of which I myself am the bearer. An idea, being something which can as little exist independently of me as my feeling of fatigue, cannot be a man, cannot look at the same field together with me, cannot see the strawberry I am holding. It is quite incredible that I should really have only my inner world instead of the whole environment, in which I am supposed to move and to act. And yet it is an inevitable consequence of the thesis that only what is my idea can be the object of my awareness. What would follow from this thesis if it were true? Would there then be other men? It would certainly be possible but I should know nothing of it. For a man cannot be my idea, consequently, if our thesis were true, he also cannot be an object of my awareness. And so the ground would be removed from under any process of thought in which I might assume that something was an object for another person as for myself, for even if this were to happen I should know nothing of it. It would be impossible for me to distinguish that of which I was the bearer from that of which I was not. In judging something not to be my idea I would make it the object of my thinking and, therefore, my idea. On this view,

---

[6] One sees a thing, one has an idea, one apprehends or thinks a thought. When one apprehends or thinks a thought one does not create it but only comes to stand in a certain relation, which is different from seeing a thing or having an idea, to what already existed beforehand.

is there a green field? Perhaps, but it would not be visible to me. For if a field is not my idea, it cannot, according to our thesis, be an object of my awareness. But if it is my idea it is invisible, for ideas are not visible. I can indeed have the idea of a green field, but this is not green for there are no green ideas. Does a shell weighing a hundred kilogrammes exist, according to this view? Perhaps, but I could know nothing of it. If a shell is not my idea then, according to our thesis, it cannot be an object of my awareness, of my thinking. But if a shell were my idea, it would have no weight. I can have an idea of a heavy shell. This then contains the idea of weight as a part-idea. But this part-idea is not a property of the whole idea any more than Germany is a property of Europe. So it follows:

Either the thesis that only what is my idea can be the object of my awareness is false, or all my knowledge and perception is limited to the range of my ideas, to the stage of my consciousness. In this case I should have only an inner world and I should know nothing of other people.

It is strange how, upon such reflections, the opposites collapse into each other. There is, let us suppose, a physiologist of the senses. As is proper for a scholarly scientist, he is, first of all, far from supposing the things he is convinced he sees and touches to be his ideas. On the contrary, he believes that in sense-impressions he has the surest proof of things which are wholly independent of his feeling, imagining, thinking, which have no need of his consciousness. So little does he consider nerve-fibres and ganglion-cells to be the content of his consciousness that he is, on the contrary, rather inclined to regard his consciousness as dependent on nerve-fibres and ganglion-cells. He establishes that light-rays, refracted in the eye, strike the visual nerve-endings and bring about a change, a stimulus, there. Some of it is transmitted through nerve-fibres and ganglion-cells. Further processes in the nervous system are perhaps involved, colour-impressions arise and these perhaps join themselves to what we call the idea of a tree. Physical, chemical and physiological occurrences insert themselves between the tree and my idea. These are immediately connected with my consciousness but, so it seems, are only occurrences in my nervous system and every spectator of the tree has his particular occurrences in his particular nervous system. Now the light-rays, before they enter my eye, may be reflected by a mirror and be spread further as if they came from a place behind the mirror. The effects on the visual nerves and all that follows will now take place just as they would if the light-rays had come from a tree behind the mirror and had been transmitted undisturbed to the eye. So an idea of a tree will finally occur even though such a tree does not exist at all. An idea, to which nothing at all corresponds, can also arise through the bending of light, with the mediation of the eye and the nervous system. But the stimulation of the visual nerves need not even happen through light. If lightning strikes near us we believe we see flames, even though we cannot see the lightning itself. In this case the visual nerve is perhaps stimulated by electric currents which originate in our body in consequence of the flash of lightning. If the visual nerve is stimulated by this means, just as it would be stimulated by light-rays coming from flames, then we believe we see flames. It just depends on the stimulation of the visual nerve, it is indifferent how that itself comes about.

One can go a step further still. This stimulation of the visual nerve is not actually immediately given, but is only a hypothesis. We believe that a thing, independent of us, stimulates a nerve and by this means produces a sense-impression, but, strictly speaking, we experience only the end of this process which projects into our consciousness. Could not this sense-impression, this sensation, which we attribute to a nerve-stimulation, have other causes also, as the same nerve-stimulation can arise in different ways? If we call what happens in our consciousness idea, then we really experience only ideas but not their causes. And if the scientist wants to avoid all mere hypothesis, then only ideas are left for him, everything resolves into ideas, the light-rays, nerve-fibres and ganglion-cells from which he started. So he finally undermines the foundations of his own construction. Is everything an idea? Does everything need a bearer, without which it could have no stability? I have considered myself as the bearer of my ideas, but am I not an idea myself? It seems to me as if I were lying in a deck-chair, as if I could see the toes of a pair of waxed boots, the front part of a pair of trousers, a waistcoat, buttons, part of a jacket, in particular sleeves, two hands, the hair of a beard, the blurred outline of a nose. Am I myself this entire association of visual impressions, this total idea? It also seems to me as if I see a chair over there. It is an idea. I am not actually much different from this myself, for am I not myself just an association of sense-impressions, an idea? But where then is the bearer of these ideas? How do I come to single out one of these ideas and set it up as the bearer of the rest? Why must it be the idea which I choose to call "I"? Could I not just as well choose the one that I am tempted to call a chair? Why, after all, have a bearer for ideas at all? But this would always be something essentially different from merely borne ideas, something independent, needing no extraneous bearer. If everything is idea, then there is no bearer of ideas. And so now, once again, I experience a change into the opposite. If there is no bearer of ideas then there are also no ideas, for ideas need a bearer without which they cannot exist. If there is no ruler, there are also no subjects. The dependence, which I found myself induced to confer on the experience as opposed to the experient, is abolished if there is no more bearer. What I called ideas are then independent objects. Every reason is wanting for granting an exceptional position to that object which I call "I."

But is that possible? Can there be an experience without someone to experience it? What would this whole play be without an onlooker? Can there be a pain without someone who has it? Being experienced is necessarily connected with pain, and someone experiencing is necessarily connected with being experienced. But there is something which is not my idea and yet which can be the object of my awareness, of my thinking, I am myself of this nature. Or can I be part of the content of my consciousness while another part is, perhaps, an idea of the moon? Does this perhaps take place when I judge that I am looking at the moon? Then this first part would have a consciousness and part of the content of this consciousness would be I myself once more. And so on. Yet it is surely inconceivable that I should be boxed into myself in this way to infinity, for then there would not be only one I but infinitely many. I am not my own idea and if I assert something about myself, *e.g.* that I do not feel any pain at this moment, then my judgment concerns something which is not a content of my consciousness, is not my idea, that is me myself. Therefore that about which I state something is not necessarily my idea. But, someone perhaps objects, if I think I have no pain at the moment, does not the word 'I' nevertheless correspond with something in the content of my consciousness and is that not an idea? That may be. A certain idea in my consciousness may be associated with the idea of the word 'I'. But then it is an idea among other ideas and I am its bearer as I am the bearer of the other ideas. I have an idea of myself but I am not identical with this idea. What is a content of my consciousness, my idea, should be sharply distinguished from what is an object of my thought. Therefore the thesis that only what belongs to the content of my consciousness can be the object of my awareness, of my thought, is false.

Now the way is clear for me to recognize another person as well as to be an independent bearer of ideas. I have an idea of him but I do not confuse it with him himself. And if I state something about my brother I do not state it about the idea that I have of my brother.

The invalid who has a pain is the bearer of this pain, but the doctor in attendance who reflects on the cause of this pain is not the bearer of the pain. He does not imagine he can relieve the pain by anaesthetizing himself. An idea in the doctor's mind may very well correspond to the pain of the invalid but that is not the pain and not what the doctor is trying to remove. The doctor might consult another doctor. Then one must distinguish: first, the pain whose bearer is the invalid, second, the first doctor's idea of this pain, third, the second doctor's idea of this pain. This idea does indeed belong to the content of the second doctor's consciousness, but it is not the object of his reflection, it is rather an aid to reflection, as a drawing can be such an aid perhaps. Both doctors have the invalid's pain, which they do not bear, as their common object of thought. It can be seen from this that not only a thing but also an idea can be the common object of thought of people who do not have the idea.

So, it seems to me, the matter becomes intelligible. If man could not think and could not take something of which he was not the bearer as the object of his thought he would have an inner world but no outer world. But may this not be based on a mistake? I am convinced that the idea I associate with the words 'my brother' corresponds to something that is not my idea and about which I can say something. But may I not be making a mistake about this? Such mistakes do happen. We then, against out will, lapse into fiction. Indeed! By the step with which I secure an environment for myself I expose myself to the risk of error. And here I come up against a further distinction between my inner and outer worlds. I cannot doubt that I have a visual impression of green but it is not so certain that I see a lime-leaf. So, contrary to widespread views, we find certainty in the inner world while doubt never altogether leaves us in our excursions into the outer world. It is difficult in many cases, nevertheless, to distinguish probability from certainty here, so we can presume to judge about things in the outer world. And we must presume this even at the risk of error if we do not want to succumb to far greater dangers.

In consequence of these last considerations I lay down the following: not everything that can be the object of my understanding is an idea. I, as a bearer of ideas, am not myself an idea. Nothing now stands in the way of recognizing other people to be bearers of ideas as I am myself. And, once given the possibility, the probability is very great, so great that it is in my opinion no longer distinguishable from certainty. Would there be a science of history otherwise? Would not every precept of duty, every law otherwise come to nothing? What would be left of religion? The natural sciences too could only be assessed as fables like astrology and alchemy. Thus the reflections I have carried on, assuming that there are other people besides myself who can take the same thing as the object of their consideration, of their thinking, remain essentially unimpaired in force.

Not everything is an idea. Thus I can also recognize the thought, which other people can grasp just as much as I, as being independent of me. I can recognize a science in which many people can be engaged in research. We are not bearers of thoughts as we are bearers of our ideas. We do not have a thought as we have, say, a sense-impression, but we also do not see a thought as we see, say, a star. So it is advisable to choose a special expression and the word 'apprehend' offers itself for the purpose. A particular mental capacity, the power of thought, must correspond to the apprehension [7] of thought. In thinking we do not produce thoughts but we apprehend them. For what I have called thought stands in the closest relation to truth. What I recognize as true I judge to be true quite independently of my recognition of its truth and of my

---

[7] The expression 'apprehend' is as metaphorical as 'content of consciousness'. The nature of language does not permit anything else. What I hold in my hand can certainly be regarded as the content of my hand but is all the same the content of my hand in quite a different way from the bones and muscles of which it is made and their tensions, and is much more extraneous to it than they are.

thinking about it. That someone thinks it has nothing to do with the truth of a thought. 'Facts, facts, facts' cries the scientist if he wants to emphasize the necessity of a firm foundation for science. What is a fact? A fact is a thought that is true. But the scientist will surely not recognize something which depends on men's varying states of mind to be the firm foundation of science. The work of science does not consist of creation but of the discovery of true thoughts. The astronomer can apply a mathematical truth in the investigation of long past events which took place when on earth at least no one had yet recognized that truth. He can do this because the truth of a thought is timeless. Therefore that truth cannot have come into existence with its discovery.

Not everything is an idea. Otherwise psychology would contain all the sciences within it or at least it would be the highest judge over all the sciences. Otherwise psychology would rule over logic and mathematics. But nothing would be a greater misunderstanding of mathematics than its subordination to psychology. Neither logic nor mathematics has the task of investigating minds and the contents of consciousness whose bearer is a single person. Perhaps their task could be represented rather as the investigation of the mind, of the mind not of minds.

The apprehension of a thought presupposes someone who apprehends it, who thinks. He is the bearer of the thinking but not of the thought. Although the thought does not belong to the contents of the thinker's consciousness yet something in his consciousness must be aimed at the thought. But this should not be confused with the thought itself. Similarly Algol itself is different from the idea someone has of Algol.

The thought belongs neither to my inner world as an idea nor yet to the outer world of material, perceptible things.

This consequence, however cogently it may follow from the exposition, will nevertheless not perhaps be accepted without opposition. It will, I think, seem impossible to some people to obtain information about something not belonging to the

inner world except by sense-perception. Sense-perception indeed is often thought to be the most certain, even to be the
sole, source of knowledge about everything that does not
belong to the inner world. But with what right? For sense-
impressions are necessary constituents of sense-perceptions
and are a part of the inner world. In any case two men do
not have the same, though they may have similar, sense-
impressions. These alone do not disclose the outer world to
us. Perhaps there is a being that has only sense-impressions
without seeing or touching things. To have visual impressions
is not to see things. How does it happen that I see the tree
just there where I do see it? Obviously it depends on the
visual impressions I have and on the particular type which
occur because I see with two eyes. A particular image arises,
physically speaking, on each of the two retinas. Another person sees the tree in the same place. He also has two retinal
images but they differ from mine. We must assume that these
retinal images correspond to our impressions. Consequently
we have visual impressions, not only not the same, but mark-
edly different from each other. And yet we move about in the
same outer world. Having visual impressions is certainly
necessary for seeing things but not sufficient. What must still
be added is non-sensible. And yet this is just what opens up
the outer world for us; for without this non-sensible something everyone would remain shut up in his inner world. So
since the answer lies in the non-sensible, perhaps something
non-sensible could also lead us out of the inner world and
enable us to grasp thoughts where no sense-impressions were
involved. Outside one's inner world one would have to
distinguish the proper outer world of sensible, perceptible
things from the realm of the nonsensibly perceptible. We
should need something non-sensible for the recognition of
both realms but for the sensible perception of things we should
need sense-impressions as well and these belong entirely to
the inner world. So that in which the distinction between the
way in which a thing and a thought is given mainly consists

is something which is attributable, not to both realms, but to the inner world. Thus I cannot find this distinction to be so great that on its account it would be impossible for a thought to be given that did not belong to the inner world.

The thought, admittedly, is not something which it is usual to call real. The world of the real is a world in which this acts on that, changes it and again experiences reactions itself and is changed by them. All this is a process in time. We will hardly recognize what is timeless and unchangeable as real. Now is the thought changeable or is it timeless? The thought we express by the Pythagorean theorem is surely timeless, eternal, unchangeable. But are there not thoughts which are true today but false in six months time? The thought, for example, that the tree there is covered with green leaves, will surely be false in six months time. No, for it is not the same thought at all. The words 'this tree is covered with green leaves' are not sufficient by themselves for the utterance, the time of utterance is involved as well. Without the time-indication this gives we have no complete thought, *i.e.* no thought at all. Only a sentence supplemented by a time-indication and complete in every respect expresses a thought. But this, if it is true, is true not only today or tomorrow but timelessly. Thus the present tense in 'is true' does not refer to the speaker's present but is, if the expression be permitted, a tense of timelessness. If we use the mere form of the indicative sentence, avoiding the word 'true', two things must be distinguished, the expression of the thought and the assertion. The time-indication that may be contained in the sentence belongs only to the expression of the thought, while the truth, whose recognition lies in the form of the indicative sentence, is timeless. Yet the same words, on account of the variability of language with time, take on another sense, express another thought; this change, however, concerns only the linguistic aspect of the matter.

And yet! What value could there be for us in the eternally unchangeable which could neither undergo effects nor have effect on us? Something entirely and in every respect inactive would be unreal and non-existent for us. Even the timeless, if it is to be anything for us, must somehow be implicated with the temporal. What would a thought be for me that was never apprehended by me? But by apprehending a thought I come into a relation to it and it to me. It is possible that the same thought that is thought by me today was not thought by me yesterday. In this way the strict timelessness is of course annulled. But one is inclined to distinguish between essential and inessential properties and to regard something as timeless if the changes it undergoes involve only its inessential properties. A property of a thought will be called inessential which consists in, or follows from the fact that, it is apprehended by a thinker.

How does a thought act? By being apprehended and taken to be true. This is a process in the inner world of a thinker which can have further consequences in this inner world and which, encroaching on the sphere of the will, can also make itself noticeable in the outer world. If, for example, I grasp the thought which we express by the theorem of Pythagoras, the consequence may be that I recognize it to be true and, further, that I apply it, making a decision which brings about the acceleration of masses. Thus our actions are usually prepared by thinking and judgment. And so thought can have an indirect influence on the motion of masses. The influence of one person on another is brought about for the most part by thoughts. One communicates a thought. How does this happen? One brings about changes in the common outside world which, perceived by another person, are supposed to induce him to apprehend a thought and take it to be true. Could the great events of world history have come about without the communication of thoughts? And yet we are inclined to regard thoughts as unreal because they appear to be without influence on events, while thinking, judging, stating, understanding and the like are facts of human life. How much more real a hammer appears compared with a thought. How different the process of handing over a hammer is from the communication of a thought. The hammer passes from one control to another, it is gripped, it undergoes pressure and on account of this its density, the disposition of its parts, is changed in places. There is nothing of all this with a thought. It does not leave the control of the communicator by being communicated, for after all a person has no control over it. When a thought is apprehended, it at first only brings about changes in the inner world of the apprehender, yet it remains untouched in its true essence, since the changes it undergoes involve only inessential properties. There is lacking here something we observe throughout the order of nature: reciprocal action. Thoughts are by no means unreal but their reality is of quite a different kind from that of things. And their effect is brought about by an act of the thinker without which they would be ineffective, at least as far as we can see. And yet the thinker does not create them but must take them as they are. They can be true without being apprehended by a thinker and are not wholly unreal even then, at least if they could be apprehended and by this means be brought into operation.[8]

---

[8] [Throughout the essay, Frege's 'wirklich' and 'Wirklichkeit' have been translated as 'real' and 'reality.' Prof. R. H. Stoothoff has suggested that a preferable rendering would be the now well-established 'actual' and 'actuality.' Ed.]

Compound Thoughts

GOTTLOB FREGE

[Translator's Note: This article, entitled 'Logische Untersuchungen. Dritter Teil: Gedankengefüge,' was published in the *Beiträge zur Philosophie des deutschen Idealismus*, III (1923), 36-51. The first two parts of these 'logical investigations' were 'Der Gedanke' (*Beiträge*, I (1918), trans. 'The Thought' in *Mind*, LXV (1956)) and 'Die Verneinung' (*Beiträge*, I (1919), trans. 'Negation' in Geach and Black (ed.), *Translations from the Philosophical Writings of Gottlob Frege*). The translation is by Prof. R. H. Stoothoff, who wishes to thank Prof. P. L. Heath for checking it.]

It is astonishing what language can do. With a few syllables it can express an incalculable number of thoughts, so that even a thought grasped by a human being for the very first time can be put into a form of words which will be understood by someone to whom the thought is entirely new. This would be impossible, were we not able to distinguish parts in the thought corresponding to the parts of a sentence, so that the structure of the sentence serves as an image of the structure of the thought. To be sure, we really talk figuratively when we transfer the relation of whole and part to thoughts; yet the analogy is so ready to hand and so generally valid that we are hardly ever bothered by the hitches which occur from time to time.

Reprinted with the kind permission of the translator and the editor from *Mind*, LXXII (1963), 1-17.

If, then, we look upon thoughts as composed of simple parts, and take these, in turn, to correspond to the simple parts of sentences, we can understand how a few parts of sentences can go to make up a great multitude of sentences, to which, in turn, there correspond a great multitude of thoughts. But the question now arises how the thought comes to be constructed, and how its parts are so combined together that the whole amounts to something more than the parts taken separately. In my article 'Negation' [37] I considered the case where a thought seems to be composed of a part needing completion (the unsaturated part, as one may also call it, represented in language by the negative term), and a thought. There can be no negation without something negated, and this is a thought. The whole owes its unity to the fact that the thought saturates the unsaturated part or, as we can also say, completes the part needing completion. And it is natural to suppose that, for logic in general, combination into a whole always comes about through the saturation of something unsaturated.[1]

But here a special case of such combination is to be considered, namely that in which two thoughts are combined to form a single thought. In the realm of language, the combination of two sentences into a whole is represented by something that likewise is a sentence. On the analogy of the grammatical term "compound sentence," I shall employ the expression "compound thought," without wishing to imply by this that every compound sentence has a compound thought as its sense, or that every compound thought is the sense of a compound sentence. By "compound thought" I shall understand a thought consisting of thoughts, but not of thoughts alone. For a thought is complete and saturated, and needs no completion in order to exist. For this reason, thoughts do not cleave to one another unless they are connected together by something that is not a thought, and it may be taken that

---

[1] Here, and in what follows, it must always be remembered that this saturating and this combining are not temporal processes.

this 'connective' is unsaturated. The compound thought must itself be a thought: that is, something either true or false (with no third alternative).

Not every sentence composed, linguistically speaking, of sentences will provide us with a serviceable example; for grammar recognises "sentences" which logic cannot acknowledge as genuine sentences because they do not express thoughts. This is illustrated in relative clauses; for in a relative clause detached from its main clause, we cannot tell what the relative pronoun is supposed to refer to. Such a clause contains no sense whose truth can be investigated; in other words, the sense of a detached relative clause is not a thought. So we must not expect a compound sentence consisting of a main and a relative clause to have as its sense a compound thought.

First Kind of Compound Thought

In language, the simplest case seems to be that of two main clauses conjoined by "and." But the matter is not so simple as it first appears, for in an assertoric sentence we must distinguish between the thought expressed and the assertion. Only the former [38] is in question here, for acts of judgement are not said to be "conjoined." [2] I therefore understand the sentences conjoined by "and" to be uttered without assertive force. Assertive force can most easily be eliminated by changing the whole into a question; for one can express the same thought in a question as in an assertoric sentence, only without asserting it. If we use "and" to conjoin two sentences, neither of which is uttered with assertive force, then we have to ask whether the sense of the resultant whole is a thought. For not only each of the component sentences, but also the

---

[2] Logicians often seem to mean by "judgement" what I call "thought." In my terminology, one judges by acknowledging a thought as true. This act of acknowledgement I call "judgement." Judgement is made manifest by a sentence uttered with assertive force. But one can grasp and express a thought without acknowledging it as true, *i.e.*, without judging it.

whole, must have a sense which can be made the content of a question. Suppose witnesses are asked: "Did the accused deliberately set fire to the pile of wood, and deliberately start a forest-fire?"; the problem then arises whether two questions are involved here, or only one. If the witnesses are free to reply affirmatively to the question about the pile of wood, but negatively to that about the forest-fire, then we have two questions, each containing a thought, and there is no question of a single thought compounded out of these two. But if—as I shall suppose—the witnesses are permitted to answer only "yes" or "no," without dividing the whole into subquestions, then this whole is a single question which should be answered affirmatively only if the accused acted deliberately both in setting fire to the pile of wood and also in starting the forest-fire; and negatively in every other case. Thus, a witness who thinks that the accused certainly set fire to the pile of wood on purpose, but that the fire then spread further and set the forest alight without his meaning it to, must answer the question in the negative. For the thought of the whole question must be distinguished from the two component thoughts: it contains, as well as the component thoughts, that which combines them together; and this is represented in language by the word "and." This word is used here in a particular way, *viz.* solely as a conjunction between two genuine sentences. I call any sentence "genuine" if it expresses a thought. But a thought is something which must be either true or false, without further option. Furthermore, the "and" now under discussion can only conjoin sentences which are uttered non-assertively. I do not mean by this to exclude the act of judgement; but if it occurs, it must relate to the compound thought as a whole. If we wish to present a compound of this first kind as true, we may use the phrase "It is true that . . . and that. . . ."

Our "and" is not meant to conjoin interrogative sentences, any more than assertoric sentences. In our example the witnesses are confronted with only one question. [39] But the thought proposed for judgement by this question is composed of two thoughts. In his reply, however, the witness must give only a single judgement. Now this may certainly seem an artificial refinement, for doesn't it really come to the same thing, whether the witness first replies affirmatively to the question "Did the accused deliberately set fire to the pile of wood?" and then to the question "Did the accused deliberately start a forest-fire?", or whether he replies affirmatively at one stroke to the whole question? This may well seem so, in case of an affirmative reply, but the difference shows up more clearly where the answer is negative. For this reason it is useful to express the thought in a single question, since then both negative and affirmative cases will have to be considered in order to understand the thought correctly.

The "and" whose mode of employment is more precisely delimited in this way seems doubly unsaturated: its saturation requires both a sentence preceding and another following. And what corresponds to "and" in the realm of sense must also be doubly unsaturated: in so far as it is saturated by thoughts, it combines them together.[3] As a mere thing, of course, the group of letters "and" is no more unsaturated than any other thing. It may be called "unsaturated" in respect of its employment as a symbol meant to express a sense, for here it can have the intended sense only when situated between two sentences: its purpose as a symbol requires completion by a preceding and a succeeding sentence. The unsaturatedness really emerges in the realm of sense, and is transferred from there to the symbol.

If "A" and "B" are both genuine sentences, uttered with neither assertive nor interrogative force, then "A and B" is likewise a genuine sentence, and its sense is a compound thought of the first kind. Hence I also say that "A and B" expresses a compound thought of the first kind.

That "B and A" has the same sense as "A and B" can be

[3] *Cf.* note 1.

seen without proof by merely taking account of the sense. Here we have a case where two linguistically different expressions correspond to the same sense. This divergence of expressive symbol and expressed thought is an inevitable consequence of the difference between spatio-temporal phenomena and the world of thoughts.[4]

Finally, we may point out an inference that holds in this connection:

A is true;[5]
B is true; therefore
(A and B) is true. [40]

Second Kind of Compound Thought

The negation of a compound of the first kind between one thought and another is itself a compound of the same two thoughts. I shall call it a "compound thought of the second kind." Whenever a compound thought of the first kind between two thoughts is false, the compound of the second kind between them is true, and conversely. A compound of the second kind is false only if each compounded thought is true, and a compound of the second kind is true whenever at least one of the compounded thoughts is false. In all this it is assumed throughout that the thoughts do not belong to fiction. By presenting a compound thought of the second kind as true, I declare the compounded thoughts to be incompatible.

Without knowing whether

$$(21/20)^{100} \text{ is greater than } \sqrt[10]{10^{21}},$$

or whether

$$(21/20)^{100} \text{ is less than } \sqrt[0]{10^{21}},$$

I can still recognise that the compound of the first kind between these two thoughts is false. Accordingly, the corre-

---

[4] Another case of this sort is that "A and A" has the same sense as "A."

[5] When I write "A is true," I mean more exactly "the thought expressed in the sentence 'A' is true." So too in analogous cases.

sponding compound of the second kind is true. Apart from the thoughts compounded, we have something that combines them, and here too the 'connective' is doubly unsaturated. The combination comes about in that the component thoughts saturate the 'connective'.

To express briefly a compound thought of this kind, I write

"not [A and B],"

where "A" and "B" are the sentences corresponding to the compounded thoughts. The 'connective' stands out more clearly in this expression: it is the sense of whatever occurs in the expression apart from the letters "A" and "B." The two gaps in the expression

"not [and   ]"

bring out the two-fold unsaturatedness. The 'connective' is the doubly unsaturated sense of this doubly unsaturated expression. By filling the gaps with expressions of thoughts, we form the expression of a compound thought of the second kind. But we really should not talk as if the compound thought originated in this way, for it is a thought and a thought does not originate.

In a compound thought of the first kind, the two thoughts may be interchanged. The same interchangeability must also hold for the negation of a compound thought of the first kind, hence for a compound thought of the second kind. If, therefore, "not [A and B]" expresses a compound thought, then "not [B and A]" expresses the same compound of the same thoughts. This interchangeability should no more be regarded as a theorem here than in the case of compounds of the first kind, for there is no difference in sense between these expressions. It is therefore self-evident [41] that the sense of the second compound sentence is true if that of the first is true—for it is the same sense.

An inference may also be mentioned for the present case:

not [A and B] is true;

A is true; therefore
B is false.

Third Kind of Compound Thought

A compound of the first kind, of the negation of one thought conjoined with the negation of another thought, is also a compound of these thoughts. I call it a "compound of the third kind" between the first thought and the second. Let the first thought, for example, be that Paul can read, and the second that Paul can write; then the compound of the third kind between these two thoughts is the thought that Paul can neither read nor write. A compound thought of the third kind is true only if each of the two compounded thoughts is false, and it is false if at least one of the compounded thoughts is true. In compound thoughts of the third kind, the component thoughts are also interchangeable. If "A" expresses a thought, then "not A" must express the negation of this thought, and similarly for "B." Hence, if "A" and "B" are genuine sentences, then the sense of

"(not A) and (not B),"

for which I also write

"neither A nor B,"

is the compound of the third kind between the two thoughts expressed by "A" and "B."

Here the 'connective' is the sense of everything in these expressions apart from the letters "A" and "B." The two gaps in

"(not) and (not),"

or in

"neither , nor ,"

indicates the two-fold unsaturatedness of these expressions, which corresponds to the two-fold unsaturatedness of the 'connective'. In that the latter is saturated by thoughts, there comes about the compound of the third kind between these thoughts.

Once again we may mention an inference:

> A is false;
> B is false; therefore
> (neither A nor B) is true.

The brackets are to make it clear that what they contain is the whole whose sense is presented as true.

Fourth Kind of Compound Thought

The negation of a compound of the third kind between two thoughts is likewise a compound of these two thoughts: it may be called a "compound thought [42] of the fourth kind." A compound of the fourth kind between two thoughts is a compound of the second kind between the negations of these thoughts. In presenting such a compound thought as true, we thereby assert that at least one of the compounded thoughts is true. A compound thought of the fourth kind is false only if each of the compounded thoughts is false. Given once again that "A" and "B" are genuine sentences, the sense of

> "not [(not A) and (not B)]"

is a compound thought of the fourth kind between the thoughts expressed by "A" and "B." The same holds of

> "not [neither A nor B],"

which may be written more briefly

> "A or B."

Taken in this sense, "or" occurs only between sentences—indeed only between genuine sentences. By acknowledging the truth of such a compound thought, I do not rule out the truth of both compounded thoughts: we have in this case the non-exclusive "or." The 'connective' is the sense of whatever occurs in "A or B" apart from "A" and "B," that is, the sense of

> "(or),"

where the gaps on both sides of "or" indicate the two-fold unsaturatedness of the 'connective'. The sentences conjoined by "or" should be regarded merely as expressions of thoughts, and not therefore as individually endowed with assertive force. The compound thought as a whole, on the other hand, can be acknowledged as true. The linguistic expression does not make this clear: each component sentence of the assertion "5 is less than 4, or 5 is greater than 4" has the linguistic form which it would also have if it were uttered separately with assertive force, whereas really only the whole compound is meant to be presented as true.

Perhaps it will be found that the sense here assigned to the word "or" does not always agree with ordinary usage. On this point it should first be noted that in determining the sense of scientific expressions we cannot undertake to concur exactly with the usage of ordinary life; the latter, indeed, is for the most part unsuited to scientific purposes, where we feel the need for more precise definition. The scientist must be allowed to diverge, in his use of the word "ear," from what is otherwise the custom. In the field of logic, assonant side-issues may be distracting. In virtue of what has been said about our use of "or," it can truly be asserted "Frederick the Great won the battle of Rossbach, or two is greater than three." This leads someone to think: "Good Heavens! What does the battle of Rossbach have to do with the nonsense that two is greater than three?" But "two is greater than three" is false, not senseless: it makes no difference to logic whether the falsity of a thought is easy or difficult to discern. In sentences conjoined by "or," we usually suppose that the sense of the one has something to do with that of the other, that there is some sort of relationship between them. [43] Such a relationship may well indeed be specifiable for any given case, but for different cases there will be different relationships, and it will therefore be impossible to specify a relationship of meaning which would always be attached to "or" and could accordingly be deemed the sense of this word. "But why does the speaker add the second sentence at all? If he wants to assert that Frederick the Great won the battle of Rossbach, then surely the first sentence would be sufficient. We may certainly assume that he does not want to claim that two is greater than three; and if he had been satisfied with just the first sentence, he would have said more with fewer words. Why, therefore, this waste of words?" These questions, too, only distract us into side-issues. Whatever may be the speaker's intentions and motives for saying just this and not that, our concern is not with these at all, but solely with what he says.

Compound thoughts of the first four kinds have this in common, that their component thoughts may be interchanged.

Here, too, follows another inference:

(A or B) is true;
A is false; therefore
B is true.

Fifth Kind of Compound Thought

By forming a compound of the first kind out of the negation of one thought and a second thought, we get a compound of the fifth kind between these two thoughts. Given that "A" expresses the first thought and "B" expresses the second, the sense of

"(not A) and B"

is such a compound thought. A compound of this kind is true if, and only if, the first compounded thought is false while the second is true. Thus, for example, the compound thought expressed by

"(not $3^2 = 2^3$) and ($2^4 = 4^2$)"

viz. the thought that 3^2 is not equal to 2^3 and 2^4 is equal to 4^2, is true. After seeing that 2^4 is equal to 4^2, someone may think that in general the exponent of a number raised to a power can be interchanged with the number itself. Someone else may then try to correct this mistake by saying "2^4 equals 4^2, but 2^3 does not equal 3^2." If it is asked what difference there is between conjunction with "and" and with "but," the answer is: with respect to what I have called the "thought" or the "sense" of the sentence, it is immaterial whether the idiom of "and" or that of "but" is chosen. The difference comes out only in what I call the "illumination" of the thought,[6] and does not belong to the province of logic.

The 'connective' in a compound thought of the fifth kind is the doubly incomplete sense of the doubly incomplete expression

"(not   ) and (   )."[44]

Here the compounded thoughts are not interchangeable, for

"(not B) and A"

does not express the same as

"(not A) and B."

The first thought does not occupy the same kind of 'position' in the compound as that of the second thought. Since I hesitate to coin a new word, I am obliged to use the word "position" with a transferred meaning. In speaking of written expressions of thoughts, "position" may be taken to have its ordinary spatial connotation. But a position in the expression of a thought must correspond to something in the thought itself, and for this I shall retain the word "position." In the present case we cannot simply allow the two thoughts to exchange their 'positions', but we can set the negation of the second thought in the 'position' of the first, and at the same time the negation of the first in the 'position' of the second. (Of course, this too must be taken with a grain of salt, for an operation in space and time is not intended.) Thus from

"(not A) and B"

we obtain

"(not (not B)) and (not A)."

But since "not (not B)" has the same sense as "B," we have here

"B and (not A),"

---

[6] *Cf.* my article 'The Thought.'

which expresses the same as

"(not A) and B."

Sixth Kind of Compound Thought

By negating a compound of the fifth kind between two thoughts we get a compound of the sixth kind between the same two thoughts. We can also say that a compound of the second kind between the negation of one thought and a second thought is a compound of the sixth kind between these two thoughts. A compound of the fifth kind is true if, and only if, when its first component thought is false, the second, on the other hand, is true. From this it follows that a compound of the sixth kind between two thoughts is false if, and only if, when its first component is false, the second again is true. Such a compound thought is therefore true given only the truth of its first component thought, regardless of whether the second is true or false. It is also true given only the falsehood of its second component thought, regardless of whether the first is true or false.

Without knowing whether

$$((21/20)^{100})^2 \text{ is greater than } 2^2,$$

or whether

$$(21/20)^{100} \text{ is greater than } 2,$$

I can still recognise as true the compound of the sixth kind [45] between these two thoughts. The negation of the first thought excludes the second thought, and *vice versa*. We can put it as follows:

"If $(21/20)^{100}$ is greater than 2,
then $((21/20)^{100})^2$ is greater than 2^2."

Instead of "compound thought of the sixth kind," I shall also speak of "hypothetical compound thought," and I shall refer to the first and second components of a hypothetical compound thought as "consequent" and "antecedent" respectively. Thus, a hypothetical compound thought is true if its consequent is true; it is also true if its antecedent is false, regardless of whether the consequent is true or false. The consequent must none the less always be a thought.

Given once again that "A" and "B" are genuine sentences, then

$$\text{"not } [\,(\text{not A}) \text{ and B}\,]\text{"}$$

expresses a hypothetical compound with the sense (thought-content) of "A" as consequent and the sense of "B" as antecedent. We may also write instead:

$$\text{"If B, then A."}$$

But here, indeed, doubts may arise. It may perhaps be maintained that this does not square with linguistic usage. In reply, it must once again be emphasized that science has to be allowed its own terminology, that it cannot always bow to ordinary language. Just here I see the greatest difficulty for philosophy: the instrument it finds available for its work, namely ordinary language, is little suited to the purpose, its formation having been governed by requirements wholly different from those of philosophy. So also logic is first of all obliged to fashion a useable instrument from those already to hand. And for this purpose it initially finds but little in the way of useable instruments available.

Many would undoubtedly declare that the sentence

$$\text{"If 2 is greater than 3, then 4 is a prime number"}$$

is nonsense; and yet, according to my stipulation it is true because the antecedent is false. To be false is not yet to be nonsense. Without knowing whether

$$\sqrt[10]{10^{21}} \text{ is greater than } (21/20)^{100},$$

we can see that

$$\text{If } \sqrt[10]{10^{21}} \text{ is greater than } (21/20)^{100},$$

$$\text{then } (\sqrt[10]{10^{21}})^2 \text{ is greater than } ((21/20)^{100})^2;$$

and nobody will see any nonsense in that. But it is false that

$$\sqrt[10]{10^{21}} \text{ is greater than } (21/20)^{100}, \text{ [46]}$$

and it is equally false that

$$(\sqrt[10]{10^{21}})^2 \text{ is greater than } ((21/20)^{100})^2.$$

If this could be apprehended as easily as the falsity of "2 is greater than 3," then the hypothetical compound thought of the present example would seem just as nonsensical as that of the previous one. Whether the falsity of a thought can be apprehended with greater or less difficulty is of no matter from a logical point of view, for the difference is a psychological one.

The thought expressed by the compound sentence

"If I own a cock which has laid eggs today, then the
Cologne cathedral will collapse tomorrow morning"

is also true. Someone will perhaps say: "But here the antecedent has no inner connection at all with the consequent." In my account, however, I required no such connection, and I ask that "If B, then A" should be understood solely in terms of what I have said and expressed in the form

"not [(not A) and B]."

It must be admitted that this conception of a hypothetical compound thought will at first be thought strange. But my account is not designed to keep in step with ordinary linguistic usage, which is generally too vague and ambiguous for the purposes of logic. Questions of all kinds arise at this point, *e.g.* the relation of cause and effect, the intention of a speaker who utters a sentence of the form "If B, then A," the grounds on which he holds its content to be true. The speaker may perhaps give hints in regard to such questions arising among his hearers. These hints are among the adjuncts which often surround the thought in ordinary language. My task here is to remove the adjuncts and thereby to pick out, as the logical kernel, a compound of two thoughts, which I have entitled "hypothetical compound thought." Insight into the structure of thoughts compounded of two thoughts must provide the foundation for consideration of multiply compounded thoughts.

What I have said about the expression "If B, then A" must

not be so understood as to imply that every compound sentence of this form expresses a hypothetical compound thought. If either "A" or "B" by itself does not completely express a thought, and is not therefore a genuine sentence, the case is altered. In the compound sentence

"If someone is a murderer, then he is a criminal,"

neither the antecedent-clause nor the consequent-clause, taken by itself, expresses a thought. Without some further clue, we cannot determine whether what is expressed in the sentence "He is a criminal" is true or false when detached from this compound; for the word "he" is not a proper name, and in the detached sentence it designates nothing. It follows that the consequent-clause expresses no thought, and is therefore not a genuine sentence. This holds of the antecedent-clause as well, for it [47] likewise has a non-designating component, namely "someone." Yet the compound sentence can none the less express a thought. The "someone" and the "he" refer to each other. Hence, and in virtue of the "If - - -, then - - -," the two clauses are so connected with one another that they together express a thought; whereas we can distinguish three thoughts in a hypothetical compound thought, namely the antecedent, the consequent, and the thought compounded of these. Thus, compound sentences do not always express compound thoughts, and it is very important to distinguish the two cases which arise for compound sentences of the form

"If B, then A."

Once again I append an inference:

(If B, then A) is true;
B is true; therefore
A is true.

In this inference, the characteristic feature of hypothetical compound thoughts stands out, perhaps in its clearest form.

The following mode of inference is also noteworthy:

(If C, then B) is true;
(If B, then A) is true; therefore

(If C, then A) is true.

I should like here to call attention to a misleading way of speaking. Many mathematical writers express themselves as if conclusions could be drawn from a thought whose truth is still doubtful. In saying "I infer A from B," or "I conclude from B that A is true," we take B for one of the premisses or the sole premiss of the inference. But prior to acknowledgement of its truth, one cannot use a thought as premiss of an inference, nor can one infer or conclude anything from it. If anyone still thinks this can be done, he is apparently confusing acknowledgement of the truth of a hypothetical compound thought with performing an inference in which the antecedent of this compound is taken for a premiss. Now acknowledgement of the truth of the sense of

"If C, then A"

can certainly depend on an inference, as in the example given above, while there may yet be a doubt about the truth of C.[7] But in this case, the thought expressed by "C" is by no means a premiss of the inference; the premiss, rather, was the sense of the sentence

"If C, then B."

If the thought-content of "C" were a premiss of the inference, then it would not occur in the conclusion: for that is just how inference works. [48]

We have seen how, in a compound thought of the fifth kind, the first thought can be replaced by the negation of the second, and the second simultaneously by the negation of the first, without altering the sense of the whole. Now since a compound thought of the sixth kind is the negation of a compound thought of the fifth kind, the same also holds for it: that is, we can replace the antecedent of a hypothetical compound by the negation of the consequent, and the consequent simultaneously by the negation of the antecedent, without

---

[7] More precisely: whether the thought expressed by "C" is true.

thereby altering its sense. (This is contraposition, the transition from *modus ponens* to *modus tollens*.)

Summary of the Six Compound Thoughts

I. A and B;   II. not [A and B];
III. (not A) and (not B); IV. not [(not A) and (not B)];
V. (not A) and B;   VI. not [(not A) and B].

It is tempting to add

A and (not B).

But the sense of "A and (not B)" is the same as that of "(not B) and A," for any genuine sentences "A" and "B." And since "(not B) and A" has the same form as "(not A) and B," we get nothing new here, but only another expression of a compound thought of the fifth kind; and in "not [A and (not B)]" we have another expression of a compound thought of the sixth kind. Thus our six kinds of compound thought form a completed whole, whose primitive elements seem here to be the first kind of compound and negation. However acceptable to psychologists, this apparent pre-eminence of the first kind of compound over the others has no logical justification: for any one of the six kinds of compound thought can be taken as fundamental and can be used, together with negation, for deriving the others; so that, for logic, all six kinds have equal justification. If, for example, we start with the hypothetical compound

If B, then C (*i.e.* not [(not C) and B]),

and replace "C" by "not A," then we get

If B, then not A (*i.e.* not [A and B]). [49]

By negating the whole, we get

not [If B, then not A] (*i.e.* A and B),

from which it follows that

"not [If B, then not A]"

says the same as

"A and B."

We have thereby derived a compound of the first kind from a hypothetical compound and negation; and since compounds of the first kind and negation together suffice for the derivation of the other compound thoughts, it follows that all six kinds of compound thought can be derived from hypothetical compounds and negation. What has been said of the first and the sixth kinds of compound holds in general of all our six kinds of compound thought, so that none has any priority over the others. Each of them can serve as a basis for deriving the others, and our choice is not governed by any considerations of logic.

A similar situation exists in the foundations of geometry. Two different geometries can be formulated in such a way that certain theorems of the one occur as axioms of the other, and conversely.

Let us now consider cases where a thought is compounded with itself rather than with some different thought. For any genuine sentence "A," "A and A" expresses the same thought as "A": the former says no more and no less than the latter. It follows that "not [A and A]" expresses the same as "not A."

Equally, "(not A) and (not A)" also expresses the same as "not A"; and consequently "not [(not A) and (not A)]" also expresses the same as "not (not A)," or "A." Now, "not [(not A) and (not A)]" expresses a compound of the fourth kind, and instead of this we can say "A or A." Accordingly, not only "A and A," but also "A or A" has the same sense as "A." [50]

It is otherwise for compounds of the fifth kind. The compound thought expressed by "(not A) and A" is false, since, of two thoughts, where one is the negation of the other, one must always be false; so that a compound of the first kind composed of them is likewise false. The compound of the sixth kind between a thought and itself, namely that expressed by "not [(not A) and A]" is accordingly true (assuming that "A" is a genuine sentence). We can also render this compound thought verbally by the expression "If A, then A": for example, "If the Schneekoppe is higher than the Brocken, then the Schneekoppe is higher than the Brocken."

In such a case the questions arise: "Does this sentence express a thought? Doesn't it lack content? Do we learn anything new upon hearing it?" Now it may happen that before hearing it someone did not know this truth at all, and had therefore not acknowledged it. To that extent one could, under certain conditions, learn something new from it. It is surely an undeniable fact that the Schneekoppe is higher than the Brocken if the Schneekoppe is higher than the Brocken. Since only thoughts can be true, this compound sentence must express a thought; and, despite its apparent senselessness, the negation of this thought is also a thought. It must always be borne in mind that a thought can be expressed without being asserted. Here we are concerned just with thoughts, and the appearance of senselessness arises only from the assertive force with which one involuntarily thinks of the sentence as uttered. But who says that anyone uttering it nonassertively does so in order to present its content as true? Perhaps he is doing it with precisely the opposite intention.

This can be generalized. Let "O" be a sentence which expresses a particular instance of a logical law, but which is not presented as true. Then it is easy for "not O" to seem senseless, but only because it is thought of as uttered assertively. The assertion of a thought which contradicts a logical law can indeed appear, if not senseless, then at least absurd; for the truth of a logical law is immediately evident from itself, *i.e.* from the sense of its expression. But a thought which contradicts a logical law may be expressed, since it may be negated. "O" itself, however, seems almost to lack content.

Each compound thought, being itself a thought, can be compounded with other thoughts. Thus, the compound expressed by "(A and B) and C" is composed of the thoughts expressed by [51] "A and B" and "C." But we can also treat it as composed of the thoughts expressed by "A" and "B" and "C." In this way compound thoughts containing three thoughts can originate.[8] Other examples of such compounds are expressed by:

"not [(not A) and (B and C)]," and
"not [(not A) and ((not B) and (not C))]."

So too it will be possible to find examples of compound thoughts containing four, five, or more thoughts.

Compound thoughts of the first kind, and negation, are together adequate for the formation of all these compounds, and any other of our six kinds of compound can be chosen instead of the first. Now the question arises whether every compound thought is formed in this way. So far as mathematics is concerned, I am convinced that it includes no compound thoughts formed in any other way. It will scarcely be otherwise in physics, chemistry, and astronomy as well; but teleological statements enjoin caution and seem to require more precise investigation. Here I shall leave this question open. Compound thoughts thus formed with the aid of negation from compounds of the first kind seem, at all events, to merit a special title. They may be called "mathematical compound thoughts." This should not be taken to mean that there are compound thoughts of any other type. Mathematical compound thoughts seem to have something else in common: for if a true component of such a compound is replaced by another true thought, the resultant compound thought is true or false according to whether the original compound is true or false. The same holds if a false component of a mathematical compound thought is replaced by another false thought. I now want to say that two thoughts have the same truth-value if they are either both true or else both false. I maintain, therefore, that the thought expressed by "A" has the same truth-value as that expressed by "B" if either "A and B" or else "(not A) and (not B)" expresses a true thought. Having established this, I can phrase my thesis in this way:

---

[8] This originating must not be regarded as a temporal process.

"If one component of a mathematical compound thought is replaced by another thought having the same truth-value, then the resultant compound thought has the same truth-value as the original."

GLOSSARY

anerkennen	acknowledge (as true)
entstehen	originate
Fügende	'connective'
Gedankengefüge	compound thought
Gefüge	compound
sättigen	saturate
Satzgefüge	compound sentence
ungesättigt	unsaturated
verbinden	conjoin
zusammenfügen	combine (together), compound
Zusammenfügung (Fügung)	combination, connection

APPENDIX C

On the Foundations of Geometry

GOTTLOB FREGE

Translator's Note: The two parts of the following essay, entitled "Über die Grundlagen der Geometrie," were published in the *Jahresbericht der deutschen Mathematiker-Vereinigung*, XII (1903), 319-324; 368-375. The translator wishes to express his thanks to Mr. P. Geach for checking the translation—(M. E. Szabo)

I

Hilbert's publication on the foundations of geometry prompted me to express to the author my divergent views. An exchange of letters ensued which, unfortunately, came to an early end. I considered the questions raised in these letters to be of more general interest, however, and was thinking of subsequently publishing them. Hilbert, on the other hand, still withholds his consent because meanwhile his own views have changed. I regret this, because studying these letters would have been the easiest way for the reader to become acquainted with the questions raised. Also, I would have been spared the trouble of rewriting the discussion. But opinions expressed on this subject seem to be so divergent and distant from a solution that I think a public discussion is called for with a view to bringing about an agreement. I should therefore like to consider a number of questions of fundamental importance, and

Reprinted with the kind permission of the translator and the editor from *The Philosophical Review*, LXIX (1960), 3-17.

I should like to do this by giving a critical exposition of Hilbert's publication. In doing so it is of no importance whatever whether Hilbert has ceased to hold the disputed views.

To begin with, I should like to discuss two questions: What is an axiom? What is a definition and in what relation do they stand to each other?

For a long time an axiom has always been taken to be a thought whose truth is known without being susceptible of proof by a logical chain of reasoning. Logical laws, too, are of this kind. Yet not everyone would agree to calling these general laws of inference "axioms." Some would rather wish to confine the name "axiom" to the basic laws of a limited field, for example, the field of geometry. But this is a question of less consequence. Let us not now enter upon a discussion of why we are justified in predicating truth of an axiom. For the axioms of geometry the usual source given is intuition.

Definition in mathematics usually means a determination of the reference of a word or symbol. Definitions are distinct from all other mathematical propositions in containing a word or symbol which up to then has had no reference; the definition now supplies one. All other mathematical propositions (theorems and ones expressing axioms) must not contain proper names, concept words, relation words or functional symbols, whose reference is not already determined.[1]

Once a word or symbol has been assigned a reference by definition, we can form a self-evident proposition from the definition, which may be used in a proof in the same way as we use basic propositions.[2] Let us suppose, for example, the references of the plus sign, and of the symbols for the num-

---

[1] Letters as a rule have no reference. (There are some exceptions: "π," "e.") They do not designate anything; they only indicate something in order to give generality to a thought. As in the case of certain formal words, we cannot look for their reference. But it must be determined in what way they contribute to the expression of a thought. I have treated in great detail of the use of letters in Bk. I, Sections 8, 9, 17, 19, 24, 25 of my *Grundgesetze der Arithmetik* (Jena, Pohle, 1893).

[2] I will here call a basic proposition a proposition whose sense is an axiom.

bers three and one, to be known; then we can assign a reference to the symbol for the number four by means of the defining equation "$3 + 1 = 4$." Once this has been done the content of this equation is trivially true and does not require a proof. It would still, however, be inept to include definitions among the basic propositions. For, initially, definitions are arbitrarily laid down and are in this way distinct from statements. Even if we go on to assert whatever has been laid down by definition, it has no greater value as a contribution to knowledge than an example of the law of identity, $a = a$. By defining we do not create knowledge, and we can only say, therefore, that although definitions which have been made into statements formally play the part of basic propositions, they are not really such. For even if, at best, we could call the law of identity itself an axiom, we should hardly wish to give the status of an axiom to every single instance of that law. Such a status really demands a greater cognitive value. No definition extends our knowledge. Definitions are only a means of reducing manifold contents to a concise word or symbol and in doing so making them easier to handle. This and only this is the use of definitions in mathematics.[3] A definition must never attempt more than that. And if, notwithstanding, it is yet meant to do more and to generate real knowledge, and one wants to avoid having to give a proof, the definition degenerates into logical thimble-rigging. One feels tempted to write in the margin beside some of the definitions one finds in mathematical writings: "If you cannot give a demonstration, regard it as an explanation." One must simply never present as a definition that which requires a proof or an intuition to establish its truth. On the other hand,

---

[3] It may be counted as part of the usefulness of a definition that it makes us more clearly conscious of a content only half-consciously associated with a word. This sometimes happens, but what is useful in this way is the act of defining rather than the definition. When the definition is once given, it is no matter in the sequel whether the defined sign is a newly invented one or already had a sense associated with it.

one can never expect basic propositions and theorems to determine the reference of a word or symbol. The rigor of mathematical investigations makes it absolutely imperative that we should not obscure the difference between definitions and all other propositions.

Axioms *do not* contradict each other because they are true; no proof is necessary to establish this fact. Definitions *must not* contradict each other. In defining we must formulate our basic propositions in such a way as to rule out any possibility of contradiction. Mainly we must avoid giving various explanations of the same symbol.[4]

The usage of the words "axiom" and "definition" as presented in this paper would seem to concur with that employed in works on the subject to date and also seems to be the most useful.

Now as far as Hilbert's publication is concerned, we are struck by a curious confusion of linguistic usage. If he says in the introduction, "For the cogent construction of geometry we require only few and simple basic facts, and these facts are called axioms of geometry," this is entirely in keeping with what has been expounded above; equally, when in Section 1, page 4, he says, "The axioms of geometry fall into five groups; each one of these groups expresses certain basic facts of our intuition that belong together." [5]

The following pronouncement (Section 3), however, seems to be based on a totally different conception: "The axioms of this group define the concept 'between.'" How can axioms define? Here we are burdening axioms with something which is really the job of definitions. The same observation is forced on us when we read in Section 6: "The axioms of this group define the concepts of congruence or movement."

Hilbert was good enough to enable me to state in what sense he has been using the word "axiom." For him axioms

---

[4] Cf. my *Grundgesetze der Arithmetik*, II, Sections 56-57.

[5] Whilst in the first sentence quoted above axioms are thoughts, in the second quotation they are expressions of thoughts, propositions.

are components of his definitions.[6] Thus the axioms II 1 to II 5, for example, are components of the definition of "between." "Between" is therefore a relation for those points on a straight line to which the axioms II 1 to II 5 apply. II 1 is thus formulated in the *Festschrift*: "If A, B, C are points on a straight line and B lies between A and C, then B also lies between C and A."

Axioms specify the notes of concepts, which would otherwise be missing from the explanations. The explanation of Section 1 of the *Festschrift* also contains the definitions of the concepts point, straight line, plane, if one includes the axioms of the axiom groups I to V, whose exposition covers the whole of the first chapter. So the first definition is as long as that. Other definitions are embedded in it, for example, that of "between," and theorems, for example, theorems of congruence. It is therefore not easy to see what parts of the first chapter belong to that definition. At least it is difficult to believe that the theorems should also be regarded as such components. This explains Hilbert's claim that axioms are defining something. But is this compatible with the view that axioms express basic facts of our intuition? If they do, then they assert something. But that means that every expression occurring in them must already be completely understood. Yet if the axioms are components of definitions, they will contain expressions, for example, "point," "straight line," whose references are not previously fixed but are just being determined. No single axiom is then independent, or conceivable at all, except in conjunction with the other axioms belonging to the same definition. If Hilbert's intention is to be met, the reference of the word "point" will only be determined on page 19 of the *Festschrift*. It is not until then that the axioms that have been set out express thoughts which are true by defi-

---

[6] As the time when Hilbert was holding this view we must take the time of his writing his *Festschrift* and the date of his letter (29, XII, 99). [I.e., *Festschrift zur Feier der Enthüllung des Gaus-Weber-Denkmals in Göttingen*. Leipzig, 1899—TRANSLATOR]

nition. But this is the very reason why they do not express basic facts of our intuition, for then their validity would be founded precisely on intuition. Let us take the following straight-forward example: the definition of "a rectangle is a parallelogram with a right angle" may be rewritten in the following way:

"Explanation: we imagine plane figures which we call rectangles.

Axiom 1. All rectangles are parallelograms.

Axiom 2. In every rectangle there is a pair of sides which are perpendicular to each other."

These two axioms must be regarded as inseparable elements of the explanation. If we omitted axiom 1, for example, we should be giving a different reference to the word "rectangle," and the remaining second axiom would receive a different sense, if one gave it the status of a statement in the completed definition, from the sense it now has as a result of its conjunction with the first axiom; that is, axiom 2 would not even be the same proposition any more, at least if one regards the thought expressed in the proposition as an essential feature of the proposition. Once the explanation including both axioms has been given, we can assert them as true. Yet their truth is not based on intuition but on the definition. For this reason they do not contain any real knowledge, as axioms in the customary sense of the word undoubtedly do.

In Chapter 2 of the *Festschrift* Hilbert discusses the questions whether the axioms are independent of each other and are free from contradiction. How are we to understand this independence? In the above example does not each axiom require the other to be what it is? We notice this in other instances too. Only by stating all axioms which, according to Hilbert, belong, for example, to the definition of a point, does the word "point" receive a sense. Accordingly, only through the totality of axioms in which the word "point" occurs, does each one of them receive its full sense. It is impossible to separate the axioms so as to regard some of them as holding and others as not holding, because in doing so we would also alter the sense of the ones we wanted to count as holding good. Thus axioms belonging to the same definitions are dependent on each other, nor are they contradictory; if they were, the definition would be unjustified. Neither can one find out whether the axioms contradict each other before the definition is completed, because only the definition gives a sense to the axioms and it is pointless to inquire whether senseless propositions are contradictory.

How then are we to understand Hilbert's approach to this question? I think we can suppose that he is not concerned with axioms as wholes,[7] but only with those of their parts which express notes of the concept that is being defined. In our example these notes are *parallelogram* and *having two perpendicular sides*. If these were contradictory, there would be no object which could be found to have these properties; in other words, there would be no rectangle. Conversely, if we can produce a rectangle, it follows that these notes are not contradictory. And this is in fact roughly the way in which Hilbert proves that his axioms are free from contradiction. In reality, however, all that has been shown is that the notes of a concept are not contradictory. Similarly with independence. If from the fact that an object has a first property we can conclude that it also has a second one, we can say that the second is dependent on the first. And if these properties are notes of a concept, then the second note is dependent on the first. This is roughly the manner in which Hilbert proves the independence of his axioms (really notes of concepts). For the time being we may view the matter in this way. Yet it is not as simple as may seem to be the case so far. If we wish to fathom the real nature of the problem, we must take a closer look at the special nature of Hilbert's definitions. This we shall do in a succeeding essay.

---

[7] As is obvious, I am here employing Hilbert's usage, as I have already been doing earlier.

II

Hilbert's definitions and explanations seem to be of a two-fold nature. The first explanation of Section 4 explains the expressions "points on a straight line lying on the same side of a point" and "points on a straight line lying on different sides of a point." Once the expressions "point on a straight line *a*" and "a point lying between a point A and a point B" are understood, this explanation enables us to know quite precisely what these expressions refer to. The explanation of Section 9 is, however, of an entirely different kind. It says: "Points on a straight line stand in a certain relation to each other, and the word 'between' in particular is used to describe that relation."

It is obvious that thereby we are not furnished with the reference of the word "between." But the explanation is also incomplete. It must be supplemented by the following axioms:

II 1. If A, B, C are points on a straight line, and B lies between A and C, then B also lies between C and A.

II 2. If A and C are two points on a straight line, then there always is at least one point B, such that it lies between A and C, and at least one point D, such that C lies between A and D.

II 3. Among any three points on a straight line there always is one and only one point that lies between the other two.

II 4. Any four points A, B, C, D on a straight line may be ordered in such a way that B lies between A and C and also between A and D, and furthermore that C lies between A and D and also between B and D.

But does the above tell us when the relation of lying-in-between occurs? It does not; but, conversely, once we have understood the relation, we realize the truth of the axioms. If we take as our basis the Gaussean definition of the congruence of numbers, we can easily decide whether 2 and 8 are congruent *modulo* 3, or what sorts of investigation we should have to make to find out. All we have to know are the expressions occurring in the definition ("difference," "one number going into another").

Let us now contrast the above with a further explanation which I have written up following Hilbert's example:

All numbers stand in certain relations to each other, and the word "congruent" in particular is used to describe that relation.

Axiom 1. Every number is congruent to itself under any modulus.

Axiom 2. If any number is congruent to any other number and that number is congruent to a third number under the same modulus, then the first number is also congruent to the third number under that modulus.

Axiom 3. If a first number is congruent to a second and a third number is congruent to a fourth under the same modulus, then the sum of the first and third numbers is also congruent to the sum of the second and fourth numbers under the same modulus, and so forth.

But would such a definition tell us that 2 is congruent to 8 *modulo* 3? Hardly! And it must be noted that in the last example we have given we have a much more favorable case than Hilbert's explanation containing the words "point" and "straight line," whose references are still unknown to us at this stage. But even if we understand these words in the sense that has been given to them in Euclidean geometry, we cannot decide, given our explanation, which of the three points lying on a straight line lies between the other two.

If we survey the whole of Hilbert's explanations and axioms, it would appear comparable to a system of equations with several unknowns; for an axiom as a rule contains several unknown expressions such as "point," "straight line," "plane," "lying," "between," and so forth, and it is not sufficient to state some axioms or groups of axioms to determine the unknowns; only by stating all the axioms can we determine the unknowns. Yet is this totality sufficient for our purpose? Who is to tell us that the system is soluble for the unknowns and that these are uniquely determined? What indeed would a solution look like, if it were possible to give one? Each of the expressions "point," "straight line," and so forth, would have to be explained severally, in a sentence in which all other words are known and understood. If such a solution to the Hilbertean system of definitions and axioms were possible, it would have to be given. But it is certainly impossible. If we want to answer the question whether an object, for example, my watch, is a point, we are at once faced with the difficulty that the first axiom already talks of two points.[8] We must therefore already know an object as a point, in order to be able to answer the question whether my watch, for example, together with that point determines a straight line. This means, however, that we must know how to interpret the word "determine," and also what counts as a straight line. Hence this axiom does not get us any further forward. And we shall find that the same applies to all axioms. When and if we have finally got them all, we still do not know whether they hold good for my watch, so that they enable us to call it a point. Nor do we know what sorts of investigation we shall have to make to answer this question.

Axiom I 7 says: "Every straight line has at least two points." Compare this with the following:

"Explanation: We imagine objects which we call gods.

Axiom 1. Every god is omnipotent.

Axiom 2. There is at least one god.

If this procedure were legitimate, then the ontological proof of God would be brilliantly vindicated. And this takes us to the core of the problem. He who sees quite clearly why such a proof is mistaken also recognizes the fundamental error contained in Hilbert's definition. The error consists in failing to distinguish first- and second-level concepts, as I shall

---

[8] "Two distinct points A, B, always determine a straight line *a*."

call them. It would appear true to say that it was I who first introduced such a rigid distinction, and Hilbert, when he wrote the *Festschrift,* must have been quite unfamiliar with my writings on this subject.[9] And many others must still be in the same position. But since, on the other hand, any deeper insight in mathematics and logic without this distinction is impossible, I will try to show very briefly what it is all about.

Let us take the proposition "two is a prime number." Linguistically we distinguish two parts: a subject "two" and a predicative part "is a prime number." With the latter we usually associate assertive force. Yet this is not essential. If an actor utters a statement on the stage, it cannot be said that he *really* asserts anything, nor is he responsible for the truth of that statement. Let us eliminate the assertive force from the predicative part, as it is inessential. The two parts of the proposition will still remain as distinctly different as they are, and it is important to grasp the point that this difference really cuts deep and must not be blurred. The first part, "two," is a proper name of a certain number, designates an object, something complete that does not require a complement.[10] The predicative part, "is a prime number," on the other hand, does require a complement, and does not designate an object. I shall also call the first part *saturated* and the second part *unsaturated.* To this distinction among the symbols there naturally corresponds an analogous distinction in realm of references: to a proper name corresponds an object, and to the predicative part corresponds what I will call a concept. This is not meant to be a definition. For the decom-

---

[9] The *Foundations of Arithmetic, a logico-mathematical investigation concerning the Concept of Number.* Breslau, Köbner, 1884, Section 53, where I use "order" for "level." *Function and Concept.* Paper given before a meeting of the Society for Medicine and Natural Science at Jena. Jena, Pohle, 1891, p. 26. *Grundgesetze der Arithmetik derived in logical symbolism,* vol. I. Jena, Pohle, 1893, Section 21 seq.

[10] Propositions with "all," "every," "some" are of a totally different kind and will not be considered here.

position into saturated and unsaturated parts must be regarded as a primitive feature of logical structure, which must simply be recognized and accepted but which cannot be reduced to something more primitive.

I am well aware that expressions like "saturated" and "unsaturated" are figurative and only serve the purpose of pointing to what we have been meaning to talk about; here we must always count on the reader's willingness to meet us halfway. Notwithstanding, we may perhaps be able to show more intelligibly why these parts must be distinct. An object, for example, the number 2, cannot logically adhere to another object, for example, Julius Caesar, without some sort of liaison; and this liaison cannot be an object but must rather be unsaturated. A logical combination into a whole can come about only if we saturate or complement an unsaturated part with one or more parts. This is somewhat similar to complementing "the capital of" with "Germany" or "Sweden"; or "half of" with "six." [11]

It now follows from the fundamental difference of objects from concepts that an object can never occur as a predicate or unsaturated expression and that a concept can never logically take the place of an object.[12] Figuratively, this point

---

[11] What one should regard linguistically as subject is determined by the form of the proposition. For logical analysis it is different. We can break down the proposition "$8 = 2^3$" into either "8" and "is 2 raised to the power of 3," or into "2" and "is something whose third power is 8," or into "3" and "is something such that raising 2 to that power has the result 8."

[12] B. Russell in Section 49 of *The Principles of Mathematics*, vol. I (Cambridge, 1903) does not wish to concede that there is a difference of kind between concepts and objects. He maintains that concepts, too, are always terms. He bases his argument on the fact that we are forced to use a concept substantivally as a term if we want to say something about it, e.g., that it is not the case that it is a term. This necessity, it seems to me, is only founded in the nature of our language and thus is not genuinely logical. On the other hand, at the bottom of p. 508. Russell seems to lean toward my contention. I have treated of this difficulty in my essay "On Concept and Object." It is obvious that we cannot represent a concept as something independent in the way we can represent an object. A concept can only occur in a complex.

may be expressed in the following way: there are different logical places; some of them can be filled only by objects and not by concepts, and others only by concepts and not by objects.

Let us now consider the proposition "there is a square root of 4." Obviously we cannot be talking about a particular square root of 4; we are rather dealing with the concept. And here too it has preserved its predicative nature. That this is so can be seen from the fact that we can rewrite the proposition in the following way: "there is something which is a square root of 4," or "it is false that, whatever *a* may be, *a* is not a square root of 4." But in this case we obviously cannot split the proposition up so that the unsaturated part is a concept and the saturated part an object. If we compare the proposition "there is something which is a prime number" with the proposition "there is something which is a square root of 4," we recognize that what they have in common is "there is something which" containing what would genuinely be called the logical predicate, whereas the parts that differ, despite their predicative, unsaturated nature, play a role analogous to that of the subject in other cases. Here there is something being predicated of a concept. But obviously there is a very great difference between the logical place of the number 2, if we predicate of it that it is a prime number, and the concept prime number, if we say that there is something which is a prime number. The first place can be filled only by objects, the second only by concepts. Not only is it linguistically improper to say "there is Africa," or "there is Charlemagne," but it is nonsensical. We may well say "there is something which is called Africa," and the words "is called Africa" signify a concept. Thus the expression *there is some-*

One might say that a concept can be distinguished within, but not separated from, the complex in which it occurs. All seeming contradictions which we meet at this juncture result from the fact that one is tempted to treat a concept as an object contrary to its unsaturated nature, which, it is true to say, language sometimes compels us to do. But this is only a point of language.

thing which is also unsaturated, but in a totally different way from *is a prime number*. In the first case we can saturate the expression only with a concept and in the second only with an object. We take account of the similarity and disparity of these cases by means of the following terminological distinction. In the proposition "2 is a prime number" we say that an object—2—falls *under* a first-level concept—prime number —whereas in the proposition "there is a prime number" we say that a first-level concept—prime number—falls *within* a certain second-level concept. Thus first-level concepts can stand to second-level concepts in a similar relation to that of objects to first-level concepts.

What applies to concepts also applies to their notes. For notes of a concept are concepts which are logical parts of the concept of which they are notes. Instead of saying "2 is the square root of 4, and 2 is positive" we can say "2 is a positive square root of 4," and then we have as the notes of the concept *is a positive square root of 4* the two partial concepts *is a square root of 4* and *is positive*. We may also call these properties of the number 2 and hence we can say: a note of a concept is a property which an object must possess if the object is to fall under the concept. Correspondingly, of course, with second-level concepts. From the above it is easy to see that first-level concepts can have only first-level notes, and second-level concepts only second-level notes. It is quite impossible to have a mixture of first- and second-level notes. This follows from the fact that the logical places of concepts do not serve for objects, nor the logical places of objects for concepts. From this it follows further that our explanation which began with the words "we imagine objects which we call gods" is inadmissible, because the note contained in the first axiom is of the first level, whereas the note contained in the second axiom is of the second level.

What consequences has all this for Hilbert's definitions? Apparently every single point is an object. From this it follows that the concept of point (*is a point*) is of the first level,

and that all its notes must consequently be of the first level.
But on a perusal of Hilbert's axioms, regarding them as parts
of the definition of a point, we find that the notes occurring
in these axioms are not of the first level, that is, properties
which an object must have in order to be a point, but of the
second level. If, therefore, they do define a concept, it can
only be a concept of the second level. Whether a concept is
really being defined must, however, seem doubtful, since it is
not only the word "point" that occurs, but also the words
"straight line" and "plane." Disregarding this difficulty for
the moment, let us suppose that with his axioms Hilbert has
defined a second-level concept. Then we would have to express the relation of the Euclidean concept of point, which is
of the first level, to the Hilbertean concept, which is of the
second level, by saying that, according to the convention we
have adopted above, the Euclidean concept of point falls
within the Hilbertean concept. It is then conceivable and
even probable that this does not apply only to the Euclidean
concept of point. Only compare what is said on page 20 (*Festschrift*): "We imagine a pair of numbers (x, y) of the domain omega as a point," and so forth. If the word "point"
had already been given a reference by the definition and the
axioms belonging to it, then this could not be done all over
again at this juncture. I believe we shall have to conceive of
the matter in the following way, that the concept *is a pair of
numbers of the domain omega* is of the first level, and, in
the same way as the Euclidean concept of point, is supposed
to fall within the Hilbertean second-level concept (if this
exists). But the use of the word "point" in both cases is somewhat disturbing, for it obviously has a different reference in
each of them.

On these principles Euclidean geometry is represented as a
special case of a more comprehensive system of knowledge
which allows for innumerably many other special cases, innumerable geometries (if that word is still permissible). And
in every one of these geometries there will be a concept of

point (first-level) and each concept will fall within the same second-level concept. If one wanted to use the word "point" in every one of those geometries, it would become ambiguous, and in order to avoid this one would have to add the name of the particular geometry one was talking about, for example, "point of the A-geometry," "point of the B-geometry," and so forth. This will apply similarly to the words "straight line" and "plane." Looked at from this angle it would seem inevitable that under these circumstances we should have to re-examine the questions whether the axioms are free from contradiction and are independent of each other, and also the question of the non-provability of propositions from certain postulates. We shall then not simply be able to say "the axiom of parallels"; since there will be a different axiom of parallels in each different geometry. If we want to use the same terminology, we can do so only by mistakenly calling the "straight line of the A-geometry," for example, simply "straight line," thus covering up the fact that the thought it really contains is different. But in doing so we cannot eliminate the difference.

Yet here we have already reached the beginning of a path leading to greater depths. Perhaps I may be allowed some time to pursue it further.

GLOSSARY

Anschauung	intuition
Bedeutung	reference
Begriff	concept
Begriff erster Stufe	first-level concept
Behauptungssatz	statement
Bestandteil	part
Eigenschaft	property
Ergänzung	complement
Erkenntniswert	cognitive value
Festschrift	"Festschrift" or publication
Formwort	formal word
Grundgesetz	basic law
Grundsatz	basic proposition
Grundtatsache	basic fact

Grundtatsache unserer Anschauung	basic fact of our intuition
Lehrsatz	theorem
Merkmal	note
Satz	proposition
Urerscheinung	primitive feature
Zeichen	symbol

Compiled with the assistance of L. Egal and G. Moor

I. Works by Frege

A. FREGE'S MAIN WORKS

1. *Begriffsschrift, eine der arithmetischen nachgebildete: Formelsprache des reinen Denkens* (Halle AS: Louis Nebert, 1879).

2. *Die Grundlagen der Arithmetik* (Breslau: Wilhelm Koebner, 1884).

3. *Function und Begriff* (Jena: Hermann Pohle, 1891). Vortrag gehalten in der Sitzung vom 9 Januar 1891 der Jenaischen Gesellschaft für Medicin und Naturwissenschaft.

4. *Grundgesetze der Arithmetik*, I (Jena: Hermann Pohle, 1893).

5. *Grundgesetze der Arithmetik*, II (Jena: Hermann Pohle, 1903).

6. "Über Sinn und Bedeutung," *Zeitschrift für Philosophie und philosophische Kritik*, C (1892), 25-50.

7. Über Begriff und Gegenstand," *Vierteljahrsschrift für wissenschaftliche Philosophie*, XVI (1892), 192-205.

8. Review of Husserl's *Philosophie der Arithmetik, Zeitschrift für Philosophie und philosophische Kritik*, CIII (1894), 313-332.

9. "Kritische Beleuchtung einiger Punkte in E. Schröder's *Vorlesungen über die Algebra der Logik*," *Archiv für systematische Philosophie*, I (1895), 433-456.

10. "Was ist eine Function?" in *Festschrift Ludwig Boltzmann gewidmet zum sechzigsten Geburtstage 20 Februar 1904* (Leipzig, 1904), 656-666.

11. "Über die Grundlagen der Geometrie," *Jahresbericht der Deutschen Mathematiker-Vereinigung*, XII (1903), 319-324, 368-375.

12. "Über die Grundlagen der Geometrie," *Jahresbericht der Deutschen Mathematiker-Vereinigung*, XV (1906), 293-309, 377-403, 423-430.

13. "Der Gedanke: Eine logische Untersuchung," *Beiträge zur Philosophie des deutschen Idealismus*, I (1918), 58-77.

14. "Die Verneinung," *Beiträge zur Philosophie des deutschen Idealismus,* I (1919), 143-157.
15. "Logische Untersuchungen. Dritter Teil: Gedankengefüge," *Beiträge zur Philosophie des deutschen Idealismus,* III (1923), 36-51.

B. TRANSLATIONS OF FREGE'S WORKS

1. *The Foundations of Arithmetic,* trans. J. L. Austin (Oxford: Blackwell, 1953). Reprinted in paperback (New York: Harper Bros., 1960).
2. *Translations from the Philosophical Writings of Gottlob Frege,* ed. P. Geach and M. Black (Oxford: Blackwell, 1960).
3. "The Foundations of Geometry," trans. M. Szabo, *The Philosophical Review,* LXIX (1950), 3-17.
4. "The Thought," trans. A. M. and Marcelle Quinton, *Mind,* LXV (1956), 289-311.
5. "Compound Thoughts," trans. R. Stoothoff, *Mind,* LXXII (1963), 1-51.
6. *The Basic Laws of Arithmetic,* trans., in part, by M. Furth (Berkeley and Los Angeles: University of California Press, 1964). Reprinted in paperback, 1967.

II. Works on Frege

A. BOOKS

1. Angelelli, Ignacio. *Studies on Gottlob Frege and Traditional Philosophy.* Dordrecht, Holland: D. Reidel, 1967.
2. Birjukov, B. V. *Two Soviet Studies on Frege,* trans. I. Angelelli. Oxford: Blackwell, 1964.
3. Grossmann, Reinhardt. *Reflections on Frege's Philosophy.* Evanston: Northwestern University Press, 1969.
4. Sternfeld, Robert. *Frege's Logical Theory.* Carbondale and Edwardsville: Southern Illinois University Press, 1966.
5. Thiel, Christian. *Sinn und Bedeutung in der Logik Gottlob Freges.* Meisenheim/Glan: Verlag Anton Hain MG, 1967. English translation forthcoming.
6. Walker, Jeremy. *A Study of Frege.* Ithaca: Cornell University Press, 1965.

B. ARTICLES

1. Anscombe, G. E. M. *An Introduction to Wittgenstein's Tractatus* (London: Hutchinson, 1959), pp. 98-112 and *passim.* Reprinted, New York: Harper and Row, 1965.

2. Bartlett, James. "On Questioning the Validity of Frege's Concept of Function," *Journal of Philosophy*, LXI (1964), 203.
3. Bergmann, Gustav. "Frege's Hidden Nominalism," *The Philosophical Review*, LXVII (1958), 437-459. Also in *Meaning and Existence* (Madison: University of Wisconsin Press, 1960), pp. 205-224.
4. Bergmann, Gustav. "Ontological Alternatives," *Giornale Critico della Filosofia Italiana*, XVII (1963). Also in *Logic and Reality* (Madison: University of Wisconsin Press, 1964), pp. 124-157, in the original English version.
5. Black, Max. "Frege on Functions," *Problems of Analysis* (Ithaca: Cornell University Press, 1954), pp. 229-254.
6. Caton, Charles E. "An Apparent Difficulty in Frege's Ontology," *The Philosophical Review*, LXXI (1962), 462-475.
7. Church, A. "A Formulation of the Logic of Sense and Denotation," in *Structure and Meaning: Essays in Honor of Henry M. Sheffer* (New York: Liberal Arts, 1951), pp. 3-24.
8. Dummett, Michael. "Frege on Functions: A Reply," *The Philosophical Review*, LXIV (1955), 96-107.
9. Dummett, Michael. "Note: Frege on Functions," *The Philosophical Review*, LXV (1956), 229-230.
10. Dummett, Michael. "Nominalism," *The Philosophical Review*, LXV (1956), 491-505.
11. Dummett, Michael. "Gottlob Frege," in *Encyclopedia of Philosophy*, ed. Paul Edwards (New York: Macmillan, 1965), III, 225-237.
12. Fisk, Milton. "A Paradox in Frege's Semantics," *Philosophical Studies*, XIV (1963), 56-63.
13. Furth, Montgomery. "Editor's Introduction" to Frege's *Basic Laws of Arithmetic* (Berkeley and Los Angeles: University of California Press, 1964), pp. v-lvii.
14. Geach, Peter T. "Quine on Classes and Properties," *The Philosophical Review*, LXII (1953), 409-412.
15. Geach, Peter T. "Class and Concept," *The Philosophical Review*, LXIV (1955), 561-570.
16. Geach, Peter T. "On Frege's Way Out," *Mind*, LXV (1956), 408-409.
17. Geach, Peter T. "Frege," in Anscombe and Geach, *Three Philosophers* (Oxford: Blackwell, 1961), pp. 127-162.
18. Grossmann, Reinhardt. "Frege's Ontology," *The Philosophical Review*, LXX (1961), 23-40. Also in Allaire *et al.*, *Essays in Ontology* (Iowa City: University of Iowa; The Hague: M. Nijhoff, 1963), pp. 106-120.

19. Jackson, Howard. "Frege's Ontology," *The Philosophical Review*, LXIX (1960), 394-395.
20. Jackson, Howard. "Frege on Sense-Functions," *Analysis*, XXIII (1962-63), 84-87.
21. Jones, E. E. C. "Mr. Russell's Objection to Frege's Analysis of Propositions," *Mind*, XIX (1910), 379-386.
22. Jørgensen, Jørgen. *A Treatise of Formal Logic* (New York: Russell and Russell, 1962), I, 145-175.
23. Klemke, E. D. "Professor Bergmann and Frege's 'Hidden Nominalism'," *The Philosophical Review*, LXVIII (1959), 507-514.
24. Kneale, William. "Gottlob Frege and Mathematical Logic," in Ayer *et al.*, *The Revolution in Philosophy* (New York: St. Martin's Press, 1957), pp. 26-40.
25. Kneale, W., and M. Kneale. *The Development of Logic* (Oxford: Oxford University Press, 1962), Chs. VII-XI *passim*.
26. Marshall, William. "Frege's Theory of Functions and Objects," *The Philosophical Review*, LXII (1953), 374-390.
27. Marshall, William. "Sense and Reference: A Reply," *The Philosophical Review*, LXV (1956), 342-361.
28. Nidditch, P. H. "Frege's Logic," in *The Development of Mathematical Logic* (London: Routledge and Kegan Paul, 1962), pp. 59-66.
29. Nidditch, P. H. "Peano and the Recognition of Frege," *Mind*, LXXII (1963), 103-110.
30. Passmore, John. *A Hundred Years of Philosophy*, 2nd edition (New York: Basic Books, 1967), pp. 149-157.
31. Pivcevic, E. "Husserl *versus* Frege," *Mind*, LXXVI (1967), 155-165.
32. Quine, W. V. "On Frege's Way Out," *Mind*, LXIV (1955), 145-159. Also in *Selected Logic Papers* (New York: Random House, 1966).
33. Rudner, Richard. "On *Sinn* as a Combination of Physical Properties," *Mind*, LXI (1952), 82-84.
34. Russell, Bertrand. *The Principles of Mathematics*, revised ed. (New York: W. W. Norton, 1964), Appendix A.
35. Searle, J. R. "Russell's Objections to Frege's Theory of Sense and Reference," *Analysis*, XVIII (1957-58), 137-143.
36. Smart, H. R. "Frege's Logic," *The Philosophical Review*, LIV (1945), 489-505.
37. Sternfeld, Robert. "A Restriction on Frege's Use of the Term 'True'," *Philosophical Studies*, VI (1955), 58-64.
38. Stoothoff, R. H. "Note on a Doctrine of Frege," *Mind*, LXXII (1963), 406-408.

39. Urmson, J. O. (ed.), *The Concise Encyclopedia of Western Philosophy and Philosophers* (New York: Hawthorn Books, 1960), pp. 147-150.
40. Wells, Rulon S. "Frege's Ontology," *Review of Metaphysics,* IV (1951), 537-573.
41. Wells, Rulon S. "Is Frege's Concept of Function Valid?" *Journal of Philosophy,* LX (1963), 719-730.
42. Wienpahl, P. D. "Frege's *Sinn und Bedeutung,*" *Mind,* LIX (1950), 483-494.

C. REVIEWS

1. Black, Max. Review of Frege's *Foundations of Arithmetic, Journal of Symbolic Logic,* XVI (1951), 67.
2. Dummett, Michael. Review of Geach and Black, *Translations from the Philosophical Writings of Gottlob Frege, Mind,* LXIII (1954), 162-165.
3. Geach, P. T. "Frege's *Grundlagen,*" *The Philosophical Review,* LX (1951), 535-544.
4. Kneale, W. Review of Frege's *Foundations of Arithmetic, Mind,* LIX (1950), 395-399.
5. McRea, W. H. Review of Frege's *Foundations of Arithmetic, Philosophy,* XXVI (1951), 178-180.

INDEX

ILLINI BOOKS

Also available in clothbound editions.

IB-19	Black Hawk: An Autobiography	Donald Jackson, ed.	$
IB-20	Mexican Government in Transition	Robert E. Scott	$
IB-21	John Locke and the Doctrine of Majority-Rule	Willmoore Kendall	$
IB-22	The Framing of the Fourteenth Amendment	Joseph B. James	$
IB-23	The Mind and Spirit of John Peter Altgeld: Selected Writings and Addresses	Henry M. Christman, ed.	$
IB-24	A History of the United States Weather Bureau	Donald R. Whitnah	$
IB-25	Freedom of the Press in England, 1476-1776: The Rise and Decline of Government Controls	Fredrick Seaton Siebert	$
IB-26	Freedom and Communications	Dan Lacy	$
IB-27	The Early Development of Henry James	Cornelia Pulsifer Kelley, with an introduction by Lyon N. Richardson	$
IB-28	*Law in the Soviet Society	Wayne R. LaFave, ed.	$
IB-29	Beyond the Mountains of the Moon: The Lives of Four Africans	Edward H. Winter	$
IB-30	*The History of Doctor Johann Faustus	H. G. Haile	$
IB-31	One World	Wendell L. Willkie, with an introduction by Donald Bruce Johnson	$
IB-32	William Makepeace Thackeray: Contributions to the Morning Chronicle	Gordon N. Ray, ed.	$
IB-33	Italian Comedy in the Renaissance	Marvin T. Herrick	$
IB-34	Death in the Literature of Unamuno	Mario J. Valdés	$
IB-35	*Port of New York: Essays on Fourteen American Moderns	Paul Rosenfeld, with an introductory essay by Sherman Paul	$
IB-36	*How to Do Library Research	Robert B. Downs	$
IB-37	Henry James: Representative Selections, with Introduction, Bibliography, and Notes	Lyon N. Richardson	$

* Also available in clothbound editions.

B-38	*Symbolic Crusade: Status Politics and the American Temperance Movement	Joseph R. Gusfield	$1.75
B-39	*Genesis and Structure of Society	Giovanni Gentile, translated by H. S. Harris	$1.95
B-40	The Social Philosophy of Giovanni Gentile	H. S. Harris	$2.45
B-41	*As We Saw the Thirties: Essays on Social and Political Movements of a Decade	Rita James Simon, ed.	$2.45
B-42	The Symbolic Uses of Politics	Murray Edelman	$2.45
B-43	White-Collar Trade Unions: Contemporary Developments in Industrialized Societies	Adolf Sturmthal, ed.	$3.50
B-44	*The Labor Arbitration Process	R. W. Fleming	$2.45
B-45	*Edmund Wilson: A Study of Literary Vocation in Our Time	Sherman Paul	$2.45
B-46	*George Santayana's America: Essays on Literature and Culture	James Ballowe, ed.	$2.25
B-47	*The Measurement of Meaning	Charles E. Osgood, George J. Suci, and Percy H. Tannenbaum	$3.45
B-48	*The Miracle of Growth	Foreword by Arnold Gesell	$1.75
B-49	*Information Theory and Esthetic Perception	Abraham Moles	$2.45
B-50	Outlawing the Spoils: A History of the Civil Service Reform Movement, 1865-1883	Ari Hoogenboom	$2.95
B-51	*Community Colleges: A President's View	Thomas E. O'Connell	$1.95
B-52	*The Joys and Sorrows of Recent American Art	Allen S. Weller	$3.95
B-53	*Dimensions of Academic Freedom	Walter P. Metzger, Sanford H. Kadish, Arthur DeBardeleben, and Edward J. Bloustein	$ .95
B-54	*Essays on Frege	E. D. Klemke, ed.	$3.95
B-55	The Fine Hammered Steel of Herman Melville	Milton R. Stern	$2.95

* Also available in clothbound editions.

University of Illinois Press   Urbana, Chicago, and London